T0392527

THE ROUTLEDGE HANDBOOK OF CORPORA AND ENGLISH LANGUAGE TEACHING AND LEARNING

The Routledge Handbook of Corpora and English Language Teaching and Learning provides a wide-ranging and authoritative overview of the latest developments and innovations in how corpus approaches, corpus technologies, and corpus data can inform and transform English language teaching and learning.

Featuring a broad range of international experts, the *Handbook* presents state-of-the-art scholarship and inspires new avenues for research focusing on six key areas:

- English language teaching and learning informed by language corpora;
- corpora in syllabus and materials design;
- corpora and English for specific and academic purposes;
- learner corpora for English language teaching;
- data-driven learning; and
- corpora and corpus tools for language teaching.

Unique to this pioneering volume, the authors cover key areas at the cross-roads of corpus research and English language teaching by drawing on cutting-edge corpus applications, methods, and pedagogical approaches, hence, bridging the research–practice gap in the field.

This *Handbook* is a collection of novel contributions offering essential reading for those researching and studying English language teaching and learning through the application of corpus approaches.

Reka R. Jablonkai is an award-winning Associate Professor in Education and Applied Linguistics at the University of Bath. Her research interests include corpus-based discourse analysis, corpora in language teaching, and multilingual educational contexts. Her research projects were funded by the British Association for International & Comparative Education and the British Council. She has published in edited volumes and journals (e.g. *English for Specific Purposes, ESP Today*) and regularly presents at international conferences (e.g. EuroCALL, TALC, Corpora and Discourse International Conference). She is Chair of the CorpusCALL SIG of EuroCALL. She worked as a teacher trainer and visiting scholar in various contexts, for example, Italy, Lithuania, Germany, Slovenia, and Turkey.

Eniko Csomay is Professor of Applied Linguistics at San Diego State University. She applies corpus-based methods to text analysis, with a primary interest in discourse and language use at the university including English Medium Instruction (EMI) settings. Her main focus has been various aspects of university classroom discourse as well as student writing. Her articles appeared in highly ranked international journals, for example, *Applied Linguistics*, *Journal of English for Academic Purposes*, the *International Journal of Corpus Linguistics*, and *Register Studies*. She is an editor for the *Journal of Corpora and Discourse Studies*, and an editorial board member for *English for Specific Purposes* and the *Journal of English for Academic Purposes*. In addition to her edited volumes, she also co-authored a textbook (*Doing Corpus Linguistics* with Routledge). She was awarded multiple international fellowships (e.g. Soros-Oxford, British Council, Fulbright, English Language Specialist) and worked with pre- and in-service teachers and teacher trainers in several countries including Hungary, Georgia, Mexico, Morocco, and Singapore.

Routledge Handbooks in Applied Linguistics

Routledge Handbooks in Applied Linguistics provide comprehensive overviews of the key topics in applied linguistics. All entries for the handbooks are specially commissioned and written by leading scholars in the field. Clear, accessible and carefully edited *Routledge Handbooks in Applied Linguistics* are the ideal resource for both advanced undergraduates and postgraduate students.

The Routledge Handbook of Forensic Linguistics
Second Edition
Edited by Malcolm Coulthard, Alison May and Rui Sousa-Silva

The Routledge Handbook of Corpus Approaches to Discourse Analysis
Edited by Eric Friginal and Jack A. Hardy

The Routledge Handbook of World Englishes
Second Edition
Edited by Andy Kirkpatrick

The Routledge Handbook of Language, Gender and Sexuality
Edited by Jo Angouri and Judith Baxter

The Routledge Handbook of Plurilingual Language Education
Edited by Enrica Piccardo, Aline Germain-Rutherford and Geoff Lawrence

The Routledge Handbook of the Psychology of Language Learning and Teaching
Edited by Tammy Gregersen and Sarah Mercer

The Routledge Handbook of Language Testing
Second Edition
Edited by Glenn Fulcher and Luke Harding

The Routledge Handbook of Corpus Linguistics
Second Edition
Edited by Anne O'Keeffe and Michael J. McCarthy

The Routledge Handbook of Materials Development for Language Teaching
Edited by Julie Norton and Heather Buchanan

The Routledge Handbook of Corpora and English Language Teaching and Learning
Edited by Reka R. Jablonkai and Eniko Csomay

The Routledge Handbook of Language and the Global South(s)
Edited by Sinfree Makoni, Anna Kaiper-Marquez and Lorato Mokwena

For a full list of titles in this series, please visit www.routledge.com/Routledge-Handbooks-in-Applied-Linguistics/book-series/RHAL

THE ROUTLEDGE HANDBOOK OF CORPORA AND ENGLISH LANGUAGE TEACHING AND LEARNING

Edited by
Reka R. Jablonkai and Eniko Csomay

LONDON AND NEW YORK

Cover image: © Getty Images

First published 2023
by Routledge
4 Park Square, Milton Park, Abingdon, Oxon OX14 4RN

and by Routledge
605 Third Avenue, New York, NY 10158

Routledge is an imprint of the Taylor & Francis Group, an informa business

British Library Cataloguing-in-Publication Data
A catalogue record for this book is available from the British Library

Library of Congress Cataloging-in-Publication Data
A catalog record has been requested for this book

ISBN: 978-0-367-43395-6 (hbk)
ISBN: 978-1-032-23062-7 (pbk)
ISBN: 978-1-003-00290-1 (ebk)

DOI: 10.4324/9781003002901

Typeset in Bembo
by KnowledgeWorks Global Ltd.

CONTENTS

List of figures   *xi*
List of tables   *xiii*
List of contributors   *xv*
Acknowledgements   *xxii*
List of corpora and corpus tools   *xxiii*

Introduction   1
Reka R. Jablonkai and Eniko Csomay

PART I
English language teaching and learning informed by language corpora   **9**

1 A historical overview of using corpora in English language teaching   11
   Jiajin Xu

2 Corpora and second language acquisition   26
   Magali Paquot

3 Corpora and teaching vocabulary and phraseology   41
   Paweł Szudarski

4 Corpus analysis of grammar-in-discourse for English language teaching   56
   Stefan Frazier

5 Corpora in instructed second language pragmatics   71
   Kathleen Bardovi-Harlig and Sabrina Mossman

Contents

6   Corpora and speaking skills   89
    William J. Crawford

7   Corpora for teaching social conversation   102
    Michael McCarthy and Jeanne McCarten

8   Corpora for teaching culture and intercultural communication   116
    Tania Fahey Palma

9   Corpora for materials design   131
    Eric Friginal and Jennifer Roberts

10 Corpora for English language learning textbook evaluation   147
    Mike Nelson

11 English as a Lingua Franca corpora and English language teaching   161
    Xue Wu and Lei Lei

PART II
Corpora and English for specific purposes and English for
academic purposes   **175**

12 Corpus analysis of disciplinary variation and the teaching of ESP/EAP   177
    Paul Thompson

13 Corpora for teaching and learning vocabulary in ESP   193
    Averil Coxhead

14 Corpora for teaching collocations in ESP   206
    Clarence Green

15 Lexical bundles in EAP   220
    Viviana Cortes

16 Corpora for EAP writing   234
    Lynne Flowerdew

17 Corpora and EAP listening comprehension   248
    Belinda Crawford Camiciottoli

18 Corpora and feedback in EAP   264
    Hilary Nesi and Benet Vincent

PART III
Learner corpora for English language teaching 279

19 Written learner corpora to inform teaching 281
   Gaëtanelle Gilquin

20 Spoken learner corpora for language teaching 296
   Dana Gablasova and Raffaella Bottini

21 Learner corpora to inform testing and assessment 311
   Sandra Götz

PART IV
Data-driven learning 327

22 DDL pedagogy, participants, and perspectives 329
   Fiona Farr and Petter Hagen Karlsen

23 Revamping DDL: Affordances of digital technology 344
   Fanny Meunier

24 Multimodal corpora and concordancing in DDL 361
   Francesca Coccetta

25 DDL for younger learners 377
   Peter Crosthwaite

26 How learners use corpora 390
   Pascual Pérez-Paredes

27 Corpora and autonomous language learning 406
   Maggie Charles

28 DDL for English language teaching in perspective 420
   Ivor Timmis and Jane Templeton

PART V
Corpora and corpus tools for English language teaching 435

29 Evaluating corpus analysis tools for the classroom 437
   Clinton Hendry and Emily Sheepy

Contents

30 Building corpora for ELT   460
    Reka R. Jablonkai

31 Parallel corpora in ELT   478
    Laura M. Hartwell and Olivier Kraif

32 Automated syntactic analysis for ELT   495
    Xiaofei Lu, J. Elliott Casal and Yingying Liu

33 Training teachers and learners to use corpora   509
    Agnieszka Leńko-Szymańska

Index   *525*

FIGURES

2.1	Granger's (2015) CIA^2	32
2.2	The Integrated Contrastive Model (Gilquin, 2000, p. 100, adapted from Granger, 1996, p. 100)	32
3.1	Frequency-based typology of vocabulary adapted from Schmitt and Schmitt (2014)	44
3.2	A lexical profile of a text created via VocabProfiler (with the BNC/COCA 25 list used as a reference corpus)	47
4.1	Grammatical subjects connected to 241 one-word modals in the USTVRI Corpus	63
4.2	Frequency of agent-oriented vs. speaker-oriented modals in the USTVRI Corpus	64
4.3	Comparison between all modals and the modal *should* as used in questions in the USTVRI Corpus	66
5.1	MICASE KWIC lines for *I was wondering* (in mostly interactive texts)	76
5.2	MICASE KWIC lines for *I was wondering* (in highly interactive texts)	77
5.3	MICASE KWIC for *apologize*	78
5.4	Default search page for MICASE	81
5.5	Display of frequency results for *what I mean* in MICASE	81
8.1	Refugee representation in British newspapers	122
8.2	Humour in the refugee classroom	124
9.1	WordandPhrase.Info screen interface (version 1, June 2018)	140
9.2	Sample vocabulary lists provided by WordandPhrase.Info (version 1, June 2018)	140
16.1	Concordance lines for "delimiting the case under consideration" (adapted from Weber 2001, p. 17)	239
17.1	Multimodal ensemble "I don't mean to be utterly dismissive of the objection"	257
17.2	Metaphoric hand waving gesture detail	258
20.1	Teaching about disagreement (adapted from Gablasova & Brezina, 2017, p. 85)	304
23.1	The framework for digital competences for educators (Redecker, 2017, p. 8)	350
23.2	Screenshot from Phrasalstein	354
24.1	Some concordance lines for *teaser* from iWeb (https://www.english-corpora.org/iweb/)	363

24.2	Categories of concordances (Baldry & Thibault, 2008, p. 14)	363
24.3	Some concordance lines for *as you can see* from the TCSE (Hasebe, 2015; https://yohasebe.com/tcse/)	366
24.4	Example of dual co-texts in OpenMWSWeb platform	368
24.5	Hands menu labelling options in the House Corpus	369
24.6	Example of dashboard style of corpus-search results obtained with OpenMWS	370
26.1	Tracking learners' uses of corpora, based on Pérez-Paredes *et al.* (2011)	396
26.2	Search patterns in DDL, based on Pérez-Paredes *et al.* (2012)	397
26.3	An instance of a pattern C mixed search, adapted from Pérez-Paredes *et al.* (2012)	398
26.4	An ecological micro system for DDL	402
29.1	The concordancer for COCA (Davies, 2008)	440
29.2	Lextutor VocabProfile output	448
29.3	Concordancer menu from Lextutor (2020)	449
29.4	Lextutor concordancer results for the word *vocabulary* in the Academic General corpus	449
29.5	AntConc word list output	450
29.6	AntConc Keyword List output	451
29.7	AntConc concordance output	451
29.8	AntConc Collocates output	452
29.9	LancsBox words output	453
29.10	LancsBox keyword analysis output	454
29.11	LancsBox KWIC output	454
29.12	LancsBox GraphColl output	455
30.1	Main steps of corpus design and creation	463
30.2	Framework for corpus building	466
33.1	Selected concordances from the answers to an open question on the reasons for not using corpora in the classroom (Tribble, 2015, p. 56)	511
33.2	A DDL vocabulary task	517
33.3	Example of a guided discovery task on making and modifying claims (Charles, 2015, p. 154)	519

TABLES

4.1	Five tokens of *could* from a spoken corpus for illustration of vertical vs. horizontal readings	60
8.1	Refugee classroom word frequency list	123
8.2	Topic frequency in Mumsnet advice threads	127
9.1	Commercially-available CL in classroom textbooks, from 2007 to 2018	135
11.1	Lexical features examined in ELFA written discourse	165
11.2	Category and examples of non-conventional use of lexical forms in ELFA writing (based on Luzon, 2018 and Rozycki & Johnson, 2013)	166
11.3	Different lexical patterns of some hedging modal verbs in ELF and ENL research articles (summarized by Mur-Dueñas, 2017, p. 168)	166
11.4	Features of syntactic structures/patterns in long sentences of ELF research articles (based on Wu et al., 2020)	168
11.5	Featured syntactic patterns with coordination phrases in ELF research articles	169
11.6	Different syntactic patterns used in complex nominals	169
13.1	The 15 most and least frequent items in the Plumbing Word List (Coxhead & Demecheleer, 2018)	200
14.1	The Word Association Lists (Green & Lambert, 2018)	214
15.1	Common functions of lexical bundles in academic prose (adapted from Biber et al., 2004, pp. 384–388)	224
15.2	Common functions of lexical bundles in research articles, theses, and dissertations (Hyland, 2008, pp. 13–14)	225
15.3	PRAC sub-section used for three-word bundle analyses	227
15.4	Structural classification of three-word lexical bundles	228
15.5	Functional classification of three-word lexical bundles	229
17.1	Markers of lecturer attitude	256
21.1	Three approaches to using learner corpora in LTA (slightly adapted from Callies et al., 2014, p. 76)	316
21.2	Orthographic control snapshot grid for B2/C1 French-speaking learners of English (Thewissen, 2012, p. 273; corrections of errors are put right behind the errors between $-signs)	317
23.1	Check-list for revamped DDL activities	351

23.2	Using the check-list for a TTS tool in DDL activities	352
23.3	Using the check-list for Google as a concordancer in DDL activities	353
23.4	Using the check-list for film and series transcripts as data sources for DDL	353
23.5	Using the check-list for animated clips as part of DDL activities	354
23.6	Using the check-list for digital games as DDL activities	356
29.1	Usability heuristics adapted from Nielsen (1995)	443
29.2	Instructional goals and benchmark tasks for the heuristic evaluation	446
29.3	Overall negotiated ratings for Lextutor using Nielsen's (1995) usability heuristic framework	447
29.4	Overall negotiated ratings for AntConc using Nielsen's (1995) usability heuristic framework	450
29.5	Overall negotiated ratings for LancsBox using Nielsen's (1995) usability heuristic framework	453
29.6	Comparison of Lextutor, AntConc, and LancsBox	456
30.1	A framework for corpus building	465
31.1	Lexical comparison	487
32.1	Syntactic complexity indices from Lu et al. (2020)	502

CONTRIBUTORS

Kathleen Bardovi-Harlig is a Professor of Second Language Studies at Indiana University, where she teaches and conducts research on second language acquisition, L2 pragmatics, and tense-aspect systems. Her work on teaching formulaic language in L2 pragmatics using corpora has appeared in *Language Teaching Research, Language Learning & Technology*, and edited volumes.

Raffaella Bottini is a doctoral researcher at the ESRC Centre for Corpus Approaches to Social Science, Lancaster University. Her research interests include corpus linguistics, statistics and data visualization, second language acquisition, language teaching and testing. She focuses on the application of corpus methods to the analysis of vocabulary in spoken learner corpora.

J. Elliott Casal is a postdoctoral scholar in the Case Western Reserve University Department of Cognitive Science. His research interests include corpus linguistics and corpus-based writing pedagogies, English for Academic Purposes, and second language writing. His recent work appears in the *Journal of Second Language Writing, Journal of English for Academic Purposes, Language Learning and Technology*, and *System*.

Maggie Charles taught EAP for many years at Oxford University, where she devised and taught a corpus-based course in academic writing. Her main research interests lie in the analysis of academic discourse and corpus use in EAP pedagogy. She has published widely on these topics, including articles in *Applied Linguistics, English for Specific Purposes*, and the *Journal of English for Academic Purposes*. Her recent books include *Corpora in ESP/EAP writing instruction: Preparation, exploitation, analysis* with Ana Frankenberg-Garcia (Routledge, 2021) and *Introducing English for Academic Purposes* with Diane Pecorari (Routledge, 2015).

Francesca Coccetta is a tenured Assistant Professor at Ca' Foscari University of Venice in English Language and Translation and holds a doctorate in English Linguistics from Padua University where she specialized in multimodal corpus studies. Her research interests centre on multimodal discourse analysis of domain-specific discourses, video corpus construction and annotation, English language teaching, and computer-assisted language learning. Her publications testify both to her long-standing interest in corpus-based multimodal analysis of video genres and to her special interest in scientific and medical English. She has published in several journals including *ReCALL*, *System*, and *Lingue e Linguaggi*.

Viviana Cortes is a Associate Professor of Applied Linguistics at Georgia State University, where she teaches courses in corpus-based discourse analysis and descriptive English grammar. Her research interests focus on the study of formulaic language, particularly lexical bundles, in academic and specialized written registers. Her publications can be found in top journals in the field, such as *Applied Linguistics*, the *Journal of English for Academic Purposes*, and *English for Specific Purposes*.

Averil Coxhead is a Professor of Applied Linguistics in the School of Linguistics and Applied Language Studies, Victoria University of Wellington, New Zealand. She is the co-author of *Measuring native speaker vocabulary size* (John Benjamins, 2021) with Paul Nation and *English for vocational purposes* (Coxhead, Parkinson, Mackay & McLaughlin, 2020, Routledge). Her current research interests include technical vocabulary in trades education, measuring knowledge of technical vocabulary, and vocabulary in English for Specific Purposes and English for Academic Purposes.

Belinda Crawford Camiciottoli is Associate Professor of English Language and Linguistics at the University of Pisa. Her research focuses on corpus-assisted analysis of discourse in academic, professional, and digital settings. She has published in leading journals, including *Journal of Pragmatics, Intercultural Pragmatics, Discourse & Communication, Text & Talk, Discourse, Context & Media,* and *English for Specific Purposes.*

William J. Crawford is a Professor of Applied Linguistics at Northern Arizona University. His main research areas are in corpus linguistics, second language acquisition, L2 writing, and pedagogical grammar. His most recent research applies corpus linguistic approaches to second language data (both spoken and written) with the goal of describing learner performance in order to inform both theory and pedagogy. He also has extensive teacher-training experience in several countries, including China, Georgia, Thailand, and the United States.

Peter Crosthwaite is a Senior Lecturer in the School of Languages and Cultures at the University of Queensland (since 2017), having formerly been an assistant professor at the Centre for Applied English Studies (CAES), University of Hong Kong (since 2014). His areas of research and supervisory expertise include corpus linguistics and the use of corpora for language learning (known as "data-driven learning"), as well as English for General and Specific Academic Purposes. He is the author of the monograph *Learning the language of dentistry: Disciplinary corpora in the teaching of English for specific academic purposes* as part of Benjamins' Studies in Corpus Linguistics series (with Lisa Cheung, published 2019), as well as the edited volumes *Data driven learning for the next generation: Corpora and DDL for pre-tertiary learners* (published 2019) and *Referring in a second language: Reference to person in a multilingual world* (with Jonathon Ryan, published 2020) with Routledge.

Eniko Csomay is a Professor of Applied Linguistics at San Diego State University. She applies corpus-based methods to text analysis, with a primary interest in discourse and language use at the university including English Medium Instruction (EMI) settings. Her main focus has been various aspects of university classroom discourse as well as student writing. Her articles appeared in highly ranked international journals, for example, *Applied Linguistics, Journal of English for Academic Purposes,* the *International Journal of Corpus Linguistics,* and *Register Studies.*

She is an editor for the *Journal of Corpora and Discourse Studies*, and an editorial board member for *English for Specific Purposes* and the *Journal of English for Academic Purposes*. In addition to her edited volumes, she also co-authored a textbook (*Doing Corpus Linguistics* with Routledge). She was awarded multiple international fellowships (e.g. Soros-Oxford, British Council, Fulbright, English Language Specialist) and worked with pre- and in-service teachers and teacher trainers in several countries including Hungary, Georgia, Mexico, Morocco, and Singapore.

Tania Fahey Palma is an award-winning lecturer in Linguistics at the University of Aberdeen. An expert in Workplace Discourse and Intercultural Communication, she has developed over 15 courses and two masters programmes integrating interdisciplinary and mixed method approaches to understanding communication in context.

Fiona Farr is a Associate Professor of Applied Linguistics and TESOL at the University of Limerick, Ireland. Her key areas of expertise are teacher education, reflective practice, applied corpus linguistics, and technology-enhanced language learning. She is author of *Teaching practice feedback: An investigation of spoken and written modes* (2011, Routledge), *Practice in TESOL* (2015, EUP), and *Social interaction in language teacher education* (with Angela Farrell and Elaine Riordan, 2019, EUP), and in 2022 her co-authored book (with Angela Farrell) *The reflective cycle of the teaching practicum* will be published. She is co-editor (with Bróna Murphy) of the *EUP textbooks in TESOL series*, and is Associate Editor of the journal *Second Language Teacher Education*. She is also co-editor (with Liam Murray) of the *Routledge handbook of language learning and technology* (2016).

Lynne Flowerdew is currently an Honorary Visiting Research Fellow in the Department of Applied Linguistics and Communication, Birkbeck, University of London. Her main research and teaching interests include corpus linguistics, discourse analysis, EAP/ESP, and disciplinary writing. She has published widely in these areas in international journals and prestigious edited collections and has also authored and co-edited several books.

Stefan Frazier is an Associate Professor in and Chair of the Department of Linguistics and Language Development at San José State University. His research interests include corpus pragmatics, grammar-in-discourse, grammar-in-interaction, non-native English speaking teacher issues, and the study of multilingual / multicultural populations at U.S. universities.

Eric Friginal is a Professor of Applied Linguistics and Head of Department of English and Communication at The Hong Kong Polytechnic University. Professor of Applied Linguistics at the Department of Applied Linguistics and ESL and Director of International Programs at the College of Arts and Sciences, Georgia State University. He specializes in applied corpus linguistics, quantitative research, language policy and planning, technology and language teaching, sociolinguistics, cross-cultural communication, discipline-specific writing, and the analysis of spoken professional discourse in the workplace. His recent publications include *The Routledge handbook of corpus approaches to discourse analysis* (2020), co-edited with Jack Hardy; *Advances in corpus-based research on academic writing: Effects of discipline, register, and writer expertise*, co-edited with Ute Römer and Viviana Cortes (Benjamins, 2020); and *English in global Aviation: Context, research, and pedagogy*, with Elizabeth Mathews and Jennifer Roberts (Bloomsbury, 2019). He is the founding co-editor-in-chief of *Applied Corpus Linguistics* (ACORP) journal (with Paul Thompson).

Dana Gablasova is a Senior Lecturer in the Department of Linguistics and English Language and a member of the ESRC Centre for Corpus Approaches to Social Science at Lancaster

University. Her research focuses on building corpora representing L2 English and on corpus-based approaches to language learning, teaching, and testing. She has developed the *Trinity Lancaster Corpus of L2 spoken English* and the *British Council Lancaster APTIS corpus*. She is the lead developer of the *Corpus for Schools project* which focuses on the creation of corpus-based teaching materials for English.

Gaëtanelle Gilquin is a Professor of English Language and Linguistics at the University of Louvain, Belgium. She is one of the editors of the *Cambridge handbook of learner corpus research* and the director of several corpus projects, including the Process Corpus of English in Education (PROCEED), a corpus showing the writing process through keylogging and screencasting. Her research interests include corpus linguistics and its applications, as well as its links with other frameworks such as contact linguistics or cognitive linguistics.

Sandra Götz is a Professor for the Didactics and Linguistics of English at Philipps University Marburg, Germany. Her research is mainly focused on fluency and syntax of learners of English and (South Asian) varieties of English using corpora and quantitative methods. She has served on the board of the Learner Corpus Association between 2014 and 2021 and is a co-editor of the *International Journal of Learner Corpus Research*.

Clarence Green currently lectures in the School of Education, Federation University Australia. He holds a PhD in linguistics and a Master of Applied Linguistics (University of Melbourne). His areas of expertise include corpus linguistics, vocabulary, literacy, psycholinguistics, EAP and ESP. His research has appeared in journals such as *English for Specific Purposes*, the *Journal of English for Academic Purposes*, *Language Learning and Technology*, *System*, *Cognitive Linguistics*, and *Lingua*.

Laura M. Hartwell is a Full Professor of English Studies at the University Toulouse Capitole and Director of the Lairdil laboratory in Toulouse, France. Her research interests include numerical language resources and English for legal purposes. She obtained a French HDR diploma at the University of Grenoble Alpes (Lidilem) and a Doctoral degree at the University of Toulouse (Lairdil), both on academic English and its teaching.

Clinton Hendry is a PhD candidate of Education specializing in Applied Linguistics at Concordia University. His research focuses on the pedagogical use of corpora and speech technologies (text-to-speech synthesis and speech recognition) and their effects on language learning.

Reka R. Jablonkai is an award-winning Associate Professor in Education and Applied Linguistics at the University of Bath. She is Chair of the CorpusCALL SIG of EuroCALL. Her research interests include corpus-based discourse analysis, corpora in language teaching, and multilingual educational contexts. Her research projects were funded by the British Association for International & Comparative Education (BAICE) and the British Council. She has published in edited volumes and journals (e.g. *English for Specific Purposes*, *Applied Linguistics Review*) and regularly presents at international conferences (e.g. EuroCALL, TALC, Corpora and Discourse International Conference). She worked as a teacher trainer and visiting scholar in various contexts in, for example, Italy, Lithuania, Germany, Slovenia, and Turkey.

Petter Hagen Karlsen is a doctoral student at the Inland Norway University of Applied Sciences and part of the Faculty of Education, Department of Humanities. He has a master's degree in the didactics of English language and culture, and is at present enrolled in the program "PhD in Teaching and Teacher Education" (PROFF). His research interests include applied corpus linguistics, data-driven learning, teacher education, technology-enhanced education, and inquiry-based education.

Olivier Kraif is a Full Professor in Grenoble at the Université Grenoble Alpes (UGA) and a member of LiDiLEM laboratory. He teaches in the fields of computer science, computational linguistics, and natural language processing. He has a specific interest in text corpora processing, especially related to multilingual corpora (comparable as well as parallel). His research aims at developing techniques and tools to investigate linguistic phenomena from various points of view: lexicon, phraseology, contrastive analysis, and translational studies.

Lei Lei is a Professor at the School of Foreign Languages, Shanghai Jiao Tong University, China. His research interests include corpus linguistics, academic English, and learners English. He has published extensively in home and international journals such as *Applied Linguistics*, *International Journal of Corpus Linguistics*, *Journal of English for Academic Purposes*, and *Journal of Quantitative Linguistics*. He also co-authored a book entitled *Using Corpora for Language Learning and Teaching* with TESOL Press.

Agnieszka Leńko-Szymańska is Assistant Professor at the Institute of Applied Linguistics at the University of Warsaw. Her research interests are primarily in second language acquisition and corpus linguistics, especially in learner corpus research into second language lexis and phraseology. She has published a number of papers on the acquisition of second language vocabulary and formulaic language and on explorations of learner corpora. She teaches courses in BA and MA programmes which include applied linguistics, foreign language teaching methodology, and second language acquisition as well as corpus linguistics and data-driven learning.

Yingying Liu is a Ph.D. candidate in the Department of Applied Linguistics at The Pennsylvania State University. Her research interests include corpus linguistics, English for Academic Purposes, English phraseology, and lexicography. Her work appeared in the *Journal of English for Academic Purposes*, *Language Teaching*, and *System*.

Xiaofei Lu is a Professor of Applied Linguistics and Asian Studies at The Pennsylvania State University. His research interests include corpus linguistics, English for Academic Purposes, second language writing, second language acquisition, and intelligent computer-assisted language learning. He is the author of *Computational Methods for Corpus Annotation and Analysis* (2014, Springer) and co-editor of *Computational and Corpus Approaches to Chinese Language Learning* (2019, Springer).

Jeanne McCarten has been involved in ELT/ESL for many years as a teacher, editor, publisher, and materials writer and has worked in Sweden, France, Malaysia, and the UK. Currently a freelance ELT author, corpus researcher, and occasional teacher, her ongoing professional interests lie in applying corpus insights to learning materials. She is co-author of the corpus-informed print, online, and blended courses *Touchstone* and *Viewpoint*, and *Grammar for Business*.

Michael McCarthy is an Emeritus Professor of Applied Linguistics, University of Nottingham. He is author/co-author/editor of 53 books, including *Touchstone*, *Viewpoint*, the *Cambridge*

Grammar of English, English Grammar Today, From Corpus to Classroom, The Routledge Handbook of Corpus Linguistics, Innovations and Challenges in Grammar, and *English Grammar: The Basics.* He was co-founder of the CANCODE and CANBEC spoken English corpora.

Fanny Meunier is a Professor of English Language, Linguistics and Didactics at UCLouvain, Belgium. Her research interests include fundamental, applied, and instructed Second Language Acquisition; bi-, multi-, and plurilingualism; and multiliteracies (including digital and corpus literacies). She has also been active in pre- and in-service teacher training since 2000.

Sabrina Mossman is an Assistant Professor of Practice at the University of Texas at El Paso, where she directs the ESOL program, leads the TESOL certificate program, and conducts research on L2 pragmatics, L2 acquisition of modality, and instructed and uninstructed second language acquisition. She is co-author of publications appearing in *Language Teaching Research, TESOL Journal, Studies in Second Language Acquisition, Language Learning and Technology* as well as edited volumes.

Mike Nelson is a Director of the Centre for Language and Communication Studies at the University of Turku, Finland. He has a long-held interest in corpus-based research and has advocated and implemented the use of corpus data in teaching materials since creating the Business English Corpus in the late 1990s. This experience provided the impetus and inspiration for his chapter.

Hilary Nesi is a Professor of English Language at Coventry University. Her research activities mostly concern corpus development and analysis, the discourse of English for academic purposes, and the design and use of dictionaries and reference tools. She is Editor-in-Chief of *Journal of English for Academic Purposes,* and she was Principal Investigator for the projects to create the BASE corpus of British Academic Spoken English and the BAWE corpus of British Academic Written English.

Magali Paquot is a Research Associate of Fund for Scientific Research (F.R.S.-FNRS) at the Centre for English Corpus Linguistics, UCLouvain, Belgium. She specializes in the use of learner corpora to study key topics in second language acquisition and is particularly interested in methodological issues. She is co-editor in chief of the *International Journal of Learner Corpus Research* and one of the founding members of the Learner Corpus Association.

Pascual Pérez-Paredes is a Professor of Applied Linguistics and Linguistics at the University of Murcia. His main research interests are learner language variation, the use of corpora and technology in language education and corpus-assisted discourse analysis. He is Assistant Editor of *ReCALL* published by Cambridge University Press.

Jennifer Roberts is the Aviation English Program Coordinator at Embry-Riddle Aeronautical University – Worldwide campus. She is an aviation safety advocate who works to develop and deliver aviation English training and testing programs that adhere to academic best practices. She holds an MA in Applied Linguistics and ESL from Georgia State University and serves on the Board of the International Civil Aviation English Association (ICAEA) and as Chair Elect of TESOL's English for Specific Purposes Interest Section. Her research interests are in the pedagogical applications of corpus linguistics, language policy and planning, and curriculum development in English for specific purposes settings.

Emily Sheepy is an instructional designer, educational media producer, and researcher with experience in higher education and in the educational technology industry. Her research examines the impact of usability on learner behaviour in instructional systems, and explores applications of corpus analysis methods to the development of personalized learning experiences.

Paweł Szudarski is an Assistant Professor in Applied Linguistics at the University of Nottingham. He works in the areas of second language acquisition, corpus linguistics, and TESOL, focusing in particular on the acquisition of vocabulary and phraseology by second/foreign language learners. His other interests include corpus-based analysis, replication research, and distance learning.

Jane Templeton is a Lecturer in EAP at the University of Leeds. Her main research interests are in the practical application of corpus linguistics in the language classroom and the development of learner autonomy. She has presented on these topics at conferences and seminars. Currently she is working with students and academic and support staff to develop discipline-specific support with academic literacy development in the School of Chemical and Process Engineering.

Paul Thompson is a reader in Applied Corpus Linguistics, and Deputy Director of the Centre for Corpus Research at the University of Birmingham. From 2009 to 2018, he was a co-editor-in-chief of the *Journal of English for Academic Purposes* and is currently co-editor of the *Applied Corpus Linguistics* journal. He taught EFL and EAP for twenty years in Japan and the UK.

Ivor Timmis is an Emeritus Professor of English Language Teaching at Leeds Beckett University. He has been involved in ELT for over 30 years, during which time he has been a teacher, teacher educator, materials developer, and researcher. His main interests are in the relevance of corpus findings to ELT, materials development, and, more recently, historical spoken language research. He has published in all these areas.

Benet Vincent is an Assistant Professor in Applied Linguistics at Coventry University. His research uses corpus techniques to investigate language and language learning, including Data-driven Learning (DDL). He leads the BAWE Quicklinks project with Hilary Nesi. He is also involved in the Communicating Covid project and the Clockwork Orange Translation Project.

Xue Wu is an Associate Professor of English at School of Foreign Languages at Huazhong University of Science and Technology in China. Her major research interests lie in English as a lingua franca in academic settings and corpus linguistics.

Jiajin Xu is a Professor of Linguistics at the National Research Centre for Foreign Language Education, Beijing Foreign Studies University as well as Secretary General of the Chinese Society of Corpus Linguistics. He obtained his Ph.D., specializing in corpus-based discourse studies, from Beijing Foreign Studies University, China. From 2008 to 2009, he was Post-Doctoral Researcher in the Department of Linguistics and English Language at Lancaster University. He has published a number of English papers in international journals including *Across Languages and Cultures, Chinese Language and Discourse, Corpus Linguistics and Linguistic Theory, Discourse & Society, ICAME Journal, Journal of Quantitative Linguistics,* and *Language Sciences.* He has constructed more than twenty corpora over the last ten years, and actively experimented with the corpus approach in learner dictionary compilation and ELT materials development in China.

ACKNOWLEDGEMENTS

We would like to thank our contributors and the anonymous reviewers for their dedicated and timely work on the manuscripts during an especially challenging time.

Reproduced with kind permission from John Benjamins Publication Company: Chapter 2 Figure of Granger's (2015) CIA² (https://www.benjamins.com/catalog/ijlcr) and The Integrated Contrastive Model (Gilquin, 2000, p. 100, adapted from Granger, 1996, p. 100) (https://www.benjamins.com/catalog/lic).

CORPORA AND CORPUS TOOLS

Bitextes anglais-français corpus: http://rali.iro.umontreal.ca/rali/?q=fr/BAF

BNCweb (A web-based interface to the British National Corpus) http://corpora.lancs.ac.uk/BNCweb/

British Academic Spoken English (BASE) www.coventry.ac.uk/base

British Academic Written English (BAWE) www.coventry.ac.uk/bawe

British National Corpus (BNC) http://www.natcorp.ox.ac.uk/

Canadian Parliament Hansards: https://www.isi.edu/natural-language/download/hansard/

CARLA https://carla.umn.edu/speechacts/index.html

Collins WordBanks Online https://wordbanks.harpercollins.co.uk/

Common Language Resources and Technology Infrastructure: www.clarin.eu/content/language-resource-inventory

Compara: www.linguateca.pt/COMPARA

Corpus of Academic Learner English (CALE) (https://blogs.uni-bremen.de/cale/corpus-design/

Corpus of Contemporary American English (COCA) https://www.english-corpora.org/coca/

Deepl: https://www.deepl.com

EIIDA: https://corpora.aiakide.net/scientext20/?do=SQ.setView&view=corpora

The Corpus of English as a Lingua Franca in Academic Settings (ELFA). (2008). Retrieved September 10, 2020, from https://www.helsinki.fi/en/researchgroups/english-as-a-lingua-franca-in-academic-settings/research/elfa-corpus

English-Norwegian Parallel corpus: https://tekstlab.uio.no/glossa2/saml?licence=ACA-NC-LOC-LRT-ND_OMC;back=https%3a%2f%2ftekstlab.uio.no%2fglossa2%2fomc4

European Commission's Translation Memory: https://data.europa.eu/euodp/en/data/dataset/dgt-translation-memory

European Language Resources Association: www.elra.info/en/about/elra/

European Parliament corpus: https://ec.europa.eu/jrc/en/language-technologies/dcep

European Research Infrastructure Consortium: https://www.clarin.eu/resource-families/parallel-corpora

European Science Foundation Second Language SLA Bank: https://slabank.talkbank.org/access/Multiple/ESF/

French Learner Language Oral Corpora (FLLOC): http://www.flloc.soton.ac.uk/

ICNALE Learner Essays with Feedback Comments https://www.gsk.or.jp/en/catalog/gsk2019-b

International Corpus of English http://ice-corpora.net/ice/index.html

International Corpus of Learner English. Available https://uclouvain.be/en/research-institutes/ilc/cecl/icle.html

Japanese Learner English Corpus https://alaginrc.nict.go.jp/nict_jle/index_E.html#download

Konan-JIEM Learner Corpus Sixth Edition https://www.gsk.or.jp/en/catalog/gsk2019-a

Languages and Social Networks Abroad Project (LANGSNAP): http://langsnap.soton.ac.uk

LeaP https://sourceforge.net/projects/leapcorpus/)

Learner corpora around the world https://uclouvain.be/en/research-institutes/ilc/cecl/learner-corpora-around-the-world.html

Lextutor https://lextutor.ca/conc/eng/

Linguistic Data Consortium: www.ldc.upenn.edu/about

Michigan Corpus of Academic Spoken English (MICASE) https://quod.lib.umich.edu/m/micase/

Michigan Corpus of Upper-level Student Papers (MICUSP) https://elicorpora.info/

MyMemory: https://mymemory.translated.net/

Online Corpus of Academic Lectures http://www.oncal.sci.waseda.ac.jp/index.aspx

OPUS: http://opus.nlpl.eu/

ParaSHS: http://phraseotext.univ-grenoble-alpes.fr/lexicoscope_2.0

Russian Learner Translator Corpus: https://rus-ltc.org/static/html/about.html

Sketch Engine for Language Learners (SkELL) https://www.sketchengine.eu/skell/

Sketch Engine https://www.sketchengine.eu/

Sketch Engine https://www.sketchengine.eu/guide/setting-up-parallel-corpora/

Spanish Learner Language Oral Corpora (SPLLOC): http://www.splloc.soton.ac.uk

Spoken Open American National Corpus (SOANC) http://www.anc.org/data/oanc/contents/

Statistical Natural Language Processing Group https://www.cl.uni-heidelberg.de/statnlpgroup/

Tatoeba: https://tatoeba.org/eng

Translation Automation User Society: https://data-app.taus.net/

Translation Equivalents Database: http://portal.clarin.nl/node/18403

Trinity-Lancaster Corpus (TLC) http://cass.lancs.ac.uk/trinity-lancaster-corpus/

UM-corpus: http://nlp2ct.cis.umac.mo/um-corpus/index.html

United Nations corpus: https://conferences.unite.un.org/UNCORPUS/en/Download Overview

Varieties of English for Specific Purposes dAtabase (VESPA) (https://uclouvain.be/en/research-institutes/ilc/cecl/vespa.html

The Vienna-Oxford International Corpus of English (VOICE). (2013). (version 2.0 Online). https://www.univie.ac.at/voice/page/index.php

Web Align Toolkit: http://phraseotext.univ-grenoble-alpes.fr/webAlignToolkit

INTRODUCTION

Reka R. Jablonkai and Eniko Csomay

While relatively large paper-based text collections were used to create lexical frequency lists, idiom lists, and syntax lists for language teaching purposes already in the late 19th and early 20th century (Xu, this volume), advances in technology enabled the creation of electronic corpora in the 1960s. These early electronic corpora were primarily designed and used for linguistic analyses. Soon after, however, several aspects of English language teaching were informed by findings of corpus analysis (e.g. Biber *et al.*, 1999), and teaching approaches were developed to give language learners direct access to corpus data mostly in the form of data-driven learning (DDL), as coined by Johns (1991). Recognizing the potential of corpora for English language teaching and learning, researchers in the field anticipated a transformative change (Leech, 1997), professing a corpus revolution (e.g. Conrad, 2000) that can potentially transform language education. In the process of this transformative change, the last two decades have seen a gradual increase in published research in the field. However, there still seems to be a gap between corpus research and teaching practices using corpora (Chambers, 2019). The goal of the *Handbook of Corpora and English Language Teaching and Learning* is to contribute to filling this gap by providing an overview of state-of-the-art research, key approaches, and current practice at the cross-roads of corpus linguistics and English language teaching and learning.

The role of corpora in English language learning and teaching

A simple way to look at corpora is to view them as collections of texts. However, by today's definition of what constitutes a corpus, not all collections of texts can be considered a corpus. Definitions of corpora formulate essential features that make a text collection a linguistic corpus: it is a principled, computerized collection of naturally occurring texts that are systematically selected to represent language use or a language variety (Biber *et al.*, 1998; Friginal, 2018; McEnery *et al.*, 2006). Texts in the early days of corpus building were primarily written texts with some transcribed spoken texts. Technological advances made it possible that the latest generations of corpora are multimodal, hence include audio and video recordings aligned with their transcriptions (Coccetta, this volume; Crawford Camiciottoli, this volume). At the same time, as all kinds of texts are now available in digital formats (e.g. journal articles, student papers, transcripts of academic lectures as well as TV shows, websites),

DOI: 10.4324/9781003002901-1

corpus creation that required a laborious team effort in the 1960s can be done by anyone with access to a computer and the internet. Easy and largely free access to texts in electronic formats led to a dramatic increase in the number of corpora compiled by scholars as well as instructors. It also facilitated the creation of new types of corpora, some of which are freely available, over the decades.

What is most relevant to this volume among these new types of corpora are specialized and parallel corpora as well as pedagogic and learner corpora. We discuss each in turn. Research goals in the late 1980s aimed at representing English language use in general, hence, a corpus included texts from as many spoken and written registers as possible. While this trend continues in order to meet such research goals (see collections such as the British National Corpus [BNC] or the Corpus of Contemporary American English [COCA]), more recently, and driven by different research aims, specialized corpora have also been created to represent different language varieties used in specific contexts such as, academic disciplines and professional settings. At the same time, other research goals, for example, to investigate translations, have facilitated the development of parallel corpora. Parallel corpora include English texts (or texts in one language) and their translations in another language. The purpose of such corpora was primarily to undertake linguistic analyses (Tognini-Bonelli, 2001) but have often been used for teaching purposes as well. In the 1990s, the concept of a pedagogic or teaching-oriented corpus was also introduced. This type of corpus was created with language teaching purposes in mind and aimed to satisfy the needs of specific learner groups. At the same time, learner corpora were also compiled to investigate various aspects of written and spoken productions of language learners, for example, patterns of errors of a group of learners, cross-linguistic similarities and differences of interlanguage, and fossilization (Gablasova & Bottini, this volume; Gilquin, this volume; Götz, this volume; Granger, 1998). In addition, a few corpora were built from language used in language learning textbooks to compare the English language represented in them to corpora that represent naturally occurring texts (Nelson, this volume). More recently, learners have also been encouraged to create their own micro corpora, self-compiled, or do-it-yourself (DIY) corpora and consult them in class (Fahey Palma, this volume) or autonomously (Charles, this volume).

In discussing the role that corpora play in English language teaching, three main approaches can be distinguished: (1) corpus-informed teaching, (2) integrated corpus-supported teaching and learning, and (3) self-directed DDL. These approaches differ in the extent that learners have direct access to the actual corpus data. In the case of corpus-informed teaching, it is the teacher, materials designer, or textbook writer who accesses different types of corpora to identify learning goals based on, for example, typical errors identified in learner corpora, or target lexical items based on a discipline-specific specialized corpus. Integrated corpus-supported teaching and learning can take the form of hands-on and hands-off DDL (Boulton, 2012). In this approach, corpus data is accessed as part of language instruction with varying levels of guidance and scaffolding from teachers. For hands-off, or paper-based DDL, teachers usually prepare selected concordance lines from corpora with activities that direct the learner's attention to specific aspects of the language use. In the case of hands-on DDL, learners access corpus data directly by using various corpus analysis tools (Ackerley, 2017; Boulton, 2012). However, as Pérez-Paredes (2019) points out, studies on DDL rarely discuss the integration of DDL and the use of corpora into syllabi. More often than not, studies report on the effects of stand-alone workshops in corpus consultation (Chen & Flowerdew, 2018; Boulton & Vyatkina, 2021) or semester-long corpus-based courses or series of DDL-based lessons (e.g. Ackerley, 2017; Jablonkai & Čebron, 2021). Finally, corpora have great potential as tools for self-directed or autonomous language learning. In this approach, learners are encouraged to consult corpora outside the language classroom. Corpora in this case are often publicly available or are self-compiled that include texts that represent specific genres or registers relevant for the learners (Charles, 2014; Lee & Swales, 2006).

In this volume, we bring together as wide a range of corpus applications in English language teaching and learning as possible so as to capture the most recent findings in terms of what corpus data and corpus consultation can offer to the teaching practice and thus aim to bridge the "research-practice gap" (Chamber, 2019). The *Handbook* is framed through the English language learning and teaching lens and includes themes such as, what corpora can provide for language learning and teaching research and practice, what implications corpus findings have on language teaching and learning theory and practice, and how our understanding of the English language with the help of corpora shape our understanding of English language learning and teaching. The structure of the *Handbook* reflects these areas by including chapters that discuss the role of corpora in teaching vocabulary, grammar in discourse, speaking, writing and listening skills, and implications of corpus research into disciplinary discourse and learner corpora. In addition to these frequently discussed topics, the *Handbook* also features chapters on areas that have received less attention in books and edited volumes on corpus linguistics and language teaching, for example, corpus research into developing pragmatic and intercultural competence, corpus applications for feedback, a critical discussion of corpus tools, and using parallel corpora in English language teaching.

Organization of the *Handbook*

The starting point for parts and chapters in the *Handbook* are aspects of language teaching and learning and provide an overview of research unlocking the added value of corpora for these teaching aspects. The *Handbook* has five major parts, each discussing particular aspects of corpora and English language teaching and learning (ELT). Each chapter starts with an introduction and definitions relevant to the chapter's theme followed by a review of the current state of research. Subsequently, the core issues and topics within the chapter's focal area are discussed showcasing critical issues and debates. In the next section of each chapter, depending on the theme, current contributions or recommendations for practice are outlined reporting on the latest findings or presenting exemplary studies relevant to the area. This is followed by one or two case studies to demonstrate innovative applications. The last two sections in each chapter then point us to future directions of research and list three to five further readings with the author's notes on each.

The 11 chapters in Part I, *English language teaching and learning informed by language corpora*, focus on particular relationships between language corpora and English language teaching and learning. In his chapter titled "A historical overview of using corpora in English language teaching", Xu discusses how corpora have been used for applied linguistics research and for teaching ELT from pre-electronic times to the cloud-computing age, and how applying corpora in these settings has been advanced by technological innovations. In "Corpora and Second Language Acquisition", Paquot offers a critical overview of the ways in which corpora have contributed to second language acquisition research, paying special attention to research methodologies used in this area. In his chapter titled "Corpora in the teaching of vocabulary and phraseology", Szudarski describes state-of-the-art corpus-based analyses of vocabulary, with special attention to the identification and description of various types of vocabulary and their relationship to the teaching of vocabulary and phraseology. Frazier's chapter, "Corpus analysis of grammar-in-discourse for English language teaching" discusses how a discourse perspective to the teaching of grammar would enhance students' understanding of such complex grammatical notions as tense and modality, showing the relationship between corpus linguistics and pragmatics. With the same perspective on the relationship between discourse and pragmatics, in their chapter titled "Corpora in instructed second language pragmatics", Bardovi-Harlig and Mossman illustrate how the teaching of pragmatics is aided by corpora while also pointing out some of the limitations of corpora for materials development in that area. The discussion by Crawford in "Corpora and speaking skills" remains within the area of spoken discourse but the focus this time is on how corpora can be used to help teachers and researchers address the development of speaking skills for second language learners. Still within the topic of spoken discourse, in "Corpora for teaching social conversation", McCarthy and McCarten outline how the availability of corpora of everyday social interaction helps develop a syllabus for the teaching of social conversation. They look at how speakers manage their own talk, consider other participants in the conversation, show active listenership, and manage conversation. Another area of interest in how language corpora can inform the teaching and learning of English centers around intercultural communication and the teaching of culture. Fahey Palma's chapter, "Corpora for teaching culture and intercultural communication", illustrates how corpus linguistics can inform critical discourse analysis, and how students applying this approach can undertake meaningful analyses of social contexts to explore the impact of representations particular to refugees and the LGBTQ+ community. Friginal and Roberts' chapter titled "Corpora for materials design" synthesizes ideas and suggestions for using corpora to develop teaching materials for English language learners and exemplifies materials development with those for Aviation English. Nelson's chapter, "Corpora for English language learning textbook evaluation", argues that while the creation of dictionaries and reference books have been heavily influenced by corpora in the past decades, only a few writers rely on corpora as they compile their textbooks. He presents a case study examining the differences between actual Business English and Business English as represented in textbooks. The final chapter in this section "English as a Lingua Franca corpora and English language teaching" by Wu and Lei looks at the teaching of English from an ELF perspective. Focusing on English as the international language of scientific communication and of the academia (English as a Lingua Franca Academic, ELFA), they discuss the lexical and syntactic features of ELFA and demonstrate how ELF corpora can inform English academic writing teaching.

Part II in the handbook, *Corpora and English for Specific and Academic Purposes*, contains seven chapters, each taking a different perspective within one of the most intensively researched areas of corpora, that is, in the study of English for Specific and Academic Purposes. Thompson, for example, looks at disciplinary variation in his chapter titled "Corpus analysis of disciplinary variation and the teaching of ESP/EAP". He provides an overview of such studies in the academic context outlining the relevant types of corpora developed and tools used. He also surveys published EAP/ESP corpus-informed materials closing by discussions on how teachers have used corpora in their teaching in the academic context. The two subsequent chapters, "Corpora for teaching and learning vocabulary in ESP" and "Corpora for teaching collocations in ESP" focus on English for Specific Purposes while the rest of the chapters in this section zoom in on English for Academic Purposes. The first chapter on ESP is written by Coxhead, who discusses the core issues of corpus-based vocabulary research and teaching in ESP (e.g. identifying what words to teach and how to best learn to use specialized vocabulary) with illustrations via several case studies in the ESP context. Green, the author of the other chapter on ESP, provides details on how corpus research into collocations has informed teaching and learning ESP. The remaining four chapters in this section look at various perspectives of corpora and EAP. Drawing on the conceptual distinction between corpus-based and corpus-driven linguistic studies, Cortes, in "Lexical bundles in EAP", first introduces the concept of lexical bundles followed by an in-depth discussion of lexical bundle research in EAP closing with hands-on activities exemplifying the teaching of them. Flowerdew, in "Corpora for EAP writing", first provides a rationale for using corpora for research and teaching EAP writing followed by an introduction of fundamental developments in EAP research and pedagogic applications, ending the chapter with calling for future research (and practice) into students using corpora for their writing outside the classroom. In the following chapter "Corpora and EAP listening comprehension", Crawford Camiciottoli stresses the importance of corpora to the teaching of academic listening skills in English, highlighting the significance of the various types of spoken language that could be used for academic listening activities. She ends with a case study demonstrating how a multimodal spoken corpus fosters a more effective academic listening experience. Nesi and Vincent's chapter, "Corpora and feedback in EAP", reviews developments in the use of corpora as a means to deliver feedback in EAP contexts, focusing on the most recent developments in terms of the ubiquitous use of virtual learning environments at universities. The chapter reviews research into corpus-informed feedback and considers ways in which current practices could be further developed including most recent technological advances in this area.

Part III, *Learner corpora for English language teaching*, includes three chapters outlining how different types of learner corpora have informed language teaching, testing, and assessment. More specifically, Gilquin, in "Written learner corpora to inform teaching", discusses ways in which written learner corpora have been used for teaching purposes, considers direct and indirect uses of learner corpora especially in the compilation of dictionaries, grammars, textbooks, and DDL, and offers some solutions to potential difficulties with the use of learner corpora. In "Spoken learner corpora for language teaching", Gablasova and Bottini focus on ways in which spoken learner corpora can contribute to language pedagogy including current trends in the integration of spoken learner corpora in English language teaching and consider these resources to inform curriculum design, reference materials, and learners' engagement with language from these corpora. Götz, in her chapter titled "Learner corpora to inform testing and assessment", takes a different perspective and examines how learner corpora can inform English language testing and assessment particularly in the area of operationalizing proficiency in a quantitative way and across different L1s at different levels.

Part IV includes seven chapters and is engaged with the pedagogical approach that applies corpora in the classroom, *Data-driven learning*. Farr and Karlsen give a broad outlook by reviewing "DDL pedagogy, participants, and perspectives". In their discussion, they illustrate the successes of this approach in tertiary settings while their case study shows the challenges of applying this approach in one Norwegian secondary school context. Meunier's chapter titled "Revamping DDL: Affordances of digital technology" primarily discusses critical issues of DDL and proposes concrete examples of how DDL can be revitalized with the opportunities new technologies offer. Coccetta's chapter, "Multimodal corpora and concordancing in DDL" familiarizes us with research into multimodal corpora with respect to their application to DDL. Furthermore, she argues that since the learner/researcher has the agency to the fundamental principle of DDL, they are the drivers of the process of reinventing DDL through multimodal interaction. An emerging area in the discussions of corpora and DDL is that of "DDL for younger learners" as Crosthwaite's chapter describes. He discusses the opportunities that hands-on corpus use by pre-tertiary (language) learners can offer to DDL and outlines the kinds of challenges we face in successful implementation of DDL with younger learners. The next two chapters center around the learner using corpora.

Pérez-Paredes, in "How learners use corpora", examines the ways learners consult corpora in an instructed second language acquisition setting. He offers a critical analysis of the research methodology to investigate learners' corpus use, such as the role of manual logs and computer tracking of learners' activities when working with corpora. He discusses alternative research designs, new, emerging research methods, and new platforms for corpus use, such as corpus-aided writing and mobile language learning as future directions. Charles's chapter titled "Corpora and autonomous language learning" asserts that the development of autonomous learning has been a key aspect of corpus pedagogy since the beginning of corpus-related practices and DDL. Three core issues are addressed in the chapter: how learner autonomy has supported corpus-based classes, how teachers' roles have changed to more of a facilitator in these classrooms, and what role available resources play in promoting autonomous learning. The final chapter in this section by Timmis and Templeton puts "DDL for English language teaching in perspective". They critically review research into the pedagogic potential of DDL and conclude that DDL should be part of every teacher's repertoire. They caution, however, that understanding the context in which teachers apply this, or a modified version of DDL, is critical to success.

Finally, Part V, *Corpora and corpus tools for English Language Teaching,* of the *Handbook*, houses five chapters. The chapter by Hendry and Sheepy titled "Evaluating corpus analysis tools for the classroom" claims that corpus tools are often expensive and not very user-friendly, hence jeopardizing their wide application. The authors argue that evaluating the usability of corpus tools is essential before using it for instruction and they illustrate the application of usability heuristics as they evaluate three corpus analysis tools: Lextutor, AntConc, and LancsBox. In her chapter titled "Building corpora for ELT", Jablonkai proposes a comprehensive model for corpus design and corpus creation relying on theoretical and practical considerations. She takes us through corpus compilation as she outlines the multiple considerations, decisions, and steps that go into building a corpus specifically for specialized and pedagogic corpora for English language teaching. Hartwell and Karif, in their chapter titled "Parallel corpora in ELT", outline three case studies through which they illustrate how parallel corpora can be of interest to language teachers and learners. They discuss caveats of parallel corpora and conclude with reflections on technological advances stemming from artificial intelligence that offer a multitude of future opportunities and potential for parallel corpora and its use for language learning. In the chapter "Automated syntactic analysis for ELT", Lu, Casal, and Liu examine the affordances of automated syntactic analysis (ASA) for language teaching. More specifically, they present three ways that ASA can contribute to language teaching, namely, grammar acquisition (identifying, highlighting, and creating exercises on target syntactic features), parsing pedagogical texts and presenting them in a modified format to help processing, and finally, rhetorical/functional analysis of texts to aid learners' awareness of genre-specific form–function relationships. The final chapter in this section is by Leńko-Szymańska titled "Training teachers and learners to use corpora". After critically reviewing current practices of teacher and learner training based on empirical evidence, the chapter argues for a more robust model for teacher and learner training that would emphasize the integration of data-driven activities with other classroom procedures and tasks.

Concluding remarks

We hope that this *Handbook* contributes to the transformative change in English language teaching that was brought about by corpus research and applications in the past few decades. The chapters in this collection demonstrate how corpus research can inform language course syllabi and materials design and how corpus consultation can be integrated and normalized in English language teaching. Researchers new to the field might find the reviews of core issues, current debates, and further readings of individual topics useful. At the same time, we hope that the directions for further research outlined in the chapters will inspire future innovative studies. We believe that the *Handbook* will provide food for thought for both established and novice researchers as well as instructors in the field.

References

Ackerley, K. (2017). Effects of corpus-based instruction on phraseology in learner English. *Language Learning & Technology, 21*(3), 195–216. http://llt.msu.edu/issues/october2017/ackerley.pdf

Biber, D., Conrad, S., & Reppen, R. (1998). *Corpus linguistics. Investigating language structure and use.* Cambridge University Press.

Biber, D., Johansson, S., Leech, G., Conrad, S., & Finegan, E. (1999). *Longman grammar of spoken and written English.* Longman.

Boulton, A. (2012). Hands-on/hands-off: Alternative approaches to data-driven learning. In J. Thomas & A. Boulton (Eds.), *Input, process, and product: Developments in teaching and language corpora* (pp. 152–168). Masaryk University Press.

Boulton, A., & Vyatkina, N. (2021). Thirty years of data-driven learning: Taking stock and charting new directions over time. *Language Learning & Technology, 25*(3), 66–89. https://doi.org/10125/73450

Chambers, A. (2019). Towards the corpus revolution? Bridging the research-practice gap. *Language Teaching, 52*(4), 460–475. https://doi.org/10.1017/S0261444819000089

Charles, M. (2014). Getting the corpus habit: EAP students' long-term use of personal corpora. *English for Specific Purposes, 35*(1), 30–40. https://doi.org/10.1016/j.esp.2013.11.004

Chen, M., & Flowerdew, J. (2018). Introducing data-driven learning to PhD students for research writing purposes: A territory-wide project in Hong Kong. *English for Specific Purposes, 50*, 97–112. https://doi.org/10.1016/j.esp.2017.11.004

Conrad, S. (2000). Will corpus linguistics revolutionize grammar teaching in the 21st century? *TESOL Quarterly, 34*(3), 548–560. https://doi.org/10.4324/9780203905029

Friginal, E. (2018). *Corpus linguistics for English teachers.* Routledge.

Granger, S. (Ed.). (1998). *Learner English on computer.* Longman.

Jablonkai, R. R., & Čebron, N. (2021). Undergraduate students' responses to a corpus-based ESP course with DIY corpora. In M. Charles & A. Frankenberg-Garcia (Eds.), *Corpora in ESP/EAP writing instruction* (pp. 100–120). Routledge. https://doi.org/10.4324/9781003001966-5-8

Johns, T. (1991). Should you be persuaded: Two samples of data-driven learning materials. Classroom concordancing. *ELR Journal, 4*, 1–16.

Lee, D., & Swales, J. (2006). A corpus-based EAP course for NNS doctoral students: Moving from available specialized corpora to self-compiled corpora. *English for Specific Purposes, 25*(1), 56–75.

Leech, G. (1997). Teaching and language corpora: A convergence. In A. Wichmann, S. Fligelstone, & T. McEnery (Eds.), *Teaching and language corpora* (pp. 1–23). Longman.

McEnery, T., Xiao, R., & Tono, Y. (2006). *Corpus-based language studies.* Routledge.

Pérez-Paredes, P. (2019). A systematic review of the uses and spread of corpora and data-driven learning in CALL research during 2011–2015. *Computer Assisted Language Learning, 35*, 36–61. https://doi.org/10.1080/09588221.2019.1667832

Tognini-Bonelli, E. (2001). *Corpus linguistics at work.* Benjamins.

PART I

English language teaching and learning informed by language corpora

1

A HISTORICAL OVERVIEW OF USING CORPORA IN ENGLISH LANGUAGE TEACHING

Jiajin Xu

1.1 Introduction

Dating back to the late 1940s and the early 1950s, the Italian Jesuit priest Roberto Busa started to work on his *Index Thomisticus*, a machine-generated concordance of the writings of Saint Thomas Aquinas, cataloging 11 million Latin words with technical support from IBM (Busa, 1950, 1951; Winter, 1999). Another computerized biblical scholarship project was the concordance of the English Bible, namely, *Nelson's Complete Concordance of the Revised Standard Version Bible* (Ellison, 1957). Such pioneering work in the "digital humanities" was soon matched in linguistics by the ground-breaking Brown Corpus (Francis & Kučera, 1964; Kučera & Francis, 1967). This carefully sampled computer corpus of American written English has become the foundation of modern corpus linguistics and has foreseen a fast-growing area in linguistics over the last few decades. But the impetus for compiling text collections, corpora to support research and teaching materials can be traced back to the early 19th century. This chapter gives a historical overview of using corpora for English language teaching.

The provenance of corpus linguistics goes back a long way in history if we do not restrict it exclusively to the use of texts in electronic form (Johansson, 2011; Stubbs, 2018). In defining corpus linguistics, we share Fries' (1940, ix) argument that "[o]ne cannot produce a book dealing with language without being indebted to many who have earlier struggled with the problems and made great advances". Studies that adopt the representative sampling of authentic language data and make statistical claims of language will all be broadly regarded as examples of corpus research.

This chapter starts by sketching the history of corpus use in language-related projects, and then reviews the compilation of early English frequency lists in Section 1.2. Section 1.3 illustrates the application of corpora to the development of reference books, with special reference to pedagogical grammars and dictionaries. Section 1.4 concerns the preparation of course materials and methodological approaches using corpora. The final section outlines future avenues for corpus-informed English language teaching.

1.2 The compilation of English frequency lists

This section discusses the compilation of lexical frequency lists in the early 19th century to improve spelling skills (Section 1.2.1) and moves on to Thorndike's works since the 1920s

DOI: 10.4324/9781003002901-3

providing the impetus for idiom lists, syntax lists, and semantic frequency lists in light of corpus representativeness and range statistics (Section 1.2.2).

1.2.1 Early lexical frequency lists

In the field of English language teaching, the utilization of corpus-based quantitative methods relying on a large body of natural texts dates back to the early 19th century. Around 1820, John Freeman compiled an English frequency list based on the corpus of cca. 20,000 words to teach adults to read.[1] In 1838, Pitman (1843) developed two lists (one alphabetical and the other numerical) of frequently used words based on 10,000 words taken from 20 books written to train stenographers (shorthand writers). About half a century later, in 1897, a large-scale replica project of this stenographer-oriented frequency list, *Häufigkeitswörterbuch der deutschen Sprache*, or "A Frequency Dictionary of the German Language", was completed by Fredrick Kaeding (1897).

Since the 1910s, a large number of pre-electronic corpus projects have emerged with considerable momentum. Such early corpus research, mainly based in the United States and the Far East, was primarily motivated to facilitate language teaching.

Among the first projects of this kind were Ayres' (1913, 1915, 1920), who compiled a corpus of 2,000 personal and business letters from 12 sources, amounting to 110,160 running words. In the project reports, a Zipfian distribution (Ayres, 1913) of the most frequent words in correspondence was plotted. The most frequent word "I" implies that correspondence is a more colloquial genre than the most frequent word "the" in written or balanced corpora.

Ayres (1913, p. 10) concludes the paper by saying that,

> [t]his seems to be good evidence that a useful spelling list cannot be compiled by sitting at the desk and deciding which words people ought to know how to spell. What we must know is rather which are the words that ordinary people need to know how to spell.

This comment highlighted the striking difference between the 414 spelling words required by the National Education Association (NEA) of the United States at the time, and the actual vocabulary used by common people. Seventy percent of the NEA words "did not occur at all" (Ayres, 1913, p. 10) in the letters analyzed.

However, Ayres' quantitatively driven project was by no means the only one. Cook and O'Shea (1914, pp. 226–227) compared vocabulary found in a total of 200,000 words from the family correspondence of the 13 adults with three popular expert-compiled English spellers, and only 70 per cent of the speller words appeared in the letters. According to Cook and O'Shea (1914), the spellers did not place emphasis on what was most needed by "common people".

Similar cases include Jones' (1915) investigation and counting of 15,000,000 words of texts produced by 1,050 students from second to eighth grade and yielded 4,532 different words, i.e. word types in present-day corpus terms. Another characteristic of Jones' project is the grading of spelling vocabularies across grade levels.

The research purpose of the projects at this phase was primarily to address the problem of spelling, which was considered a central part of literacy education at school. During the next phase, we see more quantitative projects focusing on the language learning of both pupils and adults.

1.2.2 1920s–1940s: Thorndike (1921) and others

A widespread "Vocabulary Control Movement" (Cowie, 1999; Hornby, 1953; Howatt, 1984) emerged in the 1920s–1930s with more innovative curriculum goals and pedagogical practices, such as the teaching of reading and writing, syllabus design, materials development, and assessment, in addition to the teaching of spelling. The vocabulary limitation enterprise fell into two overarching approaches: one subjective and the other objective. The subjective approach was preferred by some British ELT scholars in the UK (Charles Ogden and I. A. Richards), Japan (Harold Palmer and A. S. Hornby), India, and Canada (Michael West). They adopted an intuitive approach, also known as an "armchair" approach, to the so-called BASIC Vocabulary (Ogden, 1930), standing for British American Scientific International Commercial, and the minimum adequate vocabulary (Swenson & West, 1934; West, 1931, 1934) or General Service List (Faucett *et al.*, 1936; West, 1953).

American scholars, on the other hand, mainly used the objective approach to obtain minimum adequate vocabularies through quantitative methods. Thorndike's (1921) *Word Book* of 10,000 words has been regarded as a pioneering, quantitatively motivated English word list based on a large collection of authentic texts. Thorndike's work served as a key impetus for more frequency lists, not only word lists, but also idiom lists, syntax lists, and semantic frequency lists. The quantitative studies in this period outperformed those before the 1920s in terms of language varieties, aspects of language (i.e. lexis, idioms, and syntax), and improvements in methodology.

The first edition of Thorndike's *Word Book* was significantly extended from 10,000 to 20,000 words (Thorndike, 1931) and further to 30,000 words (Thorndike & Lorge, 1944) as the counts were updated and additional texts were included. Education scholars in the United States, inspired by Thorndike's work on the English language, compiled a number of frequency lists of other languages, such as French (Henmon, 1924; Vander Beke, 1929), Spanish (Buchanan, 1927), German (Morgan, 1928), and Brazilian Portuguese (Brown *et al.*, 1945). This shift from mother tongue to foreign language teaching extended beyond word counts to idiom counts in French (Cheydleur, 1929), Spanish (Keniston, 1929), German (Hauch, 1929), and Brazilian Portuguese (Brown & Shane, 1951), as well as syntax counts in Spanish (Keniston, 1937) and French (Clark & Poston, 1943). Such developments in counting phraseologies and grammatical categories, however, were not reflected in the frequency counts of English.

Semantic frequency lists of English were compiled by Lorge (1937, 1949), drawing on the senses laid down in *The Oxford English Dictionary*. Lorge's semantic frequency counts were later incorporated by Faucett *et al.* (1936) in their *Interim Report on Vocabulary Selection*, and eventually published by the frequently cited West (1953) as *A General Service List of English Words: With Semantic Frequencies and a Supplementary Word-List for the Writing of Popular Science and Technology*. Moreover, the GSL (General Service List) words were set as the first two default base lists of the vocabulary tools Range (Nation, 2005) and AntWordProfiler (Anthony, 2021) developed decades later.

Almost all studies in this period took full account of text material representativeness. Keniston's Spanish corpus (1929) is a case in point as he included texts from genres such as drama, fiction, miscellaneous prose, newspapers and periodicals, and technical prose. At the same time, the sampling frame for these genres is immediately reminiscent of the widely known Brown Corpus genre categorization (Francis & Kučera, 1964), namely, press, general prose, learned (i.e. academic) writing, and fiction. In Keniston's corpus, regional varieties of Spanish (e.g. Castilian, Peninsular, and Latin American Spanish) were also considered when collecting texts. Interestingly and surprisingly, Fries (1940) stressed, in great detail, the aspects such as authenticity, demographic representativeness, scientific sampling, and the diversity of topics/situations of corpora without adopting these contemporary corpus linguistics terms.

Another consistently followed principle in text selection and counting is range. In the introductory documentation of most studies, terms like range, distribution, "widely used", "units", and "sources" were used to illustrate this range principle alongside the frequency principle. This methodological principle was implemented since the work of Thorndike (1921) and was adhered to in almost all other studies during this period. Hence, the word/idiom/syntax counts were assigned relative frequencies as well as range statistics across different text units or sources. Furthermore, Fries (1940) called our attention to the historical differences, regional differences, literary and colloquial differences, and social and class differences in English. The differences or variational patterns of grammar points were represented by raw and relative frequencies in the 41 tables of Fries' grammar. Fries (1940) saw his book as "a study of the real grammar of [p]resent-day English [which] has never been used in the schools" (p. 285) and advised that "[w]e must agree to stimulate among our pupil[s'] observation of actual usage" (p. 291).

Regarding the aspects of language, the examination of idioms and syntax steered frequency studies beyond the word level. The idioms in question refer to both conventionalized expressions (e.g. *part and parcel*), whose meaning cannot be inferred from the component words, and lexical phrases (e.g. *pick up*). The Spanish, French, and German idiom lists were all published in 1929, which apparently predates Palmer's (1933) book-length treatment of collocations in English. Moreover, the idiom lists were based on a large quantity of natural texts and were statistically tabulated; however, Palmer's *Second Interim Report on English Collocations* was a mere list of phrases without any reference to naturally occurring texts or quantitative information. The phrasal counts of Spanish and other languages involved such constructions as compound conjunctions, compound prepositions, and verbs requiring a preposition before a complement, which naturally progressed to the quantitative description of grammatical constructions. Keniston's (1937) *Spanish Syntax List*, and Clark and Poston's (1943) *French Syntax List* followed the same range and frequency principles to quantify the full array of grammatical categories in the two languages. Besides the syntax lists, Stormzand and O'Shea (1924) took a contrastive approach to diagnosing the "excess or deficiency" (Stormzand & O'Shea, 1924, p. 48) (i.e. overuse or underuse in corpus research terms) of certain grammatical categories between adults and school children or university students. Development across grade levels was tallied and compared to gauge the progress or decline in learner performance.

Now, in the current cloud-computing age, online corpora and frequency lists are more easily available. Among these are BNC (British National Corpus) frequency lists (Leech *et al.*, 2001) and the COCA (Corpus of Contemporary American English)-based frequency dictionary of American English (Davis & Gardner, 2010). They have updated similar, previously published American English word books such as those in the 1920s–1940s and rendered them significantly more stable and reliable resources given the representativeness and size of the corpora (see Coxhead, this volume; Szudarski, this volume).

1.3 Corpora for the development of reference books

This section provides the scholarly context for the writing of pedagogical grammars, covering both systemic and comprehensive pedagogical grammars as well as some smaller and more specialized grammars (Section 1.3.1). Section 1.3.2 outlines the development of corpus-informed dictionary compilation.

1.3.1 The writing of pedagogical grammars

Unlike the numerous frequency lists, corpus-based pedagogical grammars are much less prominent during this time; they are, however, by no means insignificant. Fries' (1940) pre-electronic corpus-based English grammar is a much-neglected work. Fries, as a structuralist applied linguist, produced his *American English Grammar* on the basis of a representative corpus. The grammar book was a key reference for his seminal work titled *Teaching and Learning English as a Foreign Language* (Fries, 1945). Additionally, Fries (1940) plotted the diachronic grammatical change of English, for instance, the co-occurrence of first-, second-, and third-person pronouns with *shall* and *will* use, from 1560 to 1920. Fries (1940) also made comparative tabulations of verb prepositional/particle collocations across standard and vernacular English varieties. A decade later, Fries (1952) went further to record and transcribe the conversations of speakers of standard English in the North Central United States of cca. 250,000 words, based on which he wrote a grammar many years prior to the *Survey of English Usage* project and Quirk *et al.*'s (1972, 1985) grammars.

The Quirk-led *Survey of English Usage* and its influential Longman grammar series (1972, 1973a, 1973b, 1985, 1990) have been one of the most influential pedagogical grammar projects in the latter half of the 20th century. A clearly descriptive approach was adopted to develop the grammar. However, grammar books such as that of Quirk *et al.* (1985) do not incorporate much explicit corpus information. For instance, probabilistic information is only occasionally provided for the grammatical categories described, or with reference to the so-called The Quirk Corpus.[2]

Collins COBUILD English Grammar (Sinclair, 1990) is a systemic functional linguistics-oriented pedagogical grammar informed by corpus evidence. Typical grammatical patterns of transitivity, modality, cohesion, etc., and all the example sentences were chosen from the Birmingham Collection of English texts.

Biber *et al.* (1999) described grammatical categories and also discussed them in quantitative terms as presented in the Longman Grammar of Spoken and Written English Corpus. The other novelty in Biber *et al.*'s (1999) work was the presentation of corpus-informed register variation patterns across the conversation, news, fiction, and academic discourse in both British and American English.

The three pedagogical grammar series represented by their core grammar books, that is, Quirk *et al.* (1985), Sinclair (1990), and Biber *et al.* (1999), all have their associated concise edition or classroom edition under such names as "student grammar", "student's grammar", "basic grammar", "student grammar workbook", and "concise grammar", in order to suit classroom learning and self-study scenarios.

Apart from the big three, some smaller and more specialized corpus-based grammars also figure prominently in the ELT literature. Thornbury's (2004) *Natural Grammar* is a grammar of 100-and-something grammatical or abstract words, such as *the, do, in, much,* and *thing*. The usage of the words is presented in the form of colligations/grammatical patterns, collocation/set phrases, and example sentences/concordance lines. Conrad and Biber (2009) illustrate how register variation across speech and writing can be taught with explicit grammar patterns and situationalized activities. The typical structure of the grammar activities in the book is noticing in context, discourse-based analysis, and writing- or conversation-focused practice. McCarthy *et al.* (2009) opened up an important avenue for more grammar in the field of English for specific purposes. This *Cambridge Business Corpus-based ESP* grammar organizes major grammar points as per discourse functions or activities in business English communication. For instance, how to use the passive in business correspondence, and how to use conditionals in business negotiation, etc. Common to the three grammar books is that they are communicatively focused and organize grammatical points according to their functions in authentic discourse.

1.3.2 *The development of dictionaries*

Parallel to the compilation of frequency lists and pedagogical grammar is a corpus-based approach to dictionary writing. West and Endicott's (1935) *The New Method English Dictionary* is regarded as the earliest learner's English dictionary (Cowie, 1999). The essential idea of the new method is its 1,455 most common or important defining vocabulary items (a.k.a. definition vocabulary) based on "reading counts" of language materials (West, 1935, p. 5). The New Method was also the name for a series of Longman English coursebooks and readers in which graded frequency lists were adopted to control the reading difficulty of the passages. Another equally ground-breaking learner's dictionary, *The Thorndike-Century Junior Dictionary* (Thorndike, 1935) somehow escaped lexicographical scholars' attention. Thorndike (1935) is even more corpus-informed than West and Endicott (1935) in terms of both macrostructure and microstructure arrangement. For example, entries listed in the Junior Dictionary were based on Thorndike's word books, namely, English frequency lists. At the end of each word entry, the frequency level was annotated numerically to each headword from the first thousandth (e.g. *be*...1) to the twentieth thousandth (e.g. *authorization*...20). The principle of word sense arrangement prioritizes common uses before rare uses and easily understandable uses before difficult uses, rather than in the sequence of their historical development.

The Collins COBUILD English Dictionary (Sinclair, 1987) (CCED) is probably the bona fide game changer of dictionary making in the 20th century. Corpus methodology is inherent in almost every bit of the dictionary. For instance, the selection of headwords is based on the frequency count of all English words in a 7.3-million-word corpus (initially called the Main Corpus, later referred to as Bank of English). The main innovation of the CCED is its phraseological description of the entry word. For example, the typical collocation of the word *brink*, namely, *on the brink of*, is in the first place embedded in the whole-sentence definition "If you are *on the brink of* something, usually something important, terrible, or exciting, you are just about to do it or experience it" (p. 173). The contextualized definition is itself a condensed piece of learning material. At the end of the entry, the colligational pattern is summarized as "N-SING: usu. on/to/from the N of n". The three prepositions separated by slashes are ordered according to their probability of occurrence in the corpus. Two example sentences in the same dictionary entry, namely, "Their economy is teetering *on the brink of* collapse" and "Failure to communicate had brought the two nations *to the brink of* war", were taken from the Birmingham Corpus to illustrate the characteristic uses of *on the brink of* and *to the brink of*. The co-occurrence of *brink* with *collapse* and *brink* with *war* implies the negative semantic prosody of the entry word. The extended-unit-of-meaning model, that is, the phraseological framework, has been systematically implemented in the CCED.

Recent phraseology-informed learner's English dictionaries can also be found in the EAP and ESP fields. The Louvain EAP dictionary (LEAD) (Granger & Paquot, 2015) is a web-based EAP dictionary with a special focus on collocations and recurrent phrases based on the academic component of the British National Corpus, which develops learners' awareness of discipline-specific phraseologies. The dictionary content is customizable to suit the learner's L1 background according to the information gathered from multinational learner English corpora. Discourse functions, such as defining and exemplification, are also available as starting points for dictionary lookup. Another example is Xu's (2020) work who compiled a hotel English dictionary for tourism and hotel management students, in which frequent collocational patterns serve as a key element to link words to real-life situations. For instance, *room rate*, *room service*, and *room attendant* are listed as useful phrases underneath the headword *room*. To *do one's room* is a typical colloquial expression of hotel English, as illustrated in the example sentence "When would you like me to *do your room*, sir?" A similar domain-specific corpus approach will be adopted in 17 additional ESP dictionaries.

More recently, some advances in corpus analytical technology have expedited the writing of dictionaries. Sketch Engine is a lexicographically motivated online tool that has been adopted by major publishers. The online system can sort the typical collocations of the search word according to their grammatical relations. The fine-tuned collocations help dictionary entry writers to identify the characteristic usage patterns of target entry words. Sketch Engine also has a feature called GDEX "Good Dictionary Examples", which allows users to select dictionary friendly sentences according to criteria such as sentence length and complexity, safe topics, and the presence of difficult and low-frequency words.

In summary, corpus evidence provides quantitative information to guarantee the commonness or typicality of a word and is capable of distinguishing the senses of a word in a general or specialized domain of real-life communication.

1.4 Corpus-based materials and pedagogical approaches

This section discusses the development of course materials (Section 1.4.1) as well as methodological approaches (Section 1.4.2) using corpora. The latter includes data-driven learning and the lexical approach. Finally, research on learner corpora (Section 1.4.3) is introduced.

1.4.1 The development of course materials

The ELT course materials in this discussion mainly cover core coursebooks, supplementary materials, simplified or adapted texts, and materials evaluation. What corpora can offer to materials development includes real-life language samples, vocabulary control, a phraseological approach to lexis, and grammar. *Collins COBUILD English Course (CCEC)* is a three-level series (Willis & Willis, 1988); *Touchstone* is a four-level series (targeted at The Common European Framework of Reference (CEFR): B2 – C1) (McCarthy *et al.*, 2006, 2014); *Viewpoint* is a two-level series (targeted at CEFR: A1 – B1)[3] (McCarthy *et al.*, 2012); *On Speaking Terms: Real Language for Real Life* is a two-level series (Santana-Williamson, 2010), and *Grammar and Beyond* are a four-level series (Reppen, 2012; Reppen *et al.*, 2019). They are the major English corpus-informed coursebook series currently on the market. In *On Speaking Terms*, the content is said to have been transcribed from real-life interactions. In other words, the authenticity of the language is emphasized. However, the typicality of lexis and grammar based on the quantitative analysis of corpus data is not one of the major concerns of the coursebook design, nor is explicit information on phraseology taken into account. *On Speaking Terms* is, therefore, less representative of a corpus-based English coursebook. *CCEC* and *Touchstone* adopt the corpus approach in a more systematic manner. For instance, both series rely heavily on corpus-generated frequency lists as their primary criteria for sequencing or grading lexical and grammatical content. Thus, the scope and order of vocabulary and grammar points will be in a reasonably stepwise progression in terms of linguistic complexity. The two series both use task-oriented design to engage students in communicative activities. The listening-speaking coursebook, *Touchstone*, has an "In Conversation" section in almost every unit of the book, which is an overt illustration of how frequently a linguistic item is in the corpus of naturally occurring discourse. For example, Unit 5 of the Touchstone Level 1 student book states that "*I mean* is one of the top 15 expressions" (p. 49). Two typical usages of *I mean* are interpreted by the Cambridge English Corpus, namely, "to repeat your ideas" and "to say more about something" (McCarthy, 2004, p. 15). These two most widely used discourse functions of *I mean* are presented to students as a must-know conversation strategy under the heading "Strategy Plus". The remainder of the section is composed of a dialog completion task and a role-play of the two conversational strategies of *I mean*. Similar corpus discoveries of spoken English are systematically incorporated into the six levels of the coursebook series, designed for learners from elementary to advanced proficiency levels.

The *Grammar and Beyond* series (Reppen, 2012) were designed as a grammar coursebook, but the exercises and/or tasks involved practice in all four language skills, with an emphasis on writing. Each unit starts with a "Grammar in the Real World" section to contextualize the use of the grammar point (e.g. demonstratives or possessives) with a real-life discourse sample. All instances of the grammar point are highlighted in boldface to enable noticing. Further corpus resources are presented in the "Data from the Real World" section in the form of charts or notes. For example, a bar chart is used to show the striking quantitative difference between indefinite pronouns with *-one* and *-body* in formal and informal registers (Reppen, 2012, p. 234). Students' attention is directed to the preference of indefinite pronouns with *one* (e.g. *someone, anyone,* and *everyone*) for writing and formal speaking, while indefinite pronouns ending in *-body* (e.g. *somebody, anybody,* and *everybody*) for informal speaking. The "Avoid Common Mistakes" section is based on the analysis of a learner corpus. Frequently committed grammatical mistakes by learners are marked with strikethroughs and correct uses are shown in different font colors.

One shared feature of *CCEC, Touchstone* and *Grammar and Beyond* is that authentic and typical language content is woven into a carefully crafted communicative syllabus (McCarthy, 2004).

In addition to general-purpose English coursebooks, English for Academic Purposes (EAP) coursebooks have also been developed, informed by corpus-based genre studies. Swales and Feak's (2009a, 2009b) *Michigan series in English for Academic and Professional Purposes* is a case in point. The booklets in the series focus on how to write abstracts, introductions, literature reviews, methods, results, discussions, and conclusions. The books provide a clear account of how sub-genres of research papers can be well organized by the discourse conventions of academic communities across disciplines. Language foci such as tense, reporting verb use, and genre-specific discourse strategies are summarized from authentic academic texts.

In addition to coursebook materials, corpus methods can be used in materials evaluation to measure the textual difficulty of reading passages. The Coh-Metrix (McNamara *et al.,* 2014), Range (Nation, 2005), AntWordProfiler (Anthony, 2021), and Kristopher Kyle's tools (Kyle, 2021) are popular tools for analyzing reading texts and gauging their lexical, grammatical, and even discoursal features. In many cases, major ELT publishers conduct an in-house text analysis before the coursebooks are printed. Teachers and materials evaluators can assess coursebooks using on-the-fly tools.

1.4.2 Data-driven learning, the Lexcial Syllabus, and the Lexical Approach

The use of real language data and frequency lists for vocabulary or language control in ELT had been practiced long before 1990, when more systematic discussions on corpus-based syllabus design and teaching methodology were underway. Tribble and Jones (1990) started to experiment with printed concordances in language classrooms. The approach was meant to facilitate learning, and the intake of vocabulary and grammar in an inductive manner, where linguistic meaning was derived from its context, and patterns of grammatical structures were discovered. When the approach was proposed (Johns, 1991), and later called data-driven learning (DDL), printouts of concordance lines were the primary materials for grammar and vocabulary teaching. *Collins COBUILD Concordance Samplers* (e.g. Thompson, 1995) were specifically developed for this purpose. One of the most frequently cited DDL resources is Tim Johns' Kibbitzers[4] – the language teaching materials used for EAP consultation sessions between Tim Johns and international students at Birmingham University. The dozens of the Kibbitzer cases clearly demonstrate that the DDL approach can be applied to lexical, grammatical, and discoursal levels of English teaching. Meanwhile, the native English-speaking tutor (Johns himself) did not have the final say of grammatical correctness or acceptability, but the corpus evidence, especially collocational patterns, did. The tutor and student worked together to negotiate the correct or acceptable usage against corpus resources.

The direct application of corpus resources in classrooms is connected to the Lexical Syllabus (Willis, 1990) and the Lexical Approach (Lewis, 1993). The former focuses more on the scope and sequence of lexically centered language content in ELT. The latter, however, is conceived of as an English teaching methodology parallel to the grammar-translation method, the audio-lingual method, communicative language teaching, and task-based instruction (Richards & Rodgers, 2014). Both conceptions acknowledge the relation between lexis and grammar as the two ends of a continuum. Lexis or lexical units are of central importance in English learning using this approach. Formulaic sequences or lexical phrases that are units longer than a single word are mentally stored as holistic meaning units; hence, they should be produced as a whole as well in order to achieve native-like selection and fluency (Pawley & Syder, 1983). In actual teaching, learners' awareness of formulaic sequences used in real-life discourse should be raised, and bottom-up discovery learning should be encouraged. The teaching methods are, to some extent, the blend or convergence of corpus-based phraseological analyses and task-based pedagogy.

The concordance printouts of the 1990s have now been upgraded to online DDL systems, resources, and applications. For example, web-based writing aids such as ColloCaid and Writefull, Sketch Engine for Language Learning (SkELL), Just-the-Word, StringNet, LexTutor, and Crosthwaite's short private online course (SPOC) platform, to name but a few. They can provide easy-to-generate concordances, collocational patterns, and sometimes error feedback for learners. Please refer to Part IV (Data-driven learning) in this volume for more dedicated discussions on this topic.

Earlier sections mainly focus on corpus-informed English teaching. The next section will shift to English learning in light of corpus research, especially research on learner English production.

1.4.3 Research with learner and ELF corpora

Learner corpus research (LCR) (see Part III in this volume) was initiated in Europe in the late 1980s and gained momentum in the early 1990s (Granger, 2015; Granger *et al.*, 2015). Granger and her team at the Université Catholique de Louvain have contributed to the development of learner corpus compilation[5] and research. Both the design of learner corpus construction and LCR have worked in the comparative paradigm whose primary foci are the difference in English production between learners and that of the so-called native speakers, as well as the difference in English performance among learners of different first language backgrounds. The comparative methodology of LCR encapsulated in Granger's (1996b, 2015) contrastive interlanguage analysis (CIA) is still the dominant approach to LCR. It is an integrative model of comparison with the aim of diagnosing or predicting the possible first language transfer. CIA has been updated in later years to allow for possible other dimensions (namely "reference varieties") of comparison and to accommodate the English as a Lingua Franca (ELF) view of learner English productions. Features of learner English, sometimes called errors or "foreign-soundingness" (Granger, 1996b, p. 43) in lexis, collocation, grammar, and discourse-pragmatics, can be generalized from comparisons based on corpora.

Among the most cited learner corpora in English is probably the International Corpus of Learner English (ICLE) corpus. It was built as a complementary dataset to the International Corpus of English (ICE) against a big backdrop of comparison between different varieties of English, be them native or non-native (Granger, 1996a, p. 14). Version 1 of ICLE was released in 2002, totaling 2.5 million words of essays written by learners from 11 different mother tongue backgrounds, including essays by students studying in Britain and the US. ICLE 2.0 and 3.0 were made publicly available in 2009 and 2020, respectively. A sister project, the Louvain International Database of Spoken English Interlanguage (LINDSEI), was intended to conceptualize spoken interlanguage English using a similar, comparative model, and has been extended to the Multilingual Student Translation (MUST) learner translation project, and the Longitudinal Database of Learner English (LONGDALE) project.

LCR in other regions of the world has its own localized priorities for learner corpus construction and research. For example, British and Scandinavian scholars (e.g. Nesi and Gardner, 2012 and Hasselgård, 2017, respectively) explore more research avenues of student assignments of an EAP nature. US LCR scholars (e.g. Staples *et al.*, 2018) tend to consider register variation as a central concern when constructing and investigating learner corpora.

The ELF perspective of so-called non-native English production (Wu & Lei, this volume) is of special interest in the broad sense of interlanguage analysis. Examples of these are the Seidlhofer's VOICE (Vienna-Oxford International Corpus of English), Mauranen's ELFA (spoken academic English as a lingua franca), and Ishikawa's (International Corpus Network of Asian Learners of English (ICNALE) projects. This line of research impels us to reconsider contentious issues, such as non-nativeness and errors.

1.5 Future directions in corpus-informed English language teaching

The review above provides the following insights for future work: 1) More learning-driven corpora are needed. 2) More user-friendly corpus analysis tools need to be developed. 3) Experimentation into the integration of corpus resources with overall teaching objectives is strongly recommended. 4) More research on sociocultural and/or cognitive mechanisms should be carried out to validate the effectiveness of corpus application in English language teaching.

First, to facilitate learning, there is a need for more bespoke corpora that match learners' ages, current language proficiencies, and even their individualized learning needs (Jablonkai, this volume). The first two factors can be addressed by adding labels or annotations to the text in the corpus. For instance, corpus builders can take advantage of the six levels of CEFR, A1 to C2, to suggest that they are suitable for basic, intermediate, or proficient learners. In addition to the overall difficulty of the texts, text length, vocabulary coverage, and difficult word percentage can be automatically computed and marked. This provides the option for learners to be exposed to more comprehensible input texts. To cater to learners' personalized learning needs, for example, students of nursing, management, or history should be able to work with a corpus on their respective subject, or to create a sub-corpus in a larger general-purpose corpus. Lastly, the emerging multimodal corpora (e.g. including video as well as text for spoken corpora) can offer rich contextual resources for language learning.

Second, we cannot make the best of corpora for language teaching without friendly corpus tools. The current off-the-shelf software (e.g. AntConc) and online query systems (e.g. English-Corpora.org, Sketch Engine) can serve well for research purposes, but the learning curve of the tools for students is still too steep. The ideal design of a student-friendly corpus tool should be as intuitive as possible and should not require additional instruction for use; rather, it should provide sufficient contextual clues around the language item in focus (Hendry and Sheepy, this volume). Its main functionalities should cover but not be limited to frequency lists and the distribution of linguistic items in context (e.g. collocates, genre distribution). The visualization of analytical results may also be an additional highlight of the tool. The next generation of corpus tools should work with cross-platform designs, which can be used on PCs, Macs, web browsers, and mobile applications. One last point is that no matter what tool is used for classroom hands-on tasks or self-study, it should be able to foster autonomous learning, which is an inherent property of DDL (Charles, this volume).

Third, the lack of integration into the overall English curriculum might be a major drawback of the corpus approach to language teaching. More dialog and collaboration with language educators, practitioners, and ELT materials developers should be encouraged in order to bridge rich language data, and diversified, as well as individualistic learning needs. Despite the fact that corpus resources and tools can offer multiple affordances to English teaching and learning and scaffold learners at various stages of their learning, it is still questionable whether the entire English curriculum can rely on corpora. We should strive to work out an optimal mode of integration with corpus resources, methodology, and language teaching.

Fourth, the cognitive and sociological developments of corpus application to English teaching would be worthwhile topics. This research aims to explore the strengths and inadequacies of this approach. Psycholinguistic and neurolinguistic methods (e.g. reaction time, eye-tracking, and event-related potentials) as well as user logs in a registration-based web corpus system can address the issues in due course. On the learning side, the investigation of learner English has been on the cognitive aspect of learner English; for instance, conceptual metaphors (e.g. Nacey, 2013) and constructions (Gilquin, 2010) will see more of such studies. Methodologically, the multifactorial analysis (Gries, 2018; Gries *et al.*, 2020) might engender a new wave of LCR, because it considers richer contextual variables of learner performance. Gries (2018) recommends the use of regression modeling and other multivariate statistics to upgrade previous monofactorial analyses.

Acknowledgments

The author would like to acknowledge the funding provided by the Beijing Municipal Social Science Foundation project (20YYB013) "The History of Corpus Linguistics" and the support of the National Research Centre for Foreign Language Education, and the National Research Centre for State Language Capacity at Beijing Foreign Studies University. The author is extremely grateful to the editors and anonymous reviewers for their helpful comments and suggestions. The author would also like to thank Dr. Xiuling Xu and Ms. Jialei Li for reading an early version of the chapter.

Notes

1 On page 170 of a letter to the editor of *The Phonotypic Journal*, Freeman's (1820) frequency lists were reprinted.
2 Learn about the corpus at https://www.ucl.ac.uk/english-usage/about/history.htm.

3 *Viewpoint* series is the advanced level for the *Touchstone* series; hence, *Touchstone* is used subsequently to refer to all six levels of the combined series.
4 Tim Johns' Kibbitzers can be found at https://lexically.net/TimJohns/Kibbitzer/timeap3.htm.
5 "Learner corpora around the world" bookmark page at https://uclouvain.be/en/research-institutes/ilc/cecl/learner-corpora-around-the-world.html.

Further reading

Friginal, E. (2018). *Corpus linguistics for English teachers: Tools, online resources, and classroom activities*. Routledge. This is an ELT teacher-friendly guidebook with rich classroom activities, lesson plans, and most importantly, step-by-step tutorials of corpus tools and resources.

Granger, S., Gilquin, G., & Meunier, F. (Eds.). (2015). *The Cambridge handbook of learner corpus research*. Cambridge University Press. This is a comprehensive handbook in which a few sections deal with similar issues to the present handbook, such as LCR and second language acquisition, LCR and language teaching.

Leńko-Szymańska, A., & Boulton, A. (Eds.). (2015). *Multiple affordances of language corpora for data-driven learning*. Benjamins. This is a collection of papers that addresses the direct use of corpora in the classroom context. The applications reported concern the improvement of speaking, writing, and translating skills, lexical and grammatical knowledge, as well as English for academic competence in light of corpora.

McCarthy, M. J., McCarten, J., & Sandiford, H. (2005). *Touchstone teacher's edition 1 with audio CD*. Cambridge University Press. This teacher's book contains the full content of *Touchstone Student's Book level 1*, the rationale for how corpus methodology is implemented in the compilation of the coursebook series, and implications for classroom use.

References

Anthony, L. (2021). AntWordProfiler (Version 1.5.1) [Computer Software]. http://www.antlab.sci.waseda.ac.jp

Ayres, L. (1913). *The spelling vocabularies of personal and business letters*. Russell Sage Foundation.

Ayres, L. (1915). *A measuring scale for ability in spelling*. Russell Sage Foundation.

Ayres, L. (1920). The spelling vocabularies of personal and business letters. *The Journal of Education*, 77(10), 261–262, 270.

Biber, D., Johansson, S., Leech, G., Conrad, S., & Finegan, E. (1999). *Longman spoken and written English grammar*. Pearson.

Brown, C., & Shane, M. (1951). *Brazilian Portuguese idiom list: Selected on the basis of range and frequency of occurrence*. Vanderbilt University Press.

Brown, C., Carr, W., & Shane, M. (1945). *A graded word book of Brazilian Portuguese*. Crofts & Co., Inc.

Buchanan, M. (1927). *A graded Spanish word book*. The University of Toronto Press.

Busa, R. (1950). Complete index verborum of works of St. Thomas. *Speculum*, *XXV*(1), 424–425.

Busa, R. (1951). *Sancti Thomae Aquinatis hymnorum ritualium varia specimina concordantiarum: Primo saggio di indici di parole automaticamente composti e stampati da macchine IBM a schede perforate* (A first example of word index automatically compiled and printed by IBM punched card machines). Fratellei Bocca.

Cheydleur, F. (1929). *French idiom list: Based on a count of 1,183,000 running words*. The MacMillan Company.

Clark, R., & Poston, L. (1943). *French syntax list: A statistical study of grammatical usage in contemporary French prose on the basis of range and frequency*. H. Holt and Company.

Conrad, S., & Biber, D. (2009). *Real grammar: A corpus-based approach to English*. Pearson Education.

Cook, W., & O'Shea, M. (1914). *The child and his spelling*. The Bobbs-Merrill Company.

Cowie, A. (1999). *English dictionaries for foreign learners: A history*. Oxford University Press.

Davis, M., & Gardner, D. (2010). *A frequency dictionary of American English: Word sketches, collocates, and thematic lists*. Routledge.

Ellison, J. (1957). *Nelson's complete concordance of the revised standard version Bible*. Thomas Nelson & Sons.

Faucett, L., Palmer, H., Thorndike, E., & West, M. (1936). *Interim report on vocabulary selection*. P. S. King & Son, Ltd.

Francis, W., & Kučera, H. (1964). *Manual of information to accompany a standard corpus of present-day edited American English, for use with digital computers*. Brown University.

Fries, C. (1940). *American English Grammar: The grammatical structure of present-day American English with especial reference to social differences or class dialects*. D. Appleton-Century-Crofts.

Fries, C. (1945). *Teaching and learning English as a foreign language*. The University of Michigan Press.

Fries, C. (1952). *The structure of English: An introduction to the construction of English sentences*. Harcourt, Brace and Company.

Gilquin, G. (2010). *Corpus, cognition and causative constructions*. Benjamins. https://doi.org/10.1075/scl.39

Granger, S. (1996a). Learner English around the world. In S. Greenbaum (Ed.), *Comparing English worldwide* (pp. 13–24). Clarendon Press.

Granger, S. (1996b). From CA to CIA and back: An integrated approach to computerized bilingual and learner corpora. In K. Aijmer, B. Altenberg, & M. Johansson (Eds.), *Languages in contrast* (pp. 37–51). Lund University Press.

Granger, S. (2015). Contrastive interlanguage analysis: A reappraisal. *International Journal of Learner Corpus Research*, *1*(1), 7–24. https://doi.org/10.1075/ijlcr.1.1.01gra.

Granger, S., Gilquin, G., & Meunier, F. (Eds.). (2015). *The Cambridge handbook of learner corpus research*. Cambridge University Press.

Granger, S., & Paquot, M. (2015). Electronic lexicography goes local: Design and structures of a needs-driven online academic writing aid. *Lexicographica - International Annual for Lexicography*, *31*(1), 118–141.

Gries, S. T. (2018). On over- and underuse in learner corpus research and multifactoriality in corpus linguistics more generally. *Journal of Second Language Studies*, *1*(2), 277–309. https://doi.org/10.1075/jsls.00005.gri.

Gries, S. T., Barbara, S., Liebig, J., & Deshors, S. C. (2020). There's more to alternations than the main diagonal of a 2×2 confusion matrix: Improvements of MuPDAR and other classificatory alternation studies. *ICAME Journal*, *44*(1), 69–96.

Hasselgård, H. (2017). Stating the obvious: Signals of shared knowledge in Norwegian-produced academic English. In P. de Haan, R. de Vries, & S. van Vuuren (Eds.), *Language, learners and levels: Progression and variation* (pp. 23–44). Presses Universitaires de Louvain.

Hauch, E. (1929). *German idiom list: Selected on the basis of frequency and range of occurrence*. The MacMillan Company.

Henmon, V. (1924). *A French word book based on a count of 400,000 running words*. University of Wisconsin.

Hornby, A. S. (1953). Vocabulary control—History and principles. *ELT Journal*, *VIII*(1), 15–21.

Howatt, A. (1984). *A history of English language teaching*. Oxford University Press.

Johansson, S. (2011). A multilingual outlook of corpora studies. In V. Viana, S. Zyngier, & G. Barnbrook (Eds.), *Perspectives on corpus linguistics* (pp. 115–129). Benjamins. https://doi.org/10.1075/scl.48.08joh

Johns, T. (1991). From printout to handout: Grammar and vocabulary teaching in the context of data-driven learning. *ELR Journal*, *4*, 27–45.

Jones, W. (1915). *Concrete investigation of the material of English spelling*. The University of South Dakota.

Kaeding, F. (1897). *Häufigkeitswörterbuch der deutschen Sprache*. Self-published.

Keniston, H. (1929). *Spanish idiom list: Selected on the basis of range and frequency of occurrence*. MacMillan.

Keniston, H. (1937). *Spanish syntax list: A statistical study of grammatical usage in contemporary Spanish prose on the basis of range and frequency*. H. Holt and Company.

Kučera, H., & Francis, W. (1967). *Computational analysis of present day American English*. Brown University Press.

Leech, G., Rayson, P., & Wilson, A. (2001). *Word frequencies in written and spoken English: Based on the British National Corpus*. Longman.

Lewis, M. (1993). *The lexical approach: The state of ELT and a way forward*. Language Teaching Publications.

Lorge, I. (1937). The English semantic count. *Teachers College Record*, *39*(1), 65–77.

Lorge, I. (1949). *The semantic count of the 570 commonest English words*. Teachers College, Columbia University.

McCarthy, M. (2004). *Touchstone: From corpus to course book*. Cambridge University Press.

McCarthy, M., McCarten, J., Clark, D., & Clark, R. (2009). *Grammar for business*. Cambridge University Press.

McCarthy, M., McCarten, J., & Sandiford, H. (2006). *Touchstone student book level 1*. Cambridge University Press.

McCarthy, M., McCarten, J., & Sandiford, H. (2012). *Viewpoint level 1 student's book*. Cambridge University Press.

McCarthy, M., McCarten, J., & Sandiford, H. (2014). *Touchstone student book level 1* (2nd ed.) Cambridge University Press.

McNamara, D. S., Graesser, A. C., McCarthy, P. M., & Cai, Z. (2014). *Automated evaluation of text and discourse with Coh-Metrix*. Cambridge University Press.

Morgan, B. (1928). *German frequency word book: Based on Kaeding's Häufigkeitswörterbuch der deutschen Sprache*. MacMillan.

Nacey, S. (2013). *Metaphors in learner English*. Benjamins.

Nation, I. (2005). Range [Computer Software]. https://www.wgtn.ac.nz/lals/resources/paul-nations-resources

Nesi, H., & Gardner, S. (2012). *Genres across the disciplines: Student writing in higher education*. Cambridge University Press.

Ogden, C. (1930). *The basic vocabulary: A statistical analysis*. Kegan Paul, Trench, Trubner & Co, Ltd.

Palmer, H. (1933). *Second interim report on English collocations*. The Institute for Research in English Teaching, Department of Education.

Pawley, A., & Syder, F. (1983). Two puzzles for linguistic theory: Nativelike selection and nativelike fluency. In J. C. Richards & R. W. Schmidt (Eds.), *Language and communication* (pp. 191–226). Longman.

Pitman, I. (1843). List of words from which grammalogues may be selected. *The Phonotypic Journal*, *2*(23), 161–163.

Quirk, R., & Greenbaum, S. (1973a). *A university grammar of English*. Longman.

Quirk, R., & Greenbaum, S. (1973b). *A concise grammar of contemporary English*. Harcourt Brace Jovanovich.

Quirk, R., & Greenbaum, S. (1990). *A student's grammar of the English language*. Longman.

Quirk, R., Greenbaum, S., Leech, G., & Svartvik, J. (1972). *The grammar of contemporary English*. Longman.

Quirk, R., Greenbaum, S., Leech, G., & Svartvik, J. (1985). *The comprehensive grammar of the English language*. Longman.

Reppen, R. (2012). *Grammar and beyond level 1 student's book*. Cambridge University Press.

Reppen, R., Blass, L., Iannuzzi, S., Savage, A., Bunting, J. D., & Diniz, L. (2019). *Grammar and beyond essentials*. Cambridge University Press.

Richards, J. C., & Rodgers, T. S. (2014). *Approaches and methods in language teaching*. Cambridge University Press.

Santana-Williamson, E. (2010). *On speaking terms 1: Real language for real life*. Cengage Learning.

Sinclair, J. (1987). *Collins COBUILD dictionary of English language*. Collins.

Sinclair, J. (1990). *Collins COBUILD English grammar*. Collins.

Staples, S., Biber, D., & Reppen, R. (2018). Using corpus-based register analysis to explore the authenticity of high-stakes language exams: A register comparison of TOEFL iBT and disciplinary writing tasks. *The Modern Language Journal*, *102*(2), 310–332. https://doi.org/10.1111/modl.12465.

Stormzand, M., & O'Shea, M. (1924). *How much English grammar? An investigation of the frequency of usage of grammatical constructions in various types of writing together with a discussion of the teaching of grammar in the elementary and the high school*. Warwick & York, Inc.

Stubbs, M. (2018). The (very) long history of corpora, concordances, collocations and all that. In A. Čermáková & M. Mahlberg (Eds.), *The corpus linguistics discourse: In honour of Wolfgang Teubert* (pp. 9–33). Benjamins. https://doi.org/10.1075/scl.87.02stu

Swales, J., & Feak, C. (2009a). *Abstracts and the writing of abstracts*. The University of Michigan Press.

Swales, J., & Feak, C. (2009b). *Telling a research story: Writing a literature review*. The University of Michigan Press.

Swenson, E., & West, M. (1934). *On the counting of new words in textbooks for teaching foreign languages*. The University of Toronto Press.

Thompson, G. (1995). *Collins COBUILD concordance samplers: Reporting*. HarperCollins Publishers Ltd.

Thornbury, S. (2004). *Natural grammar: The keywords of English and how they work*. Oxford University Press.

Thorndike, E. (1921). *The teacher's word book.* Columbia University.

Thorndike, E. (1931). *A teacher's word book of the twenty thousand words: Found most frequently and widely in general reading for children and young people.* Columbia University.

Thorndike, E. (1935). *The Thorndike-century junior dictionary.* D. Appleton-Century-Crofts.

Thorndike, E., & Lorge, I. (1944). *The teacher's word book of 30,000 words.* Columbia University.

Tribble, C., & Jones, G. (1990). *Concordances in the classroom.* Longman.

Vander Beke, G. (1929). *French word book.* MacMillan.

West, M. (1931). Notes, news and clippings. *The Modern Language Journal, 15*(8), 638–647.

West, M. (1934). English as a world language. *American Speech, 9*(3), 163–174.

West, M. (1935). *Definition vocabulary.* University of California, Davis.

West, M. (1953). *A general service list of English words: With semantic frequencies and a supplementary word-list for the writing of popular science and technology.* Longmans, Green.

West, M., & Endicott, J. (1935). *The new method English dictionary.* Longman.

Willis, D. (1990). *The lexical syllabus: A new approach to language teaching.* Collins.

Willis, J., & Willis, D. (1988). *Collins COBUILD English course: Student's book 1.* Collins.

Winter, T. (1999). Roberto Busa, S.J., and the invention of the machine-generated concordance. *The Classical Bulletin, 75*(1), 3–20.

Xu, J. (2020). *Xin shidai zhiye yingyu jiudian yingyu cihui shouce* [New era vocational English word book: Hotel English]. Foreign Language Teaching and Research Press.

2

CORPORA AND SECOND LANGUAGE ACQUISITION

Magali Paquot

2.1 Introduction

Taking its contemporary roots in studies by Corder and Selinker in the late 1960s and early 1970s, the field of Second Language Acquisition (SLA) investigates "the human capacity to learn languages other than the first, during late childhood, adolescence or adulthood, and once the first language or languages have been acquired" (Ortega, 2009, p. 2). Its overarching goal is to understand the nature of second language knowledge (with 'second' referring to any language learned after the first has been acquired) and the processes through which this knowledge is developed, stored, and used. To that end, SLA is concerned with a wide variety of (potentially interacting) influencing factors (e.g. age, first language, motivation, learning styles) and complex phenomena (e.g. syntactic processing, second language development, fossilization, interaction and negotiation for meaning, incidental learning) that contribute to the "puzzling range of possible outcomes when learning an additional language in a variety of contexts" (ibid.).

SLA is also characterized by theoretical diversity, with linguistic, cognitive, interactionist, sociolinguistic, and sociocultural approaches pursuing different research agendas and thereby often focusing on different facets of SLA and adopting different views on the nature of language, the language learning process, and language learners and their role in the acquisition process (Mitchell *et al.*, 2019; Myles, 2013). As put by Rothman and VanPatten (2013), "SLA is still an emergent area of research and hypothesis creation" (p. 243), that is, no one approach to date has succeeded in capturing all its dimensions and providing explanations to the wide range of empirical observations reported in the field. For example, how do we explain that learners come to know more than what they are exposed to in the input or that second language learning is variable in its outcome? (VanPatten & Williams, 2015). This lack of a unified theory, however, is largely viewed positively as the various theoretical families "have all enriched our understanding of specific aspects of this complex phenomenon, and they complement each other by focusing on different theoretical and empirical agendas" (Myles, 2013, p. 70).

With the multiplicity of research agendas and theories also comes a variety of data and research methods. To collect SLA observations, researchers interested in the influence of the social context on second language development will not use the same methodologies as researchers who want to study the developing linguistic system or the learning mechanisms

DOI: 10.4324/9781003002901-4

involved in the SLA process and what impact upon them. Thus, depending on the research questions, data can be collected in the lab, the classroom, or in the wild. SLA study designs can take the form of experimental studies, interventionist quasi-experimental studies, observational studies, case studies, etc., and rely on a wide array of data collection techniques and methodologies, including formal theory-based methodologies (grammatical acceptability judgment and interpretation tasks), psycholinguistic methodologies (e.g. self-paced reading and listening tasks, eye-tracking techniques), neurolinguistic methodologies (e.g. event-related potentials and functional magnetic resonance imaging), and corpus linguistic methodologies (Mackey & Gass, 2012).

In SLA, researchers have been collecting and analyzing collections of production data that range in size from very small (e.g. a case study of one learner in one interview) to larger samples (e.g. the European Science Foundation Second Language Database) since the beginning of the field. However, it is only recently that they have started analyzing large, machine-readable corpora with the help of corpus linguistic methods and tools. The main objective of this chapter is to provide a critical overview of the ways in which corpora have contributed to the SLA research agenda so far. It discusses the extent to which corpus linguistics and its offshoot, learner corpus research, have informed SLA theories, broadened the scope of SLA research instruments, and brought new perspectives on key SLA research questions related to the underlying L2 knowledge system of learner language and its development and what impacts them. Special attention is devoted to the current active development of research methodologies that aim to address the complexity of learner language data as typically found in learner corpora. Finally, the chapter evaluates what it will take for (learner) corpora to become maximally useful in future SLA research.

2.2 Review of current state of research

SLA researchers today make use of two main types of computerized corpora: learner corpora and reference corpora. Learner corpora are electronic collections of natural to near-natural data produced by foreign or second language learners and assembled according to explicit design criteria. As discussed by Granger (2017), the term 'near-natural' is used here to highlight the "need for data that reflects as closely as possible 'natural' language use (i.e. language that is situationally and interactionally authentic) while recognizing that the limitations facing the collection of such data often obligate researchers to resort to clinically elicited data (for example, by using pedagogic tasks)" (Ellis & Barkhuizen, 2005, p. 7). As a result, many learner corpora include products of pedagogical tasks where learners are free to choose their own wording. Such tasks can vary in how constrained they are and range from argumentative essays and semi-structured interviews to picture-based narrative tasks with discourse prompts that trigger the use of specific grammatical structures (Tracy-Ventura & Myles, 2015). Learner corpora are also typically accompanied by metadata that characterize the learner (e.g. first language, age, sex) and the task (mode, genre, timed or untimed, etc.). Over the last 30 years or so, learner corpora have been used extensively to describe learner language varieties (typically English as written by a variety of L1 specific learner populations such as French, German, and Chinese speakers), most particularly within the framework of learner corpus research (LCR), a research strand with a strong applied orientation that emerged in the late 1980s as an offshoot of corpus linguistics (Granger *et al.*, 2015). LCR studies have generated a rich set of pedagogically relevant findings, perhaps most particularly for the teaching and learning of English for Academic Purposes. Among other things, LCR studies have shown that, when writing an academic essay, English as a Foreign Language (EFL) learners tend to use a limited lexical repertoire and infelicitous word combinations, misuse certain connectors, lack register awareness, favor sentence-initial positioning of adverbs, and are influenced by their first language even at intermediate and advanced proficiency levels (Gilquin *et al.*, 2007; Granger *et al.*, 2015; Paquot, 2010). Importantly, these descriptive studies often examined the use of linguistic features that until recently had rarely been the focus of SLA, most particularly lexical and discourse features (e.g. collocations, formulaic language, connectors). By contrast, attempts at answering some of the key SLA questions with learner corpus data and corpus linguistic techniques have been relatively limited. As will be demonstrated in Section 2.3 however, this has started to change, most notably with the development and increased availability of more and different learner corpora (e.g. spoken learner corpora, longitudinal learner corpora, learner corpora with a wider range of metadata).

Examples of well-known and often-used reference corpora include the British National Corpus (BNC) and the Corpus of Contemporary American English (COCA). Reference corpora are typically used for two main purposes in SLA. First, they are used as a source of linguistic material to inform researchers about the frequency and idiomaticity of language patterns in specific language varieties and design instruments of various types. Recent research on learners' use and processing of formulaic language is a case in point: corpora are used to identify idioms and collocations with different distributional properties (more or less frequent formulaic sequences, with more or less associated elements) to design experiments such as off-line judgment tasks, online reaction-time tasks, or classroom studies following a pre-test, post-test design. For example, Vilkaitė (2017) extracted target verb–noun collocations from COCA based on two frequency criteria (all collocations should have a raw frequency ≥50 and all their elements should belong to the 3,000 most frequent lemmas in English) and a collocation strength criterion (all target collocations should have a Mutual Information (MI) score of ≥3) in a classroom study that set out to investigate whether collocations could be learned incidentally if encountered with words intervening between collocates. Similarly, Siyanova-Chanturia *et al.* (2011) designed an eye-tracking study to investigate whether native and non-native English speakers were sensitive to the frequency with which phrases occur in language. They extracted a set of 42 three-word binomial expressions (*bride and groom*) and their reversed forms (*groom and bride*) from the BNC. These expressions were, thus, matched in frequency of the individual words, length, and part-of-speech but crucially differed in phrasal frequency. The BNC was also used to identify two types of fillers (e.g. *fluid and fumes, tennis and badminton*) that were not binomials but were used in the experiment to prevent participants from noticing the binomials, and in particular, their reversed forms, which might catch the participants' attention due to their low frequency.

Second, linguistic information derived from reference corpora is also used to describe and analyze learner production, either in the form of direct comparisons between reference corpora and learner corpora (see Section 2.4 for more details), or through the use of research procedures that rely on corpus-derived frequencies, association measures, and other types of indices to characterize learner texts. This is particularly the case in lexical richness or lexical complexity research where some of the most frequently used indices of lexical sophistication are based on corpus-derived word frequency counts (Kyle *et al.*, 2018). Thus, Kyle and Crossley (2015) computed a variety of word frequency lists, range indices, and n-gram indices on the basis of corpora such as the BNC and the SUBTLEXus corpus, a 51 million word corpus of subtitles from 8,388 American films and television series. Together with other indices of lexical sophistication (e.g. word information indices such as familiarity, concreteness, and imageability), the measures served to explain 47.5% of the variance in holistic scores of lexical proficiency in writing samples and 48.7% of the variance in holistic scores of speaking proficiency in independent tasks from the TOEFL public use data set. Another area where measures derived from reference corpora are frequently used to describe learner language is the study of phraseological competence. Durrant and Schmitt (2009), for example, assigned to each noun/adjective + noun sequence extracted from a corpus of L2 texts its MI score as computed on the basis of a large native reference corpus. They showed that, compared to native writers, L2 writers of English tend to underuse less common, strongly associated items as identified by high MI scores (e.g. *densely populated, bated breath, preconceived notions*). This seminal paper was followed by many others that further developed the approach and contributed to our current understanding of learners' use of word combinations (e.g. Garner *et al.*, 2019; Granger & Bestgen, 2014; Paquot, 2019).

2.3 Core issues and topics

One core issue that has been raised repeatedly in the literature when discussing the use of corpora in SLA is to what extent modern corpora and corpus linguistic tools and techniques – which were typically used to describe learner language varieties – can contribute to SLA theory building and knowledge creation (Myles, 2005, 2015). According to Van Patten and Williams (2015), SLA theories need to be able to explain a number of observed phenomena, which include:

1. a good deal of SLA happens incidentally
2. learners come to know more than what they have been exposed to in the input
3. learners' output (speech) often follows predictable paths with predictable stages in the acquisition of a given structure
4. second language learning is variable in its outcome
5. second language learning is variable across linguistic subsystems
6. there are limits on the effects of a learner's first language on SLA
7. exposure to input is necessary for SLA
8. there are limits on the effects of frequency on SLA
9. there are limits on the effects of output (learner production) on language acquisition
10. there are limits on the effects of instruction on SLA

(Van Patten & Williams, 2015, p. 9–11)

Until recently, efforts to provide an underlying explanation for such observations and test corresponding hypotheses were typically made with data types other than (learner) corpora. The critical issue here is whether corpus data, alone or as a complement to experimental data, can provide a sound empirical basis for testing (at least some SLA) hypotheses and developing theories. Recent research suggests that this is the case. Over the last years, there has been an increasing number of studies that have put SLA claims, often made on the basis of relatively small language samples, to the test of large-scale learner corpora. For example, Murakami and Alexopoulou (2015) used approximately 10,000 error-tagged written exam scripts from the Cambridge Learner Corpus to revisit the claim according to which there is a universal order in the acquisition of grammatical morphemes by first and second language learners. They investigated the L2 acquisition order of six English grammatical morphemes (articles, past tense -*ed*, plural -*s*, possessive '*s*, progressive -*ing*, and third person -*s*) by learners from seven L1 groups across five proficiency levels. They found L1 influence on the absolute accuracy of morphemes and their acquisition order, therefore demonstrating that the accuracy order of

L2 English grammatical morphemes is not universal but varies across learners with different L1 backgrounds. They also showed that L1 influence is morpheme-specific, with morphemes encoding language-specific concepts (e.g. definiteness) most prone to L1 influence.

One set of related theories that have relied extensively on corpora to advance the theory is usage-based accounts of language learning. These accounts rest on the assumption that successful language learning depends, among other things, on input learners receive and output they produce. Quite naturally, proponents of such theories have turned to corpora to investigate what the properties of the input are that make it learnable (e.g. Ellis & Wulff, 2015). Over the last years, corpus-based studies that adopted a usage-based approach to SLA have provided converging evidence that human language processing and acquisition respond to a variety of input properties (frequency and distribution, functional prototypicality, recency, salience, and contingency of form-function mappings). Ellis *et al.* (2016), for example, studied L2 processing of Verb-Argument Constructions (VACs) and showed that L2 speakers, like L1 speakers, are sensitive to the statistics of usage in terms of verb exemplar type-token frequency distribution, VAC-verb contingency, and VAC-verb semantic prototypicality. Similarly, proponents of Complex Dynamic System Theory (CDST) have started to compile and use longitudinal learner corpora with dense data collection points by a limited number of learners to explore individual learners' trajectories. They have also started to provide corroborative evidence for the CDST tenet that language development is a highly individual and emerging process due to the dynamic and non-linear interaction of related subsystems, for example, linguistic subsystems such as grammar and vocabulary, but also individual factors such as degrees of motivation, willingness to communicate, or anxiety. CDST studies have also documented the extent to which variability (non-linear growth) and interacting variables play a role in the emergence of new forms and self-organization of the linguistic system (Verspoor *et al.*, 2011; Verspoor & Lowie, 2021).

Many of the observations listed by Van Patten and Williams (2015) are still in need of further explanation. Some of them focus on topics that are at the core of corpus linguistics (e.g. frequency, variability). Therefore, and as illustrated above, it just seems appropriate that corpora be used to explore issues related to variability in learners' production or the effects of frequency and other distributional properties on SLA (Gries & Ellis, 2015). By doing so, corpus studies are also answering repeated calls in the field for quantifying findings and integrating empirical evidence produced across a variety of methodological paradigms into a more robust process of theorizing (e.g. Fuchs & Werner, 2018).

A related core issue centers around the extent to which corpora and corpus linguistic techniques can help the field of SLA address its current concerns for replicability, validity, and reliability (Abbuhl & Mackey, 2008). Again, recent work shows that corpus linguistics can contribute to SLA challenges and debates in at least some of these areas. To illustrate, one cause of concern in SLA is internal validity, i.e. the degree to which study results are attributable to the independent variable(s) and not some confounding variable(s) (Abbuhl & Mackey, 2008, p. 102). As further demonstrated in the next section, methods are currently being used and/or developed in the field of LCR to analyze learner corpus data in multifactorial study designs to explore the effects of several independent variables and their interactions on learner language. These methodological advancements are made possible (but also necessary, see Section 2.4) thanks to the often rich metadata (learner variables, task variables) that are typically collected with learner corpora, as well as the size of such data types, which allows for the study of linguistic phenomena that are frequent enough to crosstabulate variables and examine their interactions. This characteristic of learner corpora has the potential to shed new light on at least some unresolved issues in SLA such as the effect of constraints (e.g. proficiency, markedness) on L1 influence (Jarvis, 2000).

Another area of much concern is the validity of constructs that are at the core of SLA research (Norris & Ortega, 2003). For example, one construct that has been the focus of ongoing debate is that of complexity (Ortega, 2012). Studies of L2 writing development have traditionally measured grammatical complexity by means of T-units and clausal subordination, assuming that increased subordination was a sign of more proficient writing. On the basis of a corpus analysis of 28 grammatical features in academic writing and conversation, Biber *et al.* (2011) challenged this practice by showing that 1) clausal subordination is actually more characteristic of conversation than academic writing and 2) the grammatical complexity of academic writing is better characterized in terms of complex noun phrase constituents and complex phrases. Based on these findings, they hypothesized a sequence of developmental stages for student writing that has been confirmed since then in several studies (Biber *et al.*, 2020; Kreyer & Schaub, 2018). Other key SLA constructs have been revisited or further developed based on corpus data and/or corpus techniques. Wulff and Gries (2011) proposed a usage-based measure of accuracy that is based on corpus-derived (conditional) probability/ frequency of usage and involves "the selection of a construction (...) in its preferred context within a particular target variety and genre" (p. 70). Jarvis (2013) made use of human judgments and corpus data in a first attempt to validate new measurable properties of lexical diversity in accordance with how well they actually measure the construct of lexical diversity.

2.4 Main research methods

As mentioned above, a variety of corpora have been used in SLA. For lack of space, this section will focus on a selected set of research methods that place learner corpora at the core of their inquiry. See, for example, Dang (2019) for more information about the use of reference corpora in L2 vocabulary research.

Learner corpora often come with metadata about the learner characteristics and task settings. Until recently, however, learner corpus researchers have mainly used just one learner variable, i.e. first language (Granger, 2021). The variable has often not been used as a dependent variable among others, but as a grouping factor to compile L1 specific learner corpora to be analyzed within the methodological framework of Contrastive Interlanguage Analysis (CIA; Granger, 1996, 2015). CIA is a twofold comparative framework that involves:

• a comparison of native and non-native production of the same language that aims to identify non-native features of learner writing and speech (not only errors but also instances of under- and over-representation of words, phrases, and structures)
• a comparison of different interlanguages of the same language, i.e. the English of French learners, Spanish learners, Dutch learners, etc. that will help "differentiate between features which are shared by several learner populations and are therefore more likely to be developmental and those which are peculiar to one national group and therefore possibly L1-dependent" (Granger, 2002, p. 13).

In its revised version (Granger, 2015), CIA[2] places more emphasis on variation by explicitly broadening the range of reference points against which learner data can be compared (see Figure 2.1). Importantly, and to answer one of the major criticisms leveled against CIA in the past, Reference Language Varieties (RLVs) do not necessarily need to represent a norm. Depending on the research objectives, corpora of English as a first language varieties (British English, American English, Australian English, etc.), English as a second language varieties (Indian English, Singaporean English, etc.), or English as a Lingua Franca varieties may be

Magali Paquot

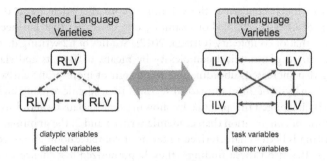

Figure 2.1 Granger's (2015) CIA²

used as RLVs for an EFL learner corpus. In line with the current state of the art in second language research, CIA² also recognizes the highly variable nature of interlanguage by introducing the term 'Interlanguage Varieties' and encouraging comparisons across learner variables and task variables. Crosthwaite *et al.* (2016), for example, relied on the revised CIA framework to analyze non-numerical quantificational NPs (NNQs, i.e. 'some people') produced by Mandarin and Korean L2 English learners.

The combination of CIA and contrastive analysis (CA) as proposed in the Integrated Contrastive Model (ICM; Gilquin, 2000; Granger, 1996) aims to help researchers explain interlanguage behavior based on performance data in the first language. Figure 2.2 shows that this can be done in two ways. From CA to CIA, the approach is predictive as it involves formulating CA-based predictions about L2 production that will then be checked against

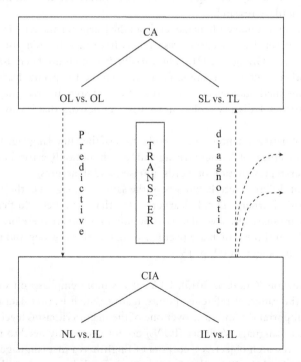

Figure 2.2 The Integrated Contrastive Model (Gilquin, 2000, p. 100, adapted from Granger, 1996, p. 100)

CIA data. From CIA to CA, the approach is diagnostic as it aims to explain CIA findings, i.e. errors but also overuse and underuse, in the light of CA descriptions. Thus, the terms 'predictive' and 'diagnostic' refer to working hypotheses that will be confirmed or refuted by corpus data analysis (Granger, 1996, p. 46). Compared to CIA, and despite its explanatory potential, however, the ICM has not been used extensively in learner corpus studies, perhaps because some of the most recent crosslinguistic influence studies have adopted Jarvis's (2000) unified framework for the study of L1 influence instead (e.g. Golden *et al.*, 2017; Paquot, 2017).

Recent methodological developments have built on the ICM and CIA frameworks to propose techniques that aim to move away from primarily descriptive and monofactorial form-based analyses of errors, overuse, and underuse, toward study designs that are more context-sensitive, multifactorial, explanatory, and grounded in current SLA theory (Deshors & Gries, 2021). These new techniques largely come from studies that seek to explore foreign language and foreign language learning from a usage-based perspective (see Section 2.3). One of the most recent additions to LCR methodological apparatus is an approach called MuPDAR(F) (for Multifactorial Prediction and Deviation Analysis using Regression/random forests) (Gries & Adelman, 2014; Gries & Deshors, 2014).[1] Conceptually, this method is based on missing-data imputation: for every linguistic choice made by a learner, one imputes what the 'reference' speaker (e.g. a native speaker, a speaker of a dialectal variety, an expert writer) would have selected given identical contextual conditions. MuPDAR(F) focuses on probabilistic differences that result in different speaker choices and involves the following three steps:

- predict the choices that the reference speakers make with regard to the linguistic phenomenon of interest; this is typically done by fitting a regression/random forest *R(F)1* on data points extracted from a reference corpus
- predict what the reference speakers would have done in the place of the learners by applying the results of *R(F)1* to the learner data points
- explore how the learners' choices differ from those of the reference speakers by fitting a regression/random forest *R(F)2*: predictors that are significant in this new model help identify where the learners make choices that are not those of the reference speakers.

MuPDAR(F) is increasingly applied in learner corpus research for its rich descriptive and explanatory power. For example, Gries and Deshors (2014) introduced this method in a study that explored the effect of a total of 16 co-occurring semantic and morpho-syntactic features on the use of the modals *may* and *can* by native and non-native speakers of English and examined systematic deviations between the two groups at an unprecedented degree of granularity. For example, they found that learners' choices of *may* with state verbs are significantly more on target than those with other verb types, but also that, in general, learners' use of *may* is still a long way from the NSs' patterning, especially with animate subjects. Similarly, with this technique, Lester (2019) showed that native speakers use more instances of the relativizer *that* in complex and disfluent environments, while learners show the exact opposite tendency.

Recently Wulff and Gries (2021) further extended the approach by illustrating how models can be obtained that allow for the study of inter-speaker variation. There are two major reasons why examining inter-speaker variation more carefully is of utmost importance for future LCR. First, it allows to "determine to what extent the quantitative summary (e.g. a measure of central tendency such as the mean) can be used to represent the language produced by individual users in the corpus" (Gablasova *et al.*, 2017, p. 138). With rich metadata, it should also help to explore whether individual differences (e.g. age, personality, motivation, language aptitude, learning styles, learning strategies) can explain interspeaker variation.

Not all linguistic features, however, lend themselves well to the MuPDAR(F) framework, which seems to be best suited for the analysis of alternations and other phenomena that involve a choice between a limited number of items. Another limitation of MuPDAR(F) is its reliance on a reference language variety (in that sense, it does not study learner languages in their own right, something that some SLA specialists have argued against very strongly). The added value of MuPDAR(F), however, is in its recognition that no single linguistic phenomenon and no language learning situation can be explained with just one variable/predictor (Gries, 2018). Indeed, with or without the use of MuPDAR(F), the successful use of learner corpora in SLA will most probably rest, among other things, in its capacity to pursue its research agenda in a context-sensitive and multifactorial way (Gries, 2018; Paquot & Plonsky, 2017). There are at least two main reasons for this. First, the nature of learner corpora makes it a prerequisite because:

1. learner corpora often include language data from a heterogeneous set of learners (e.g. learners differ in age, proficiency, L1 background, L2 exposure, other spoken L2, motivation, etc.)
2. learner corpora can also be very complex in their design (with several texts produced by the same learner, different collection points, different L2s, etc.)
3. tasks included in corpora represent the most open-ended types of learner language and learners are free to produce the language they want, which means that the linguistic context of production will be different from one learner to the next.

Second, and as argued by Gries (2018), even a monofactorial hypothesis should be approached with a multifactorial design "to determine either (a) whether it adds anything to what we already know about the phenomenon (by statistically controlling for what we already know) or (b) whether it replaces (parts of) what we already know about the phenomenon" (Gries, 2018, p. 296).

2.5 Future directions of research

After many years of relatively independent research and development, the fields of second language acquisition and learner corpus research (and corpus linguistics more generally) have recently started to interact more (Le Bruyn & Paquot, 2021; Tracy-Ventura & Paquot, 2021). Specialists in SLA have gained a better understanding of what type of research questions can be answered with learner corpus data and what corpus techniques are needed to extract linguistic phenomena of interest. Learner corpus researchers have also started to address core issues in SLA, notably by operationalizing key SLA constructs (e.g. crosslinguistic influence, complexity, fluency) or revisiting SLA evidence and theories through the lens of learner corpus data.

As mentioned above, many key issues in SLA concern empirical evidence that the field needs to explain. So far, corpus data have only been used to address a limited number of the observations listed by Van Patten and Williams (2015). While I am certainly not claiming that learner corpus data can be used to explain them all, I believe that more can be done with learner corpora, especially perhaps in the context of mixed-method studies that combine learner corpora and experimental data (Gilquin, 2021), or in studies that aim to test SLA hypotheses or replicate SLA observations. Next to the issues of validity and reliability already discussed in Section 2.2, two critical issues in SLA are generalizability and ecological validity (Plonsky, 2014; Plonsky & Gonulal, 2015). Learner corpora can serve to test the generalizability of (some) SLA findings under different, more natural, conditions. For this to happen, however, and as discussed in more detail in Tracy-Ventura *et al.* (2021), there is a need for further improvements in a number of areas.

First, there is still much we can do to improve the design, collection, and preparation of learner corpora so that they better meet the needs of SLA researchers. In large part due to convenience, a vast majority of learner corpora to date are collections of texts (often essays or texts representing another academic register) written by educated adults over the age of 18 who are intermediate or advanced English as a Foreign Language instructed learners. If we are to better understand the process of second/foreign language acquisition from beginning to end, it is, therefore, essential that we expand our focus and collect learner data that represent:

- different languages, especially typologically distant languages
- the whole spectrum of second/foreign language competence, from complete beginners to successful multilingual speakers
- second/foreign language use by young(er) learners as well as middle-aged and older adults
- second/foreign language as spoken in a variety of settings (e.g. different instructional settings such as Content and Language Integrated Language Learning [CLIL], but also informal naturalistic contexts such as authentic interactions with members of a social network)
- second/foreign language as it develops over time.

These needs have been emphasized repeatedly in the field (e.g. Meunier, 2015; Myles, 2005, 2015) and there have already been some welcome developments as evidenced by the wider variety of learner corpora listed on the Learner Corpora around the World webpage (see References for details) managed by the Centre for English Corpus Linguistics (CECL), UCLouvain, Belgium. New types of learner corpora of particular interest for SLA include corpora of classroom interactions (Ziegler & Mackey, 2021) and learner corpora such as the PROcess Corpus of English in EDucation (PROCEED) whose compilation involves capturing the keyboard and screen activity by means of keystroke logging and screencasting so as to keep a record of all the steps involved in the writing process (Gilquin, 2020, and this volume). As a field, we would also benefit from the development of multilingual corpora of various types (e.g. corpora that include data from speakers naturally engaging in codeswitching and translanguaging; corpora of L1 and L2 language produced by the same learners/users) as a way to answer repeated calls for situating SLA research against the changing nature of language learning and teaching in a multilingual world (The Douglas Fir Group, 2016).

Learner corpora will also become more useful for advancing the SLA research agenda if they are accompanied with a wider variety of metadata, especially those variables tapping into individual differences (Wulff & Gries, 2021). As argued in Tracy-Ventura *et al.* (2021), there is also a need for more validly and reliably operationalized variables. For example, in earlier learner corpora, foreign language competence was often assessed based on institutional status, but recently more attention has been placed on the provision of reliable and valid measures of proficiency (Carlsen, 2012). More generally, Granger and Paquot (2017) called for collaborative work toward the development of some kind of shared protocol for collecting metadata that would include a minimal list of required variables and recommendations as to how to operationalize them best.

Reference corpora have been used in SLA on the ground that "a sufficiently large and adequately representative corpus can give us an indication of the types and regularity of input a language user is likely to have been exposed to" (Wolter & Gyllstad, 2013, p. 457). While this is generally true, reference corpora such as the British National Corpus (BNC) or the Corpus of Contemporary American English (COCA) are still not ideal as they do not provide direct evidence of the language that learners are exposed to. There is a need for more genuine input corpora such as the corpus compiled in Myles and Mitchell's (2012) Young Learners Project which consists of full video recordings of a set of French lessons taught to early learners with English L1 background. Such corpora are essential for investigating questions about the role of input in second/foreign language acquisition (see also Crossley *et al.*, 2016). Other important points related to corpus collection, design, and preparation discussed in Tracy-Ventura *et al.* (2021) include considering different perspectives on what a control corpus is, diversifying the kinds of corpora and experimental data collected, and increasing transparency in data transcription and annotation.

Second, the practice of sharing learner corpora is already present but should be encouraged more. The field needs to embrace Open Science practices more closely and this should happen hand in hand with increased recognition of methodological expertise. Corpus compilation is extremely time-consuming and requires expertise in a variety of areas which are often not described and discussed sufficiently (e.g. protocols for data collections, ethical/legal procedures, transcription guidelines, data annotation guidelines). The intrinsic value of all these tasks should be better recognized by the community, for example, through data reports and other types of methodological publications in top scientific journals. This is particularly important as methodological transparency and data sharing are prerequisites for reproducibility and replication studies that are considered by many to be fundamental for the progress of science (Marsden & Plonsky, 2018). As a result, Tracy-Ventura *et al.* (2021) also called for more standardization and the development of best practices and shared protocols for data collection and annotation.

Finally, we need to raise our game when using corpus linguistic methods, natural language processing (NLP) tools, and statistics to analyze learner corpora. Tracy-Ventura *et al.* (2021) offer a brief review of corpus techniques that have been used to examine SLA research questions but also to open up new domains of inquiry (e.g. collostructional analysis, multidimensional analysis); they call for more awareness of current developments in corpus linguistics and NLP. Here, we will only focus on two areas related to study design where the field needs to improve. On the one hand, a large majority of the learner corpus studies published so far have investigated the effect of just one independent variable on learner language. The focus has typically been on non-nativeness in comparisons of language samples produced by native and non-native speakers, or on first language in comparisons of learner populations with different mother tongues (e.g. English as a foreign language as produced by French vs. Dutch learners). The influence of many other learner- and task-related variables has remained largely unexplored despite the availability of relevant metadata in several learner corpora (Granger, 2021). As discussed above, the impact of these variables (and their interactions) should also be explored in multifactorial study designs (Gries, 2018). In addition, learner corpus studies have often adopted a group perspective, focusing on the language of, for instance, French speakers of English, and analyzing large samples of language from a variety of speakers without considering individual variation. This led to the "commonplace misconception among non-corpus linguists that corpora only contain massive pools of data collapsed over anonymized speakers, with no option to tie data points to the individual speaker who produced them" (Wulff & Gries, 2021, p. 193). Recent studies such as Lester (2019), Crossley *et al.* (2019), or Wulff and Gries (2021), however, have shown that, with the right study design and statistical method, it is possible to 1) explore the main effects and interaction effects of a wider range of variables, and 2) explore individual variation within and between corpora, or at least control for individual variation even though individual differences are not the primary focus (see also Gudmestad, 2021; Kerz & Wiechmann, 2021). As put in Tracy-Ventura *et al.* (2021), "this is essential given the complexity of our object of study, i.e. language use, and the complexity of the phenomenon we are trying to explain, i.e. second language acquisition" (p. 419).

Note

1 Note that the term 'deviation' is to be understood in its statistical meaning; it is not meant as a norm-based evaluation of learners' production (Gries, p.c.).

Further reading

Fuchs, R., & Werner, V. (Eds.). (2018). Tense and aspect in second language acquisition and learner corpus research. Special Issue of the *International Journal of Learner Corpus Research, 4*(2), 143–163. This special issue is entirely devoted to the study of L2 acquisition of tense and aspect on the basis of learner corpus data.

Le Bruyn, B., & Paquot, M. (Eds.). (2021). *Learner corpus research meets second language acquisition*. Cambridge University Press. This volume illustrates how recent advances in learner corpus research can serve to explore a broad range of key topics in SLA, such as tense and aspect, complexity, universal processes, crosslinguistic influence, and variability.

Tracy-Ventura, N., & Paquot, M. (Eds.). (2021). *The Routledge handbook of second language acquisition and corpora*. Routledge. The main objective of this handbook is to take stock of how L1 and L2 corpora have been used to address SLA core topics and issues. It places strong emphasis on methodological and theoretical contributions to the study of learner language using corpora.

References

Abbuhl, R., & Mackey, A. (2008). Second language acquisition research methods. In N. H. Hornberger (Ed.), *Encyclopedia of language and education* (pp. 3301–3313). Springer US. https://doi. org/10.1007/978-0-387-30424-3_248

Biber, D., Gray, B., & Poonpon, K. (2011). Should we use characteristics of conversation to measure grammatical complexity in L2 writing development? *TESOL Quarterly, 45,* 5–35.

Biber, D., Reppen, R., Staples, S., & Egbert, J. (2020). Exploring the longitudinal development of grammatical complexity in the disciplinary writing of L2-English university students. *International Journal of Learner Corpus Research, 6*(1), 38–71. doi: https://doi.org/10.1075/ijlcr.18007.bib.

Carlsen, C. (2012). Proficiency level—A fuzzy variable in computer learner corpora. *Applied Linguistics, 33*(2), 161–183. doi: https://doi.org/10.1093/applin/amr047.

Crossley, S., Kyle, K., & Salsbury, T. (2016). A usage-based investigation of L2 lexical acquisition: The role of input and output. *The Modern Language Journal, 100*(3), 702–715.

Crossley, S., Skalicky, S., Kyle, K., & Monteiro, K. (2019). Absolute frequency effects in second language lexical acquisition. *Studies in Second Language Acquisition, 41*(4), 721–744.

Crosthwaite, P., Choy, L. L. Y., & Bae, Y. (2016). 'Almost people' : A learner corpus account of L2 use and misuse of non-numerical quantification. *Open Linguistics, 2*(1), 317–336. doi: https://doi. org/10.1515/opli-2016-0015.

Dang, T. N. Y. (2019). Corpus-based word lists in second language vocabulary research, learning, and teaching. In S. Webb (Ed.), *The Routledge handbook of vocabulary studies* (pp. 288–303). Routledge.

Deshors, S., & Gries, S. T. (2021). Comparing corpora. In N. Tracy-Ventura, & M. Paquot (Eds.), *The Routledge handbook of second language acquisition and corpora* (pp. 105–118). Routledge.

Durrant, P., & Schmitt, N. (2009). To what extent do native and non-native writers make use of collocations? *IRAL: International Review of Applied Linguistics in Language Teaching*, 47, 157–177.

Ellis, N., Römer, U., & O'Donnell, M. (2016). *Usage-based approaches to language acquisition and processing: Cognitive and corpus investigations of construction grammar*. Wiley.

Ellis, N., & Wulff, S. (2015). Usage-based approaches to L2 acquisition. In B. VanPatten, & J. Williams (Eds.), *Theories in second language acquisition: An introduction* (pp. 75–93). Routledge.

Ellis, R., & Barkhuizen, G. P. (2005). *Analysing learner language*. Oxford University Press.

Fuchs, R., & Werner, V. (2018). Tense and aspect in second language acquisition and learner corpus research. Introduction to the special issue. *International Journal of Learner Corpus Research*, 4(2), 143–163.

Gablasova, D., Brezina, V., & McEnery, T. (2017). Exploring learner language through corpora: Comparing and interpreting corpus frequency information. *Language Learning*, 67(1), 130–154. doi: https://doi.org/10.1111/lang.12226.

Garner, J., Crossley, S., & Kyle, K. (2019). N-gram measures and L2 writing proficiency. *System*, *80*, 176–187. https://doi.org/10.1016/j.system.2018.12.001.

Gilquin, G. (2000). The integrated contrastive model. Spicing up your data. *Languages in Contrast*, *3*(1), 95–123.

Gilquin, G. (2020). Hic sunt dracones: Exploring some terra incognita in learner corpus research. In A. Čermáková, & M. Malá (Eds.), *Variation in time and space: Observing the world through corpora* (pp. 65–87). De Gruyter.

Gilquin, G. (2021). Combining learner corpora and experimental methods. In N. Tracy-Ventura, & M. Paquot (Eds.), *The Routledge handbook of second language acquisition and corpora* (pp. 133–144). Routledge.

Gilquin, G., Granger, S., & Paquot, M. (2007). Learner corpora : The missing link in EAP pedagogy. *Journal of English for Academic Purposes*, 6(4), 319–335.

Golden, A., Jarvis, S., & Tenfjord, K. (Eds.). (2017). *Crosslinguistic influence and distinctive patterns of language learning findings and insights from a learner corpus*. Multilingual Matters.

Granger, S. (1996). From CA to CIA and back: An integrated approach to computerized bilingual and learner corpora. In K. Aijmer, B. Altenberg, & M. Johansson (Eds.), *Languages in contrast. Text-based cross-linguistic studies* (pp. 37–51). Lund University Press.

Granger, S. (2002). A bird's-eye view of learner corpus research. In S. Granger, J. Hung, S. Petch-Tyson, & J. Hulstijn (Eds.), *Computer learner corpora, second language acquisition and foreign language teaching* (pp. 3–33). Benjamins.

Granger, S. (2015). Contrastive interlanguage analysis: A reappraisal. *International Journal of Learner Corpus Research*, 1(1), 7–24. doi: https://doi.org/10.1075/ijlcr.1.1.01gra.

Granger, S. (2017). Learner corpora in foreign language education. In S. Thorne & S. May (Eds.), *Language and technology. Encyclopedia of language and education* (Vol. 9, pp. 427–440). Springer. https://doi.org/10.1007/978-3-319-02237-6_33

Granger, S. (2021). Commentary: Have learner corpus research and second language acquisition finally met? In B. Le Bruyn & M. Paquot (Eds.), *Learner corpus research meets second language acquisition* (pp. 243–257). Cambridge University Press.

Granger, S., & Bestgen, Y. (2014). The use of collocations by intermediate vs. advanced non-native writers: A bigram-based study. *International Review of Applied Linguistics in Language Teaching*, 52(3), 229–252. doi: https://doi.org/10.1515/iral-2014-0011.

Granger, S., Meunier, F., & Gilquin, G. (Eds.). (2015). *The Cambridge handbook of learner corpus research*. Cambridge University Press.

Granger, S., & Paquot, M. (2017). Towards standardization of metadata for L2 corpora. Invited talk at the CLARIN workshop on Interoperability of Second Language Resources and Tools, 6–8 December 2017, University of Gothenburg, Sweden. https://sweclarin.se/sites/sweclarin.se/files/event_atachements/Granger_Paquot_Metadata_G%C3%B6teborg_final.pdf (accessed 19 April 2021).

Gries, S. T. (2018). On over- and underuse in learner corpus research and multifactoriality in corpus linguistics more generally. *Journal of Second Language Studies*, 1(2), 276–308.

Gries, S. T., & Adelman, A. (2014). Subject realization in Japanese conversation by native and non-native speakers: Exemplifying a new paradigm for learner corpus research. In J. Romero-Trillo (Ed.), *Yearbook of corpus linguistics and pragmatics 2014: New empirical and theoretical paradigms* (pp. 35–54). Springer.

Gries, S. T., & Deshors, S. (2014). Using regressions to explore deviations between corpus data and a standard/target: Two suggestions. *Corpora, 9*(1), 109–136.

Gries, S. T., & Ellis, N. C. (2015). Statistical measures for usage-based linguistics. *Language Learning, 65*(1), 1–28.

Gudmestad, A. (2021). Variationist approaches. In N. Tracy-Ventura & M. Paquot (Eds.), *The Routledge handbook of second language acquisition and corpora* (pp. 228–239). Routledge.

Jarvis, S. (2000). Methodological rigor in the study of transfer: Identifying L1 influence in the interlanguage lexicon. *Language Learning, 50*(2), 245–309.

Jarvis, S. (2013). Defining and measuring lexical diversity. In S. Jarvis & M. Daller (Eds.), *Vocabulary knowledge: Human ratings and automated measures* (pp. 13–44). Benjamins.

Kerz, E., & Wiechmann, D. (2021). Individual differences. In N. Tracy-Ventura & M. Paquot (Eds.), *The Routledge handbook of second language acquisition and corpora* (pp. 394–406). Routledge.

Kreyer, R., & Schaub, S. (2018). The development of phrasal complexity in German intermediate learners of English. *International Journal of Learner Corpus Research, 4*(1), 82–111. doi: https://doi.org/10.1075/ijlcr.16011.kre.

Kyle, K., & Crossley, S. A. (2015). Automatically assessing lexical sophistication: Indices, tools, findings, and application. *TESOL Quarterly, 49*(4), 757–786. doi: https://doi.org/10.1002/tesq.194.

Kyle, K., Crossley, S. A., & Berger, C. (2018). The tool for the analysis of lexical sophistication (TAALES): Version 2.0. *Behavior Research Methods, 50*(3), 1030–1046.

Learner Corpora around the World (n.d.) Centre for English Corpus Linguistics (CECL), UCLouvain, Belgium. https://uclouvain.be/en/research-institutes/ilc/cecl/learner-corpora-around-the-world.html

Le Bruyn, B., & Paquot, M. (Eds.). (2021). *Learner corpus research meets second language acquisition.* Cambridge University Press.

Lester, N. (2019). That's hard: Relativizer use in spontaneous L2 speech. *International Journal of Learner Corpus Research, 5*(1), 1–32.

Mackey, A., & Gass, S. (2012). *Research methods in second language acquisition: A practical guide.* Blackwell.

Marsden, E., & Plonsky, L. (2018). Conclusion: Data, open science, and methodological reform in second language acquisition research. In A. Gudmestad & A. Edmonds (Eds.), *Critical reflections on data in second language acquisition* (pp. 219–228). Benjamins.

Meunier, F. (2015). Developmental patterns in learner corpora. In S. Granger, G. Gilquin, & F. Meunier (Eds.), *The Cambridge handbook of learner corpus research* (pp. 379–400). Cambridge University Press.

Mitchell, R., Myles, F., & Marsden, E. (Eds.). (2019). *Second language theories* Routledge.

Murakami, A., & Alexopoulou, T. (2015). L1 influence on the acquisition order of English grammatical morphemes. *Studies in Second Language Acquisition, 38*(3), 1–37.

Myles, F. (2005). Interlanguage corpora and second language acquisition research. *Second Language Research, 21*, 373–391. https://doi.org/10.1191/0267658305sr252oa

Myles, F. (2013). Theoretical approaches. In J. Herschensohn & M. Young-Scholten (Eds.), *The Cambridge handbook of second language acquisition.* Cambridge University Press.

Myles, F. (2015). Second language acquisition theory and learner corpus research. In S. Granger, G. Gilquin, & F. Meunier (Eds.), *The Cambridge handbook of learner corpus research* (pp. 309–332). Cambridge University Press.

Myles, F., & Mitchell, R. (2012). *Learning French from ages 5, 7, and 11: An investigation into starting ages, rates, and routes of learning amongst early foreign language learners.* ESRC End of Award Report RES-062-23-1545. https://www.ripl.uk/wp-content/uploads/2017/03/EOA-Report-RES-062-23-1545.pdf (19 April 2021).

Norris, J., & Ortega, L. (2003). Defining and measuring SLA. In M. Long & C. J. Doughty (Eds.), *The handbook of second language acquisition* (p. 716–761). Wiley. https://doi.org/10.1002/9780470756492.ch21

Ortega, L. (2009). *Understanding second language acquisition.* Routledge.

Ortega, L. (2012). Interlanguage complexity a construct in search of theoretical renewal. In B. Kortmann & B. Szmrecsanyi (Eds.), *Linguistic complexity: Second language acquisition, indigenization, contact* (pp. 127–155). Mouton de Gruyter.

Paquot, M. (2010). *Academic vocabulary in learner writing: From extraction to analysis.* Continuum.

Paquot, M. (2017). L1 frequency in foreign language acquisition: Recurrent word combinations in French and Spanish EFL learner writing. *Second Language Research, 33*(1), 13–32.

Paquot, M. (2019). The phraseological dimension in interlanguage complexity research. *Second Language Research, 35*(1), 121–145. https://doi.org/10.177/0267658317694221

Paquot, M., & Plonsky, L. (2017). Quantitative research methods and study quality in learner corpus research. *International Journal of Learner Corpus Research, 3*(1), 61–94.

Plonsky, L. (2014). Study quality in quantitative L2 research (1990-2010): A methodological synthesis and call for reform. The *Modern Language Journal, 98*, 450–470. https://doi.org/10.1111/j.1540-4781.2014.12058.x

Plonsky, L., & Gönülal, T. (2015). Methodological synthesis in quantitative L2 research: A review of reviews and a case study of exploratory factor analysis. *Language Learning, 65*(1), 9–36.

Rothman, J., & VanPatten, B. (2013). On multiplicity and mutual exclusivity: The case for different SLA theories. In M. del Pilar García Mayo, M. Junkal Gutierrez Mangado, & M. Martínez Adrián (Eds.), *Contemporary approaches to second language acquisition* (pp. 243–256). Benjamins.

Siyanova-Chanturia, A., Conklin, K., & van Heuven, W. J. B. (2011). Seeing a phrase "time and again" matters : The role of phrasal frequency in the processing of multiword sequences. *Journal of Experimental Psychology: Learning, Memory, and Cognition, 37*(3), 776–784. doi: https://doi.org/10.1037/a0022531.

The Douglas Fir Group (2016). A transdisciplinary framework for SLA in a multilingual world. *The Modern Language Journal, 100*, 19–47. doi: https://doi.org/10.1111/modl.12301.

Tracy-Ventura, N., & Myles, F. (2015). The importance of task variability in the design of learner corpora for SLA research. *International Journal of Learner Corpus Research, 1*(1), 58–95. doi: https://doi.org/10.1075/ijlcr.1.1.03tra.

Tracy-Ventura, N., & Paquot, M. (Eds.). (2021). *The Routledge handbook of second language acquisition and corpora.* Routledge.

Tracy-Ventura, N., Paquot, M., & Myles, F. (2021). The future of corpora in SLA. In N. Tracy-Ventura & M. Paquot (Eds.), *The Routledge handbook of second language acquisition and corpora* (pp. 409–424). Routledge.

Van Patten, B., & Williams, J. (2015). Introduction: The nature of theories. In B. Van Patten & J. Williams (Eds.), *Theories in second language acquisition: An introduction* (pp. 1–16). Routledge.

Verspoor, M., & Lowie, W. (2021). Complex Dynamic System Theory (CDST) In N. Tracy-Ventura & M. Paquot (Eds.), *The RoutledgeRoutledge handbook of second language acquisition and corpora* (pp. 189–200). Routledge.

Verspoor, M., De Bot, K., & Lowie, W. (Eds). (2011). *A dynamic approach to second language development: Methods and techniques.* Benjamins.

Vilkaitė, L. (2017). Incidental acquisition of collocations in L2: Effects of adjacency and prior vocabulary knowledge. *International Journal of Applied Linguistics, 168*(2), 248–277. doi: https://doi.org/10.1075/itl.17005.vil.

Wolter, B., & Gyllstad, H. (2013). Frequency of input and L2 collocational processing. *Studies in Second Language Acquisition, 35*(03), 451–482. doi: https://doi.org/10.1017/S0272263113000107.

Wulff, S., & Gries, S. T. (2011). Corpus-driven methods for assessing accuracy in learner production. In P. Robinson (Ed.), *Second language task complexity: Researching the cognition hypothesis of language learning and performance* (pp. 61–87). Benjamins.

Wulff, S., & Gries, S. T. (2021). Explaining individual variation in learner corpus research: Some methodological suggestions. In B. Le Bruyn & M. Paquot (Eds.), *Learner corpus research meets second language acquisition* (pp. 191–213). Cambridge University Press.

Ziegler, N., & Mackey, A. (2021). Interaction. In N. Tracy-Ventura & M. Paquot (Eds.), *The Routledge handbook of second language acquisition and corpora* (pp. 280–292). Routledge.

3
CORPORA AND TEACHING VOCABULARY AND PHRASEOLOGY

Paweł Szudarski

3.1 Introduction

Since the mid-1980s, the advent of corpora has exerted a significant influence on the field of applied linguistics, with vocabulary studies being a prime example of this change. As attested by the growing number of specialised publications that highlight the benefits and affordances of corpus methods for the study of vocabulary (e.g. Gardner, 2013; Szudarski, 2018), there is now a sizeable body of scholarship demonstrating the inextricable link between lexical research and corpus analysis. This chapter aims to review the main strands of this research as pertinent to analysing vocabulary and phraseology. By discussing the key corpus-based findings, the chapter not only provides a state-of-the-art overview of the applications of corpora for research and teaching purposes, but also points to future directions in this fast-growing line of linguistic inquiry.

3.2 Current state of vocabulary research

In recent decades, we have experienced an unprecedented increase in the amount of interest in vocabulary as a research topic, with a great deal of new findings focusing on the description of vocabulary, its learning, processing and use across different contexts (see Webb, 2020, for a comprehensive overview). A substantial part of this research has benefited from the expansion of corpora by relying on a variety of corpus methods and by using corpus findings to delve into the nature of vocabulary knowledge. As recently emphasised by Schmitt and Schmitt (2020), the introduction of corpora and the availability of corpus tools in the latter part of the 20th century have been one of the most significant developments in vocabulary studies.

Schmitt and Schmitt (2020, p. 75) rightly point out that corpora "have revolutionized the way we view language, particularly words and their relationships with each other in context", equipping linguists with a new set of tools and insights into vocabulary and its role as a sub-level of language. As explained in more detail in Szudarski (2018), there are a number of questions relevant to the study of vocabulary which can be addressed by means of corpus-based analysis. These include, for instance, differences between high- and low-frequency words, the prevalence and significance of formulaic language, characteristic features of academic vocabulary, to name just a few. Underlining the fundamental role of corpora in vocabulary

DOI: 10.4324/9781003002901-5

studies, the following paragraphs present an overview of the key issues which have been at the forefront of corpus-based lexical research.

3.3 Core issues in corpus-based vocabulary research

For the purposes of this chapter, the main strands of lexical research have been grouped under three broad categories: 1) the use of corpus-based analysis to identify different types of vocabulary, 2) the indirect influence of corpora in syllabus design and materials development, and 3) the direct use of corpora and corpus tools in teaching vocabulary and phraseology. By reporting the latest findings and referring to specific studies, the chapter provides examples of corpus-based applications for describing and analysing vocabulary, a summary of how corpora can be employed in teaching and suggestions for further developments in this area of research.

3.3.1 Use of corpus-based analysis of vocabulary

Corpora can be applied to analyse vocabulary and its different types in several ways. These include, among others, frequency-based descriptions of vocabulary, vocabulary use in different contexts and phrasal vocabulary and formulaic language. All of these topics are discussed in detail in the subsequent sections.

3.3.1.1 Frequency-based descriptions of vocabulary

Frequency-based analysis and description of vocabulary is a prime example of how lexical research has greatly benefitted from the development of corpora. While rather simple conceptually (ranking words on the basis of their occurrence in natural discourse), frequency is a fundamental concept in all corpus and second language (L2) research. Given its significance as a key factor that drives language learning and use (e.g. Ellis, 2002; Gries & Divjak, 2012; Madlener, 2015), the value of frequency information for exploring the occurrence and co-occurrence of specific words and multiword units cannot be overstated. As emphatically summarised by Milton (2009, p. 242), "the importance of frequency to vocabulary learning is as near a fact as it is possible to get in L2 acquisition", although by no means should frequency be regarded as the only factor that mediates the process of L2 learning.

Corpus research has revealed that vocabulary use is largely characterised by Zipf's law. It reveals a clear pattern in the occurrence of words where a relatively small number of items have a very high frequency and cover most of speakers' everyday use of language. In fact, the first 2–3,000 word families[1] do most of the work in communication, making up more than 80% of all running words in spoken and written texts (Nation, 2013; O'Keeffe *et al.*, 2007). After this, the frequency of words drops off very quickly, reflecting the fact that domain-specific communication requires more precise and specialised vocabulary (e.g. technical vocabulary) that occurs in fewer contexts and is, therefore, of lower frequency (Schmitt & Schmitt, 2020). As discussed in Szudarski (2018), a Zipfian distribution suggests an inverse relationship between the occurrence of words and their rank in corpus-derived frequency lists, with the first most frequent word on a list occurring roughly twice as often as the second word and three times as often as the third one and so on. Thus, a frequency-based analysis not only points to a highly regular and patterned structure of language, but also emphasises the essential role of commonly occurring words and phrases.

Nation (2016, pp. 4–5) summarised this role by means of three generalisations that stem from Zipf's law:

- there is a relatively small number of words that have a high frequency
- there is a very large number of words that have a low frequency
- the frequency of words on a word list drops very quickly.

In light of these corpus insights, it is not surprising that vocabulary scholars have encouraged teachers, textbooks writers and learners themselves to pay particular attention to high-frequency words as the core element of linguistic competence. By way of example, Nation (2013) contends that such is the importance of high-frequency vocabulary that anything we can do to ensure that it is learned by L2 learners is indeed worth doing. This is a perfect example of how corpus-based research has had a genuine impact on language pedagogy, with figures such as the first 2–3,000 most frequent word families in English being commonly perceived as a threshold for high-frequency vocabulary and an essential ingredient of successful language use (Nation, 2006; Schmitt, 2010; Schmitt & Schmitt, 2020). Consequently, knowing vocabulary at this level has been regarded as the absolute minimum that learners need to develop as quickly as possible if they are to communicate effectively in a range of life situations. In other words, given that such high-frequency vocabulary offers learners the best chance to understand a variety of texts, the first 3,000 most frequent word families merit direct attention in the classroom and the mastery of these words needs to be prioritised in all learning contexts (Vilkaite-Lozdiene & Schmitt, 2020).

However, as important as high-frequency vocabulary may be, this knowledge alone is not sufficient to allow speakers to operate in English[2] across varied communicative situations. As demonstrated by Nation (2006), language comprehension requires specific levels of lexical knowledge or lexical coverage at different frequency levels defined as the percentage of words known in a given domain or type of text.

Put differently, a certain amount of vocabulary is necessary for the comprehension of specific types of texts, with the most frequent 8–9,000-word families required to allow L2 users an adequate understanding of a wide range of written discourse (assuming a 98 per cent coverage requirement). For spoken discourse, this requirement is lower, with 6–7,000 most frequent word families providing 98% coverage of a range of listening passages (Nation, 2006). Interestingly, for a more restricted type of listening such as everyday storytelling, van Zeeland and Schmitt (2013) found evidence that knowledge of 2–3,000 word families can provide a satisfactory level of comprehension at 95% coverage.

In practical terms, this means that the analysis and selection of lexis beyond high-frequency levels should be pedagogically informed and ought to be based on finer-grained categorisations of L2 vocabulary (Nation, 2013; O'Keeffe *et al.*, 2007). One such view of vocabulary has been proposed by Schmitt and Schmitt (2014), who used corpus findings as well as pedagogic grounds to divide English vocabulary into three main categories: high-, mid-, and low- frequency. As Figure 3.1 demonstrates, high-frequency vocabulary is understood as the first 3,000 most frequent word families essential for any language use, mid-frequency vocabulary encompasses word families between the third- and ninth-thousand band, and low-frequency vocabulary refers to any word families that go beyond the threshold of 9,000 most frequent word families in English.

This typology clearly delineates differences between the high- and low-frequency vocabulary. However, what is innovative about Schmitt and Schmitt's approach is their call for paying more attention to the "in-between" vocabulary from the mid-frequency levels, the mastery

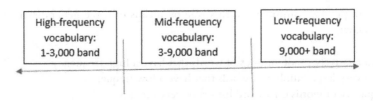

| High-frequency vocabulary: 1-3,000 band | Mid-frequency vocabulary: 3-9,000 band | Low-frequency vocabulary: 9,000+ band |

Figure 3.1 Frequency-based typology of vocabulary adapted from Schmitt and Schmitt (2014)

of which is deemed necessary to engage in authentic conversations and reach an optimal understanding of different types of texts. The authors convincingly argue that the knowledge of high-frequency and technical words is not sufficient to deal with domain-specific texts (Schmitt & Schmitt, 2014, p. 497) and therefore mid-frequency vocabulary merits consideration in its own right, in terms of both language pedagogy and materials development.

3.3.1.2 Use of vocabulary in specific contexts

Beyond simple frequency-based rankings of vocabulary, corpus tools have been employed to analyse and describe the use and behaviour of words in specific areas and registers. This has led to the identification of different types of vocabulary necessary to function in specialised contexts, such as, for instance, academic and technical vocabulary (Coxhead, this volume). The best illustration of such specialised contexts is the use of English for academic (EAP) or specific purposes (ESP), with an impressive body of evidence showing how vocabulary use in these settings differs from the use of English for general purposes (see Nesi, 2016 for an overview). In terms of academic vocabulary, a good example is Coxhead's (2000) Academic Word List (AWL), which has been one of the most influential corpus-based studies in this area. The author demonstrated how 570-word families derived from a 3.5-million-word corpus can provide a roughly 10% coverage of all words in any academic written text. However, it should be noted that the AWL is less powerful in spoken academic contexts; Dang and Webb (2014) found only 4.41% coverage of the British Academic Spoken English corpus, highlighting yet again the importance of register variation.

Similarly, there has also been a growing body of corpus-based work that focused on technical or disciplinary vocabulary defined as vocabulary with a narrow range of occurrence within a particular subject area (Coxhead, 2016). For instance, Chung and Nation (2004) illustrate how comparisons between specialised and general-purpose corpora can be an effective way of identifying disciplinary and domain-specific vocabulary. However, given that academic and technical vocabulary are subsets of general English that cut across the neat 1,000-word bands used in corpus studies (Schmitt & Schmitt, 2014), and that some high-frequency words might carry more specialised meanings when used in specific contexts, establishing the boundaries for specific bands of technical vocabulary poses a serious challenge. Consequently, vocabulary use needs to be analysed in relation to the behaviour of words as they occur in particular texts and contexts (e.g. the role of collocations and lexical patterns in building different types of discourse), supplemented with pedagogical insights gained through an analysis of learners' lexical needs (see also the following discussion of basic- and advanced-level vocabulary).

In light of the above, it can be asserted that by presenting lexis as corpus-based bands or lists of items, the task of describing the vast amount of English vocabulary and representing its various uses has become a less daunting proposition, not only for vocabulary researchers but also for teachers and other language professionals. Also, by analysing the use of vocabulary in real life and focusing on the study of language as discourse (McCarthy & Carter, 1994), corpora have shifted our attention from what is possible in language (i.e. made-up sentences produced by the "ideal" speaker) to what is typical or characteristic of specific linguistic domains, registers and types of discourse (Halliday, 1982). Put differently, frequency information, concordances and corpus outputs have shed more light on the levels of systematicity, recurrence and regularity as key characteristics of naturally occurring language. It is this highly regular and patterned aspect of language use that will be addressed in the last paragraphs of this section, with the discussion focusing on the centrality of phrasal vocabulary and formulaic sequences in corpus-based research.

3.3.1.3 Phrasal vocabulary and formulaic language

Corpora have been instrumental in underlining the importance of phraseology and multiword units, bringing to the fore the highly patterned nature of language use and showing that a large part of both written and spoken discourse consists of phraseological units. Following seminal publications in this area (Schmitt, 2004; Wray, 2002), such units have become known as "formulaic sequences"[3] and, while there are important differences between specific types of formulaic sequences, using such an umbrella term is helpful to capture and emphasise the prevalence of formulaicity as a language phenomenon.

A thorough review of corpus findings into phrasal vocabulary is beyond the scope of this chapter (see Siyanova-Chanturia & Pellicer-Sanchez, 2019; Szudarski & Barclay, 2021). However, it needs to be stressed that after many years of treating single words as the main unit of linguistic analysis, the advent of corpora has played a central part in showing that words tend to cluster together, form various kinds of lexical partnerships and, crucially, speakers and writers rely on such combinations to fulfil a number of key linguistic and pragmatic functions (e.g. building coherence). Currently, with the field experiencing an impressive growth of interest in this area, formulaic language has emerged as one of the most relevant topics in corpus-based studies and applied linguistics as a whole (Schmitt & Schmitt, 2020).

This is also true for research exploring the impact of language instruction on the knowledge of L2 formulaic sequences. As Meunier (2020) remarks, multiword units are ubiquitous linguistic constructions, the acquisition of which is dependent on a whole range of interconnected determinants, including frequency effects, meaning- and prototypicality-related aspects, form-meaning associations, salience, and specific forms of explicit and implicit learning. In light of this, it is understandable that vocabulary specialists have been rather cautious in terms of making strong recommendations on how to best enhance the knowledge of L2 formulaic sequences through classroom practice. It is clear, however, that because of L2 learners' difficulty in learning formulaic language, information on phrasal vocabulary needs to feature systematically in teaching syllabi and materials, with insights from corpora enriching and informing pedagogical decisions of teachers and textbook writers.

One example of such research is Martinez's (2013) framework for the inclusion of phraseology in mainstream language teaching, which points to the frequency and semantic transparency of phrases as the main criteria for selecting pedagogically relevant items. The framework suggests that high-frequency items ought to be targeted through explicit teaching (e.g. *take place* is more frequent than *take credit* in the BNC). However, given that frequency is not the only variable that determines the pedagogical relevance of vocabulary, Martinez suggests that the meaning and semantic compositionality of phrases should also be considered. This means that more opaque items are presented as deserving more attention in the classroom than more transparent phrases (e.g. *take time* appears easier to decode than *take place* and therefore the latter phrase may need to be prioritised in language teaching). Importantly, accepting that the selection of pedagogically relevant phrases is a matter of degree rather than absolute distinctions and stressing that this process is learner- or context-dependent, Martinez (2013) treats his framework as "a research-informed conceptual aid" (p. 190) which should assist formal language instruction. Using the judgement of learners' level and abilities, teachers and materials writers can make use of such corpus-based tools as a way to deal with the prevalence of formulaic language and draw learners' attention to these phrases that they need the most.

3.3.2 Indirect use of corpora in teaching and learning vocabulary

As regards the impact of corpus linguistics on language teaching, we can broadly talk about two main areas: 1) the use of corpus information for selecting relevant vocabulary and developing language syllabi and pedagogical materials and 2) the use of corpus data as a teaching technique. These have been referred to as "indirect" and "direct" applications of corpora, respectively (McEnery & Xiao, 2010; Römer, 2011). This section focuses on the former (see the next section for an overview of the latter) and discusses the following issues: 1) corpus-assisted analyses of the vocabulary load of different types of texts; 2) corpus-informed pedagogical approaches to learning and teaching vocabulary; and 3) the use of corpora to select appropriate vocabulary for the purposes of materials writing and syllabus design.

3.3.2.1 Corpus-assisted analysis of vocabulary and lexical profiling

Section 3.1.1 has already outlined recent corpus-based research into the notion of lexical coverage and the usefulness of frequency-based descriptions of vocabulary (see Nurmukhamedov & Webb, 2019 for a comprehensive overview). Importantly, this research has tangibly benefited and informed formal language instruction, not only with respect to lexis but, as stated by Laufer and Cobb (2020), also to language pedagogy more broadly. Specifically, corpora have produced new insights into the lexical profile of various types of discourse, the characteristics of vocabulary use across a variety of contexts and the vocabulary difficulty or load of texts representing specific domains.

By way of example, Laufer and Cobb (2020) used *Morpholex*, a piece of corpus-based software available via Lextutor (Cobb, n.d.), to explore the role of derived vocabulary in achieving reading comprehension. Specifically, by analysing the frequency of the most common derivational affixes (e.g. *-age*, *-ion*, *-ly*) and the coverage they provide in a range of authentic English texts, the authors found that the knowledge of basewords and their inflections were sufficient to reach the minimal 95% lexical threshold required for adequate reading comprehension. Knowledge of only a small number of the most frequent derivative affixes, rather than the knowledge of all derivative forms, allowed the attainment of 98% coverage, which is considered optimal for independent reading (Laufer & Ravenhorst-Kalovski, 2010). Such results then have a tangible pedagogical value, as they clearly point to specific affixes and types of vocabulary to be focused on as essential elements of L2 lexical competence.

Likewise, corpus data have been usefully applied to create lexical frequency profiles (LFP) of texts as a source of information about the quality or sophistication of vocabulary use. As Laufer (2013) notes, quantitative indices such as LFP are based on the proportion of frequent vs. nonfrequent words and, therefore, constitute a useful means of studying the lexical richness of texts, produced by both L1 and L2 users (see below for information on learner corpora) across various domains and communicative situations. For instance, in one of the first

Home > VocabProfilers > VP-Compleat Input > **Output** ('Back' preserves inputs)   FRAMEWORK IS bnc_coca Families

Freq. Level	Families (%)	Types (%)	Tokens (%)	Cumul. token (%)
K-1 :	66 (55.5)	80 (55.56)	178 (67.2)	67.2
K-2 :	25 (21.0)	29 (20.14)	32 (12.1)	79.3
K-3 :	20 (16.8)	23 (15.97)	29 (10.9)	90.2
K-4 :	2 (1.7)	2 (1.39)	2 (0.8)	91.0
K-5 :	1 (0.8)	1 (0.69)	5 (1.9)	92.9
K-6 :	2 (1.7)	3 (2.08)	7 (2.6)	95.5
Coverage 95				
K-7 :	1 (0.8)	1 (0.69)	1 (0.4)	95.9
K-8 :	1 (0.8)	1 (0.69)	5 (1.9)	97.8
Coverage 98				
K-9 :				
K-10 :				
K-11 :	1 (0.8)	1 (0.69)	2 (0.8)	98.6
K-12 :				
K-13 :				
K-14 :				
K-15 :				

Pertaining to whole text
Words in text (tokens):	265
Different words (types):	144
Type-token ratio (TTR):	0.54
Tokens per type:	1.84
Lexical density (content [166]/total [265]):	0.63

Pertaining to onlist only
Tokens:	261
Types:	141
Families:	119
Tokens per Family:	2.19
Family/token ratio (FTR):	0.46
Types per Family:	1.18
Singletons ratio Fams(n=1)[69] / total [119]	0.58

Figure 3.2   A lexical profile of a text created via VocabProfiler (with the BNC/COCA 25 list used as a reference corpus)

studies that used a vocabulary profiler as a measure of language use, Laufer and Nation (1995) investigated the written output sampled from learners representing different proficiency levels and, by comparing the lexical qualities of their output, found that more advanced learners used a higher percentage of infrequent words than lower-level learners.

In terms of how this analysis is performed, the procedure is quite simple: using corpus-based programs such as Range (Paul Nation's website) or VocabProfiler (Tom Cobb's Lextutor website), the vocabulary from a target text is compared to the vocabulary found in a reference corpus (usually a general-purpose corpus). More specifically, word lists drawn from corpora such as the BNC or COCA contain all vocabulary divided into frequency or category bands (e.g. the 1K to 25K bands in the Lextutor VocabProfiler using the BNC/COCA 25 option) and these bands are used to create a lexical profile of the text(s) under study. This produces an output similar to the one in Figure 3.2, which is a lexical profile of the current two paragraphs created via VocabProfiler.

This output demonstrates that a corpus-based profile of the text in question contains a great deal of lexical information, including information on the number of tokens (all examples of words in the text) and types (examples of distinct words in the text) at different frequency levels, the type-token ratio treated as a measure of lexical richness and other indices related to the use of vocabulary and lexical density. For instance, it can be seen that the majority of words in this text are high-frequency words that belong to the first three one-thousand-word bands (66 word families at 1K level, 25 at 2K level and 20 at 3K level). Further, the text contains only a few (seven, to be exact) mid-frequency items at the fourth–ninth levels, with only one word family at 11K level (perceived as low-frequency vocabulary). This confirms what was stated previously about the key role of high-frequency vocabulary in covering a high percentage of words in spoken and written texts. Finally, as Laufer (2013) observes, such frequency profiles can be treated as a proxy for proficiency, for they tap into writers' or speakers' lexical proficiency and the ways their lexical knowledge is put into practice (Leńko-Szymańska, 2002).

However, if our overall aim is to build a comprehensive picture of L2 vocabulary growth, such corpus-based measures of lexical proficiency should probably be complemented by information from other types of vocabulary tests. This is because while frequency plays a central part in lexical analysis, LFPs may be insufficiently granular to capture small changes in learners' lexis, particularly when we know that most texts tend to have similar percentages of the most frequent vocabulary. Further, lexical profiles do not account for the presence of homonyms or multiword units. It is, therefore, advisable to consider other variables that influence the process of L2 learning, including salience (e.g. concreteness of words), contextual distinctiveness (e.g. the range or dispersion of tokens and types across a text or corpus) and the number and quality of collocations, all of which "can be used in concert with frequency to more accurately model the sophistication of a particular lexical item" (Kyle, 2020, p. 464). With regard to the latter, Bestgen and Granger (2014) and Kyle and Crossley (2015) provide convincing evidence of how automated measures of vocabulary, including the use of multi-word units, can be effectively employed to explore proficient language production.

3.3.2.2 Corpora and pedagogical approaches to vocabulary

This part of the overview of the impact of corpora on teaching vocabulary is concerned with the role of corpus-based findings in informing the decisions and everyday practice of teachers and syllabus designers. As supported by extensive research, high-frequency vocabulary is commonly viewed as an essential element of linguistic competence and should, therefore, be targeted through formal and explicit instruction (Nation, 2013; Schmitt & Schmitt, 2020). However, L2 speakers, particularly those in foreign language contexts, face multiple challenges in developing general lexical proficiency (Levitzky-Aviad & Laufer, 2013; Nguyen & Webb, 2017; Szudarski, 2020). Consequently, the facilitation of the acquisition of the 3,000 most frequent families may constitute a tall order for both language learners and teachers. This puts a premium on applying corpus evidence as a way to deliver effective and level-appropriate language education to learners. With this in mind, the following paragraphs review the key corpus findings that pertain to the selection of L2 vocabulary, lexical syllabi and materials design.

The benefits of corpus-based analysis of vocabulary have been clearly demonstrated in pedagogically-oriented discussions of basic- and advanced-level vocabulary. For instance, McCarthy (2001) applied corpus findings to define the notion of an advanced-level vocabulary, using estimations of the relationship between L2 comprehension and lexical coverage as the basis for setting pedagogical goals. Specifically, the author stated that a 10,000-word receptive knowledge seemed a feasible goal for advanced-level learners, based on the assumption that intermediate learners already know between 4,000 and 6,000 words receptively and, therefore, learning another 4,000–5,000 words is required to get them to the advanced level of proficiency.

However, acquiring so much vocabulary is no mean feat, given the usual time constraints that characterise typical classroom teaching, particularly in EFL contexts. Therefore, rather than teaching thousands of these words explicitly, which appears an impossible task in most language classrooms anyway, McCarthy (2001) underlined the role of promoting extensive L2 reading as well as raising learners' awareness of different strategies as a way of assisting both school and out-of-school language learning. From this perspective, vocabulary teaching at higher levels is not a haphazard process aimed predominantly at introducing new bands of increasingly obscure low-frequency words. Instead, what is recommended is a research-informed and principled approach to syllabus design where lexis is organically linked to the teaching of other aspects of linguistic competence required to meet communicative goals (O'Keeffe *et al.*, 2007; Schmitt & Schmitt, 2020; see also Nation, 2007 for a four-strand model of vocabulary teaching).

3.3.2.3 Syllabus design and materials development

Corpus-based studies of vocabulary and formulaic language have also resulted in the promotion of more innovative approaches to syllabus and materials design, with series of textbooks such as *Touchstone* (McCarthy *et al.*, 2005) or *Outcomes* (Dellar & Walkley, 2015) showing that lexically-rich syllabi can be successfully implemented with learners at different proficiency levels (see Szudarski, 2012 for details on the lexical syllabus; see also Dellar and Walkley, 2016 for an overview of lexis-oriented teaching methodologies).

It is worth mentioning that recently there has been an increasing amount of work concerning the development of corpus-based lists of both single-word and phrasal vocabulary as useful tools for assisting the learning and teaching process (see Dang, 2020 for an overview). Examples of these include the New Academic Vocabulary List (Gardner & Davies, 2014) or the PHRASE List (Martinez & Schmitt, 2012). Finally, corpus findings have also informed the creation of materials aimed at teaching specialised varieties of language such as, for instance, Handford *et al.*'s (2011) *Business Advantage*, a business English textbook based on the Cambridge Business Corpus and the Cambridge and Nottingham Business English Corpus.

3.3.3 Direct use of corpora in teaching and learning vocabulary

The focus of this section is the direct use of corpora in teaching and learning vocabulary as manifested in research into data-driven learning, learner and pedagogically-oriented corpora and computer-assisted language learning (CALL).

3.3.3.1 Vocabulary and data-driven learning

Data-driven learning (DDL) is usually defined as the direct use of corpora in language teaching and constitutes another concrete manifestation of how vocabulary research has benefited from corpus analysis. In its broadest sense, DDL can be said to "consist in using the tools and techniques of corpus linguistics for pedagogical purposes" (Gilquin & Granger, 2010, p. 359), with a growing body of research supporting the direct use of corpus data in classroom instruction (e.g. O'Keeffe, 2021; see also Bardovi-Harlig & Mossman, this volume; Charles, this volume; Farr & Karlsen, this volume). Specifically, DDL allows learners to engage with concordances (authentic examples drawn from corpora) and develop the necessary autonomy and awareness to discover regularities in language.

Most encouragingly, perhaps, DDL has been shown to work as an effective pedagogical approach, resulting in gains in L2 learners' knowledge at various levels of linguistic competence. A key reference in this area is Boulton and Cobb's (2017) meta-analysis of experimental investigations of the impact of DDL on L2 learning. With 88 unique samples from 64 separate studies, DDL was found to lead to large learning effects, particularly in relation to enhancing lexical knowledge. To quote the authors' exact words, "DDL works pretty well in almost any context where it has been extensively tried" (Boulton & Cobb, 2017, p. 386), which suggests that corpora can be successfully applied in different pedagogical settings and with learners representing different proficiency levels (Crosthwaite, this volume).

Lee *et al.* (2019) and Perez-Paredes (2019) reported similarly encouraging findings, showing a positive, medium-sized effect of DDL on L2 vocabulary learning. Benefits of DDL have also been found in teaching contexts that focus on more specialised uses of language. For instance, based on a synthesis of 37 DDL studies in the area of EAP, Chen and Flowerdew (2018) revealed a range of positive trends in the use of corpus data and tools in academic writing instruction, including the use of pedagogically-oriented corpora and more specialised genre-oriented teaching approaches.

3.3.3.2 Pedagogically-oriented corpora and CALL

While still a relatively new field, research into learner English (and other languages to a lesser extent) is another robust line of linguistic inquiry that has gained popularity in recent years, with vocabulary specialists and teachers making increased use of learner and pedagogically-oriented corpora. Examples of key corpus-based findings include persistent collocational errors in learner production (Laufer & Waldman, 2011), L2 writers' overuse and underuse of important formulaic phrases (Durrant & Schmitt, 2009) and a complex relationship between lexical growth and growing L2 proficiency (Siyanova-Chanturia & Spina, 2020).

Likewise, pedagogically-oriented corpora have served an important function when it comes to delivering effective vocabulary teaching. Sometimes such corpora are also referred to as personal or do-it-yourself corpora, usually developed on the basis of a needs-analysis of specific groups of learners in specialised contexts (e.g. Charles, 2014 for details on the use of personal corpora with EAP students). For instance, personal corpora can be particularly useful in the area of teacher education, allowing a whole new level of analysis of classroom discourse, patterns of interaction and the use of language in response to specific tasks (Farr & O'Keeffe, 2019).

Further, thanks to computers and rapid technological changes, vocabulary specialists have been preoccupied with the effects of computer-assisted language learning (CALL), games and virtual learning environments on enhancing L2 learners' knowledge of both individual words and formulaic sequences (see Elgort, 2018, or Li, 2016 for comprehensive overviews of the use of technology and CALL tools for vocabulary acquisition). Also, there have been important findings into the positive effects of gaming and digital environments on enhancing lexical learning, particularly among younger learners (e.g. Sundqvist, 2019; Sylven & Sundqvist, 2012; Tang & Taguchi, 2020), showing that technology- and computer-enhanced learning begins to play an increasingly important role in contemporary language instruction.

Going forward, as language educators and materials writers, we need to be ready to capitalise on the current corpus revolution and create multimodal language learning conditions that reflect the reality and needs of our students. The ColloCaid project (Frankenberg-Garcia *et al.*, 2019) is a convincing example of how corpus data can be successfully employed to give rise to a new generation of technology-enhanced resources and learning tools. More specifically, ColloCaid is a digital text editor which supports academic writing by making real-time collocation suggestions. A key feature of this tool is that it does not distract the writing process by focusing only on errors. Rather, using corpus-derived information on common phrases, ColloCaid is responsive to the output produced by writers and by providing information on potential miscollocations and "feeding forward" (Frankenberg-Garcia, 2020), it heightens their awareness of these word combinations that may not be known or remembered during the process of "live" writing. While empirical evidence is needed before any more concrete recommendations can be made about the long-term effects of such tools, it is evident that this kind of cutting-edge research is likely to grow and make increased use of new technological developments (see Cobb, 2019, and Schmitt, 2019, for specific examples of research questions on the role of extramural exposure, CALL and corpus-informed sources of vocabulary learning).

3.4 Future directions of research

Despite many positive developments in corpus-based analysis of vocabulary outlined in this chapter, there are several areas which remain to be addressed in future research. As rightly observed by Gilmore (2015, pp. 516–517), there are at least two examples within the realm of language teaching where the uptake of corpus analysis "has been less enthusiastic". Firstly, textbook authors do not seem to make habitual use of corpus insights in the production of teaching materials (e.g. Burton, 2012) and secondly, direct applications of corpus data by language learners and teachers are still limited, widening the gap between research findings and everyday classroom practice. In fact, the issue of overcoming this disconnect and translating corpus findings into a more principled approach to materials development and vocabulary instruction has been highlighted recently by Schmitt (2019) as one of the key challenges to be tackled in future research. Likewise, in her recent commentary on the ongoing corpus revolution, Chambers (2019) called language teacher educators, materials developers and major publishers to play a much more active role in addressing the growing research-practice gap, particularly if the use of corpora is to go beyond teaching highly proficient L2 learners in academic settings and promote DDL among other populations of L2 learners (see Crosthwaite, 2020, for examples of corpus-based projects with younger learners).

Another big challenge that merits more attention is the development of corpus literacy skills and pedagogic expertise among teachers and other language practitioners. For well over a decade, a number of publications (e.g. McCarthy, 2008; O'Keeffe *et al.*, 2007) have been calling for raising the profile of corpus training in language teacher education, rendering it a necessary step for a further integration of corpora into regular classroom practice. Yet, despite all these efforts, the lack of corpus expertise and proper training in corpus analysis remains one of the biggest obstacles preventing a more ambitious implementation of corpus-based language teaching (Chambers, 2019). That said, it is encouraging to see a growing amount of work in this area, with studies such as Zareva (2017) or Leńko-Szymańska (2017) shedding more light on the mechanics of training language teachers and enabling them to explore (and benefit from) the affordances of corpora (Leńko-Szymańska, this volume).

As regards specific directions in applied corpus-based research, there is a clear need for more work describing and presenting vocabulary by means of smaller, frequency-based bands of words. For example, Dang and Webb (2016) provided a list of 800 core lemmas as a potential goal for beginner-level courses, while Kremmel (2016) advocated the use of 500-item bands for higher-frequency vocabulary and bands larger than 1,000 items for lower-frequency words, suggesting a more manageable approach to vocabulary instruction (see also Brown *et al.*, 2020, for a recent review of research into the most appropriate lexical unit for vocabulary research and pedagogy). Likewise, Vilkaite-Lozdiene and Schmitt (2020) note that "teachers should probably start focusing on the 1,000 most frequent content words first as they will have the most value for their learners" (p. 87), underlining the importance of marrying future research ambitions and classroom realities. Such ideas are a welcome proposition, as they go hand in hand with the notion of setting realistic pedagogical goals that match learners' communicative needs and capabilities at different proficiency levels.

Finally, this overview has clearly shown the importance of a principled and research-based approach to formal vocabulary instruction. As stressed several times already, it is essential that insights from corpus-based research and pedagogy are used together to create the optimal classroom conditions and assist L2 learners, not only in the sense of enhancing their lexical competence but also helping them become successful language users in a broader sense. In order to achieve this goal, what is needed is more interdisciplinary and innovative research along the lines of Simpson-Vlach and Ellis (2010), He and Godfroid (2019), or Dang *et al.* (2020), where the frequency-based descriptions and selection of vocabulary are considered in tandem with teachers' ratings of the usefulness and difficulty of words and phrases, ensuring a better level of synergy at the interface of corpus research and pedagogic practice (Chambers, 2019). It is hoped that this chapter has provided a useful summary of how these efforts can be intensified and inform our teaching approach to vocabulary as a key element of language studies.

Notes

1 Word family is a base from of a word together with all its inflections and derivatives (Schmitt & Schmitt, 2020)
2 Throughout this chapter, I will discuss and draw on corpus examples that concern English vocabulary. However, it is important to note that there are many non-English corpora available; much of the information in this chapter applies equally to such tools.
3 *Multiword units* is another term that is commonly used in the literature. Through this chapter, it will be used interchangeably with the term *formulaic sequences*.

Further reading

Schmitt, N., & Schmitt, D. (2020). *Vocabulary in language teaching*. Cambridge University Press. This volume offers a comprehensive introduction to vocabulary for language teachers with a chapter fully devoted to the use of corpora in vocabulary studies. Written by two leading specialists in the field, the book takes account of the recent developments in vocabulary research and offers a wealth of guidance on how empirical findings should inform language pedagogy.
Szudarski, P. (2018). *Corpus linguistics for vocabulary. A guide for research*. Routledge. This book is a practical introduction to the use of corpus linguistics in vocabulary research aimed at individuals with little experience in corpus analysis. The author provides a step-by-step guide on how corpus methods and tools can be applied to explore a wide range of vocabulary-related research questions.
Szudarski, P., & Barclays, S. (Eds.). (2021). *Vocabulary theory, patterning and teaching*. Multilingual Matters. This edited volume presents the current state of knowledge in the diverse field of vocabulary studies. Summarizing latest findings pertaining to vocabulary, the book presents a variety of research perspectives and showcases topics for future work in areas such as theorizing and measuring vocabulary knowledge, corpus-based analysis of vocabulary use and learning and teaching vocabulary in pedagogical settings.
Webb, S. (Ed.). (2020). *The Routledge handbook of vocabulary studies*. Routledge. This handbook constitutes a cutting-edge survey of current scholarship in the field. Featuring contributions from vocabulary specialists representing different research traditions, the book offers a comprehensive discussion of the key issues in lexical research, with the majority of chapters pointing to the fundamental role of corpora in the analysis of vocabulary.

References

Bestgen, Y., & Granger, S. (2014). Quantifying the development of phraseological competence in L2 English writing: An automated approach. *Journal of Second Language Writing, 26*, 28–41. https://doi.org/10.1016/j.jslw.2014.09.004
Boulton, A., & Cobb, T. (2017). Corpus use in language learning: A meta-analysis. *Language Learning, 67*(2), 348–393. https://doi.org/10.1111/lang.12224.
Brown, D., Stoeckel, T., Mclean, S., & Stewart, J. (2020). The most appropriate lexical unit for L2 vocabulary research and pedagogy: A brief review of the evidence. *Applied Linguistics*, Advance articles, 1–7. https://doi.org/10.1093/applin/amaa061
Burton, G. (2012). Corpora and coursebooks: Destined to be strangers forever? *Corpora, 7*(1), 91–108. https://doi.org/10.3366/cor.2012.0019.

Charles, M. (2014). Getting the corpus habit: EAP students' long-term use of personal corpora. *English for Specific Purposes, 35*, 30–40. http://dx.doi.org/10.1016/j.esp.2013.11.004

Chambers, A. (2019). Towards the corpus revolution? Bridging the research-practice gap. *Language Teaching, 52*(4), 460–475. https://doi.org/10.1017/S0261444819000089.

Chen, M., & Flowerdew, J. (2018). A critical review of research and practice in data-driven learning (DDL) in the academic writing classroom. *International Journal of Corpus Linguistics, 23*(3), 335–369. https://doi.org/10.1075/ijcl.16130.che.

Chung, T. M., & Nation, I. S. P. (2004). Identifying technical vocabulary. *System, 32*(2), 251–263. https://doi.org/10.1016/j.system.2003.11.008.

Cobb, T. (2019). From corpus to CALL. The use of technology in teaching and learning formulaic language. In A. Siyanova-Chanturia & A. Pellicer-Sanchez (Eds.), *Understanding formulaic language. A second language acquisition perspective* (pp. 192–210). Routledge.

Cobb, T. (n.d.). Lextutor. Retrieved December 30, 2020, from https://www.lextutor.ca/

Coxhead, A. (2000). A new academic word list. *TESOL Quarterly, 34*(2), 213–238. https://doi.org/10.2307/3587951.

Coxhead, A. (2016). Acquiring academic and disciplinary vocabulary. In K. Hyland & P. Shaw (Eds.), *The Routledge handbook of English for Academic Purposes* (pp. 177–190). Routledge.

Crosthwaite, P. (Ed.). (2020). *Data-driven learning for the next generation. Corpora and DDL for pre-tertiary learners.* Routledge.

Dang, T. N. Y. (2020). Corpus-based word lists in second language vocabulary research, learning, and teaching. In S. Webb (Ed.), *The Routledge handbook of vocabulary studies* (pp. 288–303). Routledge.

Dang, T. N. Y., & Webb, S. (2014). The lexical profile of academic spoken English. *English for Specific Purposes, 33*, 66–76. https://doi.org/10.1016/j.esp.2013.08.001

Dang, T. N. Y., & Webb, S. (2016). Making an essential word list for beginners. In I. S. P. Nation (Ed.), *Making and using word lists for language learning and testing* (pp. 153–167). Benjamins.

Dang, T. N. Y., Webb, S., & Coxhead, A. (2020). Evaluating lists of high-frequency words: Teachers' and learners' perspectives. *Language Teaching Research*. Early view. https://doi.org/10.1177/1362168820911189.

Dellar, H., & Walkley, A. (2015). *Outcomes: Upper intermediate.* National Geographic Learning.

Dellar, H, & Walkley, A. (2016). *Teaching lexically. Principles and practice.* Delta Publishing.

Durrant, P., & Schmitt, N. (2009). To what extent do native and non-native writers make use of collocations? *IRAL, 47*, 157–177. https://doi.org/10.1515/iral.2009.007

Elgort, I. (2018). Technology-mediated second language vocabulary development: A review of trends in research methodology. *CALICO Journal, 35*(1), 1–29. https://doi.org/10.1558/cj.34554.

Ellis, N. (2002). Frequency effects in language processing: A review with implications for theories of implicit and explicit language acquisition. *Studies in Second Language Acquisition, 24*(2), 143–188. https://doi.org/10.1017/S0272263102002024.

Farr, F., & O'Keeffe, A. (2019). Using corpus approaches in English language teacher education. In S. Walsh & S. Mann (Eds.), *The Routledge handbook of English language teacher education* (pp. 268–282). Routledge.

Frankenberg-Garcia, A. (2020). Combining user needs, lexicographic data and digital writing environments. *Language Teaching, 53*(1), 29–43. https://doi.org/10.1017/S0261444818000277.

Frankenberg-Garcia, A., Lew, R., Rees, G., Roberts, J., Sharma, N., & Butcher, P. (2019). Developing a writing assistant to help EAP writers with collocations in real time. *ReCALL, 31*(10), 23–39. https://doi.org/10.1017/S0958344018000150.

Gardner, D. (2013). *Exploring vocabulary: Language in action.* Routledge.

Gardner, D., & Davies, M. (2014). A new Academic Vocabulary List. *Applied Linguistics, 35*(3), 305–327. https://doi.org/10.1093/applin/amt015.

Gilmore, A. (2015). Research into practice: The influence of discourse studies on language description and task design in published ELT materials. *Language Teaching, 48*(4), 506–530. https://doi.org/10.1017/S0261444815000269.

Gilquin, G., & Granger, S. (2010). How can data-driven learning be used in language teaching. In A. O'Keeffe & M. McCarthy (Eds.), *The Routledge handbook of corpus linguistics* (pp. 359–370). Routledge.

Gries, S., & Divjak, D. (Eds.) (2012). *Frequency effects in language learning and processing.* De Gruyter Mouton.

Halliday, M. A. K. (1982). Linguistics in teacher education. In R. Carter (Ed.), *Linguistics and the teacher* (pp. 10–15). Routledge.

Handford, M., Lisboa, M., Koester, A., & Pitt, A. (2011). *Business advantage (Upper-intermediate).* Cambridge University Press.

He, X., & Godfroid, A. (2019). Choosing words to teach: A novel method for vocabulary selection and its practical application. *TESOL Quarterly, 53*(2), 348–371. https://doi.org/10.1002/tesq.483.

Kremmel, B. (2016). Word families and frequency bands in vocabulary tests: Challenging conversations. *TESOL Quarterly, 50*(4), 976–987. https://doi.org/10.1002/tesq.329.

Kyle, K. (2020). Measuring lexical richness. In S. Webb (Ed.), *Routledge handbook of vocabulary studies* (pp. 454–476). Routledge.

Kyle, K., & Crossley, S. A. (2015). Automatically assessing lexical sophistication: Indices, tools, findings, and application. *TESOL Quarterly, 49*(4), 757–786. https://doi.org/10.1002/tesq.194.

Laufer, B. (2013). Lexical frequency profiles. In C. A. Chapelle (Ed.), *The encyclopedia of applied linguistics*, (pp. 1–4). Wiley-Blackwell. https://doi.org/10.1002/9781405198431.wbeal0692

Laufer, B., & Cobb, T. (2020). How much knowledge of derived words is needed for reading? *Applied Linguistics, 41*(6), 971–998. https://doi.org/10.1093/applin/amz051.

Laufer, B., & Nation, I. S. P. (1995). Vocabulary size and use: Lexical richness in L2 written production. *Applied Linguistics, 16*(3), 307–322. https://doi.org/10.1093/applin/16.3.307.

Laufer, B., & Ravenhorst-Kalovski, G. C. (2010). Lexical threshold revisited: Lexical text coverage, learners' vocabulary size and reading comprehension. *Reading in a Foreign Language, 22*(1), 15–30. https://doi.org/10125/66648

Laufer, B., & Waldman, T. (2011). Verb-noun collocations in second language writing: A corpus analysis of learners' English. *Language Learning, 61*(2), 647–672. https://doi.org/10.1111/j.1467-9922.2010.00621.x

Lee, H., Warschauer, M., & Lee, J. H. (2019). The effects of corpus use on second language vocabulary learning: A multilevel meta-analysis. *Applied Linguistics, 40*(5), 721–753. https://doi.org/10.1093/applin/amy012.

Leńko-Szymańska, A. (2002). How to trace the growth of active vocabulary? A corpus-based study. In B. Kettemann & G. Marko (Eds.), *Teaching and learning by doing corpus analysis* (pp. 217–230). Brill.

Leńko-Szymańska, A. (2017). Training teachers in data driven learning: Tackling the challenge. *Language Learning and Technology, 21*(3), 217–241. https://doi.org/10125/44628

Levitzky-Aviad, T., & Laufer, B. (2013). Lexical properties in the writing of L2 learners over eight years of study: Single words and collocations. In C. Bardel, C. Lindqvist, & B. Laufer (Eds.), *L2 vocabulary acquisition, knowledge and use: New perspectives on assessment and corpus analysis* (pp. 127–147). EuroSLA.

Li, L. (2016). CALL tools for lexico-grammatical acquisition. In F. Farr & L. Murray (Eds.), *The Routledge handbook of language learning and technology* (pp. 601–621). Routledge.

Madlener, K. (2015). *Frequency effects in instructed second language acquisition.* De Gruyter Mouton.

Martinez, R. (2013). A framework for the inclusion of multi-word expressions in ELT. *ELT Journal, 67*(2), 184–198. https://doi.org/10.1093/elt/ccs100.

Martinez, R., & Schmitt, N. (2012). A phrasal expressions list. *Applied Linguistics, 33*(3), 299–320. https://doi.org/10.1093/applin/ams010.

McCarthy, M. (2001). What is an advanced level vocabulary? *SELL, 3,* 149–163.

McCarthy, M. (2008). Accessing and interpreting corpus information in the teacher education context. *Language Teaching, 41*(4), 563–574. https://doi.org/10.1017/S0261444808005247.

McCarthy, M., & Carter, R. (1994). *Language as discourse: Perspectives for language teaching.* Longman.

McCarthy, M., McCarten, J., & Sandiford, H. (2005). *Touchstone Student's Book 1.* Cambridge University Press.

McEnery, T., & Xiao, R. (2010). What corpora can offer in language teaching and learning. In E. Hinkel (Ed.), *Handbook of research in second language teaching and learning. Vol 2.* (pp. 364–380). Routledge.

Meunier, F. (2020). Resources for learning multiword items. In S. Webb (Ed.), *The Routledge handbook of vocabulary studies* (pp. 336–350). Routledge.

Milton, J. (2009). *Measuring second language vocabulary acquisition.* Multilingual Matters.

Nation, I. S. P. (2006). How large a vocabulary is needed for reading and listening? *Canadian Modern Language Review, 63*(1), 59–81. https://doi.org/10.1353/cml.2006.0049

Nation, I. S. P. (2007). The four strands. *Innovation in Language Learning and Teaching, 1*(1), 1–12.

Nation, I. S. P. (2013). *Learning vocabulary in another language* (3rd ed.). Cambridge University Press.

Nation, I. S. P. (2016). Word lists. In I. S. P. Nation (Ed.), *Making and using word lists for language learning and testing* (pp. 3–13). Benjamins.

Nesi, H. (2016). Corpus studies in EAP. In K. Hyland & P. Shaw (Eds.), *The Routledge handbook of English for academic purposes* (pp. 206–217). Routledge.

Nguyen, T. M. H., & Webb, S. (2017). Examining second language receptive knowledge of collocation and factors that affect learning. *Language Teaching Research, 21*(3), 298–320. https://doi.org/10.1177/1362168816639619

Nurmukhamedov, U., & Webb, S. (2019). Lexical coverage and profiling. *Language Teaching, 52*(2), 188–200. https://doi.org/10.1017/S0261444819000028

O'Keeffe, A. (2021). Data-driven learning – A call for a broader research gaze. *Language Teaching, 54*(2), 259–272. https://doi.org/10.1017/S0261444820000245.

O'Keeffe, A., McCarthy, M., & Carter, R. (2007). *From corpus to classroom. Language use and language teaching.* Cambridge University Press.

Perez-Paredes, P. (2019). A systematic review of the uses of spread of corpora and data-driven learning in CALL research during 2011-2015. *Computer Assisted Language Learning,* 1–27. https://doi.org/10.1080/09588221.2019.1667832

Römer, U. (2011). Corpus research applications in second language teaching. *Annual Review of Applied Linguistics, 31,* 205–225. https://doi.org/10.1017/S0267190511000055

Schmitt, N. (Ed.). (2004). *Formulaic sequences: Acquisition, processing and use.* Benjamins.

Schmitt, N. (2010). *Researching vocabulary: A vocabulary research manual.* Palgrave Macmillan.

Schmitt, N. (2019). Understanding vocabulary acquisition, instruction, and assessment: A research agenda. *Language Teaching, 52*(2), 261–274. https://doi.org/10.1017/S0261444819000053

Schmitt, N., & Schmitt, D. (2014). A reassessment of frequency and vocabulary size in L2 vocabulary teaching. *Language Teaching, 47*(4), 484–503. https://doi.org/10.1017/S0261444812000018.

Schmitt, N., & Schmitt, D. (2020). *Vocabulary in language teaching* (2nd ed.). Cambridge University Press.

Simpson-Vlach, R., & Ellis, N. (2010). An Academic Formulas List: New methods in phraseology research. *Applied Linguistics, 31*(4), 487–512. https://doi.org/10.1093/applin/amp058

Siyanova-Chanturia, A., & Pellicer-Sanchez, A. (Eds.). (2019). *Understanding formulaic language. A second language acquisition perspective.* Routledge.

Siyanova-Chanturia, A., & Spina, S. (2020). Multi-word expressions in second language writing: A large-scale longitudinal learner corpus study. *Language Learning, 70*(2), 420–463. https://doi.org/10.1111/lang.12383

Sundqvist, P. (2019). Commercial-off-the-shelf games in the digital wild and L2 learner vocabulary. *Language Learning and Technology, 23*(1), 87–113. https://doi.org/10125/44674

Sylven, L. K., & Sundqvist, P. (2012). Gaming as extramural English L2 learning and L2 proficiency among young learners. *ReCALL, 24*(3), 302–321. doi: https://doi.org/10.1017/S095834401200016X.

Szudarski, P. (2012). Lexical syllabus. In C. A. Chapelle (Ed.), *Encyclopedia of Applied Linguistics* (pp. 1–5). Wiley-Blackwell. https://doi.org/10.1002/9781405198431.wbeal0696

Szudarski, P. (2018). *Corpus linguistics for vocabulary. A guide for research.* Routledge.

Szudarski, P. (2020). Effects of data-driven learning on enhancing the phraseological knowledge of secondary school learners of L2 English. In P. Crosthwaite (Ed.), *Data-driven learning for the next generation: Corpora and DDL for pre-tertiary learners* (pp. 133–149). Routledge.

Szudarski, P., & Barclay, S. (Eds.). (2021). *Vocabulary theory, patterning and teaching.* Multilingual Matters.

Tang, X., & Taguchi, N. (2020). Designing and using a scenario-based digital game to teach Chinese formulaic expressions. *CALICO Journal, 37*(1), 1–22. https://doi.org/10.1558/cj.38574.

Van Zeeland, H., & Schmitt, N. (2013). Lexical coverage in L1 and L2 listening comprehension: The same or different from reading comprehension? *Applied Linguistics, 34*(4), 457–479. https://doi.org/10.1093/applin/ams074

Vilkaite-Lozdiene, L., & Schmitt, N. (2020). Frequency as a guide for vocabulary usefulness. High-, mid-, and low-frequency words. In S. Webb (Ed.), *The Routledge handbook of vocabulary studies* (pp. 81–96). Routledge.

Webb, S. (Ed.). (2020). *The Routledge handbook of vocabulary studies.* Routledge.

Wray, A. (2002). *Formulaic language and the lexicon.* Cambridge University Press.

Zareva, A. (2017). Incorporating corpus literacy skills into TESOL teacher training. *ELT Journal, 71*(1), 69–79. doi: https://doi.org/10.1093/elt/ccw045.

4

CORPUS ANALYSIS OF GRAMMAR-IN-DISCOURSE FOR ENGLISH LANGUAGE TEACHING

Stefan Frazier

4.1 Corpus linguistics as an avenue into analysis of grammar-in-discourse

The explosion of ever-larger language corpora over the past few decades, and the proliferation of methods used to analyze them, has made the tracking and documenting of language use much easier. Nowadays, one rarely needs to rely on intuition as a means of providing answers to questions of vocabulary use and grammar choices. Instead, anyone is able to plug vocabulary items – even entire phrases – into freely available databases online and glean basic patterns from the results. With more specifically tagged corpora (also increasingly available), even a relative novice can similarly analyze the incidence rates of particular grammar structures and vocabulary items.

This development has had profound implications for English language education. English teachers as well as English learners now have easily accessible resources available to help them track patterns of the contextual environments in which vocabulary items and grammatical structures appear (e.g. the Corpus of Contemporary American English, also known as COCA). The teachers can use this information to help them decide what to teach; the learners themselves can use it to achieve more sensitivity to which words or grammar structures to choose in certain contextual environments, based on historical past usage. When studying reporting verbs, for example, a learner can easily find out, via concordancing programs, that the verb *claim* can be followed by an infinitive verb (as well as a *that*-clause or a noun), while the same is not true for *believe*. Or, with a well-tagged corpus, a more advanced learner can determine the relative preponderance of, say, the historical present tense as it is used in many spoken narratives.

Indeed, corpus linguistics has already established its potential for language education. Also, recent special issues of journals have covered various aspects of the topic. Boulton and Pérez-Paredes, editors of the special issue of *ReCALL* (2014), for example, include a number of areas in which corpora can be used, such as comprehension and production, second-language writing feedback, acquisition of lexico-grammatical features in second-language writing, methods of discovering formulaic language, and other topics around "data-driven learning" (DDL). Vyatkina and Boulton, editors of the special issue of *Language Learning & Technology* (2017), feature work on explicit pragmatic instruction, the use of DDL for the recognition of genres, training teachers in DDL, and developing learners' awareness of fixed and semi-fixed

 DOI: 10.4324/9781003002901-6

expressions. Richards and Reppen (2016, pp. 156–157) include the use of corpora to explore texts among their 12 principles of grammar instruction. On the other hand, Huang (2018), while noting that the potential for corpus-based analytical methods in language classrooms has increased dramatically in the past few decades and presumably could be employed by everyday language teachers and students, points out that their actual direct use in classrooms is still very limited due to accessibility issues and the questionable relevance of current corpus data. Still, there are already many areas of language study in which corpora can be used directly by teachers and students to inform their teaching or their learning; and there are robust data for developing a clearer understanding of how language is used—data that can be used for educational purposes.

However, corpus linguistics still has limitations as far as describing the full range of the functions of language. Language is used not only to describe or to be propositional, but also to achieve acts, to "do things with words" (Austin, 1962). And in order to analyze what words (or phrases, or clauses, or other grammatical items) are doing, it is ultimately necessary to look beyond the very local co-textual environment and analyze also larger chunks of language—multiple paragraphs of writing, many turns at talk in conversation, or several minutes of spoken monolog.

Much analysis of that sort—at the larger discourse level—still happens with the identification and quantification of individual lexical or grammatical items, which corpus linguistics already does well. Corpus linguistics also can determine relative frequencies of those items in different genres and registers (as exemplified famously in Biber *et al.*, 1999, a key resource for English language educators). The "looking beyond", however, involves posing and answering questions such as: in what way does the choice of a certain grammatical structure at the start of a narrative affect the subsequent choices? If a certain structure is "bunched up" in certain parts of a monolog, what are they doing in those parts—narrating, explicating, posing rhetorical questions, performing a phatic function, commanding, requesting? Due to the multiple functions that any particular structure may have (e.g. a grammatical interrogative form may be a request for information or it may be mandative), many of those questions can only be addressed, yet, via human eyes looking at full transcripts and determining how people are interacting with each other or (if a written text) how a rhetorical choice at the end of a document relates to another in the middle, or at the beginning.

This chapter covers a brief history of corpus-analytic approaches to grammar-in-discourse, including a short foray into corpus pragmatics. Also included is a discussion of how corpus-informed grammar-in-discourse can be utilized in language education and a case study, on English modal verbs, to illustrate the implications of corpus research, as well as suggestions for further research.

4.2 A review of corpus-informed analyses of grammar-in-discourse

The analysis of grammar-in-discourse has its roots in functional linguistics and the functional grammar approach as best exemplified by Michael Halliday (e.g. Halliday & Matthiessen, 2014). It rests largely on the principle that a mere collection of sentences is not a unified text unless it contains elements that cause it to cohere. Those elements are, according to Halliday and Hasan (1976), generally grammatical in nature: the use of conjunctives, substitutions, reference, and ellipsis. A grammar-in-discourse approach investigates in which contexts words and structures appear, what their frequency of appearance is in those contexts, and what they're "doing" therein. A Hallidayan approach also accounts for lexicogrammar, the interplay between the words and grammar structures, on the understanding that word meaning cannot be disassociated from structure. McCarthy (2021, p. 9) notes that the term "grammar-in-discourse" is now used to refer to a range of analyses, including the functions of grammatical structures in the organization of text and in ordinary conversation, and within the field of interactional linguistics. Celce-Murcia (2016) points out that almost all grammar structures (except perhaps three: reflexive pronouns, post-prepositional gerund adverbials, and determiner-noun agreement) require knowing the context beyond a single sentence in order to understand the full reasons for a particular grammatical choice. At the same time, Hughes and McCarthy (1998) have a whole section titled "Items that Cannot be Fully Apprehended in Stand-Alone Sentences" (p. 275), adding that "grammar can move from sentence to discourse whenever the teacher, observer, or analyst wants it to and that the two are not separate levels of language that come together only when difficult problems present themselves" (p. 279).

As far as corpus linguistics has concerned itself with grammar-in-discourse, McCarthy (2021) explains that corpus-analytic approaches have challenged previous notions of the grammatical functions, in that they often more accurately explain how structures (and words) are actually used in spoken and written registers and with what frequencies (rather than relying on intuitions or anecdotal evidence). Dontcheva-Navratilova (2012) notes that analysis of grammar-in-discourse is often corpus-based and involves determining the frequency of structures within particular genres, registers, and/or contexts. Conrad (2016) argues that corpus analyses of grammar structures allow an instructor to provide not only accurate grammar, but also "appropriate and effective grammar" (p. 38), a position echoing Celce-Murcia (2015). Conrad suggests doing this by including frequency information, discerning appropriate contexts for certain structures, highlighting differences between genres and registers, and demonstrating how grammar and lexis interact. Conrad and Biber's (2009) volume is an ESL textbook that instructs students on commonly taught grammar structures, and is entirely corpus-informed. Other recent studies have investigated certain functions of specific structures (e.g. Lindley, 2020) and the affordances and drawbacks of using corpus-based approaches in grammar classes (e.g. Liu & Jiang, 2015).

The above-mentioned sources rely largely on frequency information as part of the strategy of what grammar to teach, when, and how. Celce-Murcia and Yoshida (2003), however, mention a caveat with regard to the focus on frequencies: corpora allow for the collecting of large numbers of relevant tokens, but crucial to their understanding is, in addition, a qualitative analysis (not merely the numbers). In their treatment of the English present perfect progressive tense-aspect combination (PPP), they document historical explanations of the structure that are "problematic" (p. 3) because of their failure to adequately examine the semantic properties of the particular verb in question and the resulting consequence that some verbs may assume the PPP form even when the iterative or repeated nature of the verbs might call for a different tense-aspect combination. The authors go on to present several apt examples of verbs that take the PPP that one might not have guessed, indicating the value of such a qualitative analysis. In other words, for a full understanding of how grammatical structures operate in their contexts, it is imperative, always, to consider local functions of at least several individual samples of a structure in addition to counting the instances of those functions in larger bodies of data.

McCarthy (2021), an ardent supporter and practitioner of corpus-based approaches to language study in general, notes that grammar-in-discourse has been used to supplement understandings of the functions of grammatical structures within the larger field of pragmatics. There is much overlap between the study of grammar-in-discourse and corpus pragmatics.

A brief summary of corpus pragmatics is, therefore, warranted here. Corpus pragmatics arrived later within the field of linguistics, and certainly within language education, than other areas of language study. The joining of corpus linguistics with pragmatics is well outlined in Romero-Trillo (2008), who among other things stated a "conviction that some specific language issues can be better addressed through the combination of methodologies" (p. 1) in corpus linguistics and pragmatics. Other key sources in the meantime include *Corpus Pragmatics: A Handbook* (Aijmer & Rühlemann, 2015) and the specialized journal *Corpus Pragmatics,* launched in 2017, which has since its inception published many studies related to grammar, including on the topics of modality, tense and aspect, and genre analysis.

Corpus pragmatics has striven to take up many topics and sub-topics within the standard field of pragmatics, including within grammar-in-discourse, and the lessons learned from such research lend themselves, in turn, to language educational purposes (Bardovi-Harlig *et al.*, 2017; Boulton & Tyne, 2015; Chambers, 2019). One particularly useful volume on pragmatics instruction is O'Keeffe *et al.* (2019), who reference corpus studies throughout to inform the teaching and learning of pragmatics, with a central claim that "corpora will be the biggest driver of change in both foregrounding and addressing pragmatic competence in language teaching" (p. 226); especially relevant is Chapter 9, "Pragmatics in language teaching". Granath (2009) asks, simply, "Who benefits from learning how to use corpora?" and outlines various classroom techniques, some of which include pragmatic concerns.

In the area of writing pedagogy, Park *et al.* (2019) make a compelling case for how writing style manuals from the past (e.g. Strunk & White, 1999) have perpetuated an ill-informed notion of "correctness" that is not borne out in actual language use. In second-language writing, Frodesen (2018) demonstrates (in part) the use of corpus linguistics in the teaching of grammar in second language writing specifically, assisting "English learners in gaining awareness of language use in a range of written texts, recognizing register differences between spoken and written genres, and across written genres, and developing linguistic resources needed for a range of writing tasks" (p. 3). Also, the aforementioned special issue of *Language Learning & Technology* edited by Vyatkina and Boulton (2017) covers a number of areas in which corpus linguistics can inform second-language writing pedagogy (e.g. collocational competence, genre awareness, phraseology), and many of those are within the general field of pragmatic awareness of writing conventions.

Two recent sources, in particular, are useful for the purposes of this chapter, in that they relate to a grammatical topic (modal verbs) used for exemplification in Section 4.4 below, but also—a more global purpose—illustrate the types of insights made more accessible via a corpus-pragmatic approach to grammar-in-discourse. Whitty (2019) examines the modal verbs *can* and *could* with the aim of achieving a more nuanced, pragmatics-informed categorization of their uses, which have traditionally been largely semantics-based and categorized as "ability, possibility, and permission" (p. 225). Kecskes and Kirner-Ludwig (2017) investigate the uses of the modal verbs *must* and *should* by populations of "Asian English speakers" and "native" speakers of American English via various categorization methods. Larsen-Freeman and Celce-Murcia (2016) also note that modal verbs are among the most challenging grammar topics for English learners to master, as a single one can be used for a variety of purposes depending on context. Given the often-ambiguous nature of modal verbs, it is imperative to develop a more robust method of interpreting them. Corpus pragmatics has added to that robustness.

Due to the overlap between the study of grammar-in-discourse and the burgeoning field of corpus pragmatics, there has been much mutual influence between the two sub-fields, and important principles and findings have arisen from looking liberally at both. Some of these principles and findings are cited below in Sections 4.3 and 4.4.

4.3 Core issues

One of the key ways in which corpus pragmatics differs from other sub-fields of corpus linguistics—and therefore, how it lends a broader understanding of grammar-in-discourse in any given analysis—is its attention to a "horizontal" reading of data transcripts of spoken and written text in addition to a "vertical" reading. The horizontal/vertical concept is best defined and explained in Rühlemann and Aijmer (2015). In this section, I will reproduce the explanation from that work illustrating the notions with other examples.

Corpus linguistics has traditionally examined large numbers of samples of a single lexical or grammatical item stacked one upon another, in order to observe its collocates (words or phrases that often go together) or colligates (grammar structures that often go together). Table 4.1 provides an example from a topic I will use later in this chapter, the English modal verb *could*. For illustrative purposes, it is a five-item random snapshot from the middle of a corpus of U.S. TV and radio news interviews, a corpus explained further in Section 4.4.

A quick vertical reading of the items turns up a few very basic findings which, in a properly sized analysis of far more tokens, could provide more robust conclusions: three of the five appear in the grammatical negative; three of the associated subjects are pronouns while two of them are lexical; all of the associated main verbs are highly common ones (among the top ten most common English verbs); and in no case does an adverb separate *could* from the verb. In three of five cases, the *could*-clause is subordinate to a higher clause. More could be said with more instances, and it is possible to set a computer on task to look at hundreds (or hundreds of thousands) of tokens vertically to quickly find patterns for each of these observations and many more.

But it is much less likely that automation could account for the more nuanced understanding afforded by a horizontal reading. I chose the modal verb *could* to make this point as simple as possible. *Could* has two distinct possible time frames: as a past-time form of the modal *can*, and as a hypothetical conditional marker in present and future time frames. In at least three items in the table (items 2, 3, and 5), it is not possible with the limited length of the data (one sentence each) to determine which time frame the modal pertains to. In item 5, for example, *They couldn't get to the shooter*, is the speaker relating a narrative about a past event, or discussing the outcome of a hypothetical instance? (It is the former, due to a reference

Table 4.1 Five tokens of *could* from a spoken corpus for illustration of vertical vs. horizontal readings

1. That is, these students' SAT scores suggest they	could	not do strong college work, when in fact they can.
2. Of course, he	could	n't get that with the support of his own party
3. And what really impressed me was how Begonia said that she and Delia	could	come into understanding so rapidly something she could not do with Beatriz.
4. So, I guess the president	could	say he reduced his own deficit if that's where we want to go.
5. They	could	n't get to the shooter.

Vertical reading

◄——— Horizontal reading ———►

in a previous utterance of the 1999 Columbine High School massacre in Colorado.) In all three cases, one must cross just one sentence boundary to determine the overall contextual time frame, but often, such a determination requires perusal of multiple clause or sentence boundaries.

Crossing multiple clause or sentence boundaries is actually possible with carefully pro-gramed software. It is also possible to automate the determination of frequency and positioning of pragmatic items like discourse markers which appear discretely at, say, the beginnings of turns at talk. Much more difficult, and in many cases impossible with current technology, is the automated identification of pragmatic processes like politeness or speech acts, which usu-ally involve multiple parties, complicated turn-taking behavior, hedging, and conversational repair mechanisms. Conversational organization is similarly inaccessible (as Schegloff, 1990, demonstrates) and still impossible to automate, as it requires horizontal reading to a great degree. Computer programs may eventually reach this level of sophistication, at which point the field of corpus pragmatics will have acquired automated pragmatic tagging—something that Clancy and O'Keeffe (2015, p. 251) refer to as its "holy grail".

Because of the need for integrated reading, corpus pragmatics is still limited to fairly small corpora, as Clancy and O'Keeffe (2015) also point out. Until the grand prize of automated tagging is achieved, the field still faces the challenge of using relatively limited corpora; or if using giant corpora, learning how to appropriately sample from those. Random sampling, or targeted? And if the latter, how to target? How many tokens are enough? Sampled across how many genres or sources? Do sample sizes need to be larger if comparisons are made between genres? And what kinds of features should we be searching for in the first place? How gener-alizable are they? (See, for example, Jucker *et al.*, 2018, for coverage of these questions.)

Another area of focus in the intersection between corpus pragmatics—and thus grammar-in-discourse—and language education is exactly what to do with corpora, and who should employ them. How do they best fit within the complex system of educators and learners? Corpus linguistics for educational purposes has traditionally been the realm of applied linguists, i.e. researchers, but corpora have also become increasingly accessible to language teachers as well as language learners themselves. Efforts continue, but the field still has a fair distance to go, as documented by many (Aijmer, 2009; Bardovi-Harlig & Mossman, this volume; Boulton & Tyne, 2015; Chambers, 2019; Farr & O'Keeffe, 2019). If we, as language educators, believe in empowering the student by way of maximizing the noticing required for mastery of language (Schmidt, 1990), the question of "How do we turn students into mini-discourse analysts?" is fundamental. Using the metaphor of teaching people how to cook instead of giving them food, corpus-analytic methods could be the cooking. Having achieved that goal, teachers ultimately could get away from providing just the food, i.e. the pre-crunched and pre-interpreted data. The next section offers a few corpus-informed findings in a particular grammar area, with implications for their educational purpose.

4.4 Case study: English modal verbs

All areas of English grammar benefit from corpus-informed, discourse-level exemplifica-tion, and explanation, but one of them stands out (Larsen-Freeman & Celce-Murcia, 2016): The tense-modality system. This is true in both the written and spoken realms. Learners of English coming from other languages need ultimately to become masters of understanding general time frame patterns in the flow of ongoing discourse in order to make appropriate verb tense choices (this is perhaps especially relevant when their first language does not mark tense); given how modality is accomplished cross-linguistically in very different ways (often not even through verbs), it is equally important for learners to have a holistic discourse-level comprehension of English modality for the best choices in that area too.

This section offers a summary case study of the English tense-modality system in a corpus-linguistic framework, specifically on one-word modal verbs (*can, could, may, might, must, should*). In the interest of space, the study is limited, offering merely some basic findings and insights; however, it stands as an example of the kind of findings that provide a richer understanding of tense-modality in general and what can be taught about them specifically.

The case study employs the USTVRI Corpus, a collection of TV and radio interviews from three U.S. networks, CNN (Cable News Network), Fox News, and NPR (National Public Radio), between the years 2011 and 2015. My colleague Hahn Koo and I collected the corpus originally in order to investigate how tense, aspect, and modality work within conversational contexts and how they contribute to turn-taking behavior and conversational story-telling; hence the decision to limit the spoken discourse to interviews with two or more participants. Specifically, in pursuing analyses of the English present perfect form (Frazier & Koo, 2019a) and the present progressive form (Frazier & Koo, 2019b), we examined how those forms were used in interactive contexts, as questions, requests for information, in narratives, in agreement or disagreement with a prior speaker's talk, or in helping to express a speaker's own opinion. The most easily available interactive contexts of "standard American English" talk were network interviews; we therefore decided to create a 12.2-million-word corpus of multiparty interaction (as opposed to single-person news-reading, individual commentary, or other monologic discourse).

4.4.1 Background on English modal verbs

The English modality system has been heavily documented and researched over the last several decades, both via traditional linguistic descriptions and analysis as well as through corpus-linguistic and corpus-pragmatic methods. Modal verbs are especially in need of contextual analysis, given their complexity, ambiguity, and nuanced shades of meaning. Prior research has investigated English modal verbs from a number of pragmatic directions. Although not in conversational discourse, Hoye (2008), for example, discusses the use of modal verbs (and other modal expressions like *it appears that* or *apparently*) to indicate varying degrees of evidentiality. Nokkonen (2014) analyzes the dynamic, deontic, and epistemic uses of a single modal structure—*need to*—in the British National Corpus and finds variations among different registers. Notably, *need to* appears more in dialogs than in monologs. Harrington (2017) analyzes a 48,000-word corpus of speakers of English as a Lingua Franca (ELF) at a center for asylum seekers (location unspecified) and finds that, of all the one-word modals, *can* was by far the most frequent, and the only one that appears in the first 100 most frequent words. That study provided quantitative results; however, no qualitative analysis was offered on modal use. From a pedagogical perspective, Römer (2004) notes a range of discrepancies between what is taught about modals (in German-produced textbooks) and how they are actually used, suggesting changing the order of frequency to *will/'ll → would/'d → can → could → should → might → must → may → shall → ought to* (p. 195).

Much of this kind of research is relatively easy to achieve through simple counting, as computer algorithms can be designed to locate modal verbs and their accompanying words and phrases. For example, in examining 241 single-word modal verbs in the USTVRI Corpus,

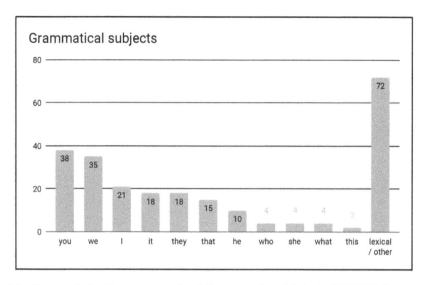

Figure 4.1   Grammatical subjects connected to 241 one-word modals in the USTVRI Corpus

we determined (through manual counting) the relative frequency of the subjects associated with each verb. This is depicted in Figure 4.1.

From this brief count, one could verify the results with far greater numbers (which would require a computer program), and then carry out an in-depth qualitative analysis asking the questions: why is the frequent use of the second person with modals? Is there an interactional purpose for conversation participants to employ modals when referring to each other? But also, why is the use of first person (the combination of *we* and *I*) far higher than any other non-lexical subject? Why is there a significantly greater use of the male pronoun *he* compared to the female *she*? All of these questions, and more, could find candidate answers with qualitative analysis of the particular interactive contexts in which the items appear, as could the finding that these 241 modals appeared overwhelmingly in the grammatical affirmative rather than the negative (207 vs. 34, respectively).

4.4.2 Agent-oriented vs. speaker-oriented modals

In corpus linguistics, while the automatic processing of the text is possible, for some research questions, an automatic functional categorization may be difficult. And for other research questions, an automatic functional categorization is currently still impossible. One such question of the latter is the determination of modal verbs as "agent-oriented" or "speaker-oriented". These categories were established in one of the definitive texts on modality, Bybee and Fleischman (1995). Unsatisfied with the previous classification of modals as either root or epistemic, the book proposed the addition of categories of agent-oriented ("all modal meanings that predicate conditions on an agent with regard to the completion of an action referred to by the main predicate, e.g. obligation, desire, ability, permission, and root possibility," p. 6) and speaker-oriented ("speech acts through which a speaker attempts to move an addressee to action," p. 6). Subsequent research has pursued this distinction in various languages (Muhaimi *et al.*, 2017; Shaffer, 2004; Šolienė, 2017).

When a modal verb is speaker-oriented, it is by definition performing pragmatic work. But how frequent are agent-oriented modal verbs compared to speaker-oriented ones?

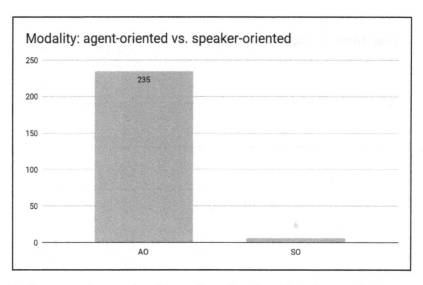

Figure 4.2   Frequency of agent-oriented vs. speaker-oriented modals in the USTVRI Corpus

For the USTVRI corpus, I hypothesized that because it is exclusive to conversations between two or more people, many of the modals might indeed be used to "move an addressee to action" (Bybee & Fleischman, 1995, p. 6). It seemed reasonable to believe that conversation participants would at least somewhat frequently attempt to verbally induce some sort of action from their co-participant. However, I was wrong, at least as far as those attempts involving modal verbs. It turns out that when I examined each of the items in their contexts within the USTVRI Corpus, only 6 of the 241 could be tagged as speaker-oriented, as shown in Figure 4.2.

While rare, it is still worth pointing out a few contexts in which speaker-oriented modals do appear. One of them fits a common understanding of modal use as a mitigating device in requests, such as in the following in an interview with film director Andrew Sarris (actually a rebroadcast from 1990):

(1) NPR
GROSS: So let me ask you to name a few of your favorite films. And you could go as far into the past as you want to—films that you *might* want to recommend to us to see, if we haven't already seen them.
SARRI: Yeah. Well, my favorite film of all time is probably "Madame de...", the Max Ophuls film with Danielle Darrieux.

The interviewer's choice of modal *might* within her request shows an orientation to not imposing excessively on her guest. Another possible context (which would need to be confirmed with further data) is a more combative one, during arguments, when a speaker makes space for a longer turn at talk. Prior to the following excerpt, there has been a marked amount of what is known as "crosstalk" in interviews, as the conversation participants talk over each other to make their points. The interviewer (Bill O'Reilly) challenges his interviewee (journalist Bob Woodward) to answer his question about a speech that U.S. President Obama had recently given.

(2) (Fox)

O'REILLY: All right but you didn't answer my question. I know it's a little bit of an esoteric question. How can the nation change in less than 30 years where we're—Ronald Reagan becomes an icon into what we have now which is 180 degrees opposite of Reagan? What changed?

WOODWARD: I think part of this I mean, looking at presidents you realize that their personal appeal and popularity is often what people vote on. And that happened to Reagan and Obama as you point out is personally popular. I think this 19-minute speech, quite frankly is going to be quickly forgotten. I mean as the old John Mitchell who is the attorney general for Nixon who said quite rightly "Don't watch what we say, watch what we do". And I think we have to see what Obama is really going to do. And of course, what the Republicans are doing. I think the other thing if I *can* dwell on it for a moment, he didn't talk about the world.

O'REILLY: No.

WOODWARD: The world is a very dangerous place and there are a lot of dangerous things going on.

Appearing toward the end of a lengthy turn at talk, the modal *can* (connoting permission) is deployed with an orientation toward the prior crosstalk (in which "dwelling" hadn't been permitted) and an upcoming extension of the turn, which indeed the speaker receives.

In further study of this phenomenon, if more examples of this sort are attested, they have implications for what English learners can do with modals. One such implication is that, in relatively focus-oriented interactions such as interviews, speakers actually rarely attempt to "move an address to action" (Bybee & Fleischman, 1995, p. 6), at least not with modals. When they do, however, it is to soften the imposition of a request or to hold the floor firmly for a longer turn at talk.

4.4.3 *Modal verb use in questions*

The use of question-asking in speech is achieved with the help of specific grammatical mechanisms and with the help of other grammatical items. In English, questions often invert the grammatical form of a standard statement, placing an auxiliary verb before the subject. Questions can also have an interactional effect when the purpose of the question is to elicit an answer from a conversation participant. But they do not always have such a purpose. Often questions are rhetorical, not intended to elicit a response. Also, questions in which a response is expected do not always take question form but they might be grammatically embedded questions that assume standard statement word order. Thus, in order to distinguish between sincere questions (intended to elicit response) and rhetorical ones (not intended to elicit response), it is not enough for a computer program to search for English grammatical question forms (sub-aux inversion).

Human eyes are, therefore, still needed to comb through transcripts of conversations to look at all question-like items and determine which type of question it actually is. A perusal of the 241 modal verb tokens in the USTVRI Corpus produced the result that overall 7.4% of modals (18/241) appeared within sincere questions. An example of a sincere question, from the corpus, is in Example (3), in which U.S. Congressman Mike Rogers is being asked regarding the condition of a prisoner at the U.S. detention center at Guantanamo Bay:

(3) (CNN)

CROWLEY: And the conditions under which he is held, what *can* you tell us about that?

ROGERS: He's being held in a, I would argue, appropriately secure environment, given the nature of his crimes against the United States.

An example of a sincere question whose modal verb is embedded within a subordinate clause is one in which the show host (Michel Martin) is asking her guest (journalist Lonnae O'Neal Parker) about the possible future of then-First Lady of the United States, Michelle Obama:

(4) (NPR)

MARTIN: But do we have any sense of—in the second term—what her priorities *might* be?
PARKER: Well, when I was talking to people for the article, some of the women I spoke with
would like to see an extension of that mom-in-chief platform.

In these kinds of questions, modals were generally used in the lower single-digit percentages (*can*, 5.5%; *could*, 6.9%; *may*, 2.3%; *might*, 2.2%; *must*, 3.2%). A general conclusion with this result is that, while news interviews may involve a lot of questioning and answering, modal verbs are not generally used to form those questions. Worthy of further study is a dual inquiry: do news interviews actually involve a lot of questions, or are responses elicited in a different manner? And if the first answer is yes, how are the questions formed if not with modal verbs?

Five of the modals—*can, could, may, might, must*—had similarly low percentages of use in questions, ranging from 2.2% to 6.9%. One modal stood out, however. *Should* appeared within questions 22.7% of the time (10/44). Figure 4.3 depicts a bar chart comparison of all modals vs. the modal *should*. This result raises the question of why the modal *should* seems to appear more often in questions than the other modals, and that is a question to be taken up in further study.

Another salient finding that arose from examining the USTVRI Corpus is the relatively high co-occurrence of the modal *should* with the preceding expressions *I* or *we* (i.e. first-person reference) *think* or *believe* in the higher clause (7/37=16%). O'Keeffe *et al.* (2019) analyze the use of *I think* by speakers of English from different language backgrounds, noting cross-cultural differences in their frequencies, and the fact that it is used "in expressing certainty/uncertainty; managing discourse; mitigating or boosting, among other functions" (p. 204). The high co-occurrence with *think* or *believe* in our data with the modal of obligation *should*

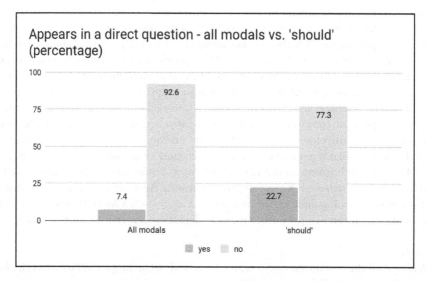

Figure 4.3 Comparison between all modals and the modal *should* as used in questions in the USTVRI Corpus

would seem to argue for its mitigating use, as in the following example from the corpus in which the interviewee (a sergeant in the U.S. Army who had survived a shooting at the Fort Hood Army base) states what measures could be taken to prevent future such incidents:

(5) (Fox)

MANNING: I think certain soldiers *should* be able to defend themselves and you should be able to carry weapons. You can conceal carry, you know, outside of the gates but as soon as you enter the gates you can't have a weapon. You know, I think in certain instances we *should* have our own weapons. We're trained soldiers, I mean, that's what we do.

One of the benefits of looking at many such instances in their various environments is the insightful questions they pose for further study. In this case, why is this mitigating use deployed with the modal *should* but not nearly as much with the even stronger *must*? Implications for such further study are useful for English language learners' mastery of the pragmatic nuances of face-to-face interaction.

4.5 Future directions of research

In reviewing the literature and performing the brief grammar analysis for this chapter, three suggestions for further research arose.

4.5.1 A unified theory of tense and aspect

The analysis of modal verbs above came up after previous work (Frazier & Koo, 2019a, 2019b) motivated by a conviction that the tense-aspect-modality system still has a distance to go in order to arrive at a comprehensive understanding. The analysis in Section 4 was presented for illustrative purposes and as examples of the many ways a corpus-analytic approach can influence grammar-in-discourse. However, it is hoped that it also contributes to such a comprehensive understanding.

This motivation is inspired by Larsen-Freeman and Celce-Murcia (2016), which outlines how phenomena of tense and aspect are employed for many other reasons than merely to mark time, for example, to perform confirmation checks or to mark personal involvement in conversation, and how modality integrates with tense and aspect in a single system (Chapter 9). The explanations come from a variety of sources and are offered piecemeal. Eventually, with enough research that explores the tripartite "form-meaning-use" model as a whole (Larsen-Freeman & Celce-Murcia, 2016, pp. 3–4), we may arrive at a unified theory that explains all of it.

4.5.2 Focus on preparing teachers-in-training for data-driven learning (DDL)

Turning language students into mini-discourse analysts (see Section 4.3) requires teachers with adequate theoretical backgrounds in corpus-linguistic methods themselves and the competence and patience to transmit practical, classroom-based versions of those methods to their students. As covered in much prior research (e.g. Boulton & Tyne, 2015; Chambers, 2019; Farr & O'Keeffe, 2019), a great deal of resources are already available to teachers, but the mere existence of materials does not mean that teachers will automatically accept and adopt data-driven approaches to teaching grammar-in-discourse (often preferring, still, grammar judgments based on intuition). Also, analyzing corpora is clearly not a panacea to teaching and learning grammar. Thus, challenges remain to understand how best to incorporate corpus linguistics in the education of grammar-in-discourse. But the potential remains clear in addition.

4.5.3 Continue working for the ultimate goal of automatic tagging of corpora for pragmatic features

In the illustrative analysis of tense-aspect-modality in Section 4.4, and from prior work by many researchers in corpus pragmatics, it is clear that some pragmatic phenomena—or at least indications of such phenomena—can be automatically tagged (or at least identified) by computer programs, namely, fixed-expression routines (e.g. Bardovi-Harlig *et al.*, 2017), discourse markers (e.g. Amador-Moreno *et al.*, 2006), or even the bunching of tense tokens at the start of interviews as demonstrated above. Other phenomena, however, are yet impossible to automatically tag as with the speaker-oriented modal verbs discussed above, or a question asked by a speaker that is answered a distant two pages of transcript later which nevertheless forms a coherent conversation (Schegloff, 1990). As Clancy and O'Keeffe (2015) point out, automatic tagging of pragmatic transcripts remains the ultimate prize, and researchers of pragmatics would do well to collaborate with computational linguists in achieving it.

Further reading

Aijmer, K., & Rühlemann, C. (Eds.). (2015). *Corpus pragmatics: A handbook*. Cambridge University Press. https://doi.org/10.1017/cbo9781139057493. This volume outlines the history of corpus pragmatics, many directions that sub-field has taken and can take, and suggestions for future research. It also provides an in-depth explanation of the integration of "vertical" and "horizontal" reading for pragmatics research, an approach that is crucial to understanding grammar-in-discourse as well.

Conrad, S. (2016). Using corpus linguistics to improve the teaching of grammar. In E. Hinkel (Ed.), *Teaching English grammar to speakers of other languages* (pp. 38–62). Routledge. https://doi.org/10.4324/9781315695273. This article explains how to make appropriate corpus-linguistic-informed choices based on the contexts in which grammatical structures appear, how to differentiate between different genres, how to integrate grammar and vocabulary, and how to directly apply corpus linguistics to grammar teaching.

McCarthy, M. (2021). *Innovations and challenges in grammar*. Routledge. https://doi.org/10.4324/9780429243561. Authored by a long-time practitioner-expert in corpus linguistics, this book features a full chapter on the value of corpus linguistics to grammar analysis as well as a fascinating history of grammar education and a strong focus on grammar-in-discourse.

References

Aijmer, K. (Ed.). (2009). *Corpora and language teaching*. Benjamins. https://doi.org/10.1075/scl.33

Aijmer, K., & Rühlemann, C. (Eds.). (2015). *Corpus pragmatics: A handbook*. Cambridge University Press. https://doi.org/10.1017/cbo9781139057493

Amador Moreno, C. P., Chambers, A., & O'Riordan, S. (2006). Integrating a corpus of classroom discourse in language teacher education: The case of discourse markers. *ReCALL*, *18*(1), 83–104. doi: https://doi.org/10.1017/S0958344006000619.

Austin, J. L. (1962). *How to do things with words*. Oxford University Press. https://doi.org/10.1093/acprof:oso/9780198245537.001.0001

Bardovi-Harlig, K., Mossman, S., & Su, Y. (2017). The effect of corpus-based instruction on pragmatic routines. *Language Learning & Technology*, *21*(3), 76–103.

Biber, D., Johansson, S., Leech, G., Conrad, S., & Finegan, E. (1999). *Longman grammar of spoken and written English*. Pearson.

Boulton, A. & Pérez-Paredes, P. (Eds.). (2014). Special Issue: Researching uses of corpora for language teaching and learning. *ReCALL, 26*(2).

Boulton, A., & Tyne, H. (2015). Corpus-based study of language and teacher education. In M. Bigelow & J. Ennser-Kananen (Eds.), *The Routledge handbook of educational linguistics* (pp. 301–312). Routledge. https://doi.org/10.1080/07268602.2016.1142869

Bybee, J., & Fleischman, S. (Eds.). (1995). *Modality in grammar and discourse*. Benjamins. https://doi.org/10.1075/tsl.32

Celce-Murcia, M. (2015). An overview of teaching grammar in ELT. In M. Christison, D. Christian, P. A. Duff, & N. Spada (Eds.), *Teaching and learning English grammar: Research findings and future directions* (pp. 3–18). Routledge. https://doi.org/10.4324/9781315719016

Celce-Murcia, M. (2016). The importance of the discourse level in understanding and teaching English grammar. In E. Hinkel (Ed.), *Teaching English grammar to speakers of other languages* (pp. 3–18). Routledge. https://doi.org/10.4324/9781315695273

Celce-Murcia, M., & Yoshida, N. (2003). Alternatives to current pedagogy for teaching the present perfect progressive. *English Teaching Forum, 41*(1), 2–10.

Chambers, A. (2019). Towards the corpus revolution? Bridging the research–practice gap. *Language Teaching, 52*, 460–475. https://doi.org/10.1017/S0261444819000089

Clancy, B., & O'Keeffe, A. (2015). Pragmatics. In D. Biber & R. Reppen (Eds.), *The Cambridge handbook of English corpus linguistics* (pp. 235–251). Cambridge University Press. https://doi.org/10.1017/cbo9781139764377.014

Conrad, S. (2016). Using corpus linguistics to improve the teaching of grammar. In E. Hinkel (Ed.), *Teaching English grammar to speakers of other languages* (pp. 38–62). Routledge. https://doi.org/10.4324/9781315695273

Conrad, S., & Biber, D. (2009). *Real grammar: A corpus-based approach to English grammar*. Pearson.

Dontcheva-Navratilova, O. (2012). Grammar and discourse. In C. A. Chapelle (Ed.), *The encyclopedia of applied linguistics* (pp. 2324–2331). Wiley. https://doi.org/10.1002/9781405198431

Farr, F., & O'Keeffe, A. (2019). Using corpus approaches in English teacher education. In S. Walsh & S. Mann (Eds.), *The Routledge handbook of English language teacher education* (pp. 268–282). Routledge. https://doi.org/10.4324/9781315659824-19

Frazier, S., & Koo, H. (2019a). Discourse-pragmatic functions of the present perfect in American English TV and radio interviews.. *Text & Talk, 39*(1), 77–98. doi: https://doi.org/10.1515/text-2018-2019.

Frazier, S., & Koo, H. (2019b). The use of the English progressive form in discourse: An analysis of a corpus of interview data. *Corpus Pragmatics, 3*(2), 145–171. doi: https://doi.org/10.1007/s41701-018-00050-9.

Frodesen, J. (2018). Grammar and second language writing. In J. Liontas (Ed.), *The TESOL encyclopedia of English language teaching* (pp. 1–7). Wiley. https://doi.org/10.1002/9781118784235.eelt0534

Granath, S. (2009). Who benefits from learning how to use corpora? In K. Aijmer (Ed.), *Corpora and language teaching* (pp. 47–66). Benjamins. https://doi.org/10.1075/scl.33.07gra

Halliday, M. A. K., & Hasan, R. (1976). *Cohesion in English*. Longman. https://doi.org/10.4324/9781315836010

Halliday, M. A. K., & Matthiessen, C. M. I. M. (2014). *Halliday's introduction to functional grammar*. Routledge. https://doi.org/10.4324/9780203431269

Harrington, K. (2017). Corpus analysis: Pragmatic conclusions. *Corpus Pragmatics, 1*, 297–326. https://doi.org/10.1007/s41701-017-0015-x

Hoye, L. F. (2008). Evidentiality in discourse: A pragmatic and empirical account. In J. Romero-Trillo (Ed.), *Pragmatics and corpus linguistics: A mutualistic entente* (pp. 151–174). De Gruyter Mouton. https://doi.org/10.1515/9783110199024.151

Huang, L. (2018). Taking stock of corpus-based instruction in teaching English as an international language. *RELC Journal, 49*(3), 381–401. doi: https://doi.org/10.1177/0033688217698294.

Hughes, R., & McCarthy, M. (1998). From sentence to discourse: Discourse grammar and English language teaching. *TESOL Quarterly, 32*(2), 263–287. doi: https://doi.org/10.2307/3587584.

Jucker, A. H., Schneider, K. P., & Bublitz, W. (Eds.). (2018). *Methods in pragmatics*. De Gruyter Mouton. https://doi.org/10.1515/9783110424928

Kecskes, I., & Kirner-Ludwig, M. (2017). "It would never happen in my country I must say": A corpus-pragmatic study on Asian English learners' preferred uses of must and should. *Corpus Pragmatics, 1*(2), 91–134. https://doi.org/10.1007/s41701-017-0007-x

Larsen-Freeman, D., & Celce-Murcia, M. (2016). *The grammar book: Form, meaning, and use for English language teachers*. National Geographic Learning.

Lindley, J. (2020). Discourse functions of *always* progressives: Beyond complaining. *Corpus Linguistics and Linguistic Theory, 16*(2), 333–361. doi: https://doi.org/10.1515/cllt-2016-0028.

Liu, D., & Jiang, P. (2015). Corpus-based lexicogrammatical approach to grammar instruction: Its use and effects in EFL and ESL contexts. In M. Christison, D. Christian, P. A. Duff, & N. Spada (Eds.), *Teaching and learning English grammar: Research findings and future directions* (pp. 103–118). Routledge. https://doi.org/10.4324/9781315719016

McCarthy, M. (2021). *Innovations and challenges in grammar.* Routledge. https://doi.org/10.4324/9780429243561

Muhaimi, L., Sribagus, & Fadjri, M. (2017). A cognitive pragmatic perspective on epistemic modality in literary discourse and its pedagogical implications. *OKARA: Jurnal Bahasa Dan Sastra, 11*(2), 215–230. doi: https://doi.org/10.19105/ojbs.v11i2.1488.

Nokkonen, S. (2014). The register variation of *need to* in spoken British English. *Neuphilologische Mitteilungen, 115*(1), 63–94.

O'Keeffe, A., Clancy, B., & Adolphs, S. (2019). *Introducing pragmatics in use* (2nd ed.). Routledge.

Park, C., Wright, E., Beard, D., & Regal, R. (2019). Rethinking the teaching of grammar from the perspective of corpus linguistics. *Linguistic Research, 36*(1), 35–65. doi: https://doi.org/10.17250/khisli.36.1.201903.002.

Richards, J. C., & Reppen, R. (2016). 12 principles of grammar instruction. In E. Hinkel (Ed.), *Teaching English grammar to speakers of other languages* (pp. 151–170). Routledge. https://doi.org/10.4324/9781315695273

Römer, U. (2004). A corpus-driven approach to modal auxiliaries and their didactics. In J. Sinclair (Ed.), *How to use corpora in language teaching* (pp. 185–199). Benjamins.

Romero-Trillo, J. (Ed.). (2008). *Pragmatics and corpus linguistics: A mutualistic entente.* De Gruyter Mouton. https://doi.org/10.1515/9783110199024

Rühlemann, C., & Aijmer, K. (2015). Corpus pragmatics: Laying the foundations. In K. Aijmer & C. Rühlemann (Eds.), *Corpus pragmatics: A handbook* (pp. 1–28). Cambridge University Press. https://doi.org/10.1017/cbo9781139057493.001

Schegloff, E. A. (1990). On the organization of sequences as a source of "coherence" in talk-in-interaction. In B. Dorval (Ed.), *Conversational organization and its development* (pp. 51–77). Ablex.

Schmidt, R. (1990). The role of consciousness in second language learning. *Applied Linguistics, 11*(2), 129–158. doi: https://doi.org/10.1093/applin/11.2.129.

Shaffer, B. (2004). Information ordering and speaker subjectivity: Modality in ASL. *Cognitive Linguistics, 15*(2), 175–195. doi: https://doi.org/10.1515/cogl.2004.007.

Šolienė, A. (2017). (Non)epistemic modality: English *must, have to* and *have got to* and their correspondences in Lithuanian. *Kalbotyra, 69,* 223–246. https://doi.org/10.15388/klbt.2016.10374

Strunk, W. Jr., & White, E. B. (1999). *The elements of style* (4th ed.). Pearson.

Vyatkina, V., & Boulton, A. (Eds). (2017). Special Issue: Corpora in language learning and teaching. *Language Learning & Technology, 21*(3).

Whitty, L. (2019). A reanalysis of the uses of *can* and *could*: A corpus-based approach. *Corpus Pragmatics, 3,* 225–247. https://doi.org/10.1007/s41701-019-00058-9

5

CORPORA IN INSTRUCTED SECOND LANGUAGE PRAGMATICS

Kathleen Bardovi-Harlig and Sabrina Mossman

5.1 Introduction

This chapter discusses how the use of corpora might contribute to the teaching of pragmatics in second and foreign language classrooms. Although instructional pragmatics is an active area of research in instructed second language acquisition (ISLA), widespread implementation of pragmatic instruction in second and foreign language classrooms has not yet been realized in English or any other language. Sykes (2013) identifies eight challenges to teaching pragmatics, namely, (1) limited theoretical support for curricular development, (2) lack of authentic input in teaching materials, (3) lack of instructor knowledge, (4) a dominant focus on micro features of language in the foreign language context, (5) time limitations in the classroom, (6) individual student differences and learner subjectivity, (7) feedback and assessment challenges, and (8) dialectal variation (Sykes, 2013, p. 73). Bardovi-Harlig (2017) identified a ninth challenge, namely, the lack of reference books and resources. In the chapter that follows, we consider how the informed use of corpora can address Challenge 2, the lack of authentic input in teaching materials, by serving as a resource for Challenge 9.

"Pragmatics" has been defined as "the study of language from the point of view of users, especially of the choices they make, the constraints they encounter in using language in social interaction and the effects their use of language has on other participants in the act of communication" (Crystal, 1997, p. 301). Colloquially, pragmatic competence can be defined as knowing how to say what to whom when (Bardovi-Harlig, 2013). Second language learners who venture, whether physically or virtually, into the real world to become second language speakers need to be able to use language that indicates an awareness of their interlocutor(s), the situations in which they find themselves, and the impact of their words on other speakers (and listeners). Even adult learners find themselves needing to learn what speech acts are appropriate for what situations in a different culture.

We distinguish two types of pragmatic knowledge, sociopragmatics and pragmalinguistics. "Sociopragmatic knowledge" is knowledge of the rules that guide the use of language in society and in speech communities. Sociopragmatic knowledge includes knowing what speech acts are appropriate in what contexts, such as accepting or refusing an offer, or deflecting or accepting thanks for a favor, or apologizing for taking someone's time or thanking them for that same time. "Pragmalinguistic knowledge" refers to knowledge of the linguistic resources speakers use for pragmatic purposes, for example, knowing that ability questions can be used for requests such as "Can you pass the salt?" when a speaker would like the salt. We can think of sociopragmatics as the knowledge of what to say to whom when and pragmalinguistics as the resources that allow a speaker to carry it out. Although one can talk about pragmatics in both spoken and written communication, in this chapter, we will focus on pragmatics for conversation whether face-to-face, by telephone, or through computer-mediated interfaces such as Zoom and Skype.

In order to address the paucity of authentic input for pragmatics instruction, we consider the use of corpora. A corpus is "an electronically available collection of texts or transcripts of audio recordings which is sampled to represent a certain language, language variety, or other linguistic domain" (Kübler & Zinsmeister, 2015). Corpora may include conversations, institutional talk, academic language, interviews, service encounters, and even television shows and movies (including fan transcriptions, close captions, and subtitles). Just considering their status as collections of authentic language use, corpora represent a resource of significant potential for pragmatics instruction. They are sizeable collections of talk that teachers, materials developers, and students can use to discover or demonstrate how people talk to each other. They exceed what language educators or single researchers can amass on their own.

Some corpora additionally have user interfaces that let users search for individual words or sequences of words and a concordance program that returns KWIC (key word in context) lines that show how the words are used in context. The searched words occur in the center of the line, often highlighted in some way, with linguistic context preceding and following. Different corpora have different user interfaces and allow users to search for attributes for which the corpus has been annotated, such as information on speakers, type of speech event, and level of interactivity (we will discuss these attributes later in this chapter), but regardless of their differences, the use of corpora addresses the issue of providing examples of authentic language use, the key concern of instructional pragmatics.

In the next section, we give a historical overview of pragmatics instruction and the current state of the field (namely robust activity in investigating the role of instruction in pragmatics but little actual pragmatics instruction in classrooms), and how using corpora can address the challenges to pragmatics instruction identified by Sykes (2013) and Bardovi-Harlig (2017). In the following section, we discuss the current state of corpora and their viability as instructional resources for pragmatics. We also discuss the types of pragmatic information that can be accessed by using corpora. Following that, we present a study that illustrates different ways in which learners and teachers may interact with a corpus and the potential benefits to the learning and teaching of pragmatics. The chapter closes by envisioning future research in terms of what the field of English language teaching needs from corpus linguists to use corpora as a resource for pragmatics instruction.

5.2 Taking stock: Historical perspectives on a relatively new field

Pragmatics researchers have always been interested in integrating pragmatics into second/ foreign language teaching. Forty years of research into interlanguage pragmatics shows that learners are not uniformly successful in acquiring L2 pragmatics on their own. This was true 20 years ago when the then current research was used as a needs assessment for teaching pragmatics (Bardovi-Harlig, 2001) and it continues to be true today. Moreover, over the years, and in fact early in the study of interlanguage pragmatics, the field was able to document that well-developed second language grammar did not guarantee pragmatic competence whether in ESL, EFL, or other ELT contexts (Bardovi-Harlig & Hartford, 1993).

Providing learners with authentic input is the single most important issue in teaching pragmatics. Outside the grammar per se, pragmatics deals with language use, and when we learn another language, we need to see and hear "how it's done." Authentic input will have to be coordinated by teachers (with the help of language specialists) because publishers have steadfastly refused over the years to be allies in raising textbook standards in the area of pragmatics. We do not make this claim to be provocative. Published comparisons of pragmatics in the form of spontaneous spoken language to the language portrayed in contemporary language textbooks began early in the study of pragmatics and language learning and have repeatedly reported the lack of authentic pragmatic input in commercially available second and foreign language textbooks (e.g. Cohen & Ishihara, 2013; Eisenchlas, 2011; Ishihara & Paller, 2016; Vellenga, 2004).

As early as 1988, *Applied Linguistics* published two ground-breaking papers, "Language taught for meetings and language used in meetings: Is there anything in common?" (Williams, 1988) and "Natural conversations as a model for textbook dialogue" (Scotton & Bernsten, 1988), which showed that the author-created materials bore little to no resemblance to authentic language use. This mismatch is so pervasive that such comparisons can be assigned to ELT teachers-in-training with guaranteed results, namely that there is always a difference. Textbook reviews and authentic language comparisons have been conducted on a range of speech acts and pragmatic features. In addition to meetings (Williams, 1988) and service encounters and direction-giving (Scotton & Bernsten, 1988), reviews have included conversation closings (Bardovi-Harlig *et al.*, 1991), pragmatic routines for agreement, disagreement, and clarification (Bardovi-Harlig *et al.*, 2015b), suggestions (Jiang, 2006), the social use of complaints (Boxer & Pickering, 1993), and repair sequences (Cheng & Cheng, 2010). The presentation of pragmatics in current commercially marketed materials has led Cohen and Ishihara (2013) to observe that, "the actual dialogues may sound awkward or stilted, and are inauthentic in that they do not represent spontaneous pragmatic language as used in natural conversation" (p. 116). In a *TESOL Quarterly* article Wolfson (1986) warned teachers that we could not invent pragmatics examples. As individuals, we do not have the perspective to know what communities say.

With the abiding lack of credible representations of pragmatics in textbooks by major publishers, materials development in pragmatics falls to teachers and language programs, and to the teacher educators and applied linguists who support them. The earliest essays on teaching pragmatics suggested the use of film (Rose, 2001), activities in which native speakers could visit classrooms and perform pragmatics live in front of students (see, e.g. the "classroom guest," Bardovi-Harlig *et al.*, 1991), and sending learners out to be their own "ethnographers" (an especially popular suggestion at conferences).

Published studies on the effects of instruction on L2 pragmatics provide a view of whether and how teachers and researchers have incorporated authentic data. Bardovi-Harlig (2015) examined the ways in which 81 instructed pragmatics studies simulated conversation in input. Sixty-three studies employed instruction that used examples. Of those, 12 used authentic conversation and 11 used authentic-scripted input such as TV shows and movies. TV shows and movies are authentic cultural artifacts created to entertain viewers; however, they lack hesitation markers (um, uh) for nondramatic purposes, so, although cultural artifacts, they lack certain features of spontaneous talk. An additional 15 instructional units included interactions elicited from native speakers, such as role-plays (role plays, like conversation, do have hesitation markers). The remaining 25 had invented or unattributed dialogs. If we assume that published instructional effects studies report the most innovative teaching in the field, then at its best, pragmatics instruction employs 36% authentic input, 40% invented input, and in the middle, 24% elicited input.

The need for authentic data and the need for a wider perspective than what any one teacher or researcher alone can know about language is a problem that we can begin to address by using corpora and corpus data. In the next section, we show how free online corpora have been used to address the instructional needs of teachers and the learning needs of students. Corpora can be used to inform instruction, textbook development, and activities and replace the made-up discourse bearing little resemblance to real spoken language that has always characterized the majority of commercial textbooks.

5.3 Current state of using corpora to teach pragmatics to language learners

Only a few studies have documented the use of corpora in pragmatics instruction. Ishihara and Cohen (2010) provide suggestions for the use of corpora in teaching pragmatics. Schauer and Adolphs (2006) highlight some of the benefits of using corpora to document the realization of thanking expressions. Bardovi-Harlig and Mossman (2016) and Bardovi-Harlig *et al.* (2015a) developed instructional units for teaching pragmatic routines using corpora, additionally testing the efficacy of such instruction (Bardovi-Harlig *et al.*, 2015b, 2017, 2019a, 2019b; they also experimented with the delivery of instruction, comparing corpus-based teacher-developed materials to teacher-supported hands-on searches by learners. Furniss (2017) developed a corpus-referred website for the teaching of pragmatic routines in Russian and tested the efficacy of the instruction (Furniss, 2016). She used clips of classic Russian films to teach pragmatic routines that were identified from the oral and multimedia subcorpora of the Russian National Corpus. The film clips supplied authentic audio-visual input and were supplemented by audio and written transcriptions. Although Furniss's work targets Russian, there is much to learn from her discussion of materials development, tests, and building the website that is relevant for the teaching of pragmatics in any setting.

The wide array of online corpora not only offer one solution to the problem of authentic data in teaching pragmatics, but the corpus tools also make it relatively easy to search a corpus for language appropriate to the instructional goal (see also Ishihara & Cohen, 2010/2014). We consider each point individually.

5.3.1 Corpora as sources of authentic language for pragmatics

Online corpora can serve as sources for authentic and authentic-scripted language. Different types of language have been collected in corpora, so authentic language can be matched with instructional goals. For example, academic spoken English can be found in the Michigan Corpus of Academic Spoken English (MICASE) (Simpson *et al.*, 2002), the British Academic Spoken English Corpus (BASE) (Nesi & Thompson, 2006), the Newcastle Corpus of Academic Spoken English (NUCASE) (Walsh, 2014), and the Limerick-Belfast Corpus of Academic Spoken English (LI-BEL) (Walsh *et al.*, 2011). Corpora of academic spoken English are also examples of specialized language corpora, particularly well-suited for EAP programs. Conversation among family and friends can be found in the Santa Barbara Corpus of Spoken American English (Du Bois *et al.*, 2000-2005) as well as the British National Spoken Corpus (Spoken BNC, 2014). Television interviews and talk shows can be found in the Corpus of Contemporary American English (COCA) (Davies, 2008). COCA and the BNC are large corpora of English that are freely-available online, but written texts comprise the majority of the language sampled. The International Corpus of English (http://ice-corpora.net/ice/index.html) when completed will have 26 or more regional varieties of English, each of which will have a spoken subcorpus.

Fan transcriptions of popular television shows also form another type of corpus. Fifty-thousand words for each of five dramas and five sitcoms were collected and organized with a concordance tool on the Compleat Lexical Tutor (Cobb, n.d.) by Tom Cobb under the heading "TV-Marlise" (http://www.lextutor.ca/conc/eng). Anyone interested in a particular television show could also locate fan transcriptions by using an online search engine. Transcripts can often be paired with the broadcast version which provides the audio and visual cues that are necessary for conversation and learning conversational pragmatics.

Corpora of spoken conversation show how speech acts are realized, as well as how discourse markers and other related expressions are used. Importantly, they also show how turns are structured both within the turns of individual speakers and across turns. Schauer and Adolphs (2006) illustrate this by examining expressions of gratitude. Using the Cambridge and Nottingham Corpus of Discourse in English (CANCODE) (McCarthy, 1998), they not only identified expressions of gratitude (including two not widely used by American speakers, *cheers* and *ta*), but importantly they demonstrate that the corpus data provide information about turn structure. Thanking expressions are often followed by other thanking expressions both in the same speaker's turn and across speakers' turns.

Pragmatic variation, whether by region, register, age, or gender (Barron & Schneider, 2009; Félix-Brasdefer & Koike, 2012), can also be addressed through the use of corpora. And although some corpora allow searches to specify speaker demographics for age and gender or otherwise provide the information, there are also some corpora that are restricted to a particular age group, such as the Corpus of London Teenage Language (COLT), now part of the BNC. Regional variation is also often addressed by separate corpora, illustrated, for example, by the list of corpora of academic spoken English from at least four different sites (Michigan, or general American, British, Newcastle, and Limerick-Dublin).

There are at least two ways to approach regional variation. One way is to identify the region that is particularly relevant to a group of English language students, selecting either the dialect(s) with which they are interacting or the dialect(s) of the locations in which they intend to study. Another way is to systematically sample various dialects for the purpose of exposing learners to the range of possibilities within the English-speaking world. In an example of the first, matching region and academic spoken English, Bardovi-Harlig *et al.* (2015a, b) identified pragmatic routines in the American Midwest (a dialect known as "General American") for use by academic learners in the American Midwest from a corpus of academic English in the same region using MICASE, thus matching both the academic environment and the regional variety.

5.3.2 Corpora as tools for instructional pragmatics

Some corpora are collections of data that one searches by downloading a concordance program or using a general search engine. In that case, the main, and most significant benefit is the spoken data itself. The Santa Barbara Corpus is one such corpus, and it downloads as multiple files. However, corpora are often not just collections of authentic data; they are collections of data that often have built-in search tools. The search tools allow us to identify data for materials development, and depending on the interface, may even allow teacher-supported searches by the learners. Examples of online corpora that are searchable on site include COCA, MICASE, and the corpora associated with Compleat Lexical Tutor. More practical information on working with corpora to develop pragmatics units and lessons can be found in Bardovi-Harlig and Mossman (2016), Ishihara and Cohen (2010/2014), and Furniss (2017).

5.3.3 Searching for pragmatic features

Speech acts are the most commonly researched and instructed pragmatic construct. Speech acts targeted in published instructional effect studies have included requests, apologies, compliments, complaints, thanking, suggestions, and refusals. Instructional effect studies have also reported on the teaching of conventional expressions (Bardovi-Harlig & Vellenga, 2012), pragmatic routines (Bardovi-Harlig *et al.*, 2015b, 2017), criticism modifiers (Nguyen, 2013), verbal back channel signals (Sardegna & Molle, 2010), bi-clausal request forms (Takahashi, 2005), downgraders in requests (Barekat, 2013), and lexical and phrasal downgraders in requests (Takimoto, 2006, inter alia).

The lexical components of speech acts are particularly easy to search, as the concordances are designed to search words and phrases. Consider the bi-clausal request forms selected for instruction by Takahashi (2005), *I was wondering if you, Is it possible to, Do you think you could,* and *If you could.* Takahashi's original treatment gave learners transcripts of native speakers' (NS-NS) and nonnative speakers' (NNS-NNS) conversations that included request forms. If we wanted to use examples from academic English as a follow-up to her activity, we would search for these forms. For this purpose, we entered "I was wondering if" in the MICASE search box (leaving the "I/you" unspecified for more examples). We searched twice, once in the mostly interactive texts (a MICASE designation indicating discourse in which interaction is occasionally interrupted with some monologic speech) (Figure 5.1) and again in the highly interactive texts (discourse that is interactive throughout) (Figure 5.2). The first search returns examples of "I was wondering if" used in requests in public interactions, mostly after lectures and interviews (MICASE, mostly interactive).

(1) Excerpt from a career planning workshop
S1: yes one or two for more questions?
S3: yes
S5: Uh this is really an extension of the last comment but *I was wondering if* you could, uh speak a little more to the pitfalls that, await junior faculty, members and mistakes that junior faculty members, tend to make...   [COL999MG053]

(2) Another speaker at the same workshop
S4: We have another question [S8: sure] over here [S8: sure] go ahead.
S9: I have a it's uh, shifting to a different topic actually. [S3: please] um, *I was wondering if* you might be able to, give some suggestions for someone, um some graduate students like me who don't get an opportunity to teach while they're in graduate school... [COL999MG053]

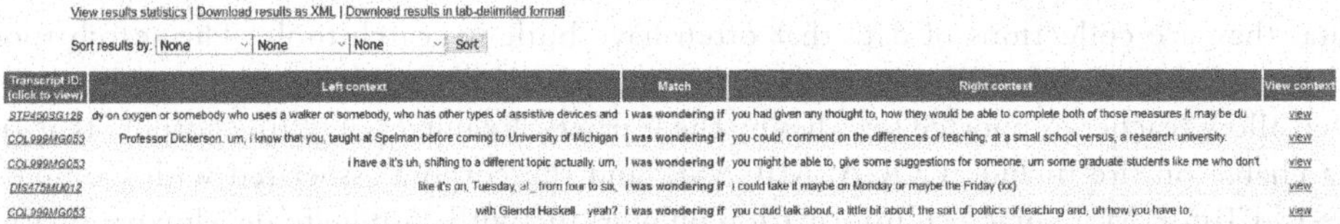

Figure 5.1   MICASE KWIC lines for *I was wondering* (in mostly interactive texts)

Figure 5.2 MICASE KWIC lines for *I was wondering* (in highly interactive texts)

If we search again in highly interactive texts, we find short turns in service encounters, advising sessions, and office hours.

(3) In the library
S28: Hello [female speaker]
S2: Hello
S28: Um, I was wondering if you could direct me to this? like where I would, find this call
   number   [SVC999MX104]

(4) Service desk 2
S3: Hi, how are you
S29: I'm actually doing a project on, these flat panel displays *I was wondering if* I could just look
   at it for a second. cuz like
S3: Sure
S29: Well, there's some information back here.
S3: Oh, okay   [SVC999MX104]

This small search illustrates a good match between the bi-clausal request form and requests. Other examples of lexically-based pragmatics instruction include conventional expressions (Bardovi-Harlig & Vellenga, 2012) and pragmatic routines for agreements, disagreement, and clarifications (Bardovi-Harlig *et al.*, 2015, 2017). What these example searches do not demonstrate, however, are two important things: first, currently, the only way to access speech acts is lexically, and second, there can be and most often is quite a bit of manual analysis that goes into determining what examples to use.

In terms of accessing speech acts lexically, the user must know key-words or phrases associated with the speech act of interest. This is where research findings play a role. Teachers can find such information easily on the CARLA (2020) speech act website (https://carla.umn.edu/speechacts/index.html). Let us start with a speech act like apologies. In American English, apologies have two main illocutionary force indicating devices (IFIDs, what Rühlemann & Aijmer, 2015, p. 10, call "speech act words"), namely, *I'm sorry* and *I apologize*. We can use those to search for apologies.

In contrast to our search for requests, this time the search returns apologies and many uses that are not apologies (Figure 5.3). Both *I'm sorry* and *I apologize* (nine instances in eight transcripts) are used as a form of *excuse me* and indicate repairs in speech. In Example (5), the speaker performs a self-repair:

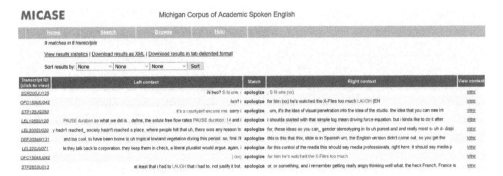

Figure 5.3 MICASE KWIC for *apologize*

(5) "such as N-two, N-one, I apologize, N-one." [Transcript ID SGR200UU125]

In contrast, an actual apology was performed during a dissertation defense in which the student apologized for including a slide in Spanish rather than English. In this example, we have annotated the excerpt by indicating the semantic formulas to show how this apology illustrates apology components.

(6) Fossil plants defense, apology (Female, NS English)
I'll apologize [IFID] this is this that this, slide is in Spanish um, [infraction]
The English version didn't come out, so you get the you get the early Spanish version [explan-ation] um, but what this basically shows is, something similar to that slide I showed you earlier, with, with vegetation types... [redress]   [Transcript ID: DEF305MX131]

A second example shows an apology-acceptance sequence.

(7) Study group
S4: I'm sorry I just kicked you.
S2: It's alright   [Transcript ID: SGR175MU126]

5.3.4 Frequency information

In addition to the authentic language examples, corpora with concordances can provide fre-quency information for teachers and students. Students can see for themselves (when provided the information or when taught how to use a corpus search) which pragmatic routines are frequent and which are not. For teaching, identifying what is infrequent can be very useful when vetting textbook "helpful expressions" that are often not helpful at all (Bardovi-Harlig *et al.*, 2015a).

5.3.5 MICASE innovations

MICASE has a companion handbook (Simpson-Vlach & Leicher, 2006) which not only is a guide to using the corpus, but also a supplement. Some of the information in the hand-book has also been programed into the search interface, such as level of interactivity or type of speech event. Particularly relevant to this chapter is the information found in Table 7 of the MICASE handbook, the pragmatic features overview (Simpson-Vlach & Leicher, 2006, pp. 70–81) and the abstracts for each of the 152 speech events that comprise the corpus. The pragmatics overview chart lists for each speech event, a limited number of speech acts (advice/ directions, disagreement, requests), humor and sarcasm, class management moves (assigning homework, returning homework or exams, review of exams, announcements), and their frequency (numerous, some, or none). This provides a guide to what is available and where to look for it for both research and pedagogy.

5.4 Current research: Testing the effects of using corpora to teach pragmatics

A number of studies have demonstrated the effectiveness of using corpora as a teaching tool for different aspects of language learning, such as vocabulary and writing development among others, as seen in this volume. For pragmatics specifically, Bardovi-Harlig *et al.* (2015b, 2017, 2019a) as well as Furniss (2016) have investigated the effectiveness of different ways of using a corpus in the classroom. One of the primary benefits of using a corpus is that it can be used as a source of authentic material for teaching pragmatics. It is especially useful for the development of activities that promote noticing of the pragmatic features of the target language that might otherwise go undetected. Through different types of focused noticing activities, learners' attention can be directed toward the targeted pragmatic forms, but there are different ways this can be carried out. Bardovi-Harlig *et al.* (2017) compared two different approaches to integrating a corpus into classroom instruction on speech acts and pragmatic routines used for academic discussions. One approach provided students with teacher-developed materials containing authentic examples of spoken language drawn from a corpus. The other had the students carry out direct searches of a corpus with the guidance of the teacher.

Each of these techniques has inherent advantages. Corpus-based materials created by teachers have the advantage of allowing the teachers to know in advance exactly what the students will encounter as they carry out the activities, and this degree of control ensures that students receive the precise input intended as a learning target. On the other hand, the guided searches are student-directed rather than teacher-directed, and the students are more autonomous, allowing them to discover the pragmatic features on their own. The cost of this autonomy is a greater degree of unpredictability at the moment of implementation, leading to some uncertainty as to exactly what exposure to the targeted pragmatic features the students will experience.

5.4.1 Method

To investigate the effectiveness of both approaches, Bardovi-Harlig *et al.* (2017) used MICASE as the source for the material used for instruction. This corpus was selected both for its ease of use and because the language in it was representative of the speech community of the learners being investigated.

The researchers collected data from 54 low-advanced ESL students from a variety of language backgrounds attending classes at a large public university in the Midwest of the United States. The students were divided into two experimental groups and a control group. The first group (n=26) was provided with corpus-based materials developed by teachers (CM). The second group (n=17) was provided with materials designed to guide the students as they carried out corpus searches themselves (CS). Both sets of materials were designed to draw the learners' attention to pragmatic routines used in academic discussion. The control group (n=11) took the pre-test and post-test but did not receive the treatment. An oral production pre-test and a post-test were used to measure gains in production of speech acts and pragmatic routines.

5.4.2 *Instruction*

The researchers created lessons designed to teach pragmatic routines used to express agreement, disagreement, self-clarification, and other-clarification, all of which are necessary to engage successfully in academic discussion. The lessons consisted of warm-up activities, focused noticing activities, metapragmatic instruction, and production activities. For the CM lessons, authentic examples of the pragmatic routines were extracted from MICASE, serving as the input for noticing activities. The excerpts from MICASE were reformatted to be more reader-friendly, and in some cases, simplified for clarity. An example of the presentation of the material using an excerpt from MICASE containing an agreement expression is illustrated in (8).

(8) Agreement Excerpt
DIALOG SET 1: These students are talking about their classes
A: Oh, it's another Chirping Sparrow
B: Yeah, you're right on those   [Transcript ID:LAB175SU026]

To encourage students to notice the agreement expression, students were asked to underline the expressions that show the students think the same thing, compelling them to attend to the specific agreement expression in the conversation.

The CS lessons had a similar format, but instead of receiving authentic texts as input for noticing activities, the students searched the corpus themselves to find the expressions in the authentic conversations. For example, in (9), students were directed to search for self-clarification expressions *what I mean* and *in other words* and record the frequency of each as indicated in the search results. A table containing the expressions in the first column was provided for the students who filled in the frequency information in the second column. The completed table is provided here, with the answers the students needed to enter in parentheses.

(9) Self-clarification frequency search

> A. Go to MICASE and search for each of the expressions in the table below and record how many times they appear.
>
> | Expression | Frequency |
> | --- | --- |
> | What I mean | (195) |
> | In other words | (229) |

To carry out the searches, the students received training in advance, but the search process in MICASE is straightforward. Once students have navigated to the search page, which is the first page accessed by default (Figure 5.4), students simply needed to type in the word or phrase they wished to search for in the "Find" box, and then click on "Submit Search."

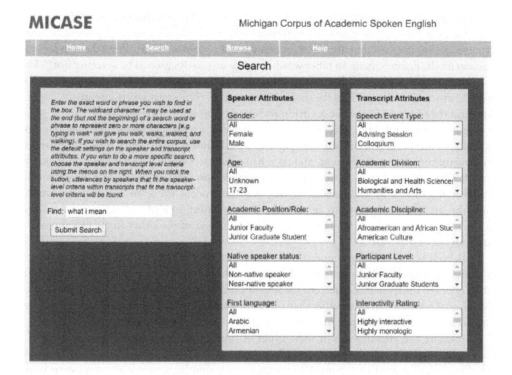

Figure 5.4 Default search page for MICASE

Once they had done so, the results were displayed with the frequency count at the top in Figure 5.5 (circled here) and a list of the entries.

In addition to recording frequencies, the CS students completed activities that directed them to look at specific entries for the expressions and identify features in the surrounding context.

The extracts from the corpus were used as a basis for providing metapragmatic information as well. For example, when teaching disagreement expressions, after a series of noticing

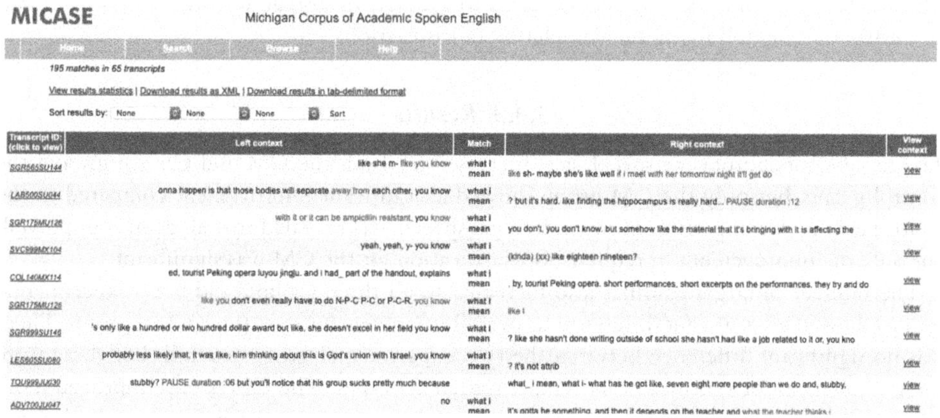

Figure 5.5 Display of frequency results for *what I mean* in MICASE

activities in which students were introduced to *I agree...but* for disagreement, the teacher provided the following information: "As you can see, people usually disagree by using the same expressions they use for agreements...except they add the word *but*. This allows them to provide a reason for the disagreement. In other words, a polite way to disagree, is by agreeing first!" The use of real-world examples to illustrate metalinguistic information provided validation for what the teacher was describing. From the students' perspective, the excerpts were essentially "proof" that what the teacher said is what occurs in real-world communication situations.

The expressions found in MICASE were also used as a basis for production activities. For example, in one of the lessons, students played a board game in which they rolled dice, landed on a square containing a statement, and then had to carry out the speech act indicated on the card they had drawn. For instance, if the student landed on a square containing the statement, *it is okay to exchange a gift for something else*, and the student drew an "other-clarification" card, the student would have to request clarification using one of the expressions covered in the lesson, such as *what do you mean by exchange* or one of the other frequent expressions encountered in MICASE.

Thus, both experimental groups received a variety of types of instruction grounded in the use of a corpus as a basis for the target input. To reiterate, the difference between the two groups was whether or not the teachers carried out the searches and curated the results to present them in an ideal format for noticing, or whether they guided the students as they engaged in these searches themselves, discovering the pragmatic routines used to carry out the speech acts directly.

To measure the effectiveness of these types of instruction, a pre/post-test consisting of a computer-delivered oral discourse completion task (DCT) was administered (see Example 10). This task consisted of a PowerPoint presentation simulating academic discussion using different scenarios requiring learners to respond by agreeing, disagreeing, clarifying a statement, and requesting clarification of a statement.

(10) Pre-test/post-test agreement item on the oral DCT
(AUDIO AND ON SCREEN): "Your group is discussing transportation and cars. You have the same opinion as your classmate."
CLASSMATE [AUDIO ONLY]: "People who take the bus are more responsible environmentally than people who drive cars."
YOU SAY:

The pre-test was administered one day prior to the start of instruction and the post-test was given one day following the completion of instruction.

5.4.3 Results

The number of appropriate speech acts increased for both the CM and CS groups and the control group, but only the CM group showed a significant improvement compared to the control group. A comparison of the individual speech acts revealed that all groups improved, but only the improvement in requests for clarification for the CM was significant.

The number of target routines also increased in all three groups, and both experimental groups showed a significant difference in overall improvement over the control group. There was no significant difference between the two experimental groups overall, but there were some differences for routines of individual speech act types. The CM group improved more on agreement routines, and the CS group improved more on disagreements and both types of clarification routines.

There are a number of conclusions that can be drawn from this study. First, there is no single "right" way to use a corpus. Both groups benefited from the type of instruction they received, improving their production of the pragmatic routines. There were some benefits, however, that were specific to each type of implementation. The presentation of corpus extracts in dialog format seems to have made the speech acts more noticeable. In contrast, when the students conducted the searches, they initially saw the KWIC lines with the highlighted vertical display of the pragmatic routines which increased their salience. In addition, students carrying out corpus searches benefited from discovering which routines were frequently used in the corpus, information not available from the CM materials. CS learners showed a dramatic improvement in high-frequency routines such as *that's right*, *that's true*, and *you're right*, for agreements, whereas the CM group preferred the less frequent but more transparent *I agree*.

The optimal implementation is probably a combination of the corpus-materials and the corpus searches by students (Bardovi-Harlig *et al.*, 2019b). Providing students with teacher-developed materials allows for input enhancement to improve salience and the noticing of certain features of the speech acts and routines. Providing students with opportunities to search the corpus themselves promotes noticing of other features, including frequency information about the different routines. Furthermore, it promotes self-discovery beyond the classroom because for many students, having access to a corpus and knowing how to use it is like a secret passageway to language they can trust to be representative of what people really say. Several students in the study reported using the corpus on their own to look up additional words and expressions outside the lessons. Students appear to appreciate the ability to "check" the language they are considering, in the same way that they like to check definitions in a dictionary.

5.5 Future directions for research

The use of corpora does not solve all of our materials development problems, of course. One issue is that even spoken language corpora are transcribed, that is, the language available for teachers and materials developers is written (see also Conversation Analysis materials that use transcripts, not recorded conversations, Bardovi-Harlig, 2015). Some of the sound files for MICASE are currently available online (https://media.talkbank.org/ca/MICASE/). The use of film (Furniss, 2016, 2017) and online TV episodes to supplement fan transcripts (Bardovi-Harlig & Mossman, 2016) can help with the audio-visual component. Revoicing the transcripts restores the audio when it is unavailable or the recordings are not clear enough for learners (Bardovi-Harlig *et al.*, 2015b, 2017; Bardovi-Harlig & Mossman, 2016; Riddiford & Newton, 2010). The matching of modality—oral input for oral production—is crucial in teaching pragmatics, just as it is in research (Bardovi-Harlig, 2018).

In addition, it must be noted for ELT as it is for corpus pragmatics that an automated search still requires substantial manual analysis (as illustrated by our short KWIC lines in which many of the lines for "I apologize" and "I'm sorry" introduced repairs rather than apologies). We have to carefully check the results of any search (Jucker, 2018). Schauer and Adolphs (2006) illustrate this in their exploration of thanking expressions in CANCODE. They searched for "cheers" and while they found 180 examples that initiated a thanking exchange, they also found 47 uses of *cheers* as a toast (which could be ruled out), and another 111 tokens following a thanking expression, which could be interpreted as reciprocal thanking or responses to thanking.

Perhaps the most significant issue is that the corpora that we can access easily (free, online corpora) can be best searched with lexical terms. That works well for pragmatic routines, conventional expressions, and illocutionary force indicating devices (IFIDs; such as *I apologize* and *I'm sorry*), which are lexical. These tend to be form-to-function searches (Aijmer, 2018). There are two problems with lexical searches. One is that the teacher has to know how the speech act is realized in the target language. If a teacher thinks that *Excuse me* or *Pardon me* is a typical apology, then more common conventions may not be explored. This is more likely with initiating speech acts than with responding speech acts. For example, if a teacher or a student thought "You're welcome" is the only appropriate response to thanking, and they searched for *thank you* (the initiating speech act), *no problem* and *my pleasure* would likely also turn up in the search. Resources such as the CARLA (2020) website (Pragmatics/Speech Acts section) provide a good starting point.

The second issue is that the lexical approach is most likely to identify direct speech acts in which the speech act is named in some way (see also Rühlemann & Aijmer, 2015). Indirect speech acts are much less likely to be returned on any search. Indirect apologies like "About last night, I shouldn't have said what I did" or a request to take out the trash such as "No allowance until your chores are done" will not show up in searches that use IFIDs or other pragmatic routines associated with direct speech acts. Thus, accessing indirect or less direct speech acts for teaching becomes problematic. This is unfortunate because the less direct a speech act is, the more challenging it is to interpret or produce.

There are at least two different approaches around this lexical conundrum. Pragmatics researchers have used key-words to find speech acts in the vicinity of where they are referred to (for example, in a novel), using metapragmatic information (Garcia McAllister, 2015; Jucker, 2018; Milà-Garcia, 2018; Weisser, 2017b). Even O'Keeffe (2018), who advocates a function-to-form approach to corpus pragmatics, uses work arounds that are essentially lexical.

In addition to being able to search for IFIDs, conventional expressions, pragmatic routines, and discourse markers, searching for speech acts would be an ideal tool not only for corpus pragmatics (Garcia McAllister, 2015; Jucker, 2018; Milà-Garcia, 2018), but especially for English language teaching. This requires a pragmatically tagged corpus (Weisser, 2015, 2017a, b, inter alia). Weisser discusses the issues involved in tagging spoken corpora pragmatically, focusing on speech act annotation (Weisser, 2015), and demonstrates the successful tagging of small sample corpora. Researchers have also discussed the pragmatic annotation of at least two other corpora, namely MICASE (Maynard & Leicher, 2007) and the Engineering Lecture Corpus (ELC www.coventry.ac.uk/elc; Alsop & Nesi, 2014). However, these visionary papers show that *pragmatics* may be interpreted in multiple ways. ELC's proposed coding includes five main categories: explaining, housekeeping, humor, storytelling, and summarizing. The 28 categories identified in the MICASE Handbook (Simpson-Vlach & Leicher, 2006) include speech acts, discourse structure, class management, and characteristics of the talk. Although these discussions reveal different conceptualizations of pragmatics, they also show that nonlexical, nonmorphosyntactic coding are being considered. Neither of these annotations have been implemented (but see the MICASE handbook).

Another promising example is found in the Online Corpus of Academic Lectures (OnCAL, n.d.; http://www.oncal.sci.waseda.ac.jp/index.aspx), a corpus of 395 lectures and 3.5 million words (Kunioshi *et al.*, 2016). The OnCAL interface offers a category "Pedagogical Function" from which a user can select Science/Chronology, Cause/Effect, Conditions, Analogy, Thought Experiment, Question, Framing Content, Linking Ideas, Clarifying, and Using Visuals. Of particular relevance to the present discussion is "Clarifying." If one selects "Clarifying" alone from the menu (without entering a lexical item), the search returns 131 instances of clarification, which, in turn, are divided into exemplifying, restating, and emphasizing. A search on *what I mean is* alone returns 17 uses, but a search that includes *what I mean is* and "clarifying" returns just those cases of *what I mean is* that are used for clarification, and not for other functions, reducing the amount of sorting that the user must do. Although the goal of the OnCAL tagging is to illuminate the language of science for teaching, as illustrated by the category "Pedagogical function," its subcategory "clarifying" provides an example of what pragmatic tagging might look like.

While we can appreciate the complexity of tagging a corpus pragmatically, from our perspective as advocates for the use of authentic input to teach pragmatics, and in particular the use of corpora in this endeavor, our desire for the future would be an interface that is as easy to use as MICASE, LexTutor, OnCAL, or COCA in which a teacher or learner could enter a speech act as a search term and it would return, for example, all apologies, both direct and indirect, which is something that currently cannot be done. Such an outcome would depend on the coding of the corpus which suggests that the coding itself should be done by multiple pragmatics researchers so that inter-rater reliability could be established.

The increasing availability of online corpora ensures that teachers have a rich source of authentic language for pragmatics and no longer need to rely on unconfirmed intuitions. Furthermore, specialized corpora also allow for the selection of contextually appropriate pragmatic input. We have seen the wide variety of potential applications for the corpus-informed teaching of pragmatics, but research in this area is still scarce, particularly on the use of corpora for the development of classroom materials. There is a great deal more to be learned about the most effective ways to use corpora for this purpose, and the next step is to expand upon the existing research by developing corresponding materials and testing their efficacy in the classroom. It is then imperative that the knowledge gained from this research be disseminated among teachers so they can employ it themselves. If we do this now, we can start the revolution of providing better pragmatic input for learners in second language classrooms.

Further reading

Bardovi-Harlig, K., & Mossman, S. (2016). Corpus-based materials development for teaching and learning pragmatic routines. In B. Tomlinson (Ed.), *SLA research and materials development for language learning* (pp. 250–267). Routledge. This chapter provides practical examples for preparing pragmatics materials using three corpora (Santa Barbara, MICASE, and TV Marlise-Compleat Lexical Tutor).

Furniss, E. (2017). Teaching pragmatics with corpus data: The development of a corpus-referred website for the instruction of routine formulas in Russian. In J. Romero-Trillo (Ed.), *Yearbook of corpus linguistics and pragmatics, Vol. 4* (pp. 129–152). Springer. Furniss provides a valuable description for building a corpus-referred instructional website which can be used for ELT.

Ishihara, N., & Cohen, A. D. (2014). *Teaching and learning pragmatics: Where language and culture meet.* Routledge. Ishihara and Cohen provide a comprehensive discussion of teaching pragmatics and include a section on using corpora.

Weisser, M. (2017b). Corpora. In A. Barron, Y. Gu, & G. Steen (Eds.), *The Routledge handbook of pragmatics* (pp. 41–52). Routledge. Weisser shows what pragmatics tagging might look like.

References

Aijmer, K. (2018). Corpus pragmatics: From form to function. In A. H. Jucker, K. P. Schneider, & W. Bublitz (Eds.), *Methods in pragmatics* (pp. 555–585). De Gruyter Mouton.

Alsop, S., & Nesi, H. (2014). The pragmatic annotation of a corpus of academic lectures. *LREC*, 1560–1563.

Bardovi-Harlig, K. (2001). Evaluating the empirical evidence: Grounds for instruction in pragmatics? In K. Rose & G. Kasper (Eds.), *Pragmatics in language teaching* (pp. 13–32). Cambridge University Press.

Bardovi-Harlig, K. (2013). Developing L2 pragmatics. *Language Learning, 63*: Supplement 1, 68–86.

Bardovi-Harlig, K. (2015). Operationalizing conversation in studies of instructional effects in L2 pragmatics. *System, 48*, 21–34.

Bardovi-Harlig, K. (2017). Acquisition of pragmatics. In S. Loewen & M. Sato (Eds.), *Handbook of instructed SLA* (pp. 224–245). Routledge.

Bardovi-Harlig, K. (2018). Matching modality in L2 pragmatics research design. *System, 75*, 13–22.

Bardovi-Harlig, K., & Hartford, B. S. (1993). Learning the rules of academic talk: A longitudinal study of pragmatic development. *Studies in Second Language Acquisition, 15*(3), 279–304.

Bardovi-Harlig, K., Hartford, B. A. S., Mahan-Taylor, R., Morgan, M. J., & Reynolds, D. W. (1991). Developing pragmatic awareness: Closing the conversation. *ELT Journal, 45*, 4–15.

Bardovi-Harlig, K., & Mossman, S. (2016). Corpus-based materials development for teaching and learning pragmatic routines. In B. Tomlinson (Ed.), *SLA research and materials development for language learning* (pp. 250–267). Routledge.

Bardovi-Harlig, K., Mossman, S., & Su, Y. (2017). The effect of corpus-based instruction on pragmatic routines. *Language Learning & Technology, 21*(3), 76–103.

Bardovi-Harlig, K., Mossman, S., & Su, Y. (2019a). Integrating instructed second language acquisition research, pragmatics, and corpus-based instruction in an intensive English program. In R. M. DeKeyser & G. P. Botana (Eds.), *Doing SLA research with implications for the classroom: Reconciling methodological demands and pedagogical applicability* (pp. 55–81). Benjamins.

Bardovi-Harlig, K., Mossman, S., & Vellenga, H. E. (2015a). Developing corpus-based materials to teach pragmatic routines. *TESOL Journal, 6*(3), 499–526.

Bardovi-Harlig, K., Mossman, S., & Vellenga, H. E. (2015b). The effect of instruction on pragmatic routines in academic discussion. *Language Teaching Research, 19*(3), 324–350.

Bardovi-Harlig, K., Mossman, S., Rothgerber, J., Su, Y., & Swanson, K. (2019b). Revisiting clarifications: Self- and other-clarifications in corpus-based pragmatics instruction. In M. Sato & S. Loewen (Eds.), *Evidence-based second language pedagogy: A collection of instructed second language acquisition studies* (pp. 52–80). Routledge.

Bardovi-Harlig, K., & Vellenga, H. E. (2012). The effect of instruction on conventional expressions in L2 pragmatics. *System, 40*, 77–89.

Barekat, B. (2013). Investigating effects of metalinguistic feedback in L2 pragmatic instruction. *International Journal of Linguistics, 5*(2), 197–208.

Barron, A., & Schneider, K. P. (2009). Variational pragmatics: Studying the impact of social factors on language use in interaction. *Intercultural Pragmatics, 6*(4), 425–442.

Boxer, D., & Pickering, L. (1993). Problems in the presentation of speech acts in ELT materials: The case of complaints. *ELT Journal, 49*, 44–58.

CARLA (2020). Regents of the University of Minnesota (https://carla.umn.edu/speechacts/index.html)

Cheng, W., & Cheng, P. (2010). Correcting others and self-correcting in business and professional discourse and textbooks. In A. Trosborg (Ed.), *Pragmatics across languages and cultures* (pp. 443–466). Mouton de Gruyter.

Cobb, T. (n.d.). Corpus Concordance English [computer program]. Accessed November 16, 2014 at http://www.lextutor.ca/conc/eng.

Cohen, A. D., & Ishihara, N. (2013). Pragmatics. In B. Tomlinson (Ed.), *Applied linguistics and materials development* (pp. 113–126). Bloomsbury Academic.

Crystal, D. (Ed.). (1997). *The Cambridge encyclopedia of language* (2nd ed.). Cambridge University Press.

Davies, M. (2008). *The Corpus of Contemporary American English.* www.english-corpora.org/coca/.

Du Bois, J. W., Chafe, W. L., Meyer, C., Thompson, S. A., Englebretson, R., & Martey, N. (2000). *Santa Barbara corpus of spoken American English, parts 1-4.* Linguistic Data Consortium. http://www.linguistics.ucsb.edu/research/santa-barbara-corpus

Eisenchlas, S. A. (2011). On-line interactions as a resource to raise pragmatic awareness. *Journal of Pragmatics, 43*(1), 51–61.

Félix-Brasdefer, J. C., & Koike, D. (Eds.). (2012). *Pragmatic variation in first and second language contexts: Methodological issues.* Benjamins.

Furniss, E. A. (2016). Teaching the pragmatics of Russian conversation using a corpus-referred website. *Language Learning & Technology, 20*(2), 38–60.

Furniss, E. (2017). Teaching pragmatics with corpus data: The development of a corpus-referred website for the instruction of routine formulas in Russian. In J. Romero-Trillo (Ed.), *Yearbook of corpus linguistics and pragmatics, Vol. 4* (pp. 129–152). Springer.

Garcia McAllister, P. (2015). Speech acts: A synchronic perspective. In K. Aijmer & C. Rühlemann (Eds.), *Corpus pragmatics: A handbook* (pp. 29–51). Cambridge University Press.

Ishihara, N., & Cohen, A. D. (2010). *Teaching and learning pragmatics: Where language and culture meet.* Longman.

Ishihara, N., & Paller, D. L. (2016). Research-informed materials for teaching pragmatics. In B. Tomlinson (Ed.), *SLA research and materials development for language learning* (pp. 87–102). Routledge.

Jiang, X. (2006). Suggestions: What should ESL students know? *System, 34*, 36–54.

Jucker, A. H. (2018). Apologies in the history of English: Evidence from the *Corpus of Historical American English* (COHA). *Corpus Pragmatics, 2*(4), 374–398.

Kübler, S., & Zinsmeister, H. (2015). *Corpus linguistics and linguistically annotated corpora.* Bloomsbury.

Kunioshi, N., Noguchi, J., Tojo, K., & Hayashi, H. (2016). Supporting English-medium pedagogy through an online corpus of science and engineering lectures. *European Journal of Engineering Education, 41*(3), 293–303.

Maynard, C., & Leicher, S. (2007). Pragmatic annotation of an academic spoken corpus for pedagogical purposes. In E. Fitzpatrick (Ed.), *Corpus linguistics beyond the word: Corpus research from phrase to discourse* (pp. 107–116). Rodopi.

McCarthy, M. J. (1998). *Spoken language and applied linguistics.* Cambridge University Press.

Milà-Garcia, A. (2018). Pragmatic annotation for a multi-layered analysis of speech acts: A methodological proposal. *Corpus Pragmatics, 2*(3), 265–287.

Nesi, H., & Thompson, P. (2006). *British Academic Spoken English Corpus,* Oxford Text Archive, http://hdl.handle.net/20.500.12024/2525.

Nguyen, T. T. M. (2013). Instructional effects on the acquisition of modifiers in constructive criticism by EFL learners. *Language Awareness, 22*(1), 76–94.

O'Keeffe, A. (2018). Corpus-based function-to-form approaches. In A. H. Jucker, K. P. Schneider, & W. Bublitz (Eds.), *Methods in pragmatics* (pp. 587–618). De Gruyter Mouton.

OnCal. (n.d.). http://www.oncal.sci.waseda.ac.jp/results_full.aspx The Online Corpus of Academic Lectures.

Riddiford, N., & Newton, J. (2010). *Workplace talk in action: An ESOL resource.* School of Linguistics and Applied Language Studies, Victoria University of Wellington.

Rose, K. R. (2001). Compliments and compliment responses in film: Implications for pragmatics research and language teaching. *IRAL, 39*(4), 309–326.

Rühlemann, C., & Aijmer, K. (2015). Corpus pragmatics: Laying the foundations. In K. Aijmer & C. Rühlemann (Eds.), *Corpus pragmatics: A handbook* (pp. 1–26). Cambridge University Press.

Sardegna, V., & Molle, D. (2010). Videoconferencing with strangers: Teaching Japanese EFL students verbal backchannel signals and reactive expressions. *Intercultural Pragmatics, 7*(2), 279–310.

Schauer, G. A., & Adolphs, S. (2006). Expressions of gratitude in corpus and DCT data: Vocabulary, formulaic sequences, and pedagogy. *System, 34*, 119–134.

Scotton, C. M., & Bernsten, J. (1988). Natural conversations as a model for textbook dialogue. *Applied Linguistics, 9*(4), 372–384.

Simpson, R. C., Briggs, S. L., Ovens, J., & Swales, J. M. (2002). *The Michigan Corpus of Academic Spoken English, MICASE.* http://quod.lib.umich.edu/m/micase

Simpson-Vlach, R., & Leicher, S. (2006). *The MICASE handbook: A resource for users of the Michigan Corpus of Academic Spoken English.* University of Michigan Press.

Spoken BNC (2014). British National Corpus. http://corpora.lancs.ac.uk/bnc2014/

Sykes, J. M. (2013). Multiuser virtual environments: Learner apologies in Spanish. In N. Taguchi & J. M. Sykes (Eds.), *Technology in interlanguage pragmatics research and teaching* (pp. 71–100). Benjamins.

Takahashi, S. (2005). Pragmalinguistic awareness: Is it related to motivation and proficiency? *Applied Linguistics, 26*(1), 90–120.

Takimoto, M. (2006). The effects of explicit feedback and form-meaning processing on the development of pragmatic proficiency in consciousness-raising tasks. *System, 34*, 601–614.

Vellenga, H. E. (2004). Learning pragmatics from ESL and EFL textbooks: How likely? *TESL-EJ, 8*(2).

Walsh, S. (2014). NUCASE: Newcastle University Corpus of Academic Spoken English.

Walsh, S., Morton, T., & O'Keeffe, A. (2011). Analyzing university spoken interaction: A corpus linguistics/conversation analysis approach. *International Journal of Corpus Linguistics, 16*(3), 326–345.

Weisser, M. (2015). Speech act annotation. In K. Aijmer & C. Rühlemann (Eds.), *Corpus pragmatics: A handbook* (pp. 84–113). Cambridge University Press.

Weisser, M. (2017a). Annotating the ICE corpora pragmatically: Preliminary issues and steps. *ICAME Journal, 41*(1), 181–214. doi: https://doi.org/10.1515/icame-2017-0008.

Weisser, M. (2017b). Corpora. In A. Barron, Y. Gu, & G. Steen (Eds.), *The Routledge handbook of pragmatics* (pp. 41–52). Routledge.

Williams, M. (1988). Language taught for meetings and language used in meetings: Is there anything in common? *Applied Linguistics, 9*(1), 45–58.

Wolfson, N. (1986). Research methodology and the question of validity. *TESOL Quarterly, 20*(4), 689–699.

6

CORPORA AND SPEAKING SKILLS

William J. Crawford

6.1 Introduction

This chapter describes how corpora can be used to help teachers and researchers address the development of speaking skills for second language learners. The chapter starts with a brief discussion of language corpora and the various components of speaking skills. Section 6.2 covers current research in the field and includes a description of six spoken learner corpora as well as a discussion of specific studies that have used these corpora. In Section 6.3, two core issues in the area of corpora and speaking skills are discussed: corpus design and the relationship between speaking skills and Second Language Acquisition (SLA). Section 6.4 presents three representative studies which highlight some of the current issues related to corpora and speaking skills. The chapter ends with a discussion of future research (Section 6.5) and then provides a list of recommendations for further exploration of speaking skills and corpora (Section 6.6).

There are two main ways that corpora can facilitate speaking development. The first uses corpora to inform our understanding of how spoken language is used by expert or proficient speakers; the second uses corpora to inform our understanding of learner language. In many studies of the second type, learner performance is compared to expert/proficient users (often called "native speakers") under the assumption that 1) the target of proficient L2 use is understood by reference to native speaker language use; and 2) such comparisons can help us understand the extent to which learners are moving toward some target. In much of the current corpus research on L2 speaking, there has been more focus on language knowledge (e.g. the representation or development of grammar or lexis in L2 learners) and less of a focus on speaking skills (i.e. the way that L2 speakers use such knowledge during performance by reference to pragmatics and pronunciation). In some cases, the distinction between these two perspectives is not so clear. For example, common in both knowledge and use perspectives, the construct of fluency has been defined by Segalowitz (2018) from three different perspectives: the cognitive processes involved in language production (cognitive fluency); the objective measures of speech, such as speech rate and duration of pauses (utterance fluency); and the judgments that listeners make about speech (perceived fluency). While cognitive fluency relates more to language knowledge, both utterance fluency and perceived fluency relate more to aspects of performance more closely aligned with pronunciation research.

DOI: 10.4324/9781003002901-8

Derwing and Munro (1997) view pronunciation as consisting of intelligibility (the degree to which the message is understood); comprehensibility (the degree to which something is easily understood); and accent (the degree to which the sound of the message adheres to the target variety of English). The overall goal of pronunciation instruction is to promote speech that can be understood without too much effort on the part of the listener (Derwing & Munro, 2009). Pragmatic ability involves the social knowledge of what is appropriate or expected in a given context and includes the cultural- and context-bound assumptions of what is considered acceptable (Wardaugh & Fuller, 2015). Because corpora contain samples of authentic language use, they can be especially helpful in aiding our understanding of what constitutes pragmatically appropriate speech. Additionally, many spoken corpora do not contain sound files or phonologically transcribed corpora and such designs do not allow for the investigation of many facets of pronunciation (e.g. stress, pitch, intonation) but are well-suited to addressing pragmatic research.

6.2 Review of current state of research

Corpus linguistics has played an important role in helping researchers and teachers understand how people use language in different settings and for different purposes. Although language corpora have been around since the 1950s, the advancement of machine-readable texts permitted a more systematic analysis of large collections of texts. Advanced statistical analyses of these texts (e.g. Biber, 1988) have shown that written and spoken language are very different from one another grammatically. These differences have led some to note that because corpus descriptions of spoken grammar are so different from those of written grammar, pedagogical approaches to the teaching of speaking skills should make explicit reference to spoken language (Carter & McCarthy, 1995). Descriptions of conversation as seen, for example, in the *Longman Grammar of Spoken and Written English* (Biber *et al.*, 1999), have identified frequent lexis and grammar representative of interactive discourse. Other spoken corpora focus on language used in higher education such as lectures, study groups, and office hours, for example, T2KSWAL (Biber *et al.*, 2002) and MICASE (Simpson *et al.*, 1999). Corpus-based descriptions of language used in authentic contexts have provided important insights into spoken language use and provided authentic material for language learning. Previous corpus-based research has illustrated how, for example, phraseological features of spoken language are used in university contexts (Biber, 2006; Römer, 2017) or how frequency information can be used to inform teaching (Biber & Reppen, 2002). Corpora have also been used as the basis for an approach to language teaching (data-driven learning) which asks students to analyze authentic examples of language use (Boulton & Cobb, 2017). Those supporting the use of corpora have also suggested the various ways that spoken corpora can be used to inform language teaching (McCarthy & O'Keeffe, 2004) and corpora and/or corpus information can promote teacher knowledge, insight, and efficiency (O'Keeffe & Farr, 2012).

In addition to corpora containing language from highly proficient users, there has also been increased interest in "interlanguage corpora" (generally referred to as learner corpora) which provide systematically collected samples of learner language. Although both types of corpora can be used to investigate a range of issues related to L2 speaking, McCarthy and O'Keefe (2004) have noted a movement away from native speaker corpora as a target for L2 teaching. Consequently, while it is certainly true that native speaking corpora can be used to inform the construct of spoken language and provide valuable insight that is crucial for language teachers, a focus on learner language as its own variety of language does not always require a comparison with native speaker models. As attested by recent handbooks on learner corpus research (Granger *et al.*, 2015; Paquot & Tracy-Ventura, 2021; Part III in this volume), learner corpora have become increasingly influential in second language acquisition and teaching research. In fact, the number of learner corpora has increased so dramatically in the past 20 years that it is becoming difficult to keep track of all available learner corpora.

For those interested in identifying existing learner corpora, two major archives of learner corpora are useful starting points: The Université Catholique de Louvain's Center for English Corpus Linguistics (CECL) list of learner corpora around the world (n.d.) and the L2 corpora portion of the Common Language Resources and Technology Infrastructure (CLARIN) organization (https://www.clarin.eu/resource-families/L2-corpora). As with native speaker corpora, the vast majority of learner corpora contain written L2 performance as well. For example, the CECL website contains descriptions of 181 corpora mentioned, 40 contain only spoken performance, and 21 contain both written and spoken performance. Of the 40 spoken corpora, there is quite a bit of variation in their design with respect to various target languages, proficiency levels, tasks, and native language backgrounds. The importance of these variables cannot be understated as corpora can be misused. One would not, for example, want to use a corpus of spoken narratives to inform the teaching of conversational language. With corpus design variables in mind, it is important to note that the current state of research using corpora for speaking skills is, like with all corpus research, entirely dependent on the corpora themselves. The clearest distinction between design variables in spoken corpora concerns the extent to which sound files are included in the corpus; those corpora without sound files or phonological annotation can be used to inform issues related to lexical, morphosyntactic, or pragmatic aspects of language but are of little use in pronunciation-based research.

To give the reader an idea of the spoken learner corpora that are currently available and the various learner variables, tasks, and language backgrounds that constitute these corpora, seven learner corpora and some representative studies are described below. These corpora are all designed to answer a wide array of research questions related to speaking ability and L2 development and include learner corpora that focus specifically on English language learners (LINDSEI, CCOT, TLC), corpora of L1 English speakers learning other languages (FLLOC, LANGSNAP, SPLLOC), and a corpora of multiple target and source languages (European Science Foundation Second Language SLA Bank).

- Louvain International Database of Spoken English Interlanguage (LINDSEI):
  https://uclouvain.be/en/research-institutes/ilc/cecl/lindsei.html
  LINDSEI is comprised of 50 speakers from 11 different language backgrounds having discussions with and interviewer in English. Each learner takes part in a discussion on a set topic, has a free discussion, and completes a picture description task. The corpus is available for purchase as is a parallel L1 English speaker corpus called LOCNEC (Louvain Corpus of Native English Conversation).

  The Corpus of Collaborative Oral Tasks (CCOT). The CCOT (see Crawford & McDonough, 2021 for a full description) contains 775 spoken tasks (268,324 words) carried out by dyads of L2 English speakers. The tasks, originally used for formative assessment purposes at a U.S. Intensive English Program, has 576 participants from different L1 backgrounds including Arabic, Chinese, Korean, Japanese, Portuguese, and Pashto (primarily Arabic and Chinese speakers) at different levels of proficiency ranging from lower intermediate to upper intermediate. The corpus contains both text and sound files for phonological analysis (unannotated) and also includes assessment ratings for each task (rated for collaboration, task completion, and style by two trained raters).

- Trinity-Lancaster Corpus (TLC): http://cass.lancs.ac.uk/trinity-lancaster-corpus/
  The most extensive of the spoken learner corpora, the TLC contains spoken inter-action between over 2000 L2 speakers of English and native English speakers who are administering a part of the Graded Examinations in Spoken English at Trinity College in London. All speakers did at least one presentation and interactive task with more highly proficient learners completing either a discussion task or a discussion and presentation task depending on their proficiency level. This corpus is freely available.
- French Learner Language Oral Corpora (FLLOC): http://www.flloc.soton.ac.uk/
  FLLOC includes a number of different sub-corpora of French as a foreign language learners doing various tasks (over 4000 different files). The corpus is freely available and includes sound files and texts (including tagged transcripts using the CHILDES format). The different corpora (described as "projects") include both younger learners and adults as well as both cross-sectional and longitudinal corpora.
- Languages and Social Networks Abroad Project (LANGSNAP): http://langsnap.soton.ac.uk
  The oral component of LANGSNAP consists of semi-structured interviews and guided story re-telling with L1 English learners of both French and Spanish. One valuable aspect of this corpus is that it also contains argumentative writing samples of the same participants so it is possible to compare written and spoken performances by the same learners. LANGSNAP is also free and contains text files, sound files, and texts that have been transcribed using the CHAT format.
- Spanish Learner Language Oral Corpora (SPLLOC): http://www.splloc.soton.ac.uk
  SPLLOC contains two sub-corpora. The first consists of L1 English speakers learning Spanish in an instructed context and includes both narratives, interviews (with L1 Spanish speakers) and other pedagogical tasks. The second corpus is designed to focus specifically on the tense/aspect system in Spanish and consists of five different tasks designed to elicit tense/aspect interlanguage performance. Both corpora are freely available and contain sound files and texts (including tagged transcripts using the CHILDES format).
- European Science Foundation Second Language SLA Bank: https://slabank.talkbank.org/access/Multiple/ESF/
  This corpus contains unplanned speech of 40 adult immigrant workers from various language backgrounds (Arabic, Finnish, Italian, Punjabi, Spanish, Turkish) interacting with L1 speakers of different languages (Dutch, German, English, French, and Swedish). The texts and sound files are freely accessible.

Although the above corpora contain sound files and would permit phonological and/or pronunciation-focused research, the majority of these corpora have been used to explore issues more reflective of the development of language knowledge than the development of speaking skills. For example, Klein and Purdue (1997) used components of the SLA Talk Bank corpus to describe a Basic Variety of L2 grammars that lack specification of both phonological and morphological components (or categories). From this perspective, learner speech features are the result of under-specified categories of representational knowledge. Data from FLLOC has been used similarly by Rule and Marsden (2006) for adolescent learners of French as an L2. The SPLLOC has been used by Domínguez *et al.* (2013) to examine the acquisition of the tense/aspect system in L2 Spanish learners and a recent article by McManus *et al.* (2021) used the LANGSNAP corpus to investigate the development of complexity, accuracy, lexis, and fluency in both French and Spanish learners participating in study abroad programs. Section 6.4 (Current contributions and research) includes a more detailed description of two studies using LINDSEI and Trinity Lancaster corpora which explore questions that are more in line with speaking skills (e.g. pragmatics and (dis)fluency).

6.3 Core issues and topics

This section covers two topics that are relevant to (learner) corpora and L2 speaking skills development: corpus design and the relationship between speaking skills and Second Language Acquisition (SLA). Some of the issues raised in this section are not restricted to corpora and speaking skills: all corpora, regardless of the language they represent, should follow sound design principles and the relationship between teaching language skills and theoretical approaches to understanding language development is not restricted to speaking. There are, however, aspects of corpus design and the relationship between teaching and pedagogy that are specific to learner corpora and speaking skills which are also addressed in this discussion.

A quick perusal of the word "corpus" in applied linguistics research will affirm that some people use the word to refer to any collection of texts. For corpus linguists, this is not an adequate definition as it does not necessarily address two main components of corpus design: 1) that the corpus contains enough texts to include some variation within a given discourse context (i.e. it is balanced); and 2) that the corpus represents the language used in a given context (Jablonkai, this volume). A third condition to define a corpus often relates to authenticity (i.e. the language in the corpus reflects actual language use relative to a specific discourse context) which raises the issue of whether the language used in classroom contexts constitutes an authentic context. This chapter adopts the position that language collected in classroom contexts or language produced in interviews or as the result of writing prompts are authentic in the sense that the contexts in which they are collected are realistic and representative of what language learners are asked to do.

As an illustration of a well-designed corpus, the LINDSEI corpus consists of 50 highly proficient L2 English speakers doing three separate interview tasks (discussion on a set topic, free discussion, and picture description). These 50 speakers are at an advanced proficiency level and from 11 different language backgrounds. The design of the LINDSEI corpus meets the criteria for a sound corpus design; namely, a) it reflects language in use; b) it contains a range of texts of language produced in a given context; and c) it is representative of the language used in a given context.

Corpus design also plays a vital role in determining what can be learned from a given corpus. LANGSNAP, for example, contains samples of the same learner doing a similar task at different time periods as well as different learners doing the same tasks which permits both longitudinal and cross-sectional research designs. LINDSEI, on the other hand, is comprised of a number of learners doing similar tasks and does not allow for a longitudinal study design. All of the corpora described in the previous section are samples of either dialogic discourse between a learner and an interviewer or monologic production by a learner such as describing a picture or telling a story. These design features mean that the corpora would be of limited use for those interested in peer interaction (two learners talking to each other) or investigating at how learners manage face to face conversations.

A final aspect related to corpus design relates to any "extra" information that is included in the corpus such as grammatical tags or phonological information (i.e. annotations). Similar to corpus design, corpus annotations determine the types of questions that can be addressed. For example, with the exception of LINDSEI and TLC, all of the above corpora have accompanying sound files which permit researchers to identify phonological features at both the segmental (vowel and consonant sounds) and suprasegmental (stress, pitch, intonation) levels.

Phonological annotation of corpora can be extremely time consuming and not many are available for use. To date, there is one learner corpus that contains phonological annotation: the LeaP corpus which is specifically designed to teach prosody to learners of English and German (https://sourceforge.net/projects/leapcorpus/). Corpora without accompanying sound files limit the types of analyses that can be done and the types of questions that can be asked; corpora with these sound files can be annotated by researchers in the absence of existing annotation. Ghanem *et al.* (2020) provide valuable information for choosing and using digital tools to aid in the construction and analysis of spoken corpora with available sound files. As for grammatical annotation, some corpora (e.g. LANGSNAP, FLLOC, SPLLOC) have grammatical tags; others that are not tagged (e.g. LINDSEI, CCOT, TLC, SLA Bank) can be tagged with the researcher's program of choice.

To date, corpora have not been as influential in informing L2 speaking skills as in other areas such as lexis and grammar acquisition. This is due not only to corpus design but also our current understanding of how speaking skills develop. Corpora have been very influential in the area of grammar learning from both a theoretical and a pedagogical perspective because we know a good deal about how grammar develops. Research in SLA has, for example, illustrated the benefit of form-focused instruction (Norris & Ortega, 2008) and corpora tell us a good deal about language form. SLA research has also found strong effects for the role of frequency in grammar acquisition (Ellis, 2002). Furthermore, as mentioned in Section 6.2, corpora are used in data-driven learning which has been shown to be an effective approach for grammar learning (Boulton & Cobb, 2017). From a more pedagogical perspective, corpora for grammar learning are also seen in corpus-based textbooks such as the *Touchstone* series (McCarthy *et al.*, 2005) and *Grammar and Beyond* (Reppen, 2012) and even teacher training materials (Crawford, 2020; Richards & Reppen, 2016). All of these examples demonstrate a clear connection between corpora, theory, and pedagogy with respect to grammar learning/teaching. Currently, this same connection between corpora, SLA, and language teaching are not reflected in the acquisition of speaking skills. Spoken corpora have been used to understand L2 pragmatic development (Bardovi-Harlig & Mossman, this volume) but the components associated with pronunciation such as intelligibility and comprehensibility are not as well represented. There are, however, strong possibilities to establish connections between corpora and the development of speaking skills beyond pragmatics. More communication between spoken corpus designers and SLA researchers interested in speaking is required to establish such connections. For example, there have been a number of excellent studies looking at linguistic correlates of comprehensibility (Saito & Akiyama, 2018; Saito *et al.*, 2017; Saito *et al.*, 2016). These studies have identified phonological features such as pitch accent and speech rate as being strongly associated with comprehensibility measures. This type of research can provide the basis for learner corpus researchers to use existing corpora or develop corpora which would permit researchers to look more closely into the relationship between specific linguistic features and comprehensibility ratings with respect to variables such as L1, proficiency, task types, or monologic/dialogic speech. Such work can then be used to help inform teaching approaches to facilitate the awareness and development of comprehensibility.

Although not specific to learner corpus research, the divide between SLA researchers and teachers has been noted by many (e.g. Chambers, 2019; Spada, 2015). There are multiple reasons for this disconnect including the need for theory building or the (in)accessibility of SLA research to many teachers but it is also the case that the relationship between the traditional language skills and SLA is not a clear one. SLA researchers have traditionally seen themselves as being concerned with the development of language by reference to lexis, morpho-syntax, phonology, and pragmatics while teaching tends to focus on language skills such as reading, writing, listening, and speaking. When focusing on the traditional skills, it is important to distinguish between the development of a given skill and the development of language ability so that specific research goals are made clear. For example, Manchón's (2011) edited volume differentiates between *learning to write* and *writing to learn* where the former focuses more on writing skill development and the latter on using writing as a type of performance to inform SLA. This same distinction is applicable in oral performance as some use spoken language to investigate L2 development (Gudmestad *et al.*, 2019) and others focus on how to get students to become better speakers (Hsu, 2016). Borrowing from Manchón, it may be useful to make a distinction between *learning to speak* (a focus on the development of speaking skills) and *speaking to learn* (a focus on using speech to understand the development of specific language abilities). It is important to acknowledge that not all research needs to inform pedagogy; however, it is useful to make distinctions between the aims of research so that even studies focusing primarily (or solely) on the development of language can sometimes be helpful to inform the teaching of a given skill.

6.4 Current contributions and research

This section presents three representative studies using spoken learner corpora to address speaking skills. The relevance of each of these studies is also discussed in relation to some of the key issues raised in the previous section as well as some of the future directions covered in the following section.

Götz (2019) used the Trinity Lancaster Corpus to investigate the use of filled pauses in spoken learner language. Filled pauses such as *eh, er, erm* are often seen as markers of disfluency but they are also indicators of fluency because they perform important communicative functions such as negotiating turn taking or showing emphasis. Götz illustrates how filled pauses are seen as both fluency and disfluency markers by showing how different functions of filled pauses are mentioned in proficiency descriptions such as the Common European Framework. At lower levels of proficiency (A1), there is reference to "much pausing to search for expressions" and "some problems with formulation resulting in pauses" (B1). At higher proficiency levels (C1), pauses are used "only to reflect on precisely the right words" (p. 164). Götz was interested in seeing if the TLC corpus reflected these different types of pauses with respect to proficiency level; that is, whether the use of filled pauses (a type of pause) varied across proficiency levels. She found significant effects for proficiency and filled pause behavior but proficiency did not explain variation as much as other variables such as country of origin and age. The study did not control for different functions of pauses (e.g. the study included the total number of pauses per 100 words but did not compare functional differences across different variables), which leaves open the issue of whether proficiency may be related to how frequent a given pause function is as opposed to how frequent filled pauses are overall. The study is notable, however, because Götz included language performances of speakers from different L1 backgrounds which raises the possibility that there may be differences in filled pause use between speakers where English has a stable, nativized variety (India) and where users are generally categorized as learners (Italy). Investigating variation across these varieties raises important issues about what native and learner language actually is and suggests the need to further research distinctions between learner and native varieties (see also Gilquin, 2015). It should also be noted that, although pausing behavior was not a strong predictor of language proficiency in both learner and nativized varieties, it may be the case that certain types of pausing behavior would have a positive, or negative, effect on the intelligibility and/ or comprehensibility of learner and nativized speech. A more in-depth investigation of the differences in filled pause use (including a comparison of functional uses of filled pauses) across varieties and proficiency levels would be of value to both teachers and researchers.

In another study using spoken learner corpora, Aijmer (2011) investigated the frequency and function of the discourse marker *well* in the Swedish component of the LINDSEI corpus and the parallel corpus LOCNEC. Aijmer noted that the use of pragmatic markers by L2 learners has been a popular area of study due to their multi-functional uses such as aiding in discourse organization, showing involvement, and expressing stance. These markers also hold different syntactic positions in an utterance and control over these positions comprise an essential part of fluent native speaker speech. Aijmer's study is notable in that her analysis compared native and learner use of *well* by function, syntactic position (turn initial, medial, final), and pause length (presumably, Aijmer was given access to the sound files). Although pause length was not quantified by a measure such as milliseconds, she did include pause length distinctions by reference to short, medium, and long pauses as well as pauses before or after well. Aijmer found that Swedish learners used well more for speech management functions and less for stance functions than native speakers. She also found that Swedish learners were more likely to combine *well* with filled pauses (both before and after) and more likely to use *well* turn initially. This study is notable for a number of reasons. First, Aijmer considered pause length (albeit measured impressionistically) in her analysis which provided some insight into the relationship between lexico-grammar and phonology. Furthermore, her study acknowledges a possible task effect by suggesting that the uses of *well* may be related to the interview format and mentions that other types of interactions (such as conversation) may result in other uses such as, attitudinal uses of well. Aijmer also raises the possibility that the native speaker comparison may not take into account the emerging functions of discourse markers in different varieties of English. This point is similar to the one raised by Götz (2019) which questions "native speaker" norms as a basis for comparison. Additionally, Aijmer makes an astute point that is not frequently raised in learner corpus research; namely, the need to account for individual variation across the learners in the corpus. Because many learner corpus researchers are concerned with overall frequency in the corpus and not individual learner variation, analyses not accounting for individual variation may not provide a clear picture of the multiple paths that learners take toward the acquisition of a given feature. Finally, Aijmer (2011) discusses specific pedagogical goals related to the learning of pragmatic markers in the language learning classroom. These are awareness raising activities that show how native speakers use *well*, including attitudinal use, how *well* functions turn initially or medially, and how *well* illustrates "active control and organization tactics deployed in the service of turn and information management under real-time" (p. 250). Such pedagogical implications along with a strong analysis of learner language illustrate the relevance of this study from both speaking to learn and learning to speak perspectives.

In addition to the two studies described above, one more recent study is notable for its inclusion of phonological variables in a corpus of peer interactions. Staples (2021) used subcomponents of the CCOT which serves as the core dataset for chapters in an edited volume (Crawford, 2021). Staples (2021) analyzed learner interactions (28 pairs; 56 speakers in total) to explore linguistic variation in two different task types (informational and argumentative). The study incorporated a wide range of linguistic features including grammatical (conditional clauses, that complement clauses) and pronunciation features which considered both fluency (speech rate, length of pauses) and pitch range as well as interactional features (turn length, backchannels). In addition to the grammatical variation across task types, Staples also found differences in pronunciation and interactional features. For example, backchannels were used more frequently in informational tasks where each speaker was expected to provide their part of the required information while the other participant listened but the argumentative task led to higher speech rates, longer runs, and shorter and fewer pauses because the task required more interaction between speakers. This study is novel not only in its inclusion of pronunciation variables in learner corpus research but it also suggests that phonological variables should be considered in studies looking at register differences. Most register studies to date are focused on lexico-grammatical variation but Staples' study provides evidence for including phonological variables as well. Furthermore, Staples notes that her study has implications for oral language assessment. As different tasks elicit different grammatical, pronunciation, and interactional features, teachers and test developers can use such information in their selection and development of tasks.

6.5 Future directions of research

Although not as common as written corpora, the increase and availability of spoken learner corpora has resulted in a deeper understanding of how learners develop their spoken language ability. In its current state, learner corpora permit study designs that range from comparing learner performance to native speaker corpora, investigating longitudinal development of spoken ability, and exploring the extent to which specific components of speaking ability relate to external proficiency measures or task performance. The future possibilities that spoken learner corpus research hold is closely related to our understanding of the constructs of spoken language, future corpus designs, and a clear understanding of differences between learner and nativized varieties.

Corpus descriptions of spoken discourse have provided empirically based evidence of lexico-grammatical features of spoken language that have been used in L2 speaking research to compare native performance with learner performance. Such comparisons allow both teachers and researchers to understand differences between learner and non-learner speech and apply knowledge of these differences to both pedagogical and theoretical pursuits. The inclusion of sound files in many learner corpora has also permitted phonological analysis to complement lexico-grammatical investigations. Due to technological advances, we can expect that a greater number of future studies will include phonological analyses. We may also expect that future corpora could include visual representations of performance, often called a multimodal corpus (Coccetta, this volume), which would permit gesture and gaze to also be included as important variables in spoken corpus research and encourage future researchers to consider interactions between lexico-grammar, phonology, and gesture/gaze. In fact, given the current conceptions of intelligibility (the degree to which the message is understood) and comprehensibility (the degree to which something is easily understood) these constructs are, by definition, reliant on perceptions of the listener. Perceptions have also been used in fluency research (Kormos & Denes, 2004) and, as mentioned above, perceptual fluency has been one important way to understand the concept of fluency (Segalowitz, 2018). The "non grammatical" constructs of phonology and gesture/gaze are surely important factors that affect such perceptions. Understanding interactions between grammar, phonology, and gesture and its effect on intelligibility, comprehensibility, and fluency also has important implications for materials development and approaches to the teaching of spoken language to L2 learners.

A second future direction in spoken learner corpora is related to the design of future corpora. Currently, there are no learner corpora constructed to investigate potential differences in monologic and dialogic production. Studies have considered how monologic and dialogic production affects linguistic performance by reference to complexity, accuracy, and/or fluency (Michel *et al.*, 2007; Tavakoli, 2016; Tavakoli & Wright, 2020) and have found evidence showing an advantage for both fluency and accuracy in dialogic task performance when compared to monologic performance. Because speaking instruction includes a focus on both monologic tasks (such as presentations or narratives) as well as dialogic tasks (such as collaborative problem solving or sharing opinions) (Goh, 2017), a more systematic understanding of how these two types of speaking are similar to and different from each other would serve to help both teachers and researchers focus their attention on the specific abilities associated with speaking under these two conditions. On a related note, future learner corpora looking at dialogic discourse would benefit from more samples of peer interaction as opposed to interaction between a native speaker/examiner and a learner. Peer interaction is at the basis of many SLA studies (Sato & Ballinger, 2016) and research has shown that interaction is a fundamental part of language learning (Mackey *et al.*, 2002). Many studies looking at collaborative interaction between peers are "one off" studies and look at patterns of interaction during specific tasks. Larger collections of these interactions could help to determine if there are more general patterns of interaction related to language. Contextual variables are certainly relevant to understand language use and development, but larger collections of data may be able to show teachers and researchers how different patterns of interaction can inform our understanding of L2 speaking abilities. It should also be noted that English is the most commonly represented target language in a majority of learner corpora with the exception of the corpora mentioned in Section 6.2 (FLLOC, LANGSNAP, SPLLOC, SLA Talk Bank). Corpus availability is also an important issue with learner corpora becoming increasingly available to the general public (free or at a cost) but corpora are often constructed in various formats with different types of annotation which leads to a potential lack of data sharing across corpora due to platform differences.

A final area for future research is a deeper understanding of how learner corpora can be used to understand potential differences between learner English and nativized varieties of English. This question was raised above in relation to Götz's (2019) study on filled pauses but more systematic investigation would provide deeper insights into this issue. Spoken corpora that include samples that vary with respect to their status as nativized varieties, or English as a Lingua Franca (Wu & Lei, this volume), would help researchers understand variation in spoken language production and the effect such variation has on comprehensibility, intelligibility, fluency, and accent. As these four constructs are (at least in part) interactionally determined between speaker and hearer, perceptions of intelligibility, comprehensibility, fluency, and accentedness often include judgments of the speakers themselves (as opposed to what they are actually saying). Such judgments have important consequences (Kang, 2010) and, unfortunately, negative perceptions of such speakers can also be extended to non-standard varieties of English (Rickford & King, 2016). As shown above, corpora that are set up to investigate the variation between learner and native varieties (such as the TLC or LINDSEI) do not contain available sound files so work in this area is currently restricted to lexico-grammatical differences and not phonological variation.

Further reading

Adolphs, S., & Carter, R. (2013). *Spoken corpus linguistics: From monomodal to multimodal.* Routledge. This excellent book is divided into two parts. The first part covers design and analysis procedures in traditional spoken corpus design with text files only. The second part of the book provides practical and useful information on designing and analyzing corpora with text, sound, and video files. Topics include alignment of audio/video to text, prosody in corpora, discourse analysis, and an initial framework for understanding gestures.

Gablasova, D., Brezina, V., & McEnery, T. (2019). The Trinity Lancaster corpus: Development, description and application. *International Journal of Learner Corpus Research, 5,* 126–158. This special issue brings together different researchers who use the TLC to conduct studies on fluency, usage-based approaches to development, tasks and proficiency, and backchannel responses. Not all papers are related to speaking skills per se but the special issue provides an excellent example of the types of studies that can be done with a single spoken learner corpora.

Ruhi, S., Haugh, M., Schmidt, T., & Wörner, K. (Eds.). (2014). *Best practices for spoken corpora in linguistic research*. Cambridge Scholars Publishing. This edited book focuses on issues related to the construction and sharing of corpora with the goal of making these practices transparent and open for debate. Although not focusing specifically on English, case studies and "discussions" on various topics range from corpus construction, annotation, and automated analyses. Topics pertinent to speaking skills include building spoken corpora to include multiple varieties of a single language and tools for both automatic and manual transcription and annotation of corpora. One strength of the book is its focus on linguistic interpretation and the need for standardized practices to promote interdisciplinary research.

Strik, H., O'Brien, M., Derwing, T., Cucchiarini, C., Hardison, D., Mixdorff, H., Thomson, R., Foote, J., & Levis, G. (2019). Directions for the future of technology in pronunciation research and teaching. *Journal of Second Language Pronunciation, 4*, 182–207. This article provides an overview of different technologies that can be used in pronunciation research and teaching. There is a specific section on learner corpora that includes a call to collect larger amounts of representative data to inform the constructs of intelligibility and comprehensibility. This paper also describes how many of the other technologies mentioned in the article can be used to analyze (automatic speech recognition) or build learner corpora (such as text to speech programs).

References

Aijmer, K. (2011). Well I'm not sure I think … The use of well by non-native speakers. *International Journal of Corpus Linguistics, 16*, 231–254. https://doi.org/10.1075/ijcl.16.2.04aij

Biber, D. (1988). *Variation across speech and writing*. Oxford University Press. https://doi.org/10.1017/CBO9780511621024

Biber, D. (2006). *University language: A corpus-based study of spoken and written registers*. Cambridge University Press.

Biber, D., Johansson, S., Leech, G., Conrad, S., & Finegan, E. (1999). *Longman grammar of spoken and written English*. Longman.

Biber, D., Conrad, S., Reppen, R., Byrd, P., & Helt, M. (2002). Speaking and writing in the university: A multidimensional comparison. *TESOL Quarterly, 36*, 9–48. https://doi.org/10.2307/3588359

Biber, D., & Reppen, R. (2002). What does frequency have to do with grammar teaching? *Studies in Second Language Acquisition, 24*, 199–208. https://doi.org/10.1017/S0272263102002048

Boulton, A., & Cobb, T. (2017). Corpus use in language learning: A meta-analysis. *Language Learning, 67*, 348–393. https://doi.org/10.1111/lang.12224

Carter, R., & McCarthy, M. (1995). Spoken grammar: What is it and how can we teach it? *ELT Journal, 49*, 207–218. https://doi.org/10.1093/elt/49.3.207

Chambers, A. (2019). Towards the corpus revolution? Bridging the research–practice gap. *Language Teaching, 52*, 460–475. https://doi.org/10.1017/S0261444819000089

Crawford, W. (2020). *Teaching grammar* (2nd ed.). TESOL Press.

Crawford, W. (2021). *Multiple perspectives on learner interaction: The corpus of collaborative oral tasks*. Mouton DeGruyter.

Crawford, W., & McDonough, K. (2021). The corpus of collaborative oral tasks. In W. Crawford (Ed.), *Multiple perspective on learner interaction: The corpus of collaborative oral tasks* (pp. 7–16). Mouton DeGruyter. https://doi.org/10.1515/9781501511370-002

Derwing, T. M., & Munro, M. J. (1997). Accent, comprehensibility and intelligibility: Evidence from four L1s. *Studies in Second Language Acquisition, 19*, 1–16.

Derwing, T., & Munro, M. J. (2009). Comprehensibility as a factor in listener interaction preferences: Implications for the workplace. *The Canadian Modern Language Review, 66*, 181–202.

Domínguez, L., Tracy-Ventura, N., Arche, M., Mitchell, R., & Myles, F. (2013). The role of dynamic contrasts in the L2 acquisition of Spanish past tense morphology. *Bilingualism: Language and Cognition, 16*, 558–577. https://doi.org/10.1017/S1366728912000363

Ellis, N. (2002). Reflections of frequency in language processing. *Studies in Second Language Acquisition*, *24*, 297–339. https://doi.org/10.1017.S0272263102002140

Ghanem, R., Edalatishams, I., Huensch, A., Puga, K., & Staples, S. (2020). The effectiveness of computer programs in the transcription and analysis of spoken discourse: towards a protocol for pronunciation corpora. *Proceedings of the 10th PSLLT conference.*

Gilquin, G. (2015). At the interface of contact linguistics and second language acquisition research: New Englishes and learner Englishes compared. *English World-Wide, 36*, 91–124. https://doi.org/10.1075/eww.36.1.05gil

Goh, C. (2017). Research into practice: Scaffolding learning processes to improve speaking performance. *Language Teaching, 50*, 247–260.

Götz, S. (2019). Filled pauses across proficiency levels, L1s and learning context variables: A multivariate exploration of the Trinity Lancaster Corpus Sample. *International Journal of Learner Corpus Research, 5*, 159–180. https://doi.org/10.1075/ijlcr.17018.got

Granger, S., Gilquin, G., & Meunier, F. (2015). *The Cambridge handbook of learner corpus research.* Cambridge University Press. https://doi.org/10.1017/CBO9781139649414

Gudmestad, A., Edmonds, A., & Metzger, T. (2019). Using variationism and learner corpus research to investigate grammatical gender marking in additional language Spanish. *Language Learning, 69*, 911–942.

Hsu, H. C. (2016). Voice blogging and L2 speaking performance. *Computer Assisted Language Learning, 29*, 968–983. https://doi.org/10.1080/09588221.2015.1113185

Kang, O. (2010). Relative salience of suprasegmental features on judgments of L2 comprehensibility and accentedness. *System, 38*, 301–315. https://doi.org/10.1016/j.system.2010.01.005

Klein, W., & Perdue, C. (1997). The basic variety (or: Couldn't natural languages be much simpler?). *Second Language Research 13*, 301–347. https://doi.org/10.1191/026765897666879396

Kormos, J., & Denes, M. (2004). Exploring measures of perceptions of fluency in the speech of second language learners. *System, 32*, 145–164. https://doi.org/10.1016/J.SYSTEM.2004.01.001

Learner corpora around the world (n.d.). The Center for English Corpus Linguistics (CECL) at Université Catholique de Louvain https://uclouvain.be/en/research-institutes/ilc/cecl/learner-corpora-around-the-world.html

Mackey, A., Philp, J., Egi, T., & Tatsumi, T. (2002). Individual differences in working memory, noticing of interactional feedback and L2 development. In P. Robinson (Ed.), *Individual differences and instructed language learning* (pp. 181–209). Benjamins.

Manchón, R. (2011). *Learning-to-write and writing-to-learn in an additional language.* Benjamins. https://doi.org/10.1075/lllt.31

McCarthy, M., McCarten, J., & Sandiford, H. (2005). *Touchstone 1–4: From corpus to course book.* Cambridge University Press.

McCarthy, M., & O'Keeffe, A. (2004). Research in the teaching of speaking. *Annual Review of Applied Linguistics, 24*, 26–43. https://doi.org/10.1017/S0267190504000029

McManus, K., Mitchell, R., & Tracy-Ventura, N. (2021). A longitudinal study of advanced learners' linguistic development before, during, and after study abroad. *Applied Linguistics, 42*(1), 136–163.

Michel, M., Kuiken, F., & Vedder, I. (2007). The influence of complexity in monologic versus dialogic tasks in Dutch. *International Review of Applied Linguistics in Language Teaching, 45*, 241–259. https://doi.org/10.1515/iral.2007.011

Norris, J., & Ortega, L. (2008). Effectiveness of L2 instruction: A research synthesis and quantitative meta-analysis. *Language Learning, 50*, 417–528.

O'Keeffe, A., & Farr, F. (2012). Using language corpora in initial teacher education: Pedagogic issues and practical applications. *TESOL Quarterly, 37*, 389–418.

Paquot, M., & Tracy-Ventura, N. (2021). *The Routledge handbook of second language acquisition and corpora.* Routledge.

Reppen, R. (2012). *Grammar and beyond.* Cambridge University Press. https://doi.org/10.1017/CBO9781139344067

Richards, J. C., & Reppen, R. (2016). 12 principles of grammar instruction. In E. Hinkle (Ed.), *Teaching English grammar to speakers of other languages* (pp. 151–170). Routledge.

Rickford, J., & King, S. (2016). Language and linguistics on trial: Hearing Rachel Jeantel (and other vernacular speakers) in the courtroom and beyond. *Language, 92*, 948–988. https://doi.org/10.1353/lan.2016.0078

Römer, U. (2017). Language assessment and the inseparability of lexis and grammar: Focus on the construct of speaking. *Language Testing, 34*, 477–492. https://doi.org/10.1177/0265532217711431

Rule, S., & Marsden, E. (2006). The acquisition of functional categories in early French second language grammars: The use of finite and non-finite verbs in negative contexts. *Second Language Research, 22*,188–218. https://doi.org/10.1191/0267658306sr265oa

Segalowitz, N. (2018). Second language fluency and its underlying cognitive and social determinants. *International Review of Applied Linguistics in Language Teaching, 54*, 79–95. https://doi.org/10.1515/iral-2016-9991

Spada, N. (2015). SLA research and L2 pedagogy: Misapplications and questions of relevance. *Language Teaching, 48*, 69–81.

Saito, K., & Akiyama, Y. (2018). Linguistic correlates of comprehensibility in second language Japanese speech. *Journal of Second Language Pronunciation, 3*(2), 199–217. https://doi.org/10.1075/jslp.3.2.02sai.

Saito, K., Trofimovich, P., & Isaacs, T. (2016). Second language speech production: Investigating linguistic correlates of comprehensibility and accentedness for learners at different ability levels. *Applied Psycholinguistics, 37*, 217–240.

Saito, K., Trofimovich, P., Isaacs, T., & Webb, S. (2017). Re-examining phonological and lexical correlates of second language comprehensibility: The role of rater experience. In T. Isaacs & P. Trofimovich (Eds.), *Second language pronunciation assessment: Interdisciplinary perspectives.* Multilingual Matters.

Sato, M., & Ballinger, S. (Eds.). (2016). *Peer Interaction and second language learning: Pedagogical potential and research agenda.* Benjamins. 10.1075/lllt.45

Simpson, R., Briggs, S., Ovens, J., & Swales, J. (1999). *The Michigan Corpus of Academic Spoken English.* University of Michigan Press.

Staples, S. (2021). Exploring the impact of situational characteristics on the linguistic features of spoken oral assessment tasks. In W. Crawford (Ed.), *Multiple perspectives on learner interaction: The corpus of collaborative oral tasks* (pp. 123–144). Mouton DeGruyter. https://doi.org/10.1515/9781501511370-007

Tavakoli, P. (2016). Fluency in monologic and dialogic task performance: Challenges in defining and measuring L2 fluency. *International Review of Applied Linguistics in Language Teaching, 54*, 133–150. https://doi.org/10.1515/iral-2016-9994

Tavakoli, P., & Wright, C. (2020). *Second language speech fluency: From research to practice.* Cambridge University Press.

Wardaugh, R., & Fuller, J. (2015). *An introduction to sociolinguistics* (7th ed.). Wiley.

7

CORPORA FOR TEACHING SOCIAL CONVERSATION

Michael McCarthy and Jeanne McCarten

7.1 Introduction

This chapter looks at the teaching of social conversation and the role spoken corpora can play in the design of syllabuses and materials to foster conversational interaction in language learning. By "social conversation", we mean everyday two- or multi-party conversations between acquaintances, friends or intimates, the primary purpose of which is the creation and maintenance of social relations. Such conversations may extend to talk among classmates, workmates, or strangers where the goal is sociability rather than just the transaction of information, goods or services. We say "just" since we acknowledge the role of sociable talk in facilitating contexts such as business transactions and other contexts of language-in-action (McCarthy, 2000). We distinguish it from speaking in the sense of the conventional four skills in language learning, since speaking can also include activities such as oral pair work to complete tasks, monologue presentations, etc.

Our concern is with the design of syllabuses and materials for the teaching of social conversation. A syllabus is a statement of the subjects and items covered in a programme of study. A syllabus also implies some notion of coherence and progression, i.e. it is not a random list of items; an organising principle must always be present. In the case of language learning syllabuses, progression is typically organised on the basis of perceived usefulness and appropriacy, linguistic complexity, difficulty of learning, or an admixture of all of those. We distinguish the syllabus from the curriculum, which is a broader conception of a programme of study informed by wider goals (e.g. a national curriculum reflecting political or cultural aims), a distinction illustrated by Nation and Macalister (2010, pp. 1–3).

In English language teaching, a general consensus exists as regards the progression of usefulness and complexity at the elementary and lower levels (simple grammatical forms, high-frequency vocabulary, basic communicative exchanges, etc.). However, at higher proficiency levels, consensus is generally less apparent and it becomes more difficult to decide on syllabus priorities (see McCarthy, 2013, for more examples). In the construction of a syllabus for social conversation, similar questions of coherence, progression and priority apply, the answers to which are considerably facilitated by having recourse to good spoken corpora.

A final question of definition which arises in discussions of the use of corpus data in language teaching contexts is that of authenticity. Invented dialogues have long been the stock-in-trade

 DOI: 10.4324/9781003002901-9

of English language teaching, and one of the arguments sometimes put forward for using corpus evidence to inform the syllabus is that good corpus data is "authentic", i.e. collected in natural contexts among users who are not performing for the purposes of displaying language features. Such data are often contrasted with the language of course books (e.g. Cullen & Kuo, 2007; Römer, 2004), where dialogues are typically composed to display target language features and voiced by actors in high-quality audio environments.

However, the term authentic can be viewed from a different angle. Widdowson (1998) refers to the authentication of language, that is, the *process* by which the language is received as authentic (or not) by the learner. If the learner cannot relate to the material presented (i.e. cannot authenticate it) and see personal relevance and usefulness, the material may fail in its aims. In this chapter, we do not assume that corpus data per se is authentic just because it is sourced from natural contexts. The data will have to be carefully selected, mediated and presented in a way informed by suitable and workable methods and techniques, with the goal of providing teachers and learners with material designed with them in mind.

7.2 Conversation in second language learning: Historical background

Any experienced language teacher is likely at some point in their career to have encountered the challenge of the conversation class. It was often with dread that the co-authors of this chapter entered classrooms over the years to deliver the item labelled on the weekly time-table as "conversation". "Getting them to talk" was the goal. Although communicative methods were already established and becoming increasingly dominant in the 1970s and early 1980s, the historical hangover of structuralism meant that teaching materials, iron-ically, offered little in terms of structure when it came to teaching and practising conver-sational English.

Spoken models of various kinds in language learning texts have a very long history over hundreds of years (see the discussion in Carter & McCarthy, 2017). In the early twentieth century, the father-figure of applied linguistics, Harold Palmer, an advocate of the teaching of the spoken language, published structured tables of language items in phonemic and ortho-graphic script, where items from any one column in the table would permutate with any item in the adjacent columns to form hundreds of correct and coherent utterances (Palmer, 1916; for examples and a discussion of Palmer's philosophy, see McCarthy, 2021).

Example (1) below is from a Berlitz Schools course book that one of the present authors used in their teaching in the mid-1960s. The Berlitz schools were a global phenomenon of the twentieth century and hundreds of thousands of language learners the world over practised with dialogues such as this one in whatever L2 they were learning.

(1)

MR. ALLEN: Today we are going to walk through Regent's Park to the Zoo, which you have not yet seen. Here is the Park.

MR. BURROWS: How tame these grey squirrels are! Why, one is feeding out of that child's hand!

MR. A.: Yes, I regret we have nothing to give them. Well, here is the Zoo.

MR. B.: These eagles and birds of prey look very miserable on their perches.

MR. A.: Yes, they do. Let us go to the Lion House. We can hear them roaring.

MR. B.: What a splendid pair of animals! I have never seen a lion with such a huge mane.   (Berlitz,1966, p. 145)

We may smile at the quaint style and content of this example in the certain knowledge that the future will find our present-day course book dialogues equally quaint and amusing. Materials writers in the 1960s had little or no access to genuine, everyday spoken language and so it is hardly surprising that the conversation comes over as wooden and more like writing. Dialogues like the one in example (1) were simply models. Students read them aloud, practised taking parts in them and, if one was lucky, were then better prepared to talk about animals and recount their experiences and opinions of zoos.

Now we have spoken corpora, with transcripts of real conversations. So perhaps we can use corpus transcripts instead of invented dialogues? However, natural conversation is messy and often difficult to follow, and the annotations transcribers add to their scripts can be very distracting. The 1966 dialogue targeted the names of animals. If we look to the Spoken British National Corpus 2014, we can find conversations about animals, but they may well look like Example (2), which is not at all untypical.

(2)
< S0421> well yeah I I saw I saw a clip and I was just like they had a tiger and they had erm an elephant and then they had this like dolphin swimming through the floor and it was just like it looked so real <pause> it's like
<S0423 overlap> oh so it's probably like your
[... seven unclear intervening turns]
< S0421> and it's like a 3D experience like when we saw that dinosaur thing and like when I went with school we watched <pause> erm like one where there was like fish swimming and it felt like you were swimming with the fish
< S0423> yeah   (Spoken BNC2014 S776)

We have unclear turns to contend with, there are pauses, overlaps, repeated words, no punctuation to guide us through the syntax, and yet, to the interlocutors, it all seems to flow perfectly normally. Such a transcript might well prove bewildering and counter-productive if presented unmediated and unedited to a class of English learners.

Before the advent of today's large spoken corpora, a pioneering piece of English language teaching material based on hours of recorded conversational data was Crystal and Davy's *Advanced Conversational English* (Crystal & Davy, 1975). The authors created the work in response to the "many teachers and advanced students who had a good command of formal English, but who were aware that there existed a conversational dimension to the language that they had little experience of ..." (p. ix). The authors collected their data in domestic environments, wanting to offer teachers and learners a realistic encounter with natural, "standard educated colloquial language" (ibid.). Crystal and Davy acknowledge that "a great deal of analysis has to be carried out before pedagogically useful generalizations can be made" (p. 1). They saw their material as an antidote to typical textbook dialogues: the "stiff imitations of the dynamic spontaneity of real life" (p. 3).

This glance back at history is not otiose; it serves to illustrate the enduring tradition of model conversations as a resource for conversational training. Tradition lives on and even the most recent course book offerings after decades of developments in communicative approaches include model dialogues. The dialogues are usually embedded in a four-skills syllabus as elements of the speaking strand and emerge from previous presentation and practice of a grammatical feature or encounter with a set of new, topic-based vocabulary. Typically, students listen to the dialogues, manipulate them in some way, e.g. re-order jumbled elements to make a coherent conversation (*Evolve*, 2019, p. 7) then practise with varying degrees of linguistic support ranging from a supply of useful phrases to being thrown in at the deep end with instructions such as "Discuss with a partner …", or "Ask your partner five questions about sports or other activities. Then tell the class" (Richards, 2017, p. 65).

So, what difference does access to everyday spoken corpus data make in the construction and delivery of dialogues for the pedagogy of social conversation? What can a spoken corpus tell us about social conversation, and what can we take from any insights into that question to inform the construction of a conversational syllabus and materials and an appropriate methodology?

7.3 Corpora and the study of conversation

7.3.1 Two research traditions

The advent of spoken corpora has revolutionised our ability to gain a more objective view of the architecture of everyday conversation. The size and composition of present-day spoken corpora such as the Spoken Open American National Corpus (hereafter SOANC) at 3.2 million words (http://www.anc.org/data/oanc/contents/) and the spoken British National Corpus (Spoken BNC2014) with over 10 million words (Love *et al.*, 2017) provide ample data for a fuller understanding of conversation.

The literature devoted to spoken corpus data is too large to survey comprehensively in this chapter; we shall just refer to works which characterise research relevant to the present context. An overview suggests two general directions in scholarship: one is the degree to which corpus insights have supported and expanded the work carried out in the conversation analysis (CA) tradition and the other is investigations approaching corpora from a lexico-grammatical perspective. Both traditions offer insights of great value to the designers of syllabuses and materials, and both feed into the four central principles for the teaching of social conversation described in this chapter. We illustrate these two approaches in the next sections.

7.3.2 Insights from CA applied to corpora

CA has contributed insights into core features of conversation such as how conversations are opened and closed, how speakers take turns, manage topics, respond appropriately or otherwise (the study of preferred and dispreferred responses in adjacency pairs), and manage the sequential organisation of the conversation as a whole (Sacks *et al.*, 1974; Schegloff, 2007; for a summary, see Sidnell, 2010). CA typically works with single transcripts of conversations which are subjected to detailed analyses revealing the unfolding talk as a sequence of meaningful social actions.

Corpus linguistics (CL) has underpinned the accomplishments of CA by showing, for example, how features of turn-taking are regular and patterned. One example is turn-openings. Sacks *et al.*'s (1974, p. 722) description of the three internal components of a speaking turn includes a first part which "addresses the relation of the turn to a prior [turn]" (see also Heritage, 2013). The opening of the speaking turn is significant in the creation and maintenance of conversational continuity and coherence, as well as participant relations. Tao (2003), using a corpus of American conversational English, showed that the turn-initial slot is typically filled by items such as *yeah, well, right, okay* and pronouns in fixed expressions such as *I think, you know, I mean, that's* + adjective (*that's right, that's true*). McCarthy (2010) built on Tao's work and analysed the British English CANCODE spoken corpus (for a description of the corpus, see McCarthy, 1998), identifying a list of items of high frequency at the beginning of speaker turns. These include lexical forms like *well* and *right* in addition to non-lexical items such as *yes, no, and, but, so,* and, as already mentioned in relation to Tao's work, *that's* + adjective. These turn-openers respond to the previous turn, hence the name *response tokens* (McCarthy, 2002, 2003), before the new speaker embarks on their own turn-agenda. Response tokens link turns cohesively and fluently, creating conversational flow or confluence (McCarthy, 2010). They show that the listener has attended to the previous speaker's turn and are, thus, key elements in the display of active listenership.

Tao's analysis is an example of how CA and CL taken together enable broad statements to be made about the structure of conversation which provides pillars for the architecture of the conversational syllabus. How speakers create conversational coherence and flow will form one such foundational element in the syllabus. How they display active listenership will be another.

CA also shows us how topic management and overall conversational management are realised, even though social conversation may appear to drift aimlessly from topic to topic and to have no pre-defined time allocated to topics or to the conversation as a whole. For a concise summary of CA work in this area, see Rühlemann (2007), whose research offers a further example of building CA insights into CL. The way speakers manage the whole interaction is another pillar in the basic architecture of conversation.

7.3.3 Lexico-grammatical insights

A number of investigations of spoken corpora have revealed aspects of grammar which are relevant to the understanding of social conversation. Carter and McCarthy (1995, 2017) argue that certain features present in their data have key roles to play in conversational interaction. These include ellipsis (the non-presence of elements normally considered obligatory), "headers" and "tails" (phrases preceding and following, but not syntactically integrated in the clause, often called left- and right-dislocated elements), and the relationship between main and subordinate clauses. Such features show how speakers attend to their listeners, using grammar appropriate to the relationship and context. Rühlemann (2007) asserts that a great proportion of what is termed spoken grammar should be better referred to as conversational grammar; it is in conversational data that the most outstanding differences between speaking and writing are observed.

Grammatical choices can contribute to the successful management of conversation. McCarthy (1998, Chapter 8), for example, showed how tense-aspect choices in reporting verbs (e.g. *say, tell*) can create a signal of newsworthiness for the listener, with turn-prefaces such as *Mary was saying that …* or *Joe was telling me …* regularly occurring in conversational data and only rarely in written data. This observation can explain the neglect of past progressive verb constructions in descriptions of speech reporting in grammars and materials based primarily on writing.

One of the principal insights conversational corpora have yielded is the ubiquity of lexico-grammatical chunks, variously known as lexical bundles, frozen formulae, formulaic sequences, among other names (Biber, 2009; Martinez & Schmitt, 2012; Schmitt, 2004; Wray, 2000). Sinclair (1991), based on corpus research, proposed the idiom principle, whereby much of language production and the creation of meaning is accomplished by ready-made chunks. Spoken corpora are particularly rich in such chunks. Martinez and Schmitt (2012, p. 313) suggest that the commonest words in corpus frequency lists are often "the tips of phraseological icebergs", and one study suggests that chunks can make up more than 50 per cent of a spoken text (Erman & Warren, 2000).

Chunks such as *it was nice talking to you* (used to close a conversation – rank 14 in the frequency list of six-word chunks in SOANC), *kind of* (used to hedge an assertion – rank 12 in the SOANC two-word chunks list) or *as a matter of fact* (used to make a point or to signal a contrast – rank 20 in the SOANC four-word chunks list) all display aspects of interactional management, showing a sensitivity to the construction of one's own turn as well as a sensitivity to the interlocutor(s) and general management of the talk.

Another example is the high frequency in conversational data of vague expressions, especially those commonly termed vague category markers (VCMs) or general extenders in the literature (Overstreet, 1999). VCMs are characterised by chunks such as *and things like that, or something like that, and stuff like that* (numbers 13, 15 and 45, respectively, in the SOANC list of four-word chunks). VCMs refer to categories the speaker assumes the listener(s) will understand; they project shared knowledge. The speaker who says "I lived in a little town south of here that is just full of old homes and uh historic old houses *and things like that*" (SOANC 107) is rarely likely to be challenged to explain themselves. Such usage is shorthand for "you and I are on the same wavelength; we share the same world". VCMs are another example of taking account of one's listener, the continuous monitoring of what one is saying vis-à-vis what one can expect the listener to understand.

Finally, there now exists a tradition of applying insights to CL from discourse analysis, in particular the study of discourse markers, whether single words (e.g. *well, right, just, so, no, actually, anyway*) or multi-word items (*of course, you know, I mean, the thing is*) and their role in the macro- (e.g. topic management, openings and closings) and micro- (e.g. prefacing dispreferred responses, signalling local agreement) organisation of the conversation. The classic study of discourse markers discussed by Schiffrin (1987) has been accompanied by a number of investigations of such items in spoken corpora (examples include Aijmer, 2015; Delahunty, 2012; Erman, 1987; Lenk, 1998).

Interlocutors' orientation towards one another using a repertoire of lexico-grammatical items emerges as another pillar of the conversational architecture. CA-based and lexico-grammatically based investigations create a jigsaw puzzle from which the syllabus and materials designer attempts to compose the bigger picture and form the framework of the syllabus, into which key items of conversational strategy can be entered and realised in the materials and classroom pedagogy.

7.4 Recommendations for practice: Corpora, conversation, and materials

The corpus-informed project described in the rest of this chapter was based on the premise that the strategies speakers employ to participate successfully in conversations (e.g. turn and topic management, good listenership, sensitivity to one's interlocutors) can form the basis of a syllabus and materials and that students can acquire both the linguistic repertoire and the strategies to create successful conversations. The steps towards this end begin with spoken corpus analysis (employing frequency lists, keyword lists, concordances, etc.). However, mediation of the data is crucial in a pedagogical context, using an appropriate methodology and various types of practice. We have argued elsewhere that natural conversational language will not simply happen or be brought about through activities which are either only loosely related to input material (Shumin, 2002) or dreamed up because the activities seem to be fun or creative, "a view often reflecting the triumph of hope over experience" (McCarthy & McCarten, 2018, p. 8).

7.4.1 Conversation and the syllabus

Above, we made a distinction between speaking and conversation. The language classroom is characterised by a wide range of speaking activities. Information-gap activities (Doughty & Pica, 1986), drama activities (Maley & Duff, 2005), discussions (Green *et al.*, 2002), recall protocols and role-plays (Golato, 2003), interviews with native-speakers (Mori, 2002), and task-based activities (Ellis, 2003) are all commonplace in English language classrooms. None of these corresponds to what we define as social conversation, and none relates directly or easily to the accounts of research in the previous sections of this chapter.

The kinds of speaking practice listed in the previous paragraph enable a degree of control, exercised either by constraints of the material, the goals of the task or the direction of the teacher. Social conversation, on the other hand, unfolds in real time and is unpredictable in terms of duration, topics, and outcomes. In the most basic sense of the word, conversation is creative (Atkins & Carter, 2012), and McCarthy and McCarten (2018) note that what we observe in corpus data is a post-facto trace of created interaction. This may at first glance appear to be a counsel of despair; however, it is the repetitive nature of corpus data, with conversational features repeated over many hundreds of recorded examples, which makes it possible to generalise for syllabus-building purposes. Having said that, we never forget the fact that social conversation is a jointly-constructed activity, a two- or multi-party chessboard on which no individual player can be wholly sure of the exact nature of the next move. On co-construction in conversation, see the discussion and examples in Clancy and McCarthy (2015).

It is clear from research in the CA and lexico-grammatical traditions that social conversation possesses its own repertoire of linguistic items and strategies distinct from writing. Vocabulary is an obvious case in point: although much of the lexicon of English is shared between speaking and writing, spoken corpus data reveal an additional lexicon that distinguishes conversation from formal writing (Buttery & McCarthy, 2012; McCarten, 2007). Social conversation is characterised by conversational flow, despite its sometimes chaotic and fragmentary appearance in corpus transcripts, which suffer from ending up as written texts that do not benefit from the co-textual syntactic and lexical support, along with punctuation, that stereotypical written do. The challenge for the syllabus and materials designer is to foster conversational fluency; the automaticity this involves (Gatbonton & Segalowitz, 1988) can be facilitated by the inclusion of the repertoire of conversational chunks (McCarthy, 2010). In fact, it is hard to conceive of conversational fluency existing at all without the ability to access a lexicon of chunks quickly and automatically.

In the next section, we outline how spoken corpus insights can be (and have been) mediated, incorporated into the syllabus and realised in teaching materials.

7.4.2 Four cornerstones of a syllabus for social conversation

The metaphor of cornerstones is apt in that we propose four macro-categories based on insights from conversational corpora to form the foundations of the syllabus. These are: (1) How conversational participants construct and organize their own talk, (2) how they take account of their listeners, (3) how they show active listenership, and (4) how they attend to the management of the conversation as a whole. These larger divisions provide a framework for subdivision where specific strategies and communicative functions (e.g. showing agreement, signalling a new stage in an anecdote) can be combined with the corpus-informed linguistic and strategic repertoire (e.g. response tokens *that's right/true*; discourse marker *anyway* for signalling a new phase of the talk).

7.4.2.1 Constructing and organizing your own talk

In this category, McCarthy and McCarten (2018) include discourse markers used in turn-construction as an example of what can be incorporated into the syllabus and materials. They give the examples of *I mean* prefacing a reiteration or an elaboration of the utterance and *the thing is* signalling an upcoming significant utterance. *Well, right*, and *really*, which are frequent turn-openers (McCarthy, 2010), are all in the top 40 most frequent words in SOANC, a notable statistic since the top ranks of any frequency list tend to be occupied by grammatical (non-lexical) items. In the case of *anyway* (word 258 in the frequency list of SOANC – still a very high rank), speakers routinely use it to move to a new segment in a narrative, to come back to a conversational topic after a digression or interruption.

7.4.2.2 Taking account of the listener(s)

High-frequency small words such as *just* (word 24 in SOANC), *probably* (word 112), *actually* (word 144) and *maybe* (word 149) also have important interactive functions in creating and maintaining relationships (*just, probably* and *maybe* as hedges or softeners; *actually* to emphasise, or to preface a dispreferred response). These small words show a sensitivity towards the listener(s); they are small, but they have big meanings in terms of the conversational architecture. Equally important are the high-frequency chunks such as *you know* and *I mean*, with which speakers monitor and project the state of shared and unshared knowledge. *You know* is number one in the frequency list of bi-grams in SOANC; *I mean* is bi-gram 13. In terms of raw frequency, *you know* occurs 35,611 times in SOANC; it is over ten times more frequent than *car(s)*, and almost 50 times more frequent than *music*. This is just to give some idea of the centrality of these chunks in the way speakers design their turns, leading us to ponder on why any course purporting to teach conversation in a second language would simply ignore or play down core items of the conversational repertoire. We mentioned vague category markers (VCMs) as a significant class of items in speaker projections of shared knowledge; *and stuff* (1,204 raw occurrences in SOANC), *or whatever* (819 occurrences), and *and things like that* (510 occurrences), all are used predominantly as VCMs, indicating a common thread of the significance of assumptions about what does and does not need to be spelt out to the listener.

7.4.2.3 Active listenership

McCarthy (2002, 2003) gives corpus-derived information on the frequency and distribution of a range of response tokens in British and American English which show engaged listenership. These may be either freestanding (i.e. single-word turns) or turn-openers to longer turns. High-frequency response tokens such as such as *absolutely, great, right, true, wow*, etc. show both understanding and engagement. They may be seen as *yes*-plus words, in that they are often found in environments where a simple *yes* would be adequate and acceptable. Speakers seem routinely to prefer to say more than just "message received" and indicate personal engagement, reciprocity of stance, enthusiasm for the topic, etc. In social conversation, the quick alternation of roles, with speakers becoming listeners and vice-versa, means that short turns, including single-word ones, are frequent and unproblematic. Turns are as long or as short as they need to be. In sum, listening is seen as an active behaviour. Labels such as listening comprehension in the syllabus may well provide useful practice in attending to and comprehending messages received through the audio channel, but this is not the same as the social-conversational skill of manifesting good listenership.

7.4.2.4 Management of the conversation as a whole

In social conversation, the usual assumption is that participants can exercise rights to manage topics, steer the conversation to particular social goals, or use sociable strategies to achieve transactional goals (McCarthy, 2000), deviate from the thread into asides and interruptions, return to the thread, decide when they have had enough and steer the conversation to pre-closure and closure. These rights are assumed to be equally distributed in well-balanced social conversation, compared with, say, a job interview or a conversation with one's superior, though power-relations generated by such factors as age, gender, social class and language competence can result in an imbalance. We have all experienced poor conversational partners who never know when enough is enough!

Discourse marking is an important key to conversational management, with markers such as *right*, *okay*, *so* and *anyway* available to signal breaks between various stages of the conversation. *Anyway* can mark a new phase in the talk, a return to a conversational thread that has been interrupted, as well as signalling a pre-closure, as in this example from an informal telephone chat: "... yeah that's true um-hum that's kind of sad well *anyway* well I guess I better go" (SOANC 580). Far less obvious is the topic management potential of *yes, no* and *yeah-no* (Burridge & Florey, 2002; Lee-Goldman, 2011), small words whose place in the syllabus is normally confined to their grammatical roles in answering polar questions. Topic management may also include referring back to an earlier phase in the talk or cross-linking to other conversations, with expressions such as *like I said (before/earlier)* and *as I/we/you was/were saying*, as in Example (3) below from the Spoken BNC2014.

(3)
[Speakers have been talking about the addictive power of TV]
... yeah like we didn't even have a TV before so it's I don't know why this is a new habit of ours yeah hm I don't know yeah but these yeah these flashing graphics which are the trend like **like I said before** I think it's the the HDTV yeah that they're just trying to brighten everything make everything dazzling...   (Spoken BNC2014 S27D)

7.4.3 From corpus to syllabus: Methodology, mediation, and materials

In this section, we refer to a project we were involved in as co-creators of a general English course at six levels (McCarthy *et al.*, 2012, 2014) with a prominent conversational syllabus strand. The present authors had taught for many years within the traditional PPP methodological paradigm of presentation – practice – production (Richards, 2006, p. 8). The input, a target language feature, was presented (often in the form of constructed sentences or an invented dialogue), then practised till a desired level of accuracy was achieved before the production phase, usually a set of prescribed activities offering varying degrees of control and freedom.

However, natural social conversation cannot be presented in exemplary sentences and needs extended samples, either in the form of the invented dialogues referred to in earlier sections, or anything ranging from unedited corpus transcripts to edited or adapted samples. If raw, natural data is chosen, the unpredictability of social conversation means that target items may only occur occasionally, or maybe only once or twice in the selected conversation; consequently, a different approach is called for to draw attention to the kinds of target items we have exemplified so far. The practice phase will also need to be different from the practising of sentence-based material. As McCarthy and McCarten (2018) point out, the target, in terms of the conversational function a particular item is performing, may not be visible or apparent at all to the learner. Finally, the third P, production ought, as well as it can, to generate natural conversation. It is clear that considerable challenges are present in teaching social conversation based on the kinds of corpus insights this chapter has highlighted via a traditional PPP framework.

Carter and McCarthy (1995) proposed a different triad for methodology with regard to unfamiliar encounters with spoken language: the three "I"s (Illustration – Interaction – Induction). In the first phase, illustration, the principle is to exemplify a target conversational feature in context, using corpus evidence, albeit corpus extracts will be edited or adapted versions of original transcripts. This does not necessarily imply always presenting entire conversations (it is often difficult in any case to define what a complete conversation is). Extracts need to be long enough to illustrate the unfolding and function of the target feature, to facilitate the process of authentication and to give learners enough context to apprehend the feature. Activities during the illustration phase can include, for example, personal reflections on the topic of the conversation, inferring relationships, meaning and intentions of speakers, offering opinions about the conversation, comparing personal experiences with those of the speakers in the conversational extracts, etc.

The second of Carter and McCarthy's three Is, Interaction, aims to promote the habit of interacting with texts, noticing and picking up on target features in natural contexts based on corpus evidence. Noticing is central here, and the activities must be designed in a way that the teacher can check that noticing has taken place before moving on to practice. We adhere to the value of noticing as an important step on the road to acquisition (Schmidt, 1990, 1993).

Example (4) shows a brief conversational extract from the Spoken BNC2014 corpus containing a typical use of the vague category marker *or something*. For reasons of space, just one extract is given here – typically, the illustration phase might include several along the same lines.

(4)
... and she starts every morning with her quiet time as she calls it so she gets up and I think
   she has er like a green tea *or something* ...

Interaction-based activities might include:

- Students choose which of a number of options the phrase *or something* might refer to, e.g. What do you think *green tea or something* means in the conversation extract? Underline the best answers.
  green tea or black tea/green tea or soda/green tea or coffee/green tea or milk
- Students offer their own suggestions as to what *green tea or something* might mean.

The third I, induction, is the process of incorporating new knowledge into existing knowledge and becoming aware of underlying principles, in the case of *or something*, the principle of creating good relations by projecting shared knowledge or shared perspectives. Here, the successful use of the target item or feature alongside language, the learner is already comfortable with in personalised practice can demonstrate whether the learners have induced its meaning and function. The combination of noticing activities during the interaction phase and the fostering of awareness in the induction phase is aimed at a more meaningful encounter with what are, for many learners, unfamiliar target items. Hughes (2002) suggests that a language-awareness based approach should be judged not by the quantity of speech learners produce but by the degree of their understanding of why speakers make the choices they do.

Putting awareness at the centre of language learning is certainly not new and has been argued for in recent decades (e.g. Clennell, 1999; O'Keeffe & Farr, 2003; Van Lier, 1998), but it is particularly important in the pedagogy of conversation since the items and features to be taught often do not correspond to traditional expectations of what will be in the syllabus. The key to the success of this pedagogy is familiarity of activity type combined with perhaps unfamiliar input which can be supported by corpus factoids to stimulate both interest and authentication of the input on the part of the learners. Corpus factoids may be small boxes on the page containing graphics showing the frequency of the target item or feature, or information on common functions of the item or feature as attested in the corpus. Learners do not need to be corpus linguists to apprehend corpus-derived statistics presented in user-friendly graphics.

7.4.4 *The syllabus: Items and features*

Corpus-based research has enabled us to describe a repertoire of items and features of social conversation. Items are the lexico-grammatical words, phrases and structures which create the conversational fabric. Features are more connected with behaviours and strategic choices. McCarthy and McCarten (2018) give the example of asking a follow-up question to keep the conversation going, a feature for which there is no pre-established set of items; what constitutes an appropriate follow-up question will be entirely dependent on the local context. On the other hand, some features can be regularly associated with particular items (e.g. *anyway* for marking conversational stages). It is here that the four pillars of conversation described above bring together the features and, wherever possible, the items that realise them, into a coherent syllabus.

The syllabus that grew out of our corpus research and informed the materials (McCarthy *et al.*, 2012, 2014) attempts to promote conversational strategies (key features and relevant items), alongside items which realise very specific functions (see also McCarthy & McCarten, 2010). For example, at the advanced level, one target conversational feature is *Softening Comments* (McCarthy *et al.*, 2012, pp. 120–121). This is supported by corpus-derived items such as *kind of, not really, slightly* and *a (little) bit*, included in listening and noticing activities. The strategic item selected for special attention is the turn-opener *yeah-no*, which we mentioned in connection with insights from spoken corpus research (Burridge & Florey, 2002; Lee-Goldman, 2011). *Yeah-no* is practised as a way of agreeing with a speaker before adding one's own comment, an interactive behaviour showing engagement and listenership, natural and efficient in terms of turn-construction, and effective in maintaining conversational flow. Corpus information is presented alongside in non-technical language, for example in graphics showing relative frequencies or simply advice notes (e.g. noting that *slightly*, as a softener, is more frequent in more formal spoken contexts). The example cited here is an advanced level lesson, but even at elementary levels, the principles can still be put into practice. For example, a simple item such as *well* to preface a dispreferred answer to a *yes-no* question or used strategically to buy time to think (McCarthy *et al.*, 2014). The corpus information accompanying the lesson tells the user that *well* is one of the top 50 words.

Conversation-focused lessons, as well as providing plenty of listening, noticing and awareness-raising activities, ideally take the learner from controlled to freer activity, with an emphasis always on personalisation, talking about one's own life and experiences. Topics of conversation should not be selected simply because they are quirky or fun; they should represent what people really do talk about, as attested in corpus data relevant to learners; otherwise, learners simply become actors playing out other people's conversations and authentication of the materials may be hindered.

7.5 Future directions of research

To achieve the aims set out in this chapter, especially that of making conversation natural, relevant and useful to learners, the compilation of spoken corpora should be targeted to the needs and experiences of the end-users of pedagogical materials. In this respect, more and more spoken corpora in natural social conversational settings are needed. And there is no doubt that multimodal corpora, with video evidence and simultaneously accessible phonological information, will offer a greatly enhanced resource for conversational pedagogy. When the present authors began compiling the syllabus for the materials cited, the transcripts were on screen; the original audio resided on cassette tapes; only later was digital audio available.

Software development needs must go hand in hand with corpus creation. At the time of writing, some automated analyses which have achieved a high level of accuracy on written data are still wanting when it comes to everyday conversational transcripts. An example is part-of-speech tagging, where items such as those we have devoted space to in this chapter (e.g. discourse markers, response tokens) are notoriously problematic in terms of the word-class labels computers are wont to attach to them. This is partly also a problem of metalanguage and terminology: attempts to fit the square pegs of written grammatical terminology into the round holes of conversational features are doomed at best to cause frustration and at worst to produce results that miss the very things which make conversation special. Finally, teacher education programmes can play an important part in disseminating knowledge and awareness of corpus developments and the insights we now have into social conversation thanks to corpora and do more than just hope that the conversation class will take care of itself.

Further reading

McCarthy, M. J., & McCarten, J. (2018). Practising conversation in second language learning. In C. Jones (Ed.), *Practice in second language learning* (pp. 7–29). Cambridge University Press. The authors consider the issues surrounding successful practice of social conversation and propose ten key criteria for achieving this.

O'Keeffe, A., McCarthy, M. J., & Carter, R. A. (2007). *From corpus to classroom, language use and language teaching.* Cambridge University Press. The authors address ways in which different types of corpus analyses can be used to investigate linguistic items and features of direct relevance to language teaching. Chapters 3, 7, 8 and 9 are particularly relevant to the present chapter.

Rühlemann, C. (2007). *Conversation in context. A corpus-driven approach.* Continuum. Bringing together a wide range of analyses of conversational data from the British National Corpus, the book covers features of conversation management, turn-taking and relational aspects of everyday conversation.

Timmis, I. (2015). *Corpus linguistics for ELT.* Routledge. This is a practical guide to corpus research and how it can inform various aspects of English Language Teaching, particularly grammar, lexis, ESP, spoken grammar and discourse.

References

Aijmer, K. (2015). Analysing discourse markers in spoken corpora: *Actually* as a case study. In P. Baker & T. McEnery (Eds.), *Corpora and discourse studies* (pp. 88–109). Palgrave Macmillan.

Atkins, S., & Carter, R. (2012). Creativity in speech. In J. P. Gee & M. Handford (Eds.), *The Routledge handbook of discourse analysis* (pp. 315–325). Routledge.

Berlitz. (1966). English First Book. Societé Internationale des Écoles Berlitz.

Biber, D. (2009). A corpus-driven approach to formulaic language: Multi-word patterns in speech and writing. *International Journal of Corpus Linguistics, 14,* 381–417.

Burridge, K., & Florey, M. (2002). Yeah-no he's a good kid: A discourse analysis of 'yeah-no' in Australian English. *Australian Journal of Linguistics, 22*(2), 149–171.

Buttery, P., & McCarthy, M. (2012). Lexis in spoken discourse. In J. P. Gee & M. Handford (Eds.), *The Routledge handbook of discourse analysis* (pp. 285–300). Routledge.

Carter, R., & McCarthy, M. (1995). Grammar and the spoken language. *Applied Linguistics, 16*(2), 141–158.

Carter, R., & McCarthy, M. (2017). Spoken grammar: Where are we and where are we going? *Applied Linguistics, 38*(1), 1–20.

Clancy, B., & McCarthy, M. (2015). Co-constructed turn-taking. In K. Aijmer & C. Rühlemann (Eds.), *Corpus pragmatics: A handbook* (pp. 430–453). Cambridge University Press.

Clennell, C. (1999). Promoting pragmatic awareness and spoken discourse skills within EAP classes. *ELT Journal, 53*, 83–91.

Crystal, D., & Davy, D. (1975). *Advanced conversational English.* Longman.

Cullen, R., & Kuo, I.-C. (2007). Spoken grammar and ELT course materials: A missing link? *TESOL Quarterly, 41*(2), 361–386.

Delahunty, G. P. (2012). An analysis of *the thing is that* sentences. *Pragmatics, 22*(1), 41–78.

Doughty, C., & Pica, T. (1986). "Information gap" tasks: Do they facilitate second language acquisition? *TESOL Quarterly, 20*(2), 305–325.

Ellis, R. (2003). *Task-based language learning and teaching.* Oxford University Press.

Erman, B. (1987). *Pragmatic expressions in English: A study of 'you know', 'you see' and 'I mean' in face-to-face conversation.* Almqvist and Wiksell.

Erman, B., & Warren, B. (2000). The idiom principle and the open choice principle. *Text, 20*(1), 29–62.

Evolve (2019) *Evolve level 1.* Cambridge University Press. Sample unit retrieved from https://assets.cambridge.org/97811084/05218/excerpt/9781108405218_excerpt.pdf

Gatbonton, E., & Segalowitz, N. (1988). Creative automatization: Principles for promoting fluency within a communicative framework. *TESOL Quarterly, 22*(3), 473–492.

Golato, A. (2003). Studying compliment responses: A comparison of DCTs and recordings of naturally occurring talk. *Applied Linguistics, 24*, 90–121.

Green, C. F., Christopher, E. R., & Lam, J. (2002). Developing discussion skills in the ESL classroom. In J. C. Richards & W. A. Renandya (Eds.), *Methodology in language teaching: An anthology of current practices* (pp. 225–233). Cambridge University Press.

Heritage, J. (2013). Turn-initial position and some of its occupants. *Journal of Pragmatics, 57*, 331–337.

Hughes, R. (2002). *Teaching and researching speaking.* Pearson.

Lee-Goldman, R. (2011). 'No' as a discourse marker. *Journal of Pragmatics, 43*, 2627–2649.

Lenk, U. (1998). Discourse markers and global coherence in conversation. *Journal of Pragmatics, 30*, 245–257.

Love, R., Dembry, C., Hardie, A., Brezina, V., & McEnery, T. (2017). The spoken BNC2014: Designing and building a spoken corpus of everyday conversations. *International Journal of Corpus Linguistics, 22*(3), 319–344.

Maley, A., & Duff, A. (2005). *Drama techniques: A resource book of communication activities for language teachers* (3rd ed.). Cambridge University Press.

Martinez, R., & Schmitt, N. (2012). A phrasal expressions list. *Applied Linguistics, 33*(3), 299–320.

McCarten, J. (2007). *Teaching vocabulary: Lessons from the corpus; lessons for the classroom.* Booklet for Cambridge University Press New York Marketing Department.

McCarten, J. (2010). Corpus-informed course book design. In A. O'Keeffe & M. McCarthy (Eds.), *The Routledge handbook of corpus linguistics* (pp. 413–427). Routledge.

McCarthy, M. (1998). *Spoken language and applied linguistics.* Cambridge University Press.

McCarthy, M. (2000). Mutually captive audiences. The discourse of close contact service encounters. In J. Coupland (Ed.), *Small talk* (pp. 84–109). Longman.

McCarthy, M. (2002). Good listenership made plain: British and American non-minimal response tokens in everyday conversation. In R. Reppen, S. Fitzmaurice, & D. Biber (Eds.), *Using corpora to explore linguistic variation* (pp. 49–71). Benjamins.

McCarthy, M. (2003). Talking back: "Small" interactional response tokens in everyday conversation. *Research on Language in Social Interaction, 36*, 33–63.

McCarthy, M. (2010). Spoken fluency revisited. English Profile Journal, 1, e4. Available online at: http://journals.cambridge.org/action/displayJournal?jid=EPJ.

McCarthy, M. (2013). Corpora and the advanced level: Problems and prospects. *English Australia Journal, 29*(1), 39–49.

McCarthy, M. (2021). *Innovations and challenges in grammar.* Routledge.

McCarthy, M., & McCarten, J. (2010). Bridging the gap between corpus and course book: The case of conversation strategies. In F. Mishan & A. Chambers (Eds.), *Perspectives on language learning materials development* (pp. 11–32). Peter Lang.

McCarthy, M., & McCarten, J. (2018). Now you're talking! Practising conversation in second language learning. In C. Jones (Ed.), *Practice in second language learning* (pp. 7–29). Cambridge University Press.

McCarthy, M., & McCarten, J. (2012). Corpora and materials design. In K. L. Hyland, M. H. Chau, & M. Handford (Eds.), *Corpus applications in applied linguistics* (pp. 225–241). Continuum.

McCarthy, M., McCarten, J., & Sandiford, H. (2012). *Viewpoint Student's book 1.* Cambridge University Press.

McCarthy, M., McCarten, J., & Sandiford, H. (2014). *Touchstone second edition levels 1-4.* Cambridge University Press.

Mori, J. (2002). Task design, plan, and development of talk-in-interaction: An analysis of a small group activity in a Japanese language classroom. *Applied Linguistics, 23*, 323–347.

Nation, I. S. P., & Macalister, J. (2010). *Language curriculum design.* Routledge.

O'Keeffe, A., & Farr, F. (2003). Using language corpora in language teacher education: Pedagogic, linguistic and cultural insights. *TESOL Quarterly, 37*, 389–418.

Overstreet, M. (1999). *Whales, candlelight and stuff like that: General extenders in English discourse.* Oxford University Press.

Palmer, H. E. (1916). *Colloquial English. Part I. Substitution tables.* W. Heffer and Sons Ltd.

Richards, J. C. (2006). *Communicative language teaching today.* Cambridge University Press.

Richards, J. C. (2017). *Introduction to interchange.* Cambridge University Press. Sample unit retrieved from https://assets.cambridge.org/97813166/20113/excerpt/9781316620113_excerpt.pdf

Römer, U. (2004). Comparing real and ideal language learner input: The use of an EFL textbook corpus in corpus linguistics and language teaching. In G. Aston, S. Bernardini, & D. Stewart (Eds.), *Corpora and language learning* (pp. 151–168). Benjamins.

Rühlemann, C. (2007). *Conversation in context. A corpus-driven approach.* Continuum.

Sacks, H., Schlegoff, E., & Jefferson, G. (1974). A simplest semantics for the organisation of turn taking for conversation. *Language, 50*(4), 696–735.

Schegloff, E. (2007). *Sequence organisation in interaction. A primer in conversation analysis.* Volume 1. Cambridge University Press.

Schiffrin, D. (1987). *Discourse markers.* Cambridge University Press.

Schmidt, R. (1990). The role of consciousness in second language learning. *Applied Linguistics, 11*, 129–158.

Schmidt, R. (1993). Awareness and second language acquisition. *Annual Review of Applied Linguistics, 13*, 206–226.

Schmitt, N. (Ed.). (2004). *Formulaic sequences.* Benjamins.

Shumin, K. (2002). Factors to consider: Developing adult EFL students' speaking abilities. In J. C. Richards & W. A. Renandya (Eds.), *Methodology in Language Teaching* (pp. 204–211). Cambridge University Press. https://doi.org/10.1017/CBO9780511667190.028

Sidnell, J. (2010). *Conversation analysis: An introduction.* Wiley-Blackwell.

Tao, H. (2003). Turn initiators in spoken English, a corpus based approach to interaction and grammar. In C. Meyer & P. Leistyna (Eds.), *Corpus analysis, language structure and language use* (pp. 187–207). Rodopi.

Van Lier, L. (1998). The relationship between consciousness, interaction and language learning. *Language Awareness, 7*, 128–145.

Widdowson, H. G. (1998). Context, community, and authentic language. *TESOL Quarterly, 32*(4), 705–16.

Wray, A. (2000). Formulaic sequences in second language teaching: Principle and practice. *Applied Linguistics, 21*, 463–489.

8

CORPORA FOR TEACHING CULTURE AND INTERCULTURAL COMMUNICATION

Tania Fahey Palma

8.1 Introduction

The development of Intercultural Communication (IC) skills has myriad benefits for students both in terms of research in the field and improving their cultural competence in the real world. The combination of using corpora in the investigation of intercultural linguistic practices while developing related IC skills is a novel approach, yet this chapter will demonstrate that it is not only possible but can be transformational to students' intercultural development. Through a discussion of various case studies, the integration of theory and practice will be demonstrated, detailing the impact of combining mixed-method corpus analysis techniques with an overarching emphasis on key areas of IC development such as critical awareness and empathy. The chosen case studies are representative examples of student-led Micro Corpus Projects which detail the cutting-edge findings from the application of mixed Corpus Linguistics (CL) and Critical Discourse Analysis (CDA) methodologies in the analysis of highly relevant, intercultural contexts.

In a world where many societies are coming to terms with the impact of discrimination on the lives and experiences of minorities and marginalised groups, it is more important than ever that educational institutions engage with material central to facilitating discussions around diversity and inclusion. Language analysis is considered central to the examination of the societal structures and institutions that have contributed to the constructed representation of social groups (Fairclough, 1989). The role of CL as a tool in identifying linguistic patterns, frequencies and the unearthing of pivotal nuances in the discourse of representation cannot be underestimated. CL is particularly relevant in the development of Intercultural Communicative Competence (ICC) skills, in that it allows students to engage with authentic discourse where representations of minority groups can be observed and analysed, thus, promoting critical awareness in the classroom. This is of particular relevance to the English language classroom, where cultural nuances central to language development can be demonstrated through authentic examples, thus, enabling students to visualise the power of language and representation first hand. The quantitative approach of CL plays an important role in identifying patterns across large data sets, however, the benefits of small, specialised corpora have also been acknowledged (Koester, 2006). This chapter will, therefore, highlight the value of familiarising students with CL tools in the development of their ICC skills through student-led

 DOI: 10.4324/9781003002901-10

Micro Corpus Projects. The case studies of the projects presented deal with complex data and consider in-group/out-group dichotomies, stereotyping and othering (Coupland, 2010) through the analysis of representations. These Micro Corpus Projects, therefore, create a space for students to critically examine and conceptualise negative representations and the possible impact of "othering discourse" in broader societal contexts. This chapter will, therefore, argue that the use of corpora in ICC development not only develops students' analytical skills through a deeper understanding of language and representation but also reinforces the values of inclusion and diversity in the classroom and beyond.

8.2 Current state of research

Through a range of scholarly perspectives and important interpretations of the human experience, the field of Intercultural Communication has grown to provide theoretical standpoints to support the development of effective communication between diverse cultural groups (Byram, 1997; Spencer-Oatey & Franklin, 2009). Drawing on the wider research of Deardorff, (2009), Spencer-Oatey & Franklin (2009), and Trompenaars, (1993), I define Intercultural Communication as interaction occurring between participants of differing cultural perspectives, cultural value points or worldviews. Courses which promote the value of IC can provide students with the skills necessary to push boundaries and engage with others in a meaningful and creative way. The teaching of ICC skills should not be limited to disciplines which specifically focus on the topic and can be subliminally taught through the instructors' influence in providing a positive interculturally open environment where students from diverse backgrounds can interact and build awareness of worldviews and ways of working. This chapter argues that English language classrooms can integrate the teaching of intercultural skills through critical engagement with representative corpora.

8.2.1 *Conceptualising intercultural communication*

Although the field of IC encompasses interaction between those pertaining to different cultural groups outside of national culture limitations, the traditional focus of IC teaching tends to be on the identification of national culture differences and even the generalisation of cultural categories based on arguably rigid models (e.g. Hofstede *et al.*, 2010). These models have allowed for the development of useful categorisations to be made in the promotion of effectively communicating in intercultural contexts bound by national differences, however, in order to consider the wider linguistic implications of IC interaction, it must be considered that intercultural sites are not limited to national culture interactions. This issue is discussed in a recent CL study by Hua *et al.* (2016). Through a rigorous corpus analysis of the discourse of Higher Education course descriptions, the authors found that many Higher Education programmes delivering IC as a core element of their offering focused on traditional models of IC communication, which do not consider context or the complexity of identity in their frameworks. The findings from this study are important as they highlight the positioning of IC development as an "en vogue" area to attract international students with little criticality considered in the design and delivery of courses in many institutions. This view of Intercultural Communication as a vehicle to focus solely on national culture differences does not capture the benefits of IC and the development of ICC in building awareness, empathy and consideration of the vast range of social groups central to our diverse cultural structures. ICC theory positioned from a Critical Intercultural Communication perspective, therefore, encapsulates the need to progress beyond limited views of "intercultural" through the national lens and also considers Postcolonialism, Transnationalism, Critical race theory, Queer theory and feminist theory (Nakayama & Halualani, 2010). In terms of addressing these issues in the language classroom, the absence of authentic resources and modern examples of cultural fluidity outside of one's own national culture presents a problem for the true advancement of cultural criticality in the vision of integrated societies. It is from this perspective that CL can lead to a rich understanding of IC relevant texts and interactions through the analysis of authentic data in context. As corpora building and analysis inherently draws on texts from a variety of representative sources (Biber, 1993), it is perfectly placed to encourage research in IC, and in this respect, also functions as a means to introduce students to a wide range of interculturally relevant issues in context.

8.3 Representations and othering

The benefits of applying CL tools to exemplify areas of negative representation and discourse that is othering of specific communities cannot be underestimated. Through the thorough analysis of corpora ranging from classroom interactions to television shows, the power of discourse in constructing negative social realities for specific groups can be demonstrated. In order to fully consider the implications of language in constructing negative identities for social groups and cultures from CL frequency and cluster analysis, it is important to determine a theoretical framework from which to position the findings.

The negative categorisation of out-groups has been extensively discussed in Coupland's (2010) work on "othering". This important piece of work emphasises the negative consequences of negative social positioning on cultural groups or communities. Coupland (2010) defines othering as "the process of representing an individual or a social group to render them distant, alien or deviant" (p. 244). This can be applied to the challenges faced by diverse minority social groups including migrants, refugees, indigenous groups and gender-fluid groups in our society. Wodak (2008) states that "exclusion is linked to power; marginalised groups tend to be discriminated against and discriminatory acts may be intended or non-intended" (p. 54). As the majority group has the voice to position minorities, they have the responsibility to construct positive representations, however the opposite tends to be true in cases where mainstream discourses render "the other" as opposing to their values and beliefs. Using the othering framework to categorise specific representational terms yielded from CL analysis, provides a tangible way for students to position their analysis and draw on important concepts in their discussions of stereotyping, suppression and other IC relevant areas central to the development of critical intercultural skills.

Considering the importance of authentic discourse in providing examples for the development of ICC skills, Sayer and Meadows (2012) detail the stereotyping behaviour by presenters on BBC's Top Gear television show. In this case study, they examine the portrayal of other cultures in mainstream media. Drawing on Wodak *et al.*'s (2009) argument on the positioning of the "other" as a representation of the "self", they exemplify how the negative depiction of the other group, in this case Mexicans and the Mexican ambassador, reinforces the notion of "Britishness" and as positive in contrast to "Mexicanness" as inferior and somewhat culturally deviant. The complexity in examining this case is found in the response positioned by the BBC. In defence of their presenters, they argue that the divisive comments were made in jest as an attribute of British humour. Sayer and Meadows, therefore, demonstrate the power of mainstream media discourse in constructing and reflecting negative representations of other cultures and groups. Offering a critical perspective on the analysis of these texts becomes a key exercise for ICC development. CL has enabled the analysis of media discourse and the institutional discourse for decades (Bednarek & Caple, 2017; Handford, 2010), furthering the categorisations of media-specific nuances such as lexical choice, turn-taking and syntactic structure. Such characteristics of discourse provide insightful information into the power dynamics at play in the text at hand. It is, therefore, intuitive that CL analysis of the representations of social groups in the mainstream media and beyond can yield fruitful results for understanding intercultural issues and through these discussions enhance ICC skills and critical awareness.

8.3.1 Combining CL and CDA to foster intercultural competence

Sayer and Meadows (2012) demonstrate the use of authentic materials and engaging resources to teach culture in the language classroom. Although they consider the data from a critical language pedagogy approach (Norton & Toohey, 2004; Osborn, 2006) the value of considering authentic data in the teaching of cultural issues is evident. Considering the complexities of culture and the challenges presented through incorrect and negative representations of minority groups across discourse contexts, it is crucial to provide students with a robust methodology to enable the development of ICC skills through engagement with authentic texts. CL has equipped researchers with the necessary tools for critical engagement across spoken and written contexts. The benefits of CL in the language learning classroom have been well documented (O'Keeffe *et al.*, 2007). From exposing students to naturally occurring language in use, to the creation of engaging and realistic exercises and examples, the value of using corpus linguistics to encourage language development cannot be underestimated. From the promotion of communicative competence to the development of grammar and syntactic skills, CL has enabled students and researchers to examine the most fundamental patterns of language in context. The role of CL in teaching IC has, thus, far been limited. Handford (2014, 2016) refers to the benefits of CL for IC development and highlights the lack of research and pedagogical advancement in this area. There has been much research on cross-cultural communication, however, the application of CL to texts and discourse in order to promote the acquisition of IC competence skills has been noticeably underdeveloped. The field of CL is widely recognised in English language teaching and for research in discourse analysis across Applied Linguistics (O'Keeffe *et al.*, 2007). CL is, however, not often considered as a core part of ICC learning in this context. The patterns and frequencies derived from CL can produce informative and indicative data for the language use of specific communities and their positioning by wider media and other cultures at large, for example, in the analysis of newspaper discourse (Bednarek, 2006). The use of CL allows for a coherent impression of the linguistic devices employed in defining and positioning outsider communities through the identification of specific identity markers such as lexical choice, naming and referencing and pronominal features uncovered in the data. It is understood that CL provides an excellent overview of large bodies of data and indeed small, specialised corpora (Biber, 1993; Handford, 2010). Although this is of utmost importance for the identification of culturally bound practices, it is also crucial to consider context from a more intricate perspective in order to truly grasp the nuanced linguistic codes at play in the discourse (Halliday, 1978).

Critical discourse analysis, originally grounded in the work of Foucault (1981), considers the impact of underlying structures of knowledge on discourse and the subsequent manifestations of power in language. The Focauldian perspective was traditionally centred on the examination of institutions and the power they imposed through the subjugation of the body. Later work by Fairclough (1989) considers the direct impact of power structures on language and considers the inextricable link between the two. CDA offers a highly relevant perspective in the investigation of the reproduction of power through language across contexts and not limited to institutions. The value of CDA in the analysis of the representation of groups and communities has been outlined by Benwell and Stokoe (2006). They consider that discourse ideologies create social representations responsible for organising the world into patterns. These patterns, in turn, enable the agendas and values of more powerful groups. The representations of social groups enabled by these power dynamics highlight the impact of language in constructing identities for groups and individuals. Language is, therefore, a powerful tool in producing and reproducing societal perspectives and even reinforcing social structures and the identities central to our societal make up (Mayr, 2004). Wodak (2008) has incorporated the use of CDA into her work on the investigation of national identities and their representations through a variety of outlets including the media. She underpins the crucial connection between language and power detailing its impact on propaganda and the positioning of minorities amongst other issues. Considering the critical lens offered by CDA in analysing the representation of social groups in context, it is clear that an approach combining CL and CDA in the examination of texts is a tangible way of capturing an encompassing perspective of the social issue at hand. The benefits of mixed methods combining CL and qualitative methods have been broadly discussed (Baker *et al.*, 2008; Handford, 2010; O'Keeffe *et al.*, 2007). These studies have focused on the importance of considering the wider linguistic patterns at play in the data while interchangeably optimising the richness offered by engaging more profoundly with data in context. Mautner (2009) advocates for the use of CDA in corpus studies as an example of this enrichment in analysis. This allows for the identification of socially enforced ideologies and representations to be identified whilst allowing for an integrated discussion of the wider patterns observable through CL tools. This CL/CDA approach to exploring interculturally relevant texts demonstrates the value of combining CL and qualitative discourse methods in capturing the intricacies of cultural issues in practice (Baker, 2006; Handford, 2014; Hua *et al.*, 2016; McEnery & Hardie, 2012).

8.4 Micro corpus CDA projects to promote ICC development

The use of CL tools to compliment and reinforce CDA findings in both analysing interculturally relevant texts and building intercultural awareness in the classroom provides a perspective on frequency patterns whilst allowing for the critical evaluation of language in context (Handford, 2016). In order to promote ICC skills, it is imperative to identify the potential barriers to positive intercultural relationships. It is, therefore, important to consider not just intercultural texts but texts that exemplify the positioning of other social groups by more powerful entities. By providing students with engaging, critical materials, they are encouraged to challenge preconceived notions of culture and cultural stereotypes, thus engaging with Byram's (1997) ICC model and developing a sense of cultural criticality. Sayer and Meadows (2012) advocate the use of texts as tools for a critical pedagogical approach in second language learning, specifically in the teaching of culture as critical for understanding language practices. They also consider the use of textual analysis in building intercultural awareness through a critical evaluation of "nationalist worldviews" rendered important to ICC development by various IC experts (Deardoff, 2009). The problematisation of culture is also considered the responsibility of the teacher by Sayer and Meadows (ibid). They argue that the teacher has the ability to guide students in the identification of problematic cultural representations in authentic texts, thus, promoting the development of intercultural awareness. The teacher's role is, therefore, central to the encouragement of reflective practice in students' engagement with ICC skills. In order to enhance students' reflective practice, it is, therefore, crucial to not only create a positive and constructive learning environment, but it is also pivotal to provide them with the resources to independently investigate cultural problems. Through the development of Micro Corpus Projects, students are equipped with the resources to critically examine the role of language in constructing representations of specific social groups. For the context of this chapter, I define Micro Corpus as a small collection of representative texts gathered to conduct a concise analysis of a specific linguistic issue in context. Unlike small, specialised corpora (Koester, 2006), micro corpora are specifically collected for the undertaking of precise research questions by students learning to engage with CL practices and develop critical thinking on ICC and societal issues. This means that a limited number of texts will be collected, however the application of corpus tools serves to expand students' interpretation of language and allows them to develop awareness of the discourse from a macro perspective. Students are provided with theoretical backgrounds in core areas for the analysis of representations and cultural identities such as Othering theory (Coupland, 2010; Wodak, 2009), Community of Practice theory (Wenger, 1998) and Identity theory (Benwell & Stokoe, 2006). The definition of cultural identity as posited by Handford (2014) is undertaken to consider its application to a range of cultural groups in encompassing their asserted and ascribed categorisations and roles such as nationality, ethnicity, religion and gender. Students undertake projects investigating the representations of cultural groups by considering the role of identity structures and othering dynamics at play in the data. CL is then applied to facilitate the top-down examination of specific examples in context whilst considering the overarching power dynamics and social structures at play through a CDA lens. In these Micro Corpus projects, a corpus-based analysis can either take place by providing a quantitative overview of searched lexical items in the data which then allows for a more in-depth discussion of context from the CDA perspective, or conversely form a secondary part of analysis after the qualitative tagging of relevant pragmatic devices to reproduce quantitative results for these findings. The topics of these Micro Corpus projects are varied, and students are encouraged to focus on discourse contexts relevant to their everyday lives and sociocultural experiences. This provides an authentic and engaging way to encourage students' reflective practice on the cultural issues framing their communicative worlds. Encouraging active engagement with these discourses to identify representation and positioning practices by specific social groups is an effective way of promoting critical cultural awareness and other ICC skills through exposing the normalisation of problematic discourses and empowering students to critically evaluate the potential issues arising from these patterns.

8.4.1 *Case studies of the Micro Corpus project*

The following section will detail examples of students' Micro Corpus Projects in order to examine the representations employed by different entities positioning of minority groups. The first case study explores the positioning of minorities focussing on the context of refugee discourse in the German "Refugee Classroom". The second case study examines the representation of the LGBTQ community through the discussion of a project focussed on the representation of trans children on the popular Mumsnet online forum. Examples are considered to highlight the benefits of a combined CL/CDA approach to the critical investigation of the representations of minority groups. The intercultural impact of engaging with these studies is evident through the students' ability to critically connect with the material at hand whilst considering the implications of context in the interpretation of socially structured representations.

8.4.1.1 Case study 1: The refugee crisis

The 2015 refugee crisis led to a media storm of debate in the UK creating a clear division in the population of those who considered the situation as a humanitarian crisis and those who perceived what were positioned as "migrants" threatening their way of life. A core element in ICC development is a clear understanding of the issue of representation and labelling. Students are taught to consider the implications of naming strategies and the potential impact of these on particular social groups. The context of media discourse provides a publicly available data set for students to examine the positioning of minority groups. Focussing on frequency of negative labels and representations of minority groups in the media can allow for rich analysis and enables students to identify core characteristics of "othering" in practice. An example of CL in demonstrating frequency patterns of representation can be seen in Figure 8.1.

This figure provides an example of the different labels applied to refugees during the 2015 crisis. The CL frequency analysis demonstrates the higher frequency of the term "migrant" across three prominent British newspapers. A further CDA investigation of these labels based on the frequency findings reveals that the overwhelming use of the term "migrant" by the Daily Mail across 20 newspaper articles can be categorised as othering as it leads to the pejoration and minoritisation (Coupland, 2010) of refugees as a social group. The prejudice experienced by refugee groups in the British media can be seen here, therefore highlighting the issues of "preferred immigrants" (Hier & Greenberg, 2002). By critically positioning research questions and data analysis, students can engage with highly relevant intercultural communication skills by cultivating cultural criticality towards their own culture, whilst acknowledging its bias, in addition to developing their discourse analysis skills. The use of CL serves to exemplify occurrences of negative representations in the data, offering a solid starting point to a novice student in the area.

The discussion around refugee representation and the subsequent need to draw awareness to the positive positioning of refugees informs the first case study. This micro corpus project titled "The Refugee Classroom" investigates the role of the language classroom in providing a space to empower and integrate refugees in Germany. Considering the context of the refugee crisis, the student collected a Micro Corpus of authentic spoken discourse from language classroom interaction. The German language corpus consisted of three hours of classroom discourse which transcribed totaled approximately 10,000 words. The German language lessons recorded were run by volunteers for refugees living in a small village. The aim of the project was to highlight the importance of pragmatic development and consider the classroom as a space for students to negotiate new identities beyond the label "refugee", thus allowing them to establish roles in their new community. Through a mixed-methods approach adopting

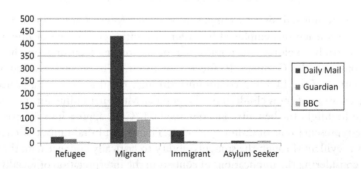

Figure 8.1 Refugee representation in British newspapers

CL and CDA, the student engaged with complex themes of identity, language, power, and integration identify key characteristics in the data. These themes, positioned in the context of the discourse of minority groups and integration, enabled the student to engage with core components of ICC frameworks including cultural criticality, awareness building and as an observer in the refugee classroom, empathy and self-awareness. In determining the importance of refugee identity, the project captured the essence of the power of language in allowing individuals to construct positive social identities in interaction. As posited by the student in their critical discussion, rather than emphasising stereotypes and creating pre-determined group identities, emphasis must be placed in on post refugee identities (Zetter, 1991). This study not only analyses the discourse of the refugee classroom, it also serves to provide a voice to the refugee community, thus fully engaging with the dynamics of IC in terms of legitimising the experience of other groups within one's community. The concept of humour is addressed as a culturally bound phenomenon (Holmes, 2006) serving to promote an interpersonal link in this intercultural context. In this study, the student not only engaged with an intercultural study as part of her research, but she developed her own intercultural awareness through a concise investigation of pragmatic devices employed in intercultural interaction. The student's own IC skills were developed through critical engagement by questioning the structure of refugee representations and working against deeply ingrained social stereotypes of the refugee community to exemplify their positive identities and interactions at play in the classroom.

Table 8.1 shows the frequency list of the refugee classroom.

The student used the corpus software AntConc (Anthony, 2015) to generate quantitative results and a larger frequency list to then inform their qualitative analysis. Table 8.1 presents the frequency list captured of the entire data set. Elements demonstrating listenership, feedback and positive reinforcement structures which are often characteristics of classroom discourse are evident from the frequency list (Dushku, 2010). Response tokens such as *okay*, *exactly*, *good* all indicate relational practice in this context. Furthering the discussion of

Table 8.1 Refugee classroom word frequency list

Rank	Frequency	German Word	English Translation
1	392	Mrs. Kaiser	Mrs Kaiser (teacher)
2	368	Mrs Meyer	Mrs. Meyer (teacher)
3	263	das	the (n); this
4	251	ja	yes
5	202	ich	I
6	192	ist	is
7	175	und	and
8	158	du	you
9	155	die	the (f)
10	121	alle	all
11	115	der	the (m)
12	103	genau	exactly
13	94	hier	here
14	90	okay	okay
15	88	gut	good
16	87	dann	then
17	87	wir	we
18	82	Marwan	Marwan (student)
19	81	nicht	not
20	80	ein	one; a

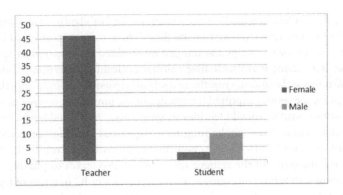

Figure 8.2 Humour in the refugee classroom

relational practice in the classroom as evidenced from the list, the student then examined the data set for instances of humour, tagging the data in order to conduct a quantitative analysis of the phenomenon in the data. As outlined in Fahey Palma (2013), humour is not easily identifiable purely through corpus frequency lists and quantitative analysis. Figure 8.2 shows the relational practice in the classroom through the use of humour by the teacher and students.

The CL quantification of the tagged humour in the data emphasises the role of the teacher in enabling the construction of positive social identities by students. As previously discussed, the teachers' role is pivotal in constructing an environment conducive to ICC learning particularly in the case minority groups. Figure 8.2 represents the frequency of humour in the classroom as illustrated by CL tools. The teacher's level of humour is clearly higher than the students' indicating the power dynamic and potential language level disparity. Based on corpus findings, the student reflected on the role of humour as a pragmatic device to foster collaboration and integration in the language classroom. It is used as a mechanism by both the teacher and students and proves an interesting phenomenon of intercultural communication in the refugee classroom. The qualitative analysis undertaken demonstrates the benefits of applying humour a means of delivering constructive feedback. The identification of humour quantitatively also allows for the rapid extraction of qualitative examples as seen in Example (1) below.

(1) Teacher-led humour

Mrs Kaiser: Excellent Marwarn
Marwan: Excuse me?
Mrs Kaiser: No
Marwan: I me?
Mrs Kaiser: No excuse me I don't understand
Marwan: Excuse me I don't stand
All (incl Marwan):   ((laughter))
Mrs Kaiser: Don't laugh
Mrs Meyer: It will be your turn soon
Mrs Kaiser: ((Laughs)) STOP
All: ((Laughter))

Although the student in the data makes a mistake, the teacher uses humour to "reprimand" the class and as the student researcher discusses in her analysis, uses humour to mitigate the face threat caused by the student's mistake. This can be considered an excellent example of teacher-led community building in the language classroom. The study also notes an example of student-led humour in the data as illustrated in Example (2) below.

(2) Student Humour

Mrs Meyer: Then ((Points to throat)) this is
Rasha: Throat
Mrs Meyer: Throat. Golam has a sore throat ((points to throat)) ouch sore throat
Hanan: Throat
Magda: Yes this is the throat ((points))
Raihana: Throat
Mrs Meyer: Throat exactly
Zeinah: Throat
Marwan: Throat. And Caroline (h)?
Caroline: Throat (h)
Marwan: ((Shows thumbs up))
All: ((Laughter))

In this example, a student in the class involves the student researcher who is present at the recording. This is a good example of how the student researcher herself is encouraged to engage interculturally with students in the refugee classroom displaying her competence in responding to the student's attempt to engage her in class interaction. Her jovial response is met with a thumbs up and laughter across the classroom. Although the aim of the research is to capture the discourse present in the refugee classroom to provide further understanding of integration mechanisms at play, the value of researcher engagement cannot be underestimated. The exposure to intercultural texts and environments when collecting data for a corpus-based project must also be considered an important process in the development of ICC skills. This example, therefore, provides a highly positive insight into the capacity of Micro Corpus Projects in enabling students to interact with diverse social groups, and, in turn, highlights the possibilities offered by IC research for the development of profound intercultural awareness through authentic experience. Through engaging with this study on the refugee classroom, the student reflected on the benefits of humour by teachers to reduce power distance in the classroom but more importantly considered the cultural role of humour in both enabling identity construction and fostering community in this context. Importantly, the student reflected on the importance of positive identity construction for refugees in a society which often positions this group in a negative light. The analysis developed within the project indicates a high level of empathy and cultural criticality as the student challenges preexisting representations and demonstrates the positive identities of refugees by amplifying and legitimising refugee voices in her analysis.

Engaging with such complex topics such as the refugee crisis and migrant representation in the media requires much consideration on the part of the student in the language classroom. The application of CDA to CL findings allows students to engage with the level of criticality needed to consider and critique the social mechanisms responsible for contributing to inequalities across contexts. Exposure to these forms of authentic texts in the language classroom has the potential to greatly enhance students' awareness of language and culture in context through displaying the power of language in constructing representations and the linguistic devices necessary in the target language to partake in positive intercultural interactions.

8.4.1.2 Case study 2: Gender minorities

The second case study presents the development of ICC competencies through critically evaluating the representation of LGBTQ groups in context. The LGBTQ community has long suffered misrepresentation and suppression across societal and discourse contexts. For this reason, the representation of the LGBTQ community becomes an important element to the progression of inclusivity in society. Providing the LGBTQ community with the same importance as the heterosexual community both legitimises the voice of the LGBTQ community and normalises a once stigmatised topic in discourse. The ability to engage with discourse which positions the LGBTQ community in a marginalised way allows students to develop their critical cultural awareness skills by determining how specific discourse strategies and language choices can be detrimental to the positive positioning of this group. For example, the use of the term *homosexual* in traditional texts to reference LGBTQ groups has been deemed highly problematic as it connotes "deviance" and negative difference (Lakoff as cited in Peters, 2014). CL investigations of this term in specific contexts such as educational textbooks, blogs or tv shows allow for the student to reflect on the current condition of discourse surrounding societally prevalent topics and enable them to contextually examine the potential inequalities experienced by minority groups. In essence, the very real impact of language as a tool to suppress or silence (Coupland, 2010) can be investigated through corpus analysis.

In addressing the lack of visibility and pejorative positioning of these groups (Coupland, 2010), the student understands the complexity of marginalisation faced by many in our society and is encouraged to reflect on impact of these practices. The next Micro Corpus project deals with the positioning of transgender children and their representations by members of the online Mumsnet community. For this CL Micro Project, the student collected over 1,000 posts from 14 "trans child" advice threads capturing data from 2017 to 2020. This amounted to a corpus of approximately 80,000 words from the publicly available forum. The data was categorised thematically in order to identify key topics for discussion. Although this project dealt predominantly with qualitative CDA analysis, CL played an important role in contributing to the framework for discussion. Corpus tools were applied to quantify topics discussed within the threads. This analysis allowed for the understanding of the structural components of the posts. Table 8.2 exemplifies the quantification of engagement with specific topics on the forum.

From the table of topics above, it is evident that the trans "condition" is one discussed on the forum from a negative viewpoint. The Mumsnet corpus exemplifies the discourse of worry, fear and distress associated with the labelling of children as trans. The data from the project allows for the student to address ongoing social and political debates on gender and sexuality through analysis of what they called "reactionary" discourse. It is clear from the posts analysed below in Example (3) however, that membership of the trans community is positioned as undesirable and even deviant in most cases. As examined by the student, the topic with the highest frequency of posts, ROGD Parent Support (Rapid Onset Gender Dysphoria) was identified as discursively belittling of trans children's experiences.

(3)

a. If a parent can support their child to overcome this phase, then of course they should. And it's very definitely a phase. In one school a dozen girls in one year group identify as boys.

Table 8.2 Topic frequency in Mumsnet advice threads

	Thread Title	*Posts*
T1.	ROGD parent support	337
T2.	My 15 year old son says he is transgender – I don't believe him.	136
T3.	12 year old daughter saying she thinks she's male	132
T4.	I think non-binary is actually reinforcing stereotypes and anti feminist?	107
T5.	Both our daughters are claiming to be trans	63
T6.	Concern for son	42
T7.	I have a transgender teenage elephant in my room	39
T8.	13 year old daughter has announced she's trans at Christmas Lunch	37
T9.	2 years on- my transgender son. I'm not coping.	29
T10.	14yo Dd now wants to be called [name]	24
T11.	Gender fluid child	22
T12.	Dealing with a transgender child who is angry with me	13
T13.	My 19YO son has just announced he is trans. How can I support him and ensure he makes good choices?	11
T14.	Need Advice my son has come out as Trans at school but not at home	5

b. When I was young it was eating disorders. More recently it was cutting. Now it's binding and gender dysphoria. I'm not discounting the genuine anguish behind these fashions but there are definitely fashions.

c. Turns out he was just a mixed-up boy in search of an identity. A decade ago, he could have been a goth.

d. Tis just a fashionable phase that the little darlings are going through. A fad. It won't last. Friends talking about it, SM [social media] full of it, the tele whispering about it in the back ground. Just another "let's jump on the bandwagon".

The threads examined in the Mumsnet corpus are an example of a negative reinforcement of broader societal biases, highlighting the importance of considering the language embedded in social institutions and how representations can be both adopted and rejected in wider public discourses. The students of this case study conclude their discussion by stating the impact of these reactionary, negative representations of the trans community in a space that has "immense influence on British civil society and public discourse". This demonstrates the developed awareness of the power of language in contributing to the representation of minorities and the value of CL projects in enabling students to further engage with critical social issues to develop their ICC skills and enhance their understanding of language in context.

The language examples presented in the case studies can be considered as having tangible real-life consequences on the lives of minority groups. Engaging with topics central to cultural representation allows students to confront societal stereotyping and stigmatisation. The analysis of the discourse of minority representations requires students to hone in on pivotal ICC skills to decipher the boundaries of generalisation and essentialism. Through applying a mixed CL/CDA framework to data analysis in Micro Corpus Projects, students are equipped with the tools to challenge the discourse of social systems and question the segregation of social groups in a tangible way.

One of the main issues found in the case studies was the level of exclusion experienced by minority groups in the media and discourse contexts examined. Suppression has been defined by Coupland (2010) as silencing cultures and groups, which can be as impactful as using pejorative language. In the media, the discourse of refugees and migrants is largely limited to negative stories leading to the reinforcement of negative stereotypes and even perpetrating fear in the general public. For this reason, student engagement with projects such as "The Refugee Classroom" is so important as they provide a much-needed voice for the positive experiences of the refugee community and allow students to challenge the negative attributes constructed for these groups. In terms of the inclusion of LGBTQ discourse in our society, further work needs to be done to reflect the positive impacts of allowing individuals the right to positive social identities. The discourse captured in the Mumsnet case study conveys resistance to the trans community even by parents. This research is fundamentally important to the progression of IC discourse and ICC skills as it reflects areas in our society, which continue to be loaded with bias and stereotyping characteristics. Through engaging with these concepts in a thorough and analytical way, we can address our own systematic failures and reinforce our vision for more progressive, workplaces, university and school systems and broader societal frameworks. Conducting a corpus analysis of particular minority representations allows students to consider complex, interculturally relevant questions and, in turn, empowers them to foster the skills necessary to be empathetic to other cultural groups and become more culturally critical of their own lived experiences. The development of Micro Corpus Projects in the teaching of ICC skills is beneficial from a range of perspectives. From the IC perspective, dealing with data of this nature allows students to experience first-hand how the language choice of institutions conveys and reproduces negative stereotypes of particular social groups even where "intentionality" can be ascertained. Understanding the role of language in manifesting bias and stigmatisation can enable and empower students to develop ICC skills through critically considering the social impact of such labels and representations. In effect, students learn to overcome some of the key barriers of IC such as stereotyping and othering in an authentic and engaging way by linguistically deconstructing divisive language.

Adopting these projects as a key point of assessment also allows students to creatively engage with data and develop corpus building skills. Students are also familiarised with corpus techniques such as tagging and the generation of frequency and cluster lists. As evidenced in the case study projects, students were not only engaging with complex material through data collection and research development, the techniques and analytical frameworks offered by CL also contributed to the identification of key linguistic features connected to representations and othering in the discourse. This is particularly relevant in the development of ICC skills for researchers that may be new to the area of CDA as CL word lists and search functions are conducive to the critical exploration of texts from a macro perspective. These functions allow students to experiment with analysis tools and can also provide a clearer picture of the overall context of the data in an immediately tangible way. This access to a wide set of indicative results is not achievable from a purely qualitative perspective. The synergies between CL and CDA foster learning through the identification of linguistic patterns in the data and the consideration of the sources of knowledge and power that have contributed to the manifestation of discourse practices in context.

8.5 Future directions of research

This chapter considers the value of empowering students to engage with self-led corpus-based projects in order to promote intercultural development and build critical cultural awareness. Promoting the discussion of minority inequalities in the classroom and utilising corpus linguistics as a means to building awareness of deep-rooted societal issues in terms of discrimination and stereotyping is fundamental to the development of critical thinking in this area. Future research addressing these benefits and considering further critical contexts for CL/CDA investigations of IC-related issues would be highly useful. These studies could reinforce awareness and criticality of the use of language by powerful institutions such as the media, education bodies, social media in order to underpin the impact of representations of social groups in the collective psyche. I suggest that future development for IC and English language classrooms should include further use of CL tools to examine highly relevant culturally critical issues. The role of the teacher in conveying the importance of inclusion and diversity in society should not be overlooked particularly in training students in the use of CL/CDA for intercultural development. When students are empowered to connect with societally relevant data in this meaningful way, they have the capacity to critically evaluate unequal power dynamics and injustices reproduced through language, whilst also considering ways in which systems and structures can be improved to reflect and maintain a more culturally equal, inclusive environment for all.

Acknowledgements

I would like to thank my incredible students for continuously inspiring me with their openness to learning and desire to improve the world we live in. Special thanks to Caroline Wotte and Esyld Scully for their permission to reflect on their thought-provoking work as case studies for this chapter.

Further reading

Coupland, N. (2010). 'Other' representation. In J. Jaspers, J. Ostman, & J. Verschueren (Eds.), *Society and language use, handbook of pragmatics highlights* (pp. 241–260). Benjamins. This chapter provides detailed descriptions and definitions for categories of "othering" in discourse which can serve as a useful framework for the examination of representation in discourse.

Handford, M. (2016). Corpus linguistics. In H. Zhu (Ed.), *Research methods in intercultural communication* (pp. 311–326). Wiley-Blackwell. In this chapter, Handford highlights the benefits of Corpus Linguistics in researching Intercultural Communication and promotes corpus tools in the development of the field.

Hua, Z., Handford, M., & Johnstone Young, T. (2016). Framing interculturality: A corpus-based analysis of online promotional discourse of higher education intercultural communication courses. *Journal of Multilingual and Multicultural Development, 38*(3), 283–300. This article delivers excellent insights into the challenges facing the field of Intercultural Communication in Higher Level institutions and applies Corpus Linguistics to conduct a thorough investigation of the area.

References

Anthony, L. (2015). *AntConc* (Version 3.4.3) [Computer Software]. Waseda University. http://www.laurenceanthony.net.

Baker, P. (2006). *Using corpora in discourse analysis*. Continuum.

Baker, P., Gabrielatos, C., Khosravinik, M., Krzyżanowski, M., McEnery, T., & Wodak, R. (2008). A useful methodological synergy? Combining critical discourse analysis and corpus linguistics to examine discourses of refugees and asylum seekers in the UK press. *Discourse and Society, 19*(3), 273–306.

Bednarek, M. (2006). *Evaluation in media discourse*. Continuum.

Bednarek, M., & Caple, H. (2017). *The discourse of news values: How news organisations create newsworthiness*. Oxford University Press.

Benwell, S., & Stokoe, E. (2006). *Discourse and identity*. Edinburgh University Press.

Biber, D. (1993). Representativeness in corpus design. *Literary and Linguistic Computing, 8*(4), 243–257.

Byram, M. (1997). *Teaching and assessing intercultural communicative competence*. Multilingual Matters.

Coupland, N. (2010). 'Other' representation. In J. Jaspers, J. Ostman, & J. Verschueren (Eds.), *Society and language use, handbook of pragmatics highlights* (pp. 241–260). Benjamins.

Deardorff, D. (2009). *The Sage handbook of intercultural competence.* Sage.

Fairclough, N. (1989). *Language and power.* Longman.

Dushku, S. (2010). Investigating engagement response tokens in spoken narrative discourse. *Classroom Discourse, 1*(2), 142–166.

Fahey Palma, T. (2013). *Investigating communicative strategies in novice professional communities of practice: A comparative study of engineering and marketing meetings.* [Doctoral Dissertation, University of Limerick]. Dspace@MIC. https://dspace.mic.ul.ie/handle/10395/2078

Foucault, M. (1981). The will to knowledge: The history of sexuality. In M.A.K. Halliday (1978). *Language as social semiotic the social interpretation of language and meaning.* Edward Arnold.

Halliday, M. A. K. (1978). *Language as social semiotic: The social interpretation of language and meaning.* Edward Arnold.

Handford, M. (2010). *The language of business meetings.* Cambridge University Press.

Handford, M. (2014). Cultural identities in international, inter-organisational meetings: A corpus-informed discourse analysis of indexical we. *Language and Intercultural Communication, 14*(1), 41–58.

Handford, M. (2016). Corpus linguistics. In H. Zhu (Ed.), *Research methods in intercultural communication* (pp. 311–326). Wiley-Blackwell.

Hier, S., & Greenberg, L. (2002). Constructing a discursive crisis: Risk, problematization and illegal Chinese in Canada. *Ethnic and Racial Studies, 25*(3), 490–513.

Hofstede, G., Hofstede, G. J., & Minkov, M. (2010). *Cultures and organizations: Software of the mind* (3rd ed.). McGraw-Hill.

Holmes, J. (2006). Sharing a laugh: Pragmatic aspects of humor and gender in the workplace. *Journal of Pragmatics, 38*, 26–50.

Hua, Z., Handford, M., & Johnstone Young, T. (2016). Framing interculturality: A corpus-based analysis of online promotional discourse of higher education intercultural communication courses. *Journal of Multilingual and Multicultural Development, 38*(3), 283–300.

Koester, A. (2006). *Investigating workplace discourse.* Routledge.

Mautner, G. (2009). Checks and balances: How corpus linguistics can contribute to CDA. In R. Wodak & M. Meyer (Eds.), *Methods of critical discourse analysis* (pp. 122–143). Sage.

Mayr, A. (2004). *Prison discourse: Language as a means of control and resistance.* Palgrave Macmillan.

McEnery, T., & Hardie, A. (2012). *Corpus linguistics.* Cambridge University Press.

Nakayama, T. K., & Halualani, R. T. (2010). *The handbook of critical intercultural communication.* Wiley-Blackwell.

Norton, B., & Toohey, K. (2004). *Critical pedagogies and language learning.* Cambridge University Press.

O'Keeffe, A., Carter, R., & McCarthy, M. (2007). *From corpus to classroom: Language use and language teaching.* Cambridge University Press.

Osborn, T. (2006). *Teaching world languages for social justice.* Lawrence Erlbaum.

Peters, W. J. (2014, April 20, 2021). The decline and fall of the 'H' word. *The New York Times.* https://www.nytimes.com/2014/03/23/fashion/gays-lesbians-the-term-homosexual.html

Sayer, P., & Meadows, B. (2012). Teaching culture beyond nationalist boundaries: National identities, stereotyping, and culture in language education. *Intercultural Education Journal, 23*(3), 265–279.

Spencer-Oatey, H., & Franklin, P. (2009). *Intercultural interaction: A multidisciplinary approach to intercultural communication.* Palgrave Macmillan.

Trompenaars, F. (1993). *Riding the waves of culture.* Irwin.

Wenger, E. (1998). *Communities of practice: Learning, meaning, and identity.* Cambridge University Press.

Wodak, R. (2008). 'Us' and 'Them' inclusion and exclusion - discrimination via discourse. In G. Delanty, P. Jones, & R. Wodak (Eds.), *Identity belonging and migration* (pp. 54–78). University of Liverpool Press.

Wodak, R., de Cilla, R., Reisigl, M., & Liebhart, K. (2009). *The discursive construction of national identity.* Edinburgh University Press.

Zetter, R. (1991). Labelling refugees: Forming and transforming a bureaucratic identity. *Journal of Refugee Studies, 4*(1), 39–62.

9

CORPORA FOR MATERIALS DESIGN

Eric Friginal and Jennifer Roberts

9.1 Introduction

Corpus linguistics (CL) is primarily a methodological research approach to the study of language, and specifically, discourse structure, patterns, and use (Biber *et al.*, 2010). Corpora serve as datasets of "systematically collected, naturally-occurring registers of texts" (Friginal & Hardy, 2014, p. 20), which are electronically stored, analyzed, and utilized for a variety of purposes by researchers and teachers, as well as learners themselves. The use of corpora has become a popular approach in the quantitative analysis of the linguistic characteristics of written and spoken language, in general, and academic and disciplinary discourse in particular. This utilization results in the development of more authentic teaching materials; accurate, frequency-based dictionaries; and textbooks that represent actual language-in-use (Friginal, 2018; Friginal & Hardy, 2014; Römer, 2011). Direct applications of corpora and corpus tools in the classroom support various language teaching and language acquisition theories and constructs especially related to learner autonomy, use of realia and authentic texts, motivation through learner-computer and learner-learner interactions, and explicit teaching of language features and patterns (Friginal *et al.*, 2020a).

The number of teachers who have utilized corpus-based materials in their classrooms has grown tremendously from the 1990s to the present. Online databases and concordancers are now easily accessible and several CL for teaching textbooks (discussed below) have been published in the past 10 years. However, as Friginal (2018), Geluso and Yamaguchi (2014), and Meunier and Reppen (2015) have noted, many teachers, even those who have received some training in corpus linguistics, are still not regularly using corpus-based activities in their classrooms for a variety of reasons, including a lack of confidence in the methodology, time constraints, questions of relevance, and the challenges in orienting their students and re-designing their courses and classrooms to incorporate corpus-based approaches.

9.1.1 Corpora for classroom activities

Bowker and Pearson (2002) identify four primary characteristics of a corpus as: 1) authentic, 2) relatively large, 3) electronic, and 4) conforms to specific design criteria. There are corpora containing multiple registers (also referred to as text types) such as

DOI: 10.4324/9781003002901-11

academic English, spoken English in job interviews, newspaper articles, novels and short stories, or legal cases with direct teaching applications. There is no specific rule regarding the size of a corpus but it should be large enough to promote a systematic analysis of relevant, target linguistic patterns, especially when utilized for materials design. With the advent of personal computers and programming tools, as well as major innovations in internet technology, corpora have been freely shared and explored for teaching purposes—available and accessible in many classrooms. One clear benefit here is that corpora allow for the observation and study of real-world language use, with relevant frequency distributions and access to actual occurrences of features, rather than relying only on limited teacher intuition (Friginal, 2018).

Considering its potential, it is easy to envision the positive contribution of corpus-based approaches and the collection of academic corpora in a variety of teaching contexts. From as early as 2005, Teubert (2005) noted that CL has been held to be the default resource in linguistic research since it reflects real language data. Learners, therefore, will benefit from the practical and pragmatic applications of corpus data as they learn about English in their classrooms. For example, corpora have contributed immensely to studies of phraseological and collocational patterns of everyday English, illustrating how such patterns can inform language learning and teaching. Phraseology is certainly not a new field, but corpus approaches have enhanced the ability of learners to understand and visualize that a word is not limited to the word itself, but also the words and phrases around it (Szudarski, this volume). Learners may more readily comprehend that the meaning and utility of a word extends even beyond the borders of its neighboring words to include various commonly co-occurring lexical chunks of bundles. As Römer (2009) observes, "language is highly patterned" (p. 140), and often, these patterns are important to highlight and teach in the classroom (Friginal *et al.*, 2020a).

9.1.2 Data-driven learning and corpora for materials design

In the broader field of language teaching across learners and settings, corpora and corpus tools have been incorporated into three primary instructional approaches: 1) educational or instructional technology-based learning, 2) computer-assisted language learning (CALL), and 3) data-driven learning (DDL). These three approaches, especially the first two, share common characteristics: both are machine-specific (i.e. use of computers) and they also align well with and support other instructional approaches such as learner-centered instruction or autonomous learning (Friginal, 2018). Specifically, the approach taken in Instructional Technology emphasizes the role of tools and their integration into the learning process; CALL focuses on learning languages with the aid of computers with a particular emphasis on software design and evaluation, and DDL highlights learners' direct discovery and use of linguistic information/data in the language classroom and beyond. These three have been the most common instructional approaches in which corpora and corpus tools have been situated across various studies over the past two decades (Friginal, 2018; Friginal *et al.*, 2020a).

Materials design with corpora appears to directly align with DDL strategies. O'Keeffe (2020) suggests that the pedagogical focus of DDL fosters the independent acquisition of linguistic knowledge (e.g. lexis, grammatical constructions, collocations, and so on). DDL allows learners to discover language structures and patterns on their own through interacting with concordancing software or with concordance-based instructional materials (Smart, 2014). This interaction presents learners with actual concordance lines of authentic language that centers on a particular word or phrase used in context. As Pérez-Paredes (2010) puts it,

> "the methods of research in corpus linguistics can be transferred to the language classroom by turning linguists' analytical procedures into a pedagogically relevant tool to increase both learners' awareness of and sensitivity to patterns of language while also enhancing language learning strategies" (p. 55).

Friginal and Hardy (2014) noted that DDL's use of concordancers "provide the user with the organized contexts of items that are searched. Often, one might be interested in exploring the words before and after a given word" (p. 39), especially when clearly explained in a particular lesson or instructional material on, for example, collocations or multi-word units of discourse. At the same time, concordancers provide the immediate elements (including punctuations) surrounding a target word or phrase. The focus is on the word or phrase of interest and its immediate context, rather than the meaning of the sentence or paragraph as a whole. This may seem confusing and limiting at first, but concordance lines typically yield enough context to inform learners and teachers of the various uses of words or phrases in relation to collocations and other multi-word patterns. The process, then, clearly provides a focus on form and meaning in short, multiple segments, showing various usages simultaneously and without the distraction of longer stretches of discourse, as emphasized in teacher-developed activities. Therefore, while the entire discourse may not be comprehensively attended to, the patterns found between words are highlighted, allowing the learners to discover nuanced meanings of the real-word language they encounter (Friginal, 2018).

9.1.3 Focal setting: CL for materials development in Aviation English

To illustrate the use of corpora and corpus-based approaches in materials development, this chapter uses Aviation English (AE) classrooms as a focal domain. Curriculum developed for AE aims to improve the language proficiency of individuals working in aviation, where accurate and concise communication is integral for safety. The aviation industry uses English in a range of communicative functions, from the language spoken by pilots and controllers over aircraft radios, to the text written in aircraft maintenance manuals for technicians in hangars all over the world. The discourse of aviation is markedly different from "natural" language in vocabulary and syntax, and proficiency is easily affected by workload, speech rate, and working memory constraints (Barshi & Farris, 2013). To successfully communicate, participants need shared operational knowledge and adequate English proficiency to complete specific communicative tasks about these topics (Friginal *et al.*, 2020b). AE is taught globally for various students and professionals in the aviation industry, especially for pilots and air traffic controllers (ATCs).

9.2 Review of current state of pedagogy

Conrad (2000), in a seminal article that asked whether CL might revolutionize grammar instruction, noted that the final decades of the 20th century brought about dramatically novel approaches that subsequently redirected grammar teaching especially for adult learners in English-medium universities. She identified renewed interest in an explicit focus on form and/or grammar instruction in the classroom (e.g. Celce-Murcia *et al.*, 1997; Ellis, 1998); new approaches to grammar pedagogy, such as teaching grammar in a discourse context (Celce-Murcia, 1991); and the design of grammatical consciousness-raising and input analysis activities (e.g. Ellis, 1995). Simultaneously, classroom technologies and computers were making it possible to conduct grammar studies of wide-ranging scope and complexity. Conrad then revealed how CL was positioned to facilitate the transfer of research data to pedagogy. At that time, Conrad noted that only one aspect of CL, concordancing, tended to be emphasized for classrooms (citing, particularly, Johns, 1994 and Cobb, 1997), but that most English as a Second Language (ESL) grammarians regarded CL as contributing to the radically changing domain of grammar research and instruction. With anticipated advances in CL, Conrad predicted that monolithic descriptions of English grammar would be replaced by register-specific descriptions; the teaching of grammar would become more integrated with the teaching of vocabulary; and, finally, the emphasis on grammar instruction would shift from structural accuracy to the appropriate conditions of use (Friginal, 2018).

In 2015, responding to Conrad (2000), Meunier and Reppen (2015) examined contemporary literature to determine whether or not Conrad's predictions had actually occurred in grammar instruction. They also explored if current teaching materials had evolved to fully incorporate register-based descriptions and data. They noted some positive changes, for example, that corpus-informed textbooks had been produced and adopted in several English courses, especially in the university setting, but they also found significant continuing limitations and areas for improvement as far as the consistency of the approach, challenges in learning to use corpus tools, and the representativeness of distributional data and corpora.

9.2.1 Current trends in corpora and materials design

Currently, the use of CL tools to help to ensure learner engagement with digital content supports the notion that digital materials provide learners (who have often been referred to as *digital learners*) a range of modified input useful in language teaching, in general, and grammar instruction, in particular. As noted earlier, the most common and most relevant corpus/digital tool for teachers and learners is the concordancer. AntConc (Anthony, 2018), WordSmith Tools (Scott, 2012), and MonoConc Pro (Barlow, 2012) are stand-alone concordancers that are easy to use and have intuitive commands in running searches and other functions. These are programs that can extract words or key words as they appear in a corpus. Concordancers are also included as built-in applications in databases such as the Michigan Corpus of Upper-Level Student Papers (MICUSP) (see Römer & O'Donnell, 2011) or the Corpus of Contemporary American English (COCA) (Davies, 2008-) and many others available online. Word or phrase frequencies can be easily obtained and the contexts within which these words are used can also be collected by taking words that appear before and after the designated key words in the corpus. This process is known as Key Word in Context or KWIC. Concordancers can also easily provide a word frequency list from the most common word to those appearing only once, n-grams, and extract common collocates of a target word or phrase.

CL tools are still not yet fully addressing the concept of gamification, i.e., the application of common elements of game play such as point scoring, competition with others, rewards upon completion of tasks, and others (Friginal, 2018), deemed as an important focus of instructional technology, but there definitely are easy options for these to be incorporated in learning materials and student handouts. Embedding questions, recommending instructional videos, responding to comments, or inserting discussion forums in content are useful add-ons to CL teaching materials. All these relate to digitized content from corpora, but also to heightened focus on project-based learning, which is a CL advantage and one of the raison d'êtres of corpus-based instruction.

Incorporating these ideas and showing the development of actual teaching materials are notable CL for teachers' textbooks published commercially in the past few years, provided in Table 9.1.

Table 9.1 Commercially-available CL in classroom textbooks, from 2007 to 2018

	Publication	Short Description
1	O'Keeffe, A., McCarthy, M., & Carter, R. (2007). *From corpus to classroom*. Cambridge University Press.	This textbook summarizes accessible corpus tools and teaching materials developed for the language classroom (from the 1990s to 2007). The authors explain how corpora could be designed to target instruction and what they tell teachers about language learning.
2	Anderson, W., & Corbett, J. (2009). *Exploring English with online corpora*. Palgrave Macmillan.	This book introduces readers to available electronic resources (up until early 2009) and demonstrates how teachers can utilize corpora in the classroom. A glossary of practical terms and topics, interactive tasks, and further readings are provided.
3	Conrad, S., & Biber, D. (2009). *Real grammar: A corpus-based approach to English*. Longman.	*Real Grammar* explicitly draws on corpus research and corpus-based comparison data "to show how 50 grammatical structures are used in speech and writing," leading to pull-out teaching materials and classroom activities.
4	Bennett, G. (2010). *Using corpora in the language learning classroom*. University of Michigan Press.	Bennet's goal was to make CL approaches accessible to teachers and to provide ideas, instructions, and sample opportunities to adapt CL tools in the classroom. A set of corpus-designed activities is presented to teach a variety of language skills.
5	Reppen, R. (2010). *Using corpora in the language classroom*. Cambridge University Press.	Reppen explains and illustrates how teachers can use corpora to create classroom materials and activities to address various learning needs. Her goal was to "demystify" CL by providing clear and simple explanations, instructions, and examples.
6	Cheng, W. (2012). *Exploring corpus linguistics: Language in action*. Routledge.	The practical aspects of CL are introduced in this book, with one chapter specifically focusing on "data-driven and corpus-driven language learning."
7	Flowerdew, L. (2012). *Corpora and language education*. Palgrave Macmillan.	Flowerdew provides a critical examination of key concepts and issues in CL, focusing on the interdisciplinary nature of the field and the role that written and spoken corpora now play in these different disciplines.
8	Timmis, I. (2015). *Corpus linguistics for ELT: Research and practice*. Routledge.	Timmis' book emphasizes a "data-rich approach" to pedagogy and how frequency-based information may contribute to effective classroom teaching.
9	Liu, D., & Lei, L. (2017). *Using corpora for language learning and teaching*. TESOL Press.	This book provides a "step-by-step hands-on introduction to the use of corpora for teaching a variety of English language skills such as grammar, vocabulary, and English academic writing."
10	Friginal, E. (2018). *Corpus linguistics for English teachers: New tools, online resources, and classroom activities*. Routledge.	Friginal describes CL and its many relevant, creative, and engaging applications to language teaching and learning for teachers and practitioners in TESOL and ESL/EFL, and graduate students in applied linguistics. Lists of new tools, sample materials, and online resources are provided.
11	Poole, R. (2018). *A guide to using corpora for English language learners*. Edinburgh University Press.	Poole focuses on a "step-by-step illustrated examples to help learners, graduate students, and language instructors visualize and understand the potential of corpus linguistics for language learning."

9.2.2 *Using corpora to develop teaching materials in the classroom*

English corpora have been put to practical use, especially in writing classrooms in universities with many L2 speakers of English. A great deal of linguistic variation exists across academic disciplines, and this can be particularly challenging for L2 English speakers working to improve their writing within a specific field. Cortes (2011) required her graduate students to compile and compare their own writing to published research articles in their disciplines to identify common organizational patterns of research articles in a particular field of study. Similarly, Lee and Swales (2006) designed an experimental course entitled "Exploring Your Own Discourse World" to help doctoral students compare their own writing to that of more established writers in their fields with the use of a concordancer. The students examined linguistic elements like common verbs and their conjugations, definite article usage, and top collocates used in their disciplines.

These types of academic English courses are particularly useful for identifying and examining patterns in specific disciplines that may differ from more general linguistic patterns found across other academic fields. By comparing their own writing to those of experts, students can identify, refine, and adapt their linguistic choices, enabling them to enhance their overall written presentation of ideas and research processes. Along this particular goal, Friginal (2013) used corpus tools to develop research report writing skills for a group of college-level students in a professional forestry program. A concordancing program was used to analyze specific linguistic patterns including linking adverbials, reporting verbs, verb tenses, and passive sentence structures. The results of the study showed improvements in the students' report writing abilities after the corpus instruction and an increased awareness for the students of the similarities and differences in their (novice) writing against those of experts in published articles.

9.2.3 *Teacher perspectives and recommendations for corpora in materials design*

Research shows a great deal of enthusiasm from teachers regarding corpus use in materials design, and there are some data, although still limited, showing that university-level learners also tend to respond positively to these types of corpus-based courses and approaches. The participants of Lee and Swales' (2006) course briefly described above found many positive applications of the corpus approach after gaining familiarity with using the tools to explore their own databases. They found corpora to be empowering as a reference tool as well as convenient because they can be accessed at any time inside or outside of the classroom. Yoon and Hirvela (2004) also confirmed students' positive attitudes regarding the use of corpus tools for developing writing skills. The authors noted, however, that the use of corpora worked more effectively with advanced learners and that teachers will have to be responsible to adequately explain the merits of corpus-based materials as supporting mechanisms to improve classroom learning.

Longitudinal research studies to confirm (or not) the efficacy of CL-based materials in the classroom are still inadequate. A sound assessment of teaching materials is critical to drawing relevant connections between language learning and corpus-based materials, but up to this point, data, especially from true experimental studies, are still significantly limited, given the clear challenges. One way to continue to contribute data is to qualitatively document and describe teacher and learner perspectives and outputs in corpus-based classrooms. Friginal *et al.* (2020a) documented and described two case studies, with two instructor-participants in semester-long courses. Case Study 1 investigated learner and instructor attitudes regarding the effectiveness of corpus-based instruction in developing academic writing skills specifically designed for a group of visiting Chinese scholars. The study took place over an eight-week English instruction class from a Faculty Mentoring Program in a university setting. Both COCA and AntConc were introduced to and used by the participants. The participants also compiled their own corpora from academic articles in their disciplines to search for field-specific linguistic patterns. The primary goal of Case Study 1 was to determine whether or not corpus materials can contribute positively to the development of professional/academic writing, editing, and research skills of the participating Chinese scholars across a range of disciplines.

Case Study 2 followed a mixed-methods, exploratory investigation into the use of a scaffolded student worksheet in order to guide learners with different levels of proficiency to use corpora and corpus tools at a non-profit, private institution based in the U.S. The worksheet was designed as an "Explorer's Daily Journal," regularly incorporating and recording learners' responses to corpus-based lessons, data, and various online and computer-based tools in the classroom or for work outside the class as homework activities. In Case Study 1, AntConc, COCA, MICASE (or Michigan Corpus of Academic Spoken English, Simpson *et al.*, 2002) and teacher-developed materials were utilized by learners. As the tools were being presented and learned during various phases of the course, student and teacher attitudes and perceptions were documented through a teacher's journal and interviews with the learners.

Friginal *et al.* (2020a) reported that instructors in both Case Studies 1 and 2 expressed that the possibilities of incorporating corpus tools in their own language classrooms were "vast and very promising" (p. 62). For the right students with specific and clear learning goals, corpus-based materials provided a practical resource to use relatively well and productively during and after the course has finished. An additional focus, then, on strategies and skills acquisition in corpus-based classrooms was deemed essential. The researchers recommended that classroom teachers should assess the needs of the students in a particular class or level of study in order to determine whether corpus-based materials were appropriate and to what extent they will have to be incorporated in various activities and modified to accommodate different skill levels. Sufficient training for students to be familiar and at ease with data and tools was necessary, and teachers needed to prepare well-developed handouts and instructions accessible outside of the classroom. Students needed to have a buy-in to the approach; this was achieved, in general, in the two case studies presented in this paper, but it took the two instructors' serious commitment, creativity, and dedication to stay the course.

9.3 Core issues and topics

9.3.1 Overview: The teaching of Aviation English

This section exemplifies how corpus-based materials could be developed and applied in the teaching of a specific subject field, Aviation English (AE). Unlike the early days of flight when accidents were prevalent, the safety record of the aviation industry has continued to improve in the past several decades (IATA, 2019). Aviation operational training for international pilots and air traffic controller (ATCs) occurs all over the world across settings and mediums of instruction (often in the student's first language outside of the English-speaking world). Along with rigorous training, technical innovations have enabled more system redundancies and operational efficiencies, resulting in most of today's accidents being attributable to human error rather than mechanical failure (Shappell & Wiegmann, 1996). One area for potential human error is communication, a fundamental task required of all pilots and ATCs to operate a flight successfully. During a single flight, hundreds or even thousands of utterances may be transmitted using a radio, becoming more frequent and complex during flights which are longer, through busier airspace, or experiencing unusual or emergency situations. To manage flight operations, pilots and ATCs use radiotelephony (abbreviated as RTF) as a highly specialized register to interact about navigation, meteorology, aircraft performance, and emergency procedures.

A majority of today's aviation professionals are L2 English speakers (Emery, 2015). With this, the United Nations' International Civil Aviation Organization (ICAO) mandates a certain level of English language proficiency required of pilots and controllers who fly or manage international air routes. Professional pilots and ATCs are rated based on ICAO's Language Proficiency Requirements (LPRs), outlined in Document 9835: Manual on the Implementation of the Language Proficiency Requirements (2nd Ed.) (ICAO, 2010). Using a six-level rating scale and six skills areas of language performance (Interaction, Fluency, Comprehension, Vocabulary, Pronunciation, and Structure), achieving Operational Level 4 is deemed the minimum requirement for safe operations and licensing. The testing/teaching of the RTF domain is unique in that its characteristics are markedly different from that of natural language, in structure, pronunciation, and pragmatic applications. In fact, on its own, RTF is much like a foreign language (Campbell-Laird, 2006). It is unlikely that an untrained individual will fully understand RTF communications between pilots and controllers (Estival *et al.*, 2016).

9.3.2 *Radiotelephony (RTF): Standardized phraseology and plain English*

Radiotelephony encompasses what is known as standardized phraseology and plain English (ICAO, 2010). Routine aviation operations are covered by standardized phraseology, which is prescribed in ICAO's Document 9432: Manual of Radiotelephony (2007). Standardized phraseology does not adhere to the grammar rules of common English, omitting many extraneous function words and using only a set of about 400 lexical items (Philps, 1991). In addition to its limited lexicon and syntactic structures, standardized phraseology is unique semantically in its rejection of ambiguity, and phonetically in its standardization of pronunciation (Lopez *et al.*, 2013). Standardized phraseology is the preferred register of use in RTF situations, but as its components are limited, aviation plain language must be used in some situations.

Non-routine situations often require the use of the less-defined plain English, described as difficult to understand, codify, or catalog, even for those expected to teach it (Lopez *et al.*, 2013). Aviation plain language is constrained on topics and should value the same features of clarity, conciseness, and precision found in standardized phraseology (ICAO, 2010; Mell, 1992). This similarity to standardized phraseology was shown in the analysis of two corpora of radiotelephony communications which illustrated that plain English utterances were relatively simple, structurally, with low type/token ratio (Prado & Tosqui-Lucks, 2017). Bieswanger (2016) found that the register of plain English also maintains structural conciseness and a restricted lexicon (similar to standardized phraseology), but he argued that these two are distinct registers which both need to be explicitly taught in schools and training facilities.

9.4 Recommendations for practice: The case of Aviation English

The English language is used differently by each individual aviation domain. Exploring the features of these domains, therefore, could greatly enhance AE materials design, enabling the development of customized training curricula which closely mimic the language used in specific operational settings (ICAO, 2010). Training curricula must include materials at a level of specification appropriate for the very different jobs, and corresponding language needs, of pilots, ATCs, and maintenance technicians (Emery, 2015; Friginal *et al.*, 2019). Although the focal materials or lessons discussed below are particularly for AE, it should be noted that these ideas also apply to other settings, especially in classroom-based English for Specific Purposes (ESP) courses or programs.

Recent corpus research in AE, such as Prado and Tosqui-Lucks' (2019) collection of the 110,000-word Radiotelephony Plain English Corpus (RTPEC) or work done with the Corpus of Pilot and Air Traffic Controller Communications or CORPAC (Friginal *et al.*, 2018) have shown important distributional patterns that could be directly adapted for instructional purposes. As noted by Bieswanger (2016), standardized phraseology and plain English are often used interchangeably in AE, so categorizing utterances within events as one or the other can be challenging, yet necessary for training. The RTPEC is based on an ICAO list of 33 different categories of "abnormal" occurrences, from bird strikes to equipment malfunctions. Prado and Tosqui-Lucks (2019) included events from each of these 33 non-routine categories and have begun analyzing the data further for patterns and insights into the use of plain language.

Guidance on approaches to teaching AE is found in ICAO Document 9835, including "Content-Based Language Training" as the recommended methodology (ICAO, 2010). However, finding the balance of content and language is delicate and deeply complicated by materials developers and teachers' potential lack of familiarity with the technical content. Professional pilots and controllers expect courses which are immediately relevant to their jobs, meaning the content must be narrowly focused on their specialty, and will gain operational, technical, and linguistic complexity as the learners advance in their careers. In addition to its relevance, the content in an AE course must also reflect the learners' English language level and the instructor's aviation familiarity (Miller, 2001).

ICAO (2010) states that pilots and controllers should be able to communicate on "common, concrete, and work-related topics" (p. 5). As there are relatively few commercial AE textbooks available, materials developers often identify these topics through news and reporting of current events, recent aircraft developments, or safety reports. Maintaining relevance in content sources promotes intrinsic motivation, but also means developers and instructors must have a certain aviation familiarity themselves. As there is currently no prescribed vocabulary list, such as the Academic Word List (AWL) (Coxhead, 2000), of frequent lexical items in the professional aviation domain, developers may not know what terms would be most useful for learners, particularly without much aviation operational experience. A more complete understanding of the aviation language in this content area would be helpful for those tasked with identifying vocabulary lists, patterns of language, and even pronunciation features as points of curricular focus.

9.4.1 Focal lesson 1: Teaching AE lexicon

The international organization Flight Safety Foundation publishes safety-related articles in their monthly magazine *AeroSafety World*. This content is not written with a L2 English speaker in mind and is likely challenging for most pilots and ATCs rated below an ICAO Expert Level 6. However, all aviation professionals need access to this content to continue learning and developing competencies in their industry, regardless of their English language proficiency. By using this authentic content, AE classes improve language proficiency and effectively teach important aviation safety information simultaneously, an attractive package to organizations looking to improve their safety management systems.

Figure 9.1 WordandPhrase.Info screen interface (version 1, June 2018)

Roberts (2018) developed a series of corpus-based materials and activities that make use of extracted texts from *Aerosafety World*. She recommends that scaffolding activities using corpus tools and databases such as WordandPhrase.Info (Davies, 2017) will allow learners to be introduced to this type of authentic, DDL content in the language learning classroom. The functionality of WordandPhrase.Info can be used to analyze written texts to identify frequent vocabulary items, guiding developers to utilize the terms in AE materials, and improve access to these important safety publications for all aviation personnel. Excerpts of Roberts' lesson materials are provided below and in Figures 9.1 and 9.2. (Note: The sample material was written for instructors, not learners.)

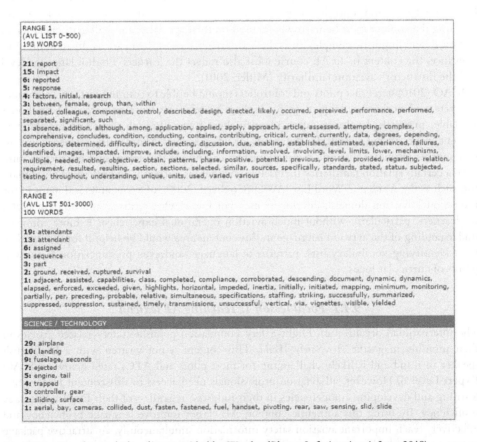

Figure 9.2 Sample vocabulary lists provided by WordandPhrase.Info (version 1, June 2018)

TASK: Analyze an authentic text to identify academic and technical vocabulary items for classroom use.

FOR THE TEACHER: When using authentic materials, unlike an ESL book, it is up to the teacher to determine which vocabulary items should be focused on in order to aid learners with both receptive and productive knowledge as related to the content. Authentic materials can be challenging for learners who may have, up until this point, dealt only with adapted or modified texts in English. Instructors can develop a range of lessons based on a single article such as one found in *Aerosafety World*, but where should they start? Through the online corpus tool WordandPhrase.Info (Davies, 2017), the article's lexical items can be revealed as categories of frequency and, even better for teachers of specific content, discipline-specific lists. The following example uses the article "Survival Factors" which discusses the National Transportation Safety Board's analysis of the Asiana Airlines Flight 214 crash.

PROCEDURE: Begin by accessing the online tool at WordandPhrase.Info. Click on "Input/ analyze texts" on the right-hand side of the screen.

Copy and paste the text to be analyzed, click on "Academic" ("All Genres" will analyze all words, not just academic words), and then "Search." The article will be displayed and color-coded to illustrate academic vocabulary words from two frequency ranges, as well as a discipline-specific color (red) as chosen by the instructor. The default setting is "All Acad," but in this case "Sci" is chosen for an aviation article (Figure 9.1).

Figure 9.1 shows the top portion of the results from clicking on "See Lists." Three vocabulary lists, Range 1 (AVL List 0 – 500), Range 2 (AVL List 501-3000), and subject-specific vocabulary (e.g., Science/Technology), are generated.

After the lists are generated, an instructor can examine the top vocabulary words in each list, and use a combination of frequency results and intuition to decide which words to focus on in classroom activities. In the FSF example, high-frequency items such as *report, impact, eject, trap, factor, sequence, fuselage,* and *initial* are useful for both receptive (e.g. comprehension or main idea questions) and productive (e.g. group discussion or summary writing) activities related to the article. Some lexical items, such as *impact,* are relevant as multiple parts of speech, and *WordandPhrase.Info* permits students to discover this distinction on their own. Alternatively, an instructor can choose which part of speech students should focus on. An instructor could further categorize the subject-specific vocabulary based on their own content knowledge. For instance, this article contains many parts of an airplane: *fuselage, engine, tail,* and *gear* (likely part of landing *gear*).

Building on Roberts (2018) analysis, a curriculum developer could take the next step of creating an entire unit by establishing further familiarity with the content topic through working with a Subject Matter Expert (SME) and gathering additional texts. These texts can be compiled into a small, specialized sub-corpus, and analyzed using tools like Lextutor (Cobb, 2019) (www.lextutor.ca). Simple frequency results and distributional data are useful for choosing lexical items which will ultimately help students comprehend the content of the themed unit. For example, the crash of Asiana Airlines Flight 214 resulted in three fatalities out of 291 passengers, a low number due largely to a successful evacuation. Both WordandPhrase. Info and Lextutor reveal vocabulary words related to *evacuation,* an appropriate and useful theme on which to develop the unit.

9.4.3 Focal lesson 2: Use of lexicon in pilot-ATC communication

Prado and Tosqui-Lucks (2017) analyzed 100 audio recordings of successful communications between pilots and ATCs in abnormal flight situations after the adoption of the LPRs in 2008. The beginnings of the recordings were marked by the first mention of the problem and concluded with its resolution. The study revealed a significant amount of softened language which is not included in standardized phraseology, such as *if you need*, *able to do*, and *do you want*, and honorifics like *sir* or *ma'am*. Even in abnormal situations, standardized phraseology prescribes conciseness and precision, leaving no room for such extraneous speech. However, this study reveals that, particularly in times of non-routine or emergency situations, aviation plain English may be the preferred choice even if standardized phraseology exists. Other related corpus studies have examined the language used in emergency situations. Pannebecker (2019) also found a departure from standardized phraseology in a corpus of emergency situations obtained from the YouTube channel VASAviation and Aviation Safety Website (https://aviation-safety.net/). While these findings do not suggest that using plain language during emergencies is the right choice, or the only choice, they do bring awareness to the register which then can inform pedagogical decisions and materials development as shown in the sample task below developed by Prado *et al.* (2019).

TASK: Teaching the correct usage of the word *right* in RTF oral communication.

LESSON DEVELOPMENT: Prado *et al.* (2019) used findings from a corpus investigation of transcripts from the National Transportation Safety Board (NTSB) to create a lesson on the polysemic word *right*. According to standardized phraseology, *right* should be used "only with the meaning of direction," but distributions from the corpus showed that *right* was used 80 percent of the time as a discourse marker, tag question, or speech act for confirmation.

To illustrate correct usage, materials should highlight *right* found in the corpus used to indicate direction, with collocates such as *deviation* or *turn*. Then, as an additional language awareness exercise, materials can also further expose students to other actual meanings of *right* from the corpus.

SAMPLE MATERIAL: Usage of *right* in the corpus and their meaning. Direct the students to run the NTSB corpus in AntConc and use the KWIC function to extract all occurrences of right. Interpret each occurrence following the three "meanings" identified in the text samples below:

… that you'll not be cleared to descend right now/you have to wait …

[An expression that means "at this moment"]

AIRPLANE/that's right and report passing position XXXX please//

[An expression that means "it is correct"]

Seven, confirm, are you making deviation to the right?

[Direction]

FOR THE TEACHER: Materials developers can use these language extracts as the foundation for discussions on the importance of standardized phraseology, ambiguous language, and resolving misunderstandings. For example, students can come up with ways to express the plain language utterances containing the term *right* using standardized phraseology and debate its effectiveness. Using non-standard phraseology in the classroom must be done with a careful approach that does not necessarily condone its use. Any data from a corpus must be interpreted by developers who have the linguistic and aviation expertise to determine if and how it can qualify as effective teaching material.

9.5 Future directions of research

Collecting corpora of AE discourse that are truly representative of the registers, not just showing features that are frequent but also what is correct or accurate, is challenging. The language which teachers or curriculum developers could teach as effective, especially outside standardized phraseology, may be rarely seen in a corpus, as most CL or DDL work being done today uses transcripts of emergency situations which are publicly available (Pacheco, 2019; Prado, 2015; Prado & Tosqui-Lucks, 2019). As miscommunication between interlocutors resulting in emergencies may not have had a successful outcome or contain inappropriate and problematic language, they may represent poor communication strategies which are not ideal teaching and learning material. The highly nuanced register of appropriate, successful RTF is very difficult, at present, to collect as a corpus due to a range of access issues. To protect stakeholders, ICAO does not allow free access to record radiotelephony transmissions, and regulations often prohibit the exchange or public use of texts without extensive permission. If a truly representative corpus of successful aviation radiotelephony communications could be collected and analyzed, certain lexico-grammatical aspects, as well as functions of the spoken language in the domain may emerge which would be useful to instructors and students (Friginal *et al.*, 2019).

Like aviation, other ESP industry areas, such as oil and gas, forestry, shipping or maritime operations, and outsourced call centers, could benefit from corpus insights into individual job roles within a single industry system. In these professional domains, corpus findings may reveal new levels of specification or surprising results about language use which can inform subsequent materials development. ESP courses in these areas could also benefit from DDL activities and corpora-informed curricula similar to that described earlier in this chapter. These approaches enable teachers and trainers to build materials that make published industry content accessible to learners without advanced language proficiency. Further, these materials are seen as worthwhile investments to stakeholders and to learners, as they contribute to safety and to professionalism. In such high-stakes teaching and learning scenarios, course efficacy cannot be compromised or overlooked. These contexts benefit from the specificity that corpus research is able to contribute to materials development and from the opportunity to expose students to actual language in use beyond that which is prescribed.

Similarly, university-level teaching materials exploring particular academic fields (e.g., engineering, history, or biology) have been introduced to students in addition to the traditional instructional focus of stylesheets or research writing tips and guidelines. In chemistry writing, for example, Robinson *et al.* (2010) published *Write Like a Chemist* which makes use of information gathered from corpus analyses of chemistry texts. This textbook was developed primarily for chemistry students in the United States, both L1 and L2 speakers of English, highlighting the use of corpus-based technology as well as the collection of specialized corpora. The authors aimed to contribute to the innovative design of writing classes that incorporate detailed descriptive data of different genres of writing. Students are exposed to the writing conventions of professionals in their own field, are given clear examples of lexico-syntactic features of various written reports and documents, and are able to focus on the nuances and skills that prepare them not only in writing, but more importantly, in reading genre-specific texts. What is clear from such publications is the need for successful collaborations between professors of various disciplines, corpus and applied linguists, and technical writing instructors in order to develop meaningful and effective corpus-based teaching materials.

Further reading

Friginal, E. (2018). *Corpus linguistics for English teachers: New tools, online resources, and classroom activities.* Routledge. Friginal's book highlights theoretical underpinnings that support the integration and use of corpora and corpus tools in the teaching of English for a variety of learners and settings. An extensive list of tools and corpus-based resources that are currently and easily available to the classroom teacher is provided and discussed, together with sample materials and activities, and lessons utilizing them. Discussions of existing and emerging theories and models of language acquisition focusing on the current and future directions of corpora in the classroom are also provided.

Liu, D., & Lei, L. (2017). *Using corpora for language learning and teaching.* TESOL Press. As a focal question in the book, Liu and Lei asks readers, "How Can You Use Corpora in Your Classroom?" The authors address the needs of today's teachers for a step-by-step hands-on introduction to the use of corpora for teaching a variety of English language skills such as grammar, vocabulary, and English academic writing. Discussions of basic, essential corpus search and teaching procedures and activities, including instructions on how to compile corpora for language instruction and research purposes are highlighted.

Poole, R. (2018). *A guide to using corpora for English language learners.* Edinburgh University Press. This book focuses on the application of various corpus searches primarily for vocabulary instruction and the teaching of academic writing. Poole also guides readers on building specialized corpora for classroom use, with a hands-on approach intended to support learners autonomously and to help instructors learn to design and implement their own corpus materials and activities. Tutorials on a range of accessible and increasingly user-friendly corpora and databases are outlined and discussed.

References

Anthony, L. (2018). *AntConc* (Version 3.4.3) [Computer Software]. Waseda University. Accessed July 9. http://www.laurenceanthony.net/

Barlow, M. (2012). *MonoConc Pro 2.2* (MP2.2) [Computer Software]. Available from http://www.monoconc.com/

Barshi, I., & Farris, C. (2013). *Misunderstandings in ATC communication: Language, cognition, and experimental methodology.* Ashgate.

Biber, D., Reppen, R., & Friginal, E. (2010). Research in corpus linguistics. In R. B. Kaplan (Ed.), *The Oxford handbook of applied linguistics* (2nd ed.) (pp. 548–570). Oxford University Press.

Bieswanger, M. (2016). Aviation English: Two distinct specialised registers. In C. Schubert & C. Sanchez-Stockhammer (Eds.), *Variational text linguistics: Revisiting register in English* (pp. 67–85). Mouton de Gruyter.

Bowker, L., & Pearson, J. (2002). *Working with specialized language: A practical guide to using corpora.* Routledge.

Campbell-Laird, K. (2006). Pedagogical approaches to aviation phraseology and communication training in collegiate flight programs. *Collegiate Aviation Review, 24*(1), 25–41.

Celce-Murcia, M. (1991). Grammar pedagogy in second and foreign language teaching. *TESOL Quarterly, 25*, 135–151.

Celce-Murcia, M., Dörnyei, Z., & Thurrell, S. (1997). Direct approaches in L2 instruction: A turning point in communicative language teaching? *TESOL Quarterly, 31*(1), 141–152.

Cobb, T. (1997). Is there any measurable learning from hands-on concordancing? *System, 25*, 301–315.

Cobb, T. (2019). Compleat Lexical Tutor v.8 [website]. Retrieved December 9, 2019 from http://lextutor.ca

Conrad, S. (2000). Will corpus linguistics revolutionize grammar teaching in the 21st century? *TESOL Quarterly, 34*(3), 548–560.

Cortes, V. (2011). Genre analysis in the academic writing class: With or without corpora? *Quaderns de Filologia-Estudis Lingüístics, 16*, 65–80.

Coxhead, A. (2000). A new academic world list. *TESOL Quarterly, 34*(2), 213–238.

Davies, M. (2008). *The Corpus of Contemporary American English (COCA): 520 million words, 1990-present.* Available online at https://corpus.byu.edu/coca/.

Davies, M. (2017). *WordandPhrase.Info* [website]. Accessed 18 Mar 2016 at corpus.byu.edu

Ellis, R. (1995). Interpretation tasks for grammar teaching. *TESOL Quarterly*, *29*(1), 87–105.

Ellis, R. (1998). Teaching and research: Options in grammar teaching. *TESOL Quarterly*, *32*(2), 39–60.

Emery, H. (2015). Aviation English for the next generation. In E. Borowska & Adrian (Eds.), *Changing perspectives on aviation English training* (pp. 8–34). University of Warsaw.

Estival, D., Farris, C., & Molesworth, B. (2016). *Aviation English: A lingua franca for pilots and air traffic controllers*. Routledge.

Friginal, E. (2013). Developing research report writing skills using corpora. *English for Specific Purposes*, *32*(4), 208–220.

Friginal, E. (2018). *Corpus linguistics for English teachers: New tools, online resources, and classroom activities*. Routledge.

Friginal, E., & Hardy, J. A. (2014). *Corpus-based sociolinguistics: A guide for students*. Routledge.

Friginal, E., Dye, P., & Nolen, M. (2020a). Corpus-based approaches in language teaching: Outcomes, observations, and teacher perspectives. *Boğaziçi University Journal of Education*, *37*(1), 43–68.

Friginal, E., Mathews, E., & Roberts, J. (2019). *English in global aviation: Context, research, and pedagogy*. Bloomsbury.

Friginal, E., Roberts, J., Pacheco, A., & Cavallet, J. (2018). Exploring the discourse of international aviation from the Corpus of Pilot and ATC Communications (CORPAC), paper presented at the *American Association for Corpus Linguistics Conference 2018*, Georgia State University.

Friginal, E., Roberts, J., Udell, R., & Schneider, A. (2020b). Pilot-ATC aviation discourse. In E. Friginal & J. Hardy (Eds.), *The Routledge handbook of corpus approaches to discourse analysis* (pp. 39–53). Routledge.

Geluso, J., & Yamaguchi, A. (2014). Discovering formulaic language through data-driven learning: Learner attitudes and efficacy. *ReCALL*, *26*(2), 225–242.

International Air Transport Association (IATA). (2019). *Safety report 2019*. *International Air Transport Association*. Retrieved from https://www.skybrary.aero/bookshelf/books/5640.pdf

International Civil Aviation Organization (ICAO) (2007). *Manual of radiotelephony (Document 9432)*. Montreal: International Civil Aviation Organization.

International Civil Aviation Organization (ICAO (2010). *Manual of implementation of the language proficiency requirements (DOC9835-AN/453* (2nd ed.). Montreal International Civil Aviation Organization.

Johns, T. (1994). From printout to handout: Grammar and vocabulary teaching in the context of data-driven learning. In T. Odlin (Ed.), *Perspectives on pedagogical grammar* (pp. 293–313). Cambridge University Press.

Lee, D., & Swales, J. (2006). A corpus-based EAP course for NNS doctoral students: Moving from available specialized corpora to self-compiled corpora. *English for Specific Purposes*, *25*(1), 56–75.

Lopez, S., Condaimines, A., Josselin-Leray, A., O'Donoghue, O., & Salmon, R. (2013). Linguistic analysis of English phraseology and plain language in air-ground communication. *Journal of Air Transport Studies*, *4*(1), 44–60.

Meunier, F., & Reppen, R. (2015). Corpus vs. non-corpus informed pedagogical materials: Grammar as the focus. In D. Biber & R. Reppen (Eds.), *The Cambridge handbook of English corpus linguistics* (pp. 498–514). Cambridge University Press.

Miller, L. (2001). English for engineers in Hong Kong. In J. Murphy & P. Byrd (Eds.), *Understanding the courses we teach: Local perspectives on English language teaching*. University of Michigan.

O'Keeffe, A. (2020). Data-driven learning – A call for a broader research gaze. *Language Teaching*, *54*(2), 259–272. doi:10.1017/S0261444820000245.

Pacheco, A. (2019). *English for aviation: Guidelines for teaching and introductory research*. EDIPUCRS.

Pannebecker, A. (2019). An analysis of the most used lexical terms in corpus-based emergency situations. In Pacheco, A. (Ed.), *English for aviation: Guidelines for teaching and introductory research*. EDIPUCRS.

Pérez-Paredes, P. (2010). Corpus linguistics and language education in perspective: Appropriation and the possibilities scenario. In T. Harris & M. Moreno Jaén (Eds.), *Corpus linguistics in language teaching* (pp. 53–73). Peter Lang.

Philps, D. (1991). Linguistic security in the syntactic structures of air traffic control English. *English World-Wide*, *12*(1), 103–124.

Prado, M. (2015). The relevance of pragmatics in the teaching of aviation English: A corpus-based study. Doctoral dissertation, Universidade de São Paulo.

Prado, M., & Tosqui-Lucks, P. (2017). Are the LPRs focusing on real life communication issues? *The Proceedings of the International Civil Aviation English Association (2017) Conference.* Retrieved from: https://commons.erau.edu/icaea-workshop/2017/tuesday/15/

Prado, M., & Tosqui-Lucks, P. (2019). Designing the radiotelephony plain English corpus (RTPEC): A specialized spoken English language corpus towards a description of aeronautical communications in non-routine situations. *Research in Corpus Linguistics, 7,* 113–128. DOI 10.32714/ricl.07.06

Prado, M., Roberts, J., Tosqui-Lucks, P., & Friginal, E. (2019). The development of aviation English programs. In E. Friginal, E. Mathews, & J. Roberts (Eds.), *English in global aviation: Context, research, and pedagogy* (pp. 215–246). Bloomsbury.

Roberts, J. (2018). Identifying and analyzing vocabulary from authentic materials in a content-based ESP class. In E. Friginal. *Corpus linguistics for English teachers: New tools, online resources, and classroom activities* (pp. 218–223). Routledge.

Robinson, M., Stoller, F., Jones, J., & Costanza-Robinson, M. (2010). *Write like a chemist.* Oxford University Press.

Römer, U. (2009). The inseparability of lexis and grammar: Corpus linguistic perspectives. *Annual Review of Cognitive Linguistics, 7,* 140–162.

Römer, U. (2011). Corpus research applications in second language teaching. *Annual Review of Applied Linguistics, 31*(2), 205–225.

Römer, U., & O'Donnell, M. B. (2011). From student hard drive to web corpus (part 1): The design, compilation and genre classification of the Michigan Corpus of Upper-level Student Papers (MICUSP). *Corpora, 6*(2), 159–177.

Scott, M. (2012). *WordSmith Tools* (Version 6). [Software]. Available from http://lexically.net/wordsmith/

Shappel, S., & Wiegmann, D. (1996). U.S. Naval aviation mishaps 1977-92: Differences between single- and dual-piloted aircraft. *Aviation, Space, and Environmental Medicine, 67,* 65–69.

Simpson, R., Briggs, S., Ovens, J., & Swales, J. (2002). *The Michigan corpus of academic spoken English.* The Regents of the University of Michigan.

Smart, J. (2014). The role of guided induction in paper-based data-driven learning. *ReCALL, 26*(02), 184–201.

Teubert, W. (2005). My version of corpus linguistics. *International Journal of Corpus Linguistics, 10*(1), 1–13.

Yoon, H., & Hirvela, A. (2004). ESL student attitudes toward corpus use in L2 writing. *Journal of Second Language Writing, 13,* 257–283.

10

CORPORA FOR ENGLISH LANGUAGE LEARNING TEXTBOOK EVALUATION

Mike Nelson

10.1 Introduction

As early as the 1500s, textbooks were being created and used to teach model dialogues to students of English and French (Becker, 2002). Nowadays, textbooks are big business for an increasingly small number of publishers in the world of English language teaching (ELT). While corpora have strongly influenced dictionaries and reference works in the last 30 years, the same phenomenon has not been observed in language learning textbook creation to quite the same extent. This lack of corpus-informed influence is reflected in reviews of ELT materials' development. In Tomlinson's "English language learning materials – a critical review" (2008) the word *corpus* is scarcely mentioned. Later, Tomlinson (2012, 2013) included some mention of corpora in materials development, but again, in Garton and Graves' (2014) review of current issues in materials in ELT it was similarly overlooked. However, despite corpus data not being used in textbook creation as much as it could have been, it has been widely used to evaluate them.

Corpus-based evaluation of language learning textbooks, particularly in the last decade, has exposed consistent linguistic misrepresentations and, therefore, the main aim of this chapter is to highlight for future researchers the issues, findings, and challenges attached to evaluating textbooks with corpora. In doing so, we ask why, what and how? Firstly, we look at why uptake of corpus-based data into textbooks has been slow and the advantages corpus data can offer their writers. For those thinking of carrying out their own research into textbooks, a good starting point is to see what has already been done; thus, the central focus of the chapter is on presenting the more recent corpus-based studies that have evaluated English language learning textbooks in terms of their grammatical, lexical, discourse and communicative accuracy. In this way, the key themes involved, and the methodological approaches taken can be made visible. In the "how" section, some of the unique elements of textbook corpus creation are discussed, followed by a case study that compares the language found in a Business English Corpus and a corpus of published Business English materials (Nelson, 2000). The chapter concludes with recommendations for the future.

DOI: 10.4324/9781003002901-12

10.2 Corpora and textbooks

Many authors point to the unique importance of course and textbooks in ELT (Lee, 2006; McCarten, 2010; Peksoy & Harmaoglu, 2017). McCarten (2010) defines coursebooks as "a carefully sequenced, graded set of teaching materials whose aim is to improve the language knowledge and performance of its users, taking them from one level to another" (p. 413). These books can be of a "global" or "local" variety as defined by Garton and Graves (2014); that is, aiming at a universal market with more general needs or a local market with more specific linguistic and functional requirements. Thus, our overview of corpus evaluation of textbooks will look at research into both global and local offerings. McCarten continued by saying that most ELT coursebooks use either American or British English; and so writers "need access to a corpus of the chosen variety to ensure their syllabus and language models accurately reflect usage in the corpus" (2010, p. 414). This seems like a perfectly reasonable statement to make; however, as we will see, there has been only limited uptake of corpus data by publishers of major ELT textbooks.

10.2.1 Calling for a corpus revolution

Timmis (2015) and Meunier and Reppen (2015) refer to Conrad's (2000) article who noted that "by the end of the 20th century … little connection had been made between the grammatical research of corpus linguistics and the rejuvenated interest in grammar teaching" (p. 549). She suggested that this connection might actually come about. However, Timmis (2015) gave a resounding negative to the question in the title of Conrad's paper asking whether corpus linguistics would revolutionise grammar teaching in the 21st century. Meunier and Reppen (2015) also found that non-corpus informed coursebooks "fail to include important information on the passive" (p. 513). Extending the revolution analogy in 2020, Le Foll (in press) still points to the lack of corpus results in teaching materials today. Thus, a substantial portion of ELT coursebooks still do not utilise corpora either at all, or to the extent that they would ensure the correct curricula and language models that accurately reflect real-life language. The reasons for this are complex and lie partly in the historical corpus data vs intuition debate where Chomskyan introspection and use of intuitive examples competed against the lexical tradition of linguistic theory represented by Firth (Stubbs, 1993), and partly in differing attitudes towards authenticity in language learning texts (Gilmore, 2007; Meunier & Reppen, 2015; Tomlinson, 2012; Widdowson, 1998). See Nelson (2000) for a fuller description of the intuition debate.

ELT author and publisher attitudes and prejudices have also played a key role, with only half of surveyed authors convinced of the benefits of corpus data when writing textbooks (Burton, 2012). It must also be noted at the outset that some textbooks writers quite justifiably place pedagogical efficacy above corpus-generated frequency. If this is done with careful thought and planning, it is, of course, acceptable, but we will see later in this chapter that for much of the time this is not the case.

10.2.2 What can corpora give textbooks?

The ways in which corpora can be utilised for pedagogical purposes, and by extension in textbook creation, have been previously well covered in the literature. The value of corpus data in language teaching, in general, and the importance of teaching collocations from corpus-generated concordance lines within a lexical approach were summarised by McEnery and

Xiao (2010). They refer to Kennedys' (2003) notion that exposure to language is key in foreign language learning and that "corpus-based teaching materials try to demonstrate how the target language is actually used in different contexts" (McEnery & Xiao, 2010, p. 368). Flowerdew (2019) concurred, saying that "concordance data can shed light on vocabulary items, e.g. the most common senses of a word or its meaning ... phraseological patterning, involving collocations, colligations and semantic preferences and prosodies" (p. 444). These themes were continued by McCarten (2010), who elucidated the advantages of corpus-informed coursebook design both in the sense of the actual data that can be mined, and also how that data can be put to use. After identifying the specific elements that corpora would need to have in order to best inform coursebook design in terms of variety, genre, age and size, she suggests that corpus data can be useful in the formulation of vocabulary and grammar syllabuses, and in identifying lexico-grammatical patterning. It can provide information on contexts of use and offer models for presentation and practice (see O'Keefe & McCarthy, 2010). More recently, Meunier and Reppen (2015), proposed a number of ways in which corpora can be used to inform materials development. They suggest that corpora can help select linguistic target features, the amount of space devoted to those features, the sequencing of materials, the inclusion of actual corpus data, the inclusion of information on register differences and in the choice of example texts, ensuring they are an accurate reflection of the target features. Thus, corpora can have an indirect impact (helping to decide what to teach and when to teach it) on language teaching (Römer, 2008).

10.3 What does corpus-based evaluation of textbooks tell us?

Before the 2010s, most evaluation of textbooks was done using a page-by-page analytical method and few used corpus-based methods (Meunier & Gouverneur, 2009). In the last ten years, corpus-based evaluation of textbooks has increased exponentially, and the following section gives an overview of this more recent research, with some reference to older studies. Analysis of these studies shows most researchers adopting a similar approach: they identify features for study, highlight limitations and make pedagogical recommendations for future textbook development. In order to organise this section, a modified version of Burton's (2012) classification of corpus-based coursebook evaluation was used creating three categories: grammar, lexis, and a broader category encompassing discourse, communication, and interaction.

10.3.1 Corpus studies of grammar in textbooks

Accurate representation of grammatical features is arguably one of the most important features textbooks should have. This first section covers a selection of research that highlights the broad lack of accuracy of grammatical usage in textbooks in a number of areas. For organisational purposes, they have been divided into examples of research into modality, use of progressives, passives, verb-tense usage, the subjunctive, conditional if-clauses, and the distribution and use of conjunctives. However, consistent under- and/or overrepresentation of grammatical features, lack of corpus data uptake and in some cases a lack of explicit teaching of important points are features that persist across these categories.

Both under- and over-representation, respectively, were found by Shortall (2007) and Bouhlal *et al.* (2018) in studies of modality found in textbooks. Shorthall used the Bank of English 20-million word spoken corpus (Brspok corpus) to study the use of the present perfect and perfective modality in a corpus of 32 widely used ELT textbooks. When 1,008 perfective sentences extracted from Brspok were compared to the textbook corpus, it was found that perfective modals, for example, *must have + participle* (2007, p.170) formed 25% of the Brspok examples to only 2% in the textbook corpus. They were, thus, infrequent in the materials and limited in scope. Similar findings were reported by Bouhlal *et al.* (2018). They drew on Römer's (2004) earlier well-known work on modality, using the BNC-COCA corpus as a reference to measure the accuracy of use of nine central modals against a corpus of nine ESL textbooks in the Secondary ESL Corpus. Analysis of the comparative distributional frequencies of *will, can, would, could, should, may must, might* and *shall* in the two corpora found that modals were over-represented in the textbook corpus. The modal *will* for example, was found to be three times higher in use than in the reference corpus. In their analysis of the semantics of four modal auxiliaries, divergence in representations of meaning was found in three out of four cases.

A similar, but more complex picture emerges in Le Foll's (in press) exploration of progressive use in textbooks, which looked at dialogues taken from 43 textbooks again using Römer (2004) as a baseline. The Spoken BNC2014 was used as the reference corpus. Unlike many studies that simply focus on frequency and under- or over-representation, Le Foll was also concerned to discover the progressive's contextual and functional use, and the lexical associations found; that is, which lexical verbs and semantic domains are significantly associated with or repelled by the progressive in textbook conversation. Taking previous studies of progressive use in textbooks (Biber & Reppen, 2002; Römer, 2005) and using Römer's study of German EFL textbooks as a comparative point of reference, Le Foll found disparity of usage in her study. Progressives, in contrast to the predictions of Biber and Reppen (2002), were slightly underrepresented, including the use of the past progressive and contracted forms. Comparison to Römer's earlier study showed that there had been some improvements in textbook accuracy, but past progressives were still found to be underrepresented in the textbooks at each level. Interestingly, although Le Foll found that even though the present progressive was overused in textbooks, it was only overused in beginner's level books and she suggested there are sound pedagogical reasons for this. In terms of lexical associations, there were differences in those verbs attracted or repelled by the progressive in the textbook and corpus and BNC, though this could possibly be attributed to corpus topic content. Further, there was evidence that phrasal verbs and discourse-structuring phrasemes typically used with progressives were underrepresented in the textbooks.

Use of the passive has also been a target of research, and two well-known studies exemplify how corpus data is not reaching textbooks. Granger (2013) examined the use of the passive in a corpus of eleven ELT grammar textbooks "with a view to assessing to what extent they integrate the insights generated by corpus-based studies" (p. 12). This was found to be lacking in many areas including a focus in the textbooks on transitive verbs, which actually cause students less problems than the intransitive, and unrealistic negative examples of passive use. Meunier and Reppen (2015) took up Granger's findings in a study of four corpus-informed and four non-corpus informed textbooks. They found that Granger's idea that "corpus-based studies have had relatively little impact on pedagogical grammars" (2015, p. 509) is confirmed in the non-corpus informed textbooks. Corpus-informed textbooks performed significantly better in terms of content, but the non-corpus books were better "in contextualisation of examples and the integration of grammar within skills" (ibid.). They do note though that integration of grammar is better in the newer corpus-based textbooks.

Over-and underrepresentation of verb tense usage was found in a 100,000-word corpus of all the English language learning coursebooks currently being used in Turkey (Peksoy & Harmaoglu, 2017). The BNC spoken corpus of 10 million words was used as the reference corpus. Of the tenses used in a positive sense, it was found that the present simple was underused, while the present continuous, simple past, past continuous, future perfect and past perfect tenses were all overrepresented. In negative verb usage, contracted negative forms were underrepresented in the coursebooks and verbs used in the negative in general were also underrepresented.

Two studies in 2006 focused on the *if-clause* in textbooks and both found it to be inaccurately represented. Lee (2006) was concerned that textbook writers "fail to acknowledge the existence of different varieties of English" (p. 80) in a corpus-based study of the subjunctive *were* and the indicative *was* in if-clauses in a corpus of twenty textbooks. Lee found that the textbooks did not accurately represent current usage and that "The observation made in many grammar practice books that in hypothetical conditions only subjunctive *were* is correct is therefore unfounded" (Lee, 2006, p. 90). Gabrielatos (2006) used a corpus of ELT coursebooks to examine usage of conditional sentences in comparison to a random sample of 1,000 if-clauses drawn from the BNC. He found that learners using the ELT coursebooks were presented with "an incomplete, and in some cases distorted, picture of if-conditionals" (p. 2).

Two of the main limitations noted above, underrepresentation and a lack of explicit tasks, this time for conjunctions, were the key findings of Philip *et al.* (2012), who examined a corpus of English language textbooks used in Malaysian schools. The 311,000-word textbook corpus was used to discover the distribution and ranking of conjunctions in comparison to data from the BNC reference corpus. They found that both correlative and subordinating conjunctions were underrepresented and explicit communicative exercises for their teaching were absent.

The research we have seen thus far highlights the often ad hoc nature by which grammatical items are presented in textbooks. Treatment of lexis in textbooks follows a similar pattern.

10.3.2 Corpus studies of lexis in textbooks

Corpus-based analysis of lexis in textbooks has seen a recent increase of interest and has yielded very similar results to studies of grammar. In this section, we look at the evaluation of lexical selection and accuracy, text coverage and vocabulary load, multiword units, and idioms and metaphors in textbooks. The key themes that emerge in this area include a lack of consistency in lexical selection, a focus on explicit rather than implicit items, a lack of reference to corpus data and failure to utilise readily-available corpus-based vocabulary lists such as the Academic Word List (Coxhead, 2000) or the Academic Vocabulary List (Gardner & Davies, 2014). Work on vocabulary load and thresholds (Hsu, 2011, 2014, 2018) offers some solutions to these issues.

Lexical selection and accuracy in textbooks at a variety of levels has been broadly investigated. Nordberg and Nordlund (2018), drawing on the tradition of Ljung (1990), created a corpus of seven English textbooks used in Swedish primary schools and compared them to the New General Service List and the VP-Kids Corpus in order to discover if the representation of everyday use of lexical verbs, adjectives and nouns was accurate. In particular, they were interested whether the textbooks supported vocabulary acquisition, if there was a consensus on how many words and their distribution found in books aiming at the same level should contain, how well the vocabulary corresponds to everyday usage, and if there is any shared approach in the books in terms of vocabulary selection (Nordberg & Nordlund, 2018). They discovered a diverse situation, where there was "an absence of a common pedagogical idea" (p. 469) and that meant that students would have different possibilities in terms of exposure to and retention of vocabulary. Despite verb usage correlating reasonably in the textbook corpus with the authentic usage found in the corpora, the lexical profile of adjectives and nouns was limited. In particular, exposure to superordinates, for example, *people, child, thing*, was distinctly lacking. They conclude by saying that their study "has provided empirical evidence of the lack of common criteria as to vocabulary size, lexical diversity and vocabulary profile in EFL textbooks used in Swedish primary schools" (p. 470).

Lack of use of available lexical resources was highlighted by Miller (2011) who compared the language found in ESL reading textbooks and the university textbooks students need to read. The research analysed vocabulary use based on the presence of AWL vocabulary (Coxhead, 2000), compression features (packing complex academic text to be as succinct as possible) and readability/complexity (sentence and word length). The ESL textbook corpora were composed of 75 reading passages from three textbooks and a 252,000-word corpus of university textbooks was created as the reference. Miller found that there was much less use of AWL vocabulary and compression features in the ESL textbooks but readability scores were similar. Importantly, his findings showed that the lexico-grammatical differences found between ESL and university textbooks were because they represent different text types: "The high frequency of nominal modification features in the university textbook excerpts is in line with their expository nature; conversely, the heavy use of adverbials and interactional features in the ESL textbook texts is in line with their narrative nature" (Miller, 2011, p. 44).

Text coverage refers to the percentage of words in a given text that are in or "covered" by a given word list. Previous corpus studies have determined a threshold for learners' understanding of texts, with 98% being considered necessary for understanding a text without a dictionary, and 95% for reasonable comprehension (Hirsh & Nation, 1992; Nation & Waring, 1997). Thus, the text coverage found in coursebooks in relation to well-established word lists is important and two studies found varying degrees of success of coverage in textbooks. Hajiyeva (2015) focused on vocabulary coverage found in eleven university-level textbooks used for the pedagogical studies of English majors. The computational tool *RANGE* was used to compare coverage in the textbooks to BNC frequency-based lists and the 570-word families found in the AWL. Hajiyeva created four subject-specific sub-corpora and found uneven frequency distribution of vocabulary across them when compared to the BNC lists. He found that 559 of the 570 AWL word families were present in the full textbook corpus (2015) though with lesser frequency than could be expected. Jahan *et al.* (2019) also used the BNC and AWL in their study of English-medium university level textbooks in a Pakistani setting. They investigated the frequency of BNC and AWL word families in a corpus of four textbooks. Results showed variations in textual coverage rates of the four textbooks when compared both to the BNC and AWL and only one book was able to achieve the desired 95% coverage rate.

In a series of pedagogically useful articles analysing university language as opposed to language teaching textbooks, Hsu studied the vocabulary load and thresholds found in business textbooks (2011), engineering textbooks (2014), and textbooks of Chinese medicine (2018). Her study of business textbooks (7.2-million-word corpus) and research articles (7.62 million word corpus) found that knowledge of the top 5,000 BNC word families should be a learning goal for EFL business majors and a prerequisite for further studies (Hsu, 2011). In order to analyse the vocabulary demands of English-medium engineering textbooks, Hsu (2014) created a corpus 100 college textbooks in use in Taiwan containing 4.57 million words. Again, the first 5,000-word families were found to be needed to form a key 95% threshold at a general level. However, the study was also able to analyse the vocabulary demands of the different engineering disciplines and key differences were found. Eight of the 20 disciplines reached

95% lexical coverage with these first 5,000 to 5,500 BNC word families. Civil and mechanical engineering needed only the top 3,500-word families to reach the threshold, whereas at the other end of the scale, marine and biochemical engineering required 8,500-word families of understanding. This would naturally place a heavy burden on students and so a further element of this research was to create an engineering wordlist for undergraduates and a 729-word list was formed. Hsu (2018), created a 13-million-word corpus of Chinese medicine textbooks and measured their vocabulary demands against the word families in the BNC and COCA. It was found that the complexity of the textbooks demanded knowledge of the first 10,000-word families from the BNC, plus proper nouns, in order to understand the textbooks adequately. Hsu created a specialised word list of just over 600-word families based on the textbook corpus that could form the basis for vocabulary study.

Vocabulary loading has also been addressed by Chen (2016) and Thiruchelvam *et al.* (2018). Chen (2016) using a corpus of three major ELT textbook series used in Taiwan analysed the reading texts of these books finding an imbalanced progression of text difficulty. Further, the increase in vocabulary-load in these texts and the structural complexity of them were also found to be uneven. Thiruchelvam *et al.* (2018) investigated vocabulary loading in civil engineering textbooks by creating a corpus of vocational textbooks and one of actual civil engineering textbooks. Text coverage of the General Service List (GSL) and AWL lexis in the authentic textbooks was high (72.2% and 10.99%) and the authors suggest this be reflected in future materials, along with specialised vocabulary lists for civil engineering.

The theme of inaccurate representation of lexis and lack of uptake of readily available corpus-based lexical resources continues with analysis of multi-word units in textbooks. Chen (2008) compared the lexical bundles and their pragmatic functions found in a corpus of introductory textbooks of engineering to those found in a corpus of ESP textbooks. She grouped the lexical bundles found in the introductory textbooks into twelve distinct types with three functional categories established by Biber et al. (2004): stance, discourse organisers and referential. Comparison with the corpus of ESP textbooks showed that the textbooks distorted the representation of the bundles, either over or under and that they "… not only lack(s) target language use, but also misrepresent(s) language use in introductory textbooks" (Chen, 2008, p. 136).

Similar findings were made by Wood and Appel (2014) who examined the formulaic language found in first-year business and engineering textbooks at a Canadian university. They identified the frequency and pedagogical treatment of multiword constructions (MWC) in a 108,000-word corpus of popular EAP textbooks in comparison to a 151,000-word corpus of first-year actual textbooks. Analysis of three- and four-word sequences in the university textbooks found that only less than half appeared in the EAP textbooks and were not specifically addressed in the materials.

Similarly, Godoy de la Rosa (2014) investigated the use of lexical formulas in a small corpus of English textbooks used in the Chilean context using the BYU-BNC and COCAS corpora as reference. Comparative frequency differences of usage were again found, with *Would you like some?* being overrepresented in the textbooks. Corpora evidence pointed to the more common use of *do you want some*, which was much less evident in the teaching materials.

The lack of context-specific target language noted by Chen was also evident in research by Coxhead *et al.* (2017). They investigated small-group academic interactions such as tutorials and laboratory sessions, which, although a key part of undergraduate life, have received little attention either in research or teaching materials. They were interested in discovering if EAP and ESP textbooks focus on this kind of vocabulary and if they do, how often the textbook patterns appear in actual labs and tutorials. A corpus comprised of 15 EAP speaking and listening coursebooks and one series of ESP textbooks was created. Analysis of the corpus showed that none of the materials focused on labs and only three of the series included vocabulary on tutorials. Of the 176 lexical patterns found in the textbooks, a comparative analysis of a spoken corpus of labs and tutorials showed that most of these 176 patterns did not appear. This "suggests that these resources contain little in the way of focus on lexis in interactive speaking" (Coxhead *et al.*, 2017, p. 74).

Idioms and metaphors are the staple stock of textbooks and three studies point to the need for a more systematic approach to their inclusion and make suggestions for more systematic lexical selection based on frequency. A small-scale study by Alavi and Rajabpoor (2015) investigated idiom usage in three advanced level textbooks used in Iran and compared it to usage in the MICASE, BNC and the Brown Corpora. Their aim was to firstly compare idiom usage in the textbooks themselves and then to the corpora. Underpinning this study was the desire to improve learning outcomes in future textbook creation. Significant differences were found across the three textbooks in terms of idiom type and token number with many low-frequency idioms in the corpora being overrepresented in the textbooks. As was seen in Nordberg and Nordlund (2018), no common approach to inclusion of important lexis, in this case idioms, was found. They suggest a more systematic approach to lexical choice and the use of actual corpus-generated lists of key lexis in the classroom (Alavi & Rajabpoor, 2015). Parizoska and Rajh (2017) studied variation in ten idioms related to competition in sport in a business English textbook. The idioms were compared with the BNC for British English and COCA for American. The results showed a degree of lexical or syntactic variation in their usage in the authentic corpora, which is not common in textbooks. They suggest incorporating idiom variation in future materials particularly at advanced levels.

Finally, the need for corpus-based evidence in the choice of metaphors for textbooks was stressed by Skorczynska Sznajder (2010) who compared a sample of metaphorical words and phrases found in a business English textbook with those in a one million-word corpus of business periodicals and articles. Metaphors related to war, health, and sports were comparatively examined and little overlap was found, with a particular lack of sports metaphors. The collocational patterns of the metaphors showed variation, and Skorczynska Sznajder (2010) suggests that this could provide material for classroom exploitation.

10.3.3 Corpus studies of discourse, communication and interaction in textbooks

Study of discourse is "a vast, multidisciplinary, and rapidly expanding area of research" (Gilmore, 2015, p. 506) and is also a crucial component of successful communication on a pragmatic level (Lam, 2010). Some coursebooks have been successful in accurately integrating discourse features, that is, where "research findings that are getting through", and some have not, where research findings are "not getting through" (Gilmore, 2015, p. 511). In these cases, ELT textbooks "often provide learners with a distorted or partial representation(s) of the language" (ibid., p. 515). Here we focus on the "not getting through".

In the following examples of research, we again see over-emphasis of explicit language and also inaccuracy in the presentation of discourse marker positioning. Four studies typify these issues. Cheng and Warren (2007) examined the teaching of interactional strategies of checking understanding by comparing usage found in sub-corpora of the Hong Kong Corpus of Spoken English (HKCSE) and a corpus of 15 school textbooks. Checking of understanding was studied from the perspectives of both the speaker and listener. Corpus evidence confirmed that whilst textbook authors placed primary responsibility for checking understanding with the hearer, the reality was that primary responsibility resided with the speaker. Further, the textbooks used language forms rarely used in real life and did not show the simpler and less explicit language found in the corpus (2007). Lam (2010) looked at discourse particles in corpus data and textbooks to investigate the use of the word *well* in a corpus of 15 upper secondary school textbooks and found considerable differences in its relative frequency. Textbook analysis showed that *well* is used commonly in discussions, but not in presentations: this was found to be false. Likewise, textbooks overwhelmingly placed *well* in sentence-initial position, whereas corpus data showed it to be common in sentence-medial position. Inaccuracy of discourse maker positioning was also evident when Tai (2016) examined their role in three corpora: junior high school English textbooks, listening workbooks, and an English test in use in Taiwan. The discourse markers most commonly used in the textbooks, roughly divided into textual and interpersonal markers, were found more commonly in dialogues than in text. They were found to be in sentence-initial position in 87% of the texts across the corpora, whereas in reality their positioning is much more flexible. As a result, Tai suggests that writers should focus more on actual "discourse marker distributions and contexts in real language use" (Tai, 2016, p. 273).

Textbook tendencies to focus on a limited number of explicit features are again seen in Deroey (2018). A comparative study of 25 lecture listening coursebooks was carried out to discover their representativeness of language, lecture authenticity and research-informedness to 160 real lectures found in the British Academic Spoken English Corpus (BASE). Deroey's analysis focused on "importance markers", that is, language that stresses the importance, relevance or significance of points. Findings were similar to those of Cheng and Warren (2007) where focus in the textbooks was on explicit forms (*the key point is*) which in reality were found to be rare in real life. Deroey argues that this indicates that authors are still not checking their materials against corpus data. The majority of coursebooks did not present authentic lectures and even when they did appear, they were shortened, slowed down and clearly structured. Most coursebooks displayed a lack of research-informedness and those that did "tended not to be incorporated in a major, systematic or obvious way" (Deroey, 2018, p. 65).

To return to the question posed in the title of this section, corpus-based evaluation of textbooks sheds light on a somewhat hit and miss approach to language presentation that often still owes more to the intuition of authors than to use of empirical data. There is, thus, more work to be done, and for anyone planning on carrying out corpus-based evaluation of textbooks, it is important to be aware of the challenges that are involved with this particular kind of research.

10.4 Case study: Published Materials Corpus

In this case study, we consider two issues related to corpora evaluation of coursebooks: the unique challenges associated with creating a textbook corpus and how they can be dealt with, and the consistency of the linguistic shortcomings in language learning textbooks. The case study focuses on the Published Materials Corpus (PMC) of 38 popular business English textbooks comprising 593,000 words, Nelson (2000).

10.4.1 Issues in creating textbook corpora

When creating a textbook corpus, a decision needs to be made on just what language in the books can be included in the corpus: that is, what constitutes actual target language? Textbooks are typically full of rubrics, exercises and word lists as well as longer texts and short one-word or phrasal examples of the target language. Indeed, some textbooks consist of little else than exercises with very few clearly discernible "texts" in the sense of separate reading/spoken texts. Few of the authors reviewed here indicated how they processed the data they gathered in textbooks, and Lam (2010, p. 264) decries the lack of advice available. However, some guidelines do exist in the literature that can help with this challenge. Hajiyeva (2015) recounts removing all bibliographies, tables, indices, and appendices from the texts and Bi (2020) pointed to the problems that mathematical, numerical and programming data can cause when calculating text coverage. Le Foll (in press) gives a detailed account of this complex process.

In line with this, in order to only include actual target language when creating the PMC, Nelson (2000) applied the following rules. Only full examples of language that purported to be examples of Business English, both written and spoken, were included. This could be in the form of exercises, examples of correspondence and longer and shorter texts. All other text was excluded: single-word word lists, all rubrics, and all exercises that were in some way gapped, i.e. where there were gaps which the student had to complete. Where there was repetition of the same phrase as part of an exercise, only one occurrence of the phrase was included in the corpus. There are also complex practical issues related to textbook formatting. Most textbooks are colourful and text is interspersed with pictures, graphs, and diagrams. If electronic-ready data is unavailable, scanners are unable to cope with this formatting and every scanned text has to be manually corrected. Additionally, books often include "hand-written" notes or text that scanners are often unable to read. These, again, must be entered by keyboarding.

As a result of these issues, subjectivity can hinder the objectivity of the process whether the researcher has to input the data by scanning or receives a digital-ready copy from the publisher. For a detailed account of textbook corpora creation see Nelson (2000; 2010, p. 60).

10.4.2 Analysis of the Published Materials Corpus

In analysing the PMC, Nelson posed the question "Can significant lexical differences be found between the language used in published Business English materials and the language actually used in business?" In order to discover the answer, Scott's (1997) notion of key words was used. Key words refer to words that appear with unusual frequency in a corpus when compared to a reference corpus, that is, they occur more or less often than might be expected. The textbook corpus was compared to the one million-word Business English Corpus (BEC) using *Wordsmith Tools* (Scott, 1997). Concordance lines were generated from the key word lists and analysis resulted in the formation of grammatical and semantic categories that could be compared between the corpora.

In terms of the lexis found in the PMC when compared to real-life business English in the BEC, Nelson found a familiar lack of accuracy in terms of over- and underrepresentation. For example, in the PMC, where the focus should be on the language of business, the lexis related to *family* and *society* was over-represented, e.g. *wife, son, doctor*. Likewise, the lexis of *food, entertaining*, and *travel* was far more prominent in the PMC than in the BEC, shown by the fact that none of these semantic categories were formed in the BEC. There was also less business-related focus in verb usage: analysis showed that the verbs over-represented in the PMC were concerned with personal and interpersonal matters – *thank, see, arrive, enjoy, dislike* – and only four business-related or sub-business verbs are over-represented – *advertise, enclose, arrange, specialise*. In a predominantly semantically positive BEC, negativity was found to be over-represented in the PMC. This was shown in both verbs – *didn't, can't, couldn't* – and in adjectives – *afraid, sorry, expensive, tiring*. However, there was less gender bias in the PMC where reference to women was more equal than in the BEC, with several lexical items related to women being key, e.g. *Mrs, ma'am* and *madam*.

Consistent with later research (Deroey, 2018), tangible, explicit lexis was also more heavily represented in the PMC in comparison to the BEC. For example, in the PMC, the key noun category of *things* consists of 95% tangible nouns, compared to 84% tangible nouns in the same category in the BEC, and there was an overrepresentation of a limited amount of job-related terminology, e.g. *manager, personnel, employee.*

A similar lack of accuracy in discourse patterns that was seen in later studies (Cheng & Warren, 2007) and was found in the PMC. For example, in textbook phone calls, direct questions were answered with direct questions, e.g. *Can you manage the 18th instead?*. In the real-life phone calls in the BEC, answers were less direct, e.g. *I just wondered how soon that one would be down? – Erm, well I would say, you know, that we've had to re-order stock so.* Unlike the PMC data, BEC language was full of hedging and hesitation devices: *erm, you know.* In contrast to PMC data, discourse in the BEC was also found not to be overly polite; for example, the seller says *just be patient,* and often checks understanding with phrases such as *OK, right* and *all right.* Several false starts and changes in mid-sentence can also be found, e.g. *Well we, I had an order.* These features were either completely missing or more limited in the PMC. See Nelson (2000) for a full description of these differences.

10.5 Future directions of research

In this chapter, we have seen examples of how the corpus data gained from evaluative studies of coursebooks can offer valuable insights into a wide variety of grammatical, lexical, and discourse-related issues. Despite increased usage of corpus data in coursebooks, notably the *In use* and *Touchstone* series by Cambridge University Press and others, evidence from the studies we have seen consistently demonstrates that there are still systematic and widespread misrepresentations of language in coursebooks that have not consulted corpus data.

The remaining gap between the research community and publishers should continue to be addressed. Römer (2006) has long called for change: she famously pointed to the need for "missionary work" in this regard "to spread the word among practitioners … to convince them that corpora can be of great use in their everyday work" (p. 128) and for an increase in comparative studies (Römer, 2008). It has been suggested that researchers may need to take things into their own hands and create their own research-led materials (Harwood, 2005).

Blueprints for the way forward do exist. McCarten (2010) made detailed suggestions on how corpus data could be included in textbook creation. Meunier and Reppen (2015) suggested the identification of certain key areas of grammar that would benefit from corpus-generated data being used in textbooks and help prioritise certain features. They mention specifically passive, conditional, and relative clauses as being prime candidates for this. They expanded this idea to include other linguistic areas and future research could focus at a meta-level on creating "checklists" of specific features of grammar, lexis and discourse that would improve textbook accuracy in pedagogical terms, rather than simply point out the discrepancies. This could be the next focus of research in order to create a clear pathway from corpus-derived data to adoption by publishers, resulting in the possibility of more accurate coursebook content and pedagogical design. Until this happens on a larger scale, we will still be waiting for Conrad's (2000) revolution.

Further reading

Burton, G. (2012). Corpora and coursebooks: Destined to be strangers forever? *Corpora,* 7(1), 91–108. This article explains publisher and author attitudes to corpus-based research and why corpus uptake has been slow.

Deroey, K. L. B. (2018). The representativeness of lecture listening coursebooks: Language, lecture authenticity, research-informedness. *Journal of English for Academic Purposes, 34,* 57–67. This article offers a model example of how to carry out corpus-based textbook research.

Meunier, F., & Gouverneur, C. (2009). New types of corpora for new educational challenges: Collecting, annotating and exploiting a corpus of textbook material. In K. Aijmer (Ed.), *Corpora and language teaching* (pp. 179–201). Benjamins. This article covers the history of coursebook analysis and shows how a coursebook corpus can be analysed.

References

Alavi, S., & Rajabpoor, A. (2015). Analyzing idioms and their frequency in three advanced ILI textbooks: A corpus-based study. *English Language Teaching, 8*(1), 170–179. https://doi.org/10.5539/elt.v8n1p170.

Becker, M. (2002). "Yf ye wyll bergayne wullen cloth or othir marchandise...". Bargaining in early modern language teaching textbooks. *Journal of Historical Pragmatics, 3*(2), 273–297. https://doi.org/10.1075/jhp.3.2.06bec.

Bi, J. (2020). How large a vocabulary do Chinese computer science undergraduates need to read English-medium specialist textbooks? *English for Specific Purposes, 58,* 77–89. https://doi.org/10.1016/j.esp.2020.01.001

Biber, D., & Reppen, R. (2002). What does frequency have to do with grammar teaching? *Studies in Second Language Acquisition, 24*(2), 199–208. https://doi.org/10.1017/S0272263102002048.

Biber, D., Conrad, S., & Cortes, V. (2004). Lexical bundles in speech and writing: An initial taxonomy. In A. Wilson, P. Rayson, & T. McEnery (Eds.), *Corpus linguistics by the Lune: A festschrift for Geoffery Leech* (pp. 71–92). Peter Lang.

Biber, D., Conrad, S., & Cortes, V. (2004). If you look at…: Lexical bundles in university teaching and textbooks. *Applied Linguistics, 25*(3), 371–405.

Bouhlal, F., Horst, M., & Martini, J. (2018). Modality in ESL textbooks: Insights from a contrastive corpus-based analysis. *Canadian Modern Language Review, 74*(2), 227–252. https://doi.org/10.3138/cmlr.3075.

Burton, G. (2012). Corpora and coursebooks: Destined to be strangers forever? *Corpora, 7*(1), 91–108. https://doi.org/10.3366/cor.2012.0019.

Chen, L. (2008). An investigation of lexical bundles in Electrical Engineering introductory textbooks and ESP text. [Unpublished Master's Thesis]. Carlton University. Ottawa, Canada.

Chen, A. C. H. (2016). A critical evaluation of text difficulty development in ELT textbook series: A corpus-based approach using variability neighbor clustering. *System, 58,* 64–81. https://doi.org/10.1016/j.system.2016.03.011

Cheng, W., & Warren, M. (2007). Checking understandings: Comparing textbooks and a corpus of spoken English in hong Kong. *Language Awareness, 16*(3), 190–207. https://doi.org/10.2167/la455.0.

Conrad, S. (2000). Will corpus linguistics revolutionize grammar teaching in the 21st century? *TESOL Quarterly, 34*(3), 548–560. https://doi.org/10.2307/3587743.

Coxhead, A. (2000). A new academic wordlist. *TESOL Quarterly, 34*(2), 213–238. https://doi.org/10.2307/3587951.

Coxhead, A., Yen Dang, T. N., & Mukai, S. (2017). Single and multi-word unit vocabulary in university tutorials and laboratories: Evidence from corpora and textbooks. *Journal of English for Academic Purposes, 30,* 66–78. https://doi.org/10.1016/j.jeap.2017.11.001

Deroey, K. L. B. (2018). The representativeness of lecture listening coursebooks: Language, lecture authenticity, research-informedness. *Journal of English for Academic Purposes, 34,* 57–67. https://doi.org/10.1016/j.jeap.2018.03.011

Flowerdew, L. (2019). Using corpora for writing instruction. In A. O'Keefe & M. McCarthy (Eds.), *The Routledge handbook of corpus linguistics* (pp. 444–470). Routledge.

Gabrielatos, C. (2006). Corpus-based evaluation of pedagogical materials: If-conditionals in ELT coursebooks and the BNC. *Paper Presented at the 7th Teaching and Language Corpora Conference Paris France 14 July 2006,* (pp. 1–4). http://eprints.lancs.ac.uk/882/

Gardner, D., & Davies (2014). A new academic vocabulary list. *Applied Linguistics, 35*(3), 305–337. https://doi.org/10.1093/applin/amt015.

Garton, S., & Graves, K. (2014). Materials in ELT: Current issues. In S. Garton & K. Graves (Eds.), *International perspectives on materials in ELT. International perspectives on English language teaching* (pp. 1–15). Palgrave Macmillan. https://doi.org/10.1057/9781137023315_1

Gilmore, A. (2007). Authentic materials and authenticity in foreign language learning. *Language Teaching, 40*(2), 97–118. https://doi.org/10.1017/S0261444807004144.

Gilmore, A. (2015). Research into practice: The influence of discourse studies on language descriptions and task design in published ELT materials. *Language Teaching, 48*(4), 506–530. https://doi.org/10.1017/S0261444815000269.

Godoy De La Rosa, W. A. (2014). Differences between ELT textbooks and English language corpora: A quick look into the Chilean context. *The Language Education and Culture Journal, 1*(1), 1–8.

Granger, S. (2013). The passive in learner English. Corpus insights and implications for pedagogical grammar. In S. Ishikawa (Ed.), *Learner corpus studies in asia and the world* (pp. 5–15). School of Languages and Communication, Kobe University.

Hajiyeva, K. (2015). A corpus-based lexical analysis of subject-specific university textbooks for English majors. *Ampersand, 2*, 136–144. https://doi.org/10.1016/j.amper.2015.10.001

Harwood, N. (2005). What do we want EAP teaching materials for. *Journal of English for Academic Purposes, 4*(2), 149–161. https://doi.org/10.1016/j.jeap.2004.07.008.

Hirsh, D., & Nation, P. (1992). What vocabulary size is needed to read unsimplified texts for pleasure. *Reading in a Foreign Language, 8*(2), 689–696.

Hsu, W. (2011). The vocabulary thresholds of business textbooks and business research articles for EFL learners. *English for Specific Purposes, 30*(4), 247–257. https://doi.org/10.1016/j.esp.2011.04.005.

Hsu, W. (2014). Measuring the vocabulary load of engineering textbooks for EFL undergraduates. *English for Specific Purposes, 33*(1), 54–65. https://doi.org/10.1016/j.esp.2013.07.001.

Hsu, W. (2018). The most frequent BNC/COCA mid- and low-frequency word families in English-medium traditional Chinese medicine (TCM) textbooks. *English for Specific Purposes, 51*, 98–110. https://doi.org/10.1016/j.esp.2018.04.001

Jahan, K., Mahmood, M., & Azhar, W. (2019). Lexical analysis of intermediate coursebooks: A corpus-based study. *International Journal of Educational Science, 24*(1), 13–22. https://doi.org/10.31901/24566322.2019/24.1-3.1071.

Kennedy, G. (2003). Amplifier collocations in the British National corpus: Implications for English language teaching. *TESOL Quarterly, 37*(3), 467–487. https://doi.org/10.2307/3588400.

Lam, P. W. Y. (2010). Discourse particles in corpus data and textbooks: The case of well. *Applied Linguistics, 31*(2), 260–281. https://doi.org/10.1093/applin/amp026.

Lee, J. (2006). Subjunctive were and indicative was: A corpus analysis for English language teachers and textbook writers. *Language Teaching Research, 10*(1), 80–93. https://doi.org/10.1191/1362168806lr185oa.

Le Foll, E. (in press). "I'm putting some salt in my sandwich." The use of the progressive in EFL textbook conversation. In S. Flach & M. Hilpert (Eds.), *Broadening the spectrum of corpus linguistics: New approaches to variability and change.* Benjamins.

Ljung, M. (1990). *A study of TEFL vocabulary.* Almqvist and Wiksell International.

McCarten, J. (2010). Corpus-informed course book design. In A. O'Keefe & M. McCarthy (Eds.), *The Routledge handbook of corpus linguistics* (pp. 413–427). Routledge.

McEnery, T., & Xiao, R. (2010). What corpora can offer in language teaching and learning. In E. Hinkel (Ed.), *Handbook of research in second language teaching and learning* (pp. 364–380). Routledge. https://doi.org/10.4324/9780203836507

Meunier, F., & Gouverneur, C. (2009). New types of corpora for new educational challenges: Collecting, annotating and exploiting a corpus of textbook material. In K. Aijmer (Ed.), *Corpora and language teaching* (pp. 179–201). Benjamins. https://doi.org/10.1075/scl.33.16meu

Meunier, F., & Reppen, R. (2015). Corpus versus non-corpus-informed pedagogical materials: Grammar as the focus. In D. Biber & R. Reppen (Eds.), *The Cambridge handbook of English corpus linguistics* (pp. 498–514). Cambridge University Press. https://doi.org/10.1017/CBO9781139764377

Miller, D. (2011). ESL reading textbooks vs. university textbooks: Are we giving our students the input they may need? *Journal of English for Academic Purposes, 10*(1), 32–46. https://doi.org/10.1016/j.jeap.2010.12.002.

Nation, P., & Waring, R. (1997). Vocabulary size, text coverage and word lists. In N. Schmitt & M. McCarthy (Eds.), *Vocabulary: Description, acquisition, and pedagogy* (pp. 6–19). Cambridge University Press.

Nelson, M. (2000). *A Corpus-Based Study of Business English and Business English Teaching Materials.* [Unpublished PhD Thesis]. University of Manchester.

Nelson, M. (2010). Building a written corpus: What are the basics? In A. O'Keefe & M. McCarthy (Eds.), *The Routledge handbook of corpus linguistics* (pp. 53–65). Routledge.

Nordberg, C., & Nordlund, M. (2018). A corpus-based study of lexis in L2 English textbooks. *Journal of Language Teaching and Research, 9*(3), 463. https://doi.org/10.17507/jltr.0903.03.

O'Keefe, A., & McCarthy, M. (Eds.) (2010). *The Routledge handbook of corpus linguistics.* Routledge.

Parizoska, J., & Rajh, I. (2017). Idiom variation in business English textbooks: A corpus-based study. *ESP Today, 5*(1), 46–67. https://doi.org/10.18485/esptoday.2017.5.1.3.

Peksoy, E., & Harmaoglu, O. (2017). Corpus based authenticity analysis of language teaching coursebooks. *International Journal of Languages' Education, 5*(4), 287–230. https://doi.org/10.18298/ijlet.2324.

Philip, A., Mukundan, J., & Nimehchisalem, V. (2012). Conjunctions in Malaysian secondary school English language textbooks. *International Journal of Applied Linguistics and English Literature, 1*(1), 1–1. https://doi.org/10.7575/ijalel.v.1n.1p.1.

Römer, U. (2004). Textbooks: A corpus-driven approach to modal auxiliaries and their didactics. In J.M. Sinclair (Ed.), *How to use corpora in language teaching* (pp. 185–199). Benjamins. https://doi.org/10.1075/scl.12

Römer, U. (2005). *Progressives, patterns, pedagogy: A corpus-driven approach to English progressive forms, functions, contexts and didactics.* Benjamins.

Römer, U. (2006). Pedagogical applications of corpora: Some reflections on the current scope and a wish list for future developments. *Zeitschrift Fur Anglistik Und Amerikanistik, 54*(2), 121–134. https://doi.org/10.1515/zaa-2006-0204.

Römer, U. (2008). Corpora and language teaching. In A. Lüdeling & M. Kytö (Eds.), *Corpus linguistics. An international handbook* (pp. 112–131). Mouton de Gruyter.

Scott, M. (1997). *Wordsmith Tools.* (Version 3.0) [Computer software]. Lexical analysis software. https://lexically.net/wordsmith/

Shortall, T. (2007). The L2 syllabus: Corpus or contrivance? *Corpora, 2*(2), 157–185.

Skorczynska Sznajder, H. (2010). A corpus-based evaluation of metaphors in a business English textbook. *English for Specific Purposes, 29*(1), 30–42. https://doi.org/10.1016/j.esp.2009.05.003.

Stubbs, J. (1993). British traditions in text analysis: From Firth to Sinclair. In M. Baker, G. Francis, & E. Tognini-Bonelli (Eds.), *Text and technology. In honour of John Sinclair* (pp. 1–36). Benjamins. https://doi.org/10.1075/z.64

Tai, T. Y. (2016). A corpus-based analysis of discourse markers in curriculum-based English textbooks and the English entrance exam in Taiwan. *The Journal of Asia TEFL, 13*(4), 297–346. http://dx.doi.org/10.18823/asiatefl.2016.13.4.2.262.

Thiruchelvam, S., Jin, N. Y., Tong, C. S., Ghazali, A., & Husin, N. B. M. (2018). The language of civil engineering: Corpus-based studies on vocational school textbooks in Malaysia. *International Journal of Engineering and Technology (UAE), 7*(4), 844–847. https://doi.org/10.14419/ijet.v7i4.35.23119.

Timmis, I. (2015). *Corpus linguistics for ELT: Research and practice.* Routledge. https://doi.org/10.4324/9781315715537

Tomlinson, B. (2012). Materials development for language learning and teaching. *Language Teaching, 45*(2), 143–179. https://doi.org/10.1017/S0261444811000528.

Tomlinson, B. (Ed.). (2013). *Developing materials for language teaching.* Bloomsbury.

Widdowson, H. G. (1998). Context, community, and authentic language. *TESOL Quarterly, 32*(4), 705–716. https://doi.org/10.2307/3588001.

Wood, D. C., & Appel, R. (2014). Multiword constructions in first year business and engineering university textbooks and EAP textbooks. *Journal of English for Academic Purposes, 15*, 1–13. https://doi.org/10.1016/j.jeap.2014.03.002

11

ENGLISH AS A LINGUA FRANCA CORPORA AND ENGLISH LANGUAGE TEACHING

Xue Wu and Lei Lei

11.1 Introduction

Although English as a Lingua Franca (ELF) as a phenomenon has existed for centuries, the teaching of ELF and ELF as a line of research have attracted researchers' attention from recent decades (Harrington & Roche, 2014; Jenkins, 2006a; Jenkins *et al.*, 2011). ELF is defined as "any use of English among speakers of different first languages for whom English is the communicative medium of choice, and often the only option" (Seidlhofer, 2011, p. 7). The main role of ELF is to facilitate cross-cultural communications in a globalized world. In this regard, ELF is different from English as a Foreign Language (EFL) which is used in a pedagogical situation that adheres to the traditional native-speaker-based English language teaching paradigm. Therefore, a typical difference between ELF and EFL is that the native norm is valued in EFL paradigm, while no specific norm is followed in the ELF paradigm.

The ELF paradigm might be more suitable for English language teaching than the EFL paradigm for three reasons. First, most English learners are non-native English speakers and they learn English to carry out effective communication with other English users who may not be native English speakers as well. In other words, communicative effectiveness rather than native norms should be prioritized in English language teaching (Canagarajah, 2014; Dewey, 2012; McKay, 2018). Second, against the backdrop of multilingualism, most English learners are bilingual or multilingual speakers whose English proficiency might approach but never reach the level of native English speakers. That is, those bilingual or multilingual speakers could make creative use of their language repertoire to achieve communicative success. In this case, the non-native English language use by English learners cannot be treated merely as negative transfer. Third, the ELF paradigm advocates usage-based language learning and emphasizes the influence of contextual factors such as genre and register which have been overlooked in language drills in the EFL paradigm.

In a word, monolingual models seem to be inadequate in the teaching of English for learners who are not native English speakers, and teaching English from an ELF perspective may serve as an alternative to replacing the widespread reliance on monolingual norms (Ortega & Carson, 2010). This chapter, therefore, attempts to shed light on the teaching of English from an ELF perspective by reviewing the corpus-based studies of English as a Lingua Franca in Academic Settings (ELFA).

DOI: 10.4324/9781003002901-13

11.2 Review of current state of research

Earlier studies suggested conceptual frameworks for ELF research, and many served as guidelines for follow-up studies. Hullen (1982), for example, first identified and reported the phenomenon of ELF. Many others (e.g. Firth, 1996; Jenkins, 1998), on the other hand, examined the phenomenon using various approaches such as conversation analysis or an intelligibility-based approach. More recently, two seminal works have caught the attention of researchers in both applied linguistics and English language instruction. One was Jenkin's (2000) investigation of the pronunciation features by ELF users. In her article, Jenkins (2000) identified some formal and functional features in ELF and argued that native English pronunciation was not optimum in ELF communication contexts based on the examined features because native speakers' pronunciation is not the most intelligible model to adopt. The other was Seidlhofer (2001) who developed the first ELF corpus, the Vienna-Oxford International Corpus of English (VOICE). Seidlhofer argued that more empirical studies were needed to describe the linguistic features of ELF for a better understanding of "speakers of lingua franca English as language users in their own right" (2001, p. 137) and for a reconsideration of native English norms as the only valid target for learners. The two works mentioned above are important to ELF research in three aspects. First, they have demonstrated the approaches to ELF studies. Second, the first ELF corpus was introduced, which is significant to subsequent ELF studies, particularly their focus on language in use. Last, they have challenged the use of native English norms as the only valid target for learners, which has consequences for the teaching of English.

More recently, a large amount of corpus-based research has been conducted to describe ELF in a comprehensive way. Those studies are roughly categorized into three types. The first type of research deals with the compilation of ELF corpora. For instance, Mauranen et al. (2003) launched the corpus of English as a Lingua Franca in Academic Settings (ELFA), and Kirkpatrick et al. (2010) developed the Asian Corpus of English (ACE). The second type of research includes empirical studies that contribute to a detailed description of the formal and functional features of ELF. For example, Mauranen (2009) analyzed recurrent patterning discernible in corpus data from ELF communications and argued that some unconventional phrases in ELF communication should be treated as emergent patterns rather than random errors. The third type focuses on the implication of ELF for English language teaching. For example, Seidlhofer (2004) identified salient features of ELF lexicogrammar in VOICE and suggested that it was not necessary to spend much time on correcting some typical "errors" in English lessons since they appeared to be unproblematic to communicative success.

The ELF research is highly situation-based due to its focus on the English language in use. That is, the use of ELF may vary in different situations. Based on previous studies in the area, this chapter aims to describe the language features in ELFA and its implications for English language teaching. It should be noted that spoken ELF in academic settings is also a relevant aspect, but the present chapter focuses on written ELFA.

11.3 Core issues and topics of ELF in academic writing

Against the backdrop of globalization, there is an active transmission of international knowledge and an upsurge of mobility in academia; therefore, English has been widely used as a lingua franca for academic purposes. Much research has been conducted to investigate the use of ELF in academic spoken discourse (Jenkins, 2011; Kecskes & Kirner-Ludwig, 2019), while research on ELF in academic written discourse is relatively rare. One possible reason could be that lexical and syntactic features in written discourse may be less noticeable indications of the English language users' identity than pronunciation in spoken discourse. Another reason might be that there is much more chance for language contact in spoken discourse. However, it should be noted that there is a steady growth in research interest on the theme of ELF academic writing since most scholars in academic publication are ELF users, especially those from countries where English has no official status but is widely used (Ingvarsdóttir & Arnbjörnsdóttir, 2013).

One of the core issues and topics of ELF in academic writing is ELF in academic publishing. As a widely used measure of academic performance, publishing in international journals is important for scholars around the world (Hyland, 2015). In the process of academic publishing, not only the authors but also the editors, reviewers, and readers might be ELF users. That is, academic writing is for an international rather than an English as a native language (ENL) community (Wu *et al.*, 2020). Therefore, exploring the use of ELF in academic publishing may shed light on intriguing questions such as what is distinctive about ELF. Previous studies in English academic writing focused either on native speakers of English or on comparisons between native English speakers and L2 learners (e.g. Casal & Lee, 2019; Martínez, 2005). With the explicit or implicit point of departure that any differences between native and non-native use of English indicate that speakers of other first languages have a problem and should be taught to adopt the ways of ENL writers. Therefore, there is a clear need to describe ELF use in ELF academic writing in its own right (Ingvarsdóttir & Arnbjörnsdóttir, 2013). More importantly, an ELF perspective can mitigate the effect of linguistic injustice which has been a concern in an increasing body of literature (e.g. Flowerdew, 1999; Hyland, 2016; Politzer-Ahles *et al.*, 2016).

Another core issue and frequently discussed topic of ELF in academic writing is the influence of genre and register. The concept of genre provides a socially informed theory to analyze the use of language in different contexts with different internal structures (Hyland, 2002). In the WrELFA (2015) corpus, genres such as academic research blogs, examiners' statements for PhD defenses, and unpublished research articles are included, which makes it convenient to describe ELF use in different text types. With a focus on the features of online ELF in academic research blogs, Luzon (2018) found that it was more important to get the meaning across than linguistic correctness in online ELF academic writing. As for the influence of register, Carey (2013) found that frequency effects were connected to the distribution of approximated chunks both in written and spoken ELFA.

Evolutionary change of language forms is also a core issue of ELF in academic writing. Biber and Gray (2016) have analyzed the historical evolution of phrasal discourse styles in academic writing, which indicates that language evolution might be the result of language contact by people with diverse linguistic and cultural backgrounds. With a focus on the evolution processes of conventional rhetorical structure used for abstracts in academic writing, Lorés-Sanz (2016) suggested that the old forms of English had been reshaped by non-Anglophone writers into new forms in innovative and creative ways. In this way, ELF writers are reshaping academic English and attempt to give expression to their own "hybrid voices" (Mauranen, 2007).

It can be summarized that the core of ELF in academic writing is that the presence and influence of non-native English writers should not be ignored. In addition, academic English reshaped by those non-native English writers is worthy of investigation in its own right.

11.4 Current contributions

Based on a large amount of language data, the use of corpora and the use of corpus analysis techniques in linguistics have made it possible to describe the salient features of language use in a specific context. For instance, with the compilation of large corpora such as the British National Corpus (BNC) and the Corpus of Contemporary American English (COCA) corpus analysis has given a good account of itself in describing the features of both learners' and native speakers' English features (Chang, 2009; Davies, 2013; Laufer & Waldman, 2011; Mur-Dueñas, 2017). In a similar vein, a few ELF corpus projects have also been launched for a legitimate description of ELF features. For instance, the Vienna-Oxford International Corpus of English (VOICE) was compiled to provide an empirical basis for a full description of spoken ELF. Another example is the development of the Corpus of English as a Lingua Franca in Academic Settings (ELFA) and the Corpus of Written English as a Lingua Franca in Academic Settings (WrELFA), both of which contribute to the use of English language in international academia. Compared to previous corpora of learner language, ELF corpora were designed to highlight the communicative role of English language rather than the "errors" or "mistakes" that learners make in the process of English language learning. Therefore, this chapter reviews corpus-based studies to summarize the communicative roles realized by lexical and syntactic features in ELFA writing.

11.4.1 Lexical features of ELFA writing

As the fundamental aspect of language, lexis in ELFA has been well investigated, especially in spoken discourse. For instance, by examining lexical features in terms of frequency and approximations of form and meaning, Mauranen (2012) found that there was a tendency to lexical simplification and variation in form and meaning in ELFA spoken interactions:

> The first corpus-based analyses indicated that ELF shows lexical simplification in similar manifestations to those observed in learner language and translations: the most frequent items tend to be even more frequent.... A major lexical process was approximation, which stemmed from connections between forms or meanings, and seemed to be a success strategy in most cases. Participants were apparently able to make sense of each other's approximations to target items, most likely because the mechanisms are shared, and the outcomes therefore comprehensible. (Mauranen, 2012, pp. 116–117)

Lexical simplification and approximation reflect the features of linguistic deviation from standard or native English norms in ELFA spoken discourse. Those features are acceptable in ELFA spoken discourse since they are motivated by the aim of attaining mutual intelligibility or achieving communicative effectiveness among interlocutors from diverse linguistic and cultural backgrounds (Smith, 2015).

Similar to spoken discourse, ELFA writing also contains a high degree of lexical variation from native English norms. Table 11.1 shows lexical features in ELFA written discourse examined by previous studies.

As is shown in Table 11.1, the corpus data used in most studies are drawn from published research articles while few from unpublished research articles or informal academic research blogs. The difference in text types leads to the different findings concerning lexical features in ELFA written discourse. For instance, Martinez (2018) found that the use of some lexical items (e.g. besides, works, in this context) in ELF and ENL research articles was different in terms of frequency, while Luzon (2018), with a focus on informal ELFA research blogs, found that the non-standard or "creative" use of lexical items (e.g. approximations of conventional English words) was quite common. It should be noted that the non-standard use of lexical forms also existed in published research articles. For instance, Rozycki and Johnson (2013)

Table 11.1 Lexical features examined in ELFA written discourse

Study	Text type	Lexical features
Lorés-Sanz (2016)	Published research articles	Simplification
Tribble (2017)	Published research articles	Non-canonical use
Rozycki and Johnson (2013)	Published research articles	Non-canonical use
Mur-Dueñas (2017)	Published research articles	Modal hedging verbs
Martinez (2018)	Published research articles	Non-native English forms
Carey (2013)	Unpublished research articles	Organizing chunks
Mauranen (Feb. 24th 2016)	Unpublished research articles	Non-canonical use
Shchemeleva (2019)	Unpublished research articles	Clusters
Luzon (2018)	Academic research blogs	Non-canonical use

detected non-standard lexical forms such as non-canonical article use, subject-verb discord, and transitive verbs used without object in published research articles by Best Paper award winners. It should be noted that the goal of advocating ELF academic writing is not to legitimize grammatical "errors", but to achieve communicative success. In other words, content is prioritized to linguistic correctness in ELFA writing.

Based on these studies, ELFA writing is featured in non-conventional use of lexical forms and accommodation to conventions in English academic writing. Non-conventional use of lexical forms and accommodation to conventions in English academic writing are discussed below.

11.4.1.1 Non-conventional use of lexical forms

The existence of non-standard or non-conventional use of lexical forms is a common feature in ELFA writing regardless of register differences. One situation where this feature appears is in the process of regularization, especially regularization of morphology, such as regularization of verbal forms by analogy with regular verbs or regularization of comparative forms. Another situation is in the process of word approximation. That is, creating a new word with recognizable features to its conventional form. Categories and examples of non-conventional use of lexical forms in ELFA writing are presented in Table 11.2.

These lexical features in ELFA writing show that ELF scholars use English language flexibly to eliminate ambiguity in written discourse. For instance, the change of word class may facilitate the readers' understanding of ELFA data (although in research articles, they will probably be corrected by reviewers and editors before publication). Since ELF users are not native English speakers, these non-conventional lexical items may be a result of exploitation of the potentialities available in their English language repertoire (Luzon, 2018; Seidlhofer, 2011). This flexible use of lexical items also indicates that ELF scholars emphasize semantic meaning rather than morphological form in ELF written interactions (Luzon, 2018).

11.4.1.2 Accommodation to conventions in English academic writing

The second lexical feature of ELFA writing is accommodation to conventions in ELFA writing. Similar to the occurrences of non-conventional lexical forms, there are also situations where the uses of the lexical patterns vary from conventional ones. For instance, Mur-Dueñas (2017) found that lexical patterns of some hedging modal verbs in research articles by

Table 11.2 Category and examples of non-conventional use of lexical forms in ELFA writing (based on Luzon, 2018 and Rozycki & Johnson, 2013)

Category	Examples
Regularization of morphology	
1 Zero third person singular marking in present tense verbs	*Technique which <u>preserve</u> the enhanced properties*
2 Regularization of verbal forms by analogy with regular verbs	*The images are <u>showed</u> in Figure 5*
3 Regularization of comparative forms	*Require <u>less resources</u> than …*
4 Regularization in the use of relatives	*The project <u>that</u> aims to support farmers…*
5 Elimination of prepositions	*<u>Apply our</u> Erasmus Mundus master*
Change of word class	
1 Noun to adjective	*Highly <u>pollutant</u> processes*
2 Adjective to noun	*One of the <u>keynotes</u> dropped*
3 Adjective to adverb	*<u>Likely</u>, other colleagues may …*
4 Adverb to adjective	*A <u>nowadays</u> example*
5 Adverb to conjunction	*The differences of the loading were attributed to higher specific surface (…), <u>meanwhile</u> the effect of the presence of ethanol…*
6 Preposition to conjunction	*Reducing the high levels of pollution <u>due to</u> hydrogen only produces water as hyproduct*
7 Preposition to adverb	*We finished the paper <u>after</u>, of course.*
8 Verb to noun	*…method presents <u>an effective converge</u> to a desired solution*
Morphological Approximation of conventional English words	*Repellent and <u>antifeedent</u> effects; A conference gathering <u>attendants</u> from around the world;*
Article deletion/insertion	*…obtained <u>for traditional</u> balanced truncation method; as described <u>in the Section II</u>…*

ELF users were different from those by native English speakers. Table 11.3 is a summary of different lexical patterns of some hedging modal verbs in ELF and ENL research articles based on Mur-Dueñas (2017).

However, most lexical items and patterns follow conventional usage (including form, frequency, and function) in ELFA writing. For instance, Mauranen (2016) found that ELFA authors preferred to use the most frequent lexis in their research articles, and Mur-Dueñas (2017) found that the use of hedging modal verbs in ELF and ENL business management research articles was similar in terms of frequency. Shchemeleva (2019) also found that there were many similarities in the distribution and functions of epistemic stance (ES) clusters in different sections of ELF academic research articles. These research findings may be of interest to researchers since lexical items such as hedging modal verbs are used differently in

Table 11.3 Different lexical patterns of some hedging modal verbs in ELF and ENL research articles (summarized by Mur-Dueñas, 2017, p. 168)

Patterns	ELF	ENL
Statement of implications (in a *that-* clause)		*may*
Attended and unattended *this/these* +hedging modal verb	*may-can-would-could-might*	*may-would*
Hedging modal verb+ *be* +adverb +adjective	*may*	*may-would*
Anticipatory *it*-pattern with a discourse verb	*may-could-can*	
Anticipatory *it*-pattern with an attitudinal adjective	*would*	

research articles across ELF users of a wide range of language backgrounds (Vold, 2006). It seems that factors such as different cultural and linguistic backgrounds of the ELF users may not affect their use of most lexical items (either in terms of frequency or function). In other words, ELFA writings, particularly research articles, seem homogeneous in lexical features. As Shchemeleva (2019) correctly argued, ELF scholars adapt their academic written outcomes to the conventions of academic writing probably due to the genre and disciplinary restrictions:

> Here, it must be noted that the functions performed by clusters of ES expressions in the texts are not different from the functions described in previous research on academic texts in English. This might be considered as further proof of the fact that L2 speakers, irrespective of their L1, create their texts in accordance with the genre and disciplinary conventions: they do the same things as everyone else in their field. (Shchemeleva, 2019, p. 39)

11.4.2 Syntactic features of ELFA writing

Previous studies have investigated the syntactic features in ELF communication. For instance, Kecskes and Kirner-Ludwig (2019) found that there were "odd structures" in ELF spoken discourse which may result in contradictory information. In ELFA written discourse, such characterized use of certain syntactic structures might result from long-term language contact with the influence of two parameters: time and language users (Pitzl, 2016). For instance, by tracking a four-century historical development of nominal structures in academic research writing, Biber and Gray (2016) found that the use of nominal structures was restricted in function and variability in the eighteenth century but became more frequent and productive in the nineteenth and twentieth centuries. One possible reason might be that English in academic writing has been reshaped by language users with different cultural and linguistic backgrounds as international knowledge transmission and collaboration across nations have been intensified since the nineteenth century.

A few studies have been conducted to describe syntactic features of academic writing (Larsson & Kaatari, 2020; Mazgutova & Kormos, 2015; Ruan, 2018), yet most of these studies focus on the description of syntactic features in English learners' or ESL/EFL speakers' academic written outcomes. For instance, Larsson and Kaatari (2020) investigated syntactic complexity in expert and learner academic prose, and Ruan (2018) compared the use of structure compression in research article abstracts by English native and Chinese EFL authors. With a focus on ELF academic writing, our description of syntactic features (particularly syntactic complexity features) in this part is mainly based on Wu *et al.* (2020).

11.4.2.1 Frequent occurrence of long sentences elaborated at a phrasal level

Compared to the impromptu nature of academic speech, academic writing leaves more time yet less space for the authors to choose the words and compose the sentences. That is, authors need to convey their scientific enquiry and academic propositions with a limited space in written discourse. In such a context, the use of long sentences might be a reasonable solution since expanded syntactic structures could be used for densified information packaging. This has been evidenced in Wu *et al.* (2020) reporting that the mean lengths of sentences and clauses in ELF research articles were significantly longer than those in native English ones. They further examined the structures and patterns in long sentences and found that embedding

Table 11.4 Features of syntactic structures/patterns in long sentences of ELF research articles (based on Wu et al., 2020)

Category	Syntactic structures/patterns
Coordinate phrases	Coordinate adjectives
	Coordinate nouns
Complex nominals	Noun + adjective phrase /possessive phrase /prepositional phrase /adjective clause /participle /appositive
	Nominal clause
	A gerund /infinitive in subject position

at the phrasal level rather than at the clausal level accounts to produce longer sentences in ELF research articles. The features of syntactic structures/patterns in longer sentences of ELF research articles based on Wu *et al.* (2020) are presented in Table 11.4.

As shown in Table 11.4, phrasal structures are characterized in longer sentences in ELF research journals. Since phrases are less complex than clauses in terms of the number of elements, they may carry similar amount of information to clauses with fewer words. In other words, the frequent use of phrasal structures in longer sentences may be motivated by the requirements of academic writing to improve efficiency of communication but maintain the economy of expression at the same time.

Earlier studies also found that embedding at the clausal level contributed to the elaborated structures in academic writing (Brown & Yule, 1983; O'Donnell, 1974). However, recent studies argued that longer sentences in academic writing were embedded with phrasal structures such as complex nominal and verb phrases (Biber & Gray, 2010; Deng *et al.*, 2020; Halliday & Martin, 2003). One possible reason is that with more ELF scholars participated, English for academic writing has been reshaped. This finding is consistent with Croft's (2000) argument that expansion into the new linguistic niche in academic written discourse resulted in more complex syntactic structures rather than completely new ones.

11.4.2.2 Enhanced clarity through coordinate phrases with similar meanings

The second syntactic feature of ELF academic writing is the use of coordinate phrases with similar meanings. In ELF communications, the participants of different language and cultural backgrounds may employ various but similar strategies to arrive at a shared understanding. For instance, self-repetition has been used in ELF conversations in academic settings to enhance the clarity of expression (Kaur, 2012). Since academic writing is much more formal in style, ELF authors choose to use coordinate phrases with similar meanings to achieve similar effect as that of self-repetition in spoken discourse. For instance, coordinate adjectives could be used to provide additional information to clarify the quality of the nouns or noun phrases (e.g. environmental and legal scientists). The featured syntactic patterns with coordination phrases in ELF research articles are summarized in Table 11.5.

As shown in Table 11.5, coordinate phrases, especially coordinate adjectives and coordinate nouns, characterize ELF research articles. These coordinate phrases contain words with similar meanings, which provide more information to help enhance clarity in ELF written discourse. It should be noted that the featured use of coordinate phrases may vary across disciplines. For instance, ELF scholars in social sciences and humanities use more coordinate adjectives with similar meaning to modify nouns or noun phrases than scholars in natural science (Wu *et al.*, 2020).

Table 11.5 Featured syntactic patterns with coordination phrases in ELF research articles

Syntactic patterns with Coordination phrases	Examples
Coordinate adjectives + noun/noun phrase	<u>secular and societal</u> missions; the <u>dominant and directive</u> role of government; <u>the emotional, spiritual or moral</u> lives
Coordinate nouns or noun phrases	<u>Self-esteem, perceived health, weight satisfaction, eating habits, physical activity, friendships, intimate relationships, smoking and substance use habits</u> can be regarded as ...

11.4.2.3 Explicitness through noun postmodifiers in complex nominals

The third syntactic feature in ELF academic writing is the use of noun postmodifiers in complex nominals (Wu *et al.*, 2020). There are different patterns of complex nominals in English writing, such as noun plus adjective, possessive, and prepositional phrase (Lu, 2011). With a detailed description of the context, a complex nominal may give the readers a more complete sense about an item than a single noun. For this reason, many complex nominals have been employed in ELF academic writings to convey more information to the readers. Among those different patterns of complex nominals, the structure noun + postmodifiers is the most frequently used one by ELF authors. Compared to other syntactic structures of complex nominals, noun +postmodifiers not only provides detailed information about the item described, but also helps raise explicitness thus prevent misunderstanding in academic written communications. For instance, the complex nominal oil from corn is more explicit in meaning than corn oil since the postmodifying prepositional phrases in the former have explicitly described the source of the oil, while the premodifying noun in the latter may blur the nature of the oil.

It should be noted that many other devices have been employed to achieve an explicit description in academic written discourse, such as the use of clauses. However, for economy purposes in expression, ELF authors prefer to use complex nominals with postmodifiers since this syntactic structure is more compressed than clauses and more explicit in meaning than noun/adjective premodifiers. For example, in Table 11.6, we changed a complex nominal (underlined) from SciELF corpus in WrELFA into different syntactic patterns. It seems that complex nominals postmodified by multilayered prepositional phrases convey similar amount of information with fewer words in comparison to those postmodified by clauses (italicized) and they may also be more explicit in meaning relations than those with multiple premodifiers (in bold).

Table 11.6 Different syntactic patterns used in complex nominals

Syntactic patterns	Examples
Complex nominal postmodified by multilayered prepositional	<u>fitness of organisms in an original habitat without natural enemies</u>
Complex nominal postmodified by clauses	fitness *that belongs to organisms* in an original habitat *where there are no natural enemies*
Complex nominal with multiple premodifiers	**organisms'** fitness in **an enemy-free original** habitat

11.4.3 Implications for English academic writing teaching

The accommodation to conventional use of lexical patterns and the frequent use of complex nominals by ELF authors may indicate that native norms are still valued in formal contexts such as English academic writing. Although native conventions may not be taken as the only appropriate norms in ELF use, they still exert norming effect in ELF communications (Prodromou, 2007). In this scenario, it seems that native norms should be placed in English academic writing syllabus. However, it would be prudent to apply native-like language as the only norm to the teaching of ELF academic writing. For one thing, ELF authors may not be that proficient in the English language. For another, their agency as a community in international academia might be belied. Under this circumstance, there seems an urgent need to set explicit norms for ELF academic writing. Since ELF is an emerging use of English, the ELF norms might contain the well-accepted or frequently occurring lexical and syntactic items from native English. That is, native norms are not the only or absolute standard but one of the norms in ELF use. Therefore, a more compatible syllabus is needed in guiding pedagogical practices in ELF academic writing. For instance, creative lexical items and "odd" structures which are intelligible and eligible should be allowed.

The second implication of the lexical and syntactic features in ELF for teaching English academic writing is a shift from a focus on teaching form to a focus on teaching meaning. Creative usage of English language from native norms is common in ELF communications, in either spoken or written discourse. Traditional theories of English language teaching treat those non-native lexical or syntactic forms as "errors", "odd structures", or interlanguage (Corder, 1981). However, creative use of lexical and syntactic forms indicates that for multilingual or at least bilingual ELF users, different languages coexist and constantly interact with each other (e.g. the language practice of translanguaging) (Mauranen, 2012; Li, 2018). Frequent language contact and bilingual/multilingual processing will probably lead to creative use of language such as lexical simplification and iterated long sentences. It is interesting to find that the creative use of language in ELF communications seldom causes misunderstanding, but may help ELF users achieve mutual understanding (e.g. lexical variations from regularization and simplification). The creative use of lexical and syntactic items in ELF academic writings shows that ELF authors exploit their English language repertoire to convey their content, their scientific enquiry, and academic propositions to their readers. That is, the function part of language is prior to the form one in ELF writing. Therefore, a shift of teaching focus from form to meaning should be considered in the case of teaching academic writing from an ELF perspective.

The last implication is that disciplinary difference should be emphasized when applying genre approaches in ELF academic English writing. Genre analysis reveals that authors from different disciplines follow different genre conventions (Hyland, 2008). The differences in frequency distribution of syntactic structures in research articles across social sciences and natural science showcase that ELF authors from different disciplines may value different kinds of argument. Moreover, since academic written communications can be carried out in contexts with different levels of formality, the instruction of ELF academic writing may also include the lexical and syntactic features in different situations. For instance, ELF users may be more tolerant to non-standard use of lexical and syntactic items in informal academic research blogs than those in formal research articles.

11.5 Future directions of research

Based on a review of ELF studies, this chapter described lexical and syntactic features characterizing ELF academic writing. As previously discussed, ELF in academic writing has displayed its own features such as lexical simplification and approximation, and long sentence structures elaborated at phrasal level. It is reasonable to assume that ELF "is being spread, developed independently, with a great deal of variation but enough stability to be viable for lingua franca communication" (Seidlhofer, 2001, p. 138) in academic writing, allowing for English in academic written discourse be shaped by international scholars.

This chapter maps out an important future direction of ELFA writing research and English language teaching. That is, a systematic linguistic description of the use of ELF is needed. ELF users are bilingual or multilingual, and for most of them, native norms cannot be achieved but approximated. Without a systematic linguistic description about ELF use (especially in written discourse), ELF users sometimes are forced to follow the acknowledged conventions in academic writing. In this case, teachers may spend a great amount of time on correcting some typical "errors" (some of which appear to be unproblematic to communicative success) in English lessons.

More corpus-based research is needed in the future to examine the use of ELFA in different contexts. Since communicative effectiveness is prioritized in ELF communication, teachers and students need to know what kind of language is appropriate in practical ELF situations. Corpus data are collected from naturally occurring situations, for instance, the sub-corpora SciELF in WrELFA comprises unpublished research articles written by English language users from various linguistic and cultural backgrounds. Therefore, the authentic material in a corpus can be used to reveal how ELF users exchange their scientific ideas and achieve communicative effectiveness with their repertoire of linguistic resources. The findings from corpus-based studies may free teachers of EAP writing from native norms since language use in large and authentic ELF corpora can serve as an alternative criterion for teachers to determine whether the "errors" should be corrected or not.

Further reading

Biber, D., & Gray, B. (2016). The historical evolution of phrasal discourse styles in academic writing. In B. Gray, & D. Biber (Eds.), *Grammatical complexity in academic English: Linguistic change in writing* (pp. 125–166). Cambridge University Press. In this book chapter, the authors found that the use of phrasal devices was different across sub-registers of academic research writing. They tracked the historical evolution of phrasal structures in a large corpus of academic writing and concluded that "specialist science research articles have changed dramatically in their use of phrasal grammatical devices associated with informational compression" (Biber & Gray, 2016, p. 166).

Cogo, A., & Dewey, M. (2012). *Analysing English as a lingua franca: A corpus-driven investigation*. Bloomsbury. Based on large corpus data, this book provides a detailed and comprehensive account of recent empirical findings in the field of English as a lingua franca (ELF). Innovative patterns of language use, especially patterns of innovation in ELF lexicogrammar, have been examined in this book. Moreover, the interrelationship between pragmatic and lexicogrammatical issues investigated in this book sheds light on how understanding is achieved in ELF.

Jenkins, J. (2006b). Points of view and blind spots: ELF and SLA. *International Journal of Applied Linguistics, 16*(2), 137–162. This article argues that the use of English as a lingua franca should be considered in mainstream SLA research. It also highlights that concepts such as interlanguage and fossilization are not suitable for ELF and proposes the need of legitimate ELF description in its own right.

References

Biber, D., & Gray, B. (2010). Challenging stereotypes about academic writing: Complexity, elaboration, explicitness. *Journal of English for Academic Purposes, 9*(1), 2–20. https://doi.org/10.1016/j.jeap.2010.01.001.

Biber, D., & Gray, B. (2016). The historical evolution of phrasal discourse styles in academic writing. In B. Gray & D. Biber (Eds.), *Grammatical complexity in academic English: Linguistic change in writing* (pp. 125–166). Cambridge University Press. https://doi.org/10.1017/CBO9780511920776.004

Brown, G., & Yule, G. (1983). *Discourse analysis*. Cambridge University Press.

Canagarajah, S. (2014). In search of a new paradigm for teaching English as an International Language. *TESOL Journal, 5*(4), 767–785.

Carey, R. (2013). On the other side: Formulaic organizing chunks in spoken and written academic ELF. *Journal of English as a Lingua Franca, 2*(2), 207–228. https://doi.org/10.1515/jelf-2013-0013.

Casal, J. E., & Lee, J. J. (2019). Syntactic complexity and writing quality in assessed first-year L2 writing. *Journal of Second Language Writing, 44*, 51–62. https://doi.org/10.1016/j.jslw.2019.03.005

Chang, H. (2009). The acquisition of articles and the L2 syntactic impairment: The latest developments of UG access research. *Journal of Foreign Languages, 6*, 35–46.

Corder, S. P. (1981). *Error analysis and interlanguage*. Oxford University Press.

Croft, W. (2000). *Explaining language change: An evolutionary approach*. Longman.

Davies, M. (2013). Google scholar and COCA-academic: Two very different approaches to examining academic English. *Journal of English for Academic Purposes, 12*(3), 155–165. https://doi.org/10.1016/j.jeap.2013.01.003

Deng, Y., Lei, L., & Liu, D. (2020). Calling for more consistency, refinement, and critical consideration in the use of syntactic complexity measures for writing. *Applied Linguistics*. https://doi.org/10.1093/applin/amz069.

Dewey, M. (2012). Towards a post-normative approach: Learning the pedagogy of ELF. *Journal of English as a Lingua Franca, 1*(1), 141–170.

Firth, A. (1996). The discursive accomplishment of normality: On 'lingua franca' English and conversation analysis. *Journal of Pragmatics, 26*(2), 237–259. https://doi.org/10.1016/0378-2166(96)00014-8.

Flowerdew, J. (1999). Problems in writing for scholarly publication in English: The case of Hong Kong. *Journal of Second Language Writing, 8*(3), 243–264. https://doi.org/10.1016/s1060-3743(99)80116-7.

Halliday, M. A. K., & Martin, J. R. (2003). *Writing science: Literacy and discursive power*. Taylor & Francis.

Harrington, M., & Roche, T. (2014). Identifying academically at-risk students in an English-as-a-Lingua-Franca university setting. *Journal of English for Academic Purposes, 15*, 37–47. https://doi.org/10.1016/j.jeap.2014.05.003

Hullen, W. (1982). Teaching a foreign language as 'lingua franca'. *Grazer Linguistische Studien, 16*, 83–88.

Hyland, K. (2002). Genre: Language, context, and literacy. *Annual Review of Applied Linguistics, 22*, 113–135.

Hyland, K. (2008). Genre and academic writing in the disciplines. *Language Teaching, 41*(4), 543–562. https://doi.org/10.1017/S0261444808005235.

Hyland, K. (2015). Genre, discipline and identity. *Journal of English for Academic Purposes, 19*, 32–43.

Hyland, K. (2016). Academic publishing and the myth of linguistic injustice. *Journal of Second Language Writing, 31*, 58–69.

Ingvarsdóttir, H., & Arnbjörnsdóttir, B. (2013). ELF and academic writing: A perspective from the expanding circle. *Journal of English as a Lingua Franca, 2*(1), 123–145. https://doi.org/10.1515/jelf-2013-0006.

Jenkins, J. (1998). Which pronunciation norms and models for English as an International Language? *ELT Journal, 52*(2), 119–126.

Jenkins, J. (2000). *The phonology of English as an international language*. Oxford University Press.

Jenkins, J. (2006a). Current perspectives on teaching World Englishes and English as a Lingua Franca. *TESOL Quarterly, 40*(1), 157–181. https://doi.org/10.2307/40264515.

Jenkins, J. (2011). Accommodating (to) ELF in the international university. *Journal of Pragmatics, 43*(4), 926–936. https://doi.org/10.1016/j.pragma.2010.05.011.

Jenkins, J., Cogo, A., & Dewey, M. (2011). Review of developments in research into English as a lingua franca. *Language Teaching, 44*(3), 281–315.

Kaur, J. (2012). Saying it again: Enhancing clarity in English as a Lingua Franca (ELF) talk through self-repetition. *Text & Talk, 32*(5), 593–613.

Kecskes, I., & Kirner-Ludwig, M. (2019). "Odd structures" in English as a lingua franca discourse. *Journal of Pragmatics, 151,* 76–90.

Kirkpatrick, A. (2010). Researching English as a Lingua Franca in Asia: The Asian Corpus of English (ACE) project. *Asian Englishes, 13*(1), 4–18.

Larsson, T., & Kaatari, H. (2020). Syntactic complexity across registers: Investigating (in)formality in second-language writing. *Journal of English for Academic Purposes, 45,* 100850. https://doi.org/10.1016/j.jeap.2020.100850

Laufer, B., & Waldman, T. (2011). Verb-noun collocations in second language writing: A corpus analysis of learners' English. *Language Learning, 61*(2), 647–672.

Li, W. (2018). Translanguaging as a practical theory of language. *Applied Linguistics, 39*(1), 9–30.

Lorés-Sanz, R. (2016). ELF in the making? Simplification and hybridity in abstract writing. *Journal of English as a Lingua Franca, 5*(1), 53–81.

Lu, X. (2011). A corpus-based evaluation of syntactic complexity measures as indices of college-level ESL writers' language development. *TESOL Quarterly, 45*(1), 36–62.

Luzon, M. (2018). Features of online ELF in research group blogs written by multilingual scholars. *Discourse, Context and Media.* Advance online publication. https://doi.org/10.1016/j.dcm.2018.01.004

Martínez, I. A. (2005). Native and non-native writers' use of first person pronouns in the different sections of biology research articles in English. *Journal of Second Language Writing, 14*(3), 174–190. https://doi.org/10.1016/j.jslw.2005.06.001.

Martinez, R. (2018). "Specially in the last years...": Evidence of ELF and non-native English forms in international journals. *Journal of English for Academic Purposes, 33,* 40–52. https://doi.org/10.1016/j.jeap.2018.01.007

Mauranen, A. (2003). The corpus of English as Lingua Franca in academic settings. *TESOL Quarterly, 37*(3), 513–527.

Mauranen, A. (2007). Hybrid voices: English as the Lingua Franca of academics. In K. Flottum (Ed.), *Language and discipline perspectives on academic discourse* (pp. 244–259). Cambridge Scholars Publishing.

Mauranen, A. (2009). Chunking in ELF: Expressions for managing interaction. *Intercultural Pragmatics, 6,* 217–233.

Mauranen, A. (2012). *Exploring ELF: Academic English shaped by non-native speakers.* Cambridge University Press.

Mauranen, A. (2016). How do we write in English as a lingua franca? Talk at the Centre for Global Englishes (CGE), University of Southampton. http://blog.soton.ac.uk/ilc/files/2016/03/Mauranen-slides_240216.pdf

Mazgutova, D., & Kormos, J. (2015). Syntactic and lexical development in an intensive English for Academic Purposes programme. *Journal of Second Language Writing, 29,* 3–15. https://doi.org/10.1016/j.jslw.2015.06.004

McKay, S. (2018). English as an International Language: What it is and what it means for pedagogy. *RELC Journal, 49*(1), 9–23.

Mur-Dueñas, P. (2017). Modal hedging verbs in English as a Lingua Franca (ELF) business management research articles. *Kalbotyra, 69*(69), 153–178. https://doi.org/10.15388/Klbt.2016.10371.

O'Donnell, R. C. (1974). Syntactic differences between speech and writing. *American Speech, 49*(1/2), 102–110.

Ortega, L., & Carson, J. (2010). Multicompetence, social context, and L2 writing research praxis. In T. Silva & P. K. Matsuda (Eds.), *Practicing theory in second language writing* (pp. 48–71). Parlor Press.

Pitzl, M. L. (2016). World Englishes and creative idioms in English as a Lingua Franca. *World Englishes, 35*(2), 293–309. https://doi.org/10.1111/weng.12196.

Politzer-Ahles, S., Holliday, J. J., Girolamo, T., Spychalska, M., & Berkson, K. H. (2016). Is linguistic injustice a myth? A response to Hyland (2016). *Journal of Second Language Writing, 34,* 3–8. https://doi.org/10.1016/j.jslw.2016.09.003

Prodromou, L. (2007). Is ELF a variety of English? *English Today, 23*(2), 47–53.

Rozycki, W., & Johnson, N. H. (2013). Non-canonical grammar in best paper award winners in engineering. *English for Specific Purposes, 32*(3), 157–169. https://doi.org/10.1016/j.esp.2013.04.002.

Ruan, Z. (2018). Structural compression in academic writing: An English-Chinese comparison study of complex noun phrases in research article abstracts. *Journal of English for Academic Purposes, 36,* 37–47. https://doi.org/10.1016/j.jeap.2018.09.001

Seidlhofer, B. (2001). Closing a conceptual gap: The case for a description of English as a lingua Franca. *International Journal of Applied Linguistics, 11*(2), 133–158. https://doi.org/10.1111/1473-4192.00011

Seidlhofer, B. (2004). Research perspectives on teaching English as a lingua franca. *Annual Review of Applied Linguistics, 24,* 209–239.

Seidlhofer, B. (2011). *Understanding English as a lingua franca.* Oxford University Press.

Shchemeleva, I. (2019). "It seems plausible to maintain that...": Clusters of epistemic stance expressions in written academic ELF texts. *ESP Today, 7*(1), 24–43. https://doi.org/10.18485/esptoday.2019.7.1.2.

Smith, L. E. (2015). English as an international language: No room for linguistic chauvinism. *Journal of English as a Lingua Franca, 4*(1), 165–171. https://doi.org/10.1515/jelf-2015-0002.

Tribble, C. (2017). ELFA vs. genre: A new paradigm war in EAP writing instruction? *Journal of English for Academic Purposes, 25,* 30–44. https://doi.org/10.1016/j.jeap.2016.10.003

Vold, E. T. (2006). Epistemic modality markers in research articles: A cross-linguistic and cross-disciplinary study. *International Journal of Applied Linguistics, 16*(1), 61–87. https://doi.org/10.1111/j.1473-4192.2006.00106.x.

Wu, X., Mauranen, A., & Lei, L. (2020). Syntactic complexity in English as a lingua franca academic writing. *Journal of English for Academic Purposes, 43,* 100798. https://doi.org/10.1016/j.jeap.2019.100798

PART II

Corpora and English for specific purposes and English for academic purposes

12

CORPUS ANALYSIS OF DISCIPLINARY VARIATION AND THE TEACHING OF ESP/EAP

Paul Thompson

12.1 Introduction

The chapter looks at the impact that the growth of corpus resources and techniques has had on English for Specific Purposes (ESP), both in expanding the research base that informs theory and practice in ESP and also in the inclusion of corpus consultation within ESP teaching and learning, with a particular emphasis on analyses of disciplinary variation. ESP, with its two sub-categories of English for Academic Purposes (EAP) and English for Occupational Purposes (EOP), is a field of English Language Teaching in which teaching focuses, to differing degrees, on the learners' academic or occupational needs (Anthony, 2018, p. 1). As is clear throughout this volume, the corpus "revolution" has had a powerful impact on English Language Teaching in general, and corpus studies and corpus techniques have been particularly influential in the field of ESP. The majority of the work that will be discussed in this chapter concerns EAP primarily, as this is where issues of disciplinary variation are most evident, but this work has had an impact on ESP more broadly.

The growth of corpus approaches is clearly related to advances in computer-based technologies. Tribble (2015), one of the pioneers of corpus-based teaching, presents his own personal experiences of changes in technology over a 30-year period, from the eighties onwards: relating, for example, how the introduction of the Amstrad 1512 personal computer in 1986 allowed him to move from manual analysis of paper-based textual data to computer analysis. Concordancing then became a possibility for language teachers with programmes such as the Longman Mini-Concordancer (Chandler, 1989), and the development of affordable OCR scanners made it possible for enthusiast teachers like Tribble to create their own corpora. These were followed by the emergence of corpus analysis tools such as Wordsmith Tools (Scott, 2021 [latest version]) in the nineties, and then the expansion of the Internet in the 2000s, with a concomitant growth in online interfaces to corpus resources. Where once researchers had to scan material by hand and then run OCR software over the scans, researchers were now able to use powerful software to batch-convert PDF documents into text documents for inclusion in a corpus, and the availability of freeware programmes such as those developed by Laurence Anthony (https://www.laurenceanthony.net/software.html) made it possible for both teachers and students to become researchers of their own texts as well as those of others.

These technological changes have facilitated a wide uptake of corpus consultation in language teaching research and practice in general. A language corpus is a source of evidence about authentic language use, and ESP is an area of language teaching in which evidence is of central importance. English for Specific Purposes teaching, as the name indicates, focuses on language in specific domains, such as the language used by flight controllers in aviation, or the language of nursing. One of the particularities of ESP teaching is that it is common for instructors to find themselves dealing with vocabulary and concepts that they are not expert in, and text types that they have no experience of producing. Similarly, the students may also not know much about the subject. A group of international EFL students who are studying Financial Management at Masters level in a British university, for example, may be unfamiliar not only with the content of the subject (the "what") but also the ways in which people talk and write about the subject (the "how"). The value of corpus analysis tools and methods is that they can be used by teachers and students to identify features that are characteristic of the texts typically produced or encountered within those specific domains of use.

A distinction is made in EAP between English for General Academic Purposes (EGAP) and English for Specific Academic Purposes (ESAP). In the latter, the focus is often on the language and practices of a perceived discipline, for example, Engineering, and of how one discipline differs from, or is similar to, another. Our concern in this chapter, therefore, is with ESAP and on how corpus studies of disciplinary variation have impacted on the teaching and learning of English for Specific (Academic) Purposes.

The research literature on ESP/EAP has burgeoned in the last few decades. Liu and Hu (2020) surveyed the two main journals in ESP (*English for Specific Purposes, Journal of English for Academic Purposes*) in the period 1980–2018 and proposed that there have been three evolutionary stages in the field: the "initial conceptualizing stage" (1970s–1990s) in which needs analysis was central; the "maturing stage" (1990s–2000s) characterised by the establishment and development of major methodological approaches; and the "flourishing stage" (2000s to the present) in which these approaches were applied to a diverse set of research interests. Two of the major methodological approaches developed in the maturing stage were genre analysis and corpus analysis, and we will see in the following sections that the two have often combined to produce a wealth of insights and have contributed to pedagogy in ways that are particular to ESP.

12.1.1 Disciplines

A search of the internet reveals that the term "disciplinary variation" itself is mainly used by EAP researchers and practitioners and is comparatively little used beyond the EAP community (Thompson & Hunston, 2019). The terms "discipline" and "disciplinary" on the other hand have much wider usage and provide useful ways to refer both to an academic field of study and to the researchers in that field, along with the conventions by which those people communicate with each other and the values that they espouse. However, the concept of discipline is often conflated with institutional groupings and structures. The Michigan Corpus of Spoken English, for example, employs a four-way split into disciplinary domain divisions that reflects faculty divisions at the University of Michigan, Ann Arbor (Biological and Health Sciences; Humanities and Arts; Social Sciences and Education; Physical Sciences and Engineering) while the corpus that Coxhead (2000) used for the compilation of the Academic Word List contains sub-corpora for the disciplines of Arts, Commerce, Law and Science. In Wikipedia, we find yet another metastructure in place: Humanities, Social Sciences, Natural Sciences, Formal Sciences and Applied Sciences (https://en.wikipedia.org/wiki/

Outline_of_academic_disciplines). In the Wikipedia system, Law is a part of the Humanities, while in Coxhead's corpus framework, it is a discipline at the same level as Science, and in yet another system, that developed by Ackerman and Chen (2013) for their Academic Collocation List project, Law is placed under Applied Sciences and Professions. Each system has its own justification, often, as we have seen, drawing on the nomenclature of institutional structures, but the variation in categorisation indicates that these are not clear, immutable groupings. Just as with the term genre, there is an array of meanings of discipline, ranging from the meta-level (Arts is a discipline), to an established core field (e.g. Physics), and to a part of a larger field (e.g. Econometrics). This can become even more complicated when names of degree programmes are considered – should students in an Agricultural Economics MA programme, for example, be considered economists or agriculture researchers? It is important, therefore, to question the labels that are placed upon groupings by researchers and the term discipline itself (Kaufhold & McGrath, 2019).

Much corpus work into disciplinary variation in ESP is influenced by the mapping of disciplines by Biglan (1973) and Becher (1989). Biglan placed disciplines along three axes: hard–soft, pure–applied and life–non-life. Of these, the first and second are most commonly referred to, and it is Becher (1989) who is often cited in relation to the two axes, rather than Biglan. Amongst corpus researchers, there has been a tendency to place disciplines within these categories, such as describing physics as hard–pure and economics as soft–pure, although Trowler (2014) cautions against what he terms an essentialist view on disciplines (that is, disciplines are distinct from each other and they have essential properties). In addition, there is a danger of overlooking diversity of practice when looking for what characterises textual practices in a grouping. As Barry *et al.* (2008, pp. 26–27) observe, "disciplines are routinely characterised by internal differences; the existence of a discipline does not always imply that there is acceptance of an agreed set of problems, objects, practices, theories or methods". This implies that corpus analysts should be alert both to variation between disciplines and to variation within a discipline.

12.1.2 Academic corpus resources

As is the case in general corpus linguistics, the majority of ESP corpora are written language data. The comparative paucity of spoken language corpora can be attributed to the high costs of recording and transcribing sufficient quantities of recorded data.

Until the late 1990s, the focus in EAP research was almost exclusively on published research articles, even though, as Dudley-Evans (1999, p. 28) pointed out, the texts that university students had to write were essays, reports and dissertations. If ESP aims to address the needs of the learners, the argument goes, then the focus of study should be on the assessed pieces of work that students most directly need to be able to produce rather than on journal articles. Towards the end of the 1990s, attention did turn to the language that students in academic settings would encounter in lectures and seminars, and the texts that they would be expected to produce, though the majority of EAP research continues to focus still on research articles. The British Academic Written English (BAWE; Nesi & Gardner, 2012) and the Michigan Corpus of Upper-Level Student Papers (MICUSP, 2009) projects both led to the development of large-scale corpora of student assessed writing that sample data from different disciplines. Both corpora and the spoken language counterparts (BASE, Thompson & Nesi, 2001; MICASE, Simpson *et al.*, 1999) used the same disciplinary domain framework: the broad domains of Arts & Humanities, Social Sciences, Physical Sciences and Life Sciences. These corpora have been used for numerous research studies (for example, Benitez-Castro, 2021;

Dang & Webb, 2014; Gardner *et al.*, 2019; Hardy & Römer, 2013) and for materials development (for example, Feak *et al.*, 2009).

Online resources which researchers and practitioners can use for investigations of disciplinary variation include:

- Sketch Engine (https://app.sketchengine.eu/) – this provides open access to both BASE and BAWE, and subscribers can also access the Cambridge Academic English corpus, containing 400 million words of written and spoken academic language at undergraduate and post-graduate level; this corpus uses the same four disciplinary domain division as BASE/BAWE, MICASE and MICUSP.
- Flax interactive learning (http://flax.nzdl.org/greenstone3/flax) – this houses a number of corpora and corpus analysis tools, with some material donated by registered users
- The academic section of the Corpus of Contemporary American (COCA, Davies, 2008)

Many ESP corpus investigations have been conducted on corpora compiled especially for the research project and these are generally not available for public access. Among the corpus analysis tools used in these studies, worthy of mention here for its flexibility and power is Laurence Anthony's freeware AntConc (Anthony, 2020) which is available in Windows, Mac and Linux versions.

12.2 Review of current state of disciplinary variation research

The disciplinary variation literature is large and only a brief overview can be given here. While it is recognised that there has been research into disciplinary variation in lecture discourse (e.g. Csomay, 2005, 2007; Csomay & Wu, 2020; Fortanet, 2004) and in seminars (e.g. Grant, 2011), we focus here on investigations of disciplinary variation on written language. Research has addressed a broad range of rhetorical and linguistic features in a variety of genres, such as the use of first-person pronouns (Harwood, 2005) and self-mentions (McGrath, 2016) in research articles; stance in research articles (Jiang & Hyland, 2015), in theses (Charles, 2003) and in undergraduate writing (Lancaster, 2016); how citation is used in interdisciplinary research articles (Muguiro, 2020) and theses (Thompson, 2005); the roles of interactive metadiscourse (Cao & Hu, 2014); the uses of lexical bundles in research article abstracts (Omidian *et al.*, 2018); and the uses of phraseological patterns in research articles and book reviews in two disciplines (Groom, 2005). Central to many of these studies are questions about how writers position themselves in relation to, firstly, the status of the propositions that they present, and, secondly, to the readers that they are communicating with.

A pivotal publication in the study of disciplinary variation was Hyland's (2000) monograph, *Disciplinary Discourses*, in which he examined disciplinary variation through different linguistic/rhetorical features in a variety of academic genres, using corpus methods. The book covers citation practices, evaluation, hedging and boosting, and metadiscourse in genres ranging from textbooks to book reviews. The corpora used in these studies represent eight disciplines: Biology, Applied Linguistics, Electronic Engineering and Mechanical Engineering, Marketing, Philosophy, Sociology and Physics. The book was influential in treating academic writing not as transactional and impersonal but, rather, as a highly complex act of social interaction with a readership. It has also served as an inspiration for further disciplinary variation studies that have developed a rich picture of preferred practices in different disciplines, both in terms of ways of working and in terms of discourse practices. It is important to note, here, a further aspect of Hyland's methodology which is the use of interviews with disciplinary insider informants (such as Philosophy lecturers to explain the observed patterns in Philosophy texts). The use of such specialist informants has a long tradition in ESP studies, where, as noted above, the researcher or practitioner may have expertise in language and textual analysis but not in the specific subject or discipline. The specialist informant can provide understandings that the researcher may not otherwise be privy to.

Hyland combines corpus analysis with a genre approach (e.g. Swales, 1990), in which emphasis is placed on the contexts of language use, the communicative purposes of authors and on the roles that such texts play within social groupings. Genre approaches have a focus on function – on what people do through language. As corpus programmes cannot of themselves interpret functions in language, the researcher has either to identify forms (individual words, or sequences) that have a particular function, or to annotate the data for function and then see what forms are used to perform given functions. Similarly, texts can be analysed for rhetorical organisation using move analysis (moves are text segments with a specific communicative function), as in Swales' (1990) Create A Research Space (CARS) model, and comparisons can be made between the typical move sequences in a given section of research articles, such as the introduction section, in two or more disciplines. Samraj (2002), for example, tested the CARS model on RA introductions in Conservation Biology and in Wildlife Behavior and found differences which she attributes to the different orientations of the two disciplines with the former being an interdisciplinary and applied field, while the latter is more theory-oriented.

Most of the work on research articles in the disciplines has focused on the empirical research article, organised using the IMRD (Introduction-Methods-Results-Discussion) structure, which is seen to be the predominant paradigm. However, some researchers have challenged this approach. Van Enk and Power (2017), for example, reported the inapplicability of the IMRD model to research articles in the field of Education. They found that trying to shoehorn articles in six sub-fields of Education into an IMRD structure was almost impossible, with the most resistant being articles in the Philosophy of Education. Thompson and Hunston (2019) found that only 7% of the articles in their sample from the interdisciplinary journal *Global Environmental Change* had an explicit IMRD structure. In brief, there is a risk that EAP corpus research overlooks the diversity that exists within the genres of research article by tending to focus on what is perceived to be the norm.

Dressen-Hammouda (2012) observes that genre and disciplinary variation studies typically focus on the average number of times that linguistic features occur in texts. For example, Hyland (2000) found an average of 104 citations per paper in Sociology as compared to 24.8 in Physics, norming the raw figures for citations to show how often citations are used per 1000 words in each discipline. Dressen-Hammouda argues that this use of mean scores has an effect of stressing convergence and that variations from perceived norms also need to be taken into account in a genre description, so that degrees of divergence can also be captured. For this, she proposes that dispersion measures such as standard deviation should be foregrounded. She also introduces an important factor into consideration of disciplinary writing, that of time. Her study examines change across a ten-year period in the writing of five geologists, from the publication of their doctoral dissertation onwards. The later writings contain more of what she terms personalisation cues, uses of first-person pronouns, evaluative adjectives and adverbs, and interpretive comments, which she attributes to the development of a voice of greater authority within the discipline. While not immediately presented as a disciplinary variation study, her paper points out the importance of recognising divergence within a grouping, with the possibility that degrees of acceptable divergence may vary from one discipline to another, and her research also "highlights the social, institutional and individual features of voice which novice writers need to become aware of when learning to construct their disciplinary voice and expertise in English" (Dressen-Hammouda, 2012, p. 194).

Attention to temporal aspects of writing in the disciplines can also be observed in Staples *et al.*'s (2016) study of academic writing development at undergraduate level. The study reports an analysis of grammatical complexity features, at both phrasal and clausal levels, in the BAWE corpus across year of study (first to third), discipline and genre. The finding across years of study was that phrasal features (for example, nominalisations, *of* genitives, pre-modifying nouns) increased in frequency, with a corresponding decrease in clausal features. At the disciplinary level, however, there were differences in the phrasal features that were more evident. Pre-modifying nouns were more frequent in the Life and Physical Sciences, while Arts and Humanities used more *of* genitives and prepositional phrases. This study is valuable both for its attention to student (rather than researcher) writing and also its insights into features of writing development from first to third year undergraduate in different disciplines.

Studies which compare disciplines tend to differentiate one from the other ("Discipline X does this, while Discipline Y does that") or to cluster disciplines into a group where similarities are found ("Disciplines X, Y and Z are soft disciplines and soft disciplines behave in this way"). Key word analysis (Scott, 1997) is often used for these purposes, although Gabrielatos (2018) has written an important critique of the statistical measures used for keyness analyses. Key word analyses typically focus on content words, but Whiteside and Wharton (2019) look at grammatical words instead, drawing on Hunston's (2008, p. 292) observation that small words "reveal a surprising amount about the epistemology and ideology of disciplines, because they reveal phraseologies that are linked to recurrent meanings and functions rather than subject matter". The patterning around five key closed-class items (*of, and, that, as* and *this*) are examined to identify what Groom (2007) terms "semantic sequences" and "semantic motifs"; an example of a semantic sequence is "OBJECT OF INTERPRETATION + NATURE OF INTER-PRETATION (PERCEPTION) + **as** + INTERPRETATION" as in the clause "they were seen largely as a single commodity". Their analysis suggests commonalities between the disciplines rather than differences in the range of sequences used. The approach has great potential as it can reveal patterns of semantic sequences at different stages of a text. Unlike IMRD research articles, essays seldom employ headings and they can resist automated identification of structure. Further work needs to be done with different disciplines, although it should also be noted that it is a time-intensive method.

In recent years, there has been a growth of interest in intradisciplinary variation, that is, the amount of variation that can be found within a discipline and also in interdisciplinary writing. Gray (2013, 2015) demonstrates that discipline is not only the factor that contributes to variation but another factor is the type of research – she distinguishes between theoretical, qualitative and quantitative studies. In other words, quantitative analysis papers in applied linguistics will look quite different from qualitative studies, an observation which is perhaps not surprising but which may be overlooked if there is too much emphasis on the so-called "conventional" paper.

As stated above, studies of disciplinary variation tend to place texts into disciplinary categories from the outset – texts from one discipline are compared with texts from another. A different approach was taken by Durrant (2015). In his study, profiles of 1558 texts in BAWE corpus were built by listing all the four-item lexical bundle sequences in each text, and then clustering texts by their profiles, in order to create what he terms "emergent disciplinary groupings". The texts cluster into four groupings which are as follows: Humanities and Social Sciences, Science and Technology, Life Sciences, and, finally, Commerce. At one level, this supports the notion of relatively distinct preferred ways of writing in broad disciplinary domains (Commerce is the one oddity), and at another level, Durrant shows that some disciplines are more heterogeneous than others (Psychology texts, for example, can be found in three of the groupings).

Omidian and Siyanova-Chanturia (2021) took a similarly inductive approach, looking at individual word-forms only. Using a 4.5-million-word corpus of articles with an IMRD (Introduction-Methods-Results-Discussion) structure, from ten disciplines, they extracted a list of high-frequency lexical items and then calculated the dispersion of these items across the corpus. Overlap between disciplines in use of words showed a clear differentiation into two groups which correspond with Biglan's hard and soft discipline groups, and, within each group, similarities were found for Business Studies and Management (in the soft disciplines) and for Chemistry and Biology (in the hard disciplines). Drilling further down, Omidian and Siyanova-Chanturia looked at vocabulary frequency for keywords across the rhetorical sections. They found that Introductions and Discussion sections had a high degree of vocabulary overlap in both Social Sciences and Humanities, but, in the Sciences, the overlap was highest in the Results and Discussion sections. This indicates, they say, "fundamental differences in how justification of findings and making claims about their significance are handled across disciplinary fields" (Omidian & Siyanova-Chanturia, 2021, p. 28).

We now turn to look at corpus-based research into academic vocabulary. The best known of word lists for EAP is Coxhead's (2000) Academic Word List (AWL) which was based upon an analysis of a 3.5-million-word corpus. While the AWL is a highly important resource in EAP, it was not aimed at describing disciplinary variation (other than to act as an index of general academic language). Hyland and Tse (2007) questioned the value of a single core vocabulary for academic study and proposed instead that EAP teaching should be based around discipline-specific vocabulary. They supported their argument through a testing of the AWL on a 3.3-million-word corpus containing a variety of disciplines and genres, which indicated that words behave in different ways across disciplines. Some word meanings were highly frequent in one domain but not in others, and meanings varied by discipline (for further discussion, see Coxhead, this volume).

Ward (2009) argued for discipline-specific word lists from a different perspective. In EAP contexts in which learners have limited knowledge of English, it is impractical to work with a 570-item word list like the AWL which contains more words than necessary for, say, an Engineering undergraduate in an EFL setting, and, therefore, he proposed the use of a smaller, discipline-specific word list. He and his colleagues created a 250,000-word corpus of Engineering textbooks, selected by lecturers from five Engineering faculties (Chemical, Civil, Electrical, Industrial and Mechanical) at his university. Based on the word frequency information for the corpus, and with the requirement that, in order for a word to be included, it had to be represented in all five subcorpora, a Basic Engineering List (BEL) was developed. Tests of the list on other data showed that BEL gave 17.2, 15.6 and 21% coverage of the tokens in three Chemical Engineering textbooks that had not been included in the original corpus, while the 570-word-family AWL gave only 11.3% coverage of the Engineering corpus. For students in a specific discipline with limited time to increase their vocabulary for studies within a discipline, Ward argued, BEL is a better resource.

In addition to the development of discipline-specific word lists, of which Ward's BEL is but one example, researchers have compiled lists of multiword units. These units can be n-grams (sequences of word-forms, where "n" indicates the number of items in the sequence – a sequence of three items would be a 3-gram) or they can be phrase-frames (semi-fixed sequences of words in which one slot is a variable, such as "it is ★ to").

Examples of phrase-frame lists developed for specific disciplines are Cunningham's (2017) for Mathematics research articles, and Lu et al.'s (2018), who used a corpus of research article introductions from six social science disciplines (Anthropology, Applied Linguistics, Economics, Political Science, Psychology and Sociology). Cunningham identified 180 p-frames of five- or six-words length, and then categorised them for function, such as "establishing the presumptions" (e.g. "suppose that ★ is a") or "completing a proof" (e.g. "this [completes|concludes] the proof of the [theorem|lemma]"). The resultant list is clearly aimed at a particular discipline (mathematics) and is of use in EAP courses for mathematics majors or students who are taking a mathematics module as part of their degree. Lu *et al.*'s list, on the other hand, takes six disciplines in order to have a broad sample of the social sciences, from which to create a list for social science students in general. Their list of 454 p-frames is divided into what are labelled as primary functions: referential, stance, discourse and multifunction, with each function further described (stance, for example, containing hedges, obligation, intention). They also asked a panel of teachers and students to evaluate a sample of 100 frames for pedagogical usefulness. While Cunningham's list is better suited to the teaching of a relatively homogeneous group of EAP students, Lu *et al.*'s list can be used in a heterogenous group of social science students.

Word lists are founded primarily on frequency and range criteria. However, as many ESP practitioners will point out, these are not the only two criteria by which words should be selected for pedagogical treatment. Otto (2021) addresses the question of word selection for Data-Driven Learning activities (DDL; see next section) in a discipline-specific ESP context. The context in question was a Civil Engineering undergraduate programme at a US university. To select the vocabulary to teach, she made use of three corpora: a practitioner corpus containing texts written by practising engineers, a learner corpus containing Civil Engineering student texts and the written components of COCA. The word list was developed in three stages:

1. A keyword analysis was conducted to identify discipline-specific words and the results were filtered to remove highly technical terms (comparing the practitioner corpus to COCA)
2. The learner corpus was compared with the practitioner corpus
3. Judgements were made about whether the items are well-suited to being taught through DDL

In the end, 18 items were selected as prime candidates for teaching through DDL. Although this may appear to be a small number, as Otto admits, with a low return for a lengthy process of selection, she argues that the process itself gave her a rich understanding of the specialised texts and it also ensured that the lexical items for study were of proven value.

12.3 Core issues in corpus-informed and corpus-based materials in ESP

In the previous sections, we have looked at research into disciplinary variation which has been conducted by researchers, predominantly by researchers at universities, few of whom are active practitioners. In this section, we look at accounts of how corpus analysis of discipline-specific texts has been used, firstly, in development of teaching materials and, secondly, by teachers and learners directly in the classroom, following a Data-Driven Learning (DDL) approach.

The direct use of corpora in ESP teaching is by no means mainstream yet, and much of what follows is the work of pioneering practitioners or "early adopters". In the UK, the British Association for Lecturers in English for Academic Purposes (BALEAP) has formulated a Competency Framework for Teachers of EAP which was first published in 2008. At time of writing, this framework does not contain any mention of corpus or DDL and this is suggestive of the current low levels of adoption of corpus-informed methods in EAP units in the UK. However, it is worthy of note that BALEAP ran a one-day Professional Issues Meeting (January 2021), with a view to introducing statements about corpora and DDL into a revised version of the Framework. In a blog post about this event (Alexander, 2021), Olwyn Alexander, former chair of BALEAP, relates how influential corpora had been in her own development as an EAP teacher and materials writer, giving as an example the extensive research that she conducted on a corpus of undergraduate business studies texts, research which fed into the textbooks, *EAP Essentials* and the *Access EAP* series (all published by Garnet Education).

This exemplifies how corpus analysis methods can assist in the preparation of EAP textbooks. Further evidence of the integration of discipline-specific corpus collection and analysis can be found in Friginal and Roberts' (this volume) account of developing materials for Aviation English and in several other recent publications. Crosthwaite and Cheung (2019), for example, present a series of analyses of a corpus of Dentistry texts containing the three key genres of Dentistry: experimental research articles, research reports (both professional and novice) and case reports. From these analyses, Crosthwaite and Cheung then determined the contents for the syllabus for a course in English for Dentistry students at Hong Kong University. This course was delivered online, with a variety of DDL activities, and logs of all the students' queries were also collected. These logs showed how long each student spent on an activity, what steps they took, and which sections of a text students spent more time on, providing rich data for further development of the materials and also for enhancing the materials developers' understanding of what students find interesting.

Dong and Lu (2020) also adopt a blended genre and corpus analysis approach to the teaching of discipline-specific English. The disciplinary corpus was created by the teacher and their group of 30 masters level students together, who saved the introduction sections of 150 Engineering research articles and compiled them into a corpus. The choice of articles was made in consultation with the students' lecturers. The teacher and the students then annotated the corpus for moves, utilising the revised Create A Research Space (CARS) model (Swales, 2004). It is worth noting at this point that both teacher and students were Chinese-as-L1 speakers and communication could be conducted in either Chinese or English. Once the corpus had been annotated, the students were then asked to conduct a series of DDL activities on the language used in the various moves, and the students were also asked to keep reflective journals throughout the course. Among the comments that students made in an end-of-course questionnaire was the following, which affords a good indication of the value of such a course:

> The class demo and my initial observation gave me an idea of the structures of RAs, but I don't think I understood everything completely. The corpus search activities provided many examples of the moves and linguistic patterns discussed in class. Reading through those examples really helped deepen my understanding of them. (Dong & Lu, 2020, p. 146)

Chang and Kuo (2011) created a corpus of 60 research articles from Computer Science and annotated each text in the entire corpus for moves using a scheme of rhetorical moves that the researchers developed from their readings of the texts. A set of teaching materials were then developed that addressed each section (abstract; introduction; methods; results; discussion; conclusions) from two perspectives – information structure and characteristic language use within those sections. Teaching was conducted both face-to-face in class and through online learning, where students had access to a concordancer, a collocation tool, and a move-and-keywords-engine. One of the many interesting observations of the researchers/practitioners was that the process of annotating the data for moves was highly generative as it gave them a much clearer understanding of the specific rhetorical features of research articles in Computer Science, rhetorical moves that differ from Swales (2004).

These two examples occur in single discipline contexts, but Cotos *et al.* (2017) report on the use of DDL with a mixed disciplinary group of students. They examine the use made by students of the online Research Writing Tutor (RWT), a resource that was created to help students produce an IMRD article. The RWT exploits a corpus of 900 research articles from 30 disciplines, and similarly blends genre and corpus approaches, with, as they argue, the genre element facilitating the identification of patterns at the discourse and organisational level, while readings of concordance lines help readers to develop bottom-up understandings of the texts. In a manner similar to the previous two projects, the researchers had annotated the corpus data for sections, steps and moves, so that students could search by those elements, and the system also provided automated feedback. This supported the development of students as active writers who are also researchers, within a highly structured environment.

12.4 Looking at practice

Data-Driven Learning (DDL) is a term coined by Tim Johns to describe "the use in the classroom of computer-generated concordances to get students to explore the regularities of patterning in the target language, and the development of activities and exercises based on concordance output" (Johns & King, 1991, p. iii). Examples of the latter can be found in the "kibbitzers" that Johns created to deal with language problems that he encountered in the writings of his EAP students and which are archived by Mike Scott at https://lexically.net/TimJohns/. Crosthwaite *et al.* (2021) expand on the definition so that it explicitly covers both paper-based and computer-based investigation of corpus data: "a pedagogical approach to technology-enhanced language learning involving either teacher-printed concordances of pre-selected corpus data for language learner mediation or learners' direct use of corpus query software to aid language acquisition" (n.p.).

Corpus tools and techniques can provide ESP teachers and learners with better access and frameworks for detecting regularities in specialised discourses than traditional resources such as textbooks, grammar books and so on (Boulton, 2012). However, DDL has not yet been adopted in mainstream ESP teaching (Boulton, 2010), and some of the reasons for this are that it is time-consuming to prepare DDL materials and activities, there are potential technical difficulties, and there is a lack of downloadable resources for teachers. Integration of DDL into ESP teaching will require resourcing in time allocated for corpus and teaching material development work and also in training for staff. There is evidence, however, that the use of, and research into, DDL is gathering pace; Boulton (2021) lists over 350 articles on DDL, and growth will be bolstered as more people graduate from MA TESOL courses with at least some training in corpus techniques. In addition, there is also now an online six-week corpus course for EAP teachers delivered by the English Language Teaching Centre at the University of Sheffield.

One of the pioneers of DDL in ESP is Maggie Charles who has used corpora in teaching at Oxford University with groups of Masters and PhD students from a variety of subject areas (e.g. Charles, 2007, 2012). An approach that she has used over several years is to give small groups of students training in corpus analysis techniques and ask them to create their own corpora. As these are research students who have a good understanding of the kinds of papers that they wish to be able to produce, they are better able to choose the kinds of papers which they aspire to write, or which talk about the same phenomena that they are interested in.

Charles (2014) looked at the long-term use of the do-it-yourself corpora. Her survey of 40 international students one year after they had taken their courses found that an impressively high proportion of them (70%) had used their personal corpus since completing the course, with 38% self-identifying as regular users (using the corpus once per week or more). The reasons they gave for using their DIY corpus was to check grammar and lexis while they were writing. Reasons for non-use included the small size of the corpus and its lack of reliability and convenience. These results provide strong support for the value of constructing DIY corpora in ESP teaching, at least with advanced students. Jablonkai and Cebron (2021) show that DIY corpora can be used with undergraduate students too, with good results. They taught a semester-long course to students majoring in English and studying Intercultural Linguistic Mediation at a Slovenian university, training students to be language professionals. The students compiled their own corpora and reported that the experience gave them a much enhanced understanding of language in specialist domains.

Charles (2018) challenges the notion that DDL is only about concordances. In several iterations of a course that she taught on "Editing your thesis with corpora", doctoral students were introduced to a range of tools in AntConc for the purposes of investigating different aspects of research articles in their personal corpora and in their own draft thesis. The tools that they used included the Dispersion tool which some students used to see how particular words were used throughout their text (thus giving them an insight into the coverage of particular topics) and the Clusters tool which helped students explore phraseology and collocation. This study is important because it expands the idea of DDL beyond the concordance line and shows greater potential for the use of different corpus analysis tools with learner-constructed corpora.

The disciplinary variation studies discussed above tend to be focused more on research than on pedagogical issues, although some do result in powerful insights or resources that can be used in teaching (for example, word lists which can be used in specifying the contents of a syllabus, see below). A small number of detailed descriptions of DDL teaching have been published in recent years, such as Friginal's (2018, pp. 187–212) chapter-length account of how he used DDL with a group of Forestry students in a semester-long course, which allow readers to see what sorts of activities were developed, how they worked, and how the teacher amended their plans in light of feedback. Similarly, Anthony (2016) discusses the issues involved in developing DDL materials and activities for a discipline-specific writing course, giving detailed examples. Such detailed accounts are important for practitioners, and there is a need for more, just as there is a need for greater access to teaching ideas, worksheets and other DDL materials. A recent publication that helps to address these needs is Karpenko-Seccombe's (2021) resource book for using corpora in teaching academic writing. Anthony and Thompson (2017) introduced AntCorGen (Anthony, 2019), a freeware tool that simplifies the collection and processing of research articles from the open-source research journal platform, *Plos One*, automatically generating individual files for each of the IMRD sections.

12.5 Future directions of research

The development of corpus analysis techniques and technologies has led to a rich diversity of studies of disciplinary variation that can inform ESP/EAP teaching. These have extended understandings of the characteristics of language use in specialised discourses in the disciplines, and, when combined with a genre approach, offer insights into the rhetorical choices exercised by writers in a variety of disciplinary settings and the language used to achieve those functions. Corpus research into disciplinary variation started with linguistic descriptions of the texts produced by expert members of the community, such as published research articles, but in the last two decades, there has been a small growth of studies of student writing in different subject areas. There is a need for more research into student writing and student speech, as this can relate more to immediate learner needs (how to write in ways acceptable within a course, how to participate more actively in seminars, how to understand lectures, etc.). As Boulton *et al.* (2012, p. 1) argue, "[c]orpus analysis provides an empirically-based understanding of the discourse and language used for specific purposes in the students' own fields, and gives them potentially greater autonomy for carrying out their professional tasks". Investment is required for building new, dynamic open-access collections of student writing and university teaching events that can complement the current corpus resources (BASE, BAWE, MICASE, MICUSP). Ideally, these collections would include data that cross regional borders – the current corpus resources reflect practices in US and UK Higher Education contexts, and EAP research and teaching communities in different national education systems need to have discussions about which data they choose to include in a corpus, in terms of what they want their corpora to represent. This is particularly true of EAP teaching in contexts in which English is taught as a Foreign Language.

Research has been conducted on student writing in the disciplines but an area that needs further investigation is that of writing development in different programmes. What are the expectations of student writers in, for example, a Political Sciences undergraduate programme in the first year of the programme, and what are the features of written work in the final year of the same programme? Corpora of writing at different years of a programme (e.g. see Csomay, 2020 or Csomay & Prades, 2018 for support composition programmes) can be created and made available, and research also needs to propose approaches to the analysis of relevant data that practitioners can use.

As noted above, it is important to explore not only variation between disciplines but also variation *within* disciplines, what we can call "intradisciplinary variation", and this is another direction for future research to take. Furthermore, as higher education moves towards greater promotion of interdisciplinary studies then research on the features of writing for an interdisciplinary audience is needed.

In closing, we have seen that corpora, constituting as they do evidence of how language is used in specific domains, are of central importance to ESP research and teaching. In relation to teaching, it is arguable that ESP studies have played a major role in driving the development of DDL in language teaching, where DDL is better suited to the learning of language for specific purposes. As yet, DDL is not a mainstream approach within ESP teaching but there is evidence of a gradual growth in adoption. There is room for further research into the effectiveness of DDL as well as further innovations in the conception and structuring of DDL activities.

Further reading

Charles, M., & Frankenberg-Garcia, A. (Eds.). (2021). *Corpora in ESP/EAP writing instruction: Preparation, exploitation, analysis.* Routledge. This collection contains papers on how corpora are built, analysed and used in EAP writing instruction.

Crosthwaite, P., & Cheung, L. (2019). *Learning the language of dentistry: Disciplinary corpora in the teaching of English for Specific and Academic Purposes.* Benjamins. This book gives an account of using corpora to develop an ESP course.

Nesi, H., & Gardner, S. (2012). *Genres across the disciplines: Student writing in higher education.* Cambridge University Press. This is an overview and description of the genres of assessed writing in British Higher Education.

References

Ackerman, K., & Chen, Y. (2013). Developing the Academic Collocation List (ACL) – A corpus-driven and expert-judged approach. *Journal of English for Academic Purposes, 12*(4), 235–247.

Alexander, O. (2021). Evidence-based teaching and learning: core corpus skills for EAP. Blog post https://eap-essentials.com/2021/01/15/evidence-based-teaching-and-learning-core-corpus-skills-for-eap/

Anthony, L. (2016). Introducing corpora and corpus tools into the technical writing classroom through Data-Driven Learning (DDL). In J. Flowerdew, & T. Costley (Eds.), *Discipline-specific writing: Theory into practice* (pp. 162–180). Routledge.

Anthony, L. (2018). *Introducing English for Specific Purposes.* Routledge.

Anthony, L. (2019). *AntCorGen (Version 1.1.2) [Computer Software].* Waseda University. Available from https://www.laurenceanthony.net/software.

Anthony, L. (2020). *AntConc (Version 3.5.9) [Computer Software].* Waseda University. Available from https://www.laurenceanthony.net/software.

Anthony, L., & Thompson, P. (2017). Automatic creation and discourse-level annotation of individualized discipline-specific corpora for the Data Driven Learning (DDL) classroom. Paper presented at Corpus Linguistics Conference, University of Birmingham, UK.

Barry, A., Born, G., & Weszkalnys, G. (2008). Logics of interdisciplinarity. *Economy and Society, 37*(1), 20–49.

Becher, T. (1989). *Academic tribes and territories: Intellectual inquiry and the cultures of disciplines.* Oxford University Press.

Benitez-Castro, M.-A. (2021). Shell-noun use in disciplinary student writing: A multifaceted analysis of problem and way in third-year undergraduate writing across three disciplines. *English for Specific Purposes, 61*, 132–149.

Biglan, A. (1973). The characteristics of subject matter in different academic areas. *Journal of Applied Psycholinguistics, 57*(3), 195–203.

Boulton, A. (2010). Data-driven learning: Taking the computer out of the equation. *Language Learning, 60*(3), 534–572.

Boulton, A. (2012). Corpus consultation for ESP: A review of empirical research. In A. Boulton, S. Carter-Thomas, & E. Rowley-Jolivet (Eds.), *Corpus-informed research and learning in ESP: Issues and applications* (pp. 261–291). Benjamins.

Boulton, A. (2021). Research in data-driven learning. In P. Pérez-Paredes & G. Mark (Eds.), *Beyond concordance lines: Corpora in language education.* Benjamins.

Boulton, A., Carter-Thomas, S., & Rowley-Jolivet, E. (2012). Issues in corpus-informed research and learning in ESP. In A. Boulton, S. Carter, E. Thomas, & Rowley-Jolivet (Eds.), *Corpus-informed research and learning in ESP: Issues and applications* (pp. 1–14). Benjamins.

Cao, F., & Hu, G. (2014). Interactive metadiscourse in research articles: A comparative study of paradigmatic and disciplinary influences. *Journal of Pragmatics, 66*, 15–31.

Chandler, B. (1989). *Longman Mini-Concordancer* [Computer Software]. Longman.

Chang, C. F., & Kuo, C. H. (2011). A corpus-based approach to online materials development for writing research articles. *English for Specific Purposes, 30*(3), 222–234.

Charles, M. (2003). "This mystery …": A corpus-based study of the use of nouns to con- struct stance in theses from two contrasting disciplines. *Journal of English for Academic Purposes, 2*(4), 313–326.

Charles, M. (2007). Reconciling top-down and bottom-up approaches to graduate writing: Using a corpus to teach rhetorical functions. *Journal of English for Academic Purposes, 6*, 289–302.

Charles, M. (2012). "Proper vocabulary and juicy collocations": EAP students evaluate do-it-yourself corpus-building. *English for Specific Purposes, 31*, 93–102.

Charles, M. (2014). Getting the corpus habit EAP students' long-term use of personal corpora. *English for Specific Purposes, 35*, 30–40.

Charles, M. (2018). Corpus-assisted editing for doctoral students: More than just concordancing. *Journal of English for Academic Purposes, 36*, 15–25.

Cotos, E., Link, S., & Huffman, S. (2017). Effects of technology on genre learning. *Language Learning & Technology, 21*(3), 104–130. Retrieved from http://llt.msu.edu/issues/october2017/cotoslinkhuffman.pdf

Coxhead, A. (2000). New Academic Word List. *TESOL Quarterly, 34*(2), 213–238.

Crosthwaite, P., & Cheung, L. (2019). *Learning the language of dentistry: Disciplinary corpora in the teaching of English for Specific and Academic Purposes.* Benjamins.

Crosthwaite, P., Luciana, & Schweinberger, M. (2021). Voices from the periphery: Perceptions of Indonesian primary vs secondary pre-service teacher trainees about corpora and data-driven learning in the L2 English classroom. *Applied Corpus Linguistics, 1*(1), 100003.

Csomay, E. (2005). Linguistic variation within university classroom talk: A corpus-based perspective. *Linguistics and Education, 15*(3), 243–274.

Csomay, E. (2007). A corpus-based look at linguistic variation in classroom interaction: Teacher talk versus student talk in American university classes. *Journal of English for Academic Purposes, 6,* 336–355.

Csomay, E. (2020). A corpus-based study of academic word use in EFL student writing. In U. Römer, V. Cortes, & E. Friginal (Eds.), *Advances in corpus-based research on academic writing* (pp. 9–32). Benjamins.

Csomay, E., & Prades, A. (2018). Academic vocabulary in ESL student papers: A corpus-based study. *Journal of English for Academic Purposes, 33,* 100–118.

Csomay, E., & Wu, S. (2020). Language variation in university classrooms: A corpus-driven geographical perspective. *Register Studies, 2*(1), 131–165.

Cunningham, K. (2017). A phraseological exploration of recent mathematics research articles through key phrase frames. *Journal of English for Academic Purposes, 25,* 71–83.

Dang, T., & Webb, S. (2014). The lexical profile of academic spoken English. *English for Specific Purposes, 33,* 66–76.

Davies, M. (2008–). *The Corpus of Contemporary American English (COCA).* Available online at https://www.english-corpora.org/coca/.

Dong, J., & Lu, X. (2020). Promoting discipline-specific genre competence with corpus-based genre analysis activities. *English for Specific Purposes, 58,* 138–154.

Dressen-Hammouda, D. (2012). Measuring the construction of discoursal expertise through corpus-based genre analysis. In A. Boulton, S. Carter-Thomas, & E. Rowley-Jolivet (Eds.), *Corpus-informed research and learning in ESP: Issues and applications* (pp. 193–212). Benjamins.

Dudley-Evans, T. (1999). The dissertation: A case of neglect. In P. Thompson (Ed.), *Issues in EAP writing research and instruction* (pp. 28–36). CALS University of Reading.

Durrant, P. (2015). Lexical bundles and disciplinary variation in university students' writing: Mapping the territories. *Applied Linguistics, 38*(2), 165–193.

Feak, C., Reinhart, S., & Rohlck, T. (2009). *Academic interactions: Communicating on campus (Michigan series in English for academic & professional purposes).* The University of Michigan Press.

Fortanet, I. (2004). The use of 'we' in university lectures: Reference and function. *English for Specific Purposes, 23,* 45–66.

Friginal, E. (2018). *Corpus linguistics for teachers: New tools, online resources, and classroom activities.* Routledge.

Gabrielatos, C. (2018). Keyness analysis: Nature, metrics and techniques. In C. Taylor & A. Marchi (Eds.), *Corpus approaches to discourse: A critical review* (pp. 225–258). Routledge.

Gardner, S., Nesi, H., & Biber, D. (2019). Discipline, level, genre: Integrating situational perspectives in a new MD analysis of university student writing. *Applied Linguistics, 40*(4), 646–674.

Grant, L. (2011). The frequency and functions of *just* in British academic spoken English. *Journal of English for Academic Purposes, 10*(3), 183–197.

Gray, B. (2013). More than discipline: Uncovering multi-dimensional patterns of variation in academic research articles. *Corpora, 8*(2), 153–181.

Gray, B. (2015). *Linguistic variation in research articles: When discipline tells only part of the story.* Benjamins.

Groom, N. (2005). Pattern and meaning across genres and disciplines: An exploratory study. *Journal of English for Academic Purposes, 4*(3), 257–277.

Groom, N. (2007). *Phraseology and epistemology in humanities writing: A corpus-driven study.* Unpublished doctoral thesis, University of Birmingham, UK.

Hardy, J., & Römer, U. (2013). Revealing disciplinary variation in student writing: A multi-dimensional analysis of the Michigan corpus of upper-level student papers (MICUSP). *Corpora, 8*(2), 183–207.

Harwood, N. (2005). "Nowhere has anyone attempted … in this article I aim to do just that": A corpus-based study of self-promotional I and we in academic writing across four disciplines. *Journal of Pragmatics*, *37*, 1207–1231.

Hunston, S. (2008). Starting with the small words. *International Journal of Corpus Linguistics*, *13*(3), 272–295.

Hyland, K. (2000). *Disciplinary discourses: Social interactions in academic writing*. Longman.

Hyland, K., & Tse, P. (2007). Is there an "Academic vocabulary"? *TESOL Quarterly*, *41*(2), 235–253.

Jablonkai, R., & Cebron, N. (2021). Undergraduate students' response to a corpus-based ESP course with DIY corpora. In M. Charles & A. Frankenberg-Garcia (Eds.), *Corpora in ESP/EAP writing instruction: Preparation, exploitation, analysis* (pp. 100–120). Routledge.

Jiang, F., & Hyland, K. (2015). "The fact that": Stance nouns in disciplinary writing. *Discourse Studies*, *17*(5), 529–550.

Johns, T., & King, P. (1991). *English Language research journal vol. 4: Classroom concordancing*. University of Birmingham.

Karpenko-Seccombe, T. (2021). *Academic writing with corpora: A Resource book for data-driven learning*. Routledge.

Kaufhold, K., & McGrath, L. (2019). Revisiting the role of 'discipline' in writing for publication in two social sciences. *Journal of English for Academic Purposes*, *40*, 115–128.

Lancaster, Z. (2016). Expressing stance in undergraduate writing: Discipline-specific and general qualities. *Journal of English for Academic Purposes*, *23*, 16–30.

Liu, Y., & Hu, G. (2020). Mapping the field of English for specific purposes (1980-2018): A co-citation analysis. *English for Specific Purposes*, *61*, 97–116.

Lu, X., Yoon, J., & Kisselev, O. (2018). A phrase-frame list for social science research article introductions. *Journal of English for Academic Purposes*, *36*, 76–85.

McGrath, L. (2016). Self-mentions in anthropology and history research articles: Variation between and within disciplines. *Journal of English for Academic Purposes*, *21*, 86–98.

Michigan Corpus of Upper-level Student Papers. (2009). The Regents of the University of Michigan.

Muguiro, N. (2020). *Citations in interdisciplinary research articles*. Cambridge University Press.

Nesi, H., & Gardner, S. (2012). *Genres across the disciplines: Student writing in higher education*. Cambridge University Press.

Omidian, T., Shahriari, H., & Siyanova-Chanturia, A. (2018). A cross-disciplinary investigation of multi-word expressions in the moves of research article abstracts. *Journal of English for Academic Purposes*, *36*, 1–14.

Omidian, T., & Siyanova-Chanturia, A. (2021). Parameters of variation in the use of words in empirical research writing. *English for Specific Purposes*, *62*, 15–29.

Otto, P. (2021). Choosing specialized vocabulary to teach with data-driven learning: An example from civil engineering. *English for Specific Purposes*, *61*, 32–46.

Samraj, B. (2002). Introductions in research articles: Variations across disciplines. *English for Specific Purposes*, *21*(1), 1–17.

Scott, M. (1997). PC analysis of key words - and key key words. *System*, *25*(2), 233–45.

Scott, M. (2021). *Wordsmith Tools*, version 8 [Computer software] https://lexically.net/wordsmith/

Simpson, R., Briggs, S., Ovens, J., & Swales, J. (1999). *The Michigan Corpus of Academic Spoken English*. The Regents of the University of Michigan.

Staples, S., Egbert, J., Biber, D., & Gray, B. (2016). Academic writing development at the university level: Phrasal and clausal complexity across level of study, discipline, and genre. *Written Communication*, *33*(2), 149–183.

Swales, J. M. (1990). *Genre analysis: English in academic and research settings*. Cambridge University Press.

Swales, J. M. (2004). *Research genres: Explorations and applications*. Cambridge University Press.

Thompson, P. (2005). Points of focus and position: Intertextual reference in PhD theses. *Journal of English for Academic Purposes*, *4*(4), 307–323.

Thompson, P., & Hunston, S. (2019). *Interdisciplinary research discourse: Corpus investigations into environment journals*. Routledge.

Thompson, P., & Nesi, H. (2001). The British Academic Spoken English (BASE) corpus project. *Language Teaching Research*, *5*(3), 263–264.

Tribble, C. (2015). Teaching and language corpora: Perspectives from a personal journey. In A. Leńko-Szymańska & A. Boulton (Eds.), *Multiple affordances of language corpora for data-driven learning* (pp. 37–62). Benjamins.

Trowler, P. (2014). Depicting and researching disciplines: Strong and moderate essentialist approaches. *Studies in Higher Education, 39*(10), 1720–1731.

Van Enk, A., & Power, K. (2017). What is a research article?: Genre variability and data selection in genre research. *Journal of English for Academic Purposes, 29*, 1–11.

Ward, J. (2009). A basic engineering English word list for less proficient foundation engineering undergraduates. *English for Specific Purposes, 28*(3), 170–182.

Whiteside, K., & Wharton, S. (2019). Semantic patterning of grammatical keywords in undergraduate academic writing from two close disciplines. *Journal of English for Academic Purposes, 39*, 1–20.

13

CORPORA FOR TEACHING AND LEARNING VOCABULARY IN ESP

Averil Coxhead

13.1 Introduction

The focus of this chapter is the use of corpora in the investigation of vocabulary teaching and learning in English for Specific Purposes (ESP), with a particular focus on technical or specialized vocabulary. Note that in this chapter, the terms *technical* and *specialized* are used as synonyms. Corpora are the main source of data for research into vocabulary (Anthony, 2018; Nation, 2016;) and specialized vocabulary in particular (Coxhead, 2018). Such corpus-based studies draw on written and increasingly spoken texts. As Woodrow (2018) points out, "The advantages of using corpora are that real, authentic usage of language can be uncovered, as opposed to what is intuitively believed to be common usage (p. 122)".

Specialized vocabulary is important in ESP for several reasons. Firstly, it is closely related to the subject area (Woodward-Kron, 2008) and people inside a specialized field are more likely to know the lexis than those outside the field (Chung & Nation, 2004). For example, fabrication (which includes welding) includes words such as *rutile, polyurethane*, and *crosspein*, which are used in that trade but are not often seen in general English (Coxhead *et al.*, 2019). Secondly, knowing and using the specialized vocabulary of a subject or profession is important for identity (see Parkinson & Mackay, 2016, for example) and community belonging (Wray, 2002). Finally, specialized vocabulary in ESP can make up a substantial proportion of the lexical items in written texts in particular (see Chung & Nation, 2003; Coxhead, 2018). This issue will be discussed in more detail below.

13.2 Review of current state of research

The development and use of corpora for research into vocabulary in ESP have caused several key shifts in the field over several decades. The key issues in this section are the amount of specialized vocabulary in ESP, frequency levels in specialized vocabulary, and counting technical words.

13.2.1 How much specialized vocabulary is there in ESP?

The first major shift is the estimation of the amount of specialized vocabulary in texts that has changed considerably from a conservative and rough 5% (Coxhead & Nation, 2001) to a much larger proportion of 37.6% of an Anatomy textbook and 16.3% of an Applied

Linguistics textbook (Chung & Nation, 2003). The study of Chung and Nation (2003) used a semantic scale, meaning that words in each of the textbooks (i.e. corpora) were identified and categorized on a scale from general and not related to the subject area through to technical. Other corpus-based studies have reached similar proportions of technical vocabulary in written texts. For example, Coxhead *et al.* (2016) found that just over 38% of written carpentry texts were technical. For learners, this means that almost four words in any line of text might be technical. This shift of understanding more about the burden of specialized vocabulary in texts is important because it highlights the amount of learning that is required for ESP learners, the need for planning for this lexis in ESP courses, and the gap in testing of technical vocabulary knowledge and development based on corpus results such as these. Without access to corpora, such studies would be much more time consuming.

13.2.2 High-, mid-, and low-frequency vocabulary and ESP

A second major shift is a categorization of vocabulary into high, mid, and low frequency, made possible by Nation's (2016) development of frequency-based word families using the British National Corpus and the Corpus of Contemporary American English. High frequency usually refers to the 1st 1,000–3rd 1,000 word families of English (Nation, 2013; Schmitt & Schmitt, 2012; Szudarski, this volume), and it is important for all language learners because it makes up the largest proportion of written and spoken texts (Nation, 2013). Mid-frequency vocabulary ranges from the 3rd or 4th 1,000 to the 8th 1,000 word families, and then low frequency vocabulary from the 9th 1,000 word families onwards.

Vocabulary in ESP can occur in high, mid, and low frequency categories (Nation, 2016). This point is important because some of the more recognizably technical vocabulary in ESP, such as *sarcoidosis, hypercalcemia, cortisol, hemorrhagic*, and *cardiomyopathy* in medicine (Quero & Coxhead, 2018), are low-frequency items that are not usually encountered in everyday English. High-frequency technical words, on the other hand, may be familiar to ESP learners because they know the general, but not specific, meanings of the words. Compare, for example, *tissue* in everyday English with *tissue* in medicine. Fraser (2009), in his research on pharmacology, refers to these kinds of lexical items (e.g. *expression* and *control*) as *cryptotechnical*. Examples related to COVID-19 include *elimination* and *eradication*.

A substantial proportion of technical words can be high frequency. Quero and Coxhead (2018) found that 15% of the 1st 1,000 word families in West's (1953) list of high-frequency words in English had a medical meaning (e.g. *cases, severe, levels*), and 10% of the 2nd 1,000 word of the GSL had a medical meaning (e.g. *lung, virus, tumor*). Coxhead (2000) did not include the 1st and 2nd 1,000 word families from West's GSL in her general academic word list (AWL). Gardiner and Davies (2014) developed their general academic vocabulary list (AVL) from scratch, meaning they included high-frequency vocabulary in their list. The AVL has a higher coverage over academic written and spoken texts than the AWL (Coxhead & Dang, 2019) partly because of these high frequency items, but also because the AVL is substantially larger than the AWL.

A final point to make about high-frequency vocabulary and ESP is that these items often have a first and second language equivalent (Anthony, 2018; Coxhead *et al.*, 2020a). Using trades-based vocabulary for example, *silicon, sewer*, and *wire* in English are *silikoni, sua*, and *uaea* in Tongan, a language of the Pacific. Low-frequency technical items, on the other hand, require specific definitions because these words do not exist in Tongan. This means that for Tongan learners and trades tutors, there is a wealth of high-frequency technical vocabulary in the first language which can be drawn on for learning the second language.

13.2.3 Counting words in corpus-based studies

In corpus-based studies on vocabulary in ESP, it is important to note the way words are counted. This is because individual words, or types, are more likely to be technical or related closely to the topic or area of study in ESP, rather than all the members of a word family (Chung & Nation, 2004; Coxhead, 2018). To take an example of types from trades education, the word *fixings* has a technical meaning in carpentry, but *fix* does not (Coxhead *et al.*, 2016). A word family contains a headword, derivations, and inflections, for example, *establish, establishes, established, establishing, establishment, re-establish*, and so on (Bauer & Nation, 1993). At a practical level, this means that teachers and learners need to focus on types that have a technical meaning in particular fields and pay attention to collocation patterns and other aspects of use such as grammatical features. Basturkmen (2006) points out that in medical texts, *present* (verb) and *with* are collocates, as in this dental example from Basturkmen (2006, pp. 63–64): *The patient presented with pain in the upper right molar.* This usage of the word *present* is grammatically and semantically different from general English, as can be seen in this example: *The winning team was presented with a trophy.* Corpus-based tools can help identify these patterns, as well as identify technical words themselves (see below).

13.3 Core issues and topics

Three core issues are explored in this section. The first issue is identifying technical vocabulary in ESP, which is important because definitions and approaches can differ. The second issue is the somewhat imbalanced nature of corpus-based research in teaching and learning in ESP whereby some areas are well served by research while others are not. The third issue is the size of a technical vocabulary and factors that affect research in this area.

13.3.1 Identifying technical vocabulary in ESP

The first issue is using corpora to identify technical vocabulary in ESP. Corpora and corpus linguistics can help identify words that appear more frequently in one field than another, in general English vs ESP, or in learner language vs first language speaking or writing (Paquot, this volume) and employ a range of statistical and other approaches to do so (Szudarski, this volume), including quantitative corpus-based principles combined with expert judgment (see Coxhead & Demecheleer, 2018, as an example). That said, analyzing corpora alone goes only part of the way towards identifying words that are worth teaching (Simpson-Vlach & Ellis, 2010).

Identifying single words as specialized vocabulary can be quite complex and decisions need to be made on what to include in a corpus and how to identify words. Ha and Hyland (2017) developed a 'technicality analysis' framework based on frequency and semantic principles. This framework is based on four factors (p. 38):

1. both general and specialized senses of a word
2. the banding of a word in reference word lists
3. the polysemy of a word
4. the literal meaning of a word

Ha and Hyland's (2017, p. 42) careful analysis of a financial corpus made up of written annual reports and spoken earnings calls transcripts resulted in categories of technical lexis from slightly (contains more meaning elements than the general English meaning, e.g. *capital*) to most technical (not able to be guessed or 'understood literally', e.g. *accretable, sub-prime*).

Moving beyond one-word to two-word combinations (for collocations, see Green, this volume), three- and four-word lexical bundles (Cortes, this volume), it is important for teaching and learning that these combinations are not seen as occurring just by chance. Also, a combination of words into a multiword unit means that they form a new meaning. Consider, for example, collocations from Aviation such as *base leg, sniffer dog,* and *black box* (Aiguo, 2007). Some of the main issues in working with multiword units for specific purposes include being able to identify all combinations of words that might make up a unit, for example, *deem necessary, deemed necessary, deem (to be/not to be) necessary, deem(ed) unnecessary* and so on.

Longer word strings often contain shorter ones, for example, *at the end of the* contains *at the end, the end of,* and *the end of the.* Wood and Appel (2014) carried out a study of university textbooks in business and engineering and multiword units. They used their textbook corpus to look closely at the root structures of multiword units, which they identified by comparing three- and four-word units to identify the most frequent pattern. Wood and Appel (2014) also identified overlaps in the multiword units before and after the root structures. They streamlined the presentation of these overlaps to show options of words on either side of the root structure like this: *(at) the end of (the).* This work is important because learners need to know how multiword units fit together and as much as possible focus on these units as a whole rather than as individual words (Wray, 2002; Boers *et al.,* 2017).

13.3.2 Imbalance in corpus-based vocabulary studies in ESP

The second issue is that we know much more about the vocabulary of some fields in ESP than we do in others. Researchers have developed technical word lists in engineering (Ward, 1999, 2009; Watson Todd, 2017), medicine (Chen & Ge, 2007; Hsu, 2013; Le & Miller, 2020; Lei & Liu, 2016) and various sub-fields of medicine such as pharmacology (Fraser, 2009), nursing (Bosher, 2013; Staples, 2019; Yang, 2015), and Traditional Chinese Medicine (Hsu, 2018; Lu & Coxhead, 2020). The variety of studies in each of these fields shows some of the richness in the different areas and how corpora can support investigations into lexis and ESP. There is variation of approaches to corpora even within one field and with a shared goal of curriculum development. Yang (2015), for example, draws on corpora to develop a technical word list of nursing, while Staples (2019) uses spoken corpora to investigate pronunciation in interactions between nurses and patients. Another example is Traditional Chinese Medicine (TCM), where Hsu (2018) investigates mid- and low-frequency vocabulary in a TCM corpus, while Lu and Coxhead (2020) look into loan words from Chinese in TCM (e.g. *yin, yang,* and *qi*) and medical vocabulary from English (e.g. *rhizome, fructus*). Both these studies draw on corpora, but in different ways. These approaches help us build our understanding of the lexis of a field.

Other areas of substantial research in ESP include Law (e.g. Bancroft-Billings, 2020; Csomay & Petrović, 2012; Hafner & Candlin, 2007; Northcott, 2013). It is good to see work in this area focusing on spoken lexis (Bancroft-Billings, 2020; Csomay & Petrović, 2012), but in different ways. Bancroft-Billings (2020), for example, investigated the vocabulary used by a university lecturer in a first-year law course on contracts and also the written texts which were used in the course. The total corpus size is nearly 685,000 running words, and a comparison corpus was also used to develop a keyword list (including, for example, *attorney, adjudicated, infringement,* and *malpractice.* Aviation is another area of research focus in vocabulary and ESP as evidenced by researchers such as Estival *et al.* (2016), Moder (2013), Aiguo (2007), and Friginal (this volume). Another productive area of research in ESP is business, see for example, Konstantakis (2007) and Nelson (n.d.) for general business studies vocabulary. More subject-based research has looked into accounting and finance (e.g. Ha & Hyland, 2017; Li & Qian, 2010; Smith, 2020; Tongpoon-Patanasorn, 2018). There is much work to do in areas in ESP beyond these mentioned so briefly here.

13.3.3 *How big is a technical vocabulary?*

The final issue is the size of a technical vocabulary in ESP (Nation, 2016). This issue is important because it points to the amount of learning that is required in English, which, in turn, affects ESP courses and independent language learning. Corpus-based studies are helpful for identifying technical vocabulary, as already mentioned. But the amount of knowledge a learner has about a topic is also an important factor to take into account. That is, someone who is studying finance, for example, with some years of experience working in banks, insurance, or business, would presumably have a head start over someone else who was starting their studies in finance as a completely new subject area. Nation (2016) points out that finding out about the size of a specialized vocabulary essentially involves dividing vocabulary knowledge into two categories. The first category is words which are technical and are part of general language knowledge. Nation (2016) uses examples of *lungs* and *penicillin* to illustrate the point that while they may not be considered as technical by some people, they are related to medical English. The second category is words that are technical and part of specialized knowledge, and he uses examples such as *xiphoid* and *hemoglobin*.

Specialized word lists or studies into vocabulary in areas such as chemistry (e.g. Valipouri & Nassaji, 2013) can help with understanding more about specialized vocabulary that is worth learning. They can also help with understanding the possible size of a learning goal for technical vocabulary (Nation, 2016) and, perhaps, indicating where beginner learners might start, through lists that are presented according to frequency, such as the Fabrication Word List (Coxhead *et al.*, 2019) with its most frequent items appearing first: *welding/weld(-s/-ed/-er/-ability)*, *work(-ing/-er(s))*, *figure(s)*, *cutting/cutter(s)/cut(s)*, *tool(s)/tooling*, *material(s)*, and *machine(s)/-ery/-ing/-ed/-ability*. Each fabrication word met the selection criteria for the word list according to frequency and meaning and was then ordered by frequency. Then all types that were related were gathered under the headword to show that these items were related and technical, for example *welding/ weld(-s/-ed/-er/-ability)* means this group includes *welding, weld, welds, welded, welder*, and *weldability*. Carrying out this work without corpora would be even more painstaking.

Technical word lists can be used to calculate coverage figures, which can tell us more about the amount of technical vocabulary in texts (see Section 2.1). These figures are useful, particularly when comparing technical vocabulary in written and spoken texts. For example, the Fabrication Word List covers a much higher proportion of pedagogical written fabrication texts (30.47%) compared to spoken fabrication texts (classroom tutor talk) at 9.19% (Coxhead *et al.*, 2019). This is important because first and second language learners in trades education learn a great deal through spoken language, demonstrations in classrooms, and talking through problems with classmates and tutors (Coxhead *et al.*, 2020b). Their reading texts contain far higher amounts of technical vocabulary, as Coxhead *et al.* (2019) show in the case of fabrication, and learners have commented that how the technical words sound and how they are written are often very different, for example, *fascia* and *scotia* in carpentry (Coxhead et al., 2016).

13.4 Current contributions and research

Two studies are discussed in this section in relation to the use of corpora for specialized vocabulary and their applications to teaching and learning. The first study is by Csomay and

Petrović (2012) who examined the possibilities of learning legal vocabulary through movies and TV programs. The second study is by Coxhead and Demecheleer (2018) and focuses on the vocabulary of plumbing. These studies were chosen because they are examples of innovation in corpus studies and ESP in the Csomay and Petrović (2012) research, and how corpus analysis can be augmented by expert judgments and push the boundaries of ESP as a field in the second study.

Csomay and Petrović (2012) began with a question of whether and what legal vocabulary might be contained in legal movies and TV programs. This kind of practical pedagogical question is typical of ESP research and is one of the cornerstones of the field. Their Movie and TV corpus quite small for this study at 128, 897 running words and the number of running words were quite different between the episodes of the TV program and the movies. Csomay and Petrović (2012) were interested in repetition of technical vocabulary, what to do with cryptotechnical legal terms such as *brief* and *party* and how much exposure learners would get to technical vocabulary in the movies (e.g. *A Few Good Men*; *Runaway Jury)* and TV programs (e.g. *Law and Order)* on the whole. They used corpus analysis and careful checking of a legal dictionary to guide decisions on legal terms to make a specialized word list of 651 types (218 families) which covered 6.2% of the whole corpus (p. 310). The list was divided into frequency bands and examples of the legal terms include *bar, arrest, constitute, deny, court, document, permit, warrant, withdraw, proceed, firearm, fingerprint, exam, and excuse.* The word list coverage differed over TV programs (3.5%) compared to movies (7.2%) and technical word families occurred roughly twice as often in the movies than in the TV episodes. Over 78% of the specialized types in the word list appear ten times or more in both the movies and the TV programs. The specialized vocabulary was not dispersed evenly between scenes, which is not surprising because movie and TV plots often involve aspects of life outside of courtrooms and law offices.

Another use of corpus tools in the study by Csomay and Petrović (2012) involved an early version of AntConc (Anthony, 2020), which was used to provide context for collocations for the legal vocabulary and to consider what learning might be available in the movie and TV corpora for the legal terms. For example, Band 1 items (5–7 encounters in the corpus) for the legal term *argue* include: *We're gonna ARGUE Great Benefit's motion to dismiss*; *I'm prepared to ARGUE the motion*; and *Let him ARGUE the case* (p. 312). These examples from the corpora illustrate patterns of use for *argue* that are different from what learners might have encountered in general English, such as *argue a motion* or *argue a case*. Other examples from the concordancing data show how specialized word families appear in the corpora, such as *depose, deposition* and *depositions* in these examples from Band 2 (8–9 encounters) from Csomay and Petrović (2012, p. 312): *I come from Memphis to DEPOSE four people*; *I'm going to DEPOSE Mr Lefkin, then I'm going to go*; *The DEPOSTION is set for next Thursday afternoon*; and *I'm going to take DEPOSITIONS from all the executives.*

It is possible to investigate items from the specialized word list from the Csomay and Petrović (2012) study using Tom Cobb's (n.d.) Compleat Lexical Tutor website which houses the British Law Report Corpus (BLaRC) and the Law section of the British National Corpus. Other specialized corpora include electrical engineering, commerce, and medicine. Laurence Anthony's (2019a) AntCorgen software allows users to create their own discipline specific corpora using the internet and carry out their own lexical analysis using other tools such as AntConc. For more on such tools, see Anthony (2019b) and Hendry and Sheepy (this volume). The Csomay and Petrović (2012) study focused on spoken language use and specialized vocabulary. This is an area that has taken more time to develop than analysis of written texts and has much to offer teachers and learners in ESP.

The second case study focuses on technical vocabulary in plumbing (Coxhead & Demecheleer, 2018), and amongst other things, identifying technical vocabulary in written and spoken pedagogical trades-based education texts in a polytechnic in Aotearoa/New Zealand. The written texts were used by tutors in plumbing courses and the spoken texts were gathered by recording plumbing tutors in classrooms or on building sites – the students in the construction trades build houses as part of the course each year. This research was part of a wider investigation on language in trades education (see Coxhead *et al.*, 2020b). One aim of the plumbing study was to find out more about specialized vocabulary in the trade through interviews with plumbing tutors. One of the key concerns was the need to build knowledge of this lexis with all students in the plumbing class, as the following quote from a tutor illustrates (Coxhead & Demecheleer, 2018, p. 91):

> First language students have a lack of knowledge - they call a pair of pipetongs [correct name] 'tongs' or 'Stilsons' [trade name]. Trade names are often used [for example] 'crescent' instead of 'shifting spanner'. [Students] need to be specific - 'go and get a drill' - is it the power drill or the drill bit?

One purpose of the study was to develop a specialized word list of plumbing to support learners in the trade, and in this case, corpus-based data were used along with expert opinion on the technicality of words. The first steps in identifying items for the word list involved an analysis of the written corpus and the application of frequency principles. The next steps involved seeking the expert opinion on the meaning of high-frequency items from the initial analysis because many of these words also had everyday meaning and the researchers were applied linguists and ESOL specialists rather than plumbing specialists. The tutors were asked to rate the technicality of a sample of words in a warm-up task whereby they awarded scores of 2 = technical meaning in plumbing, 1 = related to plumbing but not very technical, and 0 = not technical at all. Items from the warm up task included *pressure, asbestos, external, welding, flashings, earth, length,* and *openings.* The tutors then individually ranked over 300 other items from the corpus each, before the spoken corpus was then investigated for specialized plumbing lexis. Items from the spoken corpus which did not appear in the written corpus included *wingback* and *dwang.* The checking process with tutors was augmented by consulting dictionaries and glossaries for definition where possible, as well as the written and spoken corpora for evidence of how the words were used in context and technical meaning. These extra checking mechanisms were important because time spent with the tutors was precious and in short supply given their workload.

Coxhead and Demecheleer's (2018) Plumbing Word List contains 1465 types which are arranged by frequency in 14 sublists of 100 items and one list of 65 items. Table 13.1 shows the first 15 items in the most frequent sublist, beginning with *pipe(s/-ing/-ed)* and the last 15 items in the Plumbing Word List from the lowest frequency sublist, ending with *wingback.* Note the most frequent items in the column on the left include words which are commonly used in everyday English, e.g. *air, building,* and *required,* but also have a specialized meaning in plumbing. The items in the right column are not often encountered outside the field and clearly require specialized knowledge, e.g. *LOSP-treated* and *dwang.*

Hyphenated words in the Plumbing Word List include *P-trap, thermo-electrical* and *drain-in-common,* and there are many more examples in the right column in Table 13.1. Dealing with hyphenated words needs careful consideration in corpus-based studies (Nation, 2016). The Coxhead and Demecheleer (2018) study also showed that abbreviations, for example *Electromotive Force (EMF), Ethylene Propylene Diene Monomer (EPDM),* and Evapotranspiration

Table 13.1 The 15 most and least frequent items in the Plumbing Word List (Coxhead & Demecheleer, 2018)

First 15 items in Plumbing Sublist One	Final 15 items in Plumbing Sublist 15 cont.
pipe(s/-ing/-ed)	forced-draught
drain(s/-ing/-ed)	in-floor
building(s) / builder	kick-out
required / requirements	LOSP-treated
gas(es) / gaseous	mild-steel
heat(ing/er/ers/ed)	mill-finish
installation(s)/installed/ing/er	open-flued
work(ing)	oxygen-deficient
pressure(s) / pressurized	soil-pipe
valve(s)	stop-bank
air	thermo-electrical
document(s)(/-ation)	trickle-fill
connected / connection(s)	wall-mounted
supply(-ies/-iers)	dwang
vent(s/-ed/-ing / unvented)	wingback

Seepage (*ETS*) and proper nouns (e.g. *Wobbe* and *Gibault*) can also meet frequency and semantic requirements for technicality.

Differences in the amount of technical vocabulary in spoken and written texts is another important point to note from the plumbing study. Example (1) contains a short section of an interaction in class from the spoken plumbing corpus between a plumbing tutor and students in which they are discussing foul water and the Building Act of New Zealand. Items in the Plumbing Word List are highlighted in bold. There is roughly one word from the list per line, covering just over 16% of the words in the text. This coverage is higher than over the whole plumbing spoken corpus reported by Coxhead and Demecheleer (2018, p. 93) at 11.59%. Often the Plumbing Word List items are repeated, for example, *sewage* in Turns 2 and 3, and *grey* as in *grey water* in Turns 4 and 6. Note also the definitions for terms such as *waste water* being given or confirmed by the tutor and the use of humor in the final turn.

(1) A Plumbing tutor and students talk about foul water – Plumbing Word List items in bold

<Tutor:> (Turn 1) **G13 Foul** water. What does **foul** water cover? What do you think it covers?

<Student > (Turn 2) **Sewage**.

<Tutor:> (Turn 3) **Sewage** and?

<Student:> (Turn 4) **Grey** water.

<Student:> (Turn 5) **Untreated**.

<Tutor:> (Turn 6) **Grey** water or? we don't actually use the term **grey** water yet as such, so what is it? What do we call it? We are referring to the Australian **standards strictly**. **Grey** and black water. So what do we?, especially when we are referring to the **building code**, what's the **grey** water referred to?

< Student:> (Turn 7) **Untreated**?

<Tutor:> (Turn 8) No. Ok we've got **soil fixtures**, haven't we? And that would be black water, so that's your **toilets** and **urinals**, and **grey** water would be?

<Tutor:> (Turn 9) Oh your kitchen.

< Student:> (Turn 10) from the **sink**.

<Tutor:> (Turn 11) Yup. Shower, **bath**, so what do we call it? No? The **sanitary fixtures**?

< Student:> (Turn 12) **Waste** water

<Tutor:> (Turn 13) **Waste** water, exactly. That's called?... we call that **waste** water. Ok? Now, as always when you are reading the **G13**, you'll be trying to get information, where do we start?

<Student:> (Turn 14) at the start?

Note that *reading* is a cryptotechnical word in plumbing, in the sense for example of *sensors giving a reading*. In Example (1), the meaning is connected to reading an official document, the G13, which is part of the Building Code in New Zealand that deals with foul water as illustrated in Example (2). The tutor is working through the reading of that document in class to help with understanding and applying the written text in speaking.

Example (2) shows a section of the actual G13 Building Act, also with Plumbing Word List items in bold. The coverage of the word list is 37.5% over this section of written text, which is similar to Coxhead and Demecheleer's (2018) coverage figures for the whole written plumbing corpus of 34.48% (p. 93). This coverage is higher than the spoken text in Example (1) and is important because learners in the trades have large amounts of spoken input which contains less technical vocabulary than their written texts (see Coxhead *et al.*, 2020b for more).

(2) G13 Foul Water section of the Building Code (MBIE, n.d.) with Plumbing Word List items in bold

G13 **Foul** water

Requires the safe **disposal** of **foul** water to **prevent** illness and the loss of amenity due to **odor** and **accumulated** matter.

Under this **clause, buildings** in which **sanitary fixtures** and **sanitary appliances** using water-borne **waste disposal** are **installed** must be provided with **adequate plumbing** and **drainage** to **appropriate outfalls** or system for **storage/treatment**. This **safeguards** people from **infection** or **contamination** of the water **supply**.

It **sets** out **requirements** for the **construction** of **plumbing** systems and **protects** against loss of amenity due to **odor** or **accumulation** of offensive matter from **foul** water **disposal**.

Record of **amendments** is a record of changes to the **Acceptable Solutions, Verification Methods** and handbooks.

Example (2) shows examples of technical multiword units in **bold**, based around plumbing terms such *disposal* as in *water-borne waste disposal, foul water disposal* and *sanitary* as in *sanitary fixtures* and sanitary *appliances*.

13.5 Future directions of research

There are three main areas in this final section of the chapter: taking ESP corpus-based research into the classroom, using corpus-based research for testing in ESP, and the need for more replication studies in research as well as expanding the existing areas of ESP and vocabulary research using corpora.

13.5.1 *Taking corpus-based vocabulary research into ESP classrooms*

Taking corpus-based research into ESP classrooms is important because the main purpose of the research is usually to help learners and teachers in some way with the technical vocabulary of a field. The research could be focused on the use of input such as TV programs in the classroom and what they may offer learners and teachers, as in Csomay and Petrović (2012) and science fiction reading and science-related vocabulary (Rolls & Rogers, 2017), or the technical vocabulary of a particular field. It is important to consider the generalizability of research findings which have been created in one context and for a group of learners to other contexts and other groups of learners. There may be clear advantages for working with established word lists in ESP, particularly if they are designed well and fit the purposes of students, teachers, and courses. Clearly, definitions and procedures used for identifying technical vocabulary need to be clearly explained in research and be easily interpretable. Ideally, suggestions on how to use corpus-based findings in ESP course design, learning, and teaching also need to be practical, and where possible, address some of the key issues outlined in this chapter already, such as the use of types for counting words.

Careful consideration is needed when adopting or adapting research for classrooms. If, for example, a specialized word list is being considered for use in an ESP class, it is vital to know the purpose of the list, what corpora were used in the development and checking of a list, what principles were used, why, how words were counted (types, families or other), and how the list is organized. Nation (2016) sets out an evaluative framework for word lists which includes those key points as well as what word lists were actually developed along with the main list. For example, Coxhead and Demecheleer (2018) first identified words which only occurred in the spoken and written plumbing corpora and not in Nation's BNC/COCA lists. They then applied frequency and semantic principles to all the words in the corpora to identify items for inclusion in the Plumbing Word List.

13.5.2 *Using corpus-based vocabulary research for testing in ESP*

The key point in this section is that testing and vocabulary knowledge of specialized vocabulary is an area of possible development in future. There are tests, for example, of academic vocabulary knowledge using Gardner and Davies' (2014) AVL (Pecorari *et al.*, 2019). Nation (2016) points out that a test would need to be developed from lists which have been made carefully and checked. They also need to take into account the frequency of technical words, as high-frequency words with specialized meanings might well be better known than low-frequency technical words. The amount of background knowledge of learners is also an important factor to take into account, along with the fit between the corpora used to develop a word list and the needs of the learners who are being tested. Nation (2016, pp. 180–182) outlines key considerations when making vocabulary tests based on word lists.

13.5.3 *Replication studies and expanding areas of ESP and vocabulary research using corpora*

Carrying out more replication studies in corpus-based research is a valuable direction for research. Miller and Biber (2015) raise an important issue with corpora and reliability, which is that it can be difficult to replicate findings of corpus-based studies, even when applying the same principles. Their principal concerns include whether a corpus actually represents the academic or specialized domain and corpus design and content in relation to linguistic variation. They illustrate their points through carrying out a range of studies on vocabulary in university psychology textbooks, such as comparing the results of an analysis of a whole textbook and a sample of chapters. They conclude that there is a large amount of variability in the results and that they were unable to, therefore, present a word list from the textbook corpus that was reliable.

The second issue in this section is expanding the areas of vocabulary and ESP research using corpora. As noted above, some areas of ESP are well serviced in corpus-based research, while others remain relatively untouched. It would be good to see a broader range of research (for example, in areas such as aviation, human resources, sports, vocational education), a wider understanding of vocabulary in ESP and, therefore, more support for ESP learners and teachers.

Further reading

Coxhead, A., Parkinson, J., Mackay, J., & McLaughlin, E. (2020). *English for vocational purposes: Language use in trades education*. Routledge. This book focuses on corpus-based discourse and lexical analyses of written and spoken language in trades education, as well as visual analysis of texts.

Miller, D., & Biber, D. (2015). Evaluating reliability in quantitative vocabulary studies: The influence of corpus design and composition. *International Journal of Corpus Linguistics*, *20*(1), 30–53. This article is essential reading for anyone who is developing a technical word list or wanting to find out more about reliability and word list development.

Nation, I. S. P. (2016). *Making and using word lists for language learning and testing*. Benjamins. This book contains a wide-ranging discussion on word lists, with chapters on specialised vocabulary, multiword units and counting words, amongst others.

Woodrow, L. (2018). *Introducing course design in English for Specific Purposes*. Routledge. Chapter 15 of Woodrow (2018) has a list of word lists, webpages, dictionaries, corpora and concordances for ESP.

References

Aiguo, W. (2007). Teaching aviation English in the Chinese context: Developing ESP theory in a non-English speaking country. *English for Specific Purposes*, *26*, 121–128.

Anthony, L. (2018). *Introducing English for Specific Purposes*. Routledge.

Anthony, L. (2020). AntConc (Version 3.5.9) [Computer Software]. Waseda University. Available from https://www.laurenceanthony.net/software.

Anthony, L. (2019a). AntCorGen (Version 1.1.2) [Computer Software]. Waseda University. Available from https://www.laurenceanthony.net/software.

Anthony, L. (2019b). Tools and strategies for Data-Driven Learning(DDL). In K. Hyland & L. Wong (Eds.), *Specialised English: New directions in ESP and EAP research and practice* (pp. 179–194). Routledge.

Bancroft-Billings, S. (2020). Identifying spoken technical legal vocabulary in a law school classroom. *English for Specific Purposes*, *60*, 9–25.

Basturkmen, H. (2006). *Ideas and options for English for Specific Purposes*. Continuum.

Bauer, L., & Nation, I. S. P. (1993). Word families. *International Journal of Lexicography*, *6*, 253–279.

Boers, F., Dang, T. C. T., & Strong, B. (2017). Comparing the effectiveness of phrase-focused exercises: A partial replication of Boers, Demecheleer, Coxhead, and Webb (2014). *Language Teaching Research*, *21*, 362–380.

Bosher, S. (2013). English for nursing. In B. Paltridge & S. Starfield (Eds.), *The handbook of English for Specific Purposes* (pp. 263–281). Wiley-Blackwell.

Chen, Q., & C, Ge. (2007). A corpus-based lexical study on frequency and distribution of Coxhead's AWL word families in medical research articles. *English for Specific Purposes, 26*, 502–514.

Chung, T. M., & Nation, P. (2003). Technical vocabulary in specialised texts. *Reading in a Foreign Language, 15*(2), 103–116.

Chung, T. M., & Nation, P. (2004). Identifying technical vocabulary. *System, 32*(2), 251–263.

Cobb, T. (n.d.) Webb concordance – English. [Online]. Available: https://www.lextutor.ca/conc/eng/. [14 August, 2020].

Coxhead, A. (2000). A new academic word list. *TESOL Quarterly, 34*(2), 213–238.

Coxhead, A. (2018). *Vocabulary and English for Specific Purposes research: Quantitative and qualitative perspectives.* Routledge.

Coxhead, A., & Dang, T. N. Y. (2019). Vocabulary in university tutorials and laboratories: Corpora and word lists. In K. Hyland & K. Wong (Eds.), *Specialised English: New directions in ESP and EAP research* (pp. 120–134). Routledge.

Coxhead, A., & Demecheleer, M. (2018). Investigating the technical vocabulary of plumbing. *English for Specific Purposes, 51*, 84–97.

Coxhead, A., & Nation, P. (2001). The specialised vocabulary of English for academic purposes. In J. Flowerdew & M. Peacock (Eds.), *Research perspectives on English for Academic Purposes* (pp. 252–267). Cambridge University Press.

Coxhead, A., Demecheleer, M., & McLaughlin, E. (2016). The technical vocabulary of carpentry: Loads, lists and bearings. *TESOLANZ Journal, 24*, 38–71.

Coxhead, A., McLaughlin, E., & Reid, A. (2019). The development and application of a specialised word list: The case of fabrication. *Journal of Vocational Education & Training, 71*(2), 175–200.

Coxhead, A., Parkinson, J., & Tu'amoheloa, F. (2020a). Using Talanoa to develop bilingual word lists of technical vocabulary in the trades. *International Journal of Bilingual Education and Bilingualism, 23*(5), 513–533.

Coxhead, A., Parkinson, J., Mackay, J., & McLaughlin, E. (2020b). *English for vocational purposes: Language use in trades education.* Routledge.

Csomay, E., & Petrović, M. (2012). "Yes, your honor!": A corpus-based study of technical vocabulary in discipline-related movies and TV shows. *System, 40*(2), 305–315.

Estival, D., Farris, C., & Molesworth, B. (2016). *Aviation English: A lingua franca for pilots and air traffic controllers.* Routledge.

Fraser, S. (2009). Breaking down the divisions between general, academic and technical vocabulary: The establishment of a single, discipline-based word list for ESP learners. *Hiroshima Studies in Language and Language Education, 12*, 151–167.

Gardner, D., & Davies, M. (2014). A New Academic Vocabulary List. *Applied Linguistics, 35*, 305–327. https://doi.org/10.1093/applin/amt015

Ha, A. Y. H., & Hyland, K. (2017). What is technicality? A Technicality Analysis Model for EAP vocabulary. *Journal of English for Specific Purposes, 28*, 35–49.

Hafner, C., & Candlin, C. (2007). Corpus tools as an affordance to learning in professional legal education. *Journal of English for Academic Purposes, 6*, 303–318.

Hsu, W. H. (2013). Bridging the vocabulary gap for EFL medical undergraduates: The establishment of a medical word list. *Language Teaching Research, 17*(4), 454–484.

Hsu, W. (2018). The most frequent BNC/COCA mid- and low-frequency word families in English-medium traditional Chinese medicine (TCM) textbooks. *English for Specific Purposes, 51*, 98–110.

Konstantakis, N. (2007). Creating a business word list for teaching business English. *Elia, 7*, 79–102.

Le, C. N. N., & Miller, J. (2020). A corpus-based list of commonly used English medical morphemes for students learning English for specific purposes. *English for Specific Purposes, 58*, 102–121.

Lei, L., & Liu, D. L. (2016). A new medical academic word list: A corpus-based study with enhanced methodology. *Journal of English for Academic Purposes, 22*, 42–53.

Li, Y. & Qian, D. (2010). Profiling the Academic Word List (AWL) in a financial corpus. *System, 38*, 402–411.

Lu, C., & Coxhead, A. (2020). Vocabulary in traditional Chinese medicine: Insights from corpora. *ITL - International Journal of Applied Linguistics, 171*(1), 34–61.

Miller, D., & Biber, D. (2015). Evaluating reliability in quantitative vocabulary studies: The influence of corpus design and composition. *International Journal of Corpus Linguistics, 20*(1), 30–53.

Ministry of Business, Innovation and Employment (MBIE) (n.d.). [Online]. Available: https://www. building.govt.nz/building-code-compliance/g-services-and-facilities/g13-foul-water/ [14 August, 2020].

Moder, C. L. (2013). Aviation English. In B. Paltridge & S. Starfield (Eds.), *The handbook of English for Specific Purposes* (pp. 227–242). Wiley-Blackwell.

Nation, I. S. P. (2016). *Making and using word lists for language learning and testing.* Benjamins.

Nation, I. S. P. (2013). *Learning vocabulary in another language* (2nd ed.). Cambridge University Press.

Nelson, M. (n.d.) *Mike Nelson's Business English Lexis Site.* [Online]. Available: http://users.utu.fi/ micnel/business_english_lexis_site.htm. [13 August, 2020].

Northcott, J. (2013). Legal English. In B. Paltridge & S. Starfield (Eds.), *The handbook of English for Specific Purposes* (pp. 213–226). Wiley-Blackwell.

Parkinson, J., & Mackay, J. (2016). The literacy practices of vocational training in carpentry and auto-motive technology. *Journal of Vocational Education & Training, 68*(1), 33–50.

Pecorari, D., Shaw, P., & Malmström, H. (2019). Developing a new academic vocabulary test. *Journal of English for Academic Purposes, 39*, 59–71.

Quero, B., & Coxhead, A. (2018). Using a corpus-based approach to select medical vocabulary for an ESP course: The case for high-frequency vocabulary. In K. Yasemin & K. Dikilitaş (Eds.), *Key issues in English for Specific Purposes in higher education* (pp. 51–75). Springer.

Rolls, H., & Rodgers, M. P. (2017). Science-specific technical vocabulary in science fiction-fantasy texts: A case for 'language through literature'. *English for Specific Purposes, 48*, 44–56.

Schmitt, N., & Schmitt, D. (2012). A reassessment of frequency and vocabulary size in L2 vocabulary teaching. *Language Teaching, 47*(4), 484–503.

Simpson-Vlach, R., & Ellis, N. (2010). An academic formulas list: New methods in phraseology research. *Applied Linguistics, 31*(4), 487–512.

Staples, S. (2019). Using corpus-based discourse analysis for curriculum development: Creating and evaluating a pronunciation course for internationally educated nurses. *English for Specific Purposes, 53*, 13–29.

Tongpoon-Patanasorn, A. (2018). Developing a frequent technical words list for finance: A hybrid approach. *English for Specific Purposes, 51*, 45–54.

Valipouri, L., & Nassaji, H. (2013). A corpus-based study of academic vocabulary in chemistry research articles. *Journal of English for Academic Purposes, 12*, 248–263.

Ward, J. (1999). How large a vocabulary do EAP engineering students need? *Reading in a Foreign Language, 12*(2), 309–324.

Ward, J. (2009). A basic engineering English word list for less proficient foundation engineering undergraduates. *English for Specific Purposes, 28*(3), 170–182.

Watson Todd, R. (2017). An opaque engineering word list: Which words should a teacher focus on? *English for Specific Purposes, 45*, 31–39.

West, M. P. (1953). *A general service list of English words.* Longman.

Wood, D. C., & Appel, R. (2014). Multiword constructions in first year business and engineering university textbooks and EAP textbooks. *Journal of English for Academic Purposes, 15*, 1–13.

Woodrow, L. (2018). *Introducing course design in English for Specific Purposes.* Routledge.

Woodward-Kron, R. (2008). More than just jargon: The nature and role of specialist language in learning disciplinary knowledge. *Journal of English for Academic Purposes, 7*(4), 234–249.

Wray, A. (2002). *Formulaic sequences and the lexicon.* Cambridge University Press.

Yang, M.-N. (2015). A nursing academic word list. *English for Specific Purposes, 37*, 27–38.

14

CORPORA FOR TEACHING COLLOCATIONS IN ESP

Clarence Green

14.1 Introduction

Collocation refers to the systematic relationships between words in corpora (Gablasova *et al.*, 2017). Its importance as a topic is often justified through citation of Firth's (1957) observation that "you shall know a word by the company it keeps" (p. 179), a quip capturing the intuition that for any given vocabulary item the words that pattern with it often contribute to its meaning. Since Firth (1957), corpus research has confirmed this is a linguistic fact. To illustrate, in the Corpus of Contemporary American English (Davies, 2010), *student* collocates with *college, teacher, learning, university*, and in the Cambridge Dictionary Online (n.d.), *student* is defined as "a person who is *learning* at a *college* or *university*". Furthermore, English for specific purposes corpus research has shown that collocations vary by discipline and professional domain. In education samples from the same corpus above, for example, the collocations of *student* include *achievement, outcomes, retention, persistence* – important disciplinary concepts for teachers. The rich body of corpus research and its significant pedagogical implications for teaching collocations in English for Specific Purposes (ESP) are the focus of the current chapter.

As a starting point, some working definitions for English for Specific Purposes (ESP) and collocations are needed. Anthony (2018) defines ESP as "an approach to language teaching that targets the current and/or future academic or occupational needs of learners, focuses on the necessary language, genres, and skills to address these needs" (p. 1). He argues that the extensive use of corpora is essential to ESP if it is to effectively address the needs of students through discipline-specific resources and pedagogy. Green and Lambert (2018) suggest that ESP should be defined broadly, rather than conceptualized narrowly as a field within second language acquisition and tertiary-level language teaching. Teaching the language of specific disciplines or professions is important to both first and second language learners (Frankenberg-Garcia *et al.*, 2019) and relevant to educational contexts such as secondary and middle school (Greene & Coxhead, 2015).

Collocation has varying definitions and operationalizations in research. This can be challenging in that it leads to somewhat vague definitions, such as the formulation above "systematic relationships between words", yet this flexibility makes collocation a rich research area with wide scope. For example, Szudarski's (2012, 2017) working definition is the non-technical,

 DOI: 10.4324/9781003002901-17

but not unreasonable, phrase: word partnerships. This definition situates collocation within a broader "area of linguistic study dealing with larger sequences of language, formulae, idioms, proverbs, collocations and other phrases" (Szudarski, 2012, p. 3). While most would agree that collocation and these other areas of linguistic study are closely connected, precisely how and to what extent meaningful boundaries exist between them is not widely agreed upon. Boers and Webb (2018), for example, report that the greatest challenge when reviewing the research on collocation pedagogy in the classroom is "deciding how wide to cast the net" (p. 77).

Partington (1998), based on a historical overview of corpus linguistics that is still reasonable 20 years later, suggests that corpus research typically defines collocation in one of three ways: as textual, psychological, or statistical. When collocation is defined textually, it refers to a word that occurs more frequently than other words with a particular "node" (the target word whose relationships with other words are under examination) within a short span of text. The span is typically a 4–5 word "window" to the left or right of a node, a tradition deriving from Sinclair's (1991) observations that collocates within 4–5 words tend to be the ones that contribute to meaning (e.g. sense disambiguation in the node). When collocation is defined psychologically, the focus is on words with cognitive associations. A collocation is typically demonstrated to be psychological when two (or more) words have a faster reaction or production time together than when they are combined with different words, or when a word can prime another upon hearing or reading it, i.e. speed up the other word's reaction/production time. Psychological collocates are initially extracted from corpora then verified as psychologically real in the lab (Siyanova-Chanturia & Spina, 2020). When defined statistically, collocations are those words that co-occur and are textually more frequent than would be expected by chance given their distributional patterns with other words in the corpus (Gries, 2013).

Most current research into collocation in ESP uses a statistical measure of association. The two most common are Mutual Information (MI) and the t-score, though a wide range of other association statistics is available, including measures such as Delta P (Gries, 2013) which helpfully takes into account the direction of the collocation. Gablasova *et al.* (2017, p. 161) argue that MI is the most popular statistical measure of collocation. It is a logarithm of the number of co-occurrences of two words compared to their separate occurrences in a corpus, and typically an MI score of 3 or above is used to identify a meaningful collocation. MI highlights semantically coherent units and technical vocabulary, e.g. *carbon dioxide* and often excludes function words, but its drawback is that it values infrequent collocations when the collocating words have a tendency to be exclusive. Nevertheless, when carefully used with minimum frequency, range, and dispersion criteria, the MI measure has been found useful in predicting teacher ratings of the pedagogical usefulness of collocations and reaction time in psycholinguistic experiments (Simpson-Vlach & Ellis, 2010). The t-score is a measure for identifying collocation adapted from the t-test. It is computed by finding the raw frequency of a collocation, subtracting the value of random co-occurrence, and dividing by the square root of the raw frequency. The t-score correlates strongly with text frequency, and so captures more function word collocations in contrast to MI. It is typically considered more reliable than the MI, not being as problematically influenced by low-frequency relationships (Kang, 2018). However, a disadvantage is that it cannot be compared across corpora as it is computed relative to the size of the corpus under study.

In language teaching, as Boers and Webb (2018) note, developing second language (L2) collocational knowledge is essential, because collocational proficiency makes a speaker "sound right", helps them process language faster, and frees up cognitive space for other language operations during communication. Crossley *et al.* (2015) found that the accuracy of collocation use was the best statistical predictor of ratings of lexical proficiency in a corpus of 480 L2 written and spoken texts. Collocations are clearly important but can be difficult to master for L2 learners. Granger and Bestgen (2014), for example, found that in academic writing intermediate learners overuse collocations with a strong t-score, e.g. *hard work*, and underuse lower-frequency ones with a high MI score, e.g. *conscientious objectors*. They argue that this may be because pedagogical materials do not attend sufficiently to collocations. In this vein, Nelson (2006) argues that ESP materials for business students should be enhanced with information on how collocations contribute to semantic prosody. Semantic prosody refers to how collocations can add negative or positive sentiment to a target word. In a study of a business English corpus, Nelson (2006) finds that vocabulary such as *boss* has negative semantic prosody, collocating with *meanest*, *old-fashioned*, etc., while its near synonym *manager* has positive semantic prosody, collocating with words such as *good* and *excellent*. He argues that explicitly pointing to such effects of collocation in pedagogical materials can prepare students better for professional communication.

This chapter reviews current research into the use of corpora for teaching ESP collocations. It summarizes the historical trajectory of the field, which has seen a shift from single-item wordlists to those enriched with collocation information, a trend from general academic to discipline-specific collocational research, and the expansion of collocation research to include linguistic phenomena such as collocational frameworks. Also discussed are core issues in the field such as the subject-specificity of collocations and their stability across disciplines. Several research-based collocation lists available for teachers in ESP are outlined. The chapter closes with a synopsis of a series of related papers from the past few years that represent several current trends in the field and suggests possibilities for what future research is required in order to move the field forward.

14.2 Review of current research

This section provides a historical perspective of the use of corpora for teaching collocations in ESP. There are perhaps four trends that have taken place, though they do not form distinct, consecutive historical periods, and often overlap in time and continue in parallel to the present day. The first trend has been a progression from single-word vocabulary lists to those enriched with collocational information. The second trend has been from developing pedagogical resources for general academic English to collocational resources for ESP. The third trend has focused on expanding collocation resources in ESP to include collocation frameworks. The fourth trend has been the growing interest in more direct uses of corpora, incorporating data-driven learning (DDL) into the teaching of collocation in ESP.

The first trend has been motivated by the increasing awareness of language variation, lexical co-patterning in corpora, and their importance to second language proficiency (Ellis, 2019). The historical development might be seen as one from corpus-derived wordlists to phraseology lists capturing some collocational variation amongst the words within semi-fixed phrases, to academic collocational lists based on word span windows (Gablasova *et al.*, 2017). The Phrase List (Martinez & Schmitt, 2012) is perhaps the best exemplar of a phraseological wordlist resource for general English. It was produced from the BNC, generating three–five-word recurrent sequences, which were then vetted for teachability. An academic counterpart, the Academic Formulas List (AFL) (Simpson-Vlach & Ellis, 2010), was developed based on 4.2 million words of academic speech and writing with the goal to identify pedagogically useful phrases for EAP. This list was extracted based on statistical measures such as multiple regression, Mutual Information (MI) scores, and a minimum of ten occurrences per million words, followed by a careful selection of items from the list that proved useful for pedagogical purposes. While primarily fixed phrases, the Phrase and AFL report some collocational variability, such as the AFL entry *(more) likely to (be)*, where the brackets represent optional collocations, or the Phrase entry *have got (+NP)*, where the brackets indicate that a noun phrase typically follows.

Subsequent research using the window approach to identify academic collocations and list them on a pedagogical resource was undertaken by Ackermann and Chen (2013) and Lei and Liu (2018). The Academic Collocation List (Ackermann & Chen, 2013) is drawn from 37 million words of textbooks, lectures, and journal papers from 28 disciplines. It lists 2468 collocations within a span of 3 words that have an MI above 3 and a t-score above 2. It lists collocations useful for academic speaking and writing such as *educational institution* and *economic power*. Lei and Liu (2018) produced the Academic English Collocation List which enriched the 3015 single-word items on the Academic Vocabulary List (Gardner & Davies, 2014) with their most frequent academic collocations. They derived 9049 collocations from corpora such as the BNC academic, BAWE, and Jiao Da English for Science and Technology Corpus. Collocates on the pedagogical resource were limited to those within a span of five words and with a mutual information (MI) score above 3 and t-score above 2. Lei and Liu (2018) note that the primary limitation of their list and Ackermann and Chen's (2013) is that these collocation lists are not discipline-specific and "it will be of interest and importance to develop discipline-specific academic English collocation lists" (p. 235).

This brings us to the second trend directed towards developing pedagogical resources for collocations in ESP. One of the earliest relevant papers here was Durrant's (2009) exploration of whether an EAP collocation list might suffice to cover a substantial number of ESP collocations, thereby reducing the need to produce discipline-specific resources. Durrant (2009) also was early in seeing that positional variability, i.e. the window approach, was a research gap since most ESP corpus research beyond single-item wordlist resources had tended to focus on fixed phrases (Hyland & Tse, 2007), so, while *significant differences* had been studied *significant physiological differences* and *differences were not significant* had not been. Durrant (2009), therefore, analyzed a corpus of 25 million words and 3251 articles of life and social sciences, engineering, administration, the arts and humanities, and extracted 1000 collocates occurring at least once every million words. Durrant (2009) reports variation in these 1000 collocations amongst disciplines that showed the importance of the collocations on his list were not equal in all disciplines. For example, in the arts and humanities, the frequency of collocations was 40–50% fewer per million words than other disciplines. Based on this evidence, he concludes that a general EAP collocation list would not suffice to support students in ESP and concludes discipline-specific collocation resources would need to be developed.

The most recent contribution to the development of such discipline-specific collocation resources has been Jablonkai's (2020) work in the domain of EU professional communication. Jablonkai (2020) notes an imbalance in ESP research between professional and academic foci, with the former domain being less studied. She, therefore, developed a corpus-derived wordlist resource enriched with collocational information for professionals working within institutions in the European Union. A corpus was built from text samples identified as professionally relevant through interviews of 10 EU employees and 99 survey responses. The final corpus consisted of 1,174,753 words and 241 text types such as press releases, written regulations, and white papers. Jablonkai (2020) first extracts a wordlist from the corpus using criteria such as keyness, i.e. loglikelihood of 3 against BNC world, occurrence outside of the most frequent 2,000 words in the BNC-COCA, a minimum frequency of 57, use within at least 16 of 34 EU fields, and qualitative feedback on whether EU professionals would find a target word valuable. These 405-word families, named the European Union Wordlist, were then enriched with collocation information. Collocations for each target were extracted using criteria such as a mutual information (MI) score above 4, and a minimum frequency above 5 in at least 10% of the texts in the ESP corpus. The collocation list contains learning targets such as *European + parliament, community,* and *council; implement + measure, programme,* and *rule; criterion + eligibility, award,* and *selection.* Jablonkai (2020) compares the collocations to the collocations generated for the same single-word targets in a non-ESP corpus, namely, the BNC written component, and finds that many of the collocations are discipline-specific and not evident in the non-ESP corpus, thereby validating the value-added by a discipline-specific approach to collocation.

The third trend has been the broadening of the scope of collocational research and pedagogical resources to include what has been termed (amongst other nomenclature) "collocational frameworks". Collocational frameworks are the systematic patterns amongst words, grammar, and discourse, and also commonly referred to as mid-level constructions, p-frames/phrase frames, and pattern grammars (Hunston & Su, 2019). A typical collocational framework involves the collocation between a grammatical frame and a variable word, e.g. *a + N + of,* which is associated *a variety of/a number of/a series of* and accomplishes the discourse move of quantity specification. One of the earliest studies within ESP was Marco's (2000) analysis of collocational frameworks in a corpus of 100 medical research articles (298,457 words). Marco (2000) found that frequent collocation frameworks in medical papers such as *the...of, a...of,* and *be...to,* "enclose restricted sets of lexical items and that the selection of specific collocates for these frameworks is conditioned by the linguistic conventions of the genre" (p. 65). For example, the process within the word *discontinue* is not realized by the typical form for a process, namely the verb form, but by nominalization using the collocational framework *the... of,* e.g. *the discontinuation of digoxin.* Marco (2000) concludes that such frameworks should be pedagogically introduced within medical ESP and subsequently Marco's (2000) collocation frameworks were incorporated into some ESP textbooks (Swales & Feak, 2004).

More recently, Nekrasova-Beker (2019) explored the collocational frameworks of engineering, and Lu *et al.* (2018) explored the social sciences. Nekrasova-Beker (2019) takes up the issue of intra-variation amongst collocational frames within the sub-disciplines of engineering. She built an ESP corpus of 2.2 million words from textbooks in the areas of atmospheric sciences, biomedical engineering, civil and environmental engineering, electrical and computer engineering, and mechanical engineering. The analysis of the corpus identified common frames in engineering such as *the amount of *, the sum * the, can be * to* indicated that for four-word frames across the five engineering fields from 37–63% of their frames were shared. She concludes that while intra-variation in engineering exists, the amount of shared frameworks suggests that ESP teaching can usefully employ broader disciplinary/professional categories. Lu *et al.* (2018) developed a pedagogical list of collocational frameworks for social science from a corpus of 517,703 research articles in six sub-disciplinary areas to help students write introductions. Extraction criteria included 16 occurrences per million words for 5-word frames, 12 for six-word frames, a range greater than 3 texts occurrences across at least 2 social science areas. Each frame also had to collocate with two or more lexical content words. The final pedagogical list contained 270 of 5-word and 84 of 6-word frameworks. Lu *et al.* (2018) argue that collocational frameworks are possibly more useful than teaching fully specified lexical collocations. For example, rather than teaching *the aim of the study,* what can be taught is *the * of the study* frame where the variable collocate can be *aim* but also *goal, purpose, point,* all of which are variations on the same discourse move in social science research introductions.

The fourth trend to be reviewed in this section is the increased research into direct uses of corpora for teaching collocations in ESP. Direct corpus use refers to teacher and student interactions with ESP corpora in the classroom context (Crosthwaite & Cheung, 2019). Walker (2011a), for example, in the context of business English, conducted two case studies of teacher-directed use based on hypothetical classroom scenarios relating to the use of corpora for ESP collocation teaching. In case study 1, Walker (2011a) imagined a classroom scenario in which "Doctor T turns to his teacher and asks 'Should I say I run, manage or head, the Human Resources Division, or should I use a phrase like I am responsible for, or in charge of instead?'"(p. 104). How can the teacher respond in an evidence-based fashion? In the role of teacher-researcher, Walker (2011a) turns to an ESP corpus for the evidence and examines the collocates of *run, manage,* and *head* in the business subcategory of the BNC. This direct interrogation of collocates demonstrates that *manage* or *head* is to be preferred over *run* since the latter's semantic prosody is negative and suggests power, as in *run the show,* which might be taken as the communicative style of top-down management and better avoided in professional communication. In case study 2, Walker (2011a) proposed a hypothetical question related to a student looking for language that could frame a new innovation in customer invoices. The student asks if a new *system, process* or *procedure* would be the best words to use when communicating about the new innovation and wants to come across as having an inclusive management style. Direct corpus interrogation, Walker (2011a) reports, reveals *process* has negative semantic prosody, *procedure* collocates with norms and obligations such as *normal, standard, correct,* therefore, *system* is recommended in preference to the others.

While Walker (2011a) focusses on teacher-corpus interaction for enhancing collocation teaching in ESP, Crosthwaite and Cheung (2019) focus on student-corpus interaction in the field of dentistry. This book length treatment of Data Driven Learning (DDL) in dentistry reports on the design, use, and evaluation of several activities in which the student uses specialized corpora for learning the language of the profession, including enhancing collocational knowledge within the field. For example, Crosthwaite and Cheung (2019) report on an activity intended to teach how to signal the gap in literature reviews through the use of the vocabulary item *few*. To learn how to make this discourse move, students searched a specialized dentistry corpus for the node *few* and examined concordances, which would expose collocates such as *studies, attempts, articles,* i.e. the lexical possibilities for signalling the gap. In another activity, the researchers describe how dentistry students might explore the concordances of *significant* to learn about collocates such as *changes, correlation, difference.* Qualitative feedback from students obtained by Crosthwaite and Cheung (2019) on the direct use of corpora for learning collocations was positive.

14.3 Core issues and topics

This section discusses the issues and current debates in the area of corpora for teaching collocations in ESP. These core issues reflect aspects of the development of the field discussed in the previous sections. They include the discipline-specificity of collocation, which is situated within the broader EAP versus ESP debate, issues related to corpus development, and questions on what constitutes effective pedagogical uses of corpora for teaching ESP collocations.

Let us begin with the issue of the target data that goes into a corpus for effective ESP collocational analysis and teaching. It is widely accepted that needs-analysis, i.e. the language needs of the student at the point of teaching, should inform the ESP corpus sample (Anthony, 2018). However, researchers have taken different approaches to determining what these needs are. Nesi (2013) notes that the majority of ESP corpora are research articles, because they are easy to access in machine-readable form but also because of the tertiary focus in ESP and the importance of research article analysis in the field of academic writing. However, Durrant (2016) argues that overreliance on journal articles is problematic, since it implies that university students are pedagogically intended to write like published researchers in their discipline, when, instead, as he suggests, they are meant to write like successful university students. Thus, a better proxy might be a corpus of successful university student level writing in multiple disciplines such as the language represented by the BAWE (6.5 million words) or MICUSP (2.6 million words). In defense of the use of research articles, however, Gardner and Davies (2016) argue that journal article corpora can be seen as models of best-practice. They also contend that journal article corpora represent "established disciplinary writing (the target), whereas the BAWE corpus is based on emerging disciplinary writing (the process)" (p. 63). Green and Lambert (2018), in developing collocational pedagogical lists for eight different secondary school subjects, argued that a reasonable corpus proxy for the needs of secondary students would be secondary school textbooks in their subject areas, rather than tertiary-level texts. Jablonkai's (2020) collocational resources for EU professionals were based on corpus design that identified ESP needs through interviews and surveys about the text types they regularly encountered.

The specificity of collocations in ESP is also an important issue. Corpus development and the target data that is used may matter more or less depending on how variable collocations are across ESP areas, or from EAP and general English to ESP. A seminal paper by Hyland and Tse (2007) proposed that there is reason to doubt whether a single academic literacy construct exists that we can teach to and meet the language needs of learners across a range of different fields. They examined the coverage of the Academic Wordlist/AWL (Coxhead, 2000) in 3.3 million words of texts from biology, physics, engineering, computer science, business, sociology, and applied linguistics. They found that not only did AWL coverage vary significantly with up to 27% of the wordlist being infrequent in certain disciplines, but also, and more importantly for this chapter, the collocations for AWL targets also varied revealing that the targets were not used the same across disciplines. For example, an AWL word such as *strategy* collocated with *coping* in sociology up to 31% of the time, with *marketing* in business studies up to 11% of the time, and with *learning* in applied linguistics up to 9% of the time. Nevertheless, a counter to this position of putting aside EAP vocabulary corpus-work for an entirely ESP approach has recently been articulated by Dang *et al.* (2017). She suggested that it can be a progression from core meaning represented by an EAP corpus analysis to ESP corpus analysis to enrich the core meaning with any discipline-specific meaning and use.

What would need to be known then is what Gablasova *et al.* (2017) call the stability of association strength for collocations in different areas of ESP. They note that "little empirical evidence is available about the degree to which genres, registers, and modes of communication affect the strength of association between words" (p. 167). To demonstrate the need for more research in this area, they conduct a simple case study that highlights how collocation strength varies by genre, register, and mode. They looked at MI values amongst collocations in different subcomponents of the BNC, such as news, fiction, informal/formal spoken language, and academic writing, and found substantial variability. For example, the collocation *make [a] decision* ranges by subcategory from MI scores as low as 3.67 (barely meaningful association) up to 7.91 in different registers. What this variation suggests is that some collocations will be important to some areas of ESP but not to others, even though they may exist to some extent in other areas. Ward (2007) predicted that the research will show that collocations "are highly discipline-specific in a way that individual words are not" (p. 18), and the issue is not yet settled.

One final topic of interest concerns the teaching-research practice relationship. Walker (2011b), in his corpus work on business English questioned whether collocations are better taught through an emphasis on holistic memorization or through identifying general cognitive principles that motivate collocations which can then be explained to students to support their learning. For example, he examined collocational profiles of academic vocabulary targets such as *issue, aspect,* and *factor,* arguing that the cognitive explanatory principle motivating their collocations was that they often function as anaphors and cohesive devices. Walker (2011b) suggests that teaching such knowledge could facilitate collocation acquisition more than holistic memorization of word relationships as it would enable foreign language learners to better understand why native speakers use collocations in particular contexts. However, a more recent intervention study by Boers *et al.* (2017) found instead that collocations studied holistically rather than through the analysis of individual components were more effectively learned in form and meaning recall tests. Therefore, research into the topic is ongoing.

14.4 Current contributions

This section reports on a series of recent studies that focus on several of the areas under discussion in this chapter. These studies constitute not only a sample of the current research and some innovative methodologies with new findings, but also directly reflect the issues and research trends reviewed in the previous sections. For example, these studies involve the enrichment of multiple ESP wordlists with collocational information, take up the issue of collocation variability across disciplines and the extent of core collocational vocabulary, and explore collocational frameworks and their variability across disciplinary areas.

Green and Lambert (2018) offer the most extensive work yet done on collocations across disciplinary areas in secondary school, with a consistent methodology for comparing collocation stability and specificity across subjects. In this study, the researchers developed the Secondary Vocabulary and Word Association Lists, constituting approximately 53 thousand collocations for 4781 target lemmas across eight disciplines, namely biology, physics, chemistry, history, geography, mathematics, economics, and English. The researchers felt that there was a gap in that the advanced methods for ESP corpus research developed in tertiary L2 contexts were not fully leveraged in other educational contexts such as secondary schools, where the need to improve disciplinary literacy through collocational and vocabulary knowledge was just as essential.

The researchers first developed what they called the Secondary Vocabulary Lists for the eight secondary school subjects mentioned above, based on a 16.2-million-word corpus of textbooks recommended on official curriculum documents for the intended grades and subject areas. They extracted 4781 lemmas based on similar criteria previously used to develop the Academic Vocabulary List (Gardner & Davies, 2014) and the specialist Medical Academic Vocabulary List (Lei & Liu, 2016). These criteria included words with a minimum frequency of 28 per million in a subject area, a range of 50% or more in the textbook sample, a dispersion above 0.5, and which occurred at least three times more frequently in a target subject area than others. This method produced eight ESP wordlists for different secondary school subjects which were then enriched for collocational information. For each lemma on each discipline's wordlist, the researchers extracted the ten most frequent collocates for all inflected forms, with criteria that they occurred at least five times with the target word in the subject area, had an MI score above 3, and collocated in more than 20% of textbooks in the subject area corpus.

In their results, Green and Lambert (2018) found significant variation in the number of collocates for the target words on the ESP lists. For example, some words in some subject areas had no collocates that met the criteria mentioned above while others had dozens. The variation in the overall number of collocates per discipline was also notable, ranging from about three thousand collocations occurring in mathematics to over ten thousand in biology. This result suggests that the collocation learning burden may be higher in some subjects than others. The overall result of this study was the development of a pedagogical resource, named the Word Association Lists, listing approximately 53 thousand subject area collocations encountered by students in secondary school. An example of the collocations in the Word Association Lists is given in Table 14.1.

As Table 14.1 shows, the collocates enrich the target vocabulary word (underlined) substantially. There are collocates that signal related concepts in semantic networks, lexico-grammatical patterns, synonyms, antonyms, and hyponyms. For example, the technical word *adenine* collocates with *thymine* in biology because it is a *base* in *DNA* and they pair together. This is also true of the collocates *cytosine* and *guanine*. In English, *context, purpose, audience*, and *culture* collocate because of a pedagogy that uses these concepts in text analysis in secondary school, namely, when deconstructing reading or constructing writing, students are taught to consider purpose, audience, context, and culture. In physics, *rarefaction* collocates with its discipline-specific antonym *compression*. This is likely not known by many language teachers. As Nesi (2013) suggests, one of the cases that can be made for "the use of corpora in ESP in that ESP practitioners are not always conversant with the professions and disciplines of their students, and may not have much intuitive understanding of the way language is used in certain specified domains" (p. 407). The Word Association Lists also show interesting collocation variation across disciplines. Members of the same word family can vary in form and

Table 14.1 The Word Association Lists (Green & Lambert, 2018)

Chemistry	Biology	Geography	Physics
THEORETICAL (ADJ.)	ADENINE (N.)	RUNOFF (N.)	RAREFACTION (N.)
Yield (n.)	Thymine (n.)	Surface (n.)	Compression (n.)
(Freq. 1181, MI 12.0)	(Freq. 152, MI 11.99)	(Freq. 105, MI 8.65)	(Freq. 126, MI 12.26)
Percentage (n.)	Cytosine (n.)	Water (n.)	Pressure (n.)
(Freq. 37, MI 9.95)	(Freq. 128, MI 11.86)	(Freq. 36, MI 5.06)	(Freq. 43, MI 7.21)
Actual (adj.)	Guanine (n.)	Overland (n.)	Wave (n.)
(Freq. 30, MI 11.46)	(Freq. 88, MI 11.78)	(Freq. 30, MI 10.74)	(Freq. 39, MI 6.78)
Mass (n.)	Base (n.)	Infiltration (n.)	Sound (n.)
(Freq. 15, MI 5.83)	(Freq. 53, MI 8.96)	(Freq. 29, MI 10.33)	(Freq. 38, MI 7.52)
Experimental (adj.)	DNA (n.)	Flow (n.)	Regions (n.)
(Freq. 12, MI 9.87)	(Freq. 46, MI 6.23)	(Freq. 29, MI 7.44)	(Freq. 33, MI 10.77)

English	Mathematics	Economics	History
CONTEXT (N.)	CALCULATION (n.)	SHAREHOLDERS (n.)	ENFORCE (VB.)
Audience (n.)	Answer (n.)	Company (n.)	League (n.)
(Freq. 79, MI 8.18)	(Freq. 19, MI 5.89)	(Freq. 77, MI 7.59)	(Freq. 20, MI 7.28)
Purpose (n.)	Using (vb.)	Dividends (n.)	Sanctions (n.)
(Freq. 62, MI 7.92)	(Freq. 13, MI 4.33)	(Freq. 52, MI 9.91)	(Freq. 17, MI 9.92)
Word (n.)	Angle (n.)	Shares (n.)	Decisions (n.)
(Freq. 42, MI 5.98)	(Freq. 8, MI 4.22)	(Freq. 49, MI 8.06)	(Freq. 12, MI 9.75)
Text (n.)	Based (vb.)	Equity (n.)	Law (n.)
(Freq. 30, MI 5.05)	(Freq. 7, MI 7.57)	(Freq. 46, MI 8.24)	(Freq. 10, MI 8.38)
Culture (n.)	Product (n.)	Profits (n.)	Power (n.)
(Freq. 29, MI 7.77)	(Freq. 7, MI 5.44)	(Freq. 44, MI 6.97)	(Freq. 9, MI 5.63)

collocations by subject areas, such as in chemistry where *abundance* is the most common form of its word family and collocates with *relative, isotope, molecular,* and *natural*. In geography, by contrast, the most common form is *abundant* and it collocates with *supply, resources, rainfall,* and *source*.

In a follow-up study, Green and Lambert (2019) considered two-word lexical collocations at either one word to the right (R1) or left (L1) and developed a supplementary corpus-based ESP resource. This study was motivated by a gap in the research mentioned by Durrant (2009) earlier, namely that researchers either use the window approach (+/-five words from a node word) or the three–five word phraseology/lexical bundle approach to collocation, and both approaches having led to research largely overlooking the in-between type of collocation, namely the abundance of two word disciplinary terms made up of lexical content words such as *position vectors, surface area, supply curve,* and *gamma rays*. These kind of lexical collocates are understudied, but their importance to carrying conceptual structure in a discipline is well-noted (Shanahan & Shanahan, 2017). Green and Lambert (2019), therefore, extracted all R1/ L1 collocates from a corpus of 16.2 million words if the collocations consisted of combinations of nouns, verbs, adjectives, or adverbs. Criteria were used such as specifying that a collocation occurs more than 10 times for every million words of secondary school textbooks and have an MI score above 3 and a dispersion above 0.5. Further, raters with teaching experience rated the collocations for usefulness based on whether the collocations were worth teaching, difficult to spell, or conceptually important to a subject area.

Green and Lambert's (2019) final collocation list contains 7468 two-word lexical collocates across eight subject areas. This pedagogical resource lists separately noun + noun collocates, verb + noun collocates, noun + verb, adjective + noun collocates, and verb + adverb collocations. Examples amongst the top ten most frequent collocates in biology include *carbon dioxide, active transport, nervous system, water potential*; in chemistry, *hydrochloric acid, sodium hydroxide, periodic table, boiling point*, in economics, *demand curve, interest rate, aggregate demand, economic growth*; in English, *topic sentence, summary question, subject matter, body language*; and in Math, *surface area, straight line, position vector, standard deviation*. This shows the substantial variation in the most frequent lexical collocations of the different subject areas. Overall, 2413 collocations occurred in more than one subject area, but only 8 occurred in all 8 disciplines. The researchers address the issue raised in the previous section about the stability of association strength in ESP (Gablasova *et al.*, 2017), confirming that collocations are highly discipline-specific and more so than individual words. Green and Lambert (2019) found that even for shared collocates the frequency and MI varied considerably. For example, the frequency of *carbon dioxide*, which was shared by 6 of 8 disciplines, was as high as 1462 occurrences per million words in biology and as low as 13 occurrences per million words in economics. Its MI scores varied from as high as 14.55 in economics to as low as 4.97 in geography, even though it is more frequent (212 occurrences per million words) in the latter discipline. This is because geography discusses carbon in many different ways, e.g. *carbon accumulation, carbon agreement, carbon atoms, carbon compounds*, and important point for collocation teaching in the subject.

Green (2019) completed the series of studies consistent with the broadening scope of collocational research by developing a pedagogical resource that contains collocational frameworks. In this work, the collocational frameworks for the target vocabulary on the AWL (Coxhead, 2000) and the discipline-specific Secondary Vocabulary Lists/SVL (Green & Lambert, 2018) were extracted from a corpus of secondary school textbooks representing the same eight disciplines of the previous studies. For each noun and verb listed in the AWL and SVL, their collocational frameworks were automatically extracted using the Natural Language Processing system TAASC (Kyle, 2016). A set of criteria were then used to find which frameworks were possibly pedagogically useful, such as needing a collexeme value above 1.3 (a statistical measure used to determine the association between a grammatical pattern and a lexical items), containing at least three grammatical constituents, and occurring at least 5-10 times in the frame for every million words. The resources developed from these criteria are argued to be potentially useful for collocational teaching in ESP, since they show how groups of discipline-specific vocabulary are related by shared collocation frameworks, such as *absorb, catalyse, control, detect* which in biology as being associated with the framework *nsubjpass-v- agent*, that is, agentive passives.

14.5 Future directions of research

This section discusses future directions for research in the area, building on the present state-of-the art, research, and core issues reviewed in the previous sections. One main takeaway is simply that teachers should treat collocations as an important part of communicative competence in a discipline. As this chapter has shown, corpus research indicates that collocations play a significant role in the language of the disciplines and professional communication.

In terms of future research directions, the research into using corpora for teaching collocations in ESP is not yet rich enough. We need to better understand how different collocations are across subject areas and professional domains, and conversely how much of a common core there is to collocation. This research is essential to inform materials development. We also need research on collocations in spoken disciplinary discourse, which to date has been understudied. Different education levels and contexts need to be studied. For example, the research reviewed above from Green and Lambert (2018) looked at secondary school textbooks and we do not know how the collocations presented in their pedagogical lists compare to, or are useful for, tertiary level language learning in the same disciplines. Wider issues of corpus linguistics such as the appropriate measurement statistics for identifying pedagogically useful collocations, will be important in the near future. The past years have seen measures such as MI scores come under increasing critical scrutiny and it is not unreasonable to predict that it will stop being widely used at some point in the future and replaced by more rigorous statistical measures.

A research program that explores collocation variation across ESP areas would be particularly valuable. We need to measure the variation and consistency of collocations, as suggested by Gablasova *et al.* (2017), who demonstrate that collocation variation exists and is important to even broad genres represented within the BNC. It is possible, perhaps likely, that in ESP, it will exist even more so. Further, extensive pedagogical resources for collocations in ESP should be built. As this chapter has shown, currently many ESP wordlists are available but there are fewer ESP collocation lists, even though progress is being made and the number is steadily increasing (e.g. Jablonkai, 2020). These resources should be lists that take the "window approach" reviewed before, but also explore the collocational frameworks approach. The pedagogical research should also focus on the direct use of ESP corpora for teaching collocation by practitioners and students. This trend toward the direct use of corpora has begun, as exemplified by work in DDL and dentistry (Crosthewaite & Cheung, 2019), but it needs to be enriched and more professional domains and subject areas should be studied. Also of value would be research investigating collocations in learner disciplinary writing, building upon the research reviewed above using learner argumentative essays by Granger and Bestgen (2014) and Crossley *et al.* (2015). A comparison of a learner disciplinary corpus and a control corpus of expert writing would also help shed light on collocations that could be targeted in an ESP course.

We should also look at the effectiveness of using corpora for teaching collocations in ESP through intervention studies, of which there have not been enough. Little evidence exists on the outcomes of students' ESP collocation knowledge through the use of ESP corpora or the pedagogical research and resources that currently exist. The work by Green and Lambert (2018) makes a theoretical case that their collocational resources are pedagogically useful. However, what is really needed is the direct testing of such resources to see if they actually lead to gains in collocational knowledge. Building apps for ESP collocation learning based on ESP corpora is a pathway that could be explored further, again, with assessment of the effectiveness of these apps. As signaled by Walker (2011a) and Boers *et al.* (2017) continued research into the issue of whether in ESP cognitive or pedagogical generalizations can be derived from corpus analysis and communicated to students so as to promote collocational knowledge needs further classroom research before any final conclusions can be drawn.

Further reading

Barnbrook, G., Mason, O., & Krishnamurthy, R. (2013). *Collocation: Applications and implications.* Springer. In this book, the authors provide a valuable and extensive review of collocation, both from theoretical and practical perspectives. The work addresses some of the key background to current work in collocation research and details several of the most used methodologies for identifying collocations.

Coxhead, A. (2017). *Vocabulary and English for specific purposes research: Quantitative and qualitative perspectives.* Routledge. This book's treatment of ESP and vocabulary research provides an extensive overview of ESP corpus-based research and pedagogy. The book deals with collocation at several points and specifically contains a section that reviews collocations in ESP.

Hyland, K., & Tse, P. (2007). Is there an "academic vocabulary"? *TESOL Quarterly, 41*(2), 235–253. Somewhat of a classic paper that questions the extent of an academic vocabulary by computing occurrences of the AWL in different ESP corpora. Results are taken as indicating that the vocabulary needs of ESP students would not be met by a general EAP approach based on the limited frequency of AWL targets in certain disciplines and their collocational behaviour.

References

Ackermann, K., & Chen, Y. H. (2013). Developing the Academic Collocation List (ACL)–A corpus-driven and expert-judged approach. *Journal of English for Academic Purposes, 12*(4), 235–247.

Anthony, L. (2018). *Introducing English for Specific Purposes.* Routledge.

Boers, F., & Webb, S. (2018). Teaching and learning collocation in adult second and foreign language learning. *Language Teaching, 51*(1), 77–89.

Boers, F., Dang, T. C. T., & Strong, B. (2017). Comparing the effectiveness of phrase-focused exercises: A partial replication of Boers, Demecheleer, Coxhead, and Webb (2014). *Language Teaching Research, 21*(3), 362–380.

Coxhead, A. (2000). A new academic word list. *TESOL Quarterly, 34*(2), 213–238.

Crossley, S. A., Salsbury, T., & Mcnamara, D. S. (2015). Assessing lexical proficiency using analytic ratings: A case for collocation accuracy. *Applied Linguistics, 36*(5), 570–590.

Crosthwaite, P., & Cheung, L. (2019). *Learning the language of dentistry: Disciplinary corpora in the teaching of English for Specific and Academic Purposes.* Benjamins.

Dang, T. N. Y., Coxhead, A., & Webb, S. (2017). The Academic Spoken Word List. *Language Learning, 67*(4), 959–997.

Davies, M. (2010). The Corpus of ContemporaryAmerican English as the first reliable monitor corpus of English. *Literary and Linguistic Computing, 25*(4), 447–465.

Durrant, P. (2009). Investigating the viability of a collocation list for students of English for academic purposes. *English for Specific Purposes, 28*(3), 157–169.

Durrant, P. (2016). To what extent is the Academic Vocabulary List relevant to university student writing? *English for Specific Purposes, 43*, 49–61.

Ellis, N. C. (2019). Essentials of a theory of language cognition. *The Modern Language Journal*, 103, 39–60.

Firth, John R. (1957): Modes of meaning. *Papers in Linguistics, 1934-1951*. Oxford.

Frankenberg-Garcia, A., Lew, R., Roberts, J. C., Rees, G. P., & Sharma, N. (2019). Developing a writing assistant to help EAP writers with collocations in real time. *ReCALL, 31*(1), 23–39.

Gablasova, D., Brezina, V., & McEnery, T. (2017). Collocations in corpus-based language learning research: Identifying, comparing, and interpreting the evidence. *Language Learning, 67*(S1), 155–179.

Gardner, D., & Davies, M. (2014). A new academic vocabulary list. *Applied Linguistics, 35*(3), 305–327.

Gardner, D., & Davies, M. (2016). A response to "To what extent is the Academic Vocabulary List relevant to university student writing?". *English for Specific Purposes, 43*, 62–68.

Granger, S., & Bestgen, Y. (2014). The use of collocations by intermediate vs. advanced non-native writers: A bigram-based study. *International Review of Applied Linguistics in Language Teaching, 52*(3), 229–252.

Green, C. (2019). Enriching the academic wordlist and secondary vocabulary lists with lexicogrammar: Toward a pattern grammar of academic vocabulary. *System, 87*, 102–158.

Green, C., & Lambert, J. (2018). Advancing disciplinary literacy through English for academic purposes: Discipline-specific wordlists, collocations and word families for eight secondary subjects. *Journal of English for Academic Purposes, 35*, 105–115.

Green, C., & Lambert, J. (2019). Position vectors, homologous chromosomes and gamma rays: Promoting disciplinary literacy through secondary phrase lists. *English for Specific Purposes, 53*, 1–12.

Greene, J., & Coxhead, A. (2015). *Academic vocabulary for middle school students*. Brookes.

Gries, S. T. (2013). 50-something years of work on collocations: What is or should be next…. *International Journal of Corpus Linguistics, 18*(1), 137–166.

Hunston, S., & Su, H. (2019). Patterns, constructions, and local grammar: A case study of "evaluation". *Applied Linguistics, 40*(4), 567–593.

Hyland, K., & Tse, P. (2007). Is there an "academic vocabulary"? *TESOL Quarterly, 41*(2), 235–253.

Jablonkai, R. R. (2020). Leveraging professional wordlists for productive vocabulary knowledge. *ESP Today, 8*(1), 165–181.

Kang, B. M. (2018). Collocation and word association: Comparing collocation measuring methods. *International Journal of Corpus Linguistics, 23*(1), 85–113.

Kyle, K. (2016). *Measuring syntactic development in L2 writing: Fine grained indices of syntactic complexity and usage-based indices of syntactic sophistication*. Doctoral dissertation. Retrieved from: http://scholarworks.gsu.edu/alesl_diss/35

Lei, L., & Liu, D. (2016). A new medical academic word list: A corpus-based study with enhanced methodology. *Journal of English for Academic Purposes, 22*, 42–53.

Lei, L., & Liu, D. (2018). The academic English collocation list. *International Journal of Corpus Linguistics, 23*(2), 216–243.

Lu, X., Yoon, J., & Kisselev, O. (2018). A phrase-frame list for social science research article introductions. *Journal of English for Academic Purposes, 36*, 76–85.

Marco, M. J. L. (2000). Collocational frameworks in medical research papers: A genre-based study. *English for Specific Purposes, 19*(1), 63–86.

Martinez, R., & Schmitt, N. (2012). A phrasal expressions list. *Applied Linguistics, 33*(3), 299–320.

Nekrasova-Beker, T. M. (2019). Discipline-specific use of language patterns in engineering: A comparison of published pedagogical materials. *Journal of English for Academic Purposes, 41*, 100774.

Nelson, M. (2006). Semantic associations in Business English: A corpus-based analysis. *English for Specific Purposes, 25*(2), 217–234.

Nesi, H. (2013). ESP and corpus studies. In B. Paltridge & S. Starfield (Eds.), *The handbook of English for Specific Purposes* (pp. 407–426). Wiley-Blackwell.

Partington, A. (1998). *Patterns and meaning: Using corpora for English language research and teaching*. Benjamins.

Shanahan, T., & Shanahan, C. (2017). Disciplinary literacy: Just the FAQs. *Educational Leadership, 74*(5), 18–22.

Simpson-Vlach, R., & Ellis, N. C. (2010). An academic formulas list: New methods in phraseology research. *Applied Linguistics, 31*(4), 487–512.

Sinclair, J. (1991). *Corpus, concordance, collocation*. Oxford: Oxford University Press.

Siyanova-Chanturia, A., & Spina, S. (2020). Multi-word expressions in second language writing: A large-scale longitudinal learner corpus study. *Language Learning, 70*(2), 420–463.

Swales, J. M., & Feak, C. B. (2004). *Academic writing for graduate students: Essential tasks and skills* (Vol. 1). University of Michigan Press.

Szudarski, P. (2012). Effects of meaning-and form-focused instruction on the acquisition of verb-noun collocations in L2 English. *Journal of Second Language Teaching & Research, 1*(2), 3–37.

Szudarski, P. (2017). Learning and teaching L2 collocations: Insights from research. *TESL Canada Journal, 34*(3), 205–216.

Walker, C. P. (2011a). How a corpus-based study of the factors which influence collocation can help in the teaching of business English. *English for Specific Purposes, 30*(2), 101–112.

Walker, C. P. (2011b). A corpus-based study of the linguistic features and processes which influence the way collocations are formed: Some implications for the learning of collocations. *TESOL Quarterly, 45*(2), 291–312.

Ward, J. (2007). Collocation and technicality in EAP engineering. *Journal of English for Academic Purposes, 6*(1), 18–35.

15

LEXICAL BUNDLES IN EAP

Viviana Cortes

15.1 Introduction

It is undeniable that in the past two decades lexical bundles have become a salient construct in the study of formulaic language in many written and spoken English registers and especially in the study of written and spoken academic registers in English (Biber, 2006) and in other languages like Spanish and Portuguese (Berber Sardinha & Sao Bento Ferreira, 2014; Cortes, 2008). Ever since the term lexical bundles made its first appearance in the applied linguistics world introduced by Biber and his collaborators in their seminal study of English grammar (1999), lexical bundles have been granted a prominent position across the spectrum of formulaic forms. In order to identify the origin of the study of this type of corpus-driven recurrent expressions, we need to go back in time to the last decades of the twentieth century and look at the work of Allen (1975) and Altenberg (1993), who were pioneers in the identification and early analysis of this type of formulas.

Lexical bundles are one of the few linguistic features that are identified by a fully automatic empirical analysis of a corpus without any preconceptions or intuition. They are groups of three or more words that recur frequently in a register (Biber *et al.*, 1999). One of the most salient characteristics of lexical bundles is the way in which they are identified, using specially-designed computer programs that run through the texts in a corpus and flag expressions of three or more words that repeat frequently, employing a pure corpus-driven procedure. Examples of lexical bundles that have been frequently found in written academic genres are expressions such as *on the other hand, as a result of the, in the context of, the fact that the,* and *the purpose of the study is to determine,* to mention only a few. Spoken academic texts have yielded bundles such as *if you look at, going to talk about, what I want to,* and *at the same time,* among many others. As we can see from these examples, lexical bundles are not complete grammatical units and they are made up of fragmented and embedded phrases or clauses. Frequency is a very important feature of lexical bundles: in fact, it is the only quality that makes any three-word expression or any four-word expression, for example, a lexical bundle. Biber *et al.* (1999) used a frequency threshold of ten times per million words (pmw) for four-word expressions to be considered lexical bundles. Subsequent studies have used higher, more conservative frequency thresholds to ensure that the expressions are really frequent and to avoid the possibility of those words to come together by chance. Cortes (2004) used 20 times pmw as a frequency

 DOI: 10.4324/9781003002901-18

cut-off point in her study of published and university student writing in history and biology, and Biber *et al.* (2004) used 40 times pmw in their study of lexical bundles in academic lectures and textbooks.

Another measure that needs to be taken into consideration with lexical bundles is range, as it is important to avoid any idiosyncratic use of fixed expressions that could be produced by only one user or a few language users in a register. Common thresholds for range in lexical bundle studies consider occurrences of these expressions in 5 or more texts or in the case of larger corpora, a percentage of the texts in the corpus, such as 10 per cent or a higher percent. Lexical bundles are not the only type of formulaic language that is identified using this corpus-driven methodology. The methodology is also used for the identification of n-grams, that is, groups of *n* number of words (two words or bigrams, three words or trigrams, four-grams, and so on). Thus, the main difference between n-grams and bundles is a matter of frequency and range. All lexical bundles are in essence n-grams (3-grams, 4-grams, and so on) but only those n-grams that meet the frequency and range thresholds can be considered lexical bundles. We will return to the discussion of frequency and range when we analyze in detail the procedures used for the identification and analysis of lexical bundles in the following sections.

Currently, lexical bundles have been extensively studied in a wide variety of written academic registers but not so deeply studied in spoken academic registers. One of the reasons why lexical bundles have become such an important construct in academic writing can be explained in the existence and easy accessibility of many corpora of different written academic registers that are available for analysis, and in the fact that collecting written academic corpora seems to be less problematic than collecting spoken language samples, particularly when the texts are already published and can be accessed electronically (Cortes, 2013). This is not the case when collecting academic corpora that may not be produced electronically and the texts need to be converted into machine-readable texts (Cortes, 2004). There are, however, some studies that identified and analyzed lexical bundles in spoken academic registers (Biber *et al.*, 2004; Cortes & Csomay, 2007; Csomay, 2013; Csomay & Cortes, 2010). These studies contribute to the construction of formulaic profiles of academic language production. The other and perhaps more important reason for the increased saliency of lexical bundles may be related to the structural and functional characteristics of these frequent expressions that make them optimal building blocks in written academic registers. Several studies have worked on the structural and functional classification of lexical bundles and the taxonomies produced for classifications are currently used as a tool to complete standard procedures when categorizing these expressions in academic and many other registers (Biber *et al.*, 1999; Biber *et al.*, 2004; Hyland, 2008). These studies, which describe the grammatical features in lexical bundles and evaluate the functions they perform in discourse, have provided invaluable information about lexical bundles that could translate into pedagogical applications for the teaching of these expressions at different academic levels.

15.2 Review of current state of research

The analysis of formulaic language in English has moved dramatically forward with the advancements introduced by the use of computers and with the development of language analysis approaches derived from the collection of corpora. Many corpus-based research studies focused on the identification and classification of a wide variety of recurrent expressions (De Cock, 1998; Nattinger & DeCarrico, 1992; Sinclair, 1991, among many others). These studies were corpus-based in that they used expressions extracted mostly from related literature that were perceived to be frequent in different English registers as the target of their corpus analysis. In this way, researchers could verify whether these expressions were really frequent with empirical evidence by using corpus tools to search for those expressions and their frequencies in language collections. Moon (1998) compiled a list of over 6,000 expressions previously perceived as frequent from dictionaries and other sources and she used several large corpora to verify the frequency of such expressions. Moon's study tried to merge the phraseological and frequency traditions targeted to the study of formulaic language. While the phraseological tradition centers on syntactic and sematic analyses of collocations (Cowie, 1981), the frequency-based tradition focuses on the frequency and statistics of recurrent multi-word expressions (Firth, 1951; Sinclair, 1991). Moon's study was groundbreaking in that she could verify that many expressions that had been thought to be frequent and had been the center of many instructional materials for the teaching of English as a second or foreign language were in fact extremely infrequent, with some expressions never found in her corpora. One group of expressions that was very infrequent was that of obscure idioms, expressions such as *kick the bucket, over the moon,* or *shoot the breeze,* which tend to occur once every two million words or even less frequently and be restricted to only one or a few registers such as fiction.

Following the frequency tradition, several scholars tried to identify empirically the most frequent expressions produced in a given register using a collection or texts or language corpus. Out of this tradition, lexical bundles emerged as a construct in the 1990s and their study fully developed in the first decade of the new millennium. Altenberg and Eeg-Olofsoon (1990) introduced an automatic corpus-driven approach to the identification of recurrent expressions. Some years later, Biber *et al.* (1999) coined the term lexical bundles to refer to this type of recurrent word combination. The specialized computer program used to identify lexical bundles runs through a corpus of language flagging expressions of the desired length (three-word, four-word, or other) as recurrent, respecting punctuation mark boundaries. The program reads text and identifies the recurrent expressions until it encounters a punctuation mark. When this happens, the identification stops and starts again after the punctuation mark. When these flagged expressions meet the frequency and range thresholds conventionally pre-established, those expressions are raised to the lexical bundle category for further analysis. Initially, many researchers have used their own computer programs for the identification of lexical bundles (Biber *et al.*, 1999; Cortes, 2002) but there are now commercially available software such as Collocate (Barlow, 2000), among others, or freeware like AntGram and AntConc (Anthony, 2020), which can be employed for this task.

The way in which lexical bundles are identified is considered data-driven or corpus-driven (Tognini-Bonelli, 2001) because the program that identifies n-grams or bundles performs automatically and the expressions that it yields are completely empirical, deriving from the texts in a given corpus. The focus of the program is to identify all expressions of a certain length, four-words for example, starting from the first word in a text and moving one word at a time. The program identifies the first four words, stores that expression in a database and moves one word to the right identifying one new four-word expression, continuing storing the subsequent expressions, and respecting punctuation boundaries. Each time the program identifies a new expression, it goes back to the database to check whether the expression is already there. If the expression is there, it flags the expression and keeps count. The program does the same for the texts in which the expressions occur. When the program finishes processing the last word of the last text of the corpus under analysis, it selects those expressions that have reached the pre-established frequency and range thresholds and yields those as lexical bundles.

It is important to emphasize the fact that there is no pre-conceived list of expressions or intuition before the program is set to identify n-grams. The only conventions in the case of lexical bundles are the thresholds that need to be pre-established to allow their identification. As I have mentioned earlier, frequency is the only quality that raises any combination of three or more words to the lexical bundle category. For this reason, the pre-established thresholds are key in the procedure used to identify these expressions. Using appropriate cut-off points, researchers can ensure that the words that make up a lexical bundle recur together with high frequency.

The most popular written genre studied for lexical bundle use is undoubtedly, the published research article (RA) as a whole (Cortes, 2004) and its sub-sections like introductions or stand-alone literature reviews (Cortes, 2013; Wright, 2019). Other studies of lexical bundles in academic genres concentrated, for example, on MA theses and doctoral dissertations across disciplines (Hyland, 2008), dissertation abstracts (Lu & Cheng, 2019), and textbooks (Chen, 2018).

A small number of studies has focused on the function of lexical bundles in academic lectures exploring the potential of bundles for academic listening tasks. Nesi and Basturkmen (2006) analyzed lexical bundles as discourse signals in academic lectures, exploring the cohesive role that these formulaic expressions play in this particular register. Their results show that many lexical bundles that were identified in lectures often signaled different discourse relations. Sometimes these expressions were used on their own, but in some particular cases, these lexical bundles were used together with cohesive conjunctions. Nesi and Basturkmen highlighted the importance of the signaling function of lexical bundles for language learners, as recognizing the signaling power of lexical bundles and determining their function in discourse could help language learners when processing the complex discourse they are regularly exposed to in academic lectures. Cortes and Csomay (2007) and Csomay and Cortes (2010) worked with a group of bundles identified in the T2KSWAL corpus (Biber *et al.*, 2004) making connections between those bundles and vocabulary-based discourse units (VBDUs) (for a more detailed description of VBDUs, see Csomay, 2005), to investigate which lexical bundles previously identified as frequent in classroom talk appeared in the initial discourse units of university lectures and also to find the relationship between the position of the bundles in these units and the functions they were performing in the lectures. These authors discovered that the first three units in lectures made extensive use of lexical bundles to help establish the organization of the class and to provide a context for the class content about to be delivered. Csomay and Cortes (2010) extended their work to analyze lexical bundles in the first six VBDUs in those lectures with similar findings. Finally, Csomay (2013) reported on the relationship between distributional patterns and lexical bundle sub-functions (see below) in discourse structure.

15.3 Core issues and topics

Even though, as previously explained, lexical bundles are not complete structural units, they can be grouped into various basic structural types. Biber *et al.* (1999) introduced a list of four-, five-, and six-word lexical bundles extracted from two large corpora of academic writing and conversation. The lexical bundles presented in their work showed very different structural types across speech and writing. While the lexical bundles frequently occurring in conversation are more clausal in nature, made up of fragments of verb phases and verb complement clauses, bundles that frequently recur in academic prose are phrasal, consisting mostly of prepositional phases, prepositional phrase fragments, and noun phrases with new noun phrase or prepositional phrase fragments embedded in expressions such as *as a result of, at the end of the, on the other hand; the beginning of the, the difference between the,* to mention just a few examples (Biber *et al.*, 2004). There may be a small number of lexical bundles that incorporate phrasal fragments in academic prose, as in the case of expressions with anticipatory *it* + verb phrase like *it may be possible to,* or *it has been suggested that,* as well as verb phrase fragment constructions like *are shown in table, is referred to as, is one of the most, is due to the, does not mean that,* and *may be used to,* but clausal bundles are much less frequent in written academic registers than their phrasal counterparts. Academic lectures seem to be a hybrid genre when examined from a lexical bundle use perspective as this register seems to mirror academic prose in the use of phrasal lexical bundles such as *a little bit about, one of the things that,* or *the way in which,* but also includes clausal bundles that incorporate verb phrase or dependent clause fragments as in *you don't have to, what do you think,* and *if you want to,* which are more frequent in everyday conversation.

The functions that lexical bundles perform in discourse are perhaps their strongest feature because they can help convey the message that is being communicated by speakers and writers in the academic registers being described. There are two major taxonomies that have been used in the functional analysis of lexical bundles. Biber *et al.* (2003) designed a preliminary taxonomy for academic registers and conversation that they further developed for the analysis of academic textbooks and academic lectures (Biber *et al.*, 2004). Their taxonomy had three major categories: stance bundles, discourse organizers, and referential bundles. Table 15.1 shows the major categories and sub-categories introduced by Biber *et al.* (2004).

Drawing on Biber *et al.*'s (2004), Hyland designed another taxonomy focusing only on written academic registers and shaping the categories to use these functions in the analysis of lexical bundles used in published research articles and in theses and dissertations with three

Table 15.1 Common functions of lexical bundles in academic prose (adapted from Biber et al., 2004, pp. 384–388)

Major categories	Sub-categories	Sample bundles
Stance expressions	Epistemic stance (impersonal)	*are more likely to; the fact that the*
	Attitudinal/modality stance – obligation directive (impersonal)	*it is important to; it is necessary to can be used to; it is possible to*
	Attitudinal/modality stance – ability (impersonal)	
Discourse organizers	Topic introduction/focus	*in this chapter we*
	Topic elaboration/clarification	*on the other hand; as well as the*
Referential expressions	Identification focus	*is one of the; one of the most*
	Specification of attributes – quantity	*the rest of the*
	Specification of attributes – tangible framing attributes	*the size of the; in the form of in the case of; as a result of*
	Specification of attributes – intangible framing attributes	*in the United States*
	Time/place reference – place	*at the same time; at the time of*
	Time/place reference – time	*as shown in figure* *the beginning of the; the top of the*
	Time/place reference – text deixis	
	Time/place reference – multifunctional	

Table 15.2 Common functions of lexical bundles in research articles, theses, and dissertations (Hyland, 2008, pp. 13–14)

Major categories	Sub-categories	Sample bundles
Research-oriented	Location	*at the same time*
	Procedure	*the role of the*
	Quantification	*the magnitude of the*
	Description	*the structure of the*
	Topic (related to the field of research)	*the currency board system*
Text-oriented	Transition signals	*on the other hand*
	Resultative signals	*as a result of*
	Structuring signals	*in the present study*
	Framing signals	*in the presence of*
Participant-oriented	Stance features	*are likely to be*
	Engagement features (address readers directly)	*it should be noted that*

major categories: research oriented, text oriented, and participant oriented. Table 15.2 shows the major categories in Hyland's taxonomy (2008) with some examples.

Even though the labels for some of the major categories may differ, there is a large degree of overlap in the sub-categories presented in both taxonomies. For example, the lexical bundle *in the presence of* is classified as a referential bundle with a framing sub-category by Biber *et al.* (2004) and as a text-oriented framing signal by Hyland (2008).

It has been hypothesized that these structural and functional taxonomies could help analyze the discourse in the written academic registers in which lexical bundles most frequently occur, and that those analyses would eventually yield findings that could be directly transferred to the teaching of those academic registers. So far, however, little has been done to investigate the teaching of lexical bundles in academic writing and the limited number of studies that tried to measure the impact that the use of lexical bundles can have in the acquisition of academic literacy and the development of academic writing proficiency have yielded mixed results. Cortes (2006), for example, conducted a study that tried to measure lexical bundle use in university student writing, collecting data from senior undergraduate native speaker of English students' response papers written for a history class before and after a bundle-focused pedagogical intervention. Her findings only showed an increase in students' bundle function awareness but very little gains in bundle use. Kazemia *et al.* (2014) conducted a study based on Cortes (2006) in which they taught lexical bundles to a group of Iranian students in an MA program in Teaching English as a Foreign Language (TEFL). In their study, students were asked to write a passage of about 1,000 words about the importance of vocabulary in English as a foreign language reading comprehension without any formulaic expressions cues as a pre-test and using some of the bundles that had been introduced to them in the class instructional activities as post-intervention activity. Both sets of passages were corrected by a group of experienced writing instructors. The results of their study showed statistically significant gains in the post-intervention passages. In addition, students completed a questionnaire about the perceived helpfulness of lexical bundles. Students reported that they were highly impacted by the potential they had discovered in the use of lexical bundles in their academic writing assignments. They realized they could improve their writing proficiency after the lexical bundle training they had undergone.

Many studies have attempted to compare the use of lexical bundles across different academic registers studying texts produced by native speakers of English (Biber *et al.*, 1999; Biber *et al.*, 2004; Cortes, 2004; Hyland, 2008) discovering that while there are bundles that frequently recur across different text types, spoken and written, there are other bundles that are register-specific. In addition, several studies have explored the comparison in the use of lexical bundles in the academic writing and academic speech of native and non-native speakers of English (Ädel & Erman, 2012; Chen & Baker, 2010; Shin, 2019). Some of these studies suggested that non-native speakers of English usually produced less and less varied bundles than native speakers. Shin *et al.* (2018), however, explored the use of lexical bundles in a written corpus of Korean university students from their English proficiency university admission tests. They discovered that in several cases, students were not using the definite article appropriately and due to the methodological procedure used for lexical bundle identification, many incomplete expressions that were not complete bundles were left out. Uzun (2018) replicated Shin *et al.*'s study, trying to detect erroneous lexical bundles in the English production of Turkish academic writers and reported similar findings. It may be the case that non-native speakers have the intention to use those expressions but their low proficiency in the use of articles or prepositions, words that occur in many lexical bundles in academic prose, prevents them from producing the complete expression, which could be considered a lexical bundle and added to the count otherwise.

Another important issue to take into consideration in the identification of lexical bundles for comparison across corpora is the fact that normalization, a procedure often used in corpus-based investigations to adjust raw frequency counts from texts of different lengths or corpora of different sizes (Biber *et al.*, 1998), does not seem to be a reliable procedure in comparative studies of lexical bundles. The same problems arise when other statistical procedures such as chi-square or log-likelihood, which may also be unreliable, are used to evaluate these comparisons (Bestgen, 2017, 2019). It is always recommended to work with corpora of similar sizes or to use raw frequencies in lexical bundle comparisons. In addition, the identification of lexical bundles in small corpora (corpora of less than 100,000 words, for example) can also be problematic if the frequency and range thresholds are too low. The safe procedure to follow to confirm that the expressions under study are lexical bundles is to continue keeping thresholds of at least ten times for frequency and five texts or more for range even when the corpus is very small. In that way, the expressions will meet the strict frequency cut-off points used to turn any multi-word expression into a lexical bundle.

Later studies have been extending the functional analysis of LBs by investigating the evaluating prosody and semantic preference in their surrounding context (Cortes & Hardy, 2013). Furthermore, recent studies have been focusing on the relationship between lexical bundles and communicative functions as expressed by rhetorical moves. Exploring Swales' (1981, 2004) rhetorical move scheme to analyze lexical bundles, Cortes (2013) found direct connections between bundles and the moves and steps in the introduction section of research articles from six different disciplines. Her study, which looked at bundles of four to nine words, discovered some new qualities that these expressions show in context. She noticed that certain lexical bundles contained more lexical words (nouns, adjectives, etc.), which allowed them to be tied to a specific move and step in those introductions. This quality could be more widely observed in longer bundles, which clearly showed correspondence to a particular move and step. For example, the expressions *the purpose of this study is to, the objectives of this study were,* and *the aim of this paper is to,* among others, were found to occur in move 3 step 1, announcing present research descriptively and/or purposefully, and the expressions *little is known about* and *there is a need to* were used in move 2 step 1, indicating a gap. Cortes' study also explored the role that these lexical bundles played in conveying the communicative purposes they were tied to. While some trigger bundles were used to set off a move or step, other bundles were used to comment on the purpose being communicated. This relative correspondence between certain lexical bundles and the communicative purposes expressed by the moves and steps in which the bundles occur shows definite pedagogical potential that could be exploited in the design of genre-based academic courses using corpus-based research findings.

15.4 Current contribution

In this section, we will first turn our attention to research on three-word lexical bundles, a type of bundle that may have not received enough attention within the corpus-driven formulaic language spectrum in comparison to longer lexical bundles. The section will also look at the pedagogical potential of lexical bundles for the teaching of academic writing

15.4.1 Latest research on three-word lexical bundles

With few exceptions, such as Salazar (2006), who analyzed lexical bundles of different sizes including three-word bundles in native and non-native scientific writing, and Uçar (2017), who studied the use of three-word bundles in English and Turkish academic writers, most of the studies that have investigated lexical bundles in academic prose have focused on the identification and analysis of four-word bundles. There are valid reasons for this preference and most of them have to do with the fact that four-word bundles are ten times more frequent than five-word and even more frequent than longer bundles and they seem to offer a more phrasal structure for further analysis. Trying to explain why she was not analyzing three-word bundles, Cortes (2004) claimed that most three-word bundles in her corpus of expert and student academic writing in history and biology were included in the structure of the four-word bundles in her corpus. Hyland (2008) explained that "three-word bundles are extremely common and tend not to be very interesting" (p. 151).

Three-word lexical bundles, however, may bring new insights to the formulaic profile of academic texts and deserve further analysis. Many three-word lexical bundles are embedded in longer expressions. That is the case of "as a result," which can be embedded in "as a result of" or "as a result of the/a" but it can be frequently used on its own, often followed by a comma. In addition, these bundles are extremely frequent and as shorter expressions, they can be considered extended collocations. Common three-word bundles in academic prose are expressions such as *in order to, one of the, part of the, the number of, the presence of, the use of, the fact that, there is a,* and *there is no* (Biber *et al.,* 1999). Their further study may complement the current knowledge we have about longer bundles.

Using a corpus of more than four million words consisting of research articles in Biology, Business, Economics, Engineering, and History, which was a sub-section from the Published Research Article Corpus (PRAC) (Gray & Cortes, 2010), Cortes (2020) explored the use of three-word bundles. Table 15.3 shows some descriptive information of her corpus. All tables, figures, footnotes, references, and acknowledgments were deleted from the research articles in this sub-section of the corpus.

Table 15.3 PRAC sub-section used for three-word bundle analyses

Number of texts	Total number of Tokens	Average text length	Disciplines	Type/Token ratio
623	4,531,730	6,625	Biology, Business, Economics, Engineering, and History	0.017

The first important consideration was the frequency and range thresholds to be used for the three-word bundle size. As previously explained, three-word bundles tend to be ten times more frequent than four-word bundles. Thus, if most of the studies in the literature establish a base frequency cut-off point of ten times pmw for four-word bundles, the threshold for three-word bundles should be 100 or higher. As her study was exploratory, Cortes (2020) decided on a frequency threshold of 100 times in her corpus of four million words in order to check the types of three-word expressions that could result from this analysis. Range was kept at the conventional five or more texts threshold.

Using Antconc (Anthony, 2020), three-word combinations meeting the pre-established thresholds were stored in a database. Each expression was further analyzed in search of any punctuation marks that may have gone unnoticed during the software identification. This process resulted in a total number of 120 three-word lexical bundles, expressions such as *a number of, as well as, based on the, in order to, in terms of, one of the, part of the, the number of,* and *there is a* among the most frequent.

One of the major objectives of this study was to identify overlapping bundles, that is, three-word bundles that were embedded in four-word or longer bundles as well as identifying three-word bundles with no connections to longer expressions. The analysis showed that out of 120 three-word bundles, only 42 bundles (35%) were real three-word bundles, while 78 three-word expressions were embedded in four-word or longer bundles. The frequency of the highly recurrent three-word bundles identified in this corpus is extremely high, which shows the pervasiveness of this type of bundles in the research articles in the corpus. The most frequent non-embedded three-word bundle, *in order to,* occurred 1044 times in 347 texts (more than half of the texts in the corpus).

Non-embedded three-word bundles were later structurally classified using the standard procedures frequently employed in the literature (Biber *et al.*, 1999, 2004). The structural classification of these three-word lexical bundles showed that most bundles were noun phrases followed by a prepositional phrase fragment post modifying the noun and prepositional phrases. Table 15.4 shows the non-embedded three-word bundles classified structurally.

The functional classification was conducted using the categories in Biber *et al.* (2004) and new categories were created when necessary. Table 15.5 shows the functional classification.

Several three-word bundles were complex prepositions or had complex prepositions in their internal structure, which provided them with a linking function typical of single and complex prepositions complemented by noun phrases and of subordinators in adverbial clauses. That is the case of *in order to* and *according to the.* Another new category among these three-word bundles was "grammatical only." These types of expressions had been previously identified in four-word lexical bundles recurring in a corpus of academic texts in Spanish (Cortes, 2008)

Table 15.4 Structural classification of three-word lexical bundles

Structure	Bundle examples
NP + PP fragment (13)	*the probability of, the evolution of, the rate of, the set of, a set of, increase in the, analysis of the*
PP (11)	*in this study, in this paper, in this case, in the same, of the two, between the two, in the first*
Complex prep. + NP (4)	*such as the, because of the,*
Passive V construct. (3)	*used in the, is given by, compared to the*
to-inf. Construct. (3)	*to be a, to be the, to determine the,*

Table 15.5 Functional classification of three-word lexical bundles

Function	Bundle examples
Referential - Intangible framing attributes (13)	*the probability of, the evolution of, the distribution of, the degree of*
Linking Function (8)	*in order to, according to the, between the two, in other words*
Referential – Quantity Specification (5)	*the proportion of, a set of, the amount of*
Discourse Organizers – Topic introduction/focus (5)	*there is a, there is no, to determine the*
Referential (other) (5)	*used in the, compared to the, is given by*
Referential – Text reference (2)	*in this paper, in this study*
Impersonal stance markers (2)	*to be a, to be the*
Grammatical only (2)	*in which the, and in the*

but no four-word bundle had been identified before as only having a grammatical function in English, as in *and in the* and *in which the*.

Let's look at some specific examples of three-word bundles identified in the sub-section of the PRAC corpus. One of the most frequent three-word bundles was *the probability of,* which occurred 447 times and in 120 texts in the corpus. This bundle, which is used to introduce a probable outcome, was followed by a noun phrase introduced by a definite (a/an) or indefinite (the) article in 26% of its occurrences. Examples (1) and (2) are from this corpus.

(1) The sign of each coefficient shows the effect, either increasing or decreasing *the probability of* a rear-end accident.

In the majority of this bundle occurrences, however, the expression was followed by an *–ing* complement clause (46%)

(2) Of these 19 variables, 13 had impacts on *the probability of* encountering an obstacle vehicle and 6 had impacts on driver failure probabilities.

The remaining collocates were noun phrases made up of single plural or mass nouns without determiners.

Other very frequent three-word bundles are the expressions *a set of* and *the set of,* which occurred 403 times and in 169 texts and 390 times and in 104 texts, respectively, in the corpus. These bundles were often used to identify a specific group and were followed by noun phrases containing noun heads related to the methodology and procedures in the studies reported in the research articles in the corpus, such as actions, attributes, concepts, examples, individuals, instruments, observations, outcomes, samples, and variables as in example (3).

(3) In addition, the results are very sensitive to the year analyzed and *the set of* variables used as controls, suggesting that omitted variables may play an important role.

It appears that three-word bundles which are not related to longer bundles can have a unique status in the formulaic language spectrum and there may be more to three-word bundles than the simple fact that some of these expressions may be embedded in longer bundles. The findings of Cortes' (2020) study show that three-word expressions need to be carefully reviewed to complement any other lexical bundle analyses to obtain a more complete formulaic profile of research articles and other genres.

15.4.2 *Recommendations for practice: Pedagogical potential of lexical bundles*

While lexical bundles have been found to be building blocks at the sentence level, rhetorical moves and steps have been considered building blocks at the discourse level. Cortes (2013) showed that there is a strong connection between lexical bundles and rhetorical moves/steps in the introduction section of research articles, connecting these two types of building blocks, and suggested that this strong connection should be further explored due to its invaluable pedagogical potential when teaching the construction of specific genres as in the case of research articles. The recently obtained findings from the study of three-word bundles should complement previous findings of the functions and communicative purposes of longer bundles with a pedagogical purpose. There are some academic writing courses that focus on the corpus-based exploration of academic genres (Cortes, 2011). These courses, which are often designed for graduate students, would benefit from the use of materials and activities that present real examples that illustrate the connection between bundles and rhetorical moves to accomplish specific communicative purposes.

For example, Cortes (2013) found that Move 2, *Preparing for present research,* in the research articles in her study often contained lexical bundles that indicated a gap in the field or described the state of the field in preparation for the introduction of the present research, which would come in Move 3 (Swales, 1981, 2004). Expressions that show a strong connection to this move are lexical bundles such as *it is difficult to, it is necessary to, little is known about the, there is no* and *there is a need to* among others. Taking into consideration these findings and the strong connection between those lexical bundles and the communicative purposes conveyed in Move 2, a variety of scaffolding activities could be presented to students to explore those connections. First students could review a variety of examples, like the excerpts in Examples (4), (5), and (6) below, that clearly show the bundle function and its connection to a specific move as in these excerpts from the PRAC corpus (Cortes, 2020) that show bundles frequently occurring in Move 2, *Preparing for present research.*

> (4) More importantly, the extant literature does not offer insights on how actual users employ interface agents in various software environments including electronic mail systems. *Little is known about the* actual end-use experience. (International Journal of Human and Computer Studies)

> (5) Furthermore, the RFID market is comprised of product manufacturers that claim system performances that is not yet proven. Therefore, *there is a need to* determine the factors that have the potential to adversely affect this performance in the face of the growing use of this technology. (Journal of Manufacturing Systems)

> (6) This consists of sequentially adding and deleting independent variables guided by approximate asymptotic likelihood ratio tests, leading to the selection of a single model. Inference about the determinants of CHD is then made as if the selected model were the true one. *There are a number of* difficulties with this approach. The most obvious one is its inability to compare non-nested models. (Journal of the American Statistical Association)

Later, students could work on activities used to foster the production of their own examples using the bundle-move connection. The following frameworks show lexical bundles of different lengths found in Move 2 of the introduction sections of research articles. Students could use these frameworks to scaffold their writing when producing this move in their research reports.

In order to _____ *it is necessary to* _____

It should be noted that _____

The effect of the _____ *or*

_____ *the effect of the* _____

Little is known about (the) _____

_____ *there is no* _____

It is difficult to _____

There is a need to _____

There are a number of _____ *or*

_____ *there are a number of* _____

Students could also try to identify these expressions in their reading materials using corpus-based tools and at the same time, modeling the use of those bundles to convey the specific functions and purposes of a given move/step.

15.5 Further directions of research

Studies that have explored lexical bundles in academic genres have made important contributions to the descriptions that have helped empirically describe those genres from a formulaic perspective and could be directly applied to the teaching of those genres to language learners. The potential of the pedagogical application of the findings of lexical bundle use research as a teaching tool is still rather underexplored.

The most important problem is the fact that most of the studies of lexical bundles are conducted on a limited number of academic registers. As previously explained, due to the advantages of working with written corpora, the analysis of lexical bundles has focused on written academic texts. The research article, for example, both published articles or produced by students, has been vastly analyzed in terms of lexical bundle use. Other written registers such as book reviews, case reports, lab reports, or even different types of argumentative writing, however, have not been studied so extensively or still need to be investigated regarding their use of lexical bundles. The same problem arises with the exploration of spoken academic registers. The fact that spoken corpora are more difficult to collect and there are not many easily accessible corpora of spoken academic texts makes the study of these oral registers more infrequent. The identification and analysis of lexical bundles in a wide variety of written and spoken academic registers would certainly help create a more complete formulaic profile of these registers with results that could be explored from a pedagogical perspective.

Another drawback that can be foreseen relates to the soundness of the procedures used for bundle identification. It is always important to remember that, at the expression identification stage, lexical bundles have no other quality than being very frequent. Thus, when identifying bundles, it is also important to remember that even if the procedures yield a small number of expressions (due to high-frequency thresholds in smaller corpora, for example), those expressions would be meeting the frequency quality that makes them lexical bundles and could make those expressions salient in a given register. This is one of those cases in which obtaining less expressions for further analysis and ulterior pedagogical application could be more beneficial than getting an extremely high number of expressions that may get unmanageable or pointless for language description and for teaching.

There is a need for more studies that analyze the functions of lexical bundles in academic discourse investigating the contexts in which they frequently occur and their position in clauses, sentences, and longer stretches of discourse. Moreover, studies of lexical bundles that continue exploring the connection between these expressions and communicative functions will surely help raise lexical bundles to the discourse building blocks status they deserve.

Finally, studies that focus on the perceived importance that the use of lexical bundles may inflict to certain academic genres could help discover better connections between the use of these expressions and academic language proficiency.

Further reading

Biber, D. (2009). A corpus-driven approach to formulaic language in English: Multi-word patterns in speech and writing. *International Journal of Corpus Linguistics, 14,* 275–311. This article highlights the importance of corpus-driven formulas and provides some statistical parameters for the identification and analysis of lexical bundles and other formulaic expression.

Cortes, V. (2015). Situating lexical bundles in the formulaic language spectrum: Origins and functional analysis developments. In V. Cortes & E. Csomay (Eds.), *Corpus linguistics in applied linguistics: Studies in honor of Doug Biber* (pp. 197–216). Benjamins. This chapter provides a good summary of the most important advances in the identification and analysis of lexical bundles in a wide variety of genres.

Hyland, K. (2012). Bundles in academic discourse. *Annual Review of Applied Linguistics, 32,* 150–169. This article presents an earlier discussion of lexical bundles in academic speech and writing that focuses on the importance of this type of formulas in academic language production.

References

Ädel, A., & Erman, B. (2012). Recurrent word combinations in academic writing by native and non-native speakers of English. *English for Specific Purposes, 31,* 81–92.

Allen, S. (1975). *Frequency dictionary of present-day Swedish based on newspaper, 3: Collocations.* Almqvist & Wiksell.

Altenberg, B. (1993). Recurrent word combinations in spoken English. In J. D'Arcy (Ed.), *Proceedings of the fifth Nordic Association for English Studies conference* (pp. 17–27). University of Iceland.

Altenberg, B., & Eeg-Olofsson, M. (1990). Phraseology in spoken English: Presentation of a project. In J. Aarts, & W. Meijs (Eds.), *Theory and practice in corpus linguistics* (pp. 1–26). Rodopi.

Anthony, L. (2020). AntConc (Version 3.5.9) [Computer Software]. Waseda University. Available from https://www.laurenceanthony.net/software

Anthony, L. (2020). AntGram (Version 1.2.3) [Computer Software]. Waseda University. Available from https://www.laurenceanthony.net/software

Barlow, M. (2000). *MonoConc Pro.* [Software]. Athelsan.

Berber Sardinha, T., & São Bento Ferreira, T. (2014). *Working with Portuguese corpora.* Bloomsbury.

Bestgen, Y. (2019). Comparing lexical bundles across corpora of different sizes: The Zipfian problem. *Journal of Quantitative Linguistics, 27*(3), 1–19.

Bestgen, Y. (2017). Getting rid of chi-square and log-likelihood tests for analysing vocabulary differences between corpora. *Quaderns de Filologia: Estudis Lingüístics, 22,* 33–56.

Biber, D. (2006). *University language: A corpus-based study of spoken and written registers.* Benjamins.

Biber, D., Conrad, S., & Cortes, V. (2003). Towards a taxonomy of lexical bundles in speech and writing. In A. Wilson, P. Rayson, & T. McEnery (Eds.), *Corpus linguistics by the Lune: A festschrift for Geoffrey Leech* (pp. 71–92). Peter Lang.

Biber, D., Conrad, S., & Cortes, V. (2004). 'If you look at …': Lexical bundles in university teaching and textbooks. *Applied Linguistics, 25,* 371–405.

Biber, D., Conrad, S., & Reppen, R. (1998). *Corpus linguistics: Investigating language structure and use.* Cambridge University Press.

Biber, D., Johansson, S., Leech, G., Conrad, S., & Finegan, E. (1999). *Longman grammar of spoken and written English.* Pearson.

Chen, L. (2018). *Lexical bundles in Vocabulary-based Discourse Units: A corpus-based study of first year core Engineering textbooks.* [Unpublished doctoral dissertation]. Carleton University.

Chen, Y., & Baker, P. (2010). Lexical bundles in L1 and L2 academic writing. *Language Learning and Technology, 14,* 40–49.

Cortes, V. (2002). Lexical bundles in freshman composition. In R. Reppen, S. Fitzmaurice, & D. Biber (Eds.), *Using corpora to explore linguistic variation* (pp. 131–145). Benjamins.

Cortes, V. (2004). Lexical bundles in published and student disciplinary writing: Examples from history and biology. *English for Specific Purposes, 23*, 397–423.

Cortes, V. (2006). Teaching lexical bundles in the disciplines: An example from a writing intensive history class. *Linguistics and Education, 17*, 391–406.

Cortes, V. (2008). A comparative analysis of lexical bundles in academic history writing in English and Spanish. *Corpora, 3*, 43–58.

Cortes, V. (2011). Genre analysis in the academic writing class: with or without corpora? *Quaderns de Filologia Estudis Linguistcs*, XVI, 41–64.

Cortes, V. (2013). Corpora in language for specific purposes research. In C. A. Chapelle (Ed.), *The encyclopedia of applied linguistics*. Wiley Blackwell.

Cortes, V. (2020, April 28). *Lexical bundles as building blocks in discourse: The case of three-word bundles* [Webinar]. LAEL. https://youtu.be/kUpHEf2_w3I

Cortes, V., & Csomay, E. (2007). Positioning lexical bundles in university classroom discourse. In M. Campoy Cubillo, & M. J. Luzon Marco (Eds.), *Spoken corpora in applied linguistics* (pp. 57–76). Benjamins.

Cortes, V., & Hardy, J. (2013). Analyzing the semantic prosody and semantic preference of lexical bundles. In D. Belcher & G. Nelson (Eds.), *Critical and corpus-based approaches to intercultural rhetoric* (pp. 180–200). University of Michigan Press.

Cowie, A. P. (1981). The treatment of collocations and idioms in learners' dictionaries. *Applied Linguistics, 2*(3), 223–235.

Csomay, E. (2005). Linguistic variation within university classroom talk: A corpus-based perspective. *Linguistics and Education, 15*, 243–274.

Csomay, E. (2013). Lexical bundles in discourse structure: A corpus-based study of classroom discourse. *Applied Linguistics, 34*, 369–388.

Csomay, E., & Cortes, V. (2010). Lexical bundle distribution in university classroom talk. In S. Gries, S. Wulff, & M. Davies (Eds.), *Corpus linguistics applications: Current studies, new directions* (pp. 153–168). Rodopi.

De Cock, S. (1998). A recurrent word combination approach to the study of formulae in the speech of native and non-native speakers of English. *International Journal of Corpus Linguistics, 3*(1), 59–80. https://doi.org/10.1075/ijcl.3.1.04dec

Firth, J. (1951). Modes of meaning. *Essays and Studies of the English Association, NS4*, 118–149.

Gray, B., & Cortes, V. (2010). Perception vs. evidence: An analysis of this and these in academic prose. *English for Specific Purposes, 30*, 31–43.

Hyland, K. (2008). As can be seen: Lexical bundles and disciplinary variation. *English for Specific Purposes, 27*, 4–21.

Kazemia, M., Katiraeib, S., & Eslami-RAsekhc, A. (2014). The impact of teaching lexical bundles on improving Iranian EFL students' writing skill. *Social and Behavioral Sciences, 98*, 864–869.

Lu, X., & Cheng, D. (2019). With the rapid development: A contrastive analysis of lexical bundles in dissertation abstracts by Chinese and L1 doctoral students. *Journal of English for Academic Purposes, 39*, 21–36.

Moon, R. (1998). *Fixed expressions and idioms in English A corpus-based approach*. Clarendon Press.

Nattinger, J. R., & DeCarrico, J. S. (1992). *Lexical phrases and language teaching*. Oxford University Press.

Nesi, H., & Basturkmen, H. (2006). Lexical bundles and discourse signaling in academic lecturers. *International Journal of Corpus Linguistics, 11*(3), 283–304.

Salazar, D. (2006). *Lexical bundles in native and non-native scientific writing*. Benjamins.

Shin, Y. K. (2019). Do native writers always have a head start over nonnative writers? The use of lexical bundles in college students' essays. *Journal of English for Academic Purposes, 40*, 1–4.

Shin, Y. K., Cortes, V., & Yoo, I. W. (2018). Using lexical bundles as a tool to analyze definite article use in L2 academic writing. *Journal of Second Language Writing, 39*, 29–41.

Sinclair, J. (1991). *Corpus, concordance, collocation*. Oxford University Press.

Swales, J. (1981). *Aspects of article introductions*. The University of Aston, Language Studies Unit.

Swales, J. (2004). *Research genres: Exploration and applications*. Cambridge University Press.

Tognini-Bonelli, E. (2001). *Corpus linguistics at work*. Benjamins.

Uçar, S. (2017). A corpus-based study on the use of three-word lexical bundles in the academic writing by native English and Turkish non-native writers. *English Language Teaching, 10*, 28–36.

Uzun, K. (2018). The use of lexical bundles and the definite article 'the': A core expression analysis. *Cumhuriyet International Journal of Education, 7*, 269–286.

Wright, H. (2019). Lexical bundles in stand-alone literature reviews: Sections, frequencies, and functions. *English for Specific Purposes, 54*, 1–14.

16

CORPORA FOR EAP WRITING

Lynne Flowerdew

16.1 Introduction

English for Academic Purposes (EAP) has traditionally been divided into EGAP (English for General Academic Purposes) and ESAP (English for Specific Academic Purposes). However, this distinction applied to writing is somewhat rough-and-ready, and it is preferable to view EAP writing from a more nuanced perspective. One consideration relates to the main communicative purpose of the writing task, i.e., whether the writing task is assigned by the EAP tutor or whether the writing forms part of a subject-based course, regardless of the genre under investigation. For example, argumentative essays from ICLE (International Corpus of Learner English) constitute general academic writing while the written assignments in the BAWE (British Academic Written English) corpus comprise 13 genre families, one of which is essays, reflect disciplinary writing. Moreover, disciplinary writing can best be viewed on a continuum ranging from quite general meta-disciplinary writing, e.g., thesis writing for doctoral students to more subject-specific disciplinary writing, e.g., thesis writing for biochemistry students. This chapter considers both academic writing tasks set by the EAP/ESP class tutor as well as various written genres from the disciplines.

16.1.1 Why use corpora for research and teaching of EAP writing?

Corpus research into both general academic and disciplinary writing has been of great value. Wordlists of both core academic and discipline-specific lexis have been compiled with scrutiny of the co-text revealing different senses of a word or its meaning (see Coxhead, 2018, for a review of these studies). Aside from individual lexical items, one of the main affordances of corpus investigations into writing is their ability of showing what can loosely be termed phraseological patterning, involving collocations, colligations, and lexical bundles, i.e. "… sequences of words that commonly go together in natural discourse" and which are the building blocks of academic writing (Biber *et al.*, 1999, p. 990). Many studies of a phraseological nature are concerned with variation across disciplines and genres. For example, Hyland (2008) looked at four-word lexical bundles (e.g. *as a result of*) in a 3.5 million-word corpus of research articles, doctoral dissertations, and master's theses across four disciplines, finding that, compared with research articles, master's dissertations were characterised by infrequent use

DOI: 10.4324/9781003002901-19

of stance bundles, e.g. *It is possible that....* Meanwhile, Durrant (2009) investigated academic collocations in a 25-million-word corpus of journal articles across five disciplines. Corpus-based investigations of grammar, which are often considered from a lexico-grammatical perspective, not only reveal what is correct but also what is likely/unlikely in a particular written genre and discipline based on frequency information. For example, Biber *et al.* (1999) found that in the case of academic prose the verb + *that* clause structure is commonly found with the verbs *suggest* and *show*, used to report previous research often with non-human entities acting as the subject, e.g. *Reports suggest that....* Staples and Reppen (2016) carried out a lexico-grammatical analysis of first year L2 writing, connecting the patterns they found with particular functions in the texts (e.g. stance and argumentation). The research findings from both expert and learner corpora thus provide valuable information to feed into a needs analysis for designing general EAP and disciplinary writing modules, thereby enabling the class tutor to prepare tailor-made materials, which may be pen-and-paper based or "hands-on".

From a teaching perspective, corpora have principally been used in two main ways to inform writing instruction, either indirectly through a "corpus-informed" approach where pen-and-paper worksheet materials (e.g. gap-filling exercises) are derived from concordance output, or through a hands-on "corpus-driven" approach, commonly referred to as data-driven learning (DDL), which requires the student to interact directly with the corpus. Of note is that Boulton and Cobb (2017) report hands-on tasks to be more effective than paper-based activities, and, as will be seen, the corpus-driven approach is far more prevalent. Academic written genres tend to be quite conventionalised (Swales, 1990), thus allowing for generation of prototypical patterning even in quite small corpora. Having students scrutinise these recurrent expressions in concordance data promotes the "noticing" hypothesis (Schmidt, 1990). This focus on noticing is consonant with the inductive approach associated with data-driven learning (DDL), which, in turn, promotes autonomous learning as students are encouraged to work things out for themselves, so to speak.

16.2 Taking stock and moving forwards

This section provides a snapshot of key trends in both research and pedagogic applications, looking at developments in corpora, software tools, and types of enquiry. Early corpus work involving academic writing made use of the academic sub-component of the 100-million-word British National Corpus (BNC) (Aston & Burnard, 1998), consisting of books and periodicals. However, this corpus is now quite dated as it was compiled in the early 1990s; studies using the academic sub-component of the larger-scale Corpus of Contemporary American English (COCA) (Davies, 2008), made up of academic journals, feature in more recent work. Around the same time as the compilation of the BNC, the International Corpus of Learner English (ICLE) project was launched, tasked with collecting argumentative essay writing by intermediate/advanced learners of various mother tongue backgrounds (Granger, 2003). However, it was not until the early/mid-2000s that institutional initiatives to compile corpora of student disciplinary writing got off the ground. Corpora reflecting advanced learner disciplinary writing include the Varieties of English for Specific Purposes dAtabase (VESPA) and the Corpus of Academic Learner English (CALE), often compared with native-speaker writing. A very recent corpus project, Corpus of Repository of Writing (CROW) (Staples & Dilger, 2018), contains a range of student assignments in terms of proficiency level, which can be filtered according to TOEFL scores. There have also been initiatives at the individual rather than institutional level to build learner corpora, such as the compilation by Sing (2016) of a one-million-word learner corpus of business writing (see Chambers, 2015 and Flowerdew, 2015b, for further details of learner corpora and pedagogic applications of the findings).

By way of contrast, the native-speaker components of the Michigan Corpus of Upper-level Student Papers (MICUSP) (Römer, 2012) and the British Academic Written English (BAWE) Corpus (Nesi *et al.*, 2008) comprising tertiary-level student merit/distinction written assignments have been used in research studies as a control corpus to compare proficient with less proficient student writing. For example, Callies (2013) used linguistics papers written by native speakers from MICUSP for comparison with similar papers from CALE written by L1 German students to explore the area of agentivity, i.e., the construal of the author's own work and, also that of other researchers.

Apart from advances in the types of corpora compiled, there have been quite transformative developments in software tools. In the late 1980s and early 1990s, software tools such as MicroConcord (Johns, 1986), a simple KWIC (key-word-in-context) concordancing program, and WordSmith Tools (Scott, 2004), a more sophisticated suite of tools, were used for both research and teaching of academic writing. An early initiative, using a sub-corpus from the MicroConcord Corpus of Academic Texts and a learner corpus of essays from the same domain (environmental concerns), is Flowerdew's (1998) research on cause and effect markers with implications for writing pedagogy. More recently, AntConc has become the most widely used tool, one of the main reasons being that it was created specifically for classroom use by learners (see Anthony, 2018, 2019 for an overview). Other popular tools such as Tom Cobb's Lextutor either incorporate their own suite of corpora and/or have imported corpora such as BAWE. Corpora such as COCA and MICUSP come with their own tools.

A very recent, ongoing development is for tools to address difficulties students encounter with academic writing by building in some form of guidance and help. Such resources include Frankenberg-Garcia *et al.*'s (2019) Collocaid writing assistant to help EAP writers with collocations and Vincent *et al.*'s (2021) Quicklinks project based on students' "infelicitous" uses of English for which they can retrieve concordance lines to help them select more "felicitous" expressions. Another resource which greatly assists students with search queries is the Louvain EAP dictionary (LEAD) integrated with corpus tools allowing searches from meaning/concept to lexeme (onomasiological) or from lexeme to meaning (semasiological) (see Paquot, 2012). The thorny issue often raised a few years ago on how students can search a corpus if they don't know what to search for in the first place is no longer such a stumbling block to using corpora with less advanced EAP students with the recent development of more user-friendly corpus query interfaces. In addition to these user-friendly corpus-based tools to support EAP writing, various data visualisation tools have also been developed for display of concordance data. For instance, GraphColl in the #LancsBox suite of programs (Brezina *et al.*, 2018) generates collocation networks providing insights into meaning relationships and has also been used for teaching collocations in academic writing (see Liu (2021) for a study investigating the effects of DDL by comparing the use of #LancsBox, with the use of a corpus-based collocations dictionary). Also, it must be emphasised that a great deal can be achieved using existing user-friendly tools. Charles (2018) describes how students have used some hitherto under-exploited functionalities in AntConc (clusters, keywords, concordance plot etc.) for editing their theses.

As far as pedagogic applications are concerned, rhetorical functions are a key focus of attention. There is also a clear trajectory from indirect uses of corpora, i.e., where the teacher prints out concordance data, sometimes edited, to use with students, to direct uses, i.e., where students interact directly with the corpus. An example of the former approach includes the tasks in Thurstun and Candlin's (1998) textbook on argumentative essay writing, using concordance output from the one-million-word MicroConcord Corpus.

The pen-and-paper corpus-informed tasks introduce lexico-grammar according to its specific rhetorical function, e.g. referring to the literature, reporting the research of others. Within each broad function, each keyword (e.g. *claim, identify*) is examined within a chain of activities, which progress from controlled to more open-ended writing activities. An early landmark pedagogic initiative in disciplinary writing, involving comparative analyses of expert and learner corpora, is that by Lee and Swales (2006). In their 13-week course, advanced-level doctoral students were first introduced to the "corpus way" of investigating language through, for example, using context to disambiguate near-synonyms and "gaining sensitivity to norms and distributional patterns in language" (p. 62). In the final part of the course, students were required to compile their own corpora for self-initiated enquiries (see Charles, 2014, for more details on student compilation of personal corpora for their own use). With the compilation of MICUSP in 2009, writing tutors made use of this freely available corpus. For example, Diani's (2012) account illustrates how a sub-component of MICUSP (research papers in linguistics) was used to sensitise linguistics students to how rhetorical and lexical choices are used to express particular rhetorical functions, such as the use of the verb *argue* to create a negative claim, e.g. Cortazzi *argues* that narratives are introduced into turn-by-turn talk, e.g. *While very insightful, Cortazzi's model seems somewhat narrow...* (p. 57). More recent endeavours have seen collaboration between language tutors, subject specialists, and software engineers to construct online corpus query platforms incorporating specialised corpora compiled in the local context (see Wong, 2019, for the implementation of postgraduate thesis writing).

16.3 Core issues and debates in using corpora for EAP writing

Core issues in using corpora and tools for EAP writing have been raised by Ädel (2010), Anthony (2019) and Yoon (2011) with various suggestions put forward on ways to overcome these. Both Ädel and Anthony bring up the question of obtaining a suitable corpus for use by learners. However, this does not present an intractable problem as freely-available genre- and discipline-specific corpora such as MICUSP and BAWE are available. It is also possible for the class tutor to create their own corpora, or have students build their own specialised corpora using AntCorGen (Anthony, 2019), a discipline-specific corpus creation tool.

Other key issues raised include the challenge for students to interact effectively with a corpus as they may not know what to look for or be presented with large amounts of data (Ädel, 2010; Anthony, 2019). The former challenge can partly be overcome by having clearly-defined tasks and teacher-guided activities. Indeed, many corpus-based writing programmes incorporate strategy training into the module moving through a carefully-graded sequence of teacher-activities to more student-centred ones. Some corpus tools allow for deletion of concordance lines or random sampling, thus overcoming the latter obstacle of data overload. One question posed over a decade ago concerned the effectiveness of using corpora for improving EAP writing. This issue has, in the main, been addressed as there is now a fairly substantial body of experimental studies supplemented by questionnaire and interview data on learners' performance, validating the efficacy of corpus consultation in writing programs (see Flowerdew (2021) for a summary of these). However, studies on the long-term use of corpora are few and far between.

This backdrop of key trends and core issues and debates on using corpora for both general academic and disciplinary writing sets the scene for the following sections. The use of corpora for various research and instructional purposes is first discussed. The final section reviews ongoing developments and maps out future directions for research and pedagogy.

16.4 Examining contributions from research and pedagogy

Key foci for enquiry are first discussed with reference to both research-oriented and more pedagogically motivated work. These include two functional areas (citation practices and Swalesian move structure patterning) and two linguistic features (lexical bundles and keywords), although there is some overlap amongst these categories. To note is the focus on phraseological/lexico-grammatical patterning across all these categories, irrespective of the starting point of the enquiry. This is followed by a sub-section on the classroom applications of using corpora for revising and referencing purposes in EAP writing.

16.4.1 *Corpora for research and instructional purposes*

16.4.1.1 *Citation practices and reporting verbs*

Not surprisingly, citation analysis has received a lot of attention in EAP corpus analysis as it plays a key role in academic writing at both the undergraduate and graduate level (Charles, 2006; Kwon *et al.*, 2018). An early study in this area is that by Charles (2006) who investigated phraseological patterns and their functions in reporting clauses in two corpora of theses written by native speakers in contrasting disciplines (190,000 words in politics/international relations and 300,000 words in material science). The most frequently occurring pattern in both corpora was an integral citation, a human subject, and the verb group *argue* (e.g. *argue*, *note*, *suggest*) + that in present tense, e.g. "*Skinner argues* that historical texts should be read in their intellectual context." (p. 313), used by thesis writers to situate the research of others within the field, thus allowing them to position their own work in relation to it. In contrast, a common pattern in the materials science theses was a *find/show* verb group (e.g. *show*, *find*, *observe*) in the past tense, e.g. "*Cairns et al (1975) have shown that* the ability of a material to undergo successful zone annealing..." (p. 322), whereby the writer gives credit to other researchers contributing to the cumulative construction of knowledge. Simplifying Charles's (2006) rhetorical categorisation of reporting verbs (*argue*, *show*, *find*, *think*) into three categories (textual referral, self-referral, uncited or general referral), Kwon *et al.* (2018) explored their use in literature review assignments from CROW. Findings showed that while many uses by first-year students aligned with those used by more advanced academic writers, these students used a limited range of reporting verbs and many uses of self-reference, e.g. *Through reading, I found that...* and ineffective generalisations, e.g. *Students think that...* (see Shin *et al.*, 2018, for a related study using literature review drafts from the CROW corpus to examine the effectiveness of corpus-based instruction). Another important study in this area is that by Lee *et al.* (2018) who examined L2 undergraduate students' citation practices in terms of surface forms, rhetorical functions, and writer stance in a corpus of 100 source-based research papers. They found that students used a restricted range of reporting verbs and mainly adopted a non-committal stance. While all the previous studies suggest some pedagogic applications of the findings, more detailed suggestions and activities can be found in Bloch (2009) and Thompson and Tribble (2001). Bloch makes the important point that with lower level students it is necessary to control for the types of language and text that the teacher wants to focus on. To this end, he designed a program with a user-friendly interface that presented users with only a limited number of hits for each query and a limited number of criteria for querying the database, e.g., attitude towards claim, strength of claim etc. This contrasts with Thompson and Tribble's (2001) suite of activities designed for postgraduate humanities EAP students using a micro-corpus of 22 extracts from the journal *Language and Literature*.

16.4.1.2 Swalesian move structure patterning

The Swalesian tradition of genre and move structure patterning has been applied to corpus-based research of student academic essay writing. For example, Durrant and Mathews-Aydınlı (2011) extracted a sub-set of assignments from the BAWE corpus, 94 essays produced by students in social sciences MA courses. The introduction sections were first annotated for communicative functions based on Swales's (1990) concept of moves, which were then further sub-divided into steps. For instance, in the *Essay focus* move the step "describing the structure of the essay" was found in 71% of essays, regardless of discipline. However, Swales's model has mainly been applied to pedagogy, as attested by the studies reported below which combine a bottom-up lexico-grammatical approach with a more top-down genre-based perspective (Flowerdew, 2005).

An early corpus initiative, specifically formal legal essays written by undergraduates, is reported in Weber (2001). First, Weber's students were inducted into the genre of legal essays by reading through whole essays taken from the University of London LLB Examinations written by native speakers and identifying some of the prototypical rhetorical features, e.g., identifying and/or delimiting the legal principle involved in the case. They were then asked to identify any lexical expressions which seemed to correlate with the genre features. This was followed up by consulting the corpus of the legal essays to verify and pinpoint regularities in lexico-grammatical expressions. For example, items such as *assume, consider*, and *regard* in various constructions were all found to act as signals in an opening-type move, delimiting the case under consideration before the principle involved in it was defined, as exemplified by the extract below in Figure 16.1.

In an interesting departure from the usual type of ESP work, Weber's students were also exposed to corpora of different, non-legal genres in order to sensitise them to the highly specific use and patterning of certain lexical items, such as *held* and *submit*, in legal texts (see Hafner & Candlin, 2007 for pedagogic accounts of other legal genres). Other discipline-specific accounts are reported in Bianchi and Pazzaglia (2007) for psychology and Diani (2012) for linguistics.

A few initiatives concern meta-disciplinary writing rather than subject-specific instruction, mainly for the reason that the students were not a homogeneous group from the same discipline. A case in point is the workshop for postgraduate science and engineering students reported in Flowerdew (2015a) for writing up the Discussion section of a thesis. Flowerdew made use of a freely available corpus of research articles, specifically, the Discussion sections, and also MICUSP. To note is that she did not use an "exemplar" corpus of theses due to unavailability but an "analogue" corpus of research articles, a corpus as close as possible in terms of genre, discipline, etc.,

received Brian's letter.	Assuming	the offer does remain open, Brian's Thursday
proceeding on the latter	assumption	In order to discuss the law related to
to discuss. I now have to	consider	whether B's message, left on the answerphone
third party. Bata v. Bata.	Considering	first the story about The BCDs, can the ba
With	regard to	contracts *ex facie* illegal it is necessary to
second part of the story.	Regarding	the potential claim of Evangeline, it is subm

Figure 16.1 Concordance lines for "delimiting the case under consideration" (adapted from Weber 2001, p. 17)

to the student disciplinary writing (Tribble, 2011). However, it is still possible to accommodate a discipline-specific perspective within a mixed-discipline class, as reported by Cortes (2007), who compiled ten sub-corpora of research articles reflecting the disciplines of her students. Other initiatives focus on aspects of stance and voice, e.g. Charles's (2007) students investigated the two-part structure of "defending your work against criticism" and Chang's (2012) students explored devices for projecting an effective authorial stance. Corpus-based Swalesian genre pedagogy has been greatly enhanced with the aid of technology (Cotos *et al.*, 2015).

In view of the fact that PhD students are facing increasing pressure to publish, a few accounts address the burgeoning area of English for Research Publication Purposes (ERPP). Chen and Flowerdew (2018) report a 35-hour workshop in which students worked with teacher-built discipline-specific corpora using AntConc (Anthony, 2020) before constructing their own corpora. Importantly, students' evaluation of the series of workshops was also included, as well as their use of corpora eight months later. Dong and Lu's (2020) report also covers an evaluation of their course using triangulated data. Of interest is that the instructor and students collaboratively compiled a corpus which was then annotated for rhetorical moves using AntMover (Anthony, 2003) (see Moreno & Swales, 2018, for more details on annotating moves and steps). Cotos *et al.*'s (2016) initiative on writing the Discussion section of a research paper is notable for bridging the gap between research and pedagogy, as is the account in Tribble and Wingate (2013) below.

Tribble and Wingate (2013) adopt a somewhat different approach to those above, but still work within the tradition of genre-based approaches to promote academic literacy with respect to critical assignments in Applied Linguistics and lab reports in Pharmacy. In contrast to the majority of pedagogic initiatives, Wingate and Tribble use the corpus as a database drawing on it only in the second stage of development. In the first stage, a small sub-set of high- and low-rated critical assignments in Applied Linguistics and lab reports in Pharmacy were chosen in collaboration with disciplinary specialists, who also took part in identifying move structures and problematic aspects in low scoring assignments. This input was used to prepare materials in printed format for a teaching/learning cycle moving from scaffolded to independent learning. In the second stage, corpus-informed materials derived from their research of lexical bundle analyses (see following section) in the two disciplinary genres were used to help students understand linguistic knowledge at the level of phraseology.

16.4.1.3 Lexical bundles

There is a wealth of research into lexical bundles (clusters) of both expert and student writing, which, after automatic identification, are usually classified functionally (Cortes, this volume). For example, in Hyland's (2008) investigation of four-word lexical bundles in research articles, PhD theses and Master's dissertations bundles were classified according to whether they were research-oriented (helping writers to structure their activities and experiences of the real world), text-oriented (concerned with the organisation of the text) or participant-oriented (focused on the writer or reader of the text). Using Hyland's classification, Tribble (2011) investigated bundles in a corpus of advanced student writing and compared these bundles with those found in an expert exemplar corpus from the same discipline (Applied Linguistics) as well as several analogue corpora. Tribble underscores the importance of such research for EAP pedagogy as it provides valuable insights into what students "use, fail to use, underuse and overuse" (p. 102). For instance, the text-organising bundle *the extent to which*, used as a framing device whereby expert writers limit their evaluation of their own and others' research findings, was found in the expert corpus, e.g. "*The extent to which each of the criteria was fulfilled was graded on a four-point scale….*" (p. 97) but did not appear in the top 100 bundles in the apprentice corpus.

Eriksson's (2012) account of his module on teaching lexical bundles to doctoral students of biochemistry is noteworthy for bridging research and practice. He compared three-word lexical bundles (e.g. *the absence of*) across three corpora: his self-compiled corpora of articles from biochemistry, his corpus of student writing, and Hyland's list of bundles. Eriksson's pre-instructional lexical bundle analysis, thus, acts as a needs analysis to determine which bundles to teach. His analysis also provides corpus evidence for disciplinary specificity and by extension, the value of using specialised corpora, since more than half of the top fifty bundles in his two self-compiled biochemistry corpora did not appear on Hyland's academic list (see Cortes, 2006, for an evaluation of lexical bundle instruction). Byrd and Coxhead (2010) have raised the issue of why there are so few accounts of pedagogic applications of lexical bundles, suggesting that this could be due to the lack of information on their context. By way of example, they cite research using Coxhead's Academic Word List (AWL) written academic corpus to illustrate that the bundle *on the basis of* has three patterns. It was used at the beginning of a sentence to provide a transition, as an adverbial of reason when found in a passive sentence or clause or strengthened or diminished meaning when used with an adverbial. Cortes's (2013) study seeks to resolve this issue by aligning lexical bundles with moves and steps. For example, bundles found in article introduction moves, specifically "claiming centrality of the field" included *a great deal of, one of the major, the importance of the* (see Mizumoto *et al.*, 2017, for the development of an online tool applying lexical bundle analysis to move structure patterning).

16.4.1.4 Keywords

"Keywords", i.e. words of unusually high frequency when compared with a reference corpus, have been used in both research and pedagogy. For example, Aull (2017) used keyword analysis to disambiguate two common genres, argumentative and explanatory discourse, in first-year writing tasks. Another research study is that by Whiteside and Wharton (2019) who examined keywords in two close disciplines (history and politics), using essays drawn from the BAWE corpus. Their starting point was with grammatical keywords, e.g. *of, and, that,* examining the lexico-grammatical patterning in which the keywords were found. Semantic analyses revealed there to be more similarities than differences across the two disciplines. For example, a frequent semantic sequence for *of* in both disciplines was the following: process + *of* + actor, e.g. "a complete breakdown *of* effective government" (p. 6).

Lee and Chen (2009) also view grammatical keywords as a good starting point for more qualitative, phraseological analyses. In their contrastive interlanguage analysis (CIA) study, the writing of undergraduate Chinese learners' dissertations in linguistics from the Chinese Academic Written English (CAWE) (Lee, n.d.) corpus was referenced against a comparable sub-set of novice native-speaker writing from the BAWE corpus. The keywords function in WordSmith tools was used for extraction of a list of negative keywords, i.e. underused items, and positive keywords, i.e. overused items, which then underwent an n-gram (lexical bundle) analysis. A follow-up analysis of the keyword item *the* showed that the definite article commonly occurred with the nouns, *student* and *teacher*, both important topic-related nouns for linguistics. A more qualitative, phraseological analysis enabled Lee and Chen to pinpoint problematic usage, noting that "many of the Chinese learners appear not to have mastered the art of using plural nouns" (p. 287), which they discuss in relation to the higher-level skill of argumentation. They point out that students are not able to distinguish between talking about specific research subjects under study such as, *"the students in the study..."* as opposed to more general implications as in *"students will be more motivated if..."* (p. 287). Importantly, Lee and Chen emphasise that this type of research should feed into needs analyses for the preparation of EAP writing courses and, like Tribble and Wingate (2013), advocate that this type of problematic form-focused, subject-specific phraseology should be addressed in ESP courses to complement more top-down genre approaches. Lee and Chen's study underscores the value of CIA-based research for purposive pedagogic treatment – the problematic transfer of *the* may well be transfer related as Chinese does not have functional equivalents of the English definite and indefinite article.

An innovative application of keywords to pedagogy is reported in Poole (2016), whose focus is on the teaching and learning of rhetoric in an undergraduate general academic writing course. This was grounded in a controversial topic of local relevance, the proposal to build a large copper mine near the campus. Students first read and discussed a company brochure and interest group blog posts and viewed an opposition group's video. Poole's corpus-informed course made use of extracts of corpus data, selected from two self-compiled, specialised localised pedagogic corpora (the first included blog posts from an opposition group website and the second consisted of press releases from the mine company) for follow-up corpus-aided activities, using keywords selected from the two corpora. This involved discussion work around, for example, the use of the keyword *will* in sentences such as the following: "the mine will produce over 400 direct jobs and around 1600" (p. 104). A key aim of the activities was to develop in students a critical capacity to see how rhetorical choices reflect the ideologies and values embodied in various interest groups.

16.4.2 Corpora for revising and referencing purposes

While the above accounts report the use of corpora for research and practice, several initiatives focus on the use of corpora for revising and referencing purposes, especially for error correction. Xiao and Chen (2018) describe the application of COCA which runs through the three stages of the writing process in which student consultation of COCA is used at the pre-writing stage for brainstorming, at the while-writing stage to eliminate lexical errors and at the post-writing stage to correct errors from feedback given by the teacher and peers. Flowerdew (2008), meanwhile, describes a teaching cycle in which the corpus has been used by students as a self-correcting tool at different stages of the writing process, which invariably involves some kind of "pedagogic mediation" on the part of the teacher using a guided inductive approach (Flowerdew, 2009). The corpus instruction progressed through the following three stages: teacher-identified errors, student-identified errors, and student-generated queries for writing up the final project report mediated through discussion activities. Students were divided into groups and in their process of enquiry asked to discuss various questions such as which corpus or sub-corpus would be most appropriate for their enquiry and which search word they would use, facilitated by the tutor who circulated amongst the groups to guide discussion. A similar initiative is reported in Quinn (2015), who prepared students to use a corpus, in this case, the Collins WordBanks Online, through paper-based practice tasks using a guided-inductive approach. As pointed out by Gilmore (2009), this inductive approach to error correction which allows students to generate their own hypotheses "is more in line with constructivist theories of learning from developmental psychology, which see individuals as active participants in the construction of their own personal meaning from the experiences they have" (p. 3). This constructivist approach also underlies Watson-Todd's (2001) error-correction tasks which required students to build their own concordances from internet sources and induce valid patterns for self-correction. Quantitative studies to determine whether students can improve their writing in the revision stage by using the corpus as a reference tool are discussed in Flowerdew (2021).

16.5 Future directions of research

The above accounts reveal that work tends to be either research-based with implications and/ or suggestions made for writing instruction or pedagogically oriented. There are very few studies, such as the ones by Cotos *et al.* (2016), Eriksson (2012), and Tribble and Wingate (2013) which truly bridge the gap between research and pedagogy (see Chambers, 2019, for recommendations on bridging the research-practice gap). One publication which achieves this aim is the recent volume by Crosthwaite and Cheung (2019) on the language of dentistry. The authors' research on disciplinary register features and vocabulary from three key genres from the discipline of dentistry (published experimental research articles, case reports, and novice/professional research reports) is grounded in Biber's Multidimensional Analysis (MDA) model in which language is analysed across various functional dimensions, with the second part of the book applying insights from this quantitative research to the development of data-driven tasks.

Linguistic enquiries of a comparative nature are mostly of a cross-disciplinary and cross-genre nature. While Granger's CIA approach is well documented in research studies on English L1 and L2 argumentative essay writing, it is surprising that it does not feature more prominently in studies on disciplinary writing to inform needs analyses and course development. Also, ethnographic cross-contextual investigations merit more attention; research by Li and Wharton (2012) has demonstrated that the educational context, i.e., the local institutional culture and guidance students receive in EAP writing, may have a bearing on interpretation of corpus data. Cross-linguistic/cross-cultural studies are also few and far between (Lee & Casal, 2014). By way of example, Moreno's (2021) research explores whether greater effort is made to promote research in English than in Spanish in RA discussion sections in the social sciences, using the Exemplary Empirical Research Articles (EXEMPRAES) corpus. It was found that authors in English were more promotional, highlighting more positive aspects of their studies and applications of the results, while Spanish authors writing in Spanish tended to be more neutral. An innovative aspect of this research is that a survey was administered to the authors to investigate reasons for the differences identified by the corpus analysis. Such results can usefully inform pedagogic resources from a cross-cultural perspective, as noted in Moreno and Swales (2018).

The phenomenon of English as a lingua franca (ELF) in academic writing is another area where more research is expected along the lines of Wu *et al.*'s (2020) research on syntactic complexity using samples from the SciELF corpus and COCA, illustrating how ELF writers handle explicitness and conciseness to achieve effective communication (see Flowerdew, 2019, for an exploratory study on distinctions between ELF writing and learner corpora). This chapter has concentrated on L2 writers but L1 writers can also benefit from corpus instruction as they may have inadequate mastery of disciplinary discourses, as reported in the study by Friginal (2013).

Another question that has been raised in the literature concerns the effectiveness and uptake of corpus consultation. While there is now substantial experimental research showing that students do benefit from corpus consultation even over an extended period of a one-semester course, the long-term benefits are less clear in terms of autonomous use outside the classroom. More studies along the lines of those by Charles (2014) and Jablonkai and Čebron (2021) examining students' autonomous use of corpora are needed. "Outside the classroom" can also involve an online format. For example, Crosthwaite (2020) describes an online corpus-based tertiary-level writing programme, thereby scaling up DDL from face-to-face classroom-based instruction.

This chapter has showcased the multi-faceted work being carried out in corpus-based EAP research and pedagogy for writing. However, there is scope for future work to continue building bridges across the research/pedagogy paradigm, between corpus approaches and more contextual ethnographic enquiries and between students' writing needs and software development to facilitate these needs. As more and more universities across the globe embrace digital technologies and migrate to online instruction, EAP corpus-based pedagogies will no doubt follow suit, thereby promoting autonomous and self-initiated, self-directed learning and teaching.

Further readings

Chen, M., & Flowerdew, J. (2018). A critical review of research and practice in data-driven learning (DDL) in the academic writing classroom. *International Journal of Corpus Linguistics*, *23*(3), 335–369. This survey article covers both research and practice in DDL.

Karpenko-Seccombe, T. (2020). *Academic writing with corpora*. Routledge. This book provides a practical introduction to DDL, using Lextutor as well as other resources such as Sketch Engine for Language Learning (SkELL) and MICUSP.

Römer, U., Cortes, V., & Friginal, E. (Eds.). (2020). *Advances in corpus-based research on academic writing*. Benjamins. This volume includes research that combines rhetorical move structures with multi-dimensional analyses and studies that cover both fixed and variable phraseological items (lexical bundles and phrase frames). Each chapter discusses the pedagogic applications of the research study.

References

Ädel, A. (2010). Using corpora to teach academic writing: Challenges for the direct approach. In M. Campoy-Cubillo, B. Bélles-Fortuño, & M. Gea-Valor (Eds.), *Corpus-based approaches to English language teaching* (pp. 41–55). Continuum.

Anthony, L. (2003). AntMover (Version 1.1.0) [Computer Software]. Waseda University. Available from https://www.laurenceanthony.net/software.

Anthony, L. (2018). Introducing corpora and corpus tools into the technical writing classroom through data-driven learning. In J. Flowerdew & T. Costley (Eds.), *Discipline-specific writing* (pp. 162–180). Routledge.

Anthony, L. (2019). Tools and strategies for data-driven learning in the EAP writing classroom. In K. Hyland & L. Wong (Eds.), *Specialised English. New directions in ESP and EAP research and practice* (pp. 179–194). Routledge.

Anthony, L. (2019). AntCorGen (Version 1.1.2) [Computer Software]. Waseda University. https://www.laurenceanthony.net/software

Anthony, L. (2020). AntConc (Version 3.5.9) [Computer Software]. Waseda University. https://www.laurenceanthony.net/software

Aston, G., & Burnard, L. (1998). *The BNC handbook*. Edinburgh University Press.

Aull, L. (2017). Corpus analysis of argumentative versus explanatory discourse in writing task genres. *Journal of Writing Analytics*, *1*, 1–45.

Bianchi, F., & Pazzaglia, R. (2007). Student writing of research articles in a foreign language: Metacognition and corpora. In R. Facchinetti (Ed.), *Corpus linguistics 25 years on* (pp. 259–287). Rodopi.

Biber, D., Johannson, S., Leech, G., Conrad, S., & Finnegan, E. (1999). *Longman grammar of spoken and written English*. Longman.

Bloch, J. (2009). The design of an online concordancing program for teaching about reporting verbs. *Language Learning & Technology*, *13*(1), 59–78.

Boulton, A., & Cobb, T. (2017). Corpus use in language learning: A meta-analysis. *Language Learning*, *67*(2), 348–393.

Brezina, V., Timperely, M., & McEnery, T. (2018). #LancsBox (v. 4) [Computer software]. http://corpora. lancs.ac.uk/lancsbox

Byrd, P., & Coxhead, A. (2010). On the other hand: Lexical bundles in academic writing and in the teaching of EAP. *University of Sydney Papers in TESOL*, *5*, 31–64.

Callies, M. (2013). Agentivity as a determinant of lexico-grammatical variation in L2 academic writing. *International Journal of Corpus Linguistics*, *18*(3), 357–390.

Chambers, A. (2015). The learner corpus as a pedagogic corpus. In S. Granger, G. Gilquin, & F. Meunier (Eds.), *The Cambridge handbook of learner corpus research* (pp. 445–464). Cambridge University Press.

Chambers, A. (2019). Towards the corpus revolution? Bridging the research-practice gap. *Language Teaching*, *52*(1), 460–475.

Chang, P. (2012). Using a stance corpus to learn about effective authorial stance-taking. A textlinguistic approach. *ReCALL*, *24*(2), 209–236.

Charles, M. (2006). Phraseological patterns in reporting clauses used in citation: A corpus-based study of theses in two disciplines. *English for Specific Purposes*, *25*(3), 310–331.

Charles, M. (2007). Reconciling top-down and bottom-up approaches to graduate writing: Using a corpus to teach rhetorical functions. *Journal of English for Academic Purposes*, *6*(4), 289–302.

Charles, M. (2014). Getting the corpus habit: EAP students' long-term use of personal corpora. *English for Specific Purposes*, *35*, 30–40.

Charles, M. (2018). Corpus-assisted editing: More than just concordancing. *Journal of English for Academic Purposes*, *36*, 15–25.

Chen, M., & Flowerdew, J. (2018). Introducing data-driven learning to PhD students for research writing purposes: A territory wide project. *English for Specific Purposes*, *50*, 97–112.

Cobb, T. (n.d.). *Lextutor*. Online concordancer. http://lextutor.ca/conc/eng

Corpus of Academic Learner English (CALE) https://blogs.uni-bremen.de/cale/corpus-design/

Cortes, V. (2006). Teaching lexical bundles in the disciplines: An example from a writing intensive history class. *Linguistics and Education*, *17*(4), 391–406.

Cortes, V. (2007). Exploring genre and corpora in the English for academic writing class. *The ORTESOL Journal*, *25*, 8–14.

Cortes, V. (2013). The purpose of this study is to: Connecting lexical bundles and moves in research article introductions. *Journal of English for Academic Purposes*, *12*, 33–43.

Cotos, E., Huffman, S., & Link, S. (2015). Furthering and applying move/step constructs: Technology-driven marshalling of Swalesian genre theory for EAP pedagogy. *Journal of English for Academic Purposes*, *19*, 52–72.

Cotos, E., Link, S., & Huffman, S. (2016). Studying disciplinary corpora to teach the craft of discussion. *Writing & Pedagogy*, *8*(1), 33–64.

Coxhead, A. (2018). *Vocabulary and English for Specific Purposes research*. Routledge.

Crosthwaite, P. (2020). Taking DDL online: Designing, implementing and evaluating a SPOC on data-driven learning for tertiary L2 writing. *Australian Review of Applied Linguistics*, *43*(2), 169–195.

Crosthwaite, P., & Cheung, L. (2019). *Learning the language of dentistry. Disciplinary corpora in the teaching of English for specific academic purposes*. Benjamins.

Davies, M. (2008). The Corpus of Contemporary American English. http:// www.english-corpora. org/coca/.

Diani, G. (2012). Text and corpus work, EAP writing and language learners. In R. Tang (Ed.), *Academic writing in a second or foreign language* (pp. 45–66). Continuum.

Dong, J., & Lu, X. (2020). Promoting discipline specific genre competence with corpus-based genre activities. *English for Specific Purposes*, *58*, 138–154.

Durrant, P. (2009). Investigating the viability of a collocation list for students of English for academic purposes. *English for Specific Purposes*, *28*, 157–169.

Durrant, P., & Mathews-Aydınlı, J. (2011). A function-first approach to identifying formulaic language in academic writing. *English for Specific Purposes*, *30*, 58–72.

Eriksson, A. (2012). Pedagogical perspectives on bundles: Teaching bundles to doctoral students of biochemistry. In J. Thomas & A. Boulton (Eds.), *Input, process and product. Developments in teaching and language corpora* (pp. 195–211). Masaryk University Press.

Flowerdew, L. (1998). Integrating 'expert' and 'interlanguage' computer corpora findings on causality: Discoveries for teachers and learners. *English for Specific Purposes*, *17*(4), 329–345.

Flowerdew, L. (2005). An integration of corpus-based and genre-based approaches to text analysis in EAP/ESP: Countering criticisms against corpus-based methodologies. *English for Specific Purposes*, *24*(3), 321–332.

Flowerdew, L. (2008). Corpus linguistics for academic literacies mediated through discussion activities. In D. Belcher & A. Hirvela (Eds.), *The oral-literate connection: Perspectives on L2 speaking, writing and other media interactions* (pp. 268–287). University of Michigan Press.

Flowerdew, L. (2009). Applying corpus linguistics to pedagogy: A critical evaluation. *International Journal of Corpus Linguistics*, *14*(3), 393–417.

Flowerdew, L. (2015a). Using corpus-based research and online academic corpora to inform writing of the Discussion section of a thesis. *Journal of English for Academic Purposes*, *20*, 58–68.

Flowerdew, L. (2015b). Learner corpora and language for academic and specific purposes. In S. Granger, G. Gilquin, & F. Meunier (Eds.), *The Cambridge handbook of learner corpus research* (pp. 465–484). Cambridge University Press.

Flowerdew, L. (2019). English as a Lingua Franca and learner English in disciplinary writing: A corpus perspective. In K. Hyland & L. Wong (Eds.), *Specialised English. New directions in ESP and EAP research and practice* (pp. 79–90). Routledge.

Flowerdew, L. (2021). Using corpora for writing instruction. In A. O'Keeffe & M. McCarthy (Eds.), *The Routledge handbook of corpus linguistics* (2nd ed.) (pp. 443–455). Routledge.

Frankenberg-Garcia, A., Lew, R., Roberts, J., Rees, G., & Sharma, N. (2019). Developing a writing assistant to help EAP writers with collocations in real time. *ReCALL*, *31*(1), 23–39.

Friginal, E. (2013). Developing report writing skills using corpora. *English for Specific Purposes*, *32*(4), 208–220.

Gilmore, A. (2009). Using online corpora to develop students' writing skills. *ELT Journal*, *63*(4), 363–372.

Granger, S. (2003). The International Corpus of Learner English. https://uclouvain.be/en/research-institutes/ilc/cecl/icle.html

Hafner, C., & Candlin, C. (2007). Corpus tools as an affordance to learning in professional legal education. *Journal of English for Academic Purposes*, *6*(4), 303–318.

Hyland, K. (2008). Academic clusters: Text patterning in published and postgraduate writing. *International Journal of Applied Linguistics*, *18*(1), 41–62.

Jablonkai, R., & Čebron, N. (2021). Undergraduate students' response to a corpus-based ESP course with DIY corpora. In M. Charles & A. Frankenberg-Garcia (Eds.), *Corpora in EAP/ESP writing: Preparation,* (pp. 100–120). Routledge.

Kwon, H., Staples, S., & Partridge, R. S. (2018). Source work in the first-year L2 writing classroom: Undergraduate L2 writers' use of reporting verbs. *Journal of English for Academic Purposes*, *34*, 86–96.

Johns, T. (1986). MicroConcord: A language learner's research tool. *System*, *14*(2), 151–162.

Lee, Y. W. D.(Ed.) ((n.d). *The Chinese academic written English (CAWE) corpus.* City University of Hong Kong.

Lee, D., & Chen, S. (2009). Making a bigger deal of the smaller words: Function words and other key items in research writing by Chinese learners. *Journal of Second Language Writing*, *18*(4), 281–296.

Lee, D., & Swales, J. (2006). A corpus-based EAP course for NNS doctoral students: Moving from available specialized corpora to self-compiled corpora. *English for Specific Purposes*, *25*(1), 56–75.

Lee, J. J., & Casal, J. (2014). Metadiscourse in results and discussion chapters: A cross-linguistic analysis of English and Spanish thesis writers in engineering. *System*, *46*, 39–54.

Lee, J. J., Hitchcock, C., & Casal, J. (2018). Citation practices of L2 university students in first-year writing: Form, function, and stance. *Journal of English for Academic Purposes*, *33*, 1–11.

Li, T., & Wharton, S. (2012). Metadiscourse repertoire of L1 Mandarin undergraduates writing in English: A cross-contextual, cross-disciplinary study. *Journal of English for Academic Purposes*, *11*, 345–356.

Liu, T. (2021). Data-driven learning: Using #LancsBox in academic collocation learning. In P. Pérez-Paredes & G. Mark (Eds.), *Beyond concordance lines: Corpora in language education* (pp. 177-206). Benjamins.

Michigan Corpus of Upper-level Student Papers (MICUSP). (2009). The Regents of the University of Michigan.

Mizumoto, A., Hamatami, S., & Imao, Y. (2017). Applying the bundle-move connection approach to the development of an online writing support tool for research articles. *Language Learning*, *67*(4), 885–921.

Moreno, A. (2021). Selling research in RA discussion section through English and Spanish: An intercultural rhetoric approach. *English for Specific Purposes*, *63*, 1–17.

Moreno, A., & Swales, J. M. (2018). Strengthening move analysis methodology towards bridging the form-function gap. *English for Specific Purposes, 50,* 40–63.

Nesi, H., Gardner, S., Thompson, P. & Wickens P. (2008). *British Academic Written English Corpus.* Oxford Text Archive. http://hdl.handle.net/20.500.12024/2539.

Paquot, M. (2012). The LEAD dictionary-cum-writing aid: An integrated dictionary and corpus tool. In S. Granger & M. Paquot (Eds.), *Electronic lexicography* (pp. 163–185). Oxford University Press.

Poole, R. (2016). A corpus-aided approach for the teaching and learning of rhetoric in an undergraduate composition course for L2 writers. *Journal of English for Academic Purposes, 21,* 99–109.

Quinn, C. (2015). Training L2 writers to reference corpora as a self-correction tool. *ELT Journal, 69*(2), 165–177.

Römer, U. (2012). Corpora and teaching academic writing: Exploring the pedagogic potential of MICUSP. In J. Thomas & A. Boulton (Eds.), *Input, process and product. Developments in teaching and language corpora* (pp. 70–82). Masaryk University Press.

Schmidt, R. (1990). The role of consciousness in second language learning. *Applied Linguistics, 11*(2), 129–158.

Scott, M. (2004). *Wordsmith tools, version (4.0).* Oxford University Press.

Shin, J.-Y., Velazquez, A. J., Swatek, A., Staples S., & Partridge R. S. (2018). Examining the effectiveness of corpus-informed instruction of reporting verbs in L2 first-year college writing. *L2 Journal, 10*(3), 31–46.

Sing, C. (2016). Writing for specific purposes: Developing business students' ability to 'technicalise'. In S. Göpferich & I. Neumann (Eds.), *Developing and assessing academic and professional writing skills* (pp. 15–45). Peter Lang.

Staples, S., & Dilger, B. (2018). *Corpus and repository of writing.* https://crow.corporaproject.org

Staples, S., & Reppen, R. (2016). Understanding first-year writing: A lexico-grammatical analysis across L1s, genres, and language ratings. *Journal of Second Language Writing, 32,* 17–35.

Swales, J. M. (1990). *Genre analysis: English in academic and research settings.* Cambridge University Press.

Thompson, P., & Tribble, C. (2001). Looking at citations: Using corpora in English for academic purposes. *Language Learning and Technology, 5*(3), 91–105.

Thurstun, J., & Candlin, C. (1998). *Exploring academic English: A workbook for student essay writing.* NCELTR.

Tribble, C. (2011). Revisiting apprentice texts: Using lexical bundles to investigate expert and apprentice performance in academic writing. In F. Meunier, S. de Cock, G. Gilquin, & M. Paquot (Eds.), *A taste for corpora* (pp. 85–108). Benjamins.

Tribble, C., & Wingate, U. (2013). From text to corpus: A genre-based approach to academic literacy instruction. *System, 41,* 307–321.

Varieties of English for Specific Purposes dAtabase (VESPA) https://uclouvain.be/en/research-institutes/ilc/cecl/vespa.html

Vincent, B., Nesi, H., & Quinn, D. (2021). Exploiting corpora to provide guidance for academic writing: The BAWE Quicklinks project. In M. Charles & A. Frankenberg-Garcia (Eds.), *Corpora in EAP/ESP writing: Preparation,* exploitation, analysis (pp. 13–31). Routledge.

Watson-Todd, R. (2001). Induction from self-selected concordances and self-correction. *System, 29,* 91–102.

Weber, J. J. (2001). A concordance- and genre-informed approach to ESP essay writing. *ELT Journal, 55*(1), 14–20.

Whiteside, K., & Wharton, S. (2019). Semantic patterning of grammatical keywords in undergraduate writing from two close disciplines. *Journal of English for Academic Purposes, 39,* 1–20.

Wong, L. (2019). Implementing disciplinary data-driven learning for postgraduate thesis writing. In K. Hyland & L. Wong (Eds.), *Specialised English. New directions in ESP and EAP research and practice* (pp. 195–213). Routledge.

Wu, X., Mauranen, A., & Lei, L. (2020). Syntactic complexity in English as a lingua franca in academic writing. *Journal of English for Academic Purposes, 43,* 1–13.

Xiao, G., & Chen, X. (2018). Application of COCA in EFL writing instruction at the tertiary level in China. *International Journal of Emerging Technologies in Learning, 13*(9), 160–173.

Yoon, C. (2011). Concordancing in L2 writing class: An overview of research and issues. *Journal of English for Academic Purposes, 10*(3), 130–139.

17

CORPORA AND EAP LISTENING COMPREHENSION

Belinda Crawford Camiciottoli

17.1 Introduction

More than 25 years have passed since the publication of *Academic Listening. Research Perspectives* (Flowerdew, 1994), an important collection of scholarly research papers that first brought into focus the challenges of second language listening comprehension in tertiary education, as well as the need for more empirical investigations to better understand the distinctive features of aural academic discourse. On a general level, we know that the listening comprehension process involves an integration of phonological, lexical, syntactic, semantic, and pragmatic competences (Flowerdew, 1994), all of which may require much greater effort on the part of L2 listeners compared to their L1 counterparts. In higher education instructional settings, listeners (both L1 and L2) have the added task of assimilating conceptually complex content often in a highly concentrated form that requires considerable cognitive demand. In ELT, the cultural backgrounds of listeners also come into play, especially when they lack particular cultural schemata that are reflected in academic content, which may compromise their comprehension (Flowerdew & Miller, 1996). Thus, successful second language listening encompasses a wide range of variables related not only to the linguistic features of the input, but also to the cognitive and cultural characteristics of the listeners (Flowerdew & Miller, 1996; Goh, 2005). Indeed, this distinctive blend of linguistic and contextual factors involved in academic listening can create difficulties even for L2 listeners with relatively advanced listening skills (Mulligan & Kirkpatrick, 2000).

In a review of the state of research on academic listening published over a decade later, Lynch (2011) noted that despite some progress, empirical EAP studies dedicated to listening are still considerably fewer than those targeting the other three conventional language abilities of reading, writing, and speaking. Possible reasons for this discrepancy are related to the complex nature of the listening process which, in addition to the factors discussed above, can also be impacted by issues that are both internal (e.g. momentary distractions, negative perceptions of speakers) and external to the listener (e.g. accent of the speaker). Lynch (2011) discussed an important strand of academic listening research based on the analysis of lecture discourse, or "what is said and how" (p. 81), for example, examining its distinguishing linguistic and prosodic features (Pickering, 2004; Thompson, 2003). Such research can offer key insights for practitioners in terms of which features should be emphasised in academic listening tasks to improve comprehension. The role of visual and multimodal/multimedia

DOI: 10.4324/9781003002901-20

input during academic listening was also highlighted as a new topic of research. Lynch (2011), for example, suggested that the widespread use of PowerPoint slides facilitates note-taking, which can, in turn, improve comprehension. Other studies have shown that gesturing and facial expressions observed by listeners in multimodal, video-recorded classroom discourse can lead to improved comprehension (Sueyoshi & Hardison, 2005). The effective combination of diverse semiotic modes (i.e. speech, writing, visuals, body language) that may characterise a live or video-recorded academic event targeting L2 listeners constitutes an important new facet for academic listening research (Morell *et al.*, 2008).

Research on listening comprehension has stressed the importance of exposing learners to relatively large amounts of naturally occurring and authentic speech, for example, by providing them with "comprehension corpora" created from recordings of native speakers across a variety of communicative events (Mordaunt & Olson, 2010, p. 250). Authenticity is also an important aspect in the analysis of spoken academic discourse (Pickering, 2004; Thompson, 2003), which can be considered the first step towards what Vandergrift (2007, p. 199) described as "the ultimate goal of listening instruction […] to help L2 listeners understand the target language in everyday situations." According to MacDonald *et al.* (2000), the selection of materials for language teaching authenticity remains an important criterion, even if the issue of authenticity first raised by Widdowson (1979) has been widely discussed and has taken on expanded meanings in different contexts. Thus, following Dudley-Evans and St. John (1998), the in-depth analysis of authentic spoken discourse to be used in the context of academic listening is a vital component of a needs analysis in order to distinguish salient features in a "target situation analysis" (p. 123). However, to undertake such analysis in a meaningful way, it is necessary to have access to such discourse derived from the recording and transcribing of academic events, as well as tools for investigating it systematically. Fortunately, technological advances and developments in the area of corpus linguistics have greatly expanded opportunities for this type of research. Thus, the aim of this chapter is to highlight the important contribution of corpora to enhance our understanding of the multifaceted features of instructional discourse, which can then be leveraged for academic listening activities in the context of higher education ELT. Drawing on Bernstein's (1986) notion of instructional discourse as a form of pedagogic discourse used to transmit knowledge and skills, in this chapter, I use this term to broadly refer to the language used by university educators during encounters and interactions with learners.

The remainder of the chapter will be organised as follows. In Section 17.2, I provide an overview of corpus-based research (both large- and small-scale) that has targeted instructional discourse and that has implications for L2 listening comprehension.[1] Section 17.3 shifts to the more recent trend of multimodal corpora, while foregrounding their effectiveness in fostering multimodal literacy, as well as the challenges that researchers may face when working with multimodal data. Section 17.4 presents a state-of-the-art methodology that integrates traditional corpus methods with multimodal annotation software, which can then be applied to help L2 learners exploit semiotic modes beyond verbal language (e.g. visual, gestural, spatial) in the construction of complex meanings for a more effective academic listening experience.

17.2 Corpus-based research on instructional discourse

17.2.1 Large-scale projects

In the years around the turn of the 21st century, three large-scale projects to collect samples of English language produced in institutional academic settings were embarked upon in the United States and the United Kingdom, as will be discussed below. With particular reference to spoken language, the availability of large collections of recorded and transcribed instructional discourse occurred more or less in parallel to the rise of corpus linguistics as a research framework and methodology that is highly suitable for analysing it. This timely combination has resulted in a number of studies that have provided important insights into the linguistic features of authentic spoken academic English and applications for ELT, particularly in the area of listening comprehension.

The first of these projects was the Michigan Corpus of Spoken Academic English (MICASE) (Simpson *et al.*, 2002) compiled by the English Language Institute of the University of Michigan from 1997 to 2002 to represent various genres of academic talk that occur on its campus. The corpus contains over 1.8 million words from a wide range of recorded and transcribed events including lectures, seminars, discussion sections, student presentations, advising sessions, tutorials, study groups, dissertation defences, and lab sections, thus representing a continuum of monologic to dialogic instructional discourse types. As Lynch (2011) pointed out, in university settings academic listening typically refers to the ability to understand lectures as the main instructional genre (Crawford Camiciottoli & Querol-Julián, 2016; Lee, 2009). In fact, all of the scholarly contributions in the pioneering volume by Flowerdew (1994) are based on lecture discourse. However, there are also more dialogically oriented genres (e.g. small group discussions, meetings with tutors) that similarly represent target situations for L2 academic listeners and may require listening skills of a somewhat different nature.

The MICASE corpus is accessible online and includes a search interface that functions as a concordance tool and allows for targeted queries by speaker type, age, sex, nationality, event type, and disciplinary area. One of the main purposes of MICASE was to understand to what extent English academic speech might share features with everyday conversation (Swales, 2004). The significant body of research based on MICASE that followed suggested that academic speech is indeed quite similar to conversation in terms of dysfluency, informality, and interpersonal/interactional features, thus reflecting the underlying pedagogic focus of the project for applications in ELT and, in particular, the potential listening comprehension challenges for L2 learners. From this perspective, studies have been carried out over the years to investigate conversation-like features in MICASE including evaluative language (Swales & Burke, 2003), idioms (Simpson & Mendis, 2003), question tags (Pérez-Llantada, 2005), humour (Lee & Gunesekera, 2006), discourse markers (Schleef, 2008), and epistemic and attitudinal stance (Molina, 2015), to mention only a few.

Around the same timeframe, the TOEFL 2000 Spoken and Written Academic Language (T2K-SWAL) Corpus was compiled at Northern Arizona University in Flagstaff, containing 2.7 million words of language occurring at five American universities and comprising both spoken and written instructional registers such as classroom teaching, labs, office hours, textbooks, lecture notes, and study guides. Like the MICASE corpus, the T2K-SWAL is also strongly linked to ELT and aimed to provide a comprehensive description of university registers with the ultimate goal to help incoming international students to better understand the type of language that they would encounter at the university (Biber *et al.*, 2004a). The T2K-SWAL has generated a number of studies using the multidimensional analysis method (Biber *et al.*, 1998), which have provided important insights into the overall linguistic profile of university classrooms compared to other registers in the university (Biber *et al.*, 2002), as well as the distinctive features of classroom discourse, including interactivity patterns (Csomay, 2002), lexical bundles (Biber *et al.*, 2004b), stance (Biber, 2006), and directives (Kia, 2018), among others. Overall, in line with research deriving from the MICASE corpus, these studies have suggested that spoken academic language is substantially different from written academic language and can be collocated in the oral area of an oral/written cline (Biber, 2003; Csomay, 2006).

In the United Kingdom, the British Academic Spoken English Corpus (BASE) was compiled from 2000 to 2005 (Nesi & Thompson, 2006). It was envisioned as a sister corpus to the MICASE corpus (Creer & Thompson, 2004). It includes approximately 1.6 million words transcribed from audio and video recorded lectures and seminars that took place at the Universities of Warwick and Reading. The BASE corpus has similarly spawned a considerable amount of research that has shed light on key features of instructional discourse. A few examples are mitigators and metadiscourse (Grant, 2011), humour (Nesi, 2012), hedging and vagueness indicators (Lin, 2010), markers of importance (Deroey, 2015), and interpersonal features (Deroey & Taverniers, 2011).

The highly influential role of these three large corpora in research on the features of instructional discourse is also seen in studies that have either drawn on them contemporaneously as sources of data or used them in a benchmarking capacity for comparisons with other corpora of a different or more specialised nature. For example, the MICASE and TK2-SWAL corpora were analysed in studies of informal language (Barbieri, 2013), discourse structure and their linguistic correlates (Csomay, 2005a, 2005b), lexical bundles (Csomay, 2013), and turn-taking patterns (Csomay, 2012) in classroom discourse. The BASE and MICASE corpora served as data for an investigation of participial adverbs (Malá, 2008) and lexical bundles and discourse signalling (Nesi & Basturkmen, 2006). Wang (2012) compared the use of lexical bundles and personal pronouns as interpersonal features in the BASE corpus to a corpus based on TED Talks, while Miller (2020) investigated idioms in the BASE corpus vs. a corpus of written academic discourse, namely, the Oxford Corpus of Academic English (OCAE). The MICASE corpus was used by Lee and Subtirelu (2015) to compare the use of metadiscourse in university lectures in general with a self-compiled corpus of EAP classroom instruction. Reinhardt (2010) conducted a comparative analysis of directives in the MICASE corpus vs. an ad-hoc spoken learner corpus based on the speech of international teaching assistants in training.

The studies discussed above represent just a few of the wide-ranging linguistic insights that have originated from the analyses of these three corpora. However, a clear sense of their real impact on ELT research and practice is perhaps best reflected in the relatively large number of results that were retrieved in a simple Google Scholar search at the time of writing (i.e. MICASE/2,010, BASE/286, T2K-SWAL/369), while keeping in mind that T2K-SWAL is not publicly available.

17.2.2 *Small-scale research*

To conclude this section, I would like to briefly turn to the role of smaller scale corpus-based studies of spoken instructional discourse. Clearly, such studies that typically entail the analysis of small, specialised corpora cannot have the same level of influence as the three major corpora described above (Simpson-Vlach, 2013). However, it is important to recognise their value not only in contributing to the body of knowledge in relation to spoken academic discourse in general, but also in finely tuned analyses designed to respond to specific research objectives. Indeed, because of their smaller size, they are more suitable for extensive follow-up analysis of features of interest within their context of usage with respect to large corpora. In other words, such corpora are small enough to render feasible manual analysis by means of careful reading, but still large enough to generate meaningful frequencies.[2] In this sense, such smaller scale research is perhaps better characterised as corpus-assisted discourse analysis (Baker *et al.*, 2008) that implements corpus tools to first identify and retrieve features of interest and then follows up with in-depth contextual analysis to reveal distinctive patterns and trends in usage.

Small-scale corpus-based research focusing on instructional discourse may be limited to particular disciplinary areas or contexts of usage. Flowerdew (2003) identified signalling nouns (e.g. *fact, reason, process*) as important devices for establishing links across stretches of discourse to facilitate comprehension in a small corpus of 12 undergraduate biology lectures delivered by native speakers of English to L2 listeners. Crawford Camiciottoli (2007) conducted a comprehensive analysis of the linguistic and extra-linguistic features of a small corpus of 12 business studies lectures as a needs analysis phase to prepare L2 learners for lecture experiences in English medium universities (Crawford Camiciotoli, 2010). In later studies, Crawford Camiciottoli (2018, 2020) identified culture-specific references and informal expressions by means of semantic tagging software in small corpora of multi-disciplinary OpenCourseWare lectures made available by the Massachusetts Institute of Technology and Yale University. Molino (2018) investigated the use of metadiscourse in five lectures delivered in English by native speakers of Italian in an EMI (English Medium Instruction) program at an Italian university. The aim was to shed light on the L2 lecturers' awareness of the import-ance of metadiscourse in fostering understanding in EMI contexts. O'Keeffe and Walsh (2012) extracted a 50,000-word sub-corpus from the 500,000-word Limerick Belfast Corpus of Academic Spoken English which contained episodes of sustained interaction between instructors and students in the context of small group teaching. They analysed keywords, multi-word units, and patterns of interaction to explore their roles in fostering opportunities for learning in these interactions. All of these small-scale studies are testimony to the benefits of using corpus methods even when working with relatively limited quantities of linguistic data that are collected and analysed with particular communicative contexts and pedagogical applications in mind.

17.3 Multimodal instructional discourse and listening comprehension

Recent trends in the compilation and analysis of spoken corpora for applications in ELT reflect the growing consensus that communication is multimodal in nature (O'Halloran, 2011). More specifically, speech is now widely recognised as only one of the semiotic modes through which meanings are conveyed during oral communication, which may also include gestures, facial expressions, gaze direction, and body posture and positioning (Jewitt, 2013). The multimodal turn in language and education research has been fuelled by calls to pro-mote *multimodal literacy* among learners, defined by Walsh (2010) as the capacity to construct meanings through "reading, viewing, understanding, responding to and producing and interacting with multimedia and digital texts" (p. 213). As such, multimodal literacy clearly draws on the notion of multiliteracies first introduced by the New London Group (1996) to advocate for education that responds to society's new forms of communication driven by new technologies. Thus, in the context of tertiary ELT, multimodal resources should be front and centre to help learners acquire the skills to engage with authentic texts that integrate a variety of communicative modes (O'Halloran *et al.*, 2016). This becomes even more important in light of the ever-growing influence of multisemiotic digital resources both inside and outside of the classroom, and the consequent need for English language practitioners to effectively make use of them.

Building on the International Listening Association's (1995) definition of listening as "the process of receiving, constructing meaning from and responding to spoken and/or non-verbal messages" (p. 4), Campoy-Cubillo and Querol-Julián (2016) characterised multimodal listening as a process that involves both listening and watching, during which meanings are constructed from co-occurring communicative modes. Their interpretation highlights the interplay among various modes during a listening event. To effectively harness the multimodal approach to improve comprehension of instructional discourse among L2 learners, research based on multimodal corpora can greatly enhance our understanding of how different semiotic modes interact to convey meanings, while the multimodal corpora themselves can serve as the basis for innovative materials and methods for classroom listening activities.

Unlike monomodal corpora of written or spoken language, the advantage of multimodal corpora is that they reflect the "integration of textual, audio and video records of communicative events" (Knight, 2011, p. 392), thus allowing for the investigation of a variety of linguistic and extra-linguistic features. The growing interest in compiling and analysing multimodal corpora is clearly linked to continuing advances in technology that have offered improved methods for recording, storing, and analysing digital resources. As explained by Bateman (2013), the data that comprise a multimodal corpus can be distinguished into two types: non-linear data based on a spatial organisation, such as print advertisements or book pages with illustrations, and linear data based on a temporal organisation, such as recorded speech. It is the latter type of linear data in the form of video recordings that has the most relevant applications for L2 listening comprehension and will, thus, be the focus of the discussion in this section.

The development of multimodal corpora based on video recordings presents some major differences when compared to corpora that are limited to transcribed speech or written language. Specifically, such audio-visual resources represent what Adolphs (2013) described as an "embodied phenomenon" (p. 1), where there are other semiotic modes (e.g. prosody, gesturing, facial expressions, body movement) that typically appear simultaneously during speech production. According to Adolphs (2013), the need to capture all of these modes for further investigation is reflected in the three distinctive factors that come into play when working with such multimodal data: 1) recording, or preserving the embodied speech of individuals, along with the inherent technical and ethical issues that are inevitably involved in this activity, 2) representing, or making decisions about how to simultaneously display audio, visual, and verbal codes, and 3) replaying, or determining how to store and search multimodal data for analytical purposes. This last aspect, namely, how to analyse multimodal corpora, can also be challenging as they require a layered or tiered approach in order to represent the simultaneous interaction of the various multimodal elements involved. For example, there may be layers that display the soundwave of the speech that is produced, the corresponding transcript, and any number of other layers for the annotation of other features of interest (e.g. gestures, prosodic characteristics). This usually takes the form of "standoff annotation" (Bateman, 2013, p. 3) which is created and stored separately from the original audio/visual sources (vs. textual annotation embedded directly into written data or transcribed speech). To cope with these new challenges, researchers in the field of multimodality have developed accessible multimodal annotation software that allows for a clear and accurate visualisation of the different semiotic modes that contribute and interact within a particular embodied speech event, such as ELAN (ELAN, 2020) and ANVIL (Kipp, 2012).

Some recent research has begun to investigate instructional discourse from a multimodal perspective, drawing on multimodal corpora. Mattiello (2022) performed a multimodal discourse analysis of a small corpus of video-recorded Google Talks on business and economics topics, representing an interesting new digital genre with strong instructional potential that integrates aspects of traditional university lectures and popularised expository genres such as TED Talks. She showed how verbal features are combined with still and moving visuals (e.g. images, videos) and hand gestures not only to display concrete data and figures, but also to explain abstract concepts and even to engage directly with the audience. Bernad-Mechó and Fortanet-Gómez (2019) analysed organisational metadiscourse in a small corpus of social sciences lectures procured from the Yale University Open website from a multimodal perspective. Using the software Multimodal Analysis–Video developed by O'Halloran *et al.* (2012), they found that lecturers engaged with audiences by reinforcing their verbal expressions of organisational metadiscourse with distinctive patterns of intonation and pitch, gestures, body positioning, facial expressions, and directed gaze. Working with a corpus of 15 video-recorded undergraduate mathematics lectures, Fogarty-Bourget (2019) utilised the multimodal annotation software ELAN to analyse the combination of discursive and rhetorical strategies with nonverbal actions used by instructors to engage with students. The availability of an increasing selection of digital multimodal instructional resources and dedicated software for their analysis will likely lead to more research from a multimodal perspective for the benefit of L2 learners.

17.4 Integrating corpus tools with multimodal annotation

Alongside the well-known linguistic and cognitive challenges experienced by L2 learners when listening to academic lectures in English discussed in Section 17.1, interpersonal meanings that encode the lecturer's attitude towards particular aspects of the content may also create comprehension difficulties. Indeed, especially when lecturers and student audiences do not share the same language backgrounds, students may have considerable problems with "discriminative listening" (distinguishing between fact and opinion) … and "critical listening (evaluation of the message)" (Flowerdew & Miller, 2010, p. 160). In such cases, non-verbal signals (e.g. prosody, gaze direction, gestures) that accompany verbal expressions of attitude can have an important reinforcing or clarifying function, while also satisfying students' desire to understand the views of the lecturer (Northcott, 2001). Indeed, the university lecture is much more than the simple transmission of factual knowledge from expert to novice; it is also the sharing of interpersonal meanings that may arise during the course of the lecture. In this section, I briefly describe an exploratory methodology that combines tools of corpus linguistics and multimodal annotation in order to tease out the expression of attitude among lecturers represented in a small multimodal corpus.

17.4.1 *Corpus and analysis*

The multimodal corpus used for this case study contains six lectures on humanistic topics from the disciplines of philosophy, religious studies, English, history, and African-American studies that were collected from the Yale Open website (https://oyc.yale.edu/). It is articulated into six mp4 video files of the six lectures and their corresponding transcripts (37,353 words).

The analysis was undertaken in two phases. In the first phase, drawing on widely applied theoretical frameworks for exploring the linguistic expression of attitude towards propositional content (Biber *et al.*, 1999; Hyland, 2005; Martin & White, 2005; Thompson & Hunston, 2000), I used corpus techniques to analyse markers of attitude. The transcripts of the six lectures were uploaded into the corpus analysis software program Wmatrix (Rayson, 2008) and run through its semantic tagging function that automatically tags all lexical items according to pre-established semantic domains. The semantic tagset contains over 200 domains across the gamut of human experiences, such as "Life and living things", "Money and commerce", and "The world and our environment". The advantage of semantic tagging over other types of metadata annotation schemes, in particular, part-of-speech tagging, is that it is not limited to retrieving lexical items belonging to only one grammatical class (e.g. adjectives), and thus can offer a more exhaustive analysis of features of interest. After careful scrutiny of the domains, I selected those that were the most plausibly associated with the expression of attitude: A5.1 (Evaluation: good/bad), as well as series of domains reflecting emotional actions, states, and processes: E1/Emotional/Unemotional, E2/Liking/Disliking, E3/Calm/Violent/Angry, E4/Happiness or sadness, E5/Bravery and Fear, and E6/Worry and confidence.

In the second phase, I viewed the videos to locate attitude markers identified within the above domains and observed whether there were any co-occurring non-verbal resources, such as prosodic stress, gesturing, gaze direction, and body orientation, or "multimodal ensembles" (Kress, 2011, p. 38) in which multiple semiotic modes interact synergistically to shape the intended meaning. These ensembles were then visualised with the multimodal annotation software ELAN (Version 5.9) [Computer software], 2020) to code and mark features of interest (both verbal and non-verbal) in synchronisation with the streaming audio/video tracks.

17.4.2 Findings: Linguistic analysis

The semantic tagging process retrieved 201 lexical items across 48 types in the A5.1 Evaluation: good/bad domain and 239 lexical items across 132 types in the E1–E6 domains. The large number of items retrieved that could not have feasibly been identified manually is testimony to the usefulness of automated corpus methods even when working with relatively small corpora. The tagging software displays all the lexical items assigned to a given semantic domain in frequency or alphabetical lists, together with a link to open the corresponding concordance lines for further analysis in the context of usage. This feature was important in order to distinguish the markers of the lecturer's attitudes (e.g. *I loved Minute Maid orange juice*) from attitudes that were instead attributed to other actors or entities being discussed in the context of the lecture (e.g. *Ronald Reagan sees this as a great opportunity*). Given the subjective nature of this endeavour, I opted to focus only on those lexical items that could be reasonably attributed to the lecturer through the presence of co-occurring first person singular pro-forms (e.g. *I, me, my*) in relatively close proximity. This filtering process led to the identification of the relatively small number of items that encoded the lecturers' personal attitudes as shown in Table 17.1. As can be seen, the semantic tags are distinguished according to their positive (+) or negative (–) clines, as well as intensity of meaning (+++).

17.4.3 Findings: Multimodal analysis

For reasons of space, for the multimodal component of the analysis, I present a case study of one multimodal ensemble that contains the attitude marker *dismissive*, whose meaning could be challenging for some L2 listeners. In this episode from a Yale philosophy lecture entitled "The Nature of Persons: Dualism vs. Physicalism" (https://oyc.yale.edu/philosophy/phil-176/lecture-2), the lecturer introduces the philosophical objection to the idea that there is life after death. He then anticipates his sceptical attitude by stating *I don't mean to be utterly dismissive of the objection*, before going on to explain why the objection does not account for more nuanced and deeper meanings associated with the concepts of life and death.

Figure 17.1 reproduces a screenshot from the multimodal annotation software ELAN in which the multimodal ensemble corresponding to the utterance *I don't mean to be utterly dismissive of the objection* is visualised and analysed. Underneath the streaming video is the audio soundwave of the lecturer's speech together with a series of tiers created ad-hoc to capture

Table 17.1 Markers of lecturer attitude

Lexical item	Semantic tag	Context of usage
Fantastic	A5.1+	Now I know it sounds like no big deal in the age of Obama, in his fantastic run in 2008. (African American Studies)
Look bad	A5.1–	And I should say that I don't want Nevis to look bad. Actually, it
Wonderful	A5.1+	was a wonderful place to visit and the people were wonderful on that island to me. (History)
Shocking	A5.1–	I kid you not. The profound and shocking insight of Glaucon's
Chilling	E5–	story of Gyges in Plato's Republic is, in light of this contemporary research, almost chilling. (Philosophy 2)
Brilliantly	A5.1+++	And I put those in subversively for you to have a look at in your own time. They're brilliantly written and they give you insight into the various ways in which we can read the text. (Religious Studies)
Liked	E2+	And I remember the Coca-Cola boycott, mainly because I liked
Loved	E2+	Coca-Cola [...] but Coca-Cola owns Minute Maid orange juice.
Beloved	E2+	I loved Minute Maid orange juice. So replacing my beloved
Horrible	A5.1–	Minute Maid orange juice was [...] Donald Duck orange juice.
Aggrieved	E4-	It was just horrible. So I felt rather aggrieved by the boycott myself. (African American Studies)
Temperamental	E3–	Frost wishes to be so subtle [...] This guile is something temperamental, I think. (English)
Scare off	E5–	I hope that the density of today's lecture doesn't scare off too
Fun	E4+	many of you. It gets more fun after this. And I look forward to seeing many of you next week. (Philosophy 2)
Horror	E5-	He's there when King is assassinated. I can't imagine that kind of horror. (African American Studies)
Dismissive	E6+	Now I don't mean to be utterly dismissive of the objection. That's why I spent a couple of minutes trying to spell it out. (Philosophy 1)

simultaneously the various semiotic modes that come into play and that could be observed from watching the video. The verbal text is inserted in the Transcript tier in correspondence with the relative soundwave segments. The next tier labelled Prosody allows for the coding of paralinguistic stress, in this case, the second syllable of the adjective *dismissive* that appears in the soundwave as detached from the first and third syllables, reflecting its prosodic prominence. In the Verbal attitude tier, *dismissive* is annotated as a marker of an attitude of confident disregard. The Gaze tier annotates the lecturer's gaze as directed toward the audience. The Gesture description tier describes the lecturer's hand as waving away from himself while uttering the adjective *dismissive*, and the Gesture function tier classifies the gesture as having a metaphoric function (McNeill, 1992), that here figuratively represents disregarding or rejecting something as not worthy of consideration. The Body posture tier describes the lecturer as sitting with legs crossed on the desk, while the Body orientation tier notes the lecturer's open orientation towards the audience.

Figure 17.2 illustrates a multiframe visualisation of a close-up of the trajectory of the hand-waving gesture that co-occurred with the verbal expression of attitude encoded by the adjective *dismissive* at three different points from the onset of the gesture.

The multimodal ensemble illustrated in Figure 17.1 that captures linguistic, paralinguistic, and extralinguistic meanings appears to construct a multifaceted interpersonal message. On the one hand, the verbal expression of a sceptical attitude is nonverbally reinforced by

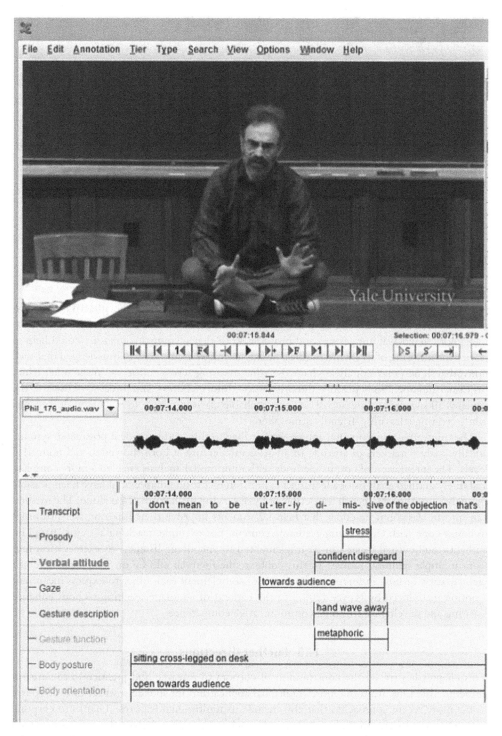

Figure 17.1   Multimodal ensemble "I don't mean to be utterly dismissive of the objection"[3]

Figure 17.2 Metaphoric hand waving gesture detail

prosodic stress and the metaphoric gesture that both co-occur with the adjective *dismissive*, in line with his status as a highly esteemed academic expert in his field. For L2 learners, the metaphoric hand-waving gesture and prosodic stress that accompany *dismissive* could help to clarify the meaning of this word in this context, although it should be acknowledged that such nonverbal signals may not always have the same meaning across cultures. On the other hand, his casual and open body posture and orientation, informal dress, and direct gaze towards the students all suggest an interactive and approachable classroom style to engage with students, while creating a learning-friendly atmosphere.

The innovative experimental approach described in this section made it possible to systematically analyse markers of attitude in an academic lecture at both the verbal and nonverbal levels. The integration of corpus methods with multimodal analysis enabled a more complete and finely grained analysis of a lecturer's expression of attitude than would have been possible by analysing either the speech transcripts or by observing the lecture video alone. The method can inform classroom practices that help L2 students improve their listening skills in order to better cope with challenging academic content. For example, teaching activities based on authentic audiovisual input can be implemented to encourage listeners to extract meanings from multiple semiotic modes. In this context, the focus should be on intersemiotic complementarity, or how different semiotic modes complement each other to express meanings, a notion introduced by Royce (2007) in the context of language teaching to both enhance learning and develop multimodal communicative competence.

17.5 Further directions

This chapter has traced the contribution of corpora to research and practice in the area of academic listening, from the more traditional applications for spoken instructional discourse to the more recent approaches that also include its multimodal features. Thanks to corpora, we have learned a great deal, but there is still much to be explored given the continuing trend towards "conversationalisation" in academic discourse (Buttery *et al.*, 2015, p. 208) and the growing impact of digital resources that can be harnessed for L2 listening comprehension, for example, OpenCourseWare lectures and TED Talks.[4] In the short term, increasingly powerful, yet user-friendly corpus software will allow for more comprehensive and finely tuned linguistic analyses to explore these trends. In the longer term, there is likely to be more research on multimodal corpora with applications in listening comprehension, as new methods and tools become available that would enable larger-scale and more empirically grounded studies (Bateman, 2013), beyond the current ones that tend to be smaller in scale. A shift towards multimodal and multimedia resources for listening comprehension will also allow researchers and practitioners to keep up with and maintain the interest of today's learners who so expertly engage with them in all aspects of their lives.

Notes

1 Corpora used for listening comprehension research and practice tend to contain mostly academic discourse. However, general and/or professional English corpora could also be applied towards this purpose, for example, the Santa Barbara Corpus of Spoken American English (https://www.linguistics.ucsb.edu/research/santa-barbara-corpus) or the Hong Kong Corpus of Spoken English (http://rcpce.engl.polyu.edu.hk/HKCSE/HKCSE.htm).
2 Following Aston (1997) and Flowerdew (2004), small corpora can range from 20,000 to 250,000 words, even if there is considerable variation in what counts as small vs. large, depending on a variety of factors, such as spoken vs. written mode or degree of specialization.
3 Shelly Kagan, Death (Yale University: Open Yale Courses), http://oyc.yale.edu (Accessed December 14, 2013). License: Creative Commons BY-NC-SA.
4 The rising importance of TED Talks is reflected in the TED Corpus Search Engine (https://yohasebe.com/tcse) designed to facilitate educators and the scientific community. TED Talks have also been usefully applied in listening comprehension research (e.g. Wingrove, 2017).

Further reading

Crawford Camiciottoli, B. (2013). Discourse and interaction: Quantitative methods. In C. Chapelle (Ed.), *The encyclopedia of applied linguistics* (pp. 1736–1743). Wiley-Blackwell. This chapter offers an illustration of how the quantitative methods of corpus linguistics can offer insights into interactional features of lecture discourse. In a step-by-step approach, it describes the various phases of analysis: identifying and accessing lecture data, preparing the data for automatic processing with corpus tools, querying and editing the data, displaying the results, and interpreting the findings. It is, thus, useful for researchers and practitioners interested in analysing lecture discourse, but who may have little experience with corpus methods.

Fortanet-Gómez, I., & Querol-Julián, M. (2010). The video corpus as a multimodal tool for teaching. In M. C. Campoy-Cubillo, B. Bellés-Fortuño, & M. L. Gea-Valor (Eds.), *Corpus-based approaches to English language teaching* (pp. 261–270). Continuum. In this chapter, the authors discuss the benefits of using a videocorpus of academic lectures delivered in English and recorded at a Spanish university to develop materials for EAP contexts. They present a case study to show how a lecture can be recorded, tagged, and subtitled, and then how to create an interface for classroom usage that implements standard video editing software. Such tools are useful for improving comprehension in relation not only to lecture content and structure, but also to pragmatic meanings that are often communicated with semiotic resources beyond verbal language.

Lynch, T. (2011). Academic listening in the 21st century: Reviewing a decade of research. *Journal of English for Academic Purposes, 10*, 79–88. This is a comprehensive review of research in the area of second language listening that addresses what the author describes as one-way listening events such as traditional lectures, as well as two-way events, such as interactive lectures and office hours. The article concludes with a discussion of future research prospects, including multimodal lectures and video resources for listening assessment.

Simpson-Vlach, R. (2013). Corpus analysis of spoken English for academic purposes. In C. Chapelle (Ed.), *The encyclopedia of applied linguistics* (pp. 452–461). Wiley-Blackwell. The author provides an in-depth overview of the development of spoken language corpora and their contribution to ELT, ESP, and ESP. She also describes significant areas of language research that have benefitted from corpus analyses, including phraseology, grammar, discourse analysis, and pragmatics, and concludes with discussion of how corpora of academic spoken English can be successfully leveraged for devising teaching materials and activities for EAP classrooms.

References

Adolphs, S. (2013). Corpora: Multimodal. In C. Chapelle (Ed.), *The encyclopedia of applied linguistics* (pp. 1–4). Wiley-Blackwell.

Aston, G. (1997). Large and small corpora in language learning. In B. Lewandowska-Tomaszczyk & P. J. Melia (Eds.), *PALC97: Practical applications in language corpora* (pp. 51–62). Łodz University Press.

Baker, P., Gabrielatos, C., Khosravinik, M., Krzyżanowski, M., McEnery, T., & Wodak, R. (2008). A useful methodological synergy? Combining critical discourse analysis and corpus linguistics to examine discourses of refugees and asylum seekers in the UK Press. *Discourse & Society, 19*(3), 273–306.

Barbieri, F. (2013). Involvement in university classroom discourse: Register variation and interactivity. *Applied Linguistics, 36*(2), 151–173.

Bateman, J. A. (2013). Multimodal corpus-based approaches. In C. Chapelle (Ed.), *The encyclopedia of applied linguistics* (pp. 1–9). Wiley-Blackwell.

Bernad-Mechó, E., & Fortanet-Gómez, I. (2019). Organizational metadiscourse across lecturing styles: Engagement beyond language. In C. Sancho Guinda (Ed.), *Engagement in professional genres* (pp. 321–340). Benjamins.

Bernstein, B. (1986). On pedagogic discourse. In J. G. Richardson (Ed.), *Handbook of theory and research for the sociology of education* (pp. 205–240). Greenwood Press.

Biber, D. (2006). Stance in spoken and written university registers. *Journal of English for Academic Purposes, 5*(2), 97–116.

Biber, D. (2003). Variation among university spoken and written registers: A new multi-dimensional analysis. In P. Leistyna & C. F. Meyer (Eds.), *Corpus analysis: Language structure and language use* (pp. 19–34). Rodopi.

Biber, D., Conrad, S., & Reppen, R. (1998). *Corpus linguistics. Investigating language structure and use.* Cambridge University Press.

Biber, D., Conrad, S., Reppen, R., Byrd, P., & Helt, M. (2002). Speaking and writing in the university: A multidimensional comparison. *TESOL Quarterly, 36*(1), 9–48.

Biber, D., Conrad, S., Reppen, R., Byrd, P., Helt, M., Clark, V., Cortes, V., Csomay, E., & Urzua, A. (2004a). *Representing language use in the university: Analysis of the TOEFL 2000 spoken and written academic language corpus.* TOEFL monograph series. Educational Testing Service.

Biber, D., Conrad, S., & Cortes, V. (2004b). If you look at…: Lexical bundles in university teaching and textbooks. *Applied Linguistics, 25*(3), 371–405.

Biber, D., Johansson, S., Leech, G., Conrad, S., & Finegan, E. (1999). *Longman grammar of spoken and written English.* Longman.

Buttery, P., McCarthy, M. J., & Carter, R. (2015). Chatting in the academy: Informality in spoken academic discourse. In M. Charles, N. Groom, & S. P. John (Eds.), *Corpora, grammar and discourse* (pp. 183–210). Benjamins.

Campoy-Cubillo, M. C., & Querol-Julián, M. (2016, May 5). *Defining the listening construct in multimodal environments.* [Paper presentation]. 13th EALTA 2016 International Conference. Assessment of what…? Revisiting the issue of construct(s). Universidad de Valencia, Spain.

Crawford Camiciottoli, B. (2007). *The language of business studies lectures: A corpus-assisted analysis.* Benjamins.

Crawford Camiciottoli, B. (2010). Meeting the challenges of European student mobility: Preparing Italian Erasmus students for business lectures in English. *English for Specific Purposes, 29*(4), 268–280.

Crawford Camiciottoli, B. (2018). Representing culture in OpenCourseWare lectures: A corpus-based semantic analysis. *Lingue e Linguaggi, 28*, 33–47.

Crawford Camiciottoli, B. (2020). The OpenCourseWare lecture: A new twist on an old genre? *Journal of English for Academic Purposes.* Advance Online Publication. https://www.sciencedirect.com/science/article/abs/pii/S1475158519306605

Crawford Camiciottoli, B., & Querol-Julián, M. (2016). Lectures. In K. Hyland & P. Shaw (Eds.), *The Routledge handbook of English for academic purposes* (pp. 309–322). Routledge.

Creer, S., & Thompson, P. (2004). Processing spoken language data: The BASE experience. *Workshop on Compiling and Processing Spoken Language Corpora, LREC 2004.* http://www.reading.ac.uk/AcaDepts/ll/base_corpus/creer_thompson_final.pdf

Csomay, E. (2002). Variation in academic lectures. Interactivity and level of instruction. In R. Reppen, S. M. Fitzgerald, & D. Biber (Eds.), *Using corpora to explore linguistic variation* (pp. 203–224). Benjamins.

Csomay, E. (2005a). Linguistic variation within university classroom talk: A corpus-based perspective. *Linguistics and Education, 15*(3), 243–274.

Csomay, E. (2005b). Linguistic variation in the lexical episodes of university classroom talk. In A. Tyler, M. Takada, Y. Kim, & D. Marinova (Eds.), *Language in use. Cognitive and discourse perspectives on language and language learning. Georgetown University Round Table (GURT) on languages and linguistics* (pp. 150–162). Georgetown University Press.

Csomay, E. (2006). Academic talk in American university classrooms: Crossing the boundaries of oral-literate discourse? *Journal of English for Academic Purposes, 5*(2), 117–135.

Csomay, E. (2012). A corpus-based look at short turns in university classroom interaction. In E. Csomay (Ed.), *Discourse and corpora.* Special issue of *Corpus Linguistics and Linguistic Theory, 8*(1), 103–128.

Csomay, E. (2013). Lexical bundles in discourse structure: A corpus-based study of classroom discourse. *Applied Linguistics, 34*(3), 369–388.

Deroey, K. L. B. (2015). Marking importance in lectures: Interactive and textual orientation. *Applied Linguistics, 36*(1), 51–72.

Deroey, K., & Taverniers, M. (2011). A corpus-based study of lecture functions. *Moderna Språk, 105*(2), 1–22.

ELAN (Version 5.9) [Computer software]. (2020). Nijmegen: Max Planck Institute for Psycholinguistics. https://archive.mpi.nl/tla/elan

Flowerdew, J. (1994). Research of relevance to L2 lecture comprehension. In J. Flowerdew (Ed.), *Academic listening. Research perspectives* (pp. 7–29). Cambridge University Press.

Flowerdew, J. (2003). Signalling nouns in discourse. *English for Specific Purposes, 22*(4), 329–346.

Flowerdew, J., & Miller, L. (1996). Lectures in a second language: Notes towards a cultural grammar. *English for Specific Purposes, (2)*, 121–140.

Flowerdew, J., & Miller, L. (2010). Listening in a second language. In D. Wolvin (Ed.), *Listening and human communication in the 21st century* (pp. 158–177). Wiley-Blackwell.

Flowerdew, L. (2004). The argument for using English specialised corpora to understand academic and professional settings. In U. Connor & T. Upton (Eds.), *Discourse in the professions: Perspectives from corpus linguistics* (pp. 11–33). John Benjamins.

Fogarty-Bourget, C. G. (2019). *Facilitating student engagement in undergraduate mathematics lectures: A multi-modal investigation* [Doctoral dissertation, Carleton University]. https://curve.carleton.ca/system/files/etd/8c658ff5-348f-4179-a74c-b5ea4769aafd/etd_pdf/c37748f722f684eccaef69f3f54fd037/fogarty-bourget-facilitatingstudentengagementinundergraduate_redacted.pdf

Goh, C. (2005). Second language listening expertise. In K. Johnson (Ed.), *Expertise in second language learning and teaching* (pp. 64–84). Palgrave Macmillan.

Grant, L. E. (2011). The frequency and functions of *just* in British academic spoken English. *Journal of English for Academic Purposes, 10*(3), 183–197.

Hyland, K. (2005). *Metadiscourse.* Continuum.

Jewitt, C. (2013). Multimodal teaching and learning. In C. A. Chapelle (Ed.), *The encyclopedia of applied linguistics* (pp. 4109–4114). Blackwell.

Kia, E. (2018). *Directive use in university classroom discourse: Variation across disciplines, academic levels, and interactivity* (Publication No. 10825653) [Doctoral dissertation, Northern Arizona University]. ProQuest Dissertations.

Kipp, M. (2012). Multimedia annotation, querying, and analysis in ANVIL. In M. Maybury (Ed.), *Multimedia information extraction. Advances in video, audio, and imagery analysis for search, data mining, surveillance and authoring* (pp. 351–368). Wiley-IEEE Computer Society.

Knight, D. (2011). The future of multimodal corpora. *Revista Brasileira de Linguística Aplicada, 11*(2), 391–415.

Kress, G. (2011). Multimodal discourse analysis. In J. P. Gee & M. Handford (Eds.), *The Routledge handbook of discourse analysis* (pp. 35–50). Routledge.

Lee, D., & Gunesekera, M. (2006). Humor in spoken academic discourse. *NUCB Journal of Language, Culture and Communication, 8*(3), 49–68.

Lee, J. J. (2009). Size matters: An exploratory comparison of small- and large-class university lecture introductions. *English for Specific Purposes, 28*, 42–57.

Lee, J. J., & Subtirelu, N. C. (2015). Metadiscourse in the classroom: A comparative analysis of EAP lessons and university lectures. *English for Specific Purposes, 37*, 52–62.

Lin, C. Y. (2010). '… that's actually sort of you know trying to get consultants in…': Functions and multifunctionality of modifiers in academic lectures. *Journal of Pragmatics, 42*(5), 1173–1183.

Lynch, T. (2011). Academic listening in the 21st century: Reviewing a decade of research. *Journal of English for Academic Purposes, 10*, 79–88.

MacDonald, M., Badger, R., & White, G. (2000). The real thing?: Authenticity and academic listening. *English for Specific Purposes, 19*(3), 253–267.

Malá, M. (2008). Participial adverbials in spoken academic corpora: "Gonna have a hard time getting through". *Discourse and Interaction, 1*(2), 53–62.

Martin, J. R., & White, P. R. (2005). *The language of evaluation. Appraisal in English.* Palgrave Macmillan.

Mattiello, E. (2022). Using Google Talks in ESP educational settings: A multimodal approach. In V. Bonsignori, B. Crawford Camiciottoli, & D. Filmer (Eds.), *Analysing multimodality in specialized discourse: Innovative research methods and applications* (pp. 65-89). Vernon Press.

McNeill, D. (1992). *Hand and mind. What gestures reveal about thought.* University of Chicago Press.

Miller, J. (2020). The bottom line: Are idioms used in English academic speech and writing. *Journal of English for Academic Purposes, 43*, 100810.

Molina, S. (2015). Epistemic and attitudinal adverbs and adjectives in MICASE: Are there differences according to disciplines? In J. R. Zamorano-Mansilla, C. Maiz, E. Dominguez, & V. Martin De la Rosa (Eds.), *Thinking modally: English and contrastive studies on modality* (pp. 271–298). Cambridge Scholars Publishing.

Molino, A. (2018). 'What I'm speaking is almost English…': A corpus-based study of metadiscourse in English-medium lectures at an Italian university. *Educational Sciences: Theory and Practice, 18*(4), 935–956.

Mordaunt, O., & Olson, D. (2010). Listen, listen, listen and listen: Building a comprehension corpus and making it comprehensible. *Educational Studies, 36*(3), 249–258.

Morell, T., Garcia, M., & Sanchez, I. (2008). Multimodal strategies for effective academic presentation in English for non-native speakers. In R. Monroy & A. Sanchez (Eds.), *25 years of applied linguistics in Spain: Milestones and challenges* (pp. 557–568). Editum.

Mulligan, D., & Kirkpatrick, A. (2000). How much do they understand? Lectures, students and comprehension. *Higher Education Research, Development, 19*(3), 311–335.

Nesi, H. (2012). Laughter in university lectures. *Journal of English for Academic Purposes, 11*(2), 79–89.

Nesi, H., & Basturkmen, H. (2006). Lexical bundles and discourse signalling in academic lectures. *International Journal of Corpus Linguistics, 11*(3), 283–304.

Nesi, H., & Thompson, P. (2006). British Academic Spoken English corpus. Oxford Text Archive. http://hdl.handle.net/20.500.12024/2525

New London Group (1996). A pedagogy of multiliteracies: Designing social futures. *Harvard Educational Review, 66*(1), 60–92.

Northcott, J. (2001). Towards an ethnography for the MBA classroom: A consideration of the role of interactive lecturing styles within the context of one MBA programme. *English for Specific Purposes, 20*(1), 15–37.

O'Halloran, K. L. (2011). Multimodal discourse analysis. In K. Hyland & B. Paltridge (Eds.), *The Bloomsbury companion to discourse analysis* (pp. 120–137). Continuum.

O'Halloran, K., Podlasov, A., & Chua, A. (2012). Interactive software for multimodal analysis. *Visual Communication, 11*(3), 363–381.

O'Halloran, K. L., Tan, S., & Smith, B. A. (2016). Multimodal approaches to English for academic purposes. In K. Hyland & P. Shaw (Eds.), *The Routledge handbook of English for academic purposes* (pp. 280–293). Routledge.

O'Keeffe, A., & Walsh, S. (2012). Applying corpus linguistics and conversation analysis in the investigation of small group teaching in higher education. In E. Csomay (Ed.), *Discourse and corpora.* Special issue of *Corpus Linguistics and Linguistic Theory, 8*(1), 159–181.

Pérez-Llantada, C. (2005). Instruction and interaction in an American lecture class. Observations from a corpus. *The ESPecialist, 26*, 205–227.

Pickering, L. (2004). The structure and function of intonational paragraphs in native and non-native speaker instructional discourse. *English for Specific Purposes, 23*, 19–43.

Rayson, P. (2008). From key words to key semantic domains. *International Journal of Corpus Linguistics, 13*(4), 519–549. https://www.jbe-platform.com/content/journals/10.1075/ijcl.13.4.06ray

Reinhardt, J. (2010). Directives in office hour consultations: A corpus-informed investigation of learner and expert usage. *English for Specific Purposes, 29*(2), 94–107.

Royce, T. D. (2007). Intersemiotic complementarity: A framework for multimodal discourse analysis. In T. D. Royce & W. L. Bowcher (Eds.), *New directions in the analysis of multimodal discourse* (pp. 63–109). Lawrence Erlbaum.

Schleef, E. (2008). The 'lecturer's OK' revisited: Changing discourse conventions and the influence of academic division. *American Speech, 83*(1), 62–84.

Simpson, R. C., Briggs, S. L., Ovens, J., & Swales, J. M. (2002). *The Michigan Corpus of Academic Spoken English*. The Regents of the University of Michigan.

Simpson, R. C., & Mendis, D. (2003). A corpus-based study of idioms in academic speech. *TESOL Quarterly, 37*(3), 419–441.

Simpson-Vlach, R. (2013). Corpus analysis of spoken English for academic purposes. In C. Chapelle (Ed.), *The encyclopedia of applied linguistics* (pp. 452–461). Wiley Blackwell.

Sueyoshi, A., & Hardison, D. M. (2005). The role of gestures and facial cues in second language listening comprehension. *Language Learning, 55*, 661–699.

Swales, J. M. (2004). Evaluation in academic speech: First forays. In G. Del Lungo Camiciotti & E. Tognini Bonelli (Eds.), *Academic discourse. New insights into evaluation* (pp. 31–53). Peter Lang.

Swales, J. M., & Burke, A. (2003). "It's really fascinating work": Differences in evaluative adjectives across academic registers. In P. Leistyna & C. F. Meyer (Eds.), *Corpus analysis: Language structure and language use* (pp. 1–18). Rodopi.

Thompson, S. (2003). Text-structuring metadiscourse, intonation and the signalling of organisation in academic lectures. *Journal of English for Academic Purposes, 2*, 5–20.

Thompson, G., & Hunston, S. (2000). Evaluation: An introduction. In S. Hunston & G. Thompson (Eds.), *Evaluation in text: Authorial stance and the construction of discourse* (pp. 1–27). Oxford University Press.

Vandergrift, L. (2007). Recent developments in second and foreign language listening comprehension research. *Language Teaching, 40*(3), 191–210.

Walsh, M. (2010). Multimodal literacy: What does it mean for classroom practice? *Australian Journal of Language and Literacy, 33*(3), 211–223.

Wang, Y. C. (2012). An exploration of vocabulary knowledge in English short talks: A corpus-driven approach. *International Journal of English Linguistics, 2*(4), 33–43.

Widdowson, H. G. (1979). *Explorations in applied linguistics*. Oxford University Press.

Wingrove, P. (2017). How suitable are TED talks for academic listening? *Journal of English for Academic Purposes, 30*, 79–95.

18

CORPORA AND FEEDBACK IN EAP

Hilary Nesi and Benet Vincent

18.1 Introduction

The purpose of an EAP programme is to enable learners to communicate effectively in an academic environment; all EAP activities, whether they focus on forms, structures, or strategies, work towards improving the way students interpret and produce academic text. Feedback is an enormously important part of this process; one of the EAP practitioner's main tasks is to help students interpret its meaning, act on its advice, and absorb from it the knowledge that will enable them to function without it in years to come.

Feedback is, however, "a complex and problematic form of communication" (Higgins, 2004, p. iii). Students can feel overwhelmed if they receive too much of it, and they can feel short-changed if they receive too little of it. Generic feedback may not address specific problems sufficiently well, while specific feedback may not perfectly fit the next context in which a similar problem arises. Moreover, the wording of feedback is prone to misinterpretation and may even run the risk of offending or alienating its recipients.

These sorts of issues will probably never entirely disappear, but the use of corpora and other electronic resources can go some way towards helping to resolve them. Feedback in the form of a link to corpus output gives learners the option to expand or reduce the amount of data they engage with, focussing on concordance lines that most closely resemble their own output or branching out to explore other forms of expression. This kind of feedback need not include any additional commentary; the corpus output can be allowed to speak for itself. The form of this type of feedback, its effectiveness, and learners' attitudes towards it are all worthy of study. Spoken or written feedback that is not linked to corpus output – the kind that learners are most likely to receive from their subject tutors – can also be gathered and analysed using corpus linguistic methods, enabling us to discover how feedback functions are typically expressed, so that we can help learners to recognise them and respond to them more effectively.

This chapter will examine the role of corpora in the presentation and interpretation of feedback, from the first days of corpus use in language teaching to the most recent applications of corpus technology.

DOI: 10.4324/9781003002901-21

18.2 Feedback before the Web 2.0 era

Two terms that are central to our study, English for Academic Purposes (EAP) and data-driven learning (DDL), were coined by Tim Johns in the 1980s. Academic researchers in computational linguistics, lexicography, and stylistics had been using concordancers on mainframes since the 1970s, but Johns was probably the first practitioner to use concordancing in English for Academic Purposes. He speculated in an early British Council publication on ESP teaching about the possibility of creating some sort of "interactive program which would give the language-learner a "user-friendly" tool for investigating problems in the target language" (Johns, 1981, p. 105). Johns went on to develop this concept into *MicroConcord*, a program he created with the needs of language learners in mind (Johns, 1986, p. 158). This eventually led to *Wordsmith Tools*, Mike Scott's corpus query program that is still in use today.

Much of Johns' use of corpora was in the English for Overseas Students Unit at the University of Birmingham, UK, where he worked from 1971 until the end of his teaching career. He centred his practice around short one-to-one sessions, where he provided feedback on work produced by students whose first language was not English. Given the time constraints, these sessions tended to deal with one specific language problem that had emerged from the student's writing. Revised and neatened versions of some of these sessions, which Johns called "kibbitzers", have since been placed online as a source of reference about tricky aspects of academic language (see https://lexically.net/TimJohns/). When the sessions first took place, however, their outcomes could not have been predicted and were as revelatory for Johns as for the student writers. As he points out, with DDL:

> the data is primary, and the teacher does not know in advance exactly what rules or patterns the learners will discover: indeed, they will often notice things that are unknown not only to the teacher, but also to the standard works of reference on the language (Johns, 1991, p. 3).

At the beginning of Kibbitzer 1, it is explained that Johns always kept his computer switched on during feedback sessions, so that lexical or syntactic choices could be checked using *MicroConcord*. Kibbitzer 31 is a typical example of John's procedure for providing feedback; it focusses on an essay written by a Japanese-speaking undergraduate student of English Literature. The student had written "It is said that she *widely read* when she was a child", and during their session, Johns and the student found enough evidence from concordance lines to distinguish between "read widely" ("read" = verb) and "widely read" (compound adjective). The published version of Kibbitzer 31 expands on this, noting that in some concordance lines the meaning was ambiguous, and that "widely read" may refer to a text (i.e. many people have read it) or to a person (i.e. (s)he has read a great deal). The Japanese student's problem was of the sort Ferris (2002) would count as "untreatable", because it is not easily resolved by consulting a dictionary or a pedagogical grammar. Nowadays, it would be a good candidate for hyperlink creation, to provide direct access to appropriate examples taken from relevant academic contexts.

Access to digitalised texts in the 1980s and 1990s was still fairly limited, however. The corpora Johns used were relatively small – sometimes containing articles from academic journals such as *Nature*, but more often serious journalism from *The New Scientist*, *The Times*, and *The Guardian*. Johns's Kibbitzers show how much information relevant to academic writing can be derived from these kinds of sources, but there must also have been areas of importance to student writers which they could not adequately represent, for example, citation forms of the type used in the humanities and social sciences and the hedging that is typical of academic argument texts. Academic corpora to fill this gap only became available in the following decades, either as private collections (usually downloads from online academic journals) or as public resources (e.g. BASE, BAWE, MICASE, MICUSP and the academic portion of COCA; see reference list).

Moreover, the technical resources to link a writer's own output to a corpus search interface had not yet been developed when Johns started holding his consultation sessions. Early use of hyperlinks for language teaching and learning was limited to the annotation of reading materials, described, for example, by Roby (1999) in his account of studies with vocabulary glosses in the 1980s and by Aust *et al.* (1993), Lyman-Hager *et al.* (1993), and Knight (1994), who experimented with texts read by learners of other languages. Levy (1990) speculates about the possible integration of concordancers into word-processing environments, but it was only in the second half of the 1990s that hyperlinks to corpora started to appear, as described in the following section.

Although individual consultations are perhaps no longer feasible in many higher education institutions, Johns's face-to-face approach to feedback still remains an attractive option. Hyperlinks to corpora allow learners to work at their own pace, with unlimited access to the resource. These advantages may not always, however, outweigh the excitement that students are likely to feel, and the depth of learning that is likely to take place, when they explore unknown corpus territory with an informed and enthusiastic teacher (or "consultant", as Johns liked to be called). Our challenge as EAP practitioners is to manage the constraints imposed by time and distance so that feedback for our students remains meaningful and motivating.

18.3 Corpora and feedback in the Web 2.0 era

"error correction is more goal-directed and could be considered an efficient starting point for novice corpus users" (Quinn, 2015, p. 174)

In recent years, numerous studies have sought to employ the affordances of corpora to provide innovative ways of giving feedback to students in EAP contexts. Almost invariably, these studies acknowledge their indebtedness to Tim Johns and the DDL approach he pioneered; they aim to develop students' language awareness as well as encourage them to be independent and take responsibility for their learning. The extent of the independence that is fostered and the degree of awareness students achieve are key issues; Johns' approach has inspired both the provision of feedback through links to ready-made corpus outputs (such as concordances, collocation lists, and common phrases) and also the training of students in the use of corpus tools to help them to correct their errors by themselves.

18.3.1 Teacher-created corpus data - Using hyperlinks to focus on errors

The idea of incorporating links to corpus data into feedback on writing has existed at least since Levy (1990) but was technically and practically challenging before the advent of Web 2.0. Milton (1997, 1998, 1999) was an early adopter, and his work is referred to by Hyland and Hyland (2006) when considering the possibility of providing feedback via links to concordance data. Research in this area typically sees itself as a first stage in widening learner (and indeed teacher) access to, and understanding of, the usefulness of corpus data for the revision of written work and the development of language awareness.

A pioneering study by Gaskell and Cobb (2004) investigated the extent to which students were able to correct grammatical errors when they were provided with links to concordances showing correct uses of relevant structures. A learner who made an error such as *I went to home* had the relevant stretch of text underlined and received a URL which led to a concordance from the 1-million-word Brown corpus (in this case based on *go* occurring within a few words before *home*). It was intended that the concordance lines would help the learner understand the mistake, correct it and transfer this knowledge to other related errors. Gaskell and Cobb stressed the importance of providing "feedback on the success of interpreting the examples" (p. 304), an example of what Carless and Boud (2018, p. 1318) refer to as "closing the feedback loop". While they reported high levels of success in correcting errors, they also emphasised that the idea was not necessarily to improve accuracy in the short term, but to raise awareness of the patterning of language in the DDL tradition. It might be said, however, that the patterning the learners were encouraged to notice – e.g. that *to* was unacceptable in *I went to home* – was fairly low-level compared to the original conception of DDL (as demonstrated by Johns's kibbitzers). The extent to which learners achieve in-depth noticing of patterns is a recurrent question in studies on feedback.

Another approach is described by Milton (1998, 1999, 2006) and Milton and Cheung (2010), who developed a toolkit which encouraged their target learners (Chinese university students in Hong Kong) to take responsibility for their own proofreading. Drawing on learner corpus research such as that of Granger and Tribble (1998) they compiled a corpus of their own students' writing, identified typical errors, and pointed students to online resources which presented typical collocation patterns and concordances from professionally written texts. Milton and Cheung claimed that their approach was effective, giving learners the confidence to attempt structures that they had previously avoided. Nevertheless, they acknowledged that teachers might be resistant to corpus approaches, and they emphasised the inadvisability of entirely replacing teacher support for learners' writing with a "deus ex machina" tool.

Work similar to and in part inspired by Milton's approach has taken two main directions. The first of these is the development of corpus-based software, recent examples of which have been reported by Blake (2018, 2020), Frankenberg-Garcia *et al.* (2019), and Bellino and Bascuñán (2020). Our discussion of this work is necessarily brief due to space limitations. Blake's "corpus-based error detector" is specifically for computer science undergraduates at a university in Japan who write dissertations in English. He used an in-house learner corpus of these dissertations to identify frequently committed and therefore predictable errors in the genre, and students use the tool to receive advice on potential issues in their writing. While Blake's work uses corpus techniques in the identification of errors, students do not detect language patterns based on corpus outputs and so his work is outside the scope of DDL. ColloCaid (Frankenberg-Garcia *et al.*, 2019), a tool that ultimately will be integrated into word-processing software, is closer to the aims of DDL in that it provides users with suggested collocations based on those found in academic corpora and academic collocations lists. Students can then make judgements on whether or not to use the suggested collocations. The WriteBetter software (Bellino & Bascuñán, 2020) is developed for similar purposes. It allows writers to refer to concordances drawn from a corpus of high-quality Wikipedia articles. Initial trials report positive results, but also the need for students to receive training to help them know what to search for and how to interpret results.

An approach which aims to support EAP teachers rather than to develop software for students is the Quicklinks project (Vincent & Nesi, 2018; Vincent *et al.*, 2021). This initiative exploits the hyperlink functionality available in Sketch Engine which makes it possible to send EAP students directly to corpus outputs, in this case retrieved from the British Academic

Written English (BAWE) corpus and filtered and sorted to facilitate the identification of patterns relevant to specific writing problems. A searchable database of links is available to teachers – mostly to concordances but also to other outputs such as collocation lists and word sketches (Vincent *et al.*, 2021). The Quicklinks project uses complex queries to create sophisticated searches, allowing a wider range of issues to be covered than in most studies discussed in this section. However, empirical data on teacher uptake and the usefulness to students is at present lacking.

Studies in this section indicate the progress that has been made towards improving the accessibility of relevant corpus-based feedback. As academic corpora have become more readily available, greater use is being made of them for this purpose. However, as Pérez-Paredes (2020) points out, research is still needed to discover what aspects of corpus output students are likely to notice; we do not yet know which approaches are most effective, and which approaches are most appealing to learners. Equally important is the question of how to involve teachers who currently do not use corpora in the provision of corpus-based feedback.

18.3.2 *Learner training on searches*

Students can also be trained to consult corpora for themselves in order to address the writing issues their instructors have identified. There have been a number of studies involving learner training in this area. These have focused on different aspects of the approach and raised questions regarding the amount of guidance and the type of training needed, what students might be expected to do, and their ability to identify patterns from corpus data.

An early study involving learner training is by Todd (2001), who investigated the ability of intermediate-level university students in Thailand to induce lexico-grammatical usage from concordances based on FAST web searches. Students worked with two lexical errors they had found in drafts of their assignments and were encouraged to retrieve relevant examples of use from the internet. These were then converted into concordance lines and consulted by the students to identify and correct their mistakes. This was a small study, involving only 25 students and only one iteration, but Todd reports some promising results; students were able to identify patterns of use and apply them to correct their errors in the majority of cases. Key barriers to success were polysemous items, words which belonged to more than one part of speech, and words which entered into more than one grammar pattern (in the sense of Hunston & Francis, 2000). These problems have also often been mentioned in subsequent studies but have rarely been given adequate attention.

The second part of the study reported by Gaskell and Cobb (2004) also aimed to test learners' ability to devise searches which could help them address grammar errors identified in their writing. Students learned how to use Cobb's online search interface, the updated version of which is to be found on the Lextutor website[1], and Gaskell and Cobb monitored the extent to which they were able to use this interface to correct their errors. This approach only proved popular with 7 out of the 20 students in the study, but these students made extensive use of the concordance and proved able to correct their own mistakes. These seem to have been the more proficient students, an observation also noted in several other studies. Gaskell and Cobb do not provide specific information about the students' searches, which would have been interesting and of potential value to users.

Yoon (2008) reported on a qualitative longitudinal study of six postgraduate students who were encouraged to use corpora when taking an academic writing course. As with other studies in this section, word and sentence-level errors were highlighted in drafts, and students attempted to correct them using the corpus after receiving training in class. The corpus interface for this study was the (now defunct) Collins COBUILD concordance and collocation sampler, chosen on the assumption that a general corpus would be appropriate for a class of students from mixed disciplines. The students claimed to find the corpus useful for expanding their knowledge of words and structures and said they had gained confidence from their new-found ability to check usage. They also appreciated the value corpus consultation added to the traditional structural focus of their classes, for example, in terms of collocation awareness. Yoon noted that the more proficient students were better able to benefit from the approach, in particular, in terms of the interpretation of corpus results.

Gilmore (2009) also trained his students to search a corpus to solve problems arising in their written production. In his study, 45 intermediate-level EAP students at a Japanese university worked with the BNC and the COBUILD concordance and collocation sampler. Gilmore underlined sentence-level, lexical, and grammatical issues in drafts written by the participants and encouraged them to "make their writing more natural" (Gilmore, 2009, p. 365). The students were given a 30-minute training session on using online corpora, and then spent one hour comparing the two corpus interfaces and trying to address their issues. The students liked the approach because of the autonomy it gave them, the ease of retrieving concordance lines, and the authenticity of the language. However, perhaps not surprisingly given the lack of time given to training and their level, they also mentioned having difficulty finding appropriate information or understanding the instances retrieved. Another issue, also noted in other studies, is that students did not always know what they should search for, especially if the error to be checked had not been clearly marked.

A further study investigating the potential of corpora to help L2 writers of English is Quinn (2015). This study involved 58 students at intermediate level (B1 in terms of the Common European Framework of Reference for Languages) who were previously unfamiliar with corpus approaches. The strength of this study is its description of, and commitment to, the training of students to benefit from corpus resources – in this case, the subscription-based Collins WordBanks Online which Quinn chose for its user-friendliness. The student participants undertook in-class activities, working together to correct sentences from peers before correcting their own mainly lexical errors, marked using a code designed for the study. Consultations were also held to give students further guidance. Quinn emphasises the amount of training involved and advises teachers on ways to introduce corpus data, for example through guiding questions. She stresses the importance of justifying to students the extra effort required to consult a corpus and of convincing them that one search might not always be enough to find an answer. As in other studies in this section, Quinn's approach had strengths but also limitations. Students welcomed the use of corpora to improve the naturalness of their writing, and as a confidence-booster. However, they struggled with the unknown vocabulary in concordance lines and could not always devise corpus queries to address the errors identified in their work.

Crosthwaite (2017) tried to address the issue of corpus query creation by showing students how to search for specific part of speech categories and how to include wildcards. This enabled them to retrieve more complex syntactic patterns, using either SkELL (Sketch Engine for Language Learners), or the BNCweb. Crosthwaite explains that the learners in this study were in a position to benefit from this more advanced training because they were all doctoral students and proficient computer users. However, he does not provide a list of the searches the students actually conducted, and it should be noted that SkELL does not allow for a wide range of query types.

An interesting aspect of this study is its description of how Crosthwaite (2017) refined his error coding technique. Almost all the other studies in this section note that students struggle to convert an indication of an error into a suitable corpus query. Crosthwaite's coding developed from highlighting a problem word, to underlining a stretch of words, and finally to underlining a stretch of words with a keyword bolded to indicate where the issue was. Despite this systematic approach to error coding, students still struggled to conduct searches addressing phrasal issues and morphosyntactic issues (e.g. tense/verb form choices). Crosthwaite concludes that there are limitations to independent corpus consultation since most students do not have the skills to compose queries which would help correct errors relating, for example, to tense or voice. Nevertheless, Crosthwaite went on to create a short private online course (SPOC) which introduces a number of search techniques to university students writing in English (Crosthwaite, 2020). A key feature of this course compared to others in this section is that it encourages the use of a corpus more appropriate to EAP students, the BAWE corpus.

In summary, students are commonly reported to benefit from interventions involving corpus-based feedback, both in terms of increased autonomy and in terms of their confidence in their ability to correct their writing problems. However, a number of questions still remain. Firstly, there is still some debate about which types of error students are able to address through corpus consultation. The type of training students should receive clearly depends on the type of issues they are judged competent to address and the sort of patterning they are considered able to detect in concordance outputs. The selection of an appropriate corpus and interface is another issue. Almost all the studies mentioned in this section opted to work with user-friendly interfaces but chose general corpora that were not entirely appropriate in terms of genre and register. Crosthwaite's choice of a corpus of high-quality student writing (the BAWE corpus) in his 2020 study makes his initiative particularly important. One further question is the extent to which students who are guided to correct their errors using corpus data are then able to apply this knowledge to other analogous language situations. These questions leave us with much still to research (see Section 18.5).

18.4 Corpora of university-level written feedback

Generally, corpus-based feedback in academic contexts aims to help students identify and correct problems of style and register, with the longer term goal of encouraging them to reflect on their language choices and gradually move towards greater autonomy. However, it is also possible for corpus analysis of feedback texts to help students, albeit indirectly, by providing insights into the way tutors comment on aspects of academic text production. In the disciplines, tutors' feedback is unlikely to relate primarily to style and register, and generally refers to organisation, content, and the development of ideas, the "higher order concerns" referred to by Keh (1990). Corpus studies of the discourse of feedback which identify the form, frequency, and distribution of recognised feedback functions can be used for instructor training purposes and can also contribute to EAP syllabus content and materials, helping students make better sense of the feedback they receive from their course tutors.

The earliest feedback study to claim the use of a corpus is that of Hyatt (2005), which analysed 60 commentaries on assignments written by Masters students in the field of Educational Studies. Hyatt placed the tutors' comments into broad categories relating to structure and style, administrative procedures, student development, the establishment and maintenance of good relationships ("phatic" comments), and study methods and assignment content. Hyatt's findings are referred to in later corpus investigations, but, although he draws attention to the benefits of corpus analysis as a means of observing "patterns of language and language use" (2005, p. 343), he makes no mention of the techniques he employed to arrive at his taxonomy, and it seems likely that these involved manual rather than corpus analysis. The lexicogrammatical features of each type of function Hyatt identifies can be guessed from the examples provided but are not explicitly described.

The same criticism could be levelled at Jones *et al.* (2017), a small study conducted by researchers in Edinburgh University Medical School, investigating a corpus of 40 dissertation feedback commentaries. The analytical approach taken in this study was derived from Hyatt's categorisation of feedback types, and the findings, which are presented only very briefly, do not seem to be the product of corpus queries. The study is interesting, however, because of its data collection method: the researchers invited feedback contributions from tutors who had been nominated by students for a "Best Feedback" award. This award not only seems like an excellent initiative to encourage the provision of high-quality feedback, but also seems to be a good way of ensuring consistent quality in a feedback corpus which has the potential to inform training materials.

A far more complete account of corpus analytical procedures and findings is provided in the work of Farr (2010), who examined post-observation feedback to trainee teachers using data from diaries and questionnaires, alongside corpora of speech and writing. Farr was interested in tutors' responses to their students' teaching methods, so her feedback framework consists of categories for direction, reflection, evaluation, and relational talk (Hyatt's "phatic" comments), but not for comments on text structure, style, or language use. She found that in comparison with her written corpus, more effort was made to manage face in her spoken corpus, with more comments relating to reflection and to relationships and greater use of hedging and boosting devices. These devices in particular were examined in her corpora of 14 face-to-face feedback sessions (81,944 words) and 171 written feedback reports (89,238 words).

Farr's observations about the role of hedging and boosting influenced the work of Spiteri (2015, 2017), who was also concerned with the way feedback was delivered to student teachers, and Lee (2013a, 2013b), who looked at written feedback given to undergraduates in the humanities. As with Farr (2010), all three of these studies included manual qualitative analyses and drew on existing frameworks to establish categories of feedback functions, using corpus analysis to identify the linguistic features associated with these functions.

Spiteri worked with written post-observation reports to trainee teachers. In her earlier study (Spiteri, 2015), her corpus was very small (7,577 words) and was marked for confirmatory, corrective, and advice categories. She examined keywords and 3-grams (continuous recurrent three-word strings such as *in my opinion*) and traced their role in the realisation of particular functions, for example, evaluative language in confirmatory comments, and the use of imperatives and modals in corrective and advisory comments. Spiteri's later study (2017) analysed a 12,378-word corpus made up of two sets of post-observation feedback and was a means of reflecting on her own practice at two points in time, separated by 10 years. No change was found in the types of feedback given, but there was greater qualification of confirmatory statements in the later data, and an increased use of questions rather than corrective statements. There was also greater use in the later data of modal constructions (*could/could have, would/would have*) and boosters as in "you *really* should have followed the coursebook" to offer alternative scenarios to students as part of corrective feedback. Overall, Spiteri notes an improvement in the quality of her supervision in the later dataset.

Lee's (2013a) doctoral thesis describes investigations of student assignment feedback. Her initial genre analysis of 84 reports built on the feedback sequence of moves, steps, and acts described by Mirador (2000) and the categories of praise, criticism, and suggestion proposed by Hyland and Hyland (2001). As in the later dataset analysed by Spiteri (2017), in Lee's corpus, negative comments tended to be embedded within positive comments in the reports (e.g. *you have read reasonably widely although you do not always make reference to your reading*), and hedging was very common while direct criticism was very rare. Lee's subsequent analysis of a corpus of 126 reports (35,941 words) focussed on the grammatical patterns associated with the most frequent nouns (e.g. *essay, analysis,* and *point(s)*), sequences of positive and negative evaluation, and the resources tutors used to downtone negativity (modal verbs, vague language, stance adverbs, and submodifiers). Lee's (2013b) study concentrates specifically on the use of modal verbs in this corpus.

Although Farr, Spiteri, and Lee do not discuss the potential application of their work to EAP, their findings have relevance to EAP practice because EAP learners tend to have problems recognising the communicative intent of heavily mitigated feedback comments. It would, therefore, be useful to draw students' attention to the forms and functions of hedging identified in these studies. As Lee points out, "Hedging probably occurs in all cultures but is expressed differently and in different proportions" (2013a, p. 438). Hedging is already an important item on most EAP syllabuses, but it is not generally introduced as a feature of feedback that students need to interpret correctly, being instead regarded primarily as a writing strategy which enables students to modify their claims.

A more technically sophisticated corpus study of feedback was conducted by Alsop and Gardner (2019), who regarded feedback as a "key driver of attainment" (2019, p. 41), and designed their corpus as a means of investigating whether there were differences in the (anonymous) provision of feedback to students from different demographic backgrounds. The study was motivated by the fact that Black, Asian, and minority ethnic (BAME) university students in the UK generally have lower levels of attainment than their White counterparts, and by the hypothesis that some feedback wording might contribute to this attainment disparity by alienating some BAME students.

Although this was only a pilot study for the purpose of framework development, and no corpus linguistic analyses were undertaken, the corpus compilation process was complex. Feedback comments had to be extracted from the institution's virtual learning environment, where they were either separated from the source text (summary) or embedded directly into the student's assignment (inline). Each comment was structurally-tagged according to its summary or inline position and annotated for its textual function, expressed in terms of a hierarchical framework developed for the project. This framework was informed by prior (non-corpus-based) studies of feedback functions, for example, Hamp-Lyons and Chen (1999) and Hughes *et al.* (2015). It is neatly binary and symmetrical, each of the five main functions of praise, critique, advice, query, and observation being further classified according to their focus and their specific or general orientation. The element praise, for example, has an idea or organisation focus, while critique has a content or form focus. Thus, a specific praise of ideas (P1A) might be *good application here*, and a general praise of ideas (P1B) might be *It is clear you have read around this subject*, while a specific critique of form (C2A) might be *page number for direct quote*, and a general critique of form (C2B) might be *rather long-winded and could have been expressed more succinctly*. One subcategory, "non-neutral observation" was a means of avoiding direct criticism and contained comments "loaded with non-explicit implications, usually recognition of an omission or a flaw" (Alsop & Gardner, 2019, p. 54). An example of a specific non-neutral observation (O2A) might be *patient centred care is a little bit more than this*, and an example of a general non-neutral observation (O2B) might be *some of this is sounding like a solution rather than analysis*.

The findings from the pilot study noted the "feedback sandwich" effect that has also been described in earlier corpus investigations, where two or three functions operate within the same comment, and the praise function is used to mitigate a critique and/or a non-neutral observation. In Alsop and Gardner's corpus, critique and praise were the most common functions, while the advice function was used least. Critique and praise tended to focus on substance (ideas and content) rather than structure (organisation and form), and this might suggest that there is scope to combine these common feedback practices with more form-focussed feedback managed through corpus links of the kind discussed in Section 18.3 above.

It is reasonable to assume that, as corpus linguistic techniques become more widely known, and as more scripts are developed to enable automatic encoding, highly annotated corpora like the one developed by Alsop and Gardner will become the norm in feedback studies. Annotation would make it much easier for researchers to plot the relationship between multiple variables that might affect feedback decisions, including others not considered in Alsop and Gardner's study but relevant in EAP contexts, such as assignment genre, and the first language and cultural background of the student. So far, however, the cost of creating highly annotated feedback corpora is proving rather prohibitive, and according to Nagata *et al.* (2020) there are almost no publicly available corpora of this kind.

Nagata *et al.* (2020) describe the creation of a corpus that might be used to inform the automatic generation of feedback. They worked with corpora that had already been fully annotated for spelling and grammatical errors and added their own annotations in the form of feedback comments in Japanese, pitched at a level to suit the proficiency of the writers. Parts of their datasets are now publicly available online (see the ICNALE Learner Essays with Feedback Comments and the Konan-JIEM Learner Corpus), but these may not be of great value to EAP practitioners because the source texts were essays produced for the purposes of English language learning, rather than for the purposes of academic study or research. Nagata *et al.*'s annotations were, therefore, restricted to comments on the mechanics of language production, such as spelling, grammatical errors, lexical choice, and organisation, and did not include the "higher order" comments that predominated in the authentic feedback analysed by Hyatt (2005), Farr (2010), Lee (2013a, 2013b), Spiteri (2015, 2017), and Alsop and Gardner (2019). These kinds of comments are probably the ones that EAP learners find most difficult to interpret, but they are also more difficult to generate automatically, because of their context-specific and interpersonal nature.

18.5 Future directions of research

As noted at various points in this chapter, we see the work we have surveyed as being ripe for development in a number of ways. Research has shown that EAP learners appreciate the incorporation of links to corpus data into feedback on writing, but we still need to investigate the extent to which they benefit from this approach. Research into the effects of feedback links might then inform interventions, targeting them more effectively to address the sorts of phenomena best treated by this means. Similar questions apply to the provision of automated feedback – qualitative studies on learner interaction with resources such as ColloCaid and automatic grammar checkers would be very useful here. It would be interesting to see if tools of this sort could incorporate more sophisticated searches based on the latest developments in such areas as phraseology, pattern grammar, and construction grammar.

An important aim of DDL, shared by EAP practitioners generally, is the development of learner autonomy (Charles, this volume). This underlies the need for further research into the way students use corpora independently in feedback contexts. As we have noted above, studies in this area do not generally report the queries undertaken by students; research into student corpus query strategies could provide useful insights into student capabilities and training needs. This work could inform efforts to encourage EAP students to develop more sophisticated searches, taking account of factors such as educational background and language proficiency. It would also be helpful to investigate whether, once students have been introduced to corpora in feedback contexts, they continue to make use of them in the longer term to resolve their language problems.

Finally, as we have indicated, the analysis of corpora of feedback comments is still a very underdeveloped field. Future work in this area might usefully focus on collecting feedback provided to EAP students and analysing it in terms of the categories mentioned in Section 18.4 above. This might provide a useful comparison with feedback provided by subject tutors and might help EAP practitioners to make more informed choices, both when providing feedback and when helping EAP learners to learn how to interpret feedback. It would be interesting to compare feedback across other variables, for example in terms of instructors' level of experience, and there is scope for the triangulation of findings from corpus studies of this sort with findings from more qualitative investigations of the way students interpret various types of feedback, both direct and indirect.

Note

1 Cobb's Compleat Lexical Tutor site (Lextutor) now includes a far wider range of corpora than when Gaskell and Cobb were writing. By keeping its relatively straightforward interface and restricting the types of query available to users, this remains a user-friendly tool for learners and teachers unfamiliar with corpora. This stands in contrast to, for example, the Sketch Engine interface used by Vincent and Nesi (2018) and Vincent *et al.* (2021), which allows more sophisticated queries but thereby excludes less expert corpus users.

Corpora and corpus interfaces referred to in the text:
British National Corpus (BNC) http://www.natcorp.ox.ac.uk/
BNCweb (A web-based interface to the British National Corpus) http://corpora.lancs.ac.uk/ BNCweb/
British Academic Spoken English (BASE) www.coventry.ac.uk/base
British Academic Written English (BAWE) www.coventry.ac.uk/bawe
Collins WordBanks Online https://wordbanks.harpercollins.co.uk/
Corpus of Contemporary American English (COCA) https://www.english-corpora.org/coca/
ICNALE Learner Essays with Feedback Comments https://www.gsk.or.jp/en/catalog/gsk2019-b
Konan-JIEM Learner Corpus Sixth Edition https://www.gsk.or.jp/en/catalog/gsk2019-a
Lextutor https://lextutor.ca/conc/eng/
Michigan Corpus of Academic Spoken English (MICASE) https://quod.lib.umich.edu/m/ micase/
Michigan Corpus of Upper-level Student Papers (MICUSP) https://elicorpora.info/
Sketch Engine https://www.sketchengine.eu/
Sketch Engine for Language Learners (SkELL) https://www.sketchengine.eu/skell/

Further reading

Alsop, S., & Gardner, S. (2019). Understanding attainment disparity: The case for a corpus-driven analysis of the language used in written feedback information to students of different backgrounds. *The Journal of Writing Analytics, 3*, 38–68. This paper provides a detailed description of the types of metadata and annotation a corpus of feedback might contain. Alsop and Gardner's categorisation of feedback functions is perhaps the most complete framework so far developed.

Crosthwaite, P. (2017). Retesting the limits of data-driven learning: Feedback and error correction. *Computer-Assisted Language Learning, 30*(6), 447–473. This paper describes the results of course to train students to use corpus resources to correct their own written errors. The paper gives some useful guidance on how to help learners identify their own errors and reports on the sorts of mistakes that this group of students were able to correct.

Johns, T. F. (1991). Should you be persuaded – two samples of data-driven learning materials. *English Language Research Journal, 4*, 1–16. This is a seminal paper that explains Tim John's approach to data-driven learning.

Quinn, C. (2015). Training L2 writers to reference corpora as a self-correction tool. *ELT Journal, 69*(2), 165–177. https://doi.org/10.1093/elt/ccu062. As the title suggests, this paper is particularly strong on the training of students to access corpus resources, providing a useful procedure which could be implemented in many different settings.

Vincent, B., & Nesi, H. (2018). The BAWE Quicklinks project: A new DDL Resource for university students. *Lidil. Revue de Linguistique et de Didactique des Langues, 58*. https://doi.org/10.4000/lidil.5306. This open-access paper describes an approach to corpus-based feedback using hyper-text links. Because BAWE is an open-access resource within SketchEngine, use of the links is not restricted to a particular institutional network. BAWE is made up of proficient university assignments in a wide range of disciplines, so the links model the kind of language EAP learners need to produce.

References

Alsop, S., & Gardner, S. (2019). Understanding attainment disparity: The case for a corpus-driven analysis of the language used in written feedback information to students of different backgrounds. *The Journal of Writing Analytics, 3*, 38–68.

Aust, R., Kelley, M. J., & Roby, W. B. (1993). The use of hyper-reference and conventional dictionaries. *Educational Technology Research and Development, 41*(4), 63–73. https://doi.org/10.1007/BF02297512

Bellino, A., & Bascuñán, D. (2020). Design and evaluation of *WriteBetter*: A corpus-based writing assistant. *IEEE Access, 8*, 70216–70233. https://doi.org/10.1109/ACCESS.2020.2982639

Blake, J. (2018). Corpus-based error detector for computer scientists. In Y. Tono & H. Isahara (Eds.), Proceedings of the Fourth Asia Pacific Corpus Linguistics Conference (pp. 50–54). Asia Pacific Corpus Linguistics Association.

Blake, J. (2020). Genre-specific error detection with multimodal feedback. *RELC Journal, 51*(1), 179–187. https://doi.org/10.1177/0033688219898282

Carless, D., & Boud, D. (2018). The development of student feedback literacy: Enabling uptake of feedback. *Assessment & Evaluation in Higher Education, 43*(8), 1315–1325. https://doi.org/10.1080/02602938.2018.1463354

Crosthwaite, P. (2017). Retesting the limits of data-driven learning: Feedback and error correction. *Computer Assisted Language Learning, 30*(6), 447–473. https://doi.org/10.1080/09588221.2017.1312462

Crosthwaite, P. (2020). Taking DDL online: Designing, implementing and evaluating a SPOC on data-driven learning for tertiary L2 writing. *Australian Review of Applied Linguistics, 43*(2), 169–195. https://doi.org/10.1075/aral.00031.cro

Farr, F. (2010). *The discourse of teaching practice feedback: A corpus-based investigation of spoken and written modes.* Routledge. https://doi.org/10.4324/9780203846742

Ferris, D. (2002). *Treatment of error in second language student writing.* University of Michigan Press. https://doi.org/10.3998/mpub.2173290

Frankenberg-Garcia, A., Lew, R., Roberts, J., Rees, G., & Sharma, N. (2019). Developing a writing assistant to help EAP writers with collocations in real time. *ReCALL, 31*(2), 23–39. https://doi.org/10.1017/S0958344018000150

Gaskell, D., & Cobb, T. (2004). Can learners use concordance feedback for writing errors? *System, 32*, 301–319. https://doi.org/10.1016/j.system.2004.04.001

Gilmore, A. (2009). Using online corpora to develop students' writing skills. *ELT Journal, 63*(4), 363–372. https://doi.org/10.1093/elt/ccn056

Granger, S., & Tribble, C. (1998). Learner corpus data in the foreign language classroom: Form-focused instruction and data-driven learning. In S. Granger (Ed.), *Learner English on computer* (pp. 199–209). Longman.

Hamp-Lyons, L., & Chen, J. (1999). An investigation into the effectiveness of teacher feedback on student writing. *English Language Teaching and Learning, 3*, 207–219.

Higgins, R. A. (2004). *The meaning and impact of assessment feedback for students in Higher Education* [Doctoral thesis, Sheffield Hallam University]. Sheffield Hallam University Research Archive (SHURA). https://shura.shu.ac.uk/19789/1/10697091.pdf

Hughes, G., Smith, H., & Creese, B. (2015). Not seeing the wood for the trees: Developing a feedback analysis tool to explore feed forward in modularised programmes. *Assessment & Evaluation in Higher Education, 40*(8), 1079–1094. https://doi.org/10.1080/02602938.2014.969193

Hyatt, D. F. (2005). 'Yes, a very good point!': A critical genre analysis of a corpus of feedback commentaries on Master of Education assignments. *Teaching in Higher Education, 10*(3), 339–353. https://doi.org/10.1080/13562510500122222

Hyland, K. & Hyland, F. (2006). Feedback on second language students' writing. *Language Teaching 39*, 83–101. https://doi.org/10.1017/S0261444806003399

Hyland, F., & Hyland, K. (2001). Sugaring the pill: Praise and criticism in written feedback. *Journal of Second Language Writing, 10*(3), 185–212. https://doi.org/10.1016/S1060-3743(01)00038-8

Johns, T. F. (1991). Should you be persuaded - two samples of data-driven learning materials. *English Language Research Journal, 4*, 1–16.

Johns, T. F. (1986). Micro-concord: A language learner's research tool. *System, 14*(2), 151–162. https://doi.org/10.1016/0346-251X(86)90004-7

Johns, T. F. (1981). The uses of an analytic generator: The computer as teacher of English for Specific Purposes. *The ESP teacher: Role, development and prospects.* ELT Documents 112 (p. 105). The British Council.

Jones, D., Lubicz-Nawrocka, T., Fawns, T., Aitken, G., & Mulherin, T. (2017). *Corpus analysis of student feedback. How is good feedback expressed?* A corpus analysis of feedback provided by Edinburgh University Students' Association Teaching Awards (Best feedback) nominees. Institute for Academic Development, University of Edinburgh.

Keh, C. L. (1990). Feedback in the writing process: A model and methods for implementation. *ELT Journal, 44*(4), 294–304. https://doi.org/10.1093/elt/44.4.294

Knight, S. (1994). Dictionary: The tool of last resort in foreign language reading? A new perspective. *The Modern Language Journal, 78*(3), 285–229.

Lee, K. Y. (2013a). Hedging expressions used in academic written feedback: A study on the use of modal verbs. *Research in Corpus Linguistics, 1*, 33–45.

Lee, K. Y. (2013b). *A genre analysis of written academic feedback* [Doctoral thesis, University of Birmingham]. https://etheses.bham.ac.uk/id/eprint/4722/1/Lee13PhD.pdf

Levy, M. (1990). Concordances and their integration into a word-processing environment for language learners. *System, 18*(2), 177–188. https://doi.org/10.1016/0346-251X(90)90052-7

Lyman-Hager, M.-A., Davis, J., Burnett, J., & Chennault, R. (1993). Une vie de boy: Interactive reading in French. In F. Borchardt, & E. Johnson (Eds.), *Proceedings of the CALICO '93 Annual Symposium on Assessment* (pp. 93–97). Duke University.

Milton, J. (1997). Providing computerized self-access opportunities for the development of writing skills. In P. Benson & P. Voller (Eds.), *Autonomy and independence in language learning* (pp. 237–248). Pearson.

Milton, J. (1998). Exploiting L1 and interlanguage corpora in the design of an electronic language learning and production environment. In S. Granger (Ed.), *Learner English on computer* (pp. 186–198). Longman.

Milton, J. (1999). Lexical thickets and electronic gateways: Making text accessible by novice writers. In C. Candlin & K. Hyland (Eds.), *Writing: Texts, processes and practices* (pp. 221–243). Routledge.

Milton, J. (2006). Resource-rich web-based feedback: Helping learners become independent writers. In K. Hyland & F. Hyland (Eds.), *Feedback in second language writing: Contexts and issues* (pp. 123–139). Cambridge University Press. https://doi.org/10.1017/CBO9781139524742.009

Milton, J., & Cheung, V. (2010). A toolkit to assist L2 writers become independent writers. Proceedings of the NAACL HLT 2010 workshop on computational linguistics and writing: writing processes and authoring aids, Association for Computational Linguistics.

Mirador, J. F. (2000). A move analysis of written feedback in higher education. *RELC Journal, 31*(1), 45–60. https://doi.org/10.1177/003368820003100103

Nagata, R., Inui, K., & Ishikawa, S. (2020). Creating corpora for research in feedback comment generation. In N. Calzolari, F. Béchet, P. Blache, K. Choukri, C. Cieri, T. Declerck, & S. Piperidis (Eds.), (LREC 2020) Proceedings of the 12th *Conference on Language Resources and Evaluation*, European Language Resources Association (pp. 123–139).

Quinn, C. (2015). Training L2 writers to reference corpora as a self-correction tool. *ELT Journal, 69*(2), 165–177. https://doi.org/10.1093/elt/ccu062

Pérez-Paredes, P. (2020). Rethinking learning in data-driven learning. Plenary talk given at the *Teaching and Language Corpora conference*, University of Perpignan.

Roby, W. (1999). What's in a gloss? *Language Learning Technology Journal, 2*(2), 94–101.

Spiteri, D. (2017). Using corpus linguistics to analyse post lesson observation feedback. *International Journal of Teaching and Education, 1*, 67–84. https://doi.org/10.20472/TE.2017.5.1.006

Spiteri, D. (2015). Counting the words that count – Using a lexical analysis tool to explore feedback to student teachers. *ELTED, 18*, 29–34.

Todd, R. W. (2001). Induction from self-selected concordances and self-correction. *System, 29*, 91–102. https://doi.org/10.1016/S0346-251X(00)00047-6

Vincent, B., & Nesi, H. (2018). The BAWE quicklinks project: A new DDL resource for university students. *Lidil. Revue de Linguistique et de Didactique des Langues, 58*. https://doi.org/10.4000/lidil.5306

Vincent, B., Nesi, H., & Quinn, D. (2021). Exploiting corpora to provide guidance for academic writing: The BAWE Quicklinks project. In M. Charles & A. Frankenberg-Garcia (Eds.), *Corpora in ESP/EAP writing instruction: Preparation, exploitation, analysis* (pp. 13–31). Routledge.

Yoon, H. (2008). More than a linguistic reference: The influence of corpus technology on L2 academic writing. *Language Learning & Technology, 12*(2), 31–48. http://dx.doi.org/10125/44142

PART III

Learner corpora for English language teaching

19

WRITTEN LEARNER CORPORA TO INFORM TEACHING

Gaëtanelle Gilquin

19.1 Introduction

This chapter deals with how written learner corpora can be used – and have been used – to inform teaching and, in particular, English language teaching (ELT). Learner corpora are corpora made up of the production of second or foreign language learners in the target language. They can consist of written, spoken, or multimodal data. However, for reasons that are partly related to the ease of compilation, written learner corpora have the lion's share. At the time of writing this chapter, the list "Learner Corpora around the World", maintained by the Centre for English Corpus Linguistics (2020), includes 64% of learner corpora exclusively made up of written data and 12% of learner corpora including both written and spoken data. When learner corpora are used to inform teaching, they are, therefore, more likely to contain written learner language. In fact, many of the pedagogical resources described in this chapter present themselves as being based on learner corpora, with no specification of the register, but they turn out to rely on written learner corpus data only. Very often, they aim to inform general English language teaching rather than specific aspects of writing.

While almost any aspect of learner writing can be investigated on the basis of a written learner corpus and can potentially be of interest for teaching purposes, it is the difficulties which learners experience with the target language that tend to be seen as the most pedagogically relevant. Among these, errors are particularly prominent. They can be retrieved from raw learner corpus data (provided they are lexically-based, e.g. *informations* or *dependent of*), ideally with the help of the teacher's or the researcher's experience of what learners usually get wrong. However, the retrieval of learners' typical errors is facilitated by prior error-tagging of the learner corpus, that is, the annotation of each error found in the corpus, often accompanied by a description of the error type and a possible correction (Lüdeling & Hirschmann, 2015). This allows for the automatic extraction of all errors, or all instances of a specific type of error (e.g. errors with modal verbs or errors with *can*).

Another way of finding out about learners' difficulties with the target language is by comparing the frequency of linguistic items in the learner corpus with that in a comparable native corpus. This makes it possible to discover cases of underuse or overuse, i.e. items that are used significantly less often or significantly more often, respectively, by learners than by native speakers. Although not wrong in the strict sense, underused or overused items contribute

DOI: 10.4324/9781003002901-23

to the non-native character of learner language and can, thus, inform teaching, especially at more advanced levels.

By identifying misuses, underuses, and overuses on the basis of learner corpora, one can provide a more reliable *description* of learner language. De Cock and Granger (2005), thus, argue that intuition-based lists of errors like Swan and Smith (1987) include misuses that are unlikely to be found among learners. The identification of problematic areas in learner corpora can also help with the *selection* of the most relevant items to include in the teaching syllabus or in pedagogical resources. Thewissen (2015, p. 201), for example, shows that punctuation errors are frequent and "improvement-resistant" in the learner corpus she investigates, which is a signal that more time could be devoted to punctuation in the English as a Foreign Language (EFL) classroom. On the other hand, learner corpora can be approached from a more positive perspective, looking at what learners get right. In Thewissen's (2015) study, adjective order errors are very infrequent, for instance, which suggests that it is probably not necessary to emphasise this aspect more in ELT. Learner corpora, therefore, provide "useful information ... on the areas of language which should be reinforced or de-emphasised" (Granger, 2015, p. 488).

Usually, learner corpora come with rich metadata about learners (e.g. their mother tongue or the number of years they have been learning the target language). This is valuable information for teaching, because it can lead to *customisation*, i.e. the adaptation of teaching or materials to the target learner population (e.g. Chinese-speaking learners, beginners). Gilquin and Granger (2021), thus, show that the phrase *as far as x* BE *concerned* is particularly common in corpus data produced by French-speaking learners, who often use it as a topic introducer at the beginning of the sentence (e.g. *As far as dreams are concerned, the same could be said*). Such a finding could lead to a pedagogical intervention specifically targeted at French-speaking learners. Metadata about learners' proficiency levels can also help with sequencing, i.e. "deciding the order in which linguistic items should be presented" (Granger, 2015, p. 488). This is the aim of the English Profile project (https://www.englishprofile.org/), which uses learner corpus data to investigate what learners at different proficiency levels of the Common European Framework of Reference for Languages (CEFR) can do. On this basis, it is possible to design pedagogical materials that take account of learners' proficiency.

Using written learner corpora to inform teaching can be done in a direct or indirect way, a distinction first introduced by Leech (1997) for corpora of native language, but later applied to learner corpora too (Granger, 2015). A direct approach means that teachers and/or their students consult learner corpora themselves to find out how learners (possibly the students themselves) use the target language. An indirect approach, on the other hand, involves researchers, pedagogical materials writers, software developers, or publishers relying on learner corpora to create resources (dictionaries, textbooks, computer programs, etc.) that are then used by teachers and/or their students. This chapter considers both direct and indirect pedagogical approaches to written learner corpora.

19.2 Review of current state of research

From the early days of corpus linguistics, it was possible to use corpora of native language to inform teaching. However, the compilation of the first learner corpora, among which the International Corpus of Learner English (ICLE; Granger, 1993) and the Longman Learners' Corpus, together with the development of the field of learner corpus research (see Granger *et al.*, 2015), certainly contributed to a growing interest in the pedagogical applications of corpora. This is due not only to the availability of a new type of corpus, but also to the fact that learner corpus research has always had strong links with the field of language teaching (Granger, 2009) and has, thus, helped draw the attention of pedagogues and pedagogically-oriented researchers to corpora and corpus linguistics. Yet, it is fair to say that learner corpora (written or otherwise, in English or in other languages) have not played a central role in language teaching so far. Flowerdew (2012, p. 207) mentions learner corpora among the "under-represented corpora for pedagogy", noting that "there is little evidence that learner corpora have had much impact on syllabus and materials design to date" (Flowerdew, 2012, p. 210). However, she also underlines "the acknowledged value in integrating learner corpora into language teaching" (Flowerdew, 2012, p. 210). In what follows, we will review some attempts at using written learner corpora directly or indirectly for ELT purposes. For the latter approach, we will consider the contribution of learner corpora to dictionaries (Section 19.2.1) and to other pedagogical resources, including grammars and textbooks (Section 19.2.2). For the direct approach, we will see how learner corpora have been used in data-driven learning (Section 19.2.3).

19.2.1 Learner dictionaries

One area that has exploited learner corpora successfully is lexicography. De Cock and Granger (2005) point out that "[t]he addition of this new resource to the lexicographer's workstation constitutes a new departure in pedagogical lexicography" (p. 72). The exploitation of learner corpora makes it possible to identify learners' main problems with the target language and to then warn them about these potential pitfalls. Error dictionaries (e.g. Turton & Heaton, 1996) and so-called "error notes" in learner dictionaries illustrate errors regularly made by learners and show how they can be corrected so as to reflect native usage, e.g.

(1) ✗ She gave me a good advice.
 ✓ She gave me some good advice.
 ✗ It is full of good advices on healthy eating.
 ✓ It is full of good advice on healthy eating.

(Turton & Heaton, 1996, p. 9)

The second edition of the *Macmillan English Dictionary for Advanced Learners* (MEDAL2; Rundell, 2007) includes 30 central pages that are meant as a guide to produce better academic writing and professional reports (Gilquin *et al.*, 2007a). The contents, which are organised around a number of rhetorical functions (such as "expressing possibility and certainty", "quoting and reporting", or "summarizing and drawing conclusions"), are entirely based on the close analysis of native and learner corpora. In addition to "Get it right" boxes, learners can find "Be careful" notes that point, among others, to words or expressions that are under- or overused by learners as indicated in Example (2). These notes also give information about words or expressions that tend to be misplaced in the sentence as with the word *therefore* discussed in Example (3), or choices that are not stylistically appropriate as shown in Example (4). Some of these notes are illustrated by means of a bar chart comparing the frequency of the items in learner writing and native writing/speech.

(2) Learners often use the preposition *in spite of*. However, *despite* is much more frequent. (Gilquin *et al.*, 2007a, p. IW20)
(3) Learners often use *therefore* at the beginning of a sentence. This use is correct, but it is much less frequent than the use of *therefore* inside the sentence. (Gilquin *et al.*, 2007a, p. IW13)

(4) Although, in informal style, *that* can be left out after very frequent reporting verbs such as *suggest*, *suppose*, and *think*, this is less frequently the case in academic writing and professional reports. (Gilquin *et al.*, 2007a, p. IW27)

As suggested by Walter (2010, p. 440), items that are overused by learners can also point to good candidates for the insertion of thesaurus-type information in dictionaries, which would provide learners with good alternatives to replace these overused items. In addition, learner corpora can help identify words that are likely to be familiar to learners and that, included in the defining vocabulary of a dictionary, would result in definitions that are understandable to most learners (Gillard & Gadsby, 1998, p. 163).

Thanks to the metadata in learner corpora, and with the support of electronic lexicography, it has also become easier to customise dictionaries according to learners' specific needs. Granger (2018) shows how the analysis of learner corpus data distinguished by learners' mother tongues (L1) can help develop a bilingualised electronic dictionary which includes L1-specific error notes. She also argues for the inclusion of such L1-specific error notes in bilingual dictionaries, where she claims they would be particularly useful given learners' preference for bilingual dictionaries over monolingual dictionaries (Granger, 2018).

19.2.2 Other pedagogical resources based on learner corpora

In addition to dictionaries, other pedagogical resources have also started to exploit learner corpora in different ways.[1] Information derived from learner corpora can help grammarians or textbook writers decide what to focus on. Thus, the corpus-informed *Cambridge Grammar of English* includes an A-Z in which the words were selected for inclusion because, among other reasons, they are "known to be difficult for learners of English and often lead to errors" (Carter & McCarthy, 2006, p. 21). In the *Objective IELTS Intermediate Workbook*, some of the exercises centre around words that learners have difficulty with, for example prepositions (Black & Sharp, 2006a), as attested by a learner corpus.

The types of error notes that have by now become quite common in learner dictionaries have also progressively made their appearance in other pedagogical resources. This is the case, for instance, in the *Common Mistakes at...* series (e.g. Moore, 2005), the *Cambridge Grammar of English* (Carter & McCarthy, 2006), and the *Viewpoint* (e.g. McCarthy *et al.*, 2012) or *Grammar and Beyond* (e.g. Reppen, 2012) textbooks, as illustrated below:

(5) [*Crucial, vital, essential, fundamental*] are 'limit' adjectives and are not normally used with *very/quite/more*, etc. To emphasise the adjective, you can use *absolutely vital/essential*, etc.: *It's absolutely essential to start off with a good business plan.* (not ~~*it's very essential*~~) (Moore, 2005, p. 42)

(6) Do not start a sentence with *Whereas* to contrast ideas with a previous sentence. *An online profile is for friends. **However,** a résumé is for employers.* (NOT ~~*Whereas*~~...)(McCarthy *et al.*, 2012, p. 18)

In addition, textbooks based on the analysis of learner corpora can include exercises related to learners' typical errors. Such exercises can take different forms. They can consist of sentences containing one or several errors that students have to correct, e.g. *Yesterday was much more funnier than the first day* (Interactive, Hadkins *et al.*, 2011, p. 39). In *Objective PET* (Hashemi & Thomas, 2010), such exercises are called "corpus spots" and they focus on specific topics, for instance pluralisation (e.g. *I look after the childs when their parents are working*, Hashemi &

Thomas, 2010, p. 21), –*ing* vs –*ed* forms in adjective positions (e.g. *She was amazed/amazing by the shops and restaurants*, Hashemi & Thomas, 2010, p. 42), or verb + noun collocations (e.g. *I hope you don't do the same mistake as me*, Hashemi & Thomas, 2010, p. 56). Some exercises go beyond isolated sentences by presenting long extracts or full texts taken from a learner corpus. This is the case in the *First Certificate Trainer* (May, 2010). Students are, for example, shown a letter written by a First Certificate candidate and asked to carry out some specific tasks:

(7) Find and correct the following (1–3):
  1. poor layout. Where should it be divided into paragraphs?
  2. two informal expressions, four contracted forms and four uses of informal punctuation. Change these to more formal language.
  3. two mistakes each in verb forms, spelling and capital letters. Correct these. (May, 2010, p. 25)

Interestingly, some learner texts are also presented as models for students. An application letter "written by Felipe, a very strong First Certificate candidate" (May, 2010, p. 26), for instance, is accompanied by notes highlighting the positive features of the candidate's letter (e.g. "correct structure for current job", "formal linking expressions", "polite to the employer") and encouraging students to write their own letter on the basis of this model.

As is the case with dictionaries based on learner corpora, customisation of other pedagogical resources is possible thanks to metadata. The *Common Mistakes at...* series mentioned above uses certain portions of the Cambridge Learner Corpus to identify errors made by learners at a certain proficiency level. *Objective PET* focuses on errors typical of the level of the Preliminary English Test (Hashemi & Thomas, 2010). Customisation according to learners' L1 is still relatively rare, but Cambridge University Press offers several of its learner-corpus-based textbooks in "English for Spanish Speakers" editions. *Objective First*, for example, has a booklet, entitled *100 Writing Tips for Cambridge English: First*, whose contents "have been informed by a study of B2 level Spanish speakers' data in the *Cambridge Learner Corpus*" (Capel, 2014, p. 1). *English in Mind, Italian Edition* (e.g. Puchta & Stranks, 2007) is informed by learner corpus data produced by Italian-speaking learners.

19.2.3 Data-driven learning and learner corpora

Data-driven learning (DDL), which involves the use of corpora in the language classroom (see Section 4 in this handbook), has mostly relied on native corpora, helping students discover how the target language should be employed. Despite a very early demonstration of the potential of learner corpora for DDL (Granger & Tribble, 1998) and several calls since then to integrate learner corpus data into DDL (e.g. Gilquin & Granger, 2010; Seidlhofer, 2002), only a handful of DDL studies so far have ventured to use learner corpora. Thus, in Chen and Flowerdew's (2018) review of empirical studies on DDL in the English for Academic Purposes classroom published between 2000 and 2017, only five studies out of thirty-seven include learner corpus data.

Doing DDL with written learner corpora means that the typical features of learner writing can be examined. Most of the time, learner corpora are used in combination with native corpora, so that students can compare the features of learner writing with those of native writing. As is the case with pedagogical resources based on learner corpora, the focus of learner-corpus-based DDL is often a problematic aspect of learner writing. Nesselhaf (2004), for example, shows how the comparison of a concordance of the verb SUGGEST in the German component of ICLE and in the Louvain Corpus of Native English Essays (LOCNESS) can make students aware of the non-standard use of SUGGEST followed by a *to*-infinitive.

While off-the-shelf learner corpora like ICLE can serve as a source of information about learner writing for DDL, most researchers or teachers who have integrated learner corpora into DDL activities have actually collected learner corpus data themselves (or sometimes asked their students to do so) in the form of a "local learner corpus" (Seidlhofer, 2002). A local learner corpus includes texts produced by the students for whom the DDL activities are meant to be designed and implemented. Moon and Oh (2017), for example, collected writing from Korean learners of English at the beginning of the school year. The analysis of this home-made learner corpus revealed learners' tendency to overgeneralise BE, producing sentences such as *He is dance very well* (Moon & Oh, 2017, p. 52). Some of the students who contributed to the learner corpus then took part in DDL activities which required them to compare concordances of *is* in the learner corpus and in a native corpus of graded reader texts, so that they could "unlearn the overgenerated *be*" (Moon & Oh, 2017, p. 54). The students, thus, examined learner corpus data produced by themselves and their classmates and they focused on a feature that had proved problematic for them. The use of a local learner corpus has the advantage of making the DDL activities particularly relevant to the learners and argu-ably more motivating for them. In Lee and Swales (2006), the relevance is even more obvious since each participant collected a learner corpus of their own writing and compared it with a corpus of expert writing in their field of study. The learner language features that they discovered by comparing the two corpora were, therefore, features which they had produced themselves and which they could correct thanks to the model of the expert corpus. As Lee and Swales (2006) underline, the comparison also brought to light the relative lack of vari-ation in students' writing, which could encourage them to look for alternative expressions or patterns in the expert corpus. The usefulness of local learner corpora in DDL is demonstrated by Cotos (2014), who compared DDL activities combining a local learner corpus and a native corpus with DDL activities involving native corpus data only, and who showed that the former is more efficient than the latter.

19.3 Critical issues

The literature review in the previous section has established that written learner corpora can inform teaching either by contributing to the production of better pedagogical resources more suited to learners' needs, or by giving learners access to authentic learner data, from which they can make their own discoveries. However, this pedagogical potential has not been exploited to the full, although, as suggested by Granger (2015), "there are clear signs that the tide is turning, albeit slowly" (p. 487). Some of the issues associated with the use of learner corpora for pedagogical purposes may explain their relative lack of uptake in foreign language teaching (Meunier, 2012).

The first issue has to do with the controversy surrounding the exposure of learners to negative evidence, that is, to erroneous forms of the target language (Flowerdew, 2001). It has been claimed that this may have a detrimental effect on learners by reinforcing (or some-times even creating) problems in their language production. However, Fuster-Márquez and Gregori-Signes (2018), dealing with the use of learner corpora in DDL, show that, provided the data are "authentic and highly specific learner data obtained from a reliable ad hoc learner corpus", "direct exposure to these data through controlled activities may cover certain learners' needs not found in textbooks" (p. 164). In addition, the potentially detrimental effect of negative evidence can be counterbalanced by positive evidence coming from a native corpus or from the learner corpus itself and by exercises that consolidate the standard form (Nesselhauf, 2004).

Another issue concerns the teacher. Despite their central role, "[t]he language teacher is an often neglected figure in learner corpora projects", as Urzúa (2015, p. 99) stresses. Meunier (2012) notes that many teachers "are not aware of the possibilities offered by (learner) corpora and of the changes that corpus methods have brought to materials that they are using" (p. 211). She also points out that most teachers receive no or very little (pre- or in-service) teacher training in the use of corpora. If they have not been trained in corpus linguistics, they are unlikely to fully benefit from learner corpora or make their students benefit from them. Urzúa (2015) describes a project in which teachers are involved in the compilation of a local learner corpus of written academic English. Thanks to the training in corpus linguistics received within the framework of this project, they are able to analyse the learner corpus data and interpret their findings on the basis of what they know about their students. By examining their students' actual usage, they are also led to re-evaluate the curriculum and rethink some of the writing tasks they give to their students. Getting teachers involved in learner corpus projects may thus have beneficial consequences, both for them and for their students. Providing them with ready-made materials (e.g. downloadable DDL worksheets) which they could use with their students in the classroom could arguably encourage them to get involved.

A third possible reason for the relative lack of uptake of learner corpus information in foreign language teaching is the conservative position of many educational publishers, who are thought to be, as Harwood (2005) puts it, "far more comfortable with rehashes of what has gone before than with something different (and refreshing)" (p. 152). Fortunately, more and more publishers have now integrated corpus data into their pedagogical materials, so that "what has gone before" is increasingly likely to be based on learner corpora. However, as Harwood (2005) also reminds us, "[m]arketability rather than pedagogical effectiveness is said to be the publishers' main concern" (ibid.). Thus, for commercial reasons rather than pedagogical ones, the publication of learner-corpus-based customised materials, in particular, L1-specific materials, is less probable simply because the market for such materials is smaller (Gilquin *et al.*, 2007b). In this respect, it is to be hoped that, in the same way as electronic lexicography has started to open new doors for the customisation of learner dictionaries, the increasing use of electronic resources in the classroom will lead educational publishers to propose innovative ways of providing students with tailor-made materials based on learner corpora.

19.4 Recommendations for practice

If we want written learner corpora to play a more prominent role in teaching, we need to address the critical issues outlined in the previous section, but we also need to make sure we adopt good practices when we use learner corpora with pedagogical aims in mind. This section offers some recommendations related to the choice of a norm (Section 19.4.1), the representativeness of the results (Section 19.4.2), and the transparency of information derived from learner corpora (Section 19.4.3).

19.4.1 Norm

When a written learner corpus is used for teaching purposes, this is often in combination with a native corpus, which makes it possible, by comparison, to identify non-native features in the learner corpus. The notions of under- and overuse, for example, necessarily imply a statistically significant difference in frequency between the learner corpus and a native corpus. As for DDL, it was emphasised earlier that native corpus data are important because they provide students with an indication of what is right in the target language. Different types of corpora can be used to represent the target language. In fact, it need not even be a native corpus: an expert corpus consisting of articles published in scientific journals (and not necessarily written by native speakers), as in Lee and Swales (2006), can constitute an excellent target for students in an English for academic purposes course. Just confining our attention to native corpora, however, there are several choices available, and one's choice may have an impact on the results (e.g. whether an item turns out to be overused or not by learners; Gilquin, 2021a).

The most important principle that should guide this choice is comparability: the native corpus should be written, like the learner corpus, but it should also correspond to the genre of the learner corpus as closely as possible. In this regard, Nesselhauf's (2004) decision to compare ICLE to LOCNESS makes perfect sense, since both corpora include argumentative and literary essays. The fact that LOCNESS includes data produced by university students, like ICLE, can be both a strength and a weakness. It is a strength in the sense that the writers are about the same age as the students represented in ICLE and they are supposed to have reached a similar cognitive development. On the other hand, as novice writers rather than expert writers, native students tend to produce language that learners would not necessarily want to imitate, as Leech (1998) already recognised.

In the MEDAL2 project described earlier (Gilquin *et al.*, 2007a), the initial decision had been to compare the ICLE data with LOCNESS. However, the first analyses made it clear that presenting students with a model primarily based on LOCNESS would not be pedagogically sound; instead, it was decided to use a corpus of academic English by expert native writers as the main reference, despite the difference in genre. When the objective involves bringing learners closer to the (ideal) target, it is important that they are mainly presented with this target and that other models are used cautiously, if at all, to avoid leading learners to commit errors that they might not have committed otherwise (e.g. the confusion between *it's* and *its*, which is quite common in novice native writing, but rarely occurs in non-native writing).

19.4.2 Representativeness

Recommendations can also be made with respect to the representativeness of the findings. If one aims to cater for a specific group of students, through the use of customised materials, the learner corpus data should represent the writing of learners whose profiles resemble those of the students as much as possible (same mother tongue background, same acquisitional context, etc.). Local learner corpora are the ultimate candidate for representativeness, since the learners represented in the corpus are also the beneficiaries of the corpus-based lessons or materials.

If one does not aim for customised materials, on the other hand, one should provide information that is as relevant as possible to the largest number of learners. Talking about error notes, Granger. (2015) rightly points out that "[i]t is counterproductive and, indeed, potentially detrimental to include warnings that are only relevant for a limited group of learners" (pp. 492–493). She gives the example of an error note in the *Cambridge Grammar of English* (Carter & McCarthy, 2006) which warns against the over-passivisation of copular verbs (e.g. *A teacher is been by her*), while this turns out to be a relatively rare phenomenon in learner corpus data, mainly found among populations with certain mother tongue backgrounds (most notably Asian languages).

In the MEDAL2 project, whose aim was to produce a resource that would be helpful to learners worldwide (and not to a specific group of learners), non-native features that were highlighted had to be both frequent and widespread. The latter criterion was operationalised by specifying that the features had to appear in at least ten L1 learner populations out of the sixteen that were investigated. In effect, this also corresponded to a spread of the features across different language families. This criterion explains why, for instance, *in fact* was not mentioned among the overused items. Although it was heavily overused by certain learner populations, the number of populations was too limited, also in terms of language families (mainly Italian- and French-speaking learners overuse *in fact*), to make it worthwhile including a "Be careful" note in the dictionary about this item.

O'Keeffe and Mark (2017), who describe methodological issues related to the English Profile project, and more particularly the English Grammar Profile, do the opposite of the MEDAL2 project: instead of looking for what learners get wrong in the learner corpus, they look for what learners get right, in order to arrive at a number of so called "grammatical competence statements", which indicate "what learners can do with grammar at each level of the CEFR based on what they have written in Cambridge exams" (O'Keeffe & Mark, 2017, p. 464). Yet, the criteria they apply are quite similar to those of the MEDAL2 project, including "frequency of use", "rate of correct uses", and "spread of first language families" (O'Keeffe & Mark, 2017, pp. 469–470). In addition, they recommend considering whether the usage is distributed across a range of individual learners, whether it is distributed across a range of contexts (e.g. letters, informative texts, essays, reports), and whether it is affected by a task (e.g. the high frequency of the pattern *Would you mind …* resulting from the task of writing a letter to ask for a different appointment). Adopting such criteria should enable all learners to benefit equally from corpus-based resources, regardless of their profiles or the context of the writing task.

19.4.3 *Transparency*

The last recommendation is for materials writers to be more transparent about the source of the information (corpus or otherwise) that they include in their pedagogical resources. Very often, the resources provide a general mention of the learner corpus that they rely on. For printed grammars and textbooks, this is typically done on the cover of the book, with a few words about the learner corpus and its general contribution to the resource. However, inside the resource, it may not always be clear what parts of the book precisely result from the analysis of the learner corpus or how exactly the corpus data have been used. In the *Cambridge Grammar of English* (Carter & McCarthy, 2006), for example, some error warnings are signalled by a special symbol. This is how these warnings are described in the introduction to the grammar:

> We also had access during the writing of this book to a large learner corpus consisting of texts produced by learners of English from a wide range of linguacultures, coded for error and inappropriate use. This, along with our own language-teaching experience and that of our reference panel, has enabled us to give warnings of common areas of potential error where appropriate. (Carter & McCarthy, 2006, p. 3)

While this confirms the use of a learner corpus, it does not necessarily seem to guarantee that this corpus was used as the (main) source of information for all the warnings. In addition, the grammar includes many crossed out sentences, as in Example (8), without it being made clear whether these come from the learner corpus.

(8) I may be free. I'll have to check my diary. ~~(I'll have got to check my diary.)~~ (Carter & McCarthy, 2006, p. 403)

In the *Objective IELTS Intermediate Student's Book* (Black & Sharp, 2006b), some exercises are said to be *based on* learner corpus data, which leaves it unclear how authentic they actually are, as illustrated by the following instructions: "Read the question below and the letter in response to it, which is <u>based on</u> an answer produced by an IELTS candidate" (Black & Sharp, 2006b, p. 57; emphasis added). It is also quite common to notice a mixture of authentic and (presumably) invented sentences, a distinction not always drawn very markedly. This mixture can be found within one and the same exercise, e.g. "Look at these sentences from job applications, <u>some of them</u> written by IELTS candidates" (Black & Sharp, 2006b, p. 57; emphasis added). It can also be found across similar exercises, for example error detection exercises in the *Objective IELTS Intermediate Workbook* (Black & Sharp, 2006a), some of which are explicitly described as taken from authentic data (e.g. "Correct the mistakes below made by IELTS candidates", Black & Sharp, 2006a, p. 49) whereas others are not (e.g. "Correct the 12 spelling mistakes in this paragraph", Black & Sharp, 2006a, p. 45). While all the pedagogical resources that rely on some learner corpus data are obviously a step in the right direction and while we cannot necessarily expect all the materials in these resources to be entirely derived from (learner) corpora, clearly signposting the contents that come from a corpus (by means of a symbol or a title, like the corpus spots in Hashemi & Thomas, 2010) would seem like a good practice to follow for materials writers.

19.5 Future directions of research

This final section considers some ways in which written learner corpora could further inform teaching in the future. The first direction is that of computer-assisted language learning (Section 19.5.1) and the second one is the study of the writing process (Section 19.5.2).

19.5.1 Computer-assisted language learning

Computer-assisted language learning (CALL) applications based on (written) learner corpora are by no means new. As early as 1992, for example, Liou *et al.* (1992) reported on a CALL project aimed at improving EFL learners' grammar, which relied on the analysis of an error-tagged corpus of essays written by Chinese students. CALL applications based on (written) learner corpora are not rare either. In fact, Granger (2015, p. 496) notes that "there is a much greater – and more diversified – use of learner corpus data in CALL materials than in other pedagogical resources". Yet, she also stresses that "[m]ost tools are still at an experimental stage and presented as prototypes" (Granger, 2015, p. 499).

Like other pedagogical resources, CALL projects based on learner corpora mostly use them as repertoires of errors typically committed by (certain populations of) learners. Lee *et al.* (2016), for example, use error-tagged learner corpora to create a CALL system that automatically generates fill-in-the-blank exercises for preposition usage. The learner corpus data also serve to create plausible distractors, which are shown through an experiment to "rival ... the quality of human-authored items" (Lee *et al.*, 2016, p. 991). Lo *et al.* (2018) describe GEC Cool Edit, a CALL system for grammatical error correction (GEC) which relies on parallel sentences taken from an error-tagged learner corpus, with the original sentence and its corrected version. The web-based system allows students to write a text and automatically receive corrective feedback. The evaluation of the system points to its "competitive performance on a number of publicly available testsets" (Lo *et al.*, 2018, p. 82) and the authors mention some avenues for further improvement of the system. These two examples should suffice to illustrate the great potential of CALL applications that rely on learner corpora, and we can only hope, as Granger (2015) does, that "the buzzing activity in the field will lead to the production of fully fledged applications in the near future" (p. 499).

19.5.2 Writing process

The resources and applications mentioned so far exploit written corpora that are made up of learners' texts, that is, the finished products of the writing act. Some learner corpora, however, seek to represent the writing process, that is, how learners go about composing a text (Gilquin, 2021b). This is the case of learner corpora which include annotations showing revisions in handwritten texts, e.g. crossed out items or elements added in superscript, as in the Marburg corpus of Intermediate Learner English (Kreyer, 2015). While not all revisions are visible in such corpora (a crossed out item may be illegible or the learner may have used correction fluid), they provide valuable information about items that the learner may have got right in the end but that caused difficulties during the process, or about elements that the learner tried to write but that eventually disappeared from the text as a result of an avoidance strategy, all of which could usefully inform teaching.

Learner corpora that include several drafts of one and the same text, like the CityU Corpus of Essay Drafts of English Language Learners (Lee *et al.*, 2015), also give snapshots of the writing process. They make it possible, for example, to examine how a text was revised and how learners addressed the feedback that they received. In terms of teaching applications, they could for instance be presented to learners to give them concrete examples of how a text can be gradually improved to reach a satisfactory result. In DDL activities, students could be asked to compare the different drafts of a text and be made to notice the improvements. They could also compare a sub-corpus made up of the first drafts with a sub-corpus made up of the final drafts and be asked to identify the differences, for example items whose frequency has significantly increased or decreased. The final versions of the texts would, thus, serve as a reference corpus, which would make it unnecessary to resort to native corpora. Multiple-draft learner corpora could also be useful for CALL. Actually, the CityU Corpus is one of the learner corpora used in Lee *et al.* (2016) to create distractors in fill-in-the-blank exercises (see Section 19.5.1). This was done by looking for prepositions that were often edited between drafts, the assumption being that "frequent editing implies a degree of uncertainty on the part of the learner as to which of these prepositions is in fact correct" (Lee *et al.*, 2016, p. 987).

Going even one step further in the representation of the writing process, the Process Corpus of English in Education (PROCEED) is a process-focused learner corpus that reproduces the whole writing process through the inclusion of keystroke logs, which contain a record of every key struck on the keyboard, and screencast videos, which show what happens on the computer screen while the learner is typing (Gilquin, 2022). Such data give an accurate picture of every revision that the text undergoes (deletion, insertion, movement, etc.) and in what order these revisions are carried out. The screencast videos make it possible to see the state of the text at each stage in the writing process and to observe its evolution second by second. The keystroke logs provide detailed statistics about the number and types of revisions, or the frequency and duration of pauses, for instance.

Process data like these offer new possibilities in terms of teaching. Gilquin (2019) describes a pedagogical intervention which used PROCEED as a local learner corpus. Students were first asked to watch at least ten minutes of their own screencast video, which they then discussed individually with the teacher. The learner and the teacher also examined the learner's keystroke report, which was compared to the report of a proficient learner and that of a native writer, thus highlighting differences in the writing process (e.g. time devoted to reviewing the whole text at the end). Finally, the teacher showed some anonymised extracts from other screencast videos illustrating successful writing strategies and asked the learner to reflect on how they could adopt some of these strategies in their own writing. Focusing on another aspect of the writing process, Gilquin and Laporte (2021) explain how videos from PROCEED were annotated as to learners' use of online writing tools (dictionaries, corpora, etc.), thus revealing, among other findings, that learners predominantly rely on bilingual tools, that they tend to look for a single word using a single tool, and that they often lack critical thinking about the information which they retrieve from online tools. These findings were then exploited to create a self-learning online platform to help learners make better use of online writing tools. The platform consists of a number of modules, each one focusing on a particular type of tool or information to search for (e.g. monolingual dictionaries, thesauri, collocations, frequency). In each module, a video introduces the topic and demonstrates some tools, with particular attention to aspects that proved problematic according to the screencast videos. Each module also includes exercises that are based on sentences or text samples from PROCEED and that involve the use of specific (combinations of) tools to improve the sentence or text.

Following this and other avenues for research, and continuing to explore paths already trodden, we can hope that written learner corpora will further enhance teaching, enabling researchers, practitioners, and ultimately learners to fully benefit from their many advantages.

Note

1 Most of the resources mentioned in this section are published by Cambridge University Press, which has been a pioneer in the production of pedagogical materials based on learner corpora. The Cambridge Learner Corpus, on which these resources rely, is primarily made up of Cambridge examination scripts (i.e. learner writing) produced by learners from a range of mother tongue backgrounds. While McCarthy (2016) points out that spoken data are gradually being added to the corpus, it is unlikely that the resources described here have already benefited from the use of such spoken data.

Further reading

Gilquin, G., Granger, S., & Paquot, M. (2007). Learner corpora: The missing link in EAP pedagogy. *Journal of English for Academic Purposes, 6*(4), 319–335. This is a plea for the inclusion of learner corpora in English for academic purposes pedagogy. It also includes a description of the MEDAL2 lexicographical project.

Granger, S., Gilquin, G., & Meunier, F. (Eds.). (2015). *The Cambridge handbook of learner corpus research.* Cambridge University Press. This handbook provides a state of the art in the field of learner corpus research. A whole section is devoted to "Learner corpus research and language teaching", including Granger's (2015) chapter on "The contribution of learner corpora to reference and instructional materials design".

McCarthy, M. (2016). Putting the CEFR to good use: Designing grammars based on learner-corpus evidence. *Language Teaching, 49*(1), 99–115. This is a convincing demonstration of the powerful evidence offered by learner corpora to inform grammar teaching. The framework for the article is that of the English Profile project.

References

Black, M., & Sharp, W. (2006a). *Objective IELTS intermediate workbook with answers.* Cambridge University Press.

Black, M., & Sharp, W. (2006b). *Objective IELTS intermediate student's book.* Cambridge University Press.

Capel, A. (2014). *Objective first, 100 writing tips for Cambridge English: First.* Cambridge University Press.

Carter, R., & McCarthy, M. (2006). *Cambridge Grammar of English: A comprehensive guide.* Cambridge University Press.

Centre for English Corpus Linguistics. (2020). Learner corpora around the world. Université Catholique de Louvain. https://uclouvain.be/en/research-institutes/ilc/cecl/learner-corpora-around-the-world.html

Chen, M., & Flowerdew, J. (2018). A critical review of research and practice in data-driven learning (DDL) in the academic writing classroom. *International Journal of Corpus Linguistics, 23*(3), 335–369. https://doi.org/10.1075/ijcl.16130.che

Cotos, E. (2014). Enhancing writing pedagogy with learner corpus data. *ReCALL, 26*(2), 202–224. https://doi.org/10.1017/S0958344014000019

De Cock, S., & Granger, S. (2005). Computer learner corpora and monolingual learners' dictionaries: The perfect match. *Lexicographica, 20,* 72–86. https://doi.org/10.1515/9783484604674.72

Flowerdew, L. (2001). The exploitation of small learner corpora in EAP materials design. In M. Ghadessy, A. Henry, & R. L. Roseberry (Eds.), *Small corpus studies and ELT: Theory and practice* (pp. 363–379). Benjamins. https://doi.org/10.1075/scl.5.21flo

Flowerdew, L. (2012). *Corpora and language education.* Palgrave Macmillan. https://doi.org/10.1057/9780230355569

Fuster-Márquez, M., & Gregori-Signes, C. (2018). Learning from learners: A non-standard direct approach to the teaching of writing skills in EFL in a university context. *Innovation in Language Learning and Teaching, 12*(2), 164–176. https://doi.org/10.1080/17501229.2016.1142549

Gillard, P., & Gadsby, A. (1998). Using a learners' corpus in compiling ELT dictionaries. In S. Granger (Ed.), *Learner English on computer* (pp. 159–171). Longman.

Gilquin, G. (2019, August 28-31). *Screencasting and keylogging as pedagogical tools to enhance writing skill development* [Paper presentation]. 27th EUROCALL conference, Louvain-la-Neuve, Belgium.

Gilquin, G. (2021a). One norm to rule them all? Corpus-derived norms in learner corpus research and foreign language teaching. *Language Teaching, 55*(1), 87–99. https://doi.org/10.1017/S0261444821000094

Gilquin, G. (2021b). Hic sunt dracones: Exploring some *terra incognita* in learner corpus research. In A. Čermáková & M. Malá (Eds.), *Variation in time and space: Observing the world through corpora* (pp. 65–86). De Gruyter.

Gilquin, G. (2022). The *Process Corpus of English in Education*: Going beyond the written text. *Research in Corpus Linguistics, 10*(1), 31–44. https://doi.org/10.32714/ricl.10.01.02

Gilquin, G., & Granger, S. (2010). How can data-driven learning be used in language teaching? In A. O'Keeffe & M. McCarthy (Eds.), *The Routledge handbook of corpus linguistics* (pp. 359–370). Routledge.

Gilquin, G., & Granger, S. (2021). The passive and the lexis-grammar interface: An inter-varietal perspective. In S. Granger (Ed.), *Perspectives on the L2 phrasicon: The view from learner corpora* (pp. 72–98). Multilingual Matters.

Gilquin, G., Granger, S., & Paquot, M. (2007a). Writing sections. In M. Rundell (Ed.), *Macmillan English dictionary for advanced learners* (2nd ed.) (pp. IW1–IW29). Macmillan.

Gilquin, G., Granger, S., & Paquot, M. (2007b). Learner corpora: The missing link in EAP pedagogy. *Journal of English for Academic Purposes, 6*(4), 319–335. https://doi.org/10.1016/j.jeap.2007.09.007

Gilquin, G., & Laporte, S. (2021). The use of online writing tools by learners of English: Evidence from a process corpus. *International Journal of Lexicography, 34*(4), 472–492. https://doi.org/10.1093/ijl/ecab012

Granger, S. (1993). The International Corpus of Learner English. In J. Aarts, P. de Haan, & N. Oostdijk (Eds.), *English language corpora: Design, analysis and exploitation* (pp. 57–69). Rodopi.

Granger, S. (2009). The contribution of learner corpora to second language acquisition and foreign language teaching: A critical evaluation. In K. Aijmer (Ed.), *Corpora and language teaching* (pp. 13–32). Benjamins. https://doi.org/10.1075/scl.33.04gra

Granger, S. (2015). The contribution of learner corpora to reference and instructional materials design. In S. Granger, G. Gilquin, & F. Meunier (Eds.), *The Cambridge handbook of learner corpus research* (pp. 485–510). Cambridge University Press. https://doi.org/10.1017/CBO9781139649414.022

Granger, S. (2018). Has lexicography reaped the full benefit of the (learner) corpus revolution? In J. Čibej, V. Gorjanc, I. Kosem, & S. Krek (Eds.), *Proceedings of the XVIII EURALEX international congress: Lexicography in global contexts* (pp. 17–24). Ljubljana University Press. https://euralex.org/category/publications/euralex-2018/

Granger, S., Gilquin, G., & Meunier, F. (Eds.). (2015). *The Cambridge handbook of learner corpus research*. Cambridge University Press. https://doi.org/10.1017/CBO9781139649414

Granger, S., & Tribble, C. (1998). Learner corpus data in the foreign language classroom: Form-focused instruction and data-driven learning. In S. Granger (Ed.), *Learner English on computer* (pp. 199–209). Longman.

Hadkins, H., Lewis, S., & Budden, J. (2011). *Interactive. Student's book 2*. Cambridge University Press.

Harwood, N. (2005). What do we want EAP teaching materials for? *Journal of English for Academic Purposes*, *4*(2), 149–161. https://doi.org/10.1016/j.jeap.2004.07.008

Hashemi, L., & Thomas, B. (2010). *Objective PET. Student's book with answers*. Cambridge University Press.

Kreyer, R. (2015). The Marburg corpus of intermediate learner English (MILE). In M. Callies & S. Götz (Eds.), *Learner corpora in language testing and assessment* (pp. 13–34). Benjamins. https://doi.org/10.1075/scl.70.01kre

Lee, D., & Swales, J. (2006). A corpus-based EAP course for NNS doctoral students: Moving from available specialized corpora to self-compiled corpora. *English for Specific Purposes*, *25*(1), 56–75. https://doi.org/10.1016/j.esp.2005.02.010

Lee, J., Sturgeon, D., & Luo, M. (2016). *A CALL system for learning preposition usage*. Proceedings of the 54th annual meeting of the association for computational linguistics, Association for Computational Linguistics (pp. 984–993). Berlin, August 7–12.

Lee, J., Yan Yeung, C., Zeldes, A., Reznicek, M., Lüdeling, A., & Webster, J. (2015). CityU corpus of essay drafts of English language learners: A corpus of textual revision in second language writing. *Language Resources and Evaluation*, *49*(3), 659–683. https://doi.org/10.1007/s10579-015-9301-z

Leech, G. (1997). Teaching and language corpora: A convergence. In A. Wichmann, S. Fligelstone, T. McEnery, & G. Knowles (Eds.), *Teaching and language corpora* (pp. 1–23). Longman.

Leech, G. (1998). Preface. In S. Granger (Ed.), *Learner English on computer* (pp. xiv–xx). Longman.

Liou, H.-C., Wang, S. H., & Hung-Yeh, Y. (1992). Can grammatical CALL help EFL writing instruction? *CALICO Journal*, *10*(1), 23–44.

Lo, Y.-C., Chen, J.-J., Yang, C.-Y., & Chang, J. S. (2018). *Cool English: A grammatical error correction system based on large learner corpora*. In *System Demonstrations*. Proceedings of the 27th international conference on computational linguistics (pp. 82–85). Santa Fe, New Mexico, August 20–26.

Lüdeling, A., & Hirschmann, H. (2015). Error annotation systems. In S. Granger, G. Gilquin, & F. Meunier (Eds.), *The Cambridge handbook of learner corpus research* (pp. 135–157). Cambridge University Press. https://doi.org/10.1017/CBO9781139649414.007

May, P. (2010). *First certificate trainer. Six practice tests with answers*. Cambridge University Press.

McCarthy, M. (2016). Putting the CEFR to good use: Designing grammars based on learner-corpus evidence. *Language Teaching*, *49*(1), 99–115. https://doi.org/10.1017/S0261444813000189

McCarthy, M., McCarten, J., & Sandiford, H. (2012). *Viewpoint 1. Student's book*. Cambridge University Press.

Meunier, F. (2012). Learner corpora in the classroom: A useful and sustainable didactic resource. In L. Pedrazzini & A. Nava (Eds.), *Learning and teaching English: Insights from research* (pp. 211–228). Polimetrica.

Moon, S., & Oh, S.-Y. (2017). Unlearning overgenerated *be* through data-driven learning in the secondary EFL classroom. *ReCALL*, *30*(1), 48–67. https://doi.org/10.1017/S0958344017000246

Moore, J. (2005). *Common mistakes at proficiency ... and how to avoid them*. Cambridge University Press.

Nesselhauf, N. (2004). Learner corpora and their potential for language teaching. In J. Sinclair (Ed.), *How to use corpora in language teaching* (pp. 125–152). Benjamins. https://doi.org/10.1075/scl.12.11nes

O'Keeffe, A., & Mark, G. (2017). The English grammar profile of learner competence: Methodology and key findings. *International Journal of Corpus Linguistics*, *22*(4), 457–489. https://doi.org/10.1075/ijcl.14086.oke

Puchta, H., & Stranks, J. (2007). *English in mind, Italian edition. Student's book 1* (2nd ed.). Cambridge University Press.

Reppen, R. (2012). *Grammar and beyond, level 1. Student's book.* Cambridge University Press.

Rundell, M. (Ed.). (2007). *Macmillan English dictionary for advanced learners* (2nd ed.). Macmillan Education.

Seidlhofer, B. (2002). Pedagogy and local learner corpora: Working with learning-driven data. In S. Granger, J. Hung, & S. Petch-Tyson (Eds.), *Computer learner corpora, second language acquisition and foreign language teaching* (pp. 213–234). Benjamins. https://doi.org/10.1075/lllt.6.14sei

Swan, M., & Smith, B. (1987). *Learner English. A teacher's guide to interference and other problems.* Cambridge University Press.

Thewissen, J. (2015). *Accuracy across proficiency levels: A learner corpus approach.* Presses Universitaires de Louvain.

Turton, N. D., & Heaton, J. B. (1996). *Longman dictionary of common errors.* Longman.

Urzúa, A. (2015). Corpora, context, and language teachers: Teacher involvement in a local learner corpus project. In V. Cortes & E. Csomay (Eds.), *Corpus-based research in applied linguistics. Studies in honor of Doug Biber* (pp. 99–122). Benjamins. https://doi.org/10.1075/scl.66.05urz

Walter, E. (2010). Using corpora to write dictionaries. In A. O'Keeffe & M. McCarthy (Eds.), *The Routledge handbook of corpus linguistics* (pp. 428–443). Routledge. https://doi.org/10.4324/9780203856949.ch31

20

SPOKEN LEARNER CORPORA FOR LANGUAGE TEACHING

Dana Gablasova and Raffaella Bottini

20.1 Introduction

When thinking about corpus-based approaches to language pedagogy, it is usually corpora representing first language (L1) speakers of the target language that come more readily to mind than learner corpora (Caines *et al.*, 2016; Huang, 2018). Despite this, learner corpora have a valid place in language teaching with their role acknowledged and highlighted repeatedly throughout the last two decades (e.g. Chambers, 2015; Huang, 2018; Mukherjee & Rohrbach, 2006; Nesselhauf, 2004). However, when it comes to the actual integration of learner corpus data into language teaching, written learner corpora have so far enjoyed considerably more attention than corpora representing spoken second language (L2) production (Friginal, 2018). This chapter discusses and illustrates issues involved in effective integration of data from spoken learner corpora into language teaching, contextualising this approach within more general trends in the use of native speaker and learner corpora in language pedagogy.

Speaking is a core means of communication and the teaching of speaking skills continues to be at the forefront of pedagogical attention of teachers and material developers (Hughes & Reed, 2017). However, despite the amount of attention and devoted effort, it remains a problematic area for learners. This is due to high demands on linguistic, cognitive, and social skills involved in producing and processing spoken communication taking place in real time, without the possibility to pause or edit the interaction (Leech, 2000). Furthermore, there still remain considerable issues related to the effectiveness of the resources available to teach spoken communication (Chan, 2017; Hughes & Reed, 2017; Wagner, 2014). For example, typical characteristics of speaking such as rephrased utterances, overlaps, and the use of discourse markers are often omitted from examples used in textbooks, and limited attention has been given to pragmatic skills (Carter & McCarthy, 2017; Hughes & Reed, 2017; Timmis, 2015). Corpora representing spoken L2 production offer an invaluable resource both for understanding the difficulties faced by L2 users in spoken communication and for developing teaching resources that can help overcome these problems.

DOI: 10.4324/9781003002901-24

20.2 Review of current state of research

This section provides an overview of research on the use of spoken learner corpora in language pedagogy. It first discusses the nature of spoken learner corpora before describing the directions in the application of data from these corpora in language teaching.

20.2.1 Spoken learner corpora

Learner corpora are specialised corpora representing language from L2 learners or L2 users. Specialised corpora, in contrast with general corpora, are characterised by a smaller size, a clearer contextualisation in terms of setting, communicative purpose, and participants, with a more narrowly defined population of language users (Friginal *et al.*, 2017). Spoken learner corpora contain transcripts of L2 learners' oral production and can also include video or audio files aligned with the transcripts. Transferring spoken language into an electronic format involves transcription of the data, which is a time-consuming and complex process, requiring a considerable degree of decision-making both before and during the transcription (De Cock, 2010; Gablasova *et al.*, 2019b). Some of the issues that need to be addressed when transcribing spoken learner production concern (interactive) language features such as overlaps, false starts, backchannelling, truncated words, unclear passages, as well as filled and unfilled pauses; others are related more specifically to learner speech and may include lexical, grammatical, and phonological errors and patterns linked to the speakers' L1 or their proficiency level (Meunier, 2016b). The following transcript illustrates some of these features. It is taken from the Trinity Lancaster Corpus (TLC) (Gablasova *et al.*, 2019b) of L2 English composed of 4.2 million words based on spoken language exams administered by Trinity College London. Each interaction recorded in the corpus involves two speakers: an L1 speaking examiner (S1) and an L2 learner (S2); in Example (1) below, the L2 speaker is an English learner from L1 Italian background and from the B1 level (lower-intermediate) of the Common European Framework of Reference for Languages (CEFR).

(1) S2: ah er I am very proud to be a Neapolitan
     S1: mm
     S2: and I know all aspect of my of my city
     S1: so
     S2: there are
     S1: why are you so proud to be Ne-Neapolitan?
     S2: erm no we are er we are funny sunny and erm
     S1: mm
     S2: we always smile
     S1: mm
     S2: yes <voc desc="laugh"/>

The extract demonstrates the occurrence of backchannel items (*mm, ah*), false starts (*Ne-Neapolitan*), filled pauses (*er, erm*), as well as non-verbal vocal sounds (*<voc desc="laugh"/>*). Elements such as these provide evidence of the real-time processing during spoken interaction which offers the speakers and listeners limited possibility of editing or controlling the language (Caines *et al.*, 2016). The extract also includes an example of a grammatical pattern that could be considered typical for lower-intermediate L2 English speakers (i.e. the lack of grammatical concord in *all aspect*). This kind of language data poses considerable challenges for corpus creation in terms of time, cost, and expertise required, likely contributing to the limited number of spoken learner corpora available (Friginal, 2018). Despite the availability of voice recognition software, manual transcription still remains the most accurate and reliable method of transcribing learner speech (e.g. Brezina *et al.*, 2019). With respect to automatic analysis of L2 language, although part-of-speech tagging of learner corpora can be considered sufficiently reliable (Van Rooy & Schäfer, 2003), features of learner language such as missing words and lexical mistakes can cause problems with automatic annotation of these corpora (Meunier, 2016b) and may require further manual input.

Compared to written learner corpora, there is still a relatively small number of spoken learner corpora available, although the number is increasing steadily. In terms of the target language, currently, most of these corpora represent L2 users and learners of English (Friginal, 2018). As regards the nature of language data, spoken learner corpora contain one or more language samples from the same speakers. In the latter case, the samples of learner production can be elicited through different speaking tasks or collected over-time (as in the Longitudinal Database of Learner English, LONGDALE; Meunier, 2016a), although longitudinal corpora of L2 speech are still rare. With respect to the different speaking tasks, language in these corpora can represent different linguistic settings and genres; for example, corpora of both monologic (e.g. picture descriptions and presentations) and dialogic (e.g. role plays and discussions) speech are available, such as the 1.9-million-word International Corpus Network of Asian Learners of English (ICNALE) (Ishikawa, 2019). The linguistic setting in which the L2 production is collected can range from informal exchanges in class (e.g. The Young Learner Corpus of English, YoLeCorE; Mattheoudakis, 2014) to formal language use during exams (e.g. the Guangwai-Lancaster Chinese Learner Corpus; Xu *et al.*, 2017), and include different genres such as academic language, as illustrated by the Multilingual Academic Corpus of Assignments: Writing and Speech (MACAWS) (Staples *et al.*, 2019).

L2 users represented in spoken learner corpora vary in relation to learner characteristics such as proficiency in the target language, first language (L1) and cultural background, age, education, and learning history. Proficiency can be determined by trained raters – as in the Trinity Lancaster Corpus (TLC), which includes speakers that range from the B1 (lower-intermediate) to the C2 (advanced) level of the CEFR – or defined institutionally – for example in the Louvain International Database of Spoken English Interlanguage (LINDSEI) (Gilquin *et al.*, 2010) whose speakers range from the upper-intermediate to the advanced level according to their university requirements. Some of these corpora are homogenous in terms of the population, for example, representing learners from a single L1 background (e.g. the Corpus of Chinese Learners of Italian, COLI; Forti & Spina, 2019) or from a specific age band (e.g. the College Learners' Spoken English Corpus of L1 Chinese; Yang & Wei, 2005), as opposed to corpora, such as the TLC, that include L2 speakers from various L1 backgrounds as well as a wide age range.

20.2.2 *Integrating spoken learner corpora into language teaching*

Two routes for integrating learner corpora into language teaching are usually distinguished (Huang, 2018; Römer, 2011). First, corpus findings can be used indirectly to develop reference materials such as dictionaries and grammar books as well as language curricula. Second, teachers and learners can work with corpus data directly, whether by accessing the corpus data online or in paper-based materials. This section describes the trends in how data from spoken learner corpora have been used, both directly and indirectly, in language pedagogy.

20.2.2.1 Indirect uses of spoken learner corpora in language pedagogy

The indirect use of spoken learner corpora in language pedagogy draws on findings from learner corpus research. Corpus-based investigations of L2 speech have been very productive so far (Friginal *et al.*, 2017) – even if most of the focus of this research has been on L2 English. Studies have examined monologic and dialogic speech (e.g. Chen & Xu, 2019; Gablasova *et al.*, 2017), different genres (e.g. Jones *et al.*, 2017 on academic language) and linguistic subsystems – such as pragmatics (e.g. Lam, 2009), lexicon (e.g. Shirato & Stapleton, 2007), formulaic language (e.g. Gilquin, 2015), and grammar (e.g. Römer & Garner, 2019). For example, De Cock (2010) reports on a study of L2 English speech from LINDSEI to examine learner use of evaluative adjectives (such as *good* and *bad*) that convey attitudes and feelings. Comparing the L2 results to L1 production, she observed that L2 speakers rarely used evaluative adjectives in sentential relative clauses to comment on a previous sentence (e.g. *I've got other people to hitch with which is good*), a structure which is favoured by L1 speakers. The author argues that teaching materials should include this type of clause to enable learners to express attitudinal stance and better manage the pressure of online processing in unplanned conversation using sentential relative clauses as an "add-on strategy". In another example, the findings from the International Teaching Assistants corpus (ITAcorp) (Thorne *et al.*, 2008) – which represents speech of advanced L2 users of English – were used to identify problematic areas (e.g. the formulation of directives) in spoken L2 communication, inspiring a change in the curriculum and leading to the introduction of new training materials (based on the L1/expert language from the Michigan Corpus of Academic Spoken English, MICASE; Simpson *et al.*, 2002). Overall, research on spoken learner corpora can be very effective in identifying and describing communicative features that are avoided or used inappropriately by (a specific group of) learners and can serve as a starting point for pedagogical interventions. However, in reality, few of the findings are picked up by practitioners or material writers (Caines *et al.*, 2016; Chambers, 2019; Granger, 2015; Huang, 2018). It should be noted that this trend is not unique to corpus-based findings; rather, it is typical of the tendency in SLA research and the gap that exists between research and practice.

Reference materials – dictionaries, pedagogical grammars, and textbooks – have seen an increase in the use of corpora to describe spoken language, although this involves mainly L1 corpora (Meunier, 2016b). An example of a textbook that used a corpus of L1 and L2 (expert) speech is *Academic Interactions* (Feak *et al.*, 2009), which includes transcripts from MICASE to assist in teaching about properties of spoken academic discourse. However, such examples are still rare and research on language coursebooks and syllabus design has highlighted the scarce use of corpus-based information, whether involving L1 or L2 corpora, especially regarding pragmatic skills and spoken language features (Hughes & Reed, 2017; Nelson, this volume; Wagner, 2014). Caines *et al.* (2016) argue that language coursebooks focus on monodirectional speaking and rarely combine listening and speaking skills in tasks that replicate real-life conversational exchanges characterised by back-channelling, turn-taking, repair, negotiation and co-construction of meaning. Having acknowledged the effectiveness of corpus-informed resources, Meunier and Reppen (2015) recommend that researchers collect findings in an accessible format and provide material writers with guidelines regarding what language aspects to prioritise in order to facilitate the integration of corpus data into reference materials.

20.2.2.2 *Direct uses of spoken learner corpora in language pedagogy*

To date, accounts of direct uses of spoken learner data have been very rare in the literature on corpus-based language teaching (Chambers, 2015; Huang, 2018). The studies so far have reported on two types of learner corpora which have made their way into language classrooms: 1) the locally developed and 2) the publicly available corpora. A local corpus is usually built purely for pedagogical purposes, using production directly relevant to a specific context and to a group of learners – for example, assignments produced by students in a particular classroom (Chambers, 2015; Huang, 2018). The major advantage of local corpora lies in the fact that they enable learners to work with language directly relevant to their learning needs and context, which can, thus, foster learning gains as well as motivation. For example, a local longitudinal learner corpus can be very effective in highlighting learners' progress (Mukherjee & Rohrbach, 2006). Whereas local written corpora may be more readily created with students' assignments submitted electronically, there are, at present, no reliable means of automatically transferring spoken language into transcripts which could facilitate the task of building local spoken corpora (Brezina *et al.*, 2019). One possible way of overcoming the issue is through integrating the transcription of spoken data into the learning process (Lynch, 2001). Describing a project that involved the creation of a local spoken corpus of L2 English with students at the University of Murcia, Pérez-Paredes (2003) notes that collaborative transcribing and editing can be particularly beneficial in guiding learners' attention to the target forms and issues in their production.

Despite the pedagogical value of local corpora, their use has been limited due to the time and effort involved in their construction, especially in the case of spoken data. It is, therefore, the publicly accessible learner corpora that have been used more often in language teaching. These corpora are created primarily for research purposes and are, thus, typically larger and more systematically built than local corpora. The learners and tasks they represent may not be directly relevant to specific learning contexts (Mukherjee & Rohrbach, 2006), but these corpora are particularly effective at highlighting and teaching patterns relevant to L2 production in general. Additionally, they can be further localised by selecting data that match the local population in terms of learner characteristics (e.g. L1 background or learner demographics such as age) and learning needs (e.g. oral presentations, topics of interests) (Ackerley & Coccetta, 2007; Nesselhauf, 2004). For example, Mukherjee and Rohrbach (2006) describe how the German component of LINDSEI (i.e. the data from 50 L1 German speakers included in the corpus) was used to analyse the distribution of discourse markers in this group; this sub-corpus could be used directly with German learners of English to look at patterns that may be, to some extent, typical of this learner group.

Spoken learner corpora have so far been integrated into the teaching of a number of areas related to pragmatic and linguistic characteristics of spoken communication, embracing both speaker and listener roles. Gablasova and Brezina (2017) and Gablasova *et al.* (2019b) drew on the Trinity Lancaster Corpus to create teaching materials on several features of spoken interactive communication in English, such as disagreeing, asking (clarifying) questions, taking an active role in the interaction, showing fluency of conversation and active listenership (the materials are available from www.trinitycollege.com). Pérez-Paredes (2003) focused on issues related to pronunciation and flow of speech (e.g. contracted forms and word linking), while Ackerley and Coccetta (2007) used the Padova Multimedia English Corpus – which includes oral communication of L2 speakers of English from a number of L1 backgrounds – to guide learners' attention towards word meanings and, more generally, to enhance their comprehension and communicative skills. In the teaching materials so far, the data from learner corpora have been presented both in the form of transcripts (e.g. Feak *et al.*, 2009; Gablasova *et al.*, 2019b; Thorne *et al.*, 2008) and in a multimodal format, with access to audio and video files (e.g. Ackerley & Coccetta, 2007; Pérez-Paredes, 2003).

20.3 Core issues and topics

This section addresses issues considered crucial for effective integration of spoken learner corpora in language teaching and discusses possible solutions that can help with overcoming these challenges.

First of all, any successful application of spoken learner corpora in language teaching has to address the general issues related to bringing corpora into the classroom (Gilquin & Granger, 2010; Schaeffer-Lacroix, 2019). Difficulties experienced by learners when working with corpus data include dealing with cut-off sentences, unfamiliar vocabulary, large amounts of data, and problems with understanding the context in which the target form appears (Chambers, 2015; Geluso & Yamaguchi, 2014). These issues may prevent learners from noticing the target patterns in language use and contribute to frustration and decreased motivation (Kaltenböck & Mehlmauer-Larcher, 2005). Many of these difficulties are likely to be even further exacerbated when working with spoken learner corpora due to the "messy" nature of spoken communication characterised by features such as overlaps, unfinished sentences, repairs, contextual references, and rapid changes in the topic of the discourse (Carter & McCarthy, 2017; Leech, 2000). It is important to acknowledge that many of the elements that could be perceived as problematic by learners do not represent a "fault" in the data but rather reflect the inherent complexity of spoken (interactive) communication which is then recorded in the corpus. Such data, therefore, offer an opportunity to expose learners to typical aspects of authentic spoken language, which are often missing from teaching materials (Hughes & Reed, 2017; McCarthy & McCarten, this volume; Wagner, 2014). This helps them successfully transfer the skills acquired in the classroom to target contexts such as conversations outside pedagogical settings, which has been identified as problematic for L2 learners (Larsen-Freeman, 2013). Further, it should be stressed that the "messy" language is not unique to L2 speech. It may be, thus, effective to create activities which compare L1 and L2 spoken production and guide learners to notice similarities, rather than drawing their attention to the differences between the two groups (as is the common practice). In addition to teaching about properties of spoken language, such activities would help learners understand that features which they may have perceived as typical of learner language (e.g. hesitations, missing words, filled/unfilled pauses, and unfinished sentences) are to a large extent typical of spoken production in general (Chan, 2017; Leech, 2000). Such awareness-raising exercises can positively influence student motivation and their willingness to communicate orally in and outside of the classroom.

Even if the complexity of spoken production as captured in corpus data is regarded as a valuable asset in teaching, it may still prove frustrating for students to encounter such language and to be asked to work with it (Chan, 2017; Wagner, 2014). Appropriate instructions and training are one way of helping students cope with corpus data and ensure the success of corpus-based teaching approaches, both in terms of linguistic outcomes and experience with the method (Leńko-Szymańska, this volume; Sripicharn, 2010). Using spoken learner production is also an effective strategy to control the complexity of language that could make the input too difficult for learners to process, thus hindering rather than fostering their learning (Wagner, 2014); for example, a high proportion of unfamiliar vocabulary items could prevent learners from noticing the target patterns. When using L2 production, language examples from appropriate proficiency levels can be selected, gradually scaffolding the input presented to learners; even using production of advanced L2 speakers can prove more accessible than that of L1 speakers and help control the range of language used (Cook, 1999). Moreover, production from L2 speakers whose linguistic and cultural background matches that of the learners can provide further scaffolding since learners can work with familiar language in terms of accent and cultural context (Hughes & Reed, 2017).

Next, there are several pedagogical issues related to working with (spoken) learner language which may contain errors or patterns not typical of L1 production. One of the key challenges lies in exposing learners to examples of language used incorrectly and thus potentially reinforcing their own use of such patterns (Chambers, 2015; Gablasova *et al.*, 2019b; Nesselhauf, 2004). This may be especially problematic when learners work with corpus data independently without direct guidance from a teacher since they may not be able to recognise erroneous patterns and know how to interpret the evidence from a learner corpus. Furthermore, learners may be reluctant to use sources that they perceive as non-authoritative and containing errors (Llurda, 2016; Timmis, 2012). Different strategies have been proposed for dealing with these difficulties, for instance, drawing explicit attention to learner errors and using them as a source of learning in the classroom (e.g. Fuster-Márquez & Gregori-Signes, 2018; Mendikoetxea *et al.*, 2010; Nesselhauf, 2004) as well as in textbooks and reference materials (e.g. Longman Dictionary of Common Learner Errors; Turton & Heaton, 1996). Working with errors – especially if directly related to learners' own learning context as in local corpora – is a powerful learning method. Nesselhauf (2004) emphasises the value of error analysis when dealing with areas of language that have not improved using other teaching methods, noting that when working with their own language, "instead of being told once again that what they are doing is wrong, learners have the opportunity to get something right, namely to identify and explain the mistake in question" (p. 140). However, the majority of studies reporting pedagogical uses of error analysis of learner corpus data have so far relied on written corpora (e.g. Fuster-Márquez & Gregori-Signes, 2018; Mendikoetxea *et al.*, 2010), despite encouraging evidence that it could be successfully applied to spoken learner data as well. For instance, Pérez-Paredes (2003) reports using spoken learner data to draw learners' attention to their pronunciation errors. Several spoken learner corpora are already error-tagged and can be used in error identification activities, such as the Guangwai-Lancaster Chinese Learner Corpus representing spoken and written production from learners of Chinese (Chen & Xu, 2019).

In addition to error analysis, Gablasova *et al.* (2019b) discuss three further strategies to establish a reference point for interpreting patterns in learner data, demonstrating each with a case study based on L2 spoken production from the Trinity Lancaster Corpus (TLC). First, learner data can be effectively contrasted with L1 spoken production and learners' attention drawn to the target features. This is a very common approach adopted both in research and in pedagogy (Chambers, 2015; Friginal, 2018; Timmis, 2015), often in combination with error analysis. The second strategy draws on comparing L2 speakers from different proficiency levels in the target language, with the production from higher proficiency levels serving as a reference point (Gablasova & Brezina, 2017). The final strategy relies on using language from "successful" L2 learners, either expert users in the target domain (e.g. academic writing) or learners who have reached a high mark in their exams (Jones *et al.*, 2017). Successful L2 spoken production can be found, for example, in the European Corpus of Academic Talk (EuroCoAT) (MacArthur *et al.*, 2014), which contains consultations between students and staff members at five European universities, or among L2 speakers who received high marks for their oral performance in the Guangwai-Lancaster and the TLC corpora. Presenting learners with "positive evidence" using spoken learner data is especially motivating since, as Mukherjee (2009) puts it,

> psychologically, learners react much more positively to the use of positive evidence obtained from learner data because they do not get the impression of learner output being treated exclusively as a hotch-potch of mistakes and errors – it is neither desirable nor useful to establish a rigid dichotomy between good and correct usage in native data on the one hand and bad and incorrect usage in learner output on the other. (p. 213)

Turning to affective and ideological factors involved in using data from spoken learner corpora, previous research has suggested that L2 learners may be reluctant to learn from non-native speakers of the target language, be it other learners or teachers (Llurda, 2016; Mukherjee & Rohrbach, 2006; Timmis, 2012; Yoshida, 2008). Arguably, working with learner data offers the opportunity to discuss such response from the students – which is often related to what is perceived as standard English in the given context – and examine it critically (Flowerdew, 2012). Further, L2 learners may benefit from exposure to "a diversity of *Englishes* in order for them to be well-prepared to understand English spoken by speakers from anywhere of the world" (Llurda, 2016, p. 57). Thus, using corpora representing the English as a Lingua Franca (ELF) and English as an International Language (EIL) populations – such as the Vienna-Oxford International Corpus of English (VOICE, 2013), the corpus of English as a Lingua Franca in Academic settings (ELFA, 2008), the ITAcorp, and the EuroCoAT – can provide models of language reference that are, from a pedagogical perspective, equally valuable as those offered by corpora representing speakers from the British or American English varieties (O'Keeffe *et al.*, 2007; Timmis, 2015).

20.4 Current contributions and recommendations for practice

This section presents a case study based on the Trinity Lancaster Corpus (TLC) to demonstrate how data from a spoken learner corpus can be integrated into language teaching, while illustrating some of the challenges and solutions discussed in Section 20.3. In this study, the corpus first serves to establish patterns in L2 production to determine what type of intervention, in terms of curriculum and target features, is appropriate; next, the data from the corpus are used to create teaching materials. Specifically, the case study focuses on (polite) disagreement in spoken, interactive English as described in Gablasova and Brezina (2017). The rationale for choosing this speech act is two-fold: to demonstrate 1) how spoken language corpora can contribute to the teaching of speaking and pragmatic skills and 2) how learner data can be used to raise awareness of variation and choice in language.

The analysis of the TLC investigated how L2 speakers at three different proficiency levels (lower-intermediate, intermediate, and advanced) expressed a particular type of disagreement, the so-called "yes, but" or "weak" disagreement due to an element of hedging already present in it by the seeming agreement. The corpus was searched for a range of surface forms conveying this type of disagreement such as *I agree but*, *yeah but*, and *you are right, however*. The results showed a clear trend in the increase of such forms of disagreements related to rising proficiency level. Moreover, higher proficiency was also linked to more complex politeness strategies accompanying these disagreements, signalled by a range of mitigating markers such as hedges, filled and unfilled pauses, delays, laughter, and hesitation markers.

	Example	Your score
A	I completely disagree with this because er I I repeat as I said …	
B	I agree with this point but don't you think maybe the fact that times are changing is a good thing?	
C	but I personally would disagree that that money would necessarily be spent on that	
D	erm no no it's not so	
E	well I'm not totally convinced but er you know I live in a really traditional family	
F	mm I can understand your opinion erm but I was still wondering …	
G	I can't agree with you	
H	er er I I think erm I I think they I I think they are wrong	
I	I think they're completely wrong	
J	no way	
K	I I I can understand what you're saying but I'm not I don't agree with that	

Figure 20.1   Teaching about disagreement (adapted from Gablasova & Brezina, 2017, p. 85)

While L2 speakers at lower-intermediate and intermediate levels used some of these markers, the advanced speech contained them systematically and in more sophisticated combinations.

These findings can inform pedagogical decisions about the intervention appropriate for different proficiency levels. For example, L2 speakers at lower proficiency levels would benefit from using some strategies to mitigate the negative impact of disagreements, while those at higher proficiency levels, who are already using these strategies consistently, could be encouraged to extend the range further. Figure 20.1 shows an exercise, developed using the TLC data from different proficiency levels, in which learners are asked to rank sentences according to how effective they are at expressing opposing views politely with the aim of raising their awareness of more/less direct disagreement strategies and the potential impact they can have on the interlocutors (see Gablasova & Brezina, 2017 for a full description of the activity). The full worksheet entitled "How to disagree politely in spoken English" can be found on the website of the *Corpus for Schools* project (wp. lancs.ac.uk/corpusforschools/) which focuses on developing resources for teaching spoken English.

This exercise illustrates spoken learner data used in offline, printed materials. While it gives learners the opportunity to work with positive evidence from learner language (Mukherjee, 2009), it is based on examples selected by the material writers, giving them control over the data presented to learners and addressing concerns about exposing learners to erroneous language use (e.g. Nesselhauf, 2004). When drawing on the corpus to develop teaching materials, examples from lower-proficiency levels were selected to demonstrate more direct, thus potentially less polite, expressions of disagreement. Speech from "successful" learners of English, defined as advanced L2 speakers, was searched in the TLC to find examples of more complex use of politeness markers. These examples were more sophisticated than those typically found at lower-intermediate and intermediate levels in the corpus, yet still remained more accessible to learners at lower levels than those from L1 speech, providing more scaffolding (Cook, 1999). Using an activity aimed at pragmatic skills also offers a suitable opportunity to discuss notions such as politeness, social norms and cultural differences in learners' L1 and L2, noting potential differences in expectations regarding linguistic marking of politeness (Flowerdew, 2012). Additionally, if allowed by the corpus, the exercise could be further localised by restricting the search to examples from speakers whose L1 and cultural background is similar to the target group of learners.

Going beyond the teaching application described in Gablasova and Brezina (2017), it is possible to (partly) replicate and expand the activity by giving learners direct access to the data in the TLC using the TLCHub (corpora.lancs.ac.uk/trinity/) (Gablasova *et al.*, 2019b), an online interface for accessing the corpus. The platform allows typing the target phrase (e.g. *yes but*) and searching for patterns in the concordance lines, while also limiting the search according to the learners' proficiency, L1 and cultural background. Learners can thus easily work with language from the more "successful" L2 speakers or contrast learners from different proficiency levels in order to identify the target patterns. This type of search gives learners greater learning autonomy and enhances their discovery learning, while allowing them to control the amount or type of language data to which they are exposed.

Further, the activity can incorporate the production of L1 speakers to be contrasted with that of L2 speakers, one of the recommended ways of using L2 data discussed in Section 20.3. This could involve paper-based or online access to the data. To do so, teachers can use BNClab (corpora.lancs.ac.uk/bnclab/) (Brezina *et al.*, 2018), a platform offering access to five million words from the British National Corpus 2014 (Love *et al.*, 2017) which represents informal spoken conversation between British English speakers. BNClab provides a pedagogically-oriented interface for searching the corpus, displaying the results according to speakers' gender, age, and social class. Searching for the same forms in BNClab and TLCHub, learners can easily access L1 and L2 examples of disagreements. As suggested in Section 20.3, the L1 speech can be used not only to identify differences, but also similarities with L2 spoken communication. Example (2) below of a "yes but" disagreement, taken from an L1 speaker of British English in BNClab, shows repetitions and unfinished sentences that could be used for such a demonstration.

(2)   I agree but they also the system shouldn't be allowing that I don't know whoever said why don't we have all of these these students being able to email their lecturers or

Such contrastive activities can help overcome the impression created by the language presented in textbooks that spoken communication is "neat and tidy, with interlocutors saying exactly what they intend to say and nothing more" (Gilmore, 2004, p. 368), thus presenting learners with "a model that is both unrealistic and unattainable" (Gilmore, 2004, p. 368; see also Wagner, 2014). An example of a teaching material focusing directly on highlighting similarities in L1 and L2 speech can be seen in the worksheet available from the Corpus for Schools website and entitled "What does spoken English *really* look like?" (italicised emphasis in the original). One of the exercises in the worksheet uses extracts from both L1 (the British National Corpus, 2014) and L2 (the TLC) spoken corpora demonstrating various disfluencies (e.g. filled pauses, unfinished sentences, lexical gaps). Learners are invited to guess which examples were taken from L1 and which from L2 speakers, raising their awareness of typical aspects of spoken communication common for both groups of speakers.

It was possible to showcase only part of the full potential of spoken learner corpora in the case study above. As shown by Pérez-Paredes (2003) and Ackerley and Coccetta (2007), in addition to accessing spoken learner corpora through transcripts, audio and video files can further enrich teaching by giving information about intonation, gestures, and facial expressions that are crucial for interpreting the meaning in interaction and for understanding the interlocutors' stance, emotions, and mood (Braun, 2005; Friginal *et al.*, 2017). Other corpora of L2 speech also include access to video/audio files that could be implemented in pedagogical practice (e.g. EuroCoAT, ITAcorp, the LONGDALE project). Practitioners and material developers are also encouraged to explore further innovative and creative ways of using spoken L2 production with learners. For example, Chan (2017) integrated transcripts of authentic L1 communication into her syllabus and contrasted them with spoken learner language from role plays in order to teach business conversation. Simpson-Vlach and Leicher (2006) and Friginal (2018) provide suggestions for activities based on spoken corpus data – such as role-playing the transcript, predicting what will happen next in the transcript, or using frequency information to infer patterns in speech – that can be readily adapted for use with spoken learner data.

20.5 Future direction of research

As discussed throughout this chapter, at present, spoken learner data represent a very small portion in corpus-based language teaching (Friginal, 2018; Gablasova et al., 2019b). Given their pedagogical value, both for direct and indirect uses in teaching, it is clearly not the lack of interest but rather issues with access and availability that have limited the role played by these resources so far (Huang, 2018). It is, thus, crucial for more spoken learner corpora to be developed and made accessible for wider use, ideally further diversifying their target languages beyond English, with good examples of such effort being the recently developed Guangwai-Lancaster corpus of L2 Chinese (Xu et al., 2017) and the COPLE2 corpus of L2 Portuguese (Mendes et al., 2016). Longitudinal records of spoken language, such as the LANGSNAP (Languages and Social Networks Abroad) corpus (Tracy-Ventura et al., 2016), would be a particularly welcome addition to the pool of spoken learner corpora that can be drawn upon in language teaching. At the same time, where possible, creators of local corpora are strongly encouraged to make these accessible to larger audiences, as the tasks and learner characteristics may make them highly relevant to similar educational settings.

While arguing for the development of further corpus resources to reflect the diversity of learners and their needs, there are already a range of spoken learner corpora available to be accessed by learners or used in teaching materials (e.g. Friginal, 2018; see also Section 20.2.1 in this chapter for examples). Given the number and range of these corpora, there has been undoubtedly much greater involvement of spoken learner corpora in teaching practice than has been reported so far; however, currently there are very few published accounts giving details of integration of spoken learner data into teaching. The field would, therefore, benefit from systematic evaluation of using spoken learner data, providing evidence of linguistic gains based on the corpora, as well as attitudes and experience of teachers and students. This would allow addressing pedagogical, ideological, or practical issues involved in using spoken learner production which may be preventing this valuable pedagogical resource from being embraced more widely.

Finally, further effort needs to be directed towards the development of tools which provide an easier way to integrate spoken corpus data into language teaching. This would make it more feasible for teachers and learners to engage with corpora (Chambers, 2015; Friginal et al., 2017; Schaeffer-Lacroix, 2019) and to inform syllabus decisions and materials design in mainstream language teaching (Pérez-Paredes, 2019). In addition to more traditional corpus platforms for corpus analysis, possible new directions have been suggested with dedicated pedagogical online corpus platforms such as TLCHub and BNClab. Further models and platforms for multimodal access through specific software should be also provided to take full advantage of the video and audio information that plays an essential part in spoken communication (Ackerley & Coccetta, 2007; Braun, 2005; Friginal et al., 2017).

Further reading

Friginal, E., Lee, J. J., Polat, B., & Roberson, A. (2017). *Exploring spoken English learner language using corpora*. Palgrave Macmillan. The book offers a useful overview of a number of spoken learner corpora of English, representing different domains and registers.

Gablasova, D., Brezina, V., & McEnery, T. (2019a). The Trinity Lancaster Corpus. Applications in language teaching and materials development. In S. Götz & J. Mukherjee (Eds.), *Learner corpora and language teaching* (pp. 7–28). Benjamins. The chapter describes and illustrates different ways in which a publicly available spoken learner corpus can be used in the development of teaching materials.

Jones, C., Byrne, S., & Halenko, N. (2017). *Successful spoken English: Findings from learner corpora*. Routledge. The book demonstrates the use of a spoken learner corpus to investigate different aspects in spoken L2 production, with special emphasis on the areas important for successful communication.

References

Ackerley, K., & Coccetta, F. (2007). Enriching language learning through a multimedia corpus. *ReCALL, 19*(3), 351–370.

Braun, S. (2005). From pedagogically relevant corpora to authentic language learning contents. *ReCALL,, 17*(1), 47–64.

Brezina, V., Gablasova, D., & McEnery, T. (2019). Corpus-based approaches to spoken L2 production. *International Journal of Learner Corpus Research, 5*(2), 119–125.

Brezina, V., Gablasova, D., & Reichelt, S. (2018). *BNClab* [electronic resource]. Lancaster University. http://corpora.lancs.ac.uk/bnclab

Caines, A., McCarthy, M., & O'Keeffe, A. (2016). Spoken language corpora and pedagogical applications. In F. Farr & L. Murray (Eds.), *The Routledge handbook of language learning and technology* (pp. 348–61). Taylor & Francis. https://doi.org/10.4324/9781315657899

Carter, R., & McCarthy, M. (2017). Spoken grammar: Where are we and where are we going? *Applied Linguistics, 38*(1), 1–20. https://doi.org/10.1093/applin/amu080

Chambers, A. (2015). The learner corpus as a pedagogic corpus. In S. Granger, G. Gilquin, & F. Meunier (Eds.), *The Cambridge handbook of learner corpus research* (pp. 445–464). Cambridge University Press.

Chambers, A. (2019). Towards the corpus revolution? Bridging the research–practice gap. *Language Teaching, 52*(4), 460–475.

Chan, C. S. (2017). Investigating a research-informed teaching idea: The use of transcripts of authentic workplace talk in the teaching of spoken business English. *English for Specific Purposes, 46*, 72–89.

Chen, H., & Xu, H. (2019). Quantitative linguistics approach to interlanguage development: A study based on the Guangwai-Lancaster Chinese Learner Corpus. *Lingua, 230*, 1–15.

Cook, V. (1999). Going beyond the native speaker in language teaching. *TESOL Quarterly, 33*(2), 185–209.

De Cock, S. (2010). Spoken learner corpora and EFL teaching. In M. C. Campoy-Cubillo, B. Bellés-Fortuno, & M. L. Gea-Valor (Eds.), *Corpus-based approaches to English language teaching* (pp. 123–137). Continuum.

ELFA (2008). The Corpus of English as a Lingua Franca in Academic Settings. Retrieved September 10, 2020, from https://www.helsinki.fi/en/researchgroups/english-as-a-lingua-franca-in-academic-settings/research/elfa-corpus

Feak, C. B., Reinhart, S. M., & Rohlck, T. N. (2009). *Academic interactions: Communicating on campus*. Michigan University Press.

Flowerdew, J. (2012). Corpora in language teaching from the perspective of English as an international language. In L. Alsagoff, S. McKay, G. Hu, & W. A. Renandya (Eds.), *Principles and practices for teaching English as an international language* (pp. 226–243). Routledge.

Forti, L., & Spina, S. (2019*).* Corpora for linguists vs. corpora for learners: Bridging the gap in Italian L2 learning and teaching. *ELLE, 8*(2), 349–362.

Friginal, E. (2018). *Corpus linguistics for English teachers: Tools, online resources, and classroom activities*. Routledge.

Fuster-Márquez, M., & Gregori-Signes, C. (2018). Learning from learners: A non-standard direct approach to the teaching of writing skills in EFL in a university context. *Innovation in Language Learning and Teaching, 12*(2), 164–176.

Gablasova, D., & Brezina, V. (2017). Disagreement in L2 spoken English: From learner corpus research to corpus-based teaching materials. In V. Brezina & L. Flowerdew (Eds.), *Learner corpus research: New perspectives and applications* (pp. 69–89). Bloomsbury.

Gablasova, D., Brezina, V., & McEnery, T. (2019b). The Trinity Lancaster corpus: Development, description and application. *International Journal of Learner Corpus Research, 5*(2), 126–158.

Gablasova, D., Brezina, V., McEnery, T., & Boyd, E. (2017). Epistemic stance in spoken L2 English: The effect of task and speaker style. *Applied Linguistics, 38*(5), 613–637.

Geluso, J., & Yamaguchi, A. (2014). Discovering formulaic language through data-driven learning: Student attitudes and efficacy. *ReCALL, 26*(2), 225–242.

Gilmore, A. (2004). A comparison of textbook and authentic interactions. *ELT Journal, 58*(4), 363–374.

Gilquin, G. (2015). The use of phrasal verbs by French-speaking EFL learners. A constructional and collostructional corpus-based approach. *Corpus Linguistics and Linguistic Theory, 11*(1), 51–88.

Gilquin, G., Cook, D., & Granger, S. (2010). *LINDSEI Louvain international database of spoken English interlanguage.* Presses Universitaires de Louvain.

Gilquin, G., & Granger, S. (2010). How can data-driven learning be used in language teaching. In A. O'Keefe & M. McCarthy (Eds.), *The Routledge handbook of corpus linguistics* (pp. 359–370). Routledge.

Granger, S. (2015). The contribution of learner corpora to reference and instructional materials design. In S. Granger, G. Gilquin, & F. Meunier (Eds.), *The Cambridge handbook of learner corpus research* (pp. 485–510). Cambridge University Press.

Huang, L. S. (2018). Taking stock of corpus-based instruction in teaching English as an international language. *RELC Journal, 49*(3), 381–401.

Hughes, R., & Reed, B. S. (2017). *Teaching and researching speaking.* Taylor & Francis.

Ishikawa, S. (2019). The ICNALE spoken dialogue: A new dataset for the study of Asian learners' performance in L2 English interviews. *English Teaching, 74*(4), 153–177.

Kaltenböck, G., & Mehlmauer-Larcher, B. (2005). Computer corpora and the language classroom: On the potential and limitations of computer corpora in language teaching. *ReCALL, 17*(1), 65–84.

Lam, P. W. (2009). The effect of text type on the use of so as a discourse particle. *Discourse Studies, 11*(3), 353–72.

Larsen-Freeman, D. (2013). Transfer of learning transformed. *Language Learning, 63,* 107–129.

Leech, G. (2000). Grammars of spoken English: New outcomes of corpus-oriented research. *Language Learning, 50*(4), 675–724.

Llurda, E. (2016). 'Native speakers', English and ELT: Changing perspectives. In G. Hall (Ed.), *The Routledge handbook of English language teaching* (pp. 51–63). Routledge.

Love, R., Dembry, C., Hardie, A., Brezina, V., & McEnery, T. (2017). The spoken BNC2014: Designing and building a spoken corpus of everyday conversations. *International Journal of Corpus Linguistics, 22*(3), 319–344.

Lynch, T. (2001). Seeing what they meant: Transcribing as a route to noticing. *ELT Journal, 55*(2), 124–132.

MacArthur, F., Alejo, R., Piquer-Piriz, A., Amador-Moreno, C., Littlemore, J., Ädel, A., Krennmayr, T., & Vaughn, E. (2014). EuroCoAT. The European Corpus of Academic Talk. http://eurocoat.es

Mattheoudakis, M. (2014). Learner Corpora of English: Glimpses into learners' L2 development. In *Assessing and Analyzing Discourses. Proceedings of 4th Postgraduate Student Conference.* University of Athens.

Mendes, A., Antunes, S., Jansseen, M., & Gonçalves, A. (2016). The COPLE2 corpus: A learner corpus for Portuguese. In N. Calzolari, K. Choukri, T. Declerck, S. Goggi, M. Grobelnik, …, & S. Piperidis (Eds.), *Proceedings of the tenth Language Resources and Evaluation Conference–LREC'16* (pp. 3207–3214). European Language Resources Association. https://www.aclweb.org/anthology/volumes/L16-1/

Mendikoetxea, A., Murcia, S., & Rollinson, P. (2010). Focus on errors: Learner corpora as pedagogical tools. In M. C. Campoy-Cubillo, B. Bellés-Fortuno, & M. L. Gea-Valor (Eds.), *Corpus-based approaches to English language teaching* (pp. 180–194). Continuum.

Meunier, F. (2016a). Introduction to the LONGDALE project. In E. Castello, K. Ackerley, & F. Coccetta (Eds.), *Studies in learner corpus linguistics. Research and applications for foreign language teaching and assessment* (pp. 123–126). Peter Lang.

Meunier, F. (2016b). Learner corpora and pedagogical applications. In F. Farr & L. Murray (Eds.), *The Routledge handbook of language learning and technology* (pp. 493–507). Taylor & Francis. https://doi.org/10.4324/9781315657899

Meunier, F., & Reppen, R. (2015). Corpus versus non-corpus-informed pedagogical materials: Grammar as the focus. In D. Biber & R. Reppen (Eds.), *The Cambridge handbook of English corpus linguistics* (pp. 498–514). Cambridge University Press. https://doi.org/10.1017/CBO9781139764377

Mukherjee, J. (2009). The grammar of conversation in advanced spoken learner English. In K. Aijmer (Ed.), *Corpora and language teaching* (pp. 203–230). Benjamins. https://doi.org/10.1075/scl.33

Mukherjee, J., & Rohrbach, J. M. (2006). Rethinking applied corpus linguistics from a language pedagogical perspective: New departures in learner corpus research. In B. Kettemann & G. Marko (Eds.), *Planing, gluing and painting corpora: Inside the applied corpus linguist's workshop* (pp. 205–232). Peter Lang.

Nesselhauf, N. (2004). Learner corpora and their potential for language teaching. In J. Sinclair (Ed.), *How to use corpora in language teaching* (pp. 125–156). Benjamins. https://doi.org/10.1075/scl.12

O'Keeffe, A., McCarthy, M., & Carter, R. (2007). *From corpus to classroom: Language use and language teaching.* Cambridge University Press. https://doi.org/10.1017/CBO9780511497650

Pérez-Paredes, P. (2003). Integrating networked learner oral corpora into foreign language instruction. In S. Granger & S. Petch-Tyson (Eds.), *Extending the scope of corpus-based research: New applications, new challenges* (pp. 249–261). Rodopi.

Pérez-Paredes, P. (2019). A systematic review of the uses and spread of corpora and data-driven learning in CALL research during 2011–2015. *Computer Assisted Language Learning, 52*(1-2), 36–61. https://doi.org/10.1080/09588221.2019.1667832

Römer, U. (2011). Corpus research applications in second language teaching. *Annual Review of Applied Linguistics, 31,* 205–225. https://doi.org/10.1017/S0267190511000055

Römer, U., & Garner, J. R. (2019). The development of verb constructions in spoken learner English. Tracing effects of usage and proficiency. *International Journal of Learner Corpus Research, 5*(2), 207–230. https://doi.org/10.1075/ijlcr.17015.rom

Schaeffer-Lacroix, E. (2019). Barriers to trainee teachers' corpus use. In P. Crosthwaite (Ed.), *Data-driven learning for the next generation: Corpora and DDL for pre-tertiary learners* (pp. 47–64). Routledge. https://doi.org/10.4324/9780429425899

Shirato, J., & Stapleton, P. (2007). Comparing English vocabulary in a spoken learner corpus with a native speaker corpus: Pedagogical implications arising from an empirical study in Japan. *Language Teaching Research, 11*(4), 393–412. https://doi.org/10.1177/1362168807080960

Simpson, R. C., Briggs, S. L., Ovens, J., & Swales, J. M. (2002). *The Michigan corpus of academic spoken English.* The University of Michigan.

Simpson-Vlach, R. C., & Leicher, S. (2006). *The MICASE handbook: A resource for users of the Michigan corpus of academic spoken English.* Michigan Publishing. https://doi.org/10.3998/mpub.101203

Sripicharn, P. (2010). How can we prepare learners for using language corpora. In A. O'Keefe & M. McCarthy (Eds.), *The Routledge handbook of corpus linguistics,* (pp. 371–384). Routledge. https://doi.org/10.4324/9780203856949

Staples, S., Novikov, A., Picoral, A., & Sommer-Farias, B. (2019–). Multilingual Academic Corpus of Assignments - Writing and Speech. https://macaws.corporaproject.org/

Thorne, S., Reinhardt, J., & Golombek, P. (2008). Mediation as objectification in the development of professional academic discourse: A corpus-informed curricular innovation. In J. Lantolf & M. Poehner (Eds.), *Sociocultural theory and the teaching of second languages* (pp. 256–284). Equinox. https://doi.org/10.1558/equinox.29291

Timmis, I. (2012). Spoken language research and ELT: Where are we now? *ELT Journal, 66*(4), 514–522. https://doi.org/10.1093/elt/ccs042

Timmis, I. (2015). *Corpus linguistics for ELT: Research and practice.* Routledge. https://doi.org/10.4324/9781315715537

Tracy-Ventura, N., Mitchell, R., & McManus, K. (2016). The LANGSNAP longitudinal learner corpus. In M. Alonso-Ramos (Ed.), *Spanish Learner corpus research: Current trends and future perspectives* (pp. 117–142). Benjamins. https://doi.org/10.1075/scl.78

Turton, N., & Heaton, J. B. (1996). *Longman dictionary of common errors* (2nd ed.). Longman.

Van Rooy, B., & Schäfer, L. (2003). An evaluation of three POS taggers for the tagging of the Tswana learner English corpus. In D. Archer, P. Rayson, A. Wilson, & T. McEnery (Eds.), *Proceedings of the Corpus Linguistics2003 conference* (pp. 835–844). Lancaster University. http://ucrel.lancs.ac.uk/cl2003/preface.pdf

VOICE. (2013). The Vienna-Oxford International Corpus of English (version 2.0 Online). https://www.univie.ac.at/voice/page/index.php

Wagner, E. (2014). Using unscripted spoken texts in the teaching of second language listening. *TESOL Journal, 5*(2), 288–311. https://doi.org/10.1002/tesj.120

Xu, H., Brezina, V., & Xiao, R. (2017). Guangwai-Lancaster Chinese Learner Corpus. Retrieved September, 10, 2020, from https://www.sketchengine.eu/guangwai-lancaster-chinese-learner-corpus/

Yang, H., & Wei, N. (2005). *Construction and data analysis of a Chinese learner spoken English corpus.* Shanghai Foreign Language Education Press.

Yoshida, R. (2008). Learners' perception of corrective feedback in pair work. *Foreign Language Annals, 41*(3), 525–541. https://doi.org/10.1111/j.1944-9720.2008.tb03310.x

21

LEARNER CORPORA TO INFORM TESTING AND ASSESSMENT

Sandra Götz

21.1 Introduction

The field of testing and assessment is an interdisciplinary one in nature. It builds on theories and definitions from the fields of linguistics, applied linguistics, (second) language acquisition, and language teaching, while at the same time applying methodologies from the disciplines of testing, measurement, and evaluation (Shohamy *et al.*, 2017). Although the terms 'testing' and 'assessment' are often used interchangeably, there is a slight difference in use, as the term testing mainly refers to assessment practices in institutional contexts, whereas the term assessment is often used to refer to a more varied process of data gathering and interpretation (Chapelle & Plakans, 2013). In the field of Language Testing and Assessment (LTA), the main goal is to build a foundation for researching, theorizing, and constructing valid language tools for assessing and judging the quality of language through reliable assessments in order to measure the language ability of a speaker or writer. These assessments are typically performed through well-designed tasks that result in test scores, which, in turn, evaluate a speaker's or writer's proficiency level in a specific language skill or task. Language tests can thus be used for different purposes, for example, there is 'placement testing' (in order to define somebody's current language-learning needs), 'diagnostic testing' (in order to discover a language learner's area(s) of weakness), or 'proficiency testing' (in order to measure a language learner's proficiency level) (Barker *et al.*, 2015). The latter types of tests are used most frequently in the field of Foreign Language Teaching (FLT) and will hence be in the spotlight in the present chapter. In these types of proficiency tests, a learner's language abilities are typically assessed by measuring the test taker's language skills (such as listening, speaking, reading, or writing) based on their performance in a standardized language test. Trained raters usually assess the outcomes of these tests and interpret them in accordance with their expectations of what learners normally "can do" at particular levels of proficiency. One very influential testing framework is the Common European Framework of Reference (CEFR; Council of Europe, 2017). For spoken language, the framework suggests descriptor scales for five basic language competences, i.e. range, accuracy, fluency, interaction, and coherence, and distinguishes between six basic competence levels ascending from descriptions of basic users (A1, A2) to independent users (B1, B2) and finally to proficient users (C1, C2). Learners are classified according to different descriptions of proficiency at each level. As the original version of the

DOI: 10.4324/9781003002901-25

CEFR was designed to apply to all (foreign) languages worldwide, the Council of Europe has encouraged the development of Reference Level Descriptions (RLDs) for national and regional languages in order to be able to adapt the descriptors to local contexts and purposes. Although the process of calibrating the exact wording of the different proficiency levels in the CEFR has been a hugely complex process (North, 2000), the resulting descriptor scales have been described as being rather vague, so that it can sometimes be difficult for language testers to distinguish between the different proficiency levels (e.g. McCarthy, 2010; North, 2014; Wisniewski, 2017a). As a result, there has been an increasing awareness among researchers and CEFR-developers of the benefits of including more specific linguistic descriptors or "criterial features" (Hawkins & Buttery, 2010; Hawkins & Filipović, 2012) which may emerge from the analysis of learner corpora, i.e. large, electronic collections of authentic written (Gilquin, this volume) or spoken (Gablasova, this volume) learner texts (Callies & Götz, 2015; McCarthy, 2016; Park, 2014). Insights gained from learner corpus analyses have, thus, recently begun to be of great use in the field of LTA, especially in order to provide descriptions of the way proficiency can be operationalized quantitatively and across first languages (L1s) at different levels (Callies & Götz, 2015b). Two of the most useful ways of how learner corpus data can inform the field of LTA are that 1) "corpora provide empirical evidence that balances teachers' and test writers' intuitions and expertise in designing and rating assessments", and that 2) learner corpora "provide real language across a range of settings, thus positively enhancing what the test purports to measure" (Barker *et al.*, 2015, p. 512).

The present chapter offers an in-depth overview of the developments and current research in the field, highlights the benefits that learner corpora can bring to the field of LTA, and provides concrete recommendations as to how learner corpora can be of (even better) use to inform the field of LTA.

21.2 Review of current state of research

Learner corpora started to emerge in the late 1980s with the development of the International Corpus of Learner English (ICLE) (Granger, 2009). The quickly emerging field of learner corpus research was, at first, mainly concerned with finding ways to analyze these new types of data, to describe learner language empirically, and to measure how learner language is different from native language empirically (Granger, 2009). Despite the obvious parallels in research questions and research desiderata between learner corpus research and its neighboring fields, it took quite some time for learner corpus researchers to widen their scope. It is only recently that we see rapprochements with the field of FLT (e.g. Götz & Mukherjee, 2019) or the field of Second Language Acquisition (SLA) (e.g. Paquot this volume; Tracy-Ventura & Paquot, 2021).

The field of LTA, on the other hand, is a comparatively old discipline that can be traced back to the imperial civil service examination system in China. The use of written examinations as a tool of selection started already in the mid-Tang dynasty (618 to 907) and the first test of English for Speakers of other Languages was introduced in 1913 with the Certificate of Proficiency in English (Barker *et al.*, 2015). Probably due to long-standing traditions and established methodologies in the field of LTA, language testers only started to make use of (native) corpora to develop or validate language tests in the 1990s. In these early applications, test developers of most of the major language tests have typically relied on native corpus data in order to extract realistic and authentic representations of how native speakers of English use language in a certain genre. These native-speaker analyses have then served as benchmarks against which a test taker's performance can be assessed (see Section 21.3.1.2). Despite running the risk of falling prey to the "comparative fallacy" (Bley-Vroman, 1983), the number of language tests that are informed by native-speaker corpora is still comparatively high, whereas applications from actual learner corpus-based studies remain surprisingly low.

The main area of application of learner corpora to the field of LTA we can witness today is how learner corpora are analyzed to inform descriptor scales such as the CEFR. This is typically done on the basis of investigating one specific language feature (e.g. a grammatical feature such as article use) and describing in detail how learners' use of this feature develops with increasing proficiency level (e.g. Díez-Bedmar, 2015; Dumont, 2017; Götz, 2015; Thewissen, 2012, 2013) (see also Section 21.3.2). These findings can then be used to refine already existing descriptor scales and fill them with more linguistic substance, or to define criterial features that differentiate learners at different proficiency levels. However, there are also more large-scale projects, such as the English Profile Project (Salamoura, 2008), that aim at describing learners' progression in different skills in very much detail (such as grammar or vocabulary) (see Section 21.4). The third type of research in this area of application is the development of L1-specific RLDs (see Section 21.1). This line of research is exemplified by the project described in Negishi *et al.* (2013), in which a fine-grained learner corpus analysis served as the database to develop a Japanese version of the CEFR called CEFR-J, i.e. an adapted version of the CEFR that reflects particular characteristics and needs of Japanese learners of English. Innovative approaches that connect the fields of learner corpus research with LTA by also taking into consideration valuable theories from the field of SLA are presented by the involvement of "quasi-longitudinal" or truly longitudinal learner corpora (see Section 21.3.1.2). Finally, with huge advances in the area of natural language processing (NLP) and machine learning, automatic assessments of test data are becoming more and more reliable, especially for written data (e.g. Marchand & Atsuku, 2015; Yannakoudakis *et al.*, 2011).

21.3 Core issues and topics

In the present chapter, I discuss the critical issues and new debates arising from the use of learner corpora in the field of LTA. First, I will present different types of learner corpora that have been/can be used to inform LTA, before I turn to different types of applications of learner corpora to the field.

21.3.1 Types of learner corpora used to inform language testing and assessment

In general, one can differentiate between different types of learner corpora that can be useful to inform LTA. The first relevant group is learner corpora that have been compiled for the very purpose of informing language testing and assessment while others have been compiled by learner corpus researchers with a view to being analyzed against a native control corpus in "contrastive (interlanguage) analyses" (Granger, 1996, 1998, 2015). I shall introduce the benefits and potential challenges of both groups in the following.

21.3.1.1 Learner corpora compiled from language tests

The first group of learner corpora discussed here is compiled from language tests or language exam material. For obvious reasons, learner corpora compiled from actual test/exam data can have a huge benefit for language testers and language test developers, either as a resource to actually generate a language test or to refine descriptor scales with what learners actually and realistically "can do" at a certain proficiency level.

The first corpus in this group is the Cambridge Learner Corpus (CLC). The corpus consists of about 56 million words of written exam scripts of over 250,000 student responses taken from the Cambridge English Language Assessment suite of exams – including the Cambridge English: First (FCE; difficulty level B2, upper intermediate), Advanced (CAE; difficulty level C1, advanced), and Proficiency (CPE; difficulty level C2, highly advanced) – and includes data from a range of L1s. The responses are from students from more than 60 countries speaking 7 different first languages. There is detailed information about each examined student available, such as their first language, their nationality, age, gender, and/or their proficiency level. Thanks to the rich metadata, the CLC can be used to find out how a specific group of students creates answers at different levels in English exams. This massive corpus formed the basis of analysis for the English Profile Project (see Section 21.4). A subset of the data is freely available (OpenCLC (v1), 2017).

The second corpus under this heading is the Trinity Lancaster Corpus (TLC) (Gablasova *et al.*, 2019). The TLC is currently the largest corpus of spoken L2 English and was compiled from 2012 to 2018 as part of the Graded Examinations in Spoken English (GESE), an exam developed and administered by Trinity College London. It was developed in collaboration between the Centre for Corpus Approaches to Social Science (CASS) at Lancaster University and Trinity College London, which represents a major international examination board. In total, the corpus contains 4.2 million words (tokens) of transcribed spoken interaction between exam candidates (L2 speakers of English) and examiners (L1 speakers of English). The learner data are comprised of over 2000 L2 speakers from different cultural and linguistic backgrounds and with a range of sociolinguistic characteristics, such as age, gender, their L1, but also their proficiency level.

A third corpus is the Japanese learner English Corpus (NICT JLE Corpus), which was compiled under the auspices of the National Institute of Information and Communications Technology in 2004. The corpus was compiled from the transcripts of the audio-recorded speech samples (1281 samples, 1.2 million words, 300 hours in total) of the English oral proficiency interview test, ACTFL-ALC SST (Standard Speaking Test). Each test taker's data includes their proficiency level based on the SST scoring method (i.e. 9 levels), which makes it possible to analyze and compare the characteristics of interlanguage of each developmental stage. One great asset of the corpus is also its rich annotation, as it includes not only metadata, but is also error-tagged for 47 different error types. A comparable subcorpus of English native speakers is also available. The corpus is freely available for download.

21.3.1.2 *General learner corpora and their application to language testing and assessment (LTA)*

The second group of corpora that I would like to mention in this context is 'general learner corpora', i.e. learner corpora that have originally not been compiled with a particular view to be applied to the area of LTA. Many of the larger general learner corpora are cross-sectional in nature, for example, the International Corpus of Learner English (ICLE) (Granger *et al.*, 2020) or the Louvain International Database of Spoken English Interlanguage (LINDSEI) (Gilquin *et al.*, 2010). The recently released third edition of the ICLE corpus includes learner essay data composed by advanced learners of English from 26 mother tongue backgrounds. LINDSEI can be considered to be the "spoken sister" of ICLE, which includes c. 1 million words of 554 interviews of advanced learners from 11 different L1 backgrounds and a rich set of learning context variables on the learners. Due to the homogeneity in composition of the different subcorpora, the extremely rigorous compilation criteria and the richness of data available in the learner profiles of general learner corpora, they have been meaningfully applied in several corpus-informed and/or corpus-based studies.

Some learner corpora are also available in an error-tagged format, i.e. each of the errors in a corpus has been manually identified and classified. Applications of such corpora have generated hugely relevant implications for LTA, especially when it comes to refining the grammatical accuracy scales of the CEFR, because in describing and discriminating proficiency levels, it has shown to be of particular relevance not only to describe what learners can do, but also what they cannot do, i.e. the types and frequencies of errors that learners commit at specific proficiency levels (Díez-Bedmar, 2015; Götz, 2015; Thewissen, 2012, 2013, 2015) (for one concrete example, see Section 21.3.2).

The last type of corpora to be introduced in this context is that of a longitudinal and quasi-longitudinal learner corpus. Two examples of truly longitudinal learner corpora are the Marburg Intermediate Learner English (MILE) corpus (Kreyer, 2015), which consists of written, error-tagged longitudinal learner data at the intermediate level, or the Longitudinal Database of Learner English (LONGDALE; Meunier & Littré, 2013), which includes spoken and written learner data of the same learners with different L1s at different proficiency levels. Such corpora allow for tracing developmental sequences in a truly longitudinal fashion and findings emerging from such projects will certainly not only inform the field of SLA, but also be of great benefit for the field of LTA. However, such longitudinal data are sometimes difficult to obtain. Learner corpora make it also possible to circumvent this problem to some extent as they also allow for quasi-longitudinal studies, that is, studies based on "samples of learner language [that] are collected from groups of different proficiency levels at a single point in time" allowing the researcher to create a "longitudinal picture (…) by comparing the devices used by the different groups" (Ellis & Barkhuizen, 2005, p. 97). Such approaches are methodologically certainly inferior to truly longitudinal studies, but they still represent a methodologically sound way that can capture overall group developments in the learning process of learners that share similar characteristics. Studies in this vein have already led to valuable findings in previous studies (Gerlach & Götz, 2021; Götz & Mukherjee, 2018; Maden-Weinberger, 2015).

All these different types of learner corpora can have different benefits for the field of LTA, and they are typically used in different research paradigms and different applications. I will introduce these applications in the following section.

21.3.2 Types of applications of learner corpora to language testing and assessment

Callies *et al.* (2014) propose a particularly useful threefold distinction of how learner corpora can be applied in LTA, by differentiating between corpus-informed, corpus-based, and corpus-driven uses of learner corpora in the field of LTA – acknowledging a certain degree of overlap between the approaches. These different types differ with respect to the way in which corpus data are actually put to use, in terms of aims and outcomes for the field of LTA, and the degree of involvement of the researcher in the actual learner corpus analysis. These three approaches are illustrated in Table 21.1 and will be exemplified in the following.

In corpus-informed applications, learner corpora typically serve as reference sources to provide test evidence (Callies *et al.*, 2014). Depending on the needs of the user and the purpose of the test, there are many possibilities in which learner corpora can inform language tests at various stages. Or, in Barker's (2010) words, "learner corpora show us what learners of a language *can do* at certain levels of proficiency, which can inform what is tested at a particular proficiency level, whether overall or at task or item level" (p. 639) (emphasis in

Table 21.1 Three approaches to using learner corpora in LTA (slightly adapted from Callies et al., 2014, p. 76)

	Corpus-informed	*Corpus-based*	*Corpus-driven*
Use	Corpus as reference source. Provides practical information on learners' language use at certain levels of proficiency	Corpus as source of data for linguistic research. Testing existing hypotheses about learner language	No preconceptions/ hypotheses prior to corpus analysis. Computer techniques for data extraction and evaluation
Aims and outcomes for LTA	Evidence used for test content and validating human ratings	Evidence used to identify a set of distinct features/ descriptors for differentiating proficiency levels	Evidence of proficiency based on automatic statistical analyses
Researcher's involvement	High	Medium	Low
Sample studies	Dumont (2017); Wisniewski (2017b)	Hawkins and Buttery (2010); Hawkins & Filipovic (2012)	Marchand and Akutsu (2015)

original). Following this, in corpus-informed applications, a learner corpus can be analyzed, for example, regarding the performance of a learner group at the B2 level. The emerging findings can then be used in order to either inform the contents of a test for the B2 level itself or to "validate" human raters' claims by revealing what learners really can do at the B2 proficiency level. One very early study that applies this approach is presented by Hargreaves (2000), who identified collocations in the Cambridge Learner Corpus and developed a new task type for a general English proficiency test. Note, however, that such approaches have not remained entirely unchallenged, because using learner corpus data that are rated for proficiency (according to certain criteria) to highlight linguistic features that may help distinguish between proficiency levels (which might end up being the very same criteria) can, of course, lead to a certain degree of circularity (e.g. Hulstijn, 2010).

Alternatively, findings from learner corpus analyses can inform language tests even on a more specific level and provide information of typical learner performance at the B2 level, e.g. in a story-retell task or according to the tenses the learners typically use at this level (Barker, 2010). To give two very illustrative examples of this approach, I would like to mention Dumont (2017), who shows how information gained by graded assessments of oral learner interviews can be combined with insights obtained from a learner corpus and corpus-based techniques. She suggests a number of criterial features for differentiating between several proficiency levels that could be further incorporated into a scale for the assessment of fluency – and also features that cannot. A second and very revealing study using this approach is Wisniewski's (2017b), which tests the empirical validity of the descriptor scales of the CEFR based on its vocabulary and fluency scales.

An already emerging new strand of corpus-based applications of learner corpus research investigates error-tagged corpora, i.e. corpora, in which each error is identified and classified. These types of studies provide valuable insights into these areas where learners still struggle with certain features at certain proficiency levels, for example in order to make recommendations for LTA and teaching (e.g. Díez-Bedmar, 2015; Götz, 2015; Thewissen, 2012, 2013, 2015). One concrete example of how a very thorough study on

Table 21.2 Orthographic control snapshot grid for B2/C1 French-speaking learners of English (Thewissen, 2012, p. 273; corrections of errors are put right behind the errors between $-signs)

	French-speaking learners of L2 English at B2/C1
Orthographic control	Spelling errors still occur at this level and can constitute more than slips of the pen. Spelling influence from French can be felt. Orthographic errors may come in the form of, e.g. substitution between two letters, unnecessary or missing doubling of consonants, erroneous splitting or joining of words, redundant or missing letters, capitalization, erroneous prefixes/suffixes.
Learner corpus-based example bank	[Substitution] exemple $example$, responsabilities $responsibilities$, negociation $negotiation$, Kuweit $Kuwait$, pityful $pitiful$, brievly $briefly$
	[Unnecessary/ missing doubling of consonants] developped $developed$, personnality $personality$, litle $little$, accomodating $accommodating$, digresions $digressions$, occured $occurred$, especialy $especially$
	[Erroneous splitting or joining of words] business man $businessman$, airpollution $air pollution$, mass-grave $mass grave$, every one $everyone$, goodhearted $good-hearted$
	[Redundant or missing letters] accompagnied $accompanied$, governement $government$, conjugual $conjugal$, advantagous $advantageous$, mecanism $mechanism$
	[Capitalisation] belgian $Belgian$, european $European$, second world war $Second World War$, christian $Christian$ duty
	[Prefixes/ suffixes] uncredible $incredible, unuseful $useless$, unpredictableness $unpredictability$, consequencies $consequences$, determinates $determines$

an error-tagged French learner corpus has suggested some refinements for more specific, L1-based RLDs to the CEFR is offered by Thewissen (2012). Zooming in on one specific, refined description she has based on her thorough analysis of the errors in the corpus on orthographic control at the B2/C1 level, including many examples from the corpus, is illustrated in Table 21.2.

While corpus-informed applications are typically the main applications that are being recognized of learner corpora to the field of LTA (Callies, 2015), Callies *et al.* (2014) suggest two further relevant applications of learner corpora to the field of LTA that deserve to be discussed in this context. In corpus-based applications, researchers make use of learner corpora in order to empirically accept or reject researchers' hypotheses. This is typically done by comparing learner data with comparable native speaker data. Examples of this type of application are Hawkins and Buttery's (2010) and Hawkins and Filipović's (2012) corpus-based identification of what they labeled "criterial features", i.e. linguistic features that clearly distinguish learners at different proficiency levels. In their work, they propose to complement the descriptor scales of the proficiency levels in the CEFR with more concrete linguistic descriptors by adding "grammatical and lexical details of English to CEFR's functional characterization of the different levels" (Hawkins & Filipović, 2012, p. 5). They propose to do so by comparing learner data (here the CLC) with native speaker data (here the *British National Corpus*) to reveal similarities and differences between learners and native speakers of certain linguistic features and usage patterns which, in turn, are considered as being a positive or negative developmental linguistic property, respectively. These properties can then be interpreted as "characteristic and indicative of L2 proficiency at each level" (ibid., p. 6), which enables examiners to make much more practical and feature-based assessments.

Finally, in corpus-driven applications, researchers rely exclusively on computer-based techniques for data extraction and discriminate between proficiency groups (or any other kind of research question they have in mind) solely on the basis of statistical analyses. As computer-based techniques of data extraction and evaluation are in the foreground here, this approach subsumes the least degree of involvement by the researcher. There are no a priori hypotheses or assumptions about the data; neither are there potential discriminators. Marchand and Akutsu (2015), for example, adopt such a purely data-driven approach to automatically assess proficiency levels. In their research, they use binary decision trees to account for the complexity, accuracy, and fluency of texts within a learner corpus automatically and compare their findings to trained rater's assessments, for example on the basis of assessing the vocabulary level according to its sophistication or the text length as predictor of a learner's fluency, etc. Although they humbly conclude from their findings that "it is too early to claim the validity of the measurement tool" (Marchand & Akutsu, 2015, p. 105), the agreement between the raters and the automatic rating tool was still "good" and their overall findings were broadly in line with their expectations. Although such types of automatic measurement methods are not yet mainstream in the field of LTA, Callies *et al.* (2014) classify this kind of approach to be "particularly useful for a 'text-centred' (Carlsen, 2012, p. 165), data-driven classification of proficiency based on linguistic descriptors, such as those that are typical of a specific register" (p. 76).

21.4 Current contributions: The English Profile Project

In the present section, a concrete example of how learner corpora can be relevant for the area of language testing is introduced. Although there are many valuable studies available, The English Profile Project (Salamoura, 2008) provides the basis for this discussion. It is one large-scale project that demonstrates particularly well how the use of learner corpora can inform descriptor scales such as the CEFR, while at the same time, the freely available online materials can prove to be highly beneficial to every researcher, language teacher, and test developer. I will describe this in the following.

The English Profile Project, as it is introduced and described on the project's website (http://www.englishprofile.org/), is not only a global research program, but also a research community consisting of researchers, academics, corpus linguists, teachers, testers, ministries of education, and other language specialists. The researchers involved in this project analyze the Cambridge Learner Corpus, a 55-million-word corpus comprising over 250,000 scripts from Cambridge English exams at all levels from over 130 countries around the world, by applying corpus-linguistic technology with a view to describing English learner language at different proficiency levels. Since the English Profile's research findings are based on data provided by real learners of English, it provides concrete evidence of what learners with different L1s really can do at each level of the CEFR. As the original version of the CEFR was designed to apply to all (foreign) languages worldwide, the Council of Europe has encouraged the development of Reference Level Descriptions (RLDs) for national and regional languages in order to adapt the descriptors to local contexts and purposes (Section 21.1). Following this recommendation, the English Profile Program has been developing the RLDs for the English language. It, thus, aims at providing detailed, language-specific guidance for users of the CEFR for English. However, the English Profile follows what the project team describes as being a 'vertical approach', i.e. they concentrate on the description of linguistic ability in specific areas of the English language (vocabulary, grammar) across all six CEFR levels, using empirical data from learner corpora and curricula to inform the framework's research findings. The project's goal is to classify, systematize and compare learners' output at different proficiency levels in order to refine the CEFR levels into English Profile's RLDs. Due to the large data set and learner corpus-based methodology, the refined levels can be referenced with much more certainty than any study preceding it. This project has, therefore, potential to inform test writers about what they can expect and what is suitable for learning at a specific proficiency level. The two main projects of the English Profile so far are the English Vocabulary Profile and the English Grammar Profile. The former investigated which words (and importantly, which meanings of those vocabulary items) are known and used by learners at each level of the CEFR. It also contains information about phrases, idioms, and collocations. The results of this analysis are freely available online (https://www.englishprofile.org/wordlists/evp). The online search tool allows the user to either generate complete word lists for a selected proficiency level, or simply generate lists of which phrasal verbs, which nouns or which adjectives learners typically know at a certain level. The tool also allows to generate lists of words of semantic fields at a certain proficiency level. For example, at the A1 level, learners know the following words in the word group "animals": *animal, bird, cat, cow, dog, fish, horse, pet, pig, sheep, zoo*. There is a British and American English version, and there is audio pronunciation available for all entries.

In a similar manner, the English Grammar Profile investigated how learners develop competence in grammatical form and meaning, as well as pragmatic appropriateness, as they move up the CEFR levels. Like the Vocabulary Profile, the English Grammar Profile disambiguates different meanings of grammatical constructions and describes in detail at which level learners of English use them correctly and appropriately. Based on a canon of grammar and on evidence the research group filtered out from the CLC, the researchers were able to compose a long list of grammar features to search for in the learner data, along with suitable can-do statements. This valuable database is also freely available online (EGP Online, 2015). For example, while A1 learners only use the past simple in affirmative forms with a range of regular and irregular verbs to talk about everyday events or states (e.g. *The people were very polite*, French, A1), at the A2-level, we can already find the past simple in *Wh-* or *Do-* questions, in negative forms, in combinations with *when* in subordinate clauses and with an increasing range of verbs (e.g. *When I arrived, the weather was horrible*, Spanish (Argentina), A2).

The results of both the Vocabulary and the Grammar Profile Project can be downloaded in .cvs format for further use. Both of these projects provide metadata in such laudable detail that it becomes easily possible for researchers, teachers, and language testers to make ideal use of these databases. The findings from the English Profile Project, therefore, make for an invaluable reference source for test developers and test raters alike.

21.5 Future directions of research

In general, learner corpora have a huge potential to make the assessment of L2 proficiency on the basis of descriptor scales much more transparent, consistent, comparable, and L1-specific. More specifically, learner corpora can be of great use to inform, validate, quantify, and advance the way L2 proficiency is described in descriptor scales such as the CEFR. However, in order to benefit even more from learner corpus-based research to inform the field of LTA, there are a variety of suggestions to move the two fields even closer together. In this final section, I would like to elaborate on four of these.

21.5.1 The nature of learner corpus data

The first issue that needs to be addressed is the nature of learner corpus data and the issue of corpus comparability. In order to ensure that the corpus under investigation contains data that are useful for testing purposes and that test and control corpora are (truly) comparable, researchers need to make sure to take inter-learner variability into account more thoroughly. For example, the variable language proficiency has been dealt with rather differently in different corpora, making comparisons between different corpora rather challenging. In some corpora, which have not initially been compiled in order to be applicable to the field of LTA (e.g. ICLE or LINDSEI), proficiency of the learners is not assessed at the time of corpus compilation, a fact that requires either post-hoc ratings of the data or other solutions (for a discussion, see, e.g. Barker *et al.*, 2015). The importance of assessing the variable of proficiency level quantitatively at the time of corpus compilation thus forms a strong desideratum for future learner corpora. Along with that, the collection of a rich variety of learning context variables will also enable future research to apply the most recent methodologically innovative techniques to the analyses of learner corpus data. The same applies to the general nature of future learner corpora that would ideally be freely available for research, longitudinal, multimodal, and include various L1s in order to apply truly useful analytical techniques to these datasets.

21.5.2 Refinement of contents in descriptor scales based on learner corpus research

Although many learner corpus-based studies have been conducted to inform descriptor scales, "the link between CEFR proficiency classifications and features of learner language is still under-researched" (Wisniewski, 2020, p. 2). The field would thus definitely benefit from more empirically-based research projects in this vein.

Another avenue of research in this area would be a continuing refinement not only of the empirical underpinnings of already known features, but also refining the contents of what is actually included in the descriptor scales, based on findings from data-driven learner-corpus analyses. Römer (2017), for example, used L1 corpora to investigate formulaic language in spoken communication and compared it to rating scales of major exams (the TOEFL iBT, IELTS, Cambridge English: Advanced exam). She found that formulaic units had a major role in spoken language in the corpora, but they were not consistently included in the construct definition and rating scales of these exams. Future truly data-driven studies in a similar vein would certainly have the power to reveal more novel features that deserve to be integrated in descriptor scales.

21.5.3 Learner corpora to develop language tests

Most corpus-based language tests use native corpora. Although there are some laudable exceptions (e.g. the Examination for the Certificate of Competency in English), I would encourage test-developers to make it common practice to consult learner corpora and not only native corpora in future test developments. Usami (2013), for example, demonstrated an innovative way how learner corpora can be applied to test development in order to improve distractors in multiple choice questions. Tests that are developed on the basis of native speaker output alone and consequently compare learner output to native speaker performance run the risk of falling prey to the comparative fallacy (Bley-Vroman, 1983) mentioned earlier, and thus neglect the very nature of interlanguage (IL) as a process (Selinker, 1972) that must be described in its own terms (Selinker, 2014). Larsen-Freeman (2014) concludes that "[b]y continuing to equate identity with idealized native speaker production as a definition of success, it is difficult to avoid seeing the learner's IL as anything but deficient" (p. 217). As interlanguage is believed to hardly ever fully reach the same level as native language, it seems to be much more appropriate to assess a test taker's performance towards the benchmark of similar test takers performance. With similar, I refer to learners with similar learner profiles (e.g. speaking the same L1, having performed the same task, having spoken to an examiner with the same gender, etc.). I will elaborate on this point in the following section.

21.5.4 *The importance of learning context variables for LTA*

Learning context variables are known to be of paramount importance for language learning in general (Norris & Ortega, 2001). Recent research has shown that such learning context variables also need to be included in learner corpus-based research studies (Mukherjee & Götz, 2015) in order to actually benefit from the typically occurring heterogeneity in learner corpus data. Taking into consideration learning context variables might be even more important when learner corpora are used to inform language tests or actual test outcomes. Within these variables, the proficiency level of the learner is obviously the first variable that comes to mind, as the empirical description of developmental stages is well documented and accepted in the field of SLA (Wisniewski, 2020). Here, future studies that empirically investigate these theoretically well-described developmental sequences based on learner corpus data would generate invaluable findings to inform the field of LTA.

Apart from the proficiency level, however, other learning context variables have also been shown to significantly impact a learner's test performance. Studies within the framework of LTA are in accordance with findings from learner corpus research, as they have shown considerable effects of certain variables on a test taker's performance. For instance, the test-taker's (Csépes, 2009; Götz, 2019a) or the interlocutor's (Götz, 2019a; O'Sullivan, 2000) gender has been shown to affect a learner's performance. Significant correlations of a learner's L1 language patterns with their L2 language patterns have also been documented (Jiránková *et al.*, 2019; Peltonen, 2018). Other variables that have proven to affect a test taker's performance either positively or negatively are the communicative style during the test (Kormos, 1999), or the task type the learners had to conduct during the test (Gráf, 2019; Porter, 1991). Due to the small scale of the aforementioned studies, they have also arrived at contrasting findings. Therefore, if descriptor scales of proficiency levels should be truly informed by authentic learner corpus data in the future, the corresponding analyses following the Council of Europe's (2017) "Reference Level Descriptions Initiative" need to account for variables other than proficiency level. Thus, another way forward in this field is certainly to extend current practices that treat 'the proficiency variable' in a learner corpus monofactorially. If, instead, we want to make use of the full potential of learner corpora to inform descriptor scales, one way to do so is to consider a defined set of typical and representative variables other than the proficiency variable. This is where learner corpora can have their largest analytic potential, because huge learner corpora along with their corresponding learner profiles are available, as well as the statistically sophisticated techniques that are necessary to analyze learner corpora in a multivariate manner (Gries, 2015, *passim*.). Using such sophisticated techniques will enable researchers to inform the field of LTA with much more thorough and robust information on what learners really can do at a certain proficiency level by controlling for other variables that are relevant for a learner's test performance. At the same time, such studies can take into consideration general test variables (such as information on the task and potentially the interlocutor), but also general learner variables (such as their L1s, their gender, age, etc.) along with their interactions with the proficiency level. In doing so, research would also be able to arrive at empirically robust criterial features that are universally valid for all learners of English, but also at those that are L1 specific for a certain learner population (e.g. Götz, 2019b; Negishi *et al.*, 2013 for Japanese learners of English).

Further reading

Callies, M., & Götz, S. (Eds.). (2015). *Learner corpora in language testing and assessment*. Benjamins. This volume features a collection of studies that are relevant for language testers on different levels: (1) studies that present new corpus resources that are tailor-made and ready for analysis in the area of language testing and assessment, (2) tools for the automatic assessment of proficiency levels in learner corpora, and (3) innovative research methodologies of how proficiency can be operationalized in learner corpus research.

Thewissen, J. (2015). *Accuracy across proficiency levels: A learner corpus approach*. Presses Universitaires de Louvain. In this research monograph, the author investigates more than 40 error types in the International Corpus of Learner English at four consecutive levels of language proficiency (B1, B2, C1, C2) of the CEFR. It provides important methodological considerations for developmental learner corpus research, presents abundantly illustrated analyses of authentic learner errors as well as some concrete suggestions for improving the descriptors of the CEFR.

Wisniewski (2017a). Empirical learner language and the levels of the *Common European Framework of Reference*. *Language Learning*, 67(1), 232–253. In this extremely thoroughly researched article, the author presents a state-of-the-art overview of why and how learner corpora can be relevant to inform descriptor scales.

References

Barker, F. (2010). How can corpora be used in language testing. In A. O'Keeffe & M. McCarthy (Eds.), *The Routledge handbook of corpus linguistics* (pp. 633–645). Routledge.

Barker, F., Salamoura, A., & Saville, N. (2015). Learner corpora and language testing. In S. Granger, G. Gilquin, & F. Meunier (Eds.), *The Cambridge handbook of learner corpus research* (pp. 511–533). Cambridge University Press.

Bley-Vroman, R. (1983). The comparative fallacy in interlanguage studies: The case of systematicity, *Language Learning*, 33, 1–17. https://doi.org/10.1111/j.1467-1770.1983.tb00983.x

Callies, M. (2015). Using learner corpora in language testing and assessment: Current practice and future challenges. In E. Castello, K. Ackerley, & F. Coccetta (Eds.), *Studies in learner corpus linguistics: Research and applications for foreign language teaching and assessment* (pp. 21–35). Peter Lang.

Callies, M., Díez-Bedmar, B., & Zaytseva, E. (2014). Using learner corpora for testing and assessing L2 proficiency. In P. Leclercq, H. Hilton, & A. Edmonds (Eds.), *Measuring L2 proficiency: Perspectives from SLA* (pp. 71–90). Multilingual Matters.

Callies, M., & Götz, S. (Eds.). (2015a). *Learner corpora in language testing and assessment*. Benjamins. https://doi.org/10.1075/scl.70

Callies, M., & Götz, S. (2015b). Learner corpora in language testing and assessment. Prospects and challenges. In M. Callies & S. Götz (Eds.), *Learner corpora in language testing and assessment* (pp. 1–9). Benjamins. https://doi.org/10.1075/scl.70.001int

Carlsen, C. (2012). Proficiency level – A fuzzy variable in computer learner corpora. *Applied Linguistics*, 33(2), 161–183. https://doi.org/10.1093/applin/amr047

Chapelle, C. A., & Plakans, L. (2013). Assessment and testing: Overview. In C. A. Chapelle (Ed.), *The encyclopedia of applied linguistics* (pp. 241–244). Wiley-Blackwell.

Council of Europe (2011). *English Profile. Introducing the CEF for English. Version 1.1*. Cambridge: Cambridge University Press. http://www.englishprofile.org/images/pdf/theenglishprofilebooklet.pdf

Council of Europe (2017). *Common European framework of reference for languages: Learning, teaching, assessment*. Cambridge University Press.

Csépes, I. (2009). *Measuring oral proficiency through paired-task performance*. Peter Lang.

Díez-Bedmar, B. (2015). Article use and criterial features in Spanish EFL writing: A pilot study from CEFRR A2 to B2 levels. In M. Callies & S. Götz (Eds.), *Learner corpora in language testing and assessment* (pp. 163–190). Benjamins. https://doi.org/10.1075/scl.70.07die

Dumont, A. (2017). The contribution of learner corpora to the substantiation of fluency levels. In P. De Haan, R. D. Vries, & S. Van Vuuren (Eds.), *Language, learners and levels: Progression and variation* (pp. 281–308). Presses Universitaires de Louvain.

Ellis, R., & Barkhuizen, G. (2005). *Analysing learner language.* Oxford University Press.

English Grammar Profile (EGP) (2015). Online. http://www.englishprofile.org/english-grammar-profile/egp-online

Gablasova, D., Brezina, V., & McEnery, T. (2019). The Trinity Lancaster corpus: Development, description and application. *International Journal of Learner Corpus Research, 5*(2), 126–158. https://doi.org/10.1075/ijlcr.19001.gab

Gerlach, D., & Götz, S. (2021). Kreatives Schreiben im Englischunterricht Eine korpuslinguistische und genreanalytische Betrachtung von Schreibprodukten der Sekundarstufe I. *ZFF- Zeitschrift für Fremdsprachenforschung, 32*(2), 203–228.

Gilquin, G., De Cock, S., & Granger, S. (2010). *Louvain International Database of Spoken English Interlanguage. Handbook and CD-ROM.* Presses Universitaires de Louvain.

Götz, S. (2015). Tense and aspect errors in spoken learner language: Implications for language testing and assessment. In M. Callies & S. Götz (Eds.), *Learner corpora in language testing and assessment* (pp. 191–215). Benjamins. https://doi.org/10.1075/scl.70.08got

Götz, S. (2019a). Do learning context variables have an effect on learners' (dis)fluency? Language-specific vs. universal patterns in advanced learners' use of filled pauses. In L. Degand, G. Gilquin, L. Meurant, & A. Catherine Simon (Eds.), *Fluency and disfluency across languages and language varieties* (pp. 177–196). Presses Universitaires de Louvain.

Götz, S. (2019b). Filled pauses across proficiency levels, L1s and learning context variables: A multivariate exploration of the Trinity Lancaster Corpus Sample. *International Journal of Learner Corpus Research, 5*(2), 159–180. https://doi.org/10.1075/ijlcr.17018.got

Götz, S., & Mukherjee, J. (2018). The effect of the study abroad variable in spoken learner language: A pseudo-longitudinal study on spoken German learner English. In V. Brezina & L. Flowerdew (Eds.), *Learner corpus research: New perspectives and applications* (pp. 47–65). Bloomsbury.

Götz, S., & Mukherjee, J. (Eds.) (2019). *Learner corpora and language teaching.* Benjamins.

Gráf, T. (2019). Speech rate revisited: The effect of task design on speech rate. In S. Götz & J. Mukherjee (Eds.), *Learner corpora and language teaching* (pp. 175–189). Benjamins. https://doi.org/10.1075/scl.92.09gra

Granger, S. (1996). From CA to CIA and back: An integrated approach to computerized bilingual and learner corpora. In K. Aijmer, B. Altenberg, & M. Johansson (Eds.), *Languages in contrast: Text-based cross-linguistic studies* (pp. 37–51). Lund University Press.

Granger, S. (1998). The computer learner corpus: A versatile new source of data for SLA research. In S. Granger (Ed.), *Learner English on computer* (pp. 3–18). Longman.

Granger, S. (2009). The contribution of learner corpora to second language acquisition and foreign language teaching: A critical evaluation. In K. Aijmer (Ed.), *Corpora and language teaching* (pp. 13–32). Benjamins. https://doi.org/10.1075/scl.33.04gra

Granger, S. (2015). Contrastive interlanguage analysis: A reappraisal. *International Journal of Learner Corpus Research, 1*(1), 7–24. https://doi.org/10.1075/ijlcr.1.1.01gra

Granger, S., Dupont, M., Meunier, F., Naets, H., & Paquot, M. (2020). *The International Corpus of Learner English* Version 3. Presses Universitaires de Louvain.

Gries, S. T. (2015). Statistical methods in learner corpus research. In G. Gilquin, S. Granger, & F. Meunier (Eds.), *The Cambridge handbook of learner corpus research* (pp. 159–181). Cambridge University Press.

Hargreaves, P. (2000). Collocation and testing. In M. Lewis (Ed.), *Teaching collocations* (pp. 203–233). Language Teaching Publications.

Hawkins, J. A., & Buttery, P. (2010). Criterial features in learner corpora: Theory and illustrations. *English Profile Journal, 1*(1), 1–23. https://doi.org/ 10.1017/S204153621000010

Hawkins, J. A., & Filipović, L. (2012). *Criterial features in L2 English: Specifying the reference levels of the Common European Framework.* Cambridge University Press.

Hulstijn, J. H. (2010). Linking L2 proficiency to L2 acquisition: Opportunities and challenges of profiling research. *EUROSLA Monographs Series, 1,* 233–238.

Japanese Learner English Corpus. https://alaginrc.nict.go.jp/nict_jle/index_E.html#download

Jiránková, L., Gráf, T., & Kvítková, A. (2019). On the relation between L1 and L2 speech rate. In A. Abel, A. Glaznieks, V. Lyding, & L. Nicolas (Eds.), *Widening the scope of learner corpus research. Selected papers from the fourth learner corpus research conference* (pp. 19–41). Presses Universitaires de Louvain.

Kormos, J. (1999). Simulating conversations in oral-proficiency assessment: A conversation analysis of role plays and non-scripted interviews in language exams. *Language Testing, 16*(2), 163–188. https://doi.org/10.1177/026553229901600203

Kreyer, R. (2015). The Marburg Corpus of Intermediate Learner English (MILE). In M. Callies & S. Götz (Eds.), *Learner corpora in language testing and assessment* (pp. 13–34). Benjamins. https://doi.org/10.1075/scl.70.01kre

Larsen-Freeman, D. 2014. Another step to be taken – Rethinking the end point of the interlanguage continuum. In Z. Han & E. Tarone (Eds.), *Interlanguage. Forty years later* (pp. 203–220). Benjamins. https://doi.org/10.1075/lllt.39.11ch9

Maden-Weinberger, U. (2015). A pseudo-longitudinal study of subjunctives in the corpus of learner German. *International Journal of Learner Corpus Research, 1*(1), 25–57. https://doi.org/10.1075/ijlcr.1.1.02mad

Marchand, T., & Akutsu, S. (2015). First steps in assigning proficiency to texts in a learner corpus of computer-mediated communication. In M. Callies & S. Götz (Eds.), *Learner corpora in language testing and assessment* (pp. 85–112). Benjamins. https://doi.org/10.1075/scl.70.04mar

McCarthy, M. (2010). Spoken fluency revisited, *English Profile Journal, 1*(1), e4. https://doi.org/10.1017/S2041536210000012

McCarthy, M. (2016). Putting the CEFR to good use: Designing grammars based on learner-corpus evidence. *Language Teaching, 49*(1), 99–115. https://doi.org/10.1017/S0261444813000189

Meunier, F., & Littré, D. (2013). Tracking learners' progress: Adopting a dual "corpus cum experimental data" approach. *The Modern Language Journal, 97*(S1), 61–76. https://doi.org/10.1111/j.1540-4781.2012.01424.x

Mukherjee, J., & Götz, S. (2015). Learner corpora and learning context. In S. Granger, G. Gilquin, & F. Meunier (Eds.), *Cambridge handbook of learner corpus research* (pp. 423–442). Cambridge University Press.

Negishi, M., Takada, T., & Tono, Y. (2013). A progress report on the development of the CEFR-J. In E. D. Galaczi & C. J. Weir (Eds.), *Exploring language frameworks* (pp. 137–165). Cambridge University Press.

North, B. (2000). *The development of a common framework scale of language proficiency.* Peter Lang.

North, B. (2014). Putting the *common European framework of reference* to good use. *Language Teaching, 47*(2), 228–249. https://doi.org/10.1017/S0261444811000206

Norris, J. M., & Ortega, L. (2001). Does type of instruction make a difference? Substantive findings from a meta-analytic review. *Language Learning, 51*(1), 157–213. https://doi.org/10.1111/j.1467-1770.2001.tb00017.x

OpenCLC (v1). (2017). Distributed by Lexical Computing Limited on behalf of Cambridge University Press and Cambridge English Language Assessment. https://www.sketchengine.eu/cambridge-learner-corpus/

O'Sullivan, B. (2000). Exploring gender and oral proficiency interview performance. *System, 28*(3), 373–386.

Park, K. (2014). Corpora and language assessment: The state of the art. *Language Assessment Quarterly, 11*(1), 27–42. https://doi.org/10.1080/15434303.2013.872647

Peltonen, P. (2018). Exploring connections between first and second language fluency: A mixed-methods approach. *The Modern Language Journal, 102*(4), 676–692. https://doi.org/10.1111/modl.12516

Porter, D. (1991). Affective factors in language testing. In J. C. Alderson & B. North (Eds.), *Language testing in the 1990s* (pp. 32–40). Macmillan.

Römer, U. (2017). Language assessment and the inseparability of lexis and grammar: Focus on the construct of speaking. *Language Testing, 34*(4), 477–492. https://doi.org/10.1177/0265532217711431

Salamoura, A. (2008). Aligning English Profile research data to the CEFR. *Cambridge ESOL: Research Notes, 33*, 5–7.

Selinker, L. (1972). Interlanguage. *IRAL. International Review of Applied Linguistics in Language Teaching, 10*(3), 209–231. https://doi.org/10.1515/iral.1972.10.1-4.209

Selinker, L. (2014). Interlanguage 40 years on. Three themes from here. In Z. Han & E. Tarone (Eds.), *Interlanguage. Forty years later* (pp. 221–246). Benjamins. https://doi.org/10.1075/lllt.39.12ch1

Shohamy, E., Or, I., & May, S. (2017). *Language testing and assessment* (3rd ed.). Springer International Publishing.

Thewissen, J. (2012). *Accuracy across proficiency levels: Insights from an error-tagged EFL learner corpus.* [Doctoral dissertation, Université catholique de Louvain].

Thewissen, J. (2013). Capturing L2 accuracy developmental patterns: Insights from an error-tagged EFL learner corpus. *The Modern Language Journal, 97*(1), 77–101. https://doi.org/10.1111/j.1540-4781.2012.01422.x

Thewissen, J. (2015). *Accuracy across proficiency levels: A learner corpus approach.* Presses Universitaires de Louvain.

Tracy-Ventura, N., & Paquot, M. (Eds.). (2021). *The Routledge handbook of SLA and corpora.* Routledge.

Usami, H. (2013). Using a learner corpus to improve distractors in multiple choice grammar questions. In S. Granger, G. Gilquin, & F. Meunier (Eds.), *Twenty years of learner corpus research: Looking back, moving ahead* (pp. 455–462). Presses Universitaires de Louvain.

Wisniewski, K. (2017a). Empirical learner language and the levels of the Common European Framework of Reference. *Language Learning, 67*(1), 232–253. https://doi.org/10.1111/lang.12223

Wisniewski, K. (2017b). The empirical validity of the Common European Framework of Reference scales. An exemplary study for the vocabulary and fluency scales in a language testing context. *Applied Linguistics, 39*(6), 933–959. https://doi-org.eres.qnl.qa/10.1093/applin/amw057

Wisniewski, K. (2020). SLA developmental stages in the CEFR-related learner corpus MERLIN. Inversion and verb-end structures in German A2 and B1 learner texts. *International Journal of Learner Corpus Research, 6*(1), 1–37. https://doi.org/10.1075/ijlcr.18008.wis

Yannakoudakis, H., Briscoe, T., & Medlock, B. (2011). A new dataset and method for automatically grading ESL texts. In *Proceedings of the 49th Annual Meeting of the Association for Computational Linguistics*, (pp. 180–189). Portland, Oregon, June 19–24, Association for Computational Linguistics.

PART IV

Data-driven learning

22

DDL PEDAGOGY, PARTICIPANTS, AND PERSPECTIVES

Fiona Farr and Petter Hagen Karlsen

22.1 Introduction

Corpus linguistics, as a research and pedagogic approach, has been with us in the world of applied linguistics for some time and given its popularity, it is most likely here to stay. Over the last 20 years, there has been a proliferation of developing corpora and corpus analysis software, resulting in robust online resources containing billions of words from a range of languages. This, in conjunction with the firmly established place of corpus findings in the publication of major reference books and course books, has secured its place for the foreseeable future (McCarthy, 2020). Language learners, teachers, researchers, and student teachers now have easy, and usually free, access to sophisticated corpus resources while corpus linguistics has also firmly established itself within the broader field of language learning and technology (Farr & Murray, 2016). As a profession, we have amassed a body of research investigating Data-Driven Learning (DDL) (Johns, 1991), the results of which are generally encouraging in terms of its positive impact. In fact, a comprehensive meta-analysis of 64 studies conducted by Boulton and Cobb (2017) suggests that the "outcomes paint an optimistic picture of the value of big language data that can be entrusted to learners themselves" (p. 382). In a more limited overview of 29 studies, with a specific focus on vocabulary, Lee *et al.* (2019) found a medium-size effect overall on L2 vocabulary learning, with a positive effect learning for those learners from intermediate level upwards. In line with the growth and evolution in general language pedagogy, research into data-driven learning (Chambers, 2010; Warren, 2016) in the English academic writing context has also expanded significantly. In a 2018 meta-analysis, Chen and Flowerdew used narrowly defined criteria to identify and review 37 studies published specifically in this area, 23 of which appeared between 2010 and 2017. The majority of the studies involve third-level undergraduate and MA students and are conducted in the North-American (N = 14), Asian (N = 12), European (N = 6), and UK (N = 5) contexts. They focus on different areas of academic writing, such as rhetorical functions and vocabulary, and utilise a range of corpora. And although it has been suggested that corpus consultation is not yet normalised in most classrooms (Chambers, 2019), it is impossible to imagine how normalisation might be measured in any systematic way. In addition, it would be difficult to argue that the integration of DDL approaches has not increased substantially in recent years, as evidenced by the number of published studies, professional organisations,

DOI: 10.4324/9781003002901-27

funded projects, focussed conferences and strands, Twitter feeds, and associated communities of practice. A specific look at the place of corpus linguistics at teaching conferences and pedagogically oriented journals by Friginal (2018) concludes that it has "grown exponentially from the mid-1990s" (p. 7), which is very much in line with our own observations over this same time period.

In addition to research, there is a pedagogically well-founded rationale for the inclusion of this approach in language learning contexts. It has been suggested that DDL has a number of advantages based on its fit with current theories of language, learning, and SLA research findings, and in relation to inductive and patterned-based approaches to learning based on rich and authentic input from corpora (Boulton & Cobb, 2017). However, there are also disadvantages cited in the literature, usually relating to one or more of the following criticisms: it requires substantial induction and training; the linguistic content in many corpora is often outside of the comfort zone of students (and often teachers), particularly at lower levels (Boulton & Tyne, 2014); it realigns and often challenges the role of the teacher; and the technology is often off-putting (Farr, 2008). The issue of lack of integration of corpus linguistics into teacher education programmes has also been cited (McCarthy, 2008), although evidence suggests that this is changing and is becoming more normalised (Farr, 2021). The question we ask in this chapter is: What are the perspectives of the learners and teachers who use corpus-based approaches? We explore the complexities around a situation where "despite undiminished enthusiasm in the research community, the application of corpus tools and resources in the classroom remains limited" (Breyer, 2009, p. 153). We also explore whether there is evidence that this situation has changed in a world where the use of technology, in general, has become much more mainstream and has never accelerated more than in the Covid lockdowns of 2020. We attempt to answer the question by briefly summarising DDL approaches reported from pedagogic contexts before exploring the perceived affordances and complexities. Following this, a recent empirical case-study is presented from the Norwegian secondary school context, exploring teacher and student perspectives. The potentially crucial role of language teacher education in helping future teachers to understand and critically apply corpus-based approaches is discussed, and we finish with an exploration of future directions. As the chapter focuses on pedagogy, it necessarily draws on research exploring both teacher and student perspectives, both of which are explored concurrently in many of the studies we discuss.

22.2 DDL in the classroom

DDL entails the direct applications of corpora in the classroom through "using the tools and techniques of corpus linguistics for pedagogic purposes" (Gilquin & Granger, 2010, p. 359). At the heart of the approach is providing learners with access to the rich, authentic data corpora can offer, most commonly through concordancer tools that let them inspect the data in systematic ways (Warren, 2016). DDL as a direct application of corpora, which involves both teachers and learners interacting with the corpus data themselves, can be distinguished from indirect applications where corpus data influence teachers and learners through the development of teaching materials, reference works, and curricula (Leech, 1997; Römer, 2011), often unknown to the end users. Although these indirect applications are highly relevant to teachers as they enter the classroom in less visible ways, it is beyond the scope of the current chapter to explore them further. In the DDL approach, the concordancer allows learners and teachers to examine keywords in context (KWIC), frequency lists, n-grams, and collocations in the corpus (Friginal, 2018). Moreover, DDL can be learner-led or teacher-directed but is essentially learner-centred (McEnery & Xiao, 2010). The approach is said to develop problem-solving and analytical skills (Vyatkina & Boulton, 2017), greater learner autonomy (Boulton & Cobb, 2017; Friginal, 2018; Vyatkina & Boulton, 2017), and increased language awareness and learner autonomy that gives the learners opportunities to follow their language interests (Bernardini, 2004; Charles, this volume; Leńko-Szymańska & Boulton, 2015). In other words, DDL not only provides new forms of linguistic data but involves educational methods that can transform pedagogic practice and classroom dynamics. For the learner, DDL entails the acquisition and development of skills such as predicting, observing, noticing, analysing, interpreting, exploring, making inferences (inductively or deductively), focusing, guessing, comparing, differentiating, theorising, hypothesising, and verifying (O'Sullivan, 2007). For the teacher, it means facilitating and scaffolding DDL activities, which requires some measure of corpus literacy, that is, understanding the basic concepts of corpus linguistics, being able to search, analyse and interpret corpus data, and creating corpus-based teaching materials (Callies, 2019; Mukherjee & Rohrbach, 2006). In addition to some corpus linguistic skills, teachers need technical and pedagogical skills related to corpora (Leńko-Szymańska, 2017).

There is a plethora of studies that show the many facets of DDL applications through a variety of approaches, corpora, and learner groups, as discussed throughout this chapter. Johns (1991) envisioned the learner as a researcher and the teacher as a director and coordinator of student-initiated research, which has been the source of much DDL research. Kennedy and Miceli (2017) find the learner-as-researcher concept problematic, however, and instead, suggest an apprenticeship approach. In this approach, the focus is on the corpus as a reference source for student writing. They suggest two techniques which align well with this approach and are conducive to the future development of research-like skills: "pattern-hunting", which entails open-ended corpus-exploration where students look for ways of expressing themselves in writing, and "pattern-refining", which involves students knowing what they want to say and searching for patterns of how to express it (Kennedy & Miceli, 2017). Similarly, Frankenberg-Garcia (2012) argues that learners do not need to possess linguist-like knowledge and data analysis; rather, they only need to be able to look up answers to their particular questions. These techniques exemplify the usefulness of both inductive and deductive approaches to corpora, while problematising the assumptions of student interest and proficiency in making learners act like researchers. Instead, they form an incremental approach to corpus consultation. Furthermore, DDL can be hands-on, where learners access corpora directly, or hands-off and where the teacher prepares printouts from corpora (Boulton, 2012; Farr & O'Keeffe, 2019; O'Keeffe & Farr, 2003). Somewhat inevitable, newer research also brings DDL to mobile devices. Pérez-Paredes *et al.* (2019) integrated DDL with Mobile Assisted Language Learning (MALL) by developing an app that allowed learners in higher education to input their texts and have the app analyse them based on word frequencies, distribution of their word use over Common European Framework of Reference for Languages (CEFR) proficiency levels, and percentages of lexical word use.

Similar to the variation of approaches to DDL, the types of corpora utilised also vary. It is beyond the scope of this chapter to cover this diversity; however, some trends and examples are highlighted. On the one hand, most studies are based on small corpora made by one or a few researchers (Chambers, 2019). On the other hand, teachers tend to use corpora representing general language use (e.g. BNC, COCA) (Tribble, 2015). Additionally, large general corpora form the basis of several guides on direct corpus application (Reppen, 2010), while specialised corpora (e.g. MICASE, Simpson *et al.*, 2002) have been especially useful in ESP and EAP (Römer, 2010). As a third option, Charles (2012) used the concordancing software AntConc with EAP university students, which allowed them to create "personal corpora" by uploading self-chosen research articles – or DIY (Do-It-Yourself) corpora (see more on DIY corpora in Jablonkai, this volume). In this way, the corpus is tailored to the individual student's needs. Another common division of corpus type is between spoken and written corpora. According to Meunier (this volume), analysis of written concordance lines still dominates DDL, but spoken and multimodal corpora appear to be on the rise (Coccetta, this volume). Naturally, corpora of written language are more common due to the required extra efforts of compiling and transcribing audio-visual material for spoken corpora. For a more comprehensive overview of corpus types and tools and their pedagogical usefulness, see Murphy and Riordan (2016) and Friginal (2018). For an indication of what corpus tools are used most by teachers, see Tribble (2015).

The last DDL trend we wish to emphasise relates to learner groups. Most teachers using DDL work in higher education (Tribble, 2015), and most studies statistically measuring the effects of corpora on language learning are conducted in tertiary education (Boulton & Cobb, 2017). For example, academic writing (Chen & Flowerdew, 2018) and teacher education (discussed further below) have been fruitful areas of application. Conversely, Pérez-Paredes (2020) claims that few learners in primary and secondary school interact with corpora. A notable exception is Braun (2007) reporting on work with the ELISA corpus, which is a multimedia corpus of topic-relevant interviews. Contemporary efforts to address the disparity between second and third-level integration are in Crosthwaite (2020, this volume) and Karlsen and Monsen (2020). We discuss the application of ELISA and present a case study by Karlsen (2021) that uses pedagogic corpora with upper secondary school students in Norway in Section 22.4.

22.3 Alignments and contentions

A great deal of fit between DDL approaches and what we currently know and believe about language acquisition is evident from the literature. As Timmis (2015) succinctly puts it, "the twin foundations of the rationale for DDL are authenticity and autonomy" (p. 135). Harmony is suggested between authentic corpus data and notions of motivation, input, exposure, preparation for real communication, and accurate and real examples of language use (Mishan & Timmis, 2015). The second pillar of autonomy is congruent with self-directed learning, evidence-based learning, noticing, learner choice, language awareness, and, generally speaking, constructivist and socio-cultural approaches to learning. The DDL marriage with constructivism seems all but impervious to divorce and "the associative link to constructivism is seen as a pedagogical hallmark for DDL" (O'Keeffe, 2020, p. 3). The inductive focus and process orientation of constructivism, at face-value at least, offer a near-perfect match with the natural affordances of corpus consultation, which is attractive to many teachers. However, there has been some criticism of an exclusive pairing of DDL with constructivism amid pragmatic discussions of the learner who does not naturally align with such an approach and who instead needs more teacher-mediation, direction, and scaffolding, notions which more naturally align with socio-cultural approaches (see Flowerdew, 2015 for a fuller account). A balanced representation of nuanced DDL approaches which nod more to constructivism or socio-cultural theory is presented by O'Keeffe (2020, p. 6), who represents the relationships on a cline from one to the other. On the socio-cultural end of the DDL cline, the teacher and learner both have instrumental roles to play, while on the constructivist end the learner operates more autonomously in a discovery-learning mode. Each position has its affordances for different learners, teachers, and contexts. Let us take the example of teaching a mature Chinese learner with no prior experience of corpus use, one-to-one, in an online context. In this scenario, a directed constructivist approach is probably most suitable, where stronger teacher input is needed and, other than the teacher, there are no other participants to help create social learning experiences. The Norwegian case study below, on the other hand, exemplifies a stronger socio-constructivist approach to the use of pedagogic corpora. There is also a third dimension related to the efficiency and efficacy afforded by the sophisticated corpus collection, transcription, extraction, reorganisation, and display tools afforded by the technology now available. All but gone are the days of dragging disks of small corpus collections to class in order to load onto learner PCs to use with appropriate, but not integrated software for analysis. There were also issues of user unfriendly interfaces, wait time, and margin for error associated with early corpus-integration attempts. Free, quick, and easy access to a range of corpora and associated pedagogically focussed support materials (for example, Friginal, 2018; O'Keeffe *et al.*, 2007; Reppen, 2010; Timmis, 2015) provide a practically solid reason for learners and teachers to adopt DDL.

Many of the alignments just discussed are also the advantages associated with the use of DDL by its various users. In the many studies where language learners' perspectives are solicited, they report benefitting from and enjoying relatively unconstrained access to real language data and being able to discover frequent words and phrases with associated contextualised examples in use. Learning language through the use of technology has also become more natural to many who can easily navigate the various interfaces that they encounter, though some still caution about the dangers of getting lost in the technology to the detriment of appropriate corpus consultation and assimilation techniques. In fact, Boulton, referring to the choice of the term DDL, suggests that

> There is some indication that Johns (2002:17) may have regretted the expression later on as DDL became, in the minds of some people, associated exclusively with its most extreme form of hands-on, autonomous, serendipitous corpus exploration, which may be difficult to implement in 'the realty of ELT classrooms' (Mukherjee 2006:14). (Boulton, 2012, p. 152)

It is precisely this classroom reality which has caused some criticism of the integration of corpus-based approaches. Users claim they do not have access to the appropriate technology, nor the time or the resources needed for effective implementation. A sense of being overwhelmed by the data is also commonplace, along with a reluctance to introduce corpus resources at lower levels. These are legitimate concerns, but they also assume that teachers do not have the ability to navigate and surmount them. As teachers and corpus users, we simply do not accept that this is the case. Technology, in many parts of the world, is no longer the impediment it once was, both because it is more widely available and also because the corpus interfaces are much more advanced and user-friendly. Most of our students need little, if any, introduction to the technology nowadays (Healey, 2016). In terms of time, this is a legitimate concern for teachers regarding all aspects of their work, not just corpus integration. However, as with all things, where there is a commitment and motivation on the part of the teacher (and learners), research has shown that appropriate corpus integration does happen and learners do benefit. Such inclinations, motivation, and commitment often stem from appropriate familiarity and support gleaned from teachers' formative experiences during teacher education programs, which have the potential to play a vital role. As Breyer (2009) puts it, "if student teachers can discover the potential of corpora for their own learning, then this may foster intrinsic motivation to make use of corpora in their profession as teachers" (p. 167) (we return to this in Section 22.5). And so, we suggest that DDL has become and will continue to fit while bringing with it its own rewards. Even more importantly DDL is accompanied by ample instructions for good usage as well as evidence of its legitimate place in the world of language pedagogy.

22.4 DDL in the upper secondary classroom: A case study from Norway

This section discusses a case study conducted by Karlsen (2021). In this study, one in-service teacher in upper secondary school collaborated with the researcher in integrating corpus resources into two of his first-year classes, students aged 15–16. As mentioned earlier, research suggests that relatively few primary and secondary school students engage with corpora (Pérez-Paredes, 2020). In Norway, Kavanagh (in press) surveyed 210 in-service English teachers in primary and secondary schools and found that 15% had never heard of corpora, 39% had little or no idea about corpora while 28% were fairly familiar with corpora, and 18% had already done some work with corpora. Only 12 teachers claimed to have used corpora either with their students or in creating teaching materials, but only seven of them had used it directly with their students. Moreover, Karlsen and Monsen (2020) interviewed four upper secondary school teachers with a semester-long corpus course in their MA backgrounds and surveyed their students (N = 154). None of these teachers had used corpora for DDL and only one of them had introduced corpora to a handful of his "brightest" students on just one occasion. Only 6% of the students claimed to have any familiarity with corpora and, when prompted, only one of these students gave a comprehensive answer to what a corpus was. These studies give credence to the claim that corpora are not used to any significant degree in Norwegian classrooms (Cardona *et al.*, 2014). Karlsen's (2021) study sought to introduce corpora in such a way that both the teacher and his learners could interact with corpus resources directly so the challenges and opportunities that arose through such interactions could be made visible.

Karlsen's (2021) Norwegian study used the pedagogic corpus resources from the *Backbone* (BB) project by Kohn *et al.* (2009), which was developed as pedagogic corpus resources in an attempt to circumvent the criticism that many corpora are made for linguists and not for learning purposes (Braun, 2007). The term "pedagogic corpora" denotes a corpus that is created and exploited for pedagogic purposes (Pérez-Paredes *et al.*, 2019), for instance, through topic-relevant language, audio-visual content, annotations based on topics and on the perceived language challenges of learners, in addition to a range of classroom materials for use by learners and teachers. The ELISA corpus (Braun, 2007) and the SACODEYL corpus (Widmann *et al.*, 2011) were early versions of pedagogic corpora targeted at younger learners. These two corpora are now available on the *Backbone* (BB) website. In addition, BB is easily accessible and available online for free, which greatly increases the feasibility of teachers integrating it in their lessons. Multimedia corpora with multiple search options like BB are congruent with constructivist ideas that providing learners with several ways of exploring data is conducive to knowledge construction (Flowerdew, 2015).

In the Norwegian case study, the learners worked in groups during all sessions to accommodate collaborative dialogue, peer scaffolding, and metatalk, which is in line with socio-cultural learning theories (see also Flowerdew, 2015). Learners (N = 69) were divided into two classes, A and B. The teacher had taught the classes in question for about one semester prior to the DDL implementation. Notably, the teacher had some corpus background from his postgraduate studies and had also participated in an interview study with other in-service teachers with similar corpus backgrounds (Karlsen & Monsen, 2020). The project collaboration entailed back-and-forth planning between the researcher and the teacher, and the research design for the project was based on the topics and curricular aims established by the teacher prior to the researcher's involvement. The lesson plans were implemented in both classes (A and B) during a two-week period that amounted to five lessons per class per week, or a total of ten lessons per class. Data were collected through classroom observations and student group interviews post-implementation. The observations were done by the researcher in person and were recorded using a camera and three audio recorders to pick up group interactions. Two semi-structured group interviews were conducted for each class, each interview had five students. During the lessons, the learners first received a couple of task sets that gave specific instructions as to how they could explore the corpora in different ways, that is, frequency lists, concordance searches, and topic searches. Each task required a search and a discussion of the results. Secondly, they could choose between one of two topics relevant to an upcoming mock exam – environmental issues or gender in education – which were worded similarly to the imminent exam except it required the students to use the multimedia corpora available on the *Backbone* website as a starting point. They were also encouraged to use the corpus resources BB and Sketch Engine for Language Learners (a free online concordancer with an easy-to-use interface intended for learners developed by Baisa & Suchomel, 2014) offer, to help their writing. By structuring the tasks in an open-ended way in the same vein as their usual process, it was hoped to minimise the novelty of the innovative approach and treat corpora as auxiliary resources to the writing process.

According to Karlsen (2021), students' impressions of the corpora were largely negative. Students disliked the look of BB, citing cluttered interfaces, off-putting colour schemes, the website's apparent age, and poor audio and video quality as central issues. These opinions show that a concordancer with many search options is a double-edged sword; on the one hand, it can facilitate knowledge construction by providing a plethora of ways to examine the data (Flowerdew, 2015; see also Section 22.2), but on the other hand, it can overwhelm users and leave them demotivated or irritated. They also show that there is an aesthetic element to websites that influences student perspectives and has the potential to affect their first impression (see more on usability in Hendry and Sheepy, this volume). Moreover, although the teacher introduced each task and despite the written guide accompanying every individual task, many of the students had wished for more teacher guidance. Several students asked for help or claimed not to understand prior to reading the whole task guide. These perspectives suggest that more teacher-mediation and scaffolding would have been preferable with these learners, as opposed to a more autonomous discovery-learning mode. In the group interviews, none of the students felt they had learned anything new. They found the frequency list searches and KWIC searches somewhat useful, with one student commenting that he found it useful to see how sentences were constructed in English. During the interviews, several students commented that they had felt like they spent more time learning the computer tool than on the language itself. However, the observer noted several learning opportunities during the sessions (Karlsen, 2021). The observed discussions and learning opportunities mostly took place when the teacher worked with the learners as a large group to ask questions and drive the conversation forward. Still, the teacher commented that he felt little ownership over the tasksets, since much of their design had been done by the researcher. It seems like a paradox that the teacher lacked a feeling of ownership over a taskset despite the collaborative nature of the study; however, the issue of teacher's busy schedules is not unique to this study and remains an issue even in collaborative work. The often-reported obstacle of the use of corpora being time consuming both during planning and implementation in higher education is arguably amplified in pre-tertiary education. Moreover, it seems that open discovery with written guides was poorly received by these students, which suggests that a more teacher-guided approach akin to Kennedy and Miceli's (2017) apprenticeship is preferable. Students' perspectives are likely influenced by their previous learning habits and the complexities of the new tasks they face, and the new learning situations, skills, and new ways of thinking that come with a corpus-based approach may therefore require an incremental acclimatization.

22.5 The teacher education context

Implementing DDL in the mainstream of language classrooms might be attributed to the fact that there is a lack of awareness and training among teachers (Boulton & Tyne, 2014). A strong argument has been made for the integration of corpus literacy in teacher education programmes as the key to cascading that implementation to a myriad of professional language teaching contexts that will provide future teaching experiences for student teachers as qualified teachers (Farr, 2010; O'Keeffe & Farr, 2003), as well as being a legitimate approach in its own right in such contexts. It is not a given that all student teachers inducted into corpus methods will go on to implement them fully in their own future teaching because of "lack of confidence, time constraints, questions of relevance, and difficulty in orienting their students (and their courses) regularly to corpus-based foci" (Friginal, 2018, p. 7). However, in a teaching world which is still strongly influenced by what Lortie (1975) termed an "apprenticeship of observation" (we often base our teaching behaviours and actions on what we have seen others do in the classroom through our years of observing them as students), there is an educated assumption that some will. There are a number of natural homes for corpus integration in teacher education programmes (Farr, 2021), including within language studies and pedagogy modules, including language learning and technology modules, for all of the reasons discussed earlier in relation to alignments with SLA theory and associated practices. In addition, arguably even more important is the use of corpora as sources of evidence to engage in reflective practice and professional development (see Farr, 2015, 2021 for more details). This type of application will provide individual teachers and teacher educators with resources and techniques to examine their own local practices and those of their students, and complements corpus-based research accounts of such contexts such as those found in Farr *et al.* (2019).

In a relatively large-scale survey of English language teacher educators (N = 106), student teachers (N = 64), and practising teachers (N = 147) across 12 universities and 30 schools representing a wide range of geographical regions in Saudi Arabia, Aljohani (2016) reports some interesting findings. In a country which is currently upskilling its educators with respect to the integration of technology, it provides a good indicator of corpus use in pedagogic contexts. According to Abdel-Latif (2020), "in the Arab world, for example, corpora and corpus-based instruction have only started to gain the attention of a few researchers recently" (p. 2). A sample from Aljohani's results shows that familiarity with corpus linguistics among this community comes primarily from attending university programmes (including on-line) in countries outside of Saudi Arabia. Divergence was apparent in knowledge of corpus linguistics reported among the three groups, with 69% of the teacher educators reporting familiarity, but only 35% of student teachers and 11% of practising teachers, and most of this understanding had been acquired since 2010. The numbers fell further when asked if they used corpus-based approaches for any aspects of their work, with only 41% of teacher educators, 33% of student teachers, and 37% of practising teachers claiming to do so, but on a relatively infrequent basis. The BNC and Google as a corpus were identified as the favoured corpus resources. The purposes for which they accessed corpora centred around three main uses:

research (47% of teacher educators, 43% of student teachers, and 0% of practising teachers); teaching (40% of teacher educators, 0% of student teachers, and 68% of practising teachers); and consultation (10% of teacher educators, 43% of student teachers, and 33% of practising teachers). These results, although encouraging, prompt a discussion about the level of integration, the disparity between reported usage in teacher education and later integration by the same student teachers as qualified teachers in their language classroom, and the reasons that might lie behind all of this.

From the studies that report teacher-educator and student-teacher perceptions, a number of common themes emerge. There seems to be a relatively high level of awareness and very positive acknowledgement of the potential uses and benefits of corpus approaches among student teachers who have direct experience of DDL as part of their teacher education programme. However, a number of issues seem to impede the translation of this positive predisposition into their own longer-term teaching practices (Abdel-Latif, 2020). For this section, we reviewed some of the few empirical studies from teacher education settings in the Arab gulf (Abdel-Latif, 2020), Canada (Naismith, 2017), Germany (Breyer, 2009; Mukherjee, 2004), Iran (Ebrahimi & Faghih, 2017), Ireland (Farr, 2008), Poland (Leńko-Szymańska, 2014, 2017), the US (Heather & Helt, 2012; Zareva, 2017), Taiwan (Lin, 2019), Turkey (Çalışkan & Kuru-Gönen, 2018), and one on-line (Ebrahimi & Faghih, 2017). The list below summarises the perceived challenges identified by (student) teachers which appear to transform into barriers for integration into their own longer-term pedagogical practices:

a. Inductive and deductive approaches

Teachers seem to harbour a reservation about abandoning the traditional presentation of grammatical rules to direct learners' understanding and acquisition. This seems to be the case especially when teaching lower-level and younger learners. Teachers in geographical contexts where traditional teacher-fronted teaching is still prevalent, such as Taiwan, also see the inductive approach espoused in DDL as an enormous challenge (Lin, 2019).

b. Exposure to real language

While there is an acknowledgement of the value of authentic language as presented in corpora, teachers also suggest that there are also many difficulties when learners attempt to comprehend its meaning. It can be difficult, messy, colloquial, distracting, and often frustrating, again often at lower levels.

c. The role of the teacher

Some teachers feel a loss of control and, therefore, confidence when allowing their learners to engage in corpus-based discovery learning. They fear not being able to mediate the content, but they also fear not being able to understand or resolve corpus content highlighted by their learners. The ultimate risk is teacher exposure and potential loss of confidence by both parties. This is also linked to the issue of lack of familiarity and training in DDL methods.

d. Corpus and access-related difficulties

The issue of finding a relevant corpus, at the correct level, which contains adequate frequencies of the linguistic item(s) under scrutiny is often cited by teachers. Some technical issues are also mentioned, such as copying concordances to word documents, but in our experience, these seem to be diminishing as the technology becomes more sophisticated and as the support resources increase (for example, the SketchEngine video tutorials). Nonetheless, as seen in the previous section, even the effort of having to register for access can be off-putting for some in today's easy access, tech world. In addition, mention was frequently made about in-class constraints in terms of access to technology and reliable internet access, particularly in technology poor educational settings such as Iran (Ebrahimi & Faghih, 2017).

e. Competition from other online resources

The use of online dictionaries and Google seem to be highlighted by many teachers as more efficient ways of checking the meaning of words and phrases. In the case of corpus-based dictionaries, the attraction is that someone else has already done the messy work of extracting and neatly packaging the corpus data in the form of a neat explanation with examples. However, there is an acknowledgement that if teachers wish to explore usage as opposed to simply meaning, they make the extra effort to use corpus-based approaches.

f. Developing corpus-based materials

Several of the studies reviewed noted that teachers identified the following issues in relation to designing corpus-based materials for use in their classrooms: very time-consuming; they may not be appropriate for the levels of the learners due to difficulties in selecting and limiting examples from the corpus; and they may not yield the results anticipated by the teacher as learners may go in other directions when they access the corpora.

22.6 Future directions

From the discussions in this chapter, and in other parts of this handbook, it is clear that while much has been achieved, there remains much to be done in terms of the effective and wider-spread applications of DDL methodologies in the language teaching classroom. We contend that the best way to achieve this is to have well-informed, resourceful, and well-supported teachers, which ideally begins at the stage of pre-service education programmes and continues through a range of professional development engagements throughout their professional careers. We fully acknowledge that this is no small or simple task. In fact, "the course of becoming a DDL teacher is a complex, radical and continuous series of transformations" (Lin, 2019, p. 70). For this reason, its integration should ideally permeate all facets of teacher education programmes to allow for maximum exposure, practice, application, and formation (Farr, 2010, 2021; Leńko-Szymańska, 2014, 2017). These various facets include language studies, theory, pedagogy and practice, professional development, and research, and it has been argued elsewhere that corpus-based methodologies lend themselves easily to all of these dimensions and the inevitable and desirable overlaps between them (Farr & O'Keeffe, 2019). We fully support the suggestion that "only extensive exposure to corpora by future teachers coupled with suitable teacher training in the applications of corpora in language education may bring a substantial change in the scope of corpus use in language classrooms in the wide educational context" (Leńko-Szymańska, 2014, p. 260), and accept that even with such an approach, transformation into the future pedagogic practices of these student teachers will inevitably incur some level of diminution.

In terms of DDL in the language classroom, we make several recommendations. We have seen how the vast majority of studies emanate from the tertiary educational context which seems to lend itself more easily to this kind of approach. This leaves a significant gap in terms of studies with a focus on pre-tertiary pedagogical settings. The Norwegian case study represents one at the pre-tertiary level, Braun's (2007) case study another, but these are few and far between. The scarcity of studies coupled with the dearth of appropriate pedagogic resources serves as another major hurdle for pre-tertiary DDL. We suggest that there are several future directions that should be considered for corpus integration. First, there is a need for up-to-date, well-designed resources. The case study presented earlier in this chapter suggests that student impressions centred largely on the perceived age of the interface and the audio-visual material, and on the resources' perceived relevance to them. This remains an enormous hurdle due to the cost and effort required to create corpora, let alone multi-media corpora, of notable size. Secondly, the case study indicated that the learners found the language aspects of the corpora somewhat useful, while they found the topics less relevant (Karlsen, 2021). Conversely, *Backbone* (and similar multimedia corpora) lack the mass of language data to represent what learners think they need for reference or exploration. Larger written corpora of topically relevant texts and user-friendly interfaces could serve this purpose alongside topic-driven multimedia corpora. Thirdly, website aesthetics played a huge role in the students' feedback, both spontaneously during the sessions and retrospectively during the interviews. Larger projects collaborating with both the intended users and professional web designers may prove fruitful going forward. Generational and age-related factors for 15-16 year olds who have very high expectations of technology and multimedia resources are obviously playing a pivotal part in their perceptions. Their constant exposure to high quality, commercially-produced games, apps, and other technologies understandably creates exceptionally high expectations among the Tik-Tok generation (Tik-Tok is an example of one such application popular among teenagers at the time of writing). This, coupled with motivational issues for non-language specialist learners at secondary level, continues to create a challenging context for the integration of corpora and DDL.

In general, perhaps greatest is the need for more qualitative studies that focus on the intricacies of classroom dynamics and other SLA variables (O'Keeffe, 2020) when corpus-based activities are introduced. These might include a sharper focus on variables such as age, gender, language level, motivation, prior learning, among others. Many studies focus either on what teachers have done or what effects corpora have on some discreet language phenomena in student learning, to the detriment of pedagogic complexities (for example the focus on vocabulary acquisition in all the studies in Lee *et al.*, 2019, as discussed in the introduction). More emphasis should be put on the teachers and students and how they operate in classroom interactions. The relationship between these groups and DDL is both interesting and paramount to our understanding of how corpora can inform education.

Further reading

Boulton, A., & Cobb, T. (2017). Corpus use in language learning: A meta-analysis. *Language Learning,* 67(2), 348–393. The authors applied systematic procedures to summarise results from 64 studies into the effectiveness of using the tools and techniques of data-driven learning. Their findings reveal that DDL approaches result in large overall effects for both control/experimental group comparisons ($d = 0.95$) and for pre/post-test designs ($d = 1.50$). They identify areas in need of further investigation and suggest that although DDL research has improved over time, further changes are recommended.

Chambers, A. (2010). What is data-driven learning? In A. O'Keeffe & M. J. McCarthy (Eds.), *The Routledge handbook of corpus linguistics* (pp. 345–358). Routledge. The author provides a reader-friendly account of the core principles and practices of corpus linguistics in a data-driven learning context. It defines the fundamental concepts and illustrates the applications of DDL through the use of various examples from a range of language learning contexts.

Flowerdew, L. (2015). Data-driven learning and language learning theories. In A. Leńko-Szymańska & A. Boulton (Eds.), *Multiple affordances of language corpora for data-driven learning* (pp. 15–36). Benjamins. The author shows the connection between DDL and different learning styles and learning theories in her chapter in Leńko-Szymańska and Boulton (2015). The chapter provides the reader with insight into DDL's fit with contemporary language learning theories, particularly the noticing hypothesis, constructivism, and socio-cultural theory, and can, therefore, offer a robust theoretical foundation and rationale for the integration of corpora as a pedagogic resource in the classroom.

Friginal, E. (2018). *Corpus linguistics for English teachers: New tools, online resources, and classroom activities.* Routledge. The author delivers a comprehensive overview of pedagogical tools, resources and approaches for teachers who would want to discover and take advantages of corpora in their own teaching practice. His book presents a multitude of corpus types, tools and resources, as well as specific lesson ideas, while providing concrete tips for the teacher along the way. In the book, he covers the basics of corpus linguistics, corpus-based pedagogy, and DDL, which makes it suitable for newcomers and advanced users alike.

O'Keeffe, A. (2020). Data-driven learning – A call for a broader research gaze. *Language Teaching, 54*(2), 259–272. The author provides a theoretical account of the relationship between DDL and various theories related to second language acquisition, such as constructivism and socio-culturalism. She maps how differentiated DDL applications fit on a cline between these two theories so that language teachers may better understand the affordances of their applications in an attempt to suit their specific contexts and learners. She goes on to recommend some more nuanced approaches to research in DDL studies in a call to raise our understandings to a higher level of sophistication in practical and theoretical terms.

References

Abdel-Latif, M. (2020). Corpus literacy instruction in language teacher education: Investigating Arab EFL student teachers' immediate beliefs and long-term practices. *ReCALL, 33*(1), 1–15. https://doi.org/10.1017/S0958344020000129

Aljohani, W. (2016). *Corpus linguistics in language teacher education: Current status and future prospects in Saudi Arabia* [Unpublished doctoral dissertation]. University of Limerick.

Baisa, V., & Suchomel, V. (2014). Sketch engine for English language learning. In A. Horák & P. Rychlý (Eds.), *Proceedings of recent advances in Slavonic natural language processing* (pp. 63–70). Lexical Computing Ltd.

Bernardini, S. (2004). Corpora and the classroom: An overview and some reflections on future developments. In J. M. Sinclair (Ed.), *How to use corpora in language teaching* (pp. 15–38). Benjamins.

Boulton, A. (2012). Hands on/hands off: Alternative approaches to data-driven learning. In A. Boulton & J. Thomas (Eds.), *Input, process and product: Developments in teaching and language corpora* (pp. 152–168). Masaryk University Press.

Boulton, A., & Cobb, T. (2017). Corpus use in language learning: A meta-analysis. *Language Learning, 67*(2), 348–393.

Boulton, A., & Tyne, H. (2014). Corpus-based study of language and teacher education. In M. Bigelow & J. Ensser-Kananen (Eds.), *The Routledge handbook of educational linguistics* (pp. 301–312). Routledge.

Braun, S. (2007). Integrating corpus work into secondary education: From data-driven learning to needs-driven corpora. *ReCALL, 19*(3), 307–328.

Breyer, Y. (2009). Learning and teaching with corpora: Reflections by student teachers. *Computer Assisted Language Learning, 22*(2), 153–172.

Çalışkan, G., & Kuru-Gönen, S. I. (2018). Training teachers on corpus-based language pedagogy: Perceptions on vocabulary instruction. *Journal of Language and Linguistic Studies, 14*(4), 190–210.

Callies, M. (2019). Integrating corpus literacy into language teacher education. In S. Götz & J. Mukherjee (Eds.), *Learner corpora and language teaching* (pp. 245–263). Benjamins.

Cardona, M. D., Didriksen, A. A., & Gjesdal, A. M. (2014). Korpusbasert undervisning i fremmedspråkene: La elevenes nysgjerrighet sette dagsorden. *Acta Didactica Norge, 8*(2), 1–26.

Chambers, A. (2010). What is data-driven learning? In A. O'Keeffe & M. J. McCarthy (Eds.), *The Routledge handbook of corpus linguistics* (pp. 345–358). Routledge.

Chambers, A. (2019). Towards the corpus revolution? Bridging the research–practice gap. *Language Learning, 52*(4), 460–475.

Charles, M. (2012). Proper vocabulary and juicy collocations': EAP students evaluate do-it-yourself corpus-building. *English for Specific Purposes, 31*, 93–102.

Chen, M., & Flowerdew, J. (2018). A critical review of research and practice in data-driven learning (DDL) in the academic writing classroom. *International Journal of Corpus Linguistics, 23*(3), 335–369.

Crosthwaite, P. (2020). *Data-driven learning for the next generation: Corpora and DDL for pre-tertiary learners.* Routledge.

Ebrahimi, A., & Faghih, E. (2017). Integrating corpus linguistics into online language teacher education programs. *ReCALL, 29*(1), 120–135.

Farr, F. (2008). Evaluating the use of corpus-based instruction in a language teacher education context: Perspectives from the users. *Language Awareness, 17*(1), 25–43.

Farr, F. (2010). How can corpora be used in teacher education. In A. O'Keeffe & M. McCarthy (Eds.), *The Routledge handbook of corpus linguistics* (pp. 620–632). Routledge.

Farr, F. (2015). *Practice in TESOL.* Edinburgh University Press.

Farr, F. (2021). How can corpora be used in teacher education? In A. O'Keeffe & M.J. McCarthy (Eds.), *The Routledge handbook of corpus linguistics.* (2nd ed.) (pp. 620–632). Routledge.

Farr, F., Farrell, A., & Riordan, E. (2019). *Social interaction in language teacher education.* Edinburgh University Press.

Farr, F., & Murray, L., (Eds.). (2016). *The Routledge handbook of language learning and technology.* Routledge.

Farr, F., & O'Keeffe, A. (2019). Using corpus approaches in English language teacher education. In S. Walsh & S. Mann (Eds.), *The Routledge handbook of English language teacher education* (pp. 268–282). Routledge.

Flowerdew, L. (2015). Data-driven learning and language learning theories. In A. Leńko-Szymańska & A. Boulton (Eds.), *Multiple affordances of language corpora for data-driven learning* (pp. 15–36). Benjamins.

Frankenberg-Garcia, A. (2012). Learners' use of corpus examples. *International Journal of Lexicography, 25*(3), 273–296.

Friginal, E. (2018). *Corpus linguistics for English teachers. New tools, online resources, and classroom activities.* Routledge.

Gilquin, G., & Granger, S. (2010). How can data-driven learning be used in language teaching. In A. O'Keeffe & M. J. McCarthy (Eds.), *The Routledge handbook of corpus linguistics* (pp. 359–370). Routledge.

Healey, D. (2016). Language learning and technology. In F. Farr & L. Murray (Eds.), *The Routledge handbook of language learning and technology* (pp. 9–23). Routledge.

Heather, J., & Helt, M. (2012). Evaluating corpus literacy training for pre-service language teachers: Six case studies. *Journal of Technology and Teacher Education, 20*(4), 415–440.

Johns, T. (1991). Should you be persuaded - two samples of data-driven learning materials. *English Language Research Journal, 4*, 1–16.

Karlsen, P. H. (2021). Integrating multimedia corpora in the secondary school classroom. Invited public lecture. Inland University of Norway Faculty of Education., March 26, 2021.

Karlsen, P. H., & Monsen, M. (2020). Corpus literacy and applications in Norwegian upper secondary schools: Teacher and learner perspectives. *Nordic Journal of English Studies, 19*(1), 118–148.

Kavanagh, B. (In press). Bridging the gap from the other side: How corpora are used by English teachers in Norwegian schools. *Nordic Journal of English Studies, 20*(1), 1–35.

Kennedy, C., & Miceli, T. (2017). Cultivating effective corpus use by language learners. *Computer Assisted Language Learning, 30*(1-2), 91–114.

Kohn, K., Hoffstaedter, P., & Widmann, J. (2009). Backbone - pedagogic corpora for content & language integrated learning [paper presentation]. EuroCALL Conference, Universidad Politecnica de Valencia, Spain.

Lee, H., Warschauer, M., & Lee, J. H. (2019). The effects of corpus use on second language vocabulary learning: A multilevel meta-analysis. *Applied Linguistics, 40*(5), 721–753.

Leech, G. (1997). Teaching and Language Corpora: A Convergence. In A. Wichmann, S. Fligelstone, T. McEnery, & G. Knowles (Eds.), *Teaching and language corpora* (pp. 1–23). Longman.

Leńko-Szymańska, A. (2014). Is this enough? A qualitative evaluation of the effectiveness of a teacher-training course on the use of corpora in language education. *ReCALL, 26*(2), 260–278.

Leńko-Szymańska, A. (2017). Training teachers in data driven learning: Tackling the challenge. *Language Learning and Technology, 21*(3), 217–241.

Leńko-Szymańska, A., & Boulton, A. (2015). Data-driven learning in language pedagogy. In A. Leńko-Szymańska & A. Boulton (Eds.), *Multiple affordances of language corpora for data-driven learning* (pp. 1–14). Benjamins.

Lin, M. H. (2019). Becoming a DDL teacher in English grammar classes: A pilot study. *The Journal of Language Learning and Teaching, 9*(1), 70–82.

Lortie, D. C. (1975). *School-teacher: A sociological study.* University of Chicago Press.

McCarthy, M. J. (2020). Fifty-five years and counting: A half-century of getting it half-right? *Language Teaching, 53*(4), 1–12.

McCarthy, M. J. (2008). Accessing and interpreting corpus information in the teacher education context. *Language Teaching, 41*(4), 563–574.

McEnery, T., & Xiao, R. (2010). *Corpus-based contrastive studies of English and Chinese.* Routledge.

Mishan, F., & Timmis, I. (2015). *Materials development for TESOL.* Edinburgh University Press.

Mukherjee, J. (2004). Bridging the gap between applied corpus linguistics and the reality of English language teaching in Germany. In U. Connor & T. A. Upton (Eds.), *Language and computers, applied corpus linguistics. A multidimensional perspective* (pp. 239–250). Rodopi.

Mukherjee, J., & Rohrbach, J. M. (2006). Rethinking applied corpus linguistics from a language-pedagogical perspective: New departures in learner corpus research. In B. Kettemann & G. Marko (Eds.), *Planing, gluing and painting corpora: Inside the applied corpus linguist's workshop* (pp. 205–232). Peter Lang.

Murphy, B., & Riordan, E. (2016). Corpus types and uses. In F. Farr & L. Murray (Eds.), *The Routledge handbook of language learning and technology* (pp. 388–403). Routledge.

Naismith, B. (2017). Integrating corpus tools on intensive Celta courses. *ELT Journal, 71*(3), 273–283.

O'Keeffe, A. (2020). Data-driven learning – A call for a broader research gaze. *Language Teaching, 54*(2), 259–272. https://doi.org/10.1017/S0261444820000245

O'Keeffe, A., & Farr, F. (2003). Using language corpora in language teacher education: Pedagogic, linguistic and cultural insights. *TESOL Quarterly, 37*(3), 389–418.

O'Keeffe, A., McCarthy, M. J., & Carter, R. (2007). *From corpus to classroom.* Cambridge University Press.

O'Sullivan, Í. (Ed.). (2007). Enhancing a process-oriented approach to literacy and language learning: The role of corpus consultation literacy. *ReCALL, 19*(3), 269–286.

Pérez-Paredes, P. (2020). Data-driven learning in the secondary classroom. In P. Crosthwaite (Ed.), *Data-driven learning for the next generation: Corpora and DDL for pre-tertiary learners* (pp. 67–87). Routledge.

Pérez-Paredes, P., Guillamón, C. O., Van de Vyver, J., Meurice, A., Jiménez, P. A., Conole, G., & Hernández, P. S. (2019). Mobile data-driven language learning: Affordances and learners' perception. *System, 84*, 145–159.

Reppen, R. (2010). *Using corpora in the language classroom.* Cambridge University Press.

Römer, U. (2010). Using general and specialized corpora in English language teaching: Past, present and future. In M. C. Campoy, B. Belles-Fortuno, & M. L. Gea-Valo (Eds.), *Corpus-based approaches to English language teaching* (pp. 18–35). Continuum.

Römer, U. (2011). Corpus research applications in second language teaching. *Annual Review of Applied Linguistics.* 31, 205–225. 10.1017/S0267190511000055

Simpson, R. C., Briggs, S. L., Ovens, J., & Swales, J. M. (2002). *The Michigan Corpus of Academic Spoken English.* Retrieved from https://quod.Lib.Umich.Edu/cgi/c/corpus/corpus?C=micase;page=simple.

Timmis, I. (2015). *Corpus linguistics for ELT: Research and practice.* Routledge.

Tribble, C. (2015). Teaching and language corpora. In A. Leńko-Szymańska & A. Boulton (Eds.), *Multiple affordances of language corpora for data-driven learning* (pp. 37–64). Benjamins.

Vyatkina, N., & Boulton, A. (2017). Corpora in language learning and teaching. *Language Learning and Technology, 21*(3), 1–8.

Warren, M. (2016). Introduction to data-driven learning. In F. Farr & L. Murray (Eds.), *The Routledge handbook of language learning and technology* (pp. 237–247). Routledge.

Widmann, J., Kohn, K., & Ziai, R. (2011). The SACODEYL search tool - exploiting corpora for language learning purposes. In A. Frankenberg-Garcia, L. Flowerdew, & G. Aston (Eds.), *New trends in teaching and language corpora* (pp. 167–178). Continuum.

Zareva, A. (2017). Incorporating corpus literacy skills into TESOL teacher training. *ELT Journal, 71*(1), 69–79.

23

REVAMPING DDL: AFFORDANCES OF DIGITAL TECHNOLOGY

Fanny Meunier

23.1 Introduction

Data-driven learning (DDL), introduced in 1990 by Tim Johns, has come in multiple guises ranging from "serendipitous corpus exploration" (Boulton, 2020, p. xiv) to focus on pre-selected linguistic aspects. When the focus is on pre-selected linguistic aspects, teachers' guidance may vary for a mere suggestion of what lexical/grammatical items to focus on to a detailed pre-processing of the raw concordance lines combined with a scaffolded pedagogical guidance in the exercises presented to their pupils or students.

Thirty years after its inception, DDL has evolved in many ways in terms of the variety of approaches used, the types of corpora used, and the targeted end users of DDL. Examples include Corino and Onesti's (2019) DDL use in Content and Language Integrated Learning; Friginal and Roberts, this volume, for the use of DDL in language for specific purposes and more specifically aviation English; Crosthwaite (2020) for an opening to less advanced learners; Boulton and Cobb (2017) for an evolution towards more online access. What has not evolved, however, is that DDL is still mainly conceptualised as the analysis of written concordance lines (even in case of transcribed speech) on screen (e.g. electronic handouts, connections to online concordancers) or on paper (e.g. classroom handouts, concordance lines in textbooks). Surprisingly, the numerous advances in digital technology over the last 20 years (e.g. multimodality, mobility, etc.) have largely been absent from DDL research and applications (Hirata, 2020; Coccetta, this volume, for exceptions). It is, thus, high time to reconsider oft-quoted definitions of DDL, such as that proposed by Gilquin and Granger (2010) saying that "Data-driven learning (DDL) consists in using the tools and techniques of corpus linguistics for pedagogical purposes" (p. 359) or by Boulton (2011), who states, "the hands-on use of authentic corpus data (concordances) by advanced, sophisticated foreign or second language learners in higher education for inductive, self-directed language learning of advanced usage" (p. 572). Such definitions have become too narrow as they limit the boundaries of DDL to the tools and techniques of corpus linguistics, and somehow exclude an opening to other tools that have strong pedagogical potential for DDL. Another issue is that such definitions seem to target mostly advanced users. Also, the focus in such definitions seems to be on corpus linguistics first and pedagogy second, whilst I believe – in line with

 DOI: 10.4324/9781003002901-28

Kolb (2017) – that it should be 'Learning First, Technology Second', or even pedagogy first, technology second.

Pushing the boundaries of DDL would in no way betray the key concepts behind data-driven learning as initially conceptualised by Johns (1990) – i.e. learning driven by data – but it would definitely no longer ignore a number of current affordances that were not available at the inception of DDL; it would also give pedagogy the central position it deserves.

In the coming sections, the fundamentals of DDL are presented (Section 23.2) together with the reasons for revamping DDL and scaling it up to include the affordances of current digital technology and pedagogy (Section 23.3). Section 23.4 presents concrete recommendations and examples for practice, and Section 23.5 suggests future directions for research.

23.2 The fundamentals of DDL

Referring to the DDL literature, Boulton (2020) lists a number of important principles at play in DDL. They include authenticity, autonomy, chunking, consciousness-raising, constructivism, critical thinking, complexity and dynamic systems theory, discovery learning, focus on form, individualisation, induction, learner-centredness, (meta-)cognitive skills, noticing, salience, task-based learning, and usage-based learning. O'Keeffe (2021), when discussing elements that are pedagogically core to DDL, points to "the aim of fostering the independent acquisition of language knowledge (lexis, grammatical constructions, collocations, and so on)" (p. 259) and to the fact that learners are encouraged, in inductive processes, to discover patterns of language. She also refers to the fostering of complex cognitive processes (such as inferencing or forming hypotheses). Whilst strongly seconding Johansson's (2009) initial plea for a greater connection between DDL and second language acquisition (SLA) research, O'Keeffe (2021) states that "few of the many worthwhile DDL studies over the years have engaged with SLA theory" (p. 259) and makes a strong case for a broadening of our research gaze.

The various principles at play presented in DDL literature can, in my view, be grouped in three fundamentals (irrespectively of the various target populations, methods, corpora, or tools used): metalinguistic awareness, proxy for frequency effects, and authenticity. Comments on those fundamentals of DDL are provided in Sections 23.2.1–23.2.3. As for the learner-centredness commonly attributed to DDL, it is questioned in Section 23.2.4.

23.2.1 Metalinguistic awareness

As stated by Roehr-Brackin (2018), researchers in applied and instructed second language acquisition "tend to conceptualise metalinguistic awareness in terms of explicit knowledge about language" and tend to "distinguish between explicit and implicit knowledge, explicit and implicit memory, and explicit and implicit learning" (p. 3) despite the limitations of such a dichotomous view. Ellis (2005), for instance, describes the dynamic interface and the cooperative nature of implicit and explicit knowledge.

By presenting learners with awareness-raising tasks to promote discovery learning, teachers using DDL activities favour what Cummins (1987) calls metalinguistic development, defined by Roehr-Brackin (2018) as "a growing awareness of certain properties of language and the ability to analyse linguistic input" (p. 3).

23.2.2 Proxy for frequency effects

By taking – usually very large – corpora as initial data source, by retrieving instances of certain linguistic features (single words, word combinations, grammatical items, constructions of various types, etc.), and by presenting them visually in the form of concordance lines (be they pre-sorted or not), DDL activities act as proxies or boosters for frequency effects. Ellis (2002) explains what these frequency effects are:

> the piecemeal learning of many thousands of constructions and the frequency-biased abstraction of regularities within them. Determinants of pattern productivity include the power law of practice, cue competition and constraint satisfaction, connectionist learning, and effects of type and token frequency. The regularities of language emerge from experience as categories and prototypical patterns. The typical route of emergence of constructions is from formula, through low-scope pattern, to construction. (p. 143)

As learners in instructed settings rarely get a sufficient amount of input to facilitate the smooth development of frequency effects, DDL's focus on metalinguistic development (defined in the above paragraph as the growing awareness of certain properties of language and the ability to analyse linguistic input) serves as a proxy for frequency effects.

23.2.3 Authenticity

Authenticity is somehow a default or bonus parameter of DDL as corpora de facto include authentic language and are meant to be representative of actual language use. Access to authentic language through DDL activities makes it possible to focus on a variety of linguistic aspects including vocabulary, grammar, syntax, discourse, pragmatics, and prosody, pronunciation or interactions in the case of spoken, and multimodal corpora. The authenticity of corpus data will not be developed further here as most chapters in the present volume discuss the value of corpora (native, learner, expert, or novice corpora) as sources of authentic language. One key question is, however, worth answering by teachers before they decide to use corpora for DDL. Does the corpus that will be used for the planned DDL activities contain the type of authentic language that the students need to be exposed to? Or, in other words, is the available data type the right choice? Asking this question has implications for what constitutes a corpus today. Coming back to the initial definition of DDL given by Johns, i.e. learning driven by data (Section 23.1), data is the key word, and data can come in many guises. Current access to massive amount of data on the web makes it possible to also extend the perception of what a corpus is/should be.

As mentioned by Krajka (2007) when referring to the implementation of DDL in classrooms, teachers should make informed choices and make sure that corpora provide "adequate coverage of genres, modes and topics" (p. 52). He argued that whilst existing corpora may be adequate for a number of language foci, there may be a need to create custom-made collections based on online materials to guarantee greater relevance of the materials. Wilkinson (2006) also points to the need for creating tailor-made corpora and the use of the web as a corpus (see also Renouf & Kehoe, 2013, on using the web as a corpus to supplement existing resources). Whilst such "do-it-yourself", "dirty", or "messy" corpora may not have been tidied up, they may be more in line with the pedagogical aims of the teachers and the needs of the users.

23.2.4 Reconsidering learner-centredness

As announced at the beginning of Section 23.2, one of the oft-cited attributes of DDL – namely its learner-centredness – can be questioned and is worth reconsidering. Learner-centred pedagogy implies that students play an active role in their learning by combining prior knowledge and new knowledge gained through active participation to create new knowledge. In DDL, the scope of the active role played by the learner is extremely variable and comes in very different degrees. In cases of self-initiated corpus consultation (for instance to improve writing accuracy) students are fully in charge of their active learning (see for instance Jablonkai & Čebron, 2020 for a discussion of corpora as tools for self-driven learning). Even if metalinguistic awareness is initially trained during courses, learners with sufficient meta-cognitive skills can become fully independent and use their corpus literacy when they feel it may be useful. In such cases, learner-centredness is rather maximal.

In much more controlled and scaffolded activities, however, learner-centredness is less prevalent as teachers have to – and quite naturally so – carefully scaffold the activity to ease the inductive path to discovery. Corino and Onesti (2019), in their very interesting DDL study, carried out in a vocational context (a school for hairdressers where learners were of different ages, displayed low motivation, and could only rely on basic language competence ranging from A1 to A2), showed that students found concordances very useful and that it helped them resolve the crossword activity they were doing more quickly than the traditional analysis of a printed text. Despite the students' interest and positive reception of DDL activities, the learner-centredness is minimal in such cases as the corpus literacy skills acquired are probably unlikely to be reinvested in non-curricular activities.

Also, DDL scholars sometimes tend to oppose "traditional teaching" (usually left unspecified as to what it actually means, but often implicitly conceived as fully teacher-centred approaches) to learner-centered DDL activities where teachers let the student become active. As clearly argued by Karlsen (2021) this binary view ignores the fact that many teachers in their everyday practice already alternate between several roles (such as giver-of-information or facilitator) and are not afraid of giving up control to let students be active, be it individually or collaboratively. In addition, learner-centredness is not exclusively experienced as positive by learners who sometimes express confusion and abandonment when left to their own devices for DDL activities. In sum, learner-centred and teacher-centred approaches should not be presented as binary choices as they actually complement each other.

Finally, most current DDL activities in instructed settings are clearly teacher-initiated, which may limit their alleged learner-centredness. Section 23.4.3 will discuss contexts in which the impetus to learn originates in the learner and is independent of curriculum guidelines, educational policy, or teacher direction.

23.3 Revamping DDL: Addressing current issues

Three critical issues calling for a revamping of DDL are discussed in this section. The following aspects are addressed in turn: a loose link with education, a lack of engagement with SLA theory, and a missed digital turn.

23.3.1 *Loose links with education*

Trying to find reasons why DDL, despite being presented as useful and effective, is not more widespread at all levels of instructed settings, Boulton (2020) suggests the following answers:

- the majority of researchers in the field are themselves university academics (also mentioned by Chambers, 2019);
- university students are being by far the most extensively studied population in second language acquisition (SLA) and applied linguistics as a whole;
- research on teaching younger learners tends to be more the domain of education than that of applied linguistics; and
- each field having its own journals and cultures, education and applied linguistics do not talk to each other very much.

The result, as Boulton argues, is that DDL work in applied linguistics remains relatively unknown in educational circles.

In earlier publications (Meunier, 2019, 2020), adopting a reversed perspective, it was shown that applied linguists promoting DDL often tend to ignore, or at least fail to comment on, key educational principles. Very few DDL studies provide information on how the activities fit in the broader curricular context in which they are carried out and this often leads to weak instructional designs that lack constructive alignment, i.e. designs where "alignment between the objectives of a course or unit and the targets for assessing student performance" (Biggs, 1996, p. 347) is absent. The lack of explicit verbalisation on how DDL activities meet curricular demands or expectations is one of the reasons for its lack of uptake in teaching contexts other than university-level courses. If, for instance, the curriculum does not promote the development or assessment of higher level-cognitive processes, it seems more difficult to convince teachers and educational stakeholders of the value and benefits of including DDL activities in the teaching activities. In addition, if school exams and teaching practices are not constructively aligned, teachers and students might not be motivated to spend time on practices that do not directly help with exam results (Szudarski, 2020).

DDL promotes and trains strategic, digital, and metacognitive sub-competences which are meant to empower communicative competence as a whole (see Ortega, 2005, for a discussion of the notion of empowerment in instructed SLA). If such sub-competences cannot be reinvested or assessed, we also run the risk of adopting inequitable and construct 'invalid' assessment policies (Ortega, 2017, 2019; Shohamy, 2011).

Section 23.4 will provide concrete examples of how DDL activities can find their place in aligned educational designs.

23.3.2 *Lack of engagement with SLA theory*

This section illustrates the lack of engagement with SLA mentioned by O'Keeffe (2021) through the lens of vocabulary learning. Two (related) aspects will be commented on: features of vocabulary knowledge and focus on students with learning disabilities.

It is fair to argue that DDL activities are mostly used to work on the depth of vocabulary knowledge rather than on the breadth of vocabulary knowledge. According to Webb (2013), depth of vocabulary knowledge "refers to how well words are known. Developing vocabulary depth typically involves the accumulation of knowledge through encountering and using words in a variety of different contexts in order to learn the forms, meanings, and uses of words" (p. 1656), whilst breadth of vocabulary knowledge broadly refers to how many words are known (as typically measured by vocabulary size tests). The DDL literature focusing on vocabulary – given that awareness-raising methodology and higher cognitive skills are implied – often focuses on a limited number of words or expressions (and hence are probably not the best types of tasks to improve the breadth of vocabulary). In contrast, depth of vocabulary is central in DDL as learners are invited to discover, for instance, the same word used in various contexts, words or types of words that occur with a given word, or patterns that can be found around that word.

When looking at Nation's (2001) list of features involved in word knowledge – subdivided into three main categories, form, meaning, use – DDL can be said to address some written formal features (how is the word written and spelled?), some features related to meaning (what meaning does this word form signal?), and some features on constraints of use (what words or types of words occur with this word? when, where, and how often can we expect to meet/use the word?). One key aspect that is conspicuously missing in DDL, however, is the spoken features of word knowledge (what does the word sound like receptively? how is the word pronounced productively?). This is surprising as SLA studies have shown the positive impact of combining various input modalities, not only aural but also visual (Hashemi & Pourgharib, 2013; Mashhadi & Jamalifar, 2015). Multimodal input (print, audio, imagery, video, etc.) has been shown to make input more comprehensible (Plass & Jones, 2005; Zarei & Khazaie, 2011). The Dual Coding Theory developed by Paivio (see his 2007 book for a discussion on the evolution and current status of the theory) basically posits that whilst verbal and non-verbal stimuli are processed by two different systems, they interact, and that their simultaneous activation results in better vocabulary recall. Recent research also reveals that multimodal input (e.g. TV viewing) benefits learners' L2 proficiency and vocabulary knowledge (Peters, 2019; Peters & Muñoz, 2020; Peters *et al.*, 2019; Puimège & Peters, 2020).

Section 23.4 will provide concrete examples of how multimodality can become part-and-parcel of DDL activities (thanks to the use of digital apps), even in cases where DDL is carried out on the basis of 'simple' written corpora (thanks to, for instance, the use if assistive technology such as text-to-speech tools).

23.3.3 Missed digital turn

As DDL activities are using electronic corpora (as data sources) and corpus tools such as concordancers (as data analysis and presentation tools), the creators of DDL activities need skills in corpus literacy. Corpus literacy is defined by Heather and Helt (2012) as "the ability to use the technology of corpus linguistics to investigate language and enhance the language development of students" (p. 417). Given the need – expressed in Section 23.1 – for scaling-up DDL, DDL specialists need broader digital competences that go beyond corpus literacy.

As explained on the European Union Science Hub the "teaching professions face rapidly changing demands, which require a new, broader and more sophisticated set of competences than before. The ubiquity of digital devices and applications, in particular, requires educators to develop their digital competence". The European Framework for the Digital Competence of Educators (Redecker, 2017) is directed towards educators at all levels of education and describes what it means for educators to be digitally competent. It provides a general reference frame to support the development of educator-specific digital competences.

As evidenced in the framework, educators' professional and pedagogic competences are key. All areas cannot possibly be commented on in the framework of this chapter, but I will focus on two areas, namely assessment strategies (4.1 in Figure 23.1) and on the fifth area,

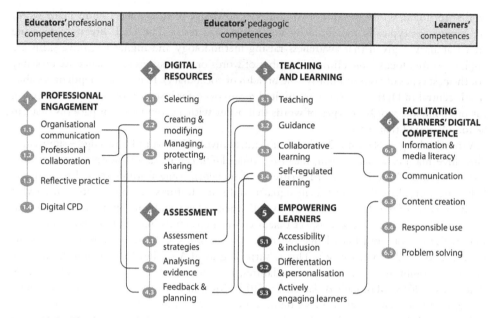

Educators' professional competences	Educators' pedagogic competences	Learners' competences

Figure 23.1 The framework for digital competences for educators (Redecker, 2017, p. 8)

empowering learners, which refers to the use of digital technologies to enhance accessibility and inclusion, differentiation and personalisation, and learners' active engagement.

In relation to assessment strategies, and beyond the need for constructive alignment already described in Section 23.3.1., it is important to "consider how digital technologies can enhance existing assessment strategies" and "how they can be used to create or to facilitate innovative assessment approaches" (Redecker, 2017, p. 21). As for the empowerment of learners, Redecker (2017, p. 22) insists that learning resources and activities:

- be made accessible and available to all learners, including those with special needs;
- address learners' diverse learning needs, by allowing learners to advance at different levels and speeds, and to follow individual learning pathways and objectives;
- foster learners' active and creative engagement with a subject matter;
- foster learners' transversal skills, deep thinking, and creative expression;
- open up learning to new, real-world contexts, which involve learners themselves in hands-on activities, scientific investigation or complex problem solving, or in other ways increase learners' active involvement in complex subject matters.

I believe that there is plenty of room for improvement in those areas for DDL. Concrete examples of how the inclusion of digital tools can help reach those aims in DDL activities are provided in the next section.

23.4 Recommendations for practice: DDL-ising teaching instead of doing stand-alone DDL activities

This section provides examples of how teachers can integrate DDL in their teaching, or, in other words, DDL-ise their teaching (Meunier, 2020). The key idea behind this concept is to keep the fundamentals of DDL (see Section 23.2) but ensure that the issues addressed in Section 23.3 are taken care of, namely ensuring more links with education and with SLA, and making better use of the affordances of digital tools. In doing so, we maximise opportunities for the inclusion of DDL at more levels of instructions, and for more learners. In sum, DDL should be revamped to:

1. integrate new input types and more multimodality;
2. be more inclusive;
3. integrate new tools (be it by using high tech or low-tech tools, or even by leveraging tools 'from the wild' into the classroom);
4. make sure that the assessment of DDL transcends purely linguistic outcomes to include strategic ones too.

Concrete examples are subdivided into three parts in the subsequent sections: high-tech DDL, low-tech DDL, and wild-tech DDL. The vocabulary focus adopted in Section 23.2 will also be kept in the examples given below. After each subsection, the same checklist will be used (Table 23.1) to see whether the elements presented above are covered, in what way, and to which degree.

Table 23.1 Check-list for revamped DDL activities

	Comments
Presence of the fundamentals of DDL (metalinguistic awareness, proxy for frequency effects, authenticity)	
Integration of additional input types	
Enhanced inclusion	
Integration of new digital tools	
Inclusion of strategic DDL skills in assessment	

23.4.1 High-tech DDL: Including multimodality

Coccetta (this volume) presents examples of DDL activities with a corpus that has been collected from the onset as a multimodal corpus. The example presented below offers suggestions for transforming DDL activities based on a written corpus. The idea is to use existing text-to-speech (TTS) technology to provide new input modalities with a view of fostering dual coding for all learners and helping learners with learning difficulties such as dyslexia (as dyslexic students find it particularly hard to decode written text, particularly when the decoding is a pre-requisite for further metalinguistic awareness-raising activities).

Svensson *et al.* (2019) show that the use of assistive technology seems to have "transfer effects on reading ability and to be supportive, especially for students with the most severe difficulties" (p. 1). In addition, it increases motivation overall. Bione and Cardoso (2020) state that SLA researchers and practitioners "have explored the pedagogical capabilities of text-to-speech (TTS) synthesisers [...] for their potential to enhance the acquisition of writing (Kirstein, 2006), vocabulary and reading (Proctor *et al.*, 2007), and pronunciation (Liakin *et al.*, 2017; Qian *et al.*, 2018; Soler-Urzua, 2011)" (p. 169). Studies have found that TTS is useful for vocabulary acquisition and reading training as it reduces decoding demands (Bione & Cardoso, 2020). Given what precedes, instead of working with written concordances lines alone, these lines can also be read by existing TTS tools. In addition to being a "vital resource for students with dyslexia to aid reading, promote comprehension, and enhance overall literacy skills" (DyslexiaHelp, 2021, online), such tools offer all students access to an additional input mode that facilitates dual coding, in this case listening-while-reading, which has been shown to promote word learning (Valentini et al., 2018).

One example[1] of TTS tools is Natural Reader (NaturalSoft, n.d.); it allows users to listen to documents from their desktop or mobile phones. The free version includes a few voices (and the paid versions include hundreds of different voices – male, female, adult, child voices) – from 16 different languages. The tool also has an option for dyslexic font (which facilitates reading for dyslexic students) and highlights the words from the text as they are being read. Speed of reading can also be tuned (from slower to more rapid spoken production of the text).

In addition to the inclusion of the tool in the DDL activity, its strategic benefits (e.g. perceived ease of use or usefulness for an enhanced comprehension for students with dyslexia) could be assessed by using the technology acceptance model (TAM) and its related questionnaires (e.g. King & He, 2006, for a meta-analysis of the TAM).

Table 23.2 presents the assessment of the use of TTS tools in DDL activities against the proposed checklist.

Table 23.2 Using the check-list for a TTS tool in DDL activities

	Comments
Presence of the fundamentals of DDL (metalinguistic awareness, proxy for frequency effects, authenticity)	YES
Integration of additional input types	YES – aural input
Enhanced inclusion	YES – for all learners: varied voices, speed / plus assistive technology for, among others, dyslexic students
Integration of new digital tools	YES – NLP technology / text-to-speech tools
Inclusion of strategic DDL skills in assessment	YES – use of the TAM to assess benefits for users

23.4.2 Low-tech DDL: Using more accessible tools

The term "low tech" has different senses ranging from basic non-electronic tools (e.g. scissors, a pen) to new technology that is designed to be as simple and accessible as possible. In the present chapter, it will be used in the latter sense and will include, for instance, simple and freely accessible digital tools which are user-friendly and do not require previous training/ knowledge to be used. Traditional DDL tasks could be nicely complemented with (or why not even replaced by) the use of free website or apps that were either not initially created to help learners acquire vocabulary or that have been created to help learners with vocabulary acquisition in innovative and fun ways.

In 2012, Boulton already questioned data types in DDL (e.g. "What data for data-driven learning?"). He suggested using Google, or any other general purpose search engine, as a concordancer – and hence the web as a corpus as data – arguing that, despite its limitations, if linguists use Google, then language learners whose requirements are less stringent than those of linguists might also use this familiar tool with a user-friendly interface. When wondering whether such uses would constitute data-driven learning, he argued that DDL is "not an all-or-nothing affair: its boundaries are fuzzy, and any identifiable cut-off point will necessarily

Table 23.3 Using the check-list for Google as a concordancer in DDL activities

	Comments
Presence of the fundamentals of DDL (metalinguistic awareness, proxy for frequency effects, authenticity)	YES
Integration of additional input types	POSSIBLE (if results are read by TTS tools)
Enhanced inclusion	YES – easy access, intuitive
Integration of new digital tools	POSSIBLE (if results are read by TTS tools)
Inclusion of strategic DDL skills in assessment	POSSIBLE (not discussed in detail in the example presented but possible if web access granted during formative or certificative assessment tasks)

be arbitrary" (Boulton, 2011, p. 575) and that whilst Johns was mainly working with corpora, he chose the term "data-driven" rather than "corpus-driven" and that "the data is primary" (Johns, 1990, p. 3).

The assessment of the use of Google as a concordance against the checklist is presented in Table 23.3.

In Meunier (2020), I described the potential of an open-access tool that can be used for oral input-based/enhanced DDL activities: the Playphraseme app (https://www.playphrase. me) or web interface (which has recently become fee-paying and limits the number of views) which allows users to search for an almost endless list of common phrases of the English language. The example given was that of *give* as initial keyword inserted in the search line which prompts the selection of more words, such as *me* and then *a*. After pressing the play button after selecting *give me a*, users are presented with very short excerpts (often a couple of seconds) of recent video clips from films or series where the characters use that phrase (137 occurrences in the present case). If students are asked by the teacher to spot expressions starting with *give me a*, they will hear, see, and read (as the transcribed text is also visible on screen) numerous examples of *give me a break*, *give me a reason*, *give me a minute*, *give me a hand*, *give me a chance*, *give me a call*, etc., in films or series like Breaking Bad, Sherlock Holmes, Game of Thrones, House, or Big Bang Theory. When working with, for instance, communicative phrasemes like *come on in* or *help yourself to*, the cognitive visualisation of the input is even stronger as users clearly see people opening doors and inviting others in (for *come on in*) or people inviting others to take the food and/or drink they want to (for *help yourself to*). Table 23.4 presents how Playphraseme measures against the checklist.

Table 23.4 Using the check-list for film and series transcripts as data sources for DDL

	Comments
Presence of the fundamentals of DDL (metalinguistic awareness, proxy for frequency effects, authenticity)	YES
Integration of additional input types	YES – aural and visual input
Enhanced inclusion	YES – multiple input sources (aural, textual, visual), connections with real life TV series and films
Integration of new digital tools	YES – open access website and mobile app
Inclusion of strategic DDL skills in assessment	Not discussed in the example presented

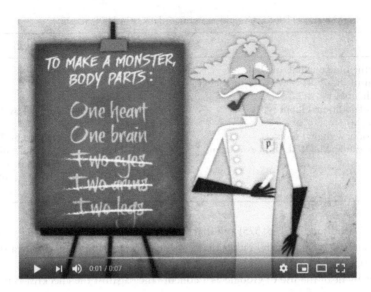

Figure 23.2 Screenshot from Phrasalstein[2]

Other tools that can be used in this category include the Phrasalverb Machine and Phrasalstein, both created by Cambridge University Press. Phrasal verbs are particularly difficult to learn for non-native speakers and are – probably subsequently – also underused by learners (Gilquin, 2015). It has also been shown that studying lists of phrasal verbs often turns out to be ineffective (Vasbieva, 2015). Taking such premises into consideration, and adding the fact that phrasal verbs are actions that can be visualised, the apps make it possible to visualise the action performed by phrasal verbs. The Phrasalverb Machine app offers animated illustrations of 100 phrasal verbs. As for Phrasalstein, it presents humorous animated videos of phrasal verbs inspired by the horror movie genre, with a touch of humour and irony. Users can scroll the dial to a verb and a preposition and hit "view". A short-animated clip is then presented and an additional window gives the meaning or translation and provides a sample sentence. Figure 23.2 above is a screenshot of *cross-out*. When played, the video shows the doctor crossing out the body parts needed to make a monster one after the other.

Such apps could be used to complement (or better illustrate) DDL activities targeting phrasal verbs. As recent research has shown, the effectiveness of mental imagery for teaching L2 formulaic sequences (Le-Thi *et al.*, 2020), concrete visualisations of phrasal verbs may come in handy in strengthening the depth of knowledge of such multiword units.

The assessment of those two apps against the checklist is given below in Table 23.5.

Table 23.5 Using the check-list for animated clips as part of DDL activities

	Comments
Presence of the fundamentals of DDL (metalinguistic awareness, proxy for frequency effects, authenticity)	YES – if the activity is scaffolded to develop metalinguistic awareness prior to the use of the app
Integration of additional input types	YES – visual input
Enhanced inclusion	YES – freely accessible mobile app
Integration of new digital tools	YES – mobile apps for learning
Inclusion of strategic DDL skills in assessment	Probably not with such apps

23.4.3 *Wild-tech DDL: Gaming*

Bell (2012) reviews recent literature in order to examine the reciprocal relationship between formulaic language and L2 language play demonstrating that language play can also create new linguistic conventions and that the use of formulaic language is needed in such contexts. Whilst Bell's research focuses on the use of play in classroom settings, other researchers have shown that gaming in non-instructed contexts can be beneficial for L2 acquisition.

Gaming is part of what Sauro and Zourou (2019) call the digital wilds (hence, the heading of the present section) defined as "informal language learning that takes place in digital spaces, communities, and networks that are independent of formal instructional contexts" (p. 2). The authors explain that the assumptions embedded in the concept of digital wilds are the following ones (Sauro & Zourou, 2019, pp. 2–3):

- learning takes place out-of-class within a digital context or community that is not governed or developed by a formally recognised school, university, or education provider;
- learning does not take place within a digital context or community with a primary goal of language teaching and learning;
- the impetus to learn in the out-of-class, digital context or community originates in the learner and not from curriculum guidelines, educational policy, or teacher direction;
- learning is not directly mediated by curriculum guidelines, educational policy, teacher practice, or norms of evaluation.

In her analysis of the uptake of affordances for language learning by young Danish children (aged 7 to 11) in their engagement with English language media in the digital wild (gaming, snapchatting etc.), Hannibal Jensen (2019) shows that most of the participants were motivated in their engagement with English by social and higher cognitive motives. Sundqvist (2019) further discusses how the use of commercial off-the-shelf games plays a role in extramural language practice, and how it helps enhance vocabulary learning. She worked with a large number of subjects, comparing and using a quantitative-dominant mixed-methods approach involving questionnaires, and productive and receptive vocabulary tests. The results of her study comparing gamers and non-gamers' vocabulary show a significant positive correlation between time played and test scores. Gamers revealed significantly higher scores at all vocabulary frequency levels and for particularly difficult words.

The advantages of gaming for language learning include[3] positive associations (fun) and engagement (playing and not studying, full user-centeredness), in-context immersive learning, multiple input and output modes (listening, reading, speaking, writing, online synchronous or asynchronous interactions), learning by doing, repetitions (repeatedly hearing, seeing, using the same words or expressions), easy access, and access to multilingualism (as many games can be tuned to be used in different languages). In addition, gaming is open to all ages, proficiency levels, and offers options for all tastes. Children can find games based on cartoon characters that can be played alone or with their parents (e.g. Nickelodeon Games, http://www.nick.tv/games/). Teenagers can use games taking music, videos, commercials, news, inspiring talks as input (e.g. FluentU, https://www.fluentu.com/, with possible access to complete interactive transcripts of the videos and options to review words and phrases from the video; or LyricsTraining, https://lyricstraining.com/app, for lovers of music videos).

Table 23.6 Using the check-list for digital games as DDL activities

	Comments
Presence of the fundamentals of DDL (metalinguistic awareness, proxy for frequency effects, authenticity)	YES – it should be noted that the metalinguistic awareness would not be guided by a teacher and would originate from the learners/users of the tools themselves
Integration of additional input types	YES – aural, visual
Enhanced inclusion	YES – mobile apps
Integration of new digital tools	YES – gaming
Inclusion of strategic DDL skills in assessment	Probably not with such games as they would mainly be used out of class in informal settings

The use of such language data and tools does not correspond to the use of a corpus in the traditional sense of the word but it constitutes authentic language use (see Section 23.2.3), learning is driven by the data, and it offers access to more adequate coverage of genres, modes, and topics in line with the pedagogical aims of the teachers and the needs of the users. Table 23.6 presents the assessment of such games against the checklist.

23.5 Future directions of research

This chapter has highlighted the needs for DDL advocates to push the boundaries of DDL to maximise opportunities of active learning driven by the data and has presented concrete ways of doing so. Boundaries can be pushed by establishing more links with education and presenting more aligned and situated DDL practices to improve uptake in more varied instructed settings.

The importance of better commenting on the benefits of using DDL for SLA has also been addressed. The call for more links with SLA expressed in this chapter also entails that the links should go far beyond a focus on a limited number of linguistic outcomes, or on whether or not users find DDL motivating or useful. The metalinguistic development that DDL promotes and the strategic skills that DDL requires are at least as important as – and probably more important than – the linguistic gains. In my view, future studies on DDL should aim to assess learners' metalinguistic skill (or metalinguistic capacity or ability – presented as synonyms by Roehr-Brackin, 2018), i.e. "the capacity to use knowledge about language as opposed to the capacity to use language" (Bialystok, 2001, p. 124). As a type of metacognition, metalinguistic awareness allows students to reflect, monitor, and control their use of language to make conscious decisions about what they can do to improve their learning. The importance of metacognition for various aspects of academic performance is now recognised (Salatas Waters & Schneider, 2010) and empirical studies suggest developmental changes in the relationship between monitoring and self-regulatory abilities, with learners being able to regulate their achievement-related behaviour. Currently, DDL proponents stress the fact that DDL promotes metalinguistic awareness but this awareness, or the actual impact it has on language use, is hardly ever assessed.

This chapter has also shown that analysing written concordance lines, be it on paper or on screen, is only one way of doing DDL. The examples given in Section 23.4 show that changing, adapting, and complementing current mainstream DDL practices by exploiting the affordances of existing digital tools does in no way question the fundamentals of DDL. The inclusion of new digital tools (be they high-tech, low-tech or wild-tech) to DDL-ise teaching makes it possible to add input modes, to be more inclusive (target much broader types of student populations, help students with learning difficulties, etc.), and to maximise opportunities for learning driven by the data in instructed and extra-mural (wild) settings. The use of wild tech DDL has also stressed the cooperative nature of implicit and explicit knowledge (Section 23.2) and the fact that – in line with Roehr-Brackin (2018) – it might be worth reconsidering a view of metalinguistic awareness as being exclusively conceptualised in terms of explicit knowledge about language.

It should also be stressed that the examples presented in Section 23.4 are only but a few illustrations and that the leading thread adopted was that of vocabulary. Many more foci (e.g. grammar, discourse, pragmatics) could also benefit from a revamped DDL view. Researchers, teachers and learners alike are strongly encouraged to share with the research and teaching communities their findings on tools and methods that can be used to revamp DDL and maximise opportunities for DDL-ised teaching and learning. A new definition for revamped DDL, or DDL 2.0, could then be learning driven by the use of aligned pedagogical practices which promote the use of authentic data – in various modalities and possibly with the help of various digital tools – to foster the metalinguistic awareness of language patterns.

Other avenues for future research that would be worth considering are a focus on studies addressing longer term linguistic gains (instead of studies focusing on the gains after only of few hours of DDL tasks) and on the long-term benefits of including multiple types of DDL tasks in learning activities.

Notes

1 For more examples of free, paid, and online TTS tools, see for instance https://www.techradar.com/best/best-text-to-speech-software
2 Short video available on https://www.youtube.com/watch?v=H4-ABIOzO8s
3 See https://www.fluentu.com/blog/language-learning-video-games/# for a convincing and lengthier discussion on the benefits of gaming. Readers might even want to pass on the link to their students to encourage them to game for language learning.

Further reading

Crosthwaite, P. (Ed.). (2020). *Data-driven learning for the next generation. Corpora and DDL for pre-tertiary learners*. Routledge. https://doi.org/10.4324/9780429425899. This edited volume targets DDL for pre-tertiary learners and includes numerous chapters stressing the importance of anchoring DDL practices in situated educational contexts.
O'Keeffe, A. (2021). Data-driven learning – A call for a broader research gaze. *Language Teaching*, *54*(2), 259–272. 10.1017/S0261444820000245. This recent chapter provides a solid rationale for more connections between DDL and SLA. It also lists areas that would deserve specific research interest.
Sauro, S., & Zourou, K. (Eds.). (2019). CALL in the digital wilds. Special issue of *Language Learning & Technology*, *23*(1). This special issue of Language Learning & Technology deepens our understanding of computer-assisted language learning practices in the digital wilds. It also offers concrete examples of how digital wilds can benefit SLA.

References

Bell, N. (2012). Formulaic language, creativity, and language play in a second language. *Annual Review of Applied Linguistics*, *32*, 189–205. https://doi.org/10.1017/S0267190512000013
Biggs, J. (1996). Enhancing teaching through constructive alignment. *Higher Education*, *32*, 347–364. https://doi.org/10.1007/BF00138871

Bialystok, E. (2001). *Bilingualism in development: Language, literacy, and cognition.* Cambridge University Press.

Bione, T., & Cardoso, W. (2020). Synthetic voices in the foreign language context. *Language Learning & Technology, 24*(1), 169–186. https://doi.org/10125/44715

Boulton, A. (2011). Data-driven learning: The perpetual enigma. In S. Goźdź-Roszkowski (Ed.), *Explorations across languages and corpora* (pp. 563–580). Peter Lang.

Boulton, A. (2020). Data-driven learning for younger learners: Obstacles and optimism. In P. Crosthwaite (Ed.), *Data-driven learning for the next generation. Corpora and DDL for pre-tertiary learners* (pp. xiv–xx). Routledge. https://doi.org/10.4324/9780429425899

Boulton, A., & Cobb, T. (2017). Corpus use in language learning: A meta-analysis. *Language Learning, 67*(2), 348–393. https://doi.org/10.1111/lang.12224

Chambers, A. (2019). Towards the corpus revolution? Bridging the research–practice gap. *Language Teaching, 52*(4), 460–475. https://doi.org/10.1017/S0261444819000089

Corino, E., & Onesti, C. (Eds.). (2019). Data-driven learning: A scaffolding methodology for CLIL and LSP teaching and learning. *Frontiers in Education, 4*(7), 1–12. https://doi.org/10.3389/feduc.2019.00007

Crosthwaite, P. (Ed.). (2020). *Data-driven learning for the next generation. Corpora and DDL for pre-tertiary learners.* Routledge. https://doi.org/10.4324/9780429425899

Cummins, J. (1987). Bilingualism, language proficiency, and metalinguistic development. In P. Homel, M. Palij, & D. Aaronson (Eds.), *Childhood bilingualism: Aspects of linguistic, cognitive, and social development* (pp. 57–73). Erlbaum.

DyslexiaHelp. (2021). *10 Helpful Text-to-Speech Readers for Back to School.* http://dyslexiahelp.umich.edu/tools/software-assistive-technology/text-to-speech-readers

Ellis, N. C. (2002). Frequency effects in language processing. A review with implications for theories of implicit and explicit language acquisition. *Studies in Second Language Acquisition, 24,* 143–188.

Ellis, N. C. (2005). At the interface: Dynamic interactions of explicit and implicit language knowledge. *Studies in Second Language Acquisition, 27,* 305–352. https://doi.org/10.1017/S027226310505014X

Gilquin, G. (2015). The use of phrasal verbs by French-speaking EFL learners. A constructional and collostructional corpus-based approach. *Corpus Linguistics and Linguistic Theory, 11*(1), 51–88.

Gilquin, G., & Granger, S. (2010). How can data-driven learning be used in language teaching. In A. O'Keeffe & M. McCarthy (Eds.), *The Routledge handbook of corpus linguistics* (pp. 359–370). Routledge.

Hannibal Jensen, S. (2019). Language learning in the wild: A young user perspective. *Language Learning & Technology, 23*(1), 72–86. https://doi.org/10125/44673

Hashemi, M., & Pourgharib, B. (2013). The effect of visual instruction on new vocabularies learning. *International Journal of Basic Science and Applied Research, 2*(6), 623–627.

Heather, J., & Helt, M. (2012). Evaluating corpus literacy training for pre-service language teachers: Six case studies. *Journal of Technology and Teacher Education, 20*(4), 415–440.

Hirata, E. (2020). The development of a multi-modal corpus for young EFL learners: A case study on the integration of DDL in teacher education. In P. Crosthwaite (Ed.), *Data driven learning for the next generation: Corpora and DDL for pre-tertiary learners* (pp. 88–105). Routledge. https://doi.org/10.4324/9780429425899-6

Jablonkai, R. R., & Čebron, N. (2020). Corpora as tools for self-driven learning: A corpus-based ESP course. In I. Management Association (Ed.), *Language learning and literacy: Breakthroughs in research and practice* (pp. 166–190). IGI Global.

Johansson, S. (2009). Some thoughts on corpora and second-language acquisition. In K. Aijmer (Ed.), *Corpora and language teaching* (pp. 33–44). Benjamins.

Johns, T. (1990). From printout to handout: Grammar and vocabulary teaching in the context of data-driven learning. *CALL Austria, 10,* 14–34.

Karlsen, P. H. (2021). Educational roles in corpus-based education: Shift or diversification? *Nordic Journal of Language Teaching and Learning, 9*(1), 1-12.

King, W., & He, J. (2006). A meta-analysis of the technology acceptance model. *Information and Management, 43,* 740–755.

Kirstein, M. (2006). *Universalizing universal design: Applying text-to-speech technology to English language learners' process writing* (Doctoral dissertation). University of Massachusetts, Boston, MA. Retrieved from https://search.proquest.com/openview/fa884a7aa83b7cdf43dc49d92e4ca645/1?pq-origsite=gscholar&cbl=18750&diss=y

Kolb, L. (2017). *Learning first, technology second: The educator's guide to designing authentic lessons.* International Society for Technology in Education.

Krajka, J. (2007). Corpora and language teachers: From ready-made to teacher-made collections. *CORELL: Computer Resources for Language Learning, 1,* 36–55.

Le-Thi, D., Dörnyei, Z., & Pellicer-Sánchez, A. (2020). Increasing the effectiveness of teaching L2 formulaic sequences through motivational strategies and mental imagery: A classroom experiment. *Language Teaching Research, 1-29.* https://doi.org/10.1177/1362168820913125

Liakin, D., Cardoso, W., & Liakina, N. (2017). The pedagogical use of mobile speech synthesis: Focus on French liaison. *Computer Assisted Language Learning, 30*(3–4), 348–365.

Mashhadi, F., & Jamalifar, G. (2015). Second language vocabulary learning through visual and textual representation. *Procedia - Social and Behavioral Sciences, 192,* 298–307. https://doi.org/10.1016/j.sbspro.2015.06.043

Meunier, F. (2019). Resources for learning multiword items. In S. Webb (Ed.), *The Routledge handbook of vocabulary studies* (pp. 336–350). Routledge.

Meunier, F. (2020). A case for constructive alignment in DDL: Rethinking outcomes, practices and assessment in (data-driven) language learning. In P. Crosthwaite (Ed.), *Data-driven learning for the next generation: Corpora and DDL for pre-tertiary learners* (pp. 13–31). Routledge. https://doi.org/10.4324/9780429425899-2

Nation, I. S. P. (2001). *Learning vocabulary in another language.* Cambridge University Press.

NaturalSoft Ltd (n.d.) *Natural Reader* [Computer Software] https://www.naturalreaders.com/index.html

O'Keeffe, A. (2021). Data-driven learning – A call for a broader research gaze. *Language Teaching, 54*(2), 259–272. https://doi:10.1017/S0261444820000245

Ortega, L. (2005). For what and for whom is our research? The ethical as transformative lens in instructed SLA. *The Modern Language Journal, 89*(3), 427–443. https://doi.org/10.1111/j.1540-4781.2005.00315.x.

Ortega, L. (2017). New CALL-SLA research interfaces for the 21st century: Towards equitable multilingualism. *CALICO Journal, 34*(3), 1–32. https://doi.org/10.1558/cj.33855

Ortega, L. (2019). SLA and the study of equitable multilingualism. *The Modern Language Journal, 103,* 23–38.

Paivio, A. (2007). *Mind and its evolution: A dual coding theoretical approach.* Erlbaum.

Peters, E. (2019). The effect of imagery and on-screen text on foreign language vocabulary learning from audiovisual input. *TESOL Quarterly, 53*(4), 1008–1032. https://doi.org/10.1002/tesq.531

Peters, E., & Muñoz, C. (2020). Introduction to the special issue: Language learning from multimodal input. *Studies in Second Language Acquisition, 42*(3), 489–497. https://doi.org/10.1017/S0272263120000212

Peters, E., Noreillie, A., Heylen, K., Bulté, B., & Desmet, P. (2019). The impact of instruction and out-of-school exposure to foreign language input on learners' vocabulary knowledge in two languages. *Language Learning, 69,* 747–782. https://doi.org/10.1111/lang.12351

Plass, J. L., & Jones, L. C. (2005). Multimedia learning in second language acquisition. In R. E. Mayer (Ed.), *The Cambridge handbook of multimedia learning* (pp. 467–488). Cambridge University Press.

Proctor, C., Dalton, B., & Grisham, D. (2007). Scaffolding English language learners and struggling readers in a universal literacy environment with embedded strategy instruction and vocabulary support. *Journal of Literacy Research, 39*(1), 71–79.

Puimège, E., & Peters, E. (2020). Learning formulaic sequences through viewing L2 television and factors that affect learning. *Studies in Second Language Acquisition, 42,* 525–549. https://doi.org/10.1017/S027226311900055X

Qian, M., Chukharev-Hudilainen, E., & Levis, J. (2018). A system for adaptive high-variability segmental perceptual training: Implementation, effectiveness, transfer. *Language Learning & Technology, 22*(1), 69–96. https://www.lltjournal.org/item/3032

Redecker, C. (2017). European framework for the digital competence of educators: DigCompEdu. In Y. Punie (Ed.), *EUR 28775 EN.* Publications Office of the European Union. https://doi.org/10.2760/159770, JRC107466

Renouf, A., & Kehoe, A. (2013). Filling the gaps: Using the WebCorp linguist's search engine to supplement existing text resources. *International Journal of Corpus Linguistics, 18*(2), 167–198.

Roehr-Brackin, K. (2018). *Metalinguistic awareness and second language acquisition.* Routledge. https://doi.org/10.4324/9781315661001

Salatas Waters, H., & Schneider, W. (Eds.). (2010). *Metacognition, strategy use, and instruction.* Guilford Press.

Sauro, S., & Zourou, K. (2019). What are the digital wilds? *Language Learning & Technology, 23*(1), 1–7. https://doi.org/10125/44666

Shohamy, E. (2011). Assessing multilingual competencies: Adopting construct valid assessment policies. *Modern Language Journal, 95*(3), 418–429.

Soler-Urzua, F. (2011). The acquisition of English /ɪ/ by Spanish speakers via text-to-speech synthesizers: A quasi-experimental study (Master's Thesis). Concordia University, Montreal, CA.

Sundqvist, P. (2019). Commercial-off-the-shelf games in the digital wild and L2 learner vocabulary. *Language Learning & Technology, 23*(1), 87–113. https://doi.org/10125/44674

Svensson, I., Nordström, T., Lindeblad, E., Gustafson, S., Björn, M., Sand, C., Almgren-Bäck, G., & Nilsson, S. (2019). Effects of assistive technology for students with reading and writing disabilities. *Disability and Rehabilitation: Assistive Technology, 16*, 1–13.

Szudarski, P. (2020). Effects of data-driven learning on enhancing the phraseological knowledge of secondary-school learners of L2 English. In P. Crosthwaite (Ed.), *Data-driven learning for the next generation: Corpora and DDL for pre-tertiary learners* (pp. 133–149). Routledge.

Valentini, A., Ricketts, J., Pye, R. E., & Houston-Price, C. (2018). Listening while reading promotes word learning from stories. *Journal of Experimental Child Psychology, 167*, 10–31. https://doi.org/10.1016/j.jecp.2017.09.022

Vasbieva, D. (2015). Teaching strategy on learning of English phrasal verbs by economics major students in Russia. *XLinguae Journal, 8*(3), 57–65.

Webb, S. (2013). Depth of vocabulary knowledge. In C. Chapelle (Ed.), *Encyclopedia of applied linguistics* (pp. 1656–1663). Wiley-Blackwell. https://doi.org/10.1002/9781405198431.wbeal1325

Wilkinson, M. (2006). Compiling corpora for use as translation resources. *Translation Journal, 10*(1). http://translationjournal.net/journal/35corpus.htm

Zarei, G. R., & Khazaie, S. (2011). L2 vocabulary learning through multimodal representations. *Procedia: Social and Behavioral Sciences, 15*, 369–375.

24

MULTIMODAL CORPORA AND CONCORDANCING IN DDL

Francesca Coccetta

24.1 Introduction

This chapter provides a state-of-the-art review of research into multimodal corpora with reference to their application in data-driven-learning (DDL). In particular, it explores their construction, annotation, and concordancing, in terms of their potential in English language teaching (ELT). DDL is historically associated with the name of Tim Johns. He described his approach as "the use in the classroom of computer-generated concordances to get students to explore the regularities of patterning in the target language, and the development of activities and exercises based on concordance output" (Johns & King, 1991, p. iii). He did so in the belief that "research is too important to be left to the researchers" (Johns, 1991a, p. 2). In the language classroom, this approach has been extensively used to explore corpora based mainly on written texts (e.g. Anthony, 2016; Bernardini, 2000; Boulton, 2010; Kettemann, 1995; Tribble & Jones, 1990). In contrast to these studies, this chapter's central concern is with the gradual but constant growth of a discovery-learning approach (Bernardini, 2002; Johns & King, 1991) in which multimodal corpora and software tools are used to help language learners become more aware of the interplay between language and other semiotic resources and to develop skills in compiling and annotating multimodal corpora that permit a more active role in the language learning process (Aston, 2002; Bianchi & Pazzaglia, 2007; Gavioli, 2005; Vasta & Baldry, 2020).

In the early 2000s, advances in technology facilitated the compilation of multimodal corpora and, since the turn of the century, researchers have been compiling multimodal corpora for both research and language teaching purposes (for spoken discourse see Ackerley & Coccetta, 2007; Adolphs & Carter, 2007; Braun, 2006; Carter & Adolphs, 2008; Knight, 2011; for podcasts Clifton *et al.*, 2020; for videos Baldry, 2004; Crawford Camiciottoli & Bonsignori, 2015; O'Halloran, 2004; for websites Baldry & O'Halloran, 2010; for translation and subtitling Taylor & Baldry, 2013). Yet, despite its potential benefits for language learners in allowing them to see how linguistic patterns interact with the other semiotic resources in discourse, the application of DDL to multimodal corpora has yet to make a strong impact on ELT. Besides potentially overcoming various reservations about the limitations of concordances (Stubbs, 2001; Widdowson, 2000), multimodal approaches provide learners with integrated visual/verbal cues that enhance language learning (Hardison & Pennington, 2021;

Kellerman, 1992; Sueyoshi & Hardison, 2005). However, the type of input and form which data can now take means that the fundamental principle of DDL, the learner as detective/researcher, has itself changed, overcoming some of the limitations that existed in the initial stages of DDL. The chapter is thus dedicated to describing how DDL is reinventing itself in the online world of multimodal interaction; it recognises, for example, that if the application of DDL to multimodal corpora is to advance in ELT, new software tools are needed to improve the search mechanisms used in concordancing that are supported by current digital technologies but which were not available when DDL was first conceived of. These include, for example, improving the ways in which DDL concordancing copes with the wide range of transcription types now present in many research corpora. In addition to transcriptions of oral and written discourse, transcriptions relating to the use of non-linguistic resources such as ambient sounds, gestures, and voice characteristics are also present (Cheng *et al.*, 2005; Lücking *et al.*, 2012).

Besides improved search mechanisms, there is also a need for a wider vision of concordancing within DDL concerned with developing specific DDL software tools that support online multimodal project-based corpus construction and annotation. While providing language learners with a source of readily available videos, the spectacular growth of video-hosting websites such as Vimeo, Dailymotion, and YouTube has not been matched by parallel developments in DDL as tools for the multimodal annotation of films. Anvil (Kipp, 2014) and Elan (Sloetjes, 2014), for example, are primarily research-oriented whereas DDL tools need to have distinctive "for students" characteristics. In this respect, Multimodal Analysis Video (O'Halloran, 2013), though not designed for multimodal DDL concordancing, is part of a suite of multimodal tools increasingly used in ELT (Vasta, 2020) that provides a significant platform of experience on which student-oriented DDL research can be based. These tools' use of multiple descriptors when exploring the interplay between different semiotic systems is particularly valuable. However, generally speaking, there is a need to overhaul and rethink the annotation and retrieval systems that underlie the various types of concordances used in DDL. To this end, three case studies are reported below which correspond to three stages in the research and development work associated with multimodal DDL.

24.2 Current contribution of research to DDL approaches to multimodal concordancing

24.2.1 Case study 1: Redefining the concordance

Can multimodal concordances exist? The concordance promoted by Johns (1991a, 1991b) was based on computer-mediated interaction where input matched output. That is, words in the corpus which corresponded to the typed-in "node word" input were presented on screen as a table of occurrences flanked on either side by a co-text providing evidence-based clues to the frequency of specific lexico-grammatical structures. Figure 24.1 shows this output in relation to the node word *teaser* in iWeb (Davies, 2018). This type of concordance is entirely lexico-grammatical and constitutes the basis for today's online lemma-based mega corpora (e.g. https://www.english-corpora.org/) that allow very accurate predictions about frequency to be made. It is also a type of concordance used in today's online concordancers specifically designed for DDL (see Section 24.2.2 in reference to WebCorp and Skell).

However, various scholars (e.g. Baldry & Thibault, 2008; Braun, 2005, 2006, 2010; Coccetta, 2008, 2011) have attempted to redefine the concordance with the goal of finding peh-TRO-kee-'n SHIRALEA SHEER-ah-lee STAR TREK: " Cost of Living " - REV. 2/03/92 - TEASER 1. STAR TREK: THE NEXT GENERATION " Cost of Living " TEASER FAL

- TEASER 1. STAR TREK: THE NEXT GENERATION " Cost of Living " TEASER FADE IN: 1 OMITTED 2 INT. BRIDGE PICARD, RIKER, DATA,

a threat? STAR TREK: " Cost of Living " - REV. 2/03/92 - TEASER 2. 3 CONTINUED: DATA Yes, sir. It is of sufficient size and

thru OMITTED 6 STAR TREK: " Cost of Living " - REV. 2/03/92 - TEASER 3. 6A EXT. SPACE - THE ASTEROID CORE (OPTICAL) A beam has

the Enterprise goes into warp drive, and away. FADE OUT. END OF TEASER STAR TREK: " Cost of Living " - 2/03/92 - ACT ONE 4.

the end The Continue reading? # No not that Accel World. Its a teaser, I say the same thing for every teaser, so you guys can just

that Accel World. Its a teaser, I say the same thing for every teaser, so you guys can just go check out my comments in previous teasers if

about it; the boogeyman needs the raiments of his occupation. He caps the teaser by pouring two shots of vodka and declaring " mir " with his adversary.

, but we're located in Nashville and we actually just put up a wedding teaser we did this weekend! # Keep up the good work & Keep in touch

Figure 24.1 Some concordance lines for *teaser* from iWeb (https://www.english-corpora.org/iweb/)

ways in which learners can analyse online multimodal texts in the light of the advances in both interface design (Baldry, 2005; O'Halloran *et al.*, 2010) and multimodal discourse analysis (Baldry & Thibault, [2006] 2010; Bateman, 2008; Kress & van Leeuwen, [1996] 2006; Machin, 2013; O'Halloran, 2004). These advances have arisen in the context of a much wider range of online text types that can be suitably analysed as text. One example illustrated in Figure 24.1 is *TEASER*, distinctively written in capitals and referring to a functional unit that introduces the conflict to be resolved in a particular episode in a TV series. In other words, just as there is a need to explore lexico-grammatical forms there is also a need to concordance functional units that make up multimodal genres such as TV films and Internet videos. To this end, as indicated by Baldry and Thibault (2008) (Figure 24.2), four general categories of concordances can be posited: 1) monomodal form-oriented concordances; 2) monomodal meaning-oriented concordances; 3) multisemiotic form-oriented concordances;

	MONOMODAL		MULTIMODAL
FORM-ORIENTED	**Type 1.** This type of concordance relates to *forms* as text-making resources retrieved from text corpora and specifically to the textual uses of *one* specific resource (e.g. a concordance of punctuation marks, symbols, lines, colours *or* ambient sounds). In practice, almost all concordances of this type are lemma-based studies of language and consist of single lines of wordings arranged in a tabular form; hence the reference in this paper to this type as *language-only, form-oriented concordances*. The examples below of *forget* are taken from the *British National Corpus* (BNC).		**Type 3.** Like *Type 1* concordances, this type relates to *forms* used as text-making resources in text corpora but, in keeping with the resource integration principle (Baldry/Thibault 2006a: 18-19), focuses on *typical combinations* of, and *relations between*, forms used at the same *point of time* in specific texts. For reasons of space, the example shown is a fragment of a single concordance which records the presence of *written, oral, vocal, visual, vectoral, spatial,* and *temporal* resources and, in part, begins to suggest their function in relation to *mini-genres* (Baldry/Thibault 2006a: 42) such as slogans and logos in a TV advert.
	FR0 3687 Sheldukher... don't	**forget** the Cell...';	**logo:** visual, vectoral and spatial resources **slogan: oral:** wording: *freedom to choose* **slogan: oral:** voice: male voice **slogan: written:** wording: *freedom to imagine* **slogan complex: written + oral overlap:** exactly synchronized **logo + slogan overlap:** exactly synchronized
	FU6 1895 I never	**forget** a face --; (He looks into the SPY's face)... not that I know yours that is.	
	FYA 859 It's it's four hundredths of don't	**forget** that times is of.	
	G0T 167 Some mornings he would rush away and	**forget** to leave anything.	
	G2W 257 Don't	**forget** to say you saw it first in Ski survey, February/March issue 1991!	
	G63 472 But er they would maybe lay it by for two or three weeks and then	**forget** for two or three weeks, and then when it came to the end of the quarter they were a whole lot of weeks behind, you know, they couldn't pay it then.	
	H7A 2505 " If you tell me to	**forget** it I will, Mr Feather.	
MEANING-ORIENTED	**Type 2.** As with *Type 1* concordances, this type relates to *forms* produced by *one* resource but *explicitly* extends the range of a concordance to *meaning* by providing information about the *functions* various forms have in specific contexts. To date, all such concordances appear to have dealt with language, taking various forms, including the two-line concordances *exemplified in Table 2*, where the first line contains actual wordings in one or more texts, the second, the functions carried out by these wordings.		**Type 4.** Like *Types 2* and *3*, this type of concordance uses *descriptive labels* to search a multimodal corpus. It focuses on meaning that derives from a combination of diverse semiotic resources. See *Table 3* for an illustration of this type of concordance and, for more complete examples, Baldry/Thibault 2001: 94-6; see also Baldry 2005a; 2006: 118-9; Baldry/Thibault 2006b).

Figure 24.2 Categories of concordances (Baldry & Thibault, 2008, p. 14)

and 4) multisemiotic meaning-oriented concordances in which the second and fourth are clearly oriented to the exploration of functional units in texts.

Rather than a statement about the current state of the art or actual feasibility, this is a research hypothesis which recognises that while all texts are multimodal, some are more overtly so compared to others and that consequently a step-by-step research procedure is required when pursuing the development of types of concordancing capable of fully embracing the relationships between form and function in multimodal texts. Already the first step, producing monomodal concordances that are function-oriented, entails a redefinition of concordances and concordancing that abandons the table-based concept of a co-text, illustrated in Figure 24.1, restricted to the words that immediately precede and follow a recurrent node word. Rather than using typed-in words, this type of concordance is produced as the result of a search typically made with descriptors selected from pre-established lists that retrieve text on the basis of a match with tags embedded in the corpus. Such concordances can retrieve all the various lexico-grammatical structures associated with a particular function. However, in addition to this, using a function/meaning-oriented descriptor has the further consequence of loosening the strict connection between input and output found in traditional node word concordances, which thus encourages the simultaneous use of various types of co-text. Hence, in addition to a co-text designed to characterise the relationship between a specific function and its multiple lexico-grammatical exponents retrieved from transcriptions of written discourse, this type of concordance will often contain an additional multimodal/multimedia co-text that reproduces the original audio or video sequence on which each transcription is based.

There are, in fact, many ways in which this type of dual co-text concordance can be realised. One early solution was provided by Braun (2005, 2006, 2010) with her work on ELISA (English Language Interview Corpus as a Second-language Application), a forerunner of SACODEYL (Widmann *et al.*, 2011) and BACKBONE (Kohn *et al.*, 2010; http://webapps. ael.uni-tuebingen.de/backbone-search/faces/search.jsp). ELISA was a small online video corpus of narrative interviews with native speakers of English about their professional careers. The interviews followed the same general pattern covering similar topics (e.g. speaker's educational background, profession, and future plans). Each interview was provided with a title, a transcription, and a brief summary which aimed to introduce learners to the content of the interviews. In Braun's view (2006), summaries were particularly useful for those learners who accessed the text through a concordance and sought further information about the text, thus contributing to overcoming Widdowson's (2000) criticism about the lack of context provided in corpus linguistics. Each interview was divided into smaller sections on the basis of the topic covered. The corpus was enriched with metadata: each sequence was annotated for the topic covered, the grammatical structures, and communicative functions used. Thanks to the online concordancer and the tags embedded in the corpus, this type of concordancing meant that teachers and learners could query the corpus, and retrieve and compare similar sections from different interviews. In "topic/function-based concordances" (Braun, 2010, p. 84), the descriptor is a topic, such as 'Introducing Oneself', which retrieves all the instances, or sections in Braun's terminology, in the corpus where speakers introduce themselves. Learners are provided with the transcripts of the sections which can be read and compared for recurrent lexical items to introduce oneself (e.g. *I am, I'm* and *my name is*). Hence the "topic/function-based approach has the (practical) advantage that it filters out irrelevant material while at the same time presenting learners with the whole gamut of relevant means of expression and giving a better idea of what it takes to introduce oneself in the

L2" (Braun, 2010, p. 88). The inclusion of the video clips of the interviews had the advantage of helping learners contextualise problematic utterances thanks to the visual, gestural, and intonational clues in the videos. The descriptor-based concordance adopted by Braun (2005, 2006, 2010), but also adopted in other projects such as those concerned with notional-functional concordancing (Ackerley & Coccetta, 2007; Coccetta, 2011), had been previously adopted by Anthony (2003) who developed a concordancer which allows users to construct their own corpus of written texts which can be analysed in terms of Swales' (1990) move model. Though restricted in other ways, it allows the user to construct their own corpora and generate concordances thanks to the use of labels that the user embeds in the written text. Anthony's project is, thus, a first stage in providing the greater learner autonomy that characterises DDL and which ultimately, and justifiably, champions both the right for users to create their own corpora, great or small as they may be, and their right to suggest what types of descriptors should be made available when designing DDL tools for the exploration of multimodal corpora (see Section 24.2.3).

24.2.2 Case study 2: Multimodal corpora go online

Can website archives and repositories be turned into multimodal corpora that are useful in ELT? This question naturally follows on from what was stated at the end of the previous section as it focuses on how learners discover patterns in texts for themselves and what types of query they want to make. The web-as-corpus approach is one possibility. This approach is used, for example, in both WebCorp (https://www.webcorp.org.uk/live/), which first appeared in 2002, and Skell (https://skell.sketchengine.eu/#home) dating from 2014, both of which foreground the type of concordance adopted by Johns, restricted to retrieving written text as monomodal form-oriented concordances, albeit with a user-friendly interface that greatly simplifies this task.

In his use of the TED Talks (https://www.ted.com/talks), Aston (2015) certainly led the way in adapting the data in video-hosting sites to the language learning needs of university students specialising in language studies who, in particular, need web concordancing that includes multimodal/multimedia co-texts. Using WordSmith Tools (Scott, 2012), Aston compiled a small corpus of 500 transcripts of TED talks aligned to their audio/video reproductions (the dual co-text principle described above) and showed how phraseological items (Wray, 2002) can be identified, interpreted, and how it can increase learners' greater phraseological awareness. The presence of two semiotic resources, explicitly separated analytically, but shown to be interdependent in the meaning-making process, is a focal point in Aston's web-as-corpus approach. One of Aston's examples is *and by the way*. By listening to random concordancing of *and by the way*, learners discovered that it started a single tone group. When enlarging the context listened to, they also found out that it was followed by laughter and concluded that it has the function of marking the beginning of a joke. Aston's approach promotes a genuinely multimodal conception of co-text (rather than a multimedia co-text) as it indicates that a co-text can include information about how different semiotic resources deictically co-reference and co-contextualise each other. Although the concordance is still form-oriented – lemma-based using the node words *and by the way* rather than a descriptor – the shift introduced by Aston and others paved the way for a redefinition of the concordance that takes a first step towards multisemiotic form-oriented concordancing (Baldry & Thibault, 2008) in which a greater focus on analysing intersemiotic resources used in co-texts is undertaken. Effectively, this increases the range of ways in which corpora can be used in the teaching and learning practices, encouraging DDL's basic principle of learner autonomy in language learning beyond the language classroom thanks to the web's empowerment. Thankfully, in the space of a few years, technological advances have led to various projects further exploring the multimodal possibilities of the TED Talks site (e.g. Hasebe, 2015; Taibi *et al.*, 2015). Of these, of particular significance is the TED Corpus Search Engine (TCSE) (https://yohasebe.com/tcse/) (Hasebe, 2015) which supports online lemma retrieval in the transcripts and translations of TED Talks. Each "hit" is associated with its corresponding video which can be instantly accessed, thus providing contextually relevant visual information. To exemplify the Ted Corpus Search Engine (TCSE)'s potential in DDL, we can take the KWIC concordances for *as you can see* shown in Figure 24.3, displayed vertically with the node words (in the original) in red and some linguistic co-text appearing before and after them.

In keeping with Aston's (2015) suggestions, these concordances can be used in DDL activities where learners can view the sequences by clicking the "view" button and can focus on the prosodic characteristics of this and other phraseological items. However, this type of access also allows learners to go beyond the analysis of prosodies and instead consider the entire set of visual-verbal semiotic resources used in the lectures. Students can read through the linguistic co-text but also reflect on the relationship of *as you can see* with the visual-verbal co-text. When the linguistic co-text seems to be suggesting that the speaker is making reference to something the viewer can see on stage/screen, this can be confirmed by viewing the multimedia co-text as the video associated with Concordance Line 1 correlates with the speaker pointing to "the graph" displayed behind her.

TED Talks have already found their place in the ELT classroom where teachers use them inter alia to foster learners' speaking skills (e.g. García-Pinar, 2019; Leopold, 2016; Pinar & Palleja, 2018). Besides providing effective examples of the use of linguistic strategies to deliver a talk, TED Talks and similar video-sharing sites can also provide learners with useful

#	ID	Line	Time					
1	48919	128 [0.49]	06:10 [12:46]	≡	❧	▶	⌀	As you can see from this graph,
2	48102	120 [0.35]	05:47 [16:52]	≡	❧	▶	⌀	So as you can see, the United States is one of the looser countries.
3	46577	86 [0.36]	05:06 [14:16]	≡	❧	▶	⌀	As you can see, this once massive glacier has already lost much of its ice.
4	43852	53 [0.18]	03:19 [17:40]	≡	❧	▶	⌀	Now as you can see I'm overnourished.
5	42946	101 [0.53]	05:11 [09:05]	≡	❧	▶	⌀	life-size sculptures as you can see behind me,
6	42488	95 [0.33]	05:13 [15:11]	≡	❧	▶	⌀	And in Copenhagen we have snow, as you can see,
7	39941	86 [0.32]	04:34 [13:33]	≡	❧	▶	⌀	because as you can see there, I hope,
8	37442	138 [0.59]	07:04 [11:53]	≡	❧	▶	⌀	As you can see, the company's work is astonishing,
9	37225	219 [0.76]	09:50 [12:41]	≡	❧	▶	⌀	as you can see here: over 200 different plants.

Figure 24.3 Some concordance lines for *as you can see* from the TCSE (Hasebe, 2015; https://yohasebe.com/tcse/)

insights into the use of hand gestures, gaze, facial expressions, intonation, and posture as hinted by the example described above. However, in the furtherance of this goal, there seems to be a need to implement what Baldry and Thibault (2008) call multisemiotic form-oriented concordances which, through the use of descriptors, explicitly enable users to query the corpus analytically in ways that show how two or more resources – one in all probability linguistic – co-contextualise each other.

In answer to the question we posed at the beginning of this section about whether website archives and repositories can be turned into multimodal corpora useful in DDL approaches to ELT, we can suggest that, based on the growing experience with multimodal corpora, research continues to promote the constant growth of multimodal DDL thanks to innovations in concordancing. However, in multimodal DDL, there is also a need for a greater focus on learner analytics, project work, and domain-specific concordancing that encourages better understanding of the typical patterns of orchestration of meaning-making resources used in specific multimodal genres, matters taken up in the third case study.

24.2.3 *Case study 3: Student-led construction of video corpora and investigation of multisemiotic genres*

Multimodal annotation is undoubtedly one of the achievements of multimodal corpora and concordancing that is particularly enticing for all ELT teachers. As Alcaraz Calero *et al.* (2010) state, "[a]nnotation plays a significant role in Data Driven Learning (DDL). If annotation is pedagogically oriented, this role may be even more relevant" (p. 233). But how can we go about annotating and then exploring multimodal corpora within carefully-defined pedagogic strategies? Freely available tools such as Anvil (Kipp, 2014), ELAN (Sloetjes, 2014), and EXMARaLDA (https://exmaralda.org/en/) allow experienced researchers to create their own annotation schemes within the framework of multimodal studies but are not in keeping with Johns' observations about students as language detectives. On the other hand, Multimodal Analysis Video (O'Halloran & Tan, 2017) that we have already mentioned above is part of a suite of multimodal tools increasingly used in ELT (Vasta, 2020) which provide a significant platform of experience on which research into multimodal DDL concordancing can be based.

Even so, as Gavioli and Aston (2001) noted, there is a tendency in ELT to "overlook the potential of corpora as tools in the hands of learners, for whom they can provide a wide range of opportunities to observe and participate in real discourse for themselves" (p. 238). Some twenty years later, when applied to the use of multimodal film and video corpora and the role of multimodal concordancing in DDL, this observation remains as valid as it was at the time when it was written. In the meantime, however, technology has changed, as have students. While many studies have ensured that multimodality has come to play a major role in ELT (Baldry & Thibault, [2006] 2010, 2020; Crawford Camiciottoli, this volume; Crawford Camiciottoli & Campoy-Cubillo, 2018; Goodman & Graddol, 1996; Vasta & Baldry, 2020), a key but as yet partly unsolved issue is learner empowerment. This requires greater attention, especially as regards the final words in Gavioli and Aston's observation quoted above, namely, for themselves.

Today, there is much greater interest in, as well as possibilities for, a hands-on approach that involves greater participation on the part of students in the construction as well as the use of corpora that is consistent with the need to explore the different functions that different resources carry out in multisemiotic texts such as videos. A basic consideration in this approach is the twinning of multimodal analysis skills with the sharpening of students' autonomous "forensic" skills in the selection, management, and interpretation of the texts and genres detectable in concordances for multisemiotic patterns. With reference to this type of concordance Baldry and Thibault (2008) explain:

> We may look on sets of multimodal concordances as records of human activity arranged so that similarities and differences are highlighted within and across texts. That is, by rearranging activities so that their patterned nature is made prominent, multimodal concordances reconstruct processes and stages in texts involving temporal and/or causal sequencing and patterns of relationships involving mergings between different activities. (p. 33)

Baldry and Thibault (2020) recently suggested in the study of multimodal ecological literacy "how temporal and/or causal sequencing and patterns" could be systematically concordanced in a way that meets "the higher-order need of understanding the ecological systems that give rise to interspecies interactions and encourages young people to articulate their thoughts about such systems" (p. 159). Apart from indicating explicitly how language is co-deployed with other resources in real discourse, this type of concordancing also provides clues as to how such co-deployments create meanings. In other words, in this conception, the patternings that concordances identify are viewed as part of the process of sharpening students' discourse analysis skills (Hunston, 2001; Stubbs, 2001), enabling them to (a) understand the sociocultural functions and implications of the texts they encounter, (b) consider what actions might be taken, and (c) reflect on how these actions might be implemented in order to improve our world – in this particular instance, our co-existence with other species.

The challenges involved in such a vision have been taken up by Baldry and Thibault (2001, 2006, 2008, [2006] 2010, 2020) working with others (Baldry *et al.*, 2020, 2022; Vasta & Baldry, 2020) including the author of this chapter (Coccetta, 2008, 2011, 2019, 2020). This group has carried out experimentation with various types of concordances, with reference initially to the House Corpus project but subsequently to the OpenMWS project. Central to the goals of these researchers' investigations are the possibilities for authorised students to construct their own video corpora and to carry out different types of searches in the corpora they have created for themselves. Accessed through the MWSWeb platform (http://mws.pa.itd.cnr.it/), the House Corpus, for example, is a scene-based corpus where dual co-texts are presented side-by-side, one a searchable written transcription of a scene in the *House M.D.* series, and the other a video clip of a specific scene (Figure 24.4). Both are used to illustrate lexico-grammatical structures using keyword searches (Taibi *et al.*, 2019).

However, students are involved in two ways: both as end users and as corpus builders. In one corpus-building task, language students from the University of Salento assisted in creating an acronym search functionality by compiling a list of all the medical acronyms used in the

Figure 24.4 Example of dual co-texts in OpenMWSWeb platform

6300 scenes in this TV series. In the form of a concordanceable search list, this allowed medical students, as end users, to understand and, more significantly, memorise these acronyms by reading scenes in which each acronym appears and by watching and listening to the video clip relating to the scenes in question. At the very same time, this task also allowed the corpus-building students enrolled in a translation and interpreting degree course to learn about the nature, frequency, and lexicogrammatical forms that acronyms and initialisms have in medical discourse in English. In particular, they learned that unlike many other languages, some medical acronyms in English can function as nouns, adjectives, and verbs (e.g. MRI'd) and can relate equally to medical facilities, equipment, or staff (Loiacono & Tursi, 2019). In another task, again under teacher supervision (Arizzi, in press), students successfully used annotation tools to group scenes into functional units thus identifying, for example, different Teaser types. This was facilitated by examining, annotating, and subsequently concordancing individual scenes in a way that established the role that hand movements and lexicogrammatical structures jointly play in structuring the recurrent patterns of conflictuality that characterise the majority of the Teasers in this series (see Figure 24.5).

The House Corpus's successor, the OpenMWS project, has extended the role of students as corpus builders (Baldry, 2021). Videos housed on in video-sharing platforms can be selected and redeveloped as a concordanceable video corpus. Currently, the OpenMWS interface (http://openmws.itd.cnr.it/) accesses and interacts with videos and podcasts hosted on YouTube and permits authorised students to transform selected videos into domain-specific corpora through which critical assessments of today's world, as represented in specific video genres, can be made. When describing the construction, within the Animal Rescue genre (Baldry & Thibault, 2020), of a subcorpus relating to animals abandoned after nuclear disasters, Taibi (2020, p. 192) has outlined a nine-step plan for student-led video corpus construction in which online annotation and concordancing are the last stages. These stages are preceded instead by preliminary steps under a teacher's guidance that introduce some of the principles to be observed in all corpus construction. They include initial agreements about text selection but also ways in which videos can be broken down into sequences that correspond to specific text functions and characteristics and which, when concordanced, illustrate how these features form patterns across the corpus so constructed.

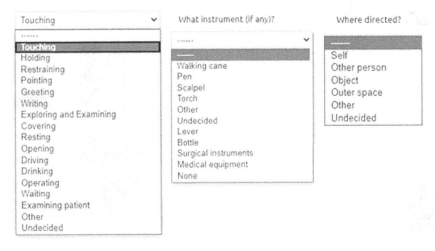

Figure 24.5 Hands menu labelling options in the House Corpus

Thanks to its annotational tools, the OpenMWS interface can incorporate complex multisemiotic function-related concordances relating, for example, to phasal analysis (Baldry & Thibault, 2008, 2020; Gregory, 2002) and generic structure potential (Hasan, 1996; Vasta & Baldry, 2020). Ultimately, this research is based on the premise that the best way of demonstrating the relevance of multimodal corpus studies and multimodal concordancing when learning to master discourse in English lies in going beyond corpus annotation and concordancing in the strict sense and embracing a far wider set of text-investigation processes that are automatically involved in the construction of corpora (Baldry *et al.*, 2011; Cambria *et al.*, 2012).

This research has promoted the principle whereby such investigation is viewed as a staged undertaking carried out by different groups of students working collaboratively, eager to compare the results obtained with other groups of students working on analogous projects (Baldry & Kantz, 2022; Baldry *et al.*, 2022). As Figure 24.6 illustrates, this more socially-committed

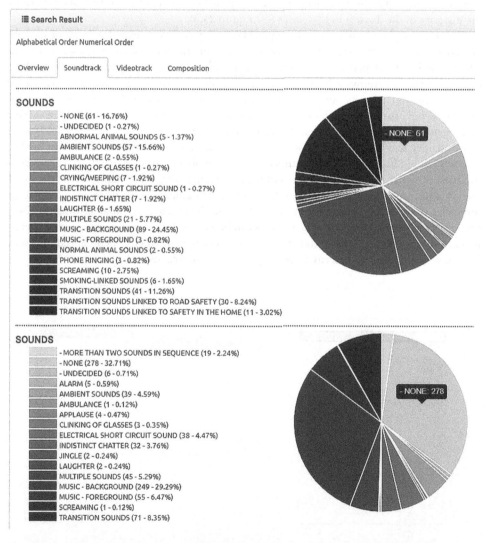

Figure 24.6 Example of dashboard style of corpus-search results obtained with OpenMWS

form of corpus investigation encourages a shift from the initial conception of concordancing as vertical KWIC co-text lists towards a dashboard style when presenting the data produced by corpus searches. This promotes a greater focus on the contribution of different semiotic resources, in this case, the nature, frequency, and distribution of types of sound. With respect to a corpus of videos about healthcare simulations, "dashboard concordancing" has allowed students to compare their corpus with the sounds prevailing in a corpus relating to videos belonging to a previous age and to a different genre (Baldry *et al.*, 2022). While the videos on virtual and augmented reality in the bottom part of Figure 24.6 clearly belong to very recent years, those in the top part relate to a corpus of 100 UK PSAs (Public Service Announcements) on the theme of home and road safety in the 1980-to-2006 period. The charts are generated automatically on the basis of corpus searches and are the result of previous stages in corpus construction and corpus annotation carried out by students.

The shift from vertical to horizontal presentation in the charts in Figure 24.6 is in keeping with criticisms made about vertical presentations and demands for new styles of screen reading that facilitate learners' tasks (e.g. Timmis, 2015) by making it easier for students to detect patterns and weigh up their significance. However, they also reflect a more fundamental change in the way analytics are used in Higher Education (Oviatt *et al.*, 2018; Taibi & Dietze, 2012). Analytics assist students by providing them with control over data; as Figure 24.6 suggests, they provide changing and constantly updated perspectives on the corpora being constructed that entertain ever-larger data sets. Thus, a further effect of this approach is to place peer and formative assessment squarely in the hands of students. Each student participating in a project is encouraged to discover how their contribution and ideas fit in with the overall trends in student-led corpus construction. Clearly, in an age in which the basic level of foreign language competence, in particular in English, is much higher than in previous decades, the shift towards investigating more domain-specific patterns of social organisation is encouraging. Put another way, what matters most in the ties between DDL and multimodal concordancing is the issue of learner autonomy (Charles, this volume), promoting in particular students' ability to engage autonomously with the world of digital multiliteracies (Cope & Kalantzis, 2015) and, above all, motivating them to explore texts and genres in ways they find attractive.

24.3 Conclusions about the current state of research

In various respects, research into multimodal DDL concordancing is concerned with creating online tools and techniques that minimise the stresses and strains all too often associated with concordancing and corpus studies. In the process of developing methods that allow greater student participation in the management of data, it is hardly surprising that the formal aspects of concordances have changed in a variety of ways such as dashboard-style presentations of concordances that facilitate learners' tasks. All this is reflected in Flowerdew's (2012) observations that "the lack of uptake of corpus-driven pedagogy" may be due to the fact that some "tools try to meet the needs of both researchers and teachers, which makes them overly complicated", a state of affairs further compounded by the fact that "learners do not possess a pedagogic grounding in exploiting corpora [since] very few accounts [exist] in the literature which touch on the question of learner training" (pp. 204-205). In other ways, as implied for example in the CFRIDiL (Sindoni *et al.*, 2019) guidelines, DDL needs to recognise that students today start out with a much wider multimodal canvas with which to engage. The evolution of online video repositories now provides access to data that can be tapped in keeping with Johns' DDL views but in terms of a much greater order of magnitude, as video hosting sites, for example, vastly increase students' ability to act as text detectives undertaking guided video discovery tasks. Moreover, generally speaking, a higher level of linguistic knowledge and multimodal literacy now exists among ELT students which need to be recognised when designing concordance and concordance-like searches just as it does even more generally when designing ELT syllabuses.

24.4 Future directions of research

As this chapter has suggested, the student-as-researcher concept is increasingly gaining ground. Though consistent with Johns' notion of the student as a detective, it adapts it to today's world. Further research into more user-friendly corpus tools that assess whether language teaching can, and should, start with multimodal input is urgently needed. In particular, postgraduate students, whether as participants in vocational training or in doctoral research programmes, need to contribute to this field by investigating the research issues suggested in this chapter. DDL was originally conceived in an age when classroom teaching was such that teachers instructed students how to explore concordances and where DDL represented a small but significant window through which the outside world of computer texts and discourse could be represented. Now, the question becomes how teachers should use DDL in an age where learner analytics (Oviatt *et al.*, 2018; Taibi & Dietze, 2012), project work (Stoller, 2002), and domain-specific corpus construction and analysis (Vasta & Baldry, 2020) are part of an online world in which students of all ages must acquire digital skills and learn how to engage with others, while defining their own identities. Can multimodal video corpora for example, as described in this chapter, provide an answer to the changing relationship between language teachers and students in this digital world? Specific issues in this respect are the role of DDL in self-presentation, translanguaging (Melo-Pfeifer, 2015; Melo-Pfeifer & Chik, 2020; Rojo, 2020), and formative and summative forms of assessment (Barker, 2013). As regards the latter, if students become researchers, issues that need investigating include: to whom do they present their work? How do they do so (video comments, podcasts, tweets)? Who provides them with feedback on their performance? Teachers? Peers? These are all matters likely to encourage the use of new forms of learner corpora in teacher training and other contexts.

Further reading

Bonsignori, V. (2018). Using films and TV series for ESP teaching: A multimodal perspective. *System*, 77, 58–69. Although not concerned with multimodal concordancing in DDL, this paper provides a description of how a corpus of clips from films and TV series where English is used in specialised domains can be used to help ESP students become more aware of the multimodal nature of communication.

Fortanet-Gómez, I., & Querol-Julián, M. (2010). The videocorpus as a multimodal tool for teaching. In M. C. Campoi, B. Bellés-Fortuno, & M. L. Gea-Valor (Eds.), *Corpus-based approaches to English language teaching* (pp. 261–270). Continuum. This book chapter presents the compilation of a multimodal corpus of Lectures in English and its annotation for the communicative functions carried out in this academic genre. It also describes how the corpus can be used in a teacher training course and the benefits of the multimodal/multimedia co-text.

Vasta, N., & Baldry, A. (Eds.). (2020). *Multiliteracy advances and multimodal challenges in ELT environments*. Forum Editrice. The volume provides case studies across primary, secondary, and tertiary education which adopt new forms of pedagogy that empower learners to analyse visual and verbal means of communication from a critical discourse perspective. Many of the case studies use software that further illustrate the principles described in this chapter.

References

Ackerley, K., & Coccetta, F. (2007). Enriching language learning through a multimedia corpus. *ReCALL, 19*(3), 351–370. https://doi.org/10.1017/S0958344007000730

Adolphs, S., & Carter, R. (2007). Beyond the word. New challenges in analysing corpora of spoken English. *European Journal of English Studies, 41*(2), 113–146.

Alcaraz Calero, J. M., Pérez-Paredes, P., & Tornero Valero, E. (2010). A generic tool for annotating tei-compliant corpora: An ELT-based approach to corpus annotation. In M. C. Campoy-Cubillo, B. Bélles-Fortuño, & M. L. Gea-Valor (Eds.), *Corpus-based approaches to English language teaching* (pp. 233–247). Continuum.

Anthony, L. (2003). *AntMover* (Version 1.1.0) [Computer Software]. Waseda University. https://www.laurenceanthony.net/software/antmover/

Anthony, L. (2016). Introducing corpora and corpus tools into the technical writing classroom through data-driven learning (DDL). In J. Flowerdew & T. Costley (Eds.), *Discipline-specific writing: Theory into practice* (pp. 162–180). Routledge.

Arizzi, C. (in press). Exploring the narrative functions of hand movement in the Teaser Phase in House MD: A corpus-assisted analysis. In K. Ackerley, E. Castello, F. Dalziel, S. Gesuato, M. T. Musacchio, & G. Palumbo (Eds.), *Thinking out of the box in English linguistics, language teaching, translation and terminology*. Proceedings of the XXIX AIA Conference. Padova University Press.

Aston, G. (2002). The learner as corpus designer. In B. Kettemann & G. Marko (Eds.), *Teaching and learning by doing corpus linguistics*. Proceedings of the fourth international conference on teaching and language corpora (pp. 9–25). Brill.

Aston, G. (2015). Learning phraseology from speech corpora. In A. Leńko-Szymańska & A. Boulton (Eds.), *Multiple affordances of language corpora for data-driven learning* (pp. 65–84). Benjamins.

BACKBONE – Corpora for Content and Language Integrated Learning. http://webapps.ael.uni-tuebingen.de/backbone-search/faces/search.jsp

Baldry, A. (2004). Phase and transition, type and instance: Patterns in media texts as seen through a multimodal concordancer. In K. O'Halloran (Ed.), *Multimodal discourse analysis: Systemic functional perspectives* (pp. 83–108). Continuum.

Baldry, A. (2005). *A multimodal approach to text studies in English. The role of MCA in multimodal concordancing and multimodal corpus linguistics*. Palladino.

Baldry, A. (2021). Multimodality and genre evolution: A decade-by-decade approach to online video genre analysis. In I. Moschini & M. G. Sindoni (Eds.), *Mediation and multimodal meaning making in digital environments* (pp. 151-167). Routledge.

Baldry, A., Coccetta, F., & Kantz, D. (2022). What if? Healthcare simulations, online searchable video corpora and formulating hypotheses. In A. Plastina (Ed.), *Analysing health discourse in digital environments*. (pp. 126–146). Cambridge Scholars Publishing.

Baldry, A., Gaggia, A., & Porta, M. (2011). Multimodal web concordancing and annotation: An overview of the MCAWEB system. In N. Vasta, A. Riem Natale, M. Bortoluzzi, & D. Saidero (Eds.), *Identities in transition in the English-speaking world* (pp. 39–60). Forum Editrice.

Baldry, A., & Kantz, D. (2022). Corpus-assisted approaches to online multimodal discourse analysis of videos. In V. Bonsignori, B. Crawford Camiciottoli, & D. Filmer (Eds.), *Analysing multimodality in specialized discourse: Innovative research methods and applications* (pp. 2-22). Vernon Press.

Baldry, A., Kantz, D., Loiacono, A., Marenzi, I., Taibi, D., & Tursi, F. (2020). The MWSWeb project: Accessing medical discourse in video-hosting websites. In E. Manca & F. Bianchi (Eds.), *Specialised languages and multimedia. Linguistic and cross-cultural issues* (pp. 433–472). Salento University Publishing. https://doi.org/10.1285/i22390359v40p433

Baldry, A., & O'Halloran, K. (2010). Research into the annotation of a multimodal corpus of university websites: An illustration of multimodal corpus linguistics. In T. Harris & M. Moreno Jaen (Eds.), *Corpus linguistics in language teaching* (pp. 177–209). Peter Lang.

Baldry, A., & Thibault, P. (2001). Towards multimodal corpora. In G. Aston & L. Burnard (Eds.), *Corpora in the description and teaching of English* (pp. 87–102). CLUEB.

Baldry, A., & Thibault, P. (2006). Multimodal corpus linguistics. In G. Thompson & S. Hunston (Eds.), *System and corpus. Exploring connections* (pp. 164–183). Equinox.

Baldry, A., & Thibault, P. (2008). Applications of multimodal concordances. *HERMES, 41*, 11–41.

Baldry, A., & Thibault, P. ([2006] 2010). *Multimodal transcription and text analysis. A multimodal toolkit and coursebook*. Equinox.

Baldry, A., & Thibault, P. (2020). Analysis a: A model for multimodal corpus construction of video genres: Phasal analysis and resource integration using *OpenMWS*. In N. Vasta & A. Baldry (Eds.), *Multiliteracy advances and multimodal challenges in ELT environments* (pp. 159–173). Forum Editrice.

Barker, F. (2013). Using corpora to design assessment. *The Companion to Language Assessment, 2*, 1013–1028.

Bateman, J. (2008). *Multimodality and genre. A foundation for the systematic analysis of multimodal documents.* Palgrave.

Bernardini, S. (2000). Systematising serendipity: Proposals for concordancing large corpora with language learners. In L. Burnard & T. McEnery (Eds.), *Rethinking language pedagogy from a corpus perspective* (pp. 225–234). Peter Lang.

Bernardini, S. (2002). Exploring new directions for discovery learning. In B. Kettemann & G. Marko (Eds.), *Teaching and learning by doing corpus analysis*. Proceedings of the fourth international conference on teaching and language corpora (pp. 165–182). Brill.

Bianchi, F., & Pazzaglia, R. (2007). Student writing of research articles in a foreign language: Metacognition and corpora. In R. Facchinetti (Ed.), *Corpus linguistics 25 years on* (pp. 259–287). Rodopi.

Boulton, A. (2010). Data-driven learning: Taking the computer out of the equation. *Language Learning, 60*(3), 534–572. https://doi:10.1111/j.1467-9922.2010.00566.x

Braun, S. (2005). From pedagogically relevant corpora to authentic language learning contents. *ReCALL, 17*(1), 47–64.

Braun, S. (2006). ELISA – A pedagogically enriched corpus for language learning purposes. In S. Braun, K. Kohn, & J. Mukherjee (Eds.), *Corpus technology and language pedagogy: New resources, new tools, new methods* (pp. 25–47). Peter Lang.

Braun, S. (2010). Getting past 'Groundhog Day': Spoken multimedia corpora for student-centred corpus exploration. In T. Harris & M. Morena Jaén (Eds.), *Corpus linguistics in language teaching* (pp. 75–98). Peter Lang.

Cambria, M., Arizzi, C., & Coccetta, F. (Eds.). (2012). *Web genres and web tools*. Ibis.

Carter, R., & Adolphs, S. (2008). Linking the verbal and visual: New directions for corpus linguistics. In C. Mair, C. Meyer, & N. Oostdijk (Eds.), *Language and computers: Studies in practical linguistics* (pp. 275–291). Rodopi.

Cheng, W., Greaves, C., & Warren, M. (2005). The creation of a prosodically transcribed intercultural corpus: The Hong Kong corpus of spoken English (prosodic). *ICAME Journal, 29*, 47–68.

Clifton, A., Reddy, S., Yu, Y., Pappu, A., Rezapour, & Jones, R. (2020). 100,000 podcasts: A spoken English document corpus. Proceedings of the 28th international conference on computational linguistics (pp. 5903–5917). https://doi.org/10.18653/v1/2020.coling-main.519

Coccetta, F. (2008). First steps towards multimodal functional concordancing. *HERMES, 41*, 43–58.

Coccetta, F. (2011). Multimodal functional-notional concordancing. In A. Frankenberg-Garcia, L. Flowerdew, & G. Aston (Eds.), *New trends in corpora and language learning* (pp. 121–138). Continuum.

Coccetta, F. (2019). Old wine in new bottles. The case of the adjacency-pair framework revisited. *Lingue e Linguaggi, 29*, 407–424. https://doi.org/10.1285/I22390359V29P407

Coccetta, F. (2020). Analysis B: The when-not-to-intervene subgenre: Awareness of ill-advised rescues. In N. Vasta & A. Baldry (Eds.), *Multiliteracy advances and multimodal challenges in ELT environments* (pp. 174–182). Forum Editrice.

Cope, B., & Kalantzis, M. (Eds.). (2015). *A pedagogy of multiliteracies: Learning by design*. Palgrave.

Crawford Camiciottoli, B., & Bonsignori, V. (2015). The Pisa audiovisual corpus project: A multimodal approach to ESP research and teaching. *ESP Today, 3*(2), 139–159.

Crawford Camiciottoli, B., & Campoy-Cubillo, M. C. (Eds.). (2018). Special issue: Multimodal perspectives on English Language Teaching in higher education. *System, 77*.

Davies, M. (2018) The iWeb Corpus. Retrieved May 7, 2021. https://english-corpora.org/iWeb/

Flowerdew, L. (2012). *Corpora and language education*. Palgrave.

Gavioli, L. (2005). *Exploring corpora for ESP learning*. Benjamins.

Gavioli, L., & Aston, G. (2001). Enriching reality: Language corpora in language pedagogy. *ELT Journal, 55*(3), 238–246. https://doi.org/10.1093/elt/55.3.238

García-Pinar, A. (2019). Getting closer to authenticity in the course of technical English: Task-based instruction and TED Talks. *English Language Teaching, 12*(11), 10–22.

Goodman, S., & Graddol, D. (Eds.). (1996). *Redesigning English: New texts, new identities*. Psychology Press.

Gregory, M. (2002). Phasal analysis within communication linguistics: Two contrastive discourses. In P. Fries, M. Cummings, D. Lockwood, & W. Sprueill (Eds.), *Relations and functions in language and discourse* (pp. 316–345). Continuum.

Hardison, D. M., & Pennington, M. (2021). Multimodal second-language communication: Research findings and pedagogical implications. *RELC Journal*, *52*(1), 62–76. https://doi.org/10.1177/0033688220966635

Hasan, R. (1996). The nursery tale as a genre. In C. Cloran, D. Butt, & G. Williams (Eds.), *Ways of saying: Ways of meaning: Selected papers of Ruqaiya Hasan* (pp. 51–72). Cassell.

Hasebe, Y. (2015). Design and implementation of an online corpus of presentation transcripts of TED Talks. *Procedia – Social and Behavioral Sciences*, *198*, 174–182.

Hunston, S. (2001). Colligation, lexis, pattern, and text. In M. Scott & G. Thompson (Eds.), *Patterns of text: In honour of Michael Hoey* (pp. 13–33). Benjamins.

Johns, T. (1991a). Should you be persuaded: Two examples of data-driven learning. *Classroom Concordancing. English Language Research Journal*, *4*, 1–16.

Johns, T. (1991b). From printout to handout: Grammar and vocabulary teaching in the context of data-driven learning. *Classroom concordancing. English Language Research Journal*, *4*, 27–45.

Johns, T., & King, P. (Eds.). (1991). Classroom concordancing. *English Language Research Journal*, *4*.

Kellerman, S. (1992). "I see what you mean": The role of kinesic behaviour in listening and implications for foreign and second language learning. *Applied Linguistics*, *13*(3), 239–258. https://doi.org/10.1093/applin/13.3.239

Kettemann, B. (1995). On the use of concordancing in ELT. *TELL&CALL*, *4*, 4–15.

Kipp, M. (2014). ANVIL: A universal video research tool. In J. Durand, U. Gut, & G. Kristofferson (Eds.), *The Oxford handbook of corpus phonology* (pp. 420–436). Oxford University Press.

Knight, D. (2011). *Multimodality and active listenership: A corpus approach*. Continuum.

Kohn, K., Hoffstaedter, P., & Widmann, J. (2010). BACKBONE – Pedagogic corpora for content & language integrated learning. In A. Gimeno Sanz (Ed.), *New trends in computer-assisted learning: Working together* (pp. 157–162). Macmillan.

Kress, G., & van Leeuwen, T. [1996] (2006). *Reading images. The grammar of visual design*. Routledge.

Leopold, L. (2016). Honing EAP learners' public speaking skills by analyzing TED Talks. *ESL Canada Journal*, *33*(2), 46–58.

Loiacono, A., & Tursi, F. (2019). Mapping medical acronyms. In A. Baldry, F. Bianchi, & A. Loiacono (Eds.), *Representing and redefining specialised knowledge: Medical discourse* (pp. 93–126). ESE University of Salento Publishing. https://doi.org/10.1285/i9788883051531

Lücking, A., Bergman, K., Hahn, F., Kopp, S., & Rieser, H. (2012). Data-based analysis of speech and gesture: The Bielefeld speech and gesture alignment corpus (SaGA) and its applications. *Journal on Multimodal User Interfaces*, *7*, 5–18. https://doi.org/10.1007/s12193-012-0106-8

Machin, D. (2013). What is multimodal critical discourse studies? *Critical Discourse Studies*, *10*(4), 347–355. https://doi.org/10.1080/17405904.2013.813770

Melo-Pfeifer, S. (2015). Multilingual awareness and heritage language education: Children's multimodal representations of their multilingualism. *Language Awareness*, *24*(3), 197–215.

Melo-Pfeifer, S., & Chik, A. (2020). Multimodal linguistic biographies of prospective foreign language teachers in Germany: Reconstructing beliefs about languages and multilingual language learning in initial teacher education. *International Journal of Multilingualism*, *10*(24), 1-24. https://doi.org/10.1080/14790718.2020.1753748

O'Halloran, K. (Ed.). (2004). *Multimodal discourse analysis*. Continuum.

O'Halloran, K. (2013). *Multimodal analysis video*. [Computer software]. Multimodal Analysis Company. http://multimodal-analysis.com/products/multimodal-analysis-video/index.html

O'Halloran, K., Tan, S., Smith, B., & Podlasov, A. (2010). Challenges in designing digital interfaces for the study of multimodal phenomena. *Information Design Journal*, *18*(1), 2–21.

O'Halloran, K., & Tan, S. (2017). Multimodal analysis for critical thinking. *Learning, Media and Technology*, *42*(2), 147–170. https://doi.org/10.1080/17439884.2016.1101003

Oviatt, S., Grafsgaard, J., Chen, L., & Ochoa, X. (2018). Multimodal learning analytics: Assessing learners' mental state during the process of learning. In S. Oviatt & B. Schuller (Eds.), *The handbook of multimodal-multisensor interfaces: Signal processing, architectures, and detection of emotion and cognition, volume 2* (pp. 331–374). Association for Comuting Machinery and Morgan & Claypool.

Pinar, A. G., & Pallejá, C. (2018). TED talks: A multimodal tool for students of technological English. *Revista Docencia e Investigación*, *29*, 6–24.

Rojo, J. L. (2020). Metatextual indicators and phraseological units in a multimodal corpus: Delimitation and essential characteristics of as the saying goes and implications for interpreting. *Translation and Translanguaging in Multilingual Contexts, 5*(3), 241–258.

Scott, M. (2012). *WordSmith Tools 6.0* [Computer software]. Lexical Analysis Software. https://lexically. net/wordsmith/downloads/

Sindoni, M. G., Adami, E., Karatza, S., Marenzi, I., Moschini, I., Petroni, S., & Rocca, M. (2019). *The common framework of reference for intercultural digital literacies. A comprehensive set of guidelines of proficiency and intercultural awareness in multimodal digital literacies.* Retrieved July 25, 2020 from https:// www.eumade4ll.eu/wp-content/uploads/2019/09/cfridil-framework-MG3_IM_4-compresso.pdf

Sloetjes, H. (2014). ELAN: Multimedia annotation application. In J. Durand, U. Gut, & G. Kristofferson (Eds.), *The Oxford handbook of corpus phonology* (pp. 305–320). Oxford University Press.

Stoller, F. (2002). Project work: A means to promote language and content. In J. Richards & W. Renandya (Eds.), *Methodology in language teaching. An anthology of current practice* (pp. 107–119). Cambridge University Press.

Stubbs, M. (2001). Text, corpora, and problems of interpretation: A response to Widdowson. *Applied Linguistics, 22*(2), 149–172.

Sueyoshi, A., & Hardison, D. M. (2005). The role of gestures and facial cues in second language listening comprehension. *Language Learning, 55*(4), 661–699. https://doi.org/10.1111/j.0023-8333. 2005.00320.x

Swales, J. (1990). *Genre analysis: English in academic and research settings.* Cambridge University Press.

Taibi, D. (2020). Analysis D: Shaping digital identities through group study: A simulated case study using online tools and videos to explore animal-human interactions. In N. Vasta & A. Baldry (Eds.), *Multiliteracy advances and multimodal challenges in ELT environments* (pp. 190–195). Forum Edizioni.

Taibi, D., Chawla, S., Dietze, S., Marenzi, I., & Fetahu, B. (2015). Exploring TED talks as linked data for education. *British Journal of Educational Technology, 46*(5), 1092–1096.

Taibi, D., & Dietze, S. (2012). Fostering analytics on learning analytics research: The LAK dataset. *LAK '15: Proceedings of the Fifth International Conference on Learning Analytics and Knowledge, 15*(3), 1–163.

Taibi, D., Marenzi, I., & Ahmad, Q. A. I. (2019). Ain't that sweet: Reflections on scene level indexing and annotation in the *House Corpus* Project. In A. Baldry, F. Bianchi, & A. Loiacono (Eds.), *Representing and redefining specialised knowledge: Medical discourse* (pp. 151–181). ESE University of Salento Publishing. https://doi.org/10.1285/i9788883051531

Taylor, C., & Baldry, A. (2013). Computer assisted text analysis and translation: A functional approach in the analysis and translation. In E. Steiner & C. Yallop (Eds.), *Exploring translation and multilingual text production: Beyond content* (pp. 277–306). De Gruyter Mouton. https://doi. org/10.1515/9783110866193.277

Timmis, I. (2015). *Corpus linguistics for ELT. Research and practice.* Routledge.

Tribble, C., & Jones, G. (1990). *Concordances in the classroom.* Longman.

Vasta, N. (2020). Advances and challenges in EFL multiliteracy environments. In N. Vasta & A. Baldry (Eds.), *Multiliteracy advances and multimodal challenges in ELT environments* (pp. 27–64). Forum Edizioni.

Vasta, N., & Baldry, A. (Eds.). (2020). *Multiliteracy advances and multimodal challenges in ELT environments.* Forum Editrice.

Widdowson, H. G. (2000). On the limitations of linguistics applied. *Applied Linguistics, 21*(1), 3–25.

Widmann, J., Kohn, K., & Ziai, R. (2011). The SACODEYL search tool – Exploring corpora for language learning purposes. In A. Frankenberg-Garcia, L. Flowerdew, & G. Aston (Eds.), *New trends in corpora and language learning* (pp. 167–178). Continuum.

Wray, A. (2002). *Formulaic language and the lexicon.* Cambridge University Press.

25

DDL FOR YOUNGER LEARNERS

Peter Crosthwaite

25.1 Introduction

Advances in the availability, functionality, and user-friendliness of language corpora have resulted in a concomitant rise in the number of Data-Driven Learning (DDL) studies focusing on young learners (YLs) in recent years, with generally positive qualitative and even quantitative results now finally reported in the literature. However, there are still a number of barriers to the implementation and integration of DDL in the primary and secondary classrooms, including the lack of "pedagogic processing" of existing (mainly adult-focused) materials, a lack of software for specific use with YLs, and a lack of corpus literacy reported for pre-/in-service teacher trainees of YLs that often leads to a reluctance to adopt DDL pedagogy. This chapter discusses the affordances of direct, hands-on corpus use by pre-tertiary (language) learners for the purposes of data-driven learning, while also outlining the challenges involved in the successful implementation of DDL with younger learners. I summarise the successes (and occasional failures) of such studies to date, while reflecting on strategies to increase the adoption of DDL for YLs in future research.

25.2 Review of current state of research

Data-driven learning typically involves direct learner engagement with language corpus data, either through the use of teacher-printed concordance materials or learner-led hands-on corpus consultation, involving concordancing software or (increasingly) the use of online multimodal corpus-based applications that allow for students to learn and internalise statistical and contextual information about language in use in the process of working as "language detectives", with "every student a Sherlock Holmes" (Johns, 1997, p. 101). DDL, as a pedagogical approach, is proposed to promote autonomous and constructivist learning in its adoptees, in that learners "learn best when they discover or can be led to discover themselves" (Cobb, 1999, p. 15). DDL provides its adoptees increased opportunities for data-enhanced, learner-centred focus-on-form (Bernardini, 2001; Long, 1991), allowing for inductive learning where the learner is responsible for the detective work, as well as allowing language teachers to aid learners' deductive reasoning through guided support and scaffolding (Flowerdew, 2009).

Doubtlessly, other chapters in this volume cover the general affordances of DDL in greater detail (Fiona & Karlsen, this volume; Meunier, this volume). Hence, the discussion now moves on to DDL for YLs (defined in the present chapter as children aged between 6 (the first grade of primary school in Australia and also in numerous other contexts) and 16 years old (the final year of secondary school in Australia and some other contexts too). While DDL studies on learners younger than six are certainly possible, it is by first grade that many children will have learned the basics of reading in their own languages, and so will have attained a key prerequisite for consulting concordance data.

Despite a large increase in the number of DDL studies in the last 10 years as corpora increase in size and accessibility and as corpus applications increase in processing power, user-friendliness, and data visualisation, there still remains a dearth of DDL research that deals with its affordances for YLs. Three recent meta-analyses of the DDL literature (Boulton & Cobb, 2017; Lee *et al.*, 2019; Pérez-Paredes, 2019a) have pointed to a severe lack of empirical data for DDL at the secondary years of education. At the time of writing, just over 5% of published studies explicitly state that they were conducted in high-school settings (Boulton, 2019), while the number of DDL studies on primary-age data "can probably be counted on one hand" (Crosthwaite & Stell, 2019, p. 150) – although I hope this is not still the case by the time this chapter goes to print. I expand on possible reasons for the lack of DDL studies with YLs in the following section.

25.3 Core issues and topics

This chapter now focuses on two main issues regarding the use of corpora and DDL with YLs. The first issue is whether YLs' ability or aptitude to engage with DDL may be different from that of older learners, while the second is related to more adult concerns – namely, whether and how DDL may be integrated by teachers into the YL classroom.

25.3.1 Younger learners and corpus consultation

For many parents who lived through the pre-internet era, the connected world they live in today is now very different from the one that they were raised in. Today, many children are learning (about) languages through internet-connected tablet devices and interactive games, are searching for information online through search engines or wikis, are viewing instructional videos online, and are communicating with others in real time via video-conferencing and chat software. While a welcome and fascinating development, we need to be careful not to assume that YLs are already equipped with the technical knowledge and ICT skills required to adopt DDL-like learning practices, as one might expect if one erroneously considers YLs as "digital natives" (Prensky, 2001). While younger children may indeed have acquired a range of ICT skills even at the primary levels of education, there may still be a gap between their technical abilities and the kind of information literacy, inductive noticing, and deductive reasoning abilities required for successful engagement with corpus data as would normally be required for DDL to be effective. For example, when exploring the affordances of the web-as-corpus with YLs, such learners have been shown to adopt an "in and out" approach to consulting online search engine data (Thompson, 2013), and it is only after a process of explicitly training YLs in deductive reasoning and query refinement that YLs can turn basic search engine consultation into a more linguistically-oriented language learning opportunity (Gatto, 2019). While adult learners also often require explicit training in these processes for DDL to be effective (Boulton, 2009), children lack the acquired contextual knowledge from which to effectively apply deductive reasoning and may lack the cognitive development required for fast induction to take place (Piaget, 1970). YLs are also developing in their L1 literacy, leaving sudden exposure to a multitude of authentic (i.e. unmodified) L1 corpus data potentially problematic (let alone L2 data), and corpus output may require significant modification to be comprehensible (see sections below). Therefore, there is still a major role to play for teachers of YLs in effectively preparing their students for DDL, and there should be no expectation that YLs will simply "pick it up themselves" if left to their own devices.

That said, if YLs are able to receive initial guidance in the basics of corpus literacy, it does not take them very long to develop autonomous and rather idiosyncratic corpus usage habits. In one of the very few studies involving primary age learners, Crosthwaite and Stell (2019) introduced the online SketchEngine for Language Learning (SKeLL, Baisa & Suchomel, 2014) corpus platform with two 5-year-old boys within a private home tutoring setting. The tutor forwarded copies of the students' writing to the researcher who provided feedback on aspects of their writing that would be amenable for corpus consultation, including certain query strings the students could use. For 10 minutes before their regular writing instruction, the students consulted SKeLL as the tutor discussed with them and made notes about their experiences. Overall, both students reacted positively towards corpora as a tool that could help them resolve lexical issues in their writing and both reported higher general self-efficacy as a result of their new-found language problem-solving skills after just five short sessions with corpora. In particular, the children took the opportunity to progress through the DDL training and revisions at their own pace, eschewed the query syntax provided by the "expert", and reported frequently accessing the corpus platform long after its introduction – something less commonly reported in studies involving adult learners. That YLs may be better at DDL than their teachers think was also a finding in a study by Kim (2019) within the Korean primary EFL context. Following the introduction of paper-based concordance materials, three teachers and eighteen 6th grade students were interviewed about their experiences. Interestingly, while the teachers were convinced that a substantial level of guidance and scaffolding would be required for their students to adopt DDL practices, the students themselves reported enjoying great progress discovering the target rules exemplified through the concordances through peer discussion with their classmates. Additionally, Liontou (2019) experimented with DDL for the teaching of idioms to intermediate level EFL learners in Greece, involving just a single hour of training in how to use the BYU-COCA corpus platform (Davies, 2009) combined with printed extension activities involving corpus data. The results of pre- and post-tests on learners' knowledge of idioms were significantly higher for students who access these materials than those who learned only through consulting school textbooks, an achievement made more impressive as a result of the very limited training time provided.

25.3.2 Issues with the integration of corpora into the YL classroom

As mentioned, the use of corpora in the primary/secondary classroom is still incredibly limited. While teachers of YLs are very familiar with the terms Computer-Assisted Language Learning (CALL) and Information and Communication Technology (ICT) (Voogt *et al.*, 2013), they are, of course, quite unfamiliar with the term DDL. A key aspect of CALL theory and research over the past 20 years has been the integration and normalisation of technology into classroom settings (e.g. Bax, 2003; Chambers *et al.*, 2004). Numerous CALL technologies including smartphones, PowerPoint, e-whiteboards have now become normalised within many teaching and learning contexts, yet the integration and normalisation of corpus technology into pre-tertiary (and even, admittedly, tertiary) classroom practice have failed to materialise, despite numerous recently reported innovations and an increase in empirical support. For such integration to occur, Eng (2005) suggests a three-phase sequence from an 'emerging' phase of infrastructure development, an 'application' phase within existing CALL/ ICT related teaching and learning processes, and an 'infusion' phase where teachers (and their students) are able to use the technology innovatively for a range of pedagogical purposes. In my introduction to the first edited volume on DDL for YLs (Crosthwaite, 2019), I argued that while the ICT infrastructure generally exists (at least in most rich Western contexts, an issue to which I return later), corpus infrastructure is not yet appropriate for general use with YLs (see also Braun, 2007). Regarding application, the current state of DDL research in pre-tertiary contexts is mostly restricted to teacher training contexts, with an incredibly small number of studies providing empirical data of corpus use with actual students. Even when introducing DDL into teacher training contexts, the results are not always positive (see below). This situation precludes there is still a long way to go before the final infusion stage outlined by Eng (2005), where teachers and students are able to use the technology in creative and unforeseen ways. As Lee (2011) suggests, "the appropriate and effective use of corpora in the classroom is partly a technical issue, but primarily a pedagogical one" (p. 159, emphasis mine).

To help overcome this situation, Whyte and Schmid (2018) suggest three current critical issues be addressed for the successful integration of CALL technology in younger (English) learner classrooms, namely (1) classroom interaction and digital interactivity, (2) design and implementation of teaching and learning tasks, and (3) challenges of orchestrating complex technology-mediated interaction with YLs. It must be said here that Whyte and Schmid are discussing CALL generally, so we must now fill in the blanks regarding the application of these recommendations for DDL.

Regarding the first issue mentioned above, teachers must learn how to apply the technical competence gained post-corpus training into appropriate didactic and dialogic opportunities for meaningful interaction between themselves, the corpus technology, and their students (Beauchamp & Kennewell, 2010; Glover *et al.*, 2007) if such learners are to appropriately develop the type of constructivist, take-charge approach to learning espoused by DDL within their current learning practices. However, corpus literacy among teacher trainees is still sorely lacking (Chen *et al.*, 2019). Many teachers of YLs also lack the technological, pedagogical, and content knowledge (TPACK, Koehler & Mishra, 2009) to integrate CALL applications (including, but not restricted to corpora) into teaching practice (Taghizadeh & Yourdshahi, 2020), and more focus needs to be given to developing teachers' use of technology that can support their own pedagogical work and core teaching performance (McKenney & Visscher, 2019).

With specific reference to teacher training for DDL, Schaeffer-Lacroix (2019) conducted a series of training sessions in DDL-focused lesson planning with trainee secondary teachers of L2 German in France. Despite 15 hours of training on technology-enhanced learning (including a number of sessions on DDL), most teachers found it difficult to design appropriate DDL tasks for younger secondary school learners, failed to incorporate all but the simplest concordance-reading activities into their lesson planning, or insisting on presenting paper-based concordances only for their learners due to doubts about the abilities of their learners to engage with corpora directly. Latif (2021) reported on DDL training for 19 secondary school teachers in the Gulf EFL context, which resulted in initially very strong support for the implementation of corpora within their teaching practice. However, when interviewed again two years later, the same teachers reported that they had not been able to successfully implement corpus use into their classroom practice to the extent they had planned to following their training. Similar concerns have also been reported in a study by Leńko-Szymańska (2017) on the experiences of pre-service teachers who were trained in DDL lesson planning over the course of a semester, with the trainees mastering only basic corpus consultation competence post-training, and lacked the pedagogic skills to put what they had learned about corpora into classroom practice. However, the learners in Schaeffer-Lacroix's (2019) and Leńko-Szymańska's (2017) studies were fortunate to at least have the opportunity to take part in extended DDL training. Generally, in-service pre-tertiary teachers appear to have very little time for extra professional development activities (Bingimlas, 2009), and my previous attempts to organise a series of workshops on how corpora can be used in EAL lesson planning and materials development in Australia were met positively during initial correspondence. However, despite invites going out to over 30 staff in Brisbane Catholic schools, only three were able to attend a single four-hour session during the busy summer period. Complications related to COVID-19 have also made further engagement more difficult.

Despite such complications, small-scale opportunities for professional development have proven effective, with Tyne (2012) working together with two secondary school teachers of L2 Spanish in France to identify specific instances of where corpora could be used to support learning outcomes in current pedagogical sequences. The teachers reported being better able to carry out their lesson and activity planning following corpus literacy training, leading Tyne to suggest that DDL techniques – with a little help – can be aligned to suit the everyday practices of "ordinary" teachers (p. 136).

Regarding the second area mentioned by Whyte and Schmid (2018) above, learner-centeredness, authentic language use, and reflective learning practices are crucial elements in the design of successful CALL teaching and learning tasks for YLs, and it is not difficult here to see the parallels between these elements and what has been proposed to occur during learners' engagement with corpora during DDL. However, regarding DDL instruction, there is still a lack of constructive alignment (Biggs, 1996) between CALL curricula, teaching methods, and assessment tasks, with learners often not playing an active nor reflective role in their own learning (as required for constructivist learning to occur); with learners' output measured mainly through cloze tasks rather than text construction/revision; and with DDL mainly limited to out-of-class experiments rather than embedded into the curriculum (Boulton, 2010; Meunier, 2019).

In the secondary classroom, Wicher (2019) suggests that the current didactics of language learning involve the well-known presentation-practice-production (PPP) models of instruction including textbooks, form-focused exercises, and pair/group communication, alongside Task-based Language Teaching (TBLT) approaches (e.g. Shintani, 2011) that combine authentic tasks with focus-on-form. Wicher believes DDL can cater for both paradigms, with concordances used at the presentation stage, learner interaction with/modification of concordance results at the practice stage, and teacher/peer discussion of concordance findings at the production stage under a PPP model. Likewise, TBLT offers "the most fertile terrain for DDL" (Wicher, 2019, p. 39) through opportunities for input enhancement at the pre-task stage and consciousness-raising focus-on-form at post-task stages. For either to succeed, and given the complexities of teaching and learning at the secondary level, Wicher suggests an increased need for flexible design including internal differentiation (see also Coffey, 2018) of input enhancement – including modifying concordances – for learners of different technical/linguistic abilities. This should help to reduce any negative consequences for weaker learners as they try DDL for the first time, and while this may result in a trade-off regarding the "authenticity" of corpus data, i.e. unmodified data obtained from a corpus containing naturally occurring language samples, and its comprehensibility, Wicher suggests that such "corpus worship" (Gabrielatos, 2005) needs to give way to internal differentiation if DDL is to be adopted by both YLs and their teachers.

As for learner-centeredness at the primary school level, traditional approaches to input enhancement and exposure to target forms in the primary L1/L2 learner classroom include teachers' read-aloud stories (Lin, 2014) and home-book reading (Roberts, 2008), along with multimodal approaches such as songs and physical gestures (Total Physical Response, Asher, 2009), and explicit teaching and rote memorisation. There are also an increasing number of apps and online games that are used both in and out of class in many contexts. Certainly, for primary-age learners, having access to multimodal forms of data for DDL is very important, given that such learners progress in their literacy development from pictures with word captions, to picture books, then on to chapter books. In particular, while all language learners benefit from repeated exposure to target language forms in context, younger L2 learners stand to benefit more from multimodal corpus consultation as they lack either the fast-mapping ability very young L1 learners have to learn new words from a single encounter (Clark, 1993) or the socio-pragmatic competence utilised for language acquisition by older learners (Goto-Butler, 2019). While there are corpora of children's chapter books available for use with traditional concordancers (Montag *et al.*, 2015) as well as corpora containing graded texts that are specifically written for learners at primary/secondary grades (e.g. the Weebit corpus, Vajjala & Meurers, 2012), there are still few concordancers designed specifically for use for primary-age students. One useful exception is the work of Eri Hirata (2016, 2019), who developed a multimodal corpus tool (or MmCT) for use with primary-age L2 English learners in the Japanese context. The MmCT boasts a MovieConc feature where learners can access video, audio, and subtitle text together on different sides of the same screen, and where the video/audio can be played at slower speeds to aid comprehension. Learners can search for target words or larger expressions and be taken directly to relevant movie clips containing these expressions. Teacher trainees reported preference towards using this multimodal resource as compared to the use of the text-only BYU-COCA online platform (Davies, 2009) in the classroom with their primary-age learners (Hirata, 2019).

Regarding the third item discussed by Whyte and Schmid (2018) , there is a paradox for YLs where engagement with CALL technology is difficult due to limited linguistic resources, but where interaction with said technology is also required to gain the relevant linguistic resources. Whyte and Schmid discuss this in relation to L2 learning, although I suggest this can apply equally to primary-age L1 learners using corpora originally designed for adults. While there have been numerous reports in the literature of adult learners (or teachers) finding corpus consultation difficult, for YLs the idea of pedagogic processing, or, in other words, the simplifying of corpus materials for use with YLs, can greatly increase the likelihood of success with YLs' initial forays into corpus consultation (Flowerdew, 2009; Pérez-Parades, 2010; Wicher, 2019). Kim (2019) reported that for younger L2 learners, it was also advantageous to have access to L1 translations or glosses for difficult/complex vocabulary, although such corpora are relatively rare. In addition, corpora designed specifically for pedagogic use with YLs – or pedagogic corpora – can have a significant advantage over commonly used online corpora such as BYU-COCA or the BAWE within SketchEngine (Alsop & Nesi, 2009) in the secondary classroom (Pérez-Parades, 2019b). While the latter was primarily designed for research purposes and L1 linguistic representativeness, pedagogic corpora are specifically designed to accommodate specific L1/L2 learners, levels, and needs. A useful example is the SACODEYL pedagogic corpus (Braun, 2007; Pérez-Parades, 2019) that is composed of data taken from video recordings of teenagers' oral interactions on everyday topics across multiple

L1s. This data allows both vertical and horizontal reading to allow learners to see more clearly how discourse is structured, while the data is segmented and annotated according to teachable discourse functions, e.g. the use of conditionals, which makes searching the corpus for particular functions much easier for teachers and learners. In addition, having the video recordings available for listening practice and other important multimodal aspects of discourse such as, gesture, provides an additional entry point into the data that may be useful for secondary learners who find reading concordances difficult.

Despite the lack of pedagogic corpora currently available, Boulton (2019) suggests there may actually be a great deal of DDL going on in pre-tertiary classrooms although this may not be in a form where students sit at a computer using a typical concordancer. Rather, Meunier (2019) suggests expanding the scope of tools and tasks commonly used in DDL activities by leveraging tools that promote constructivist learning through data consultation but that are different in form and function from traditional concordancers. By generating appropriate accompanying tasks that require the same kind of noticing and pattern-sleuthing processes as found under a more typical DDL approach (see Kennedy & Miceli, 2010 for an overview of such processes at the tertiary level), one may greatly expand their repertoire of available DDL tools to include more multimodal resources, and – crucially – tools that YLs in particular can both easily use and find appealing. Meunier uses the websites PlayPhrase.me (https://www.playphrase.me/), a web resource where students can search for phrases used in a database of film clips and see the phrases and accompanying clips together), and LyricsTraining (http://fr.lyricstraining), which presents gap-fill questions or a karaoke mode based on a database of song lyrics organised by proficiency level as potential resources that teachers looking to adopt DDL practice can try with YLs, despite these resources being very different in feel and function to traditional concordancers.

25.4 Current contributions and research

Outside of the Crosthwaite (2019) dedicated edited volume on DDL for YLs, a number of studies featuring corpus use with younger learners have been published over the last few years, and this section provides an overview of this research.

For the acquisition of collocational patterns, Boontam and Phoocharoensil (2018) used paper-based corpus materials with young fourth grade Thai EFL students at pre-intermediate levels of L2 proficiency, as they learned about the English prepositions *during, among,* and *between* through DDL. The learners read teacher-printed concordance materials containing the target items, extracting from the Graded Readers Corpus within the Compleat Lexical Tutor (http://www.lextutor.ca/, Cobb, 2005). The results of pre-/post-tests on the target items found significant improvement in learners' knowledge of these constructions at the post-test stage, measured via gap fill, sentence building, and grammaticality judgement tasks. The students themselves reported high satisfaction with the DDL approach; in particular, in gaining the ability to learn about language by themselves, while only six of thirty learners reported difficulty interpreting the selected concordances. Also covering EFL learners' development of L2 English prepositions, Özbay and Olgun (2017) compared learners' acquisition of these forms using traditional textbook-based instruction versus printed concordances on groups of high-school students in Turkey across intermediate and advanced L2 proficiency levels. The researchers found significant differences between experimental and control groups' knowledge of L2 preposition collocations following 15 weeks of instruction. Finally, Saeedakhtar *et al.* (2020) explored the use of DDL for the learning of verb-noun collocations with lower-intermediate level secondary school learners in the Iranian context. Comparing hands-on direct corpus use with hands-off DDL involving printed concordances, participants using both approaches reported learning gains over a control group not using DDL in immediate post-tests, although learners in the hands-on condition outperformed learners in the hands-off condition in delayed post-tests.

For vocabulary, Soruç and Tekin (2017) explored the development of secondary school students' L2 English lexical knowledge using DDL in the Ugandan context, comparing a paper dictionary-only control group with an experimental group who received training in understanding pre-selected concordance output before consulting a range of online corpora (the authors do not say which, unfortunately). Using a standardised pre-/post-/delayed post-test procedure, the authors report significant improvement in the experimental group over the improvement noted for the control group, as well as positive qualitative reports from the learners themselves. Tekin and Soruç (2016) also looked at L2 English vocabulary development in a Turkish high school setting using the British National Corpus (although they do not say which website was used to access the corpus). Learners received training in using the various functions of the platform together with printed concordances in order to investigate target items from the same standardised vocabulary test reported in Soruç and Tekin (2017). Semi-structured interviews with participants revealed five common themes arising from the DDL treatment, including "innovative", "autonomous", "easy and fun", and "practical" as positive aspects of corpus use, with "complex" (Soruç & Tekin, 2017, p. 1276) representing learners' negative opinions of the treatment, with the latter related to concordances being cut-off or being too difficult to decode. Overall learner satisfaction with the DDL treatment was over 75%. Also in Turkey, Yılmaz and Soruç (2017) trained twenty 14–16-year-old EFL students on how to use BYU-COCA over eight hours in a private language school setting. Again, performance on pre-/post-test vocabulary tests was significantly higher for those using corpora than a control group who did not. Also focusing on DDL for vocabulary is a study by Karras (2016) conducted in international secondary schools in the Vietnamese EFL context. A longitudinal experimental/control group training procedure on vocabulary acquisition was performed over an eight-week period, with the experimental group adopting a DDL approach through the Compleat Lexical Tutor software (Cobb, 2005), and with the control group using an online dictionary. The study is notable for its distinct treatment of EFL students at international schools as either non-local 'third culture kids' (TCKs) from a range of countries or 'educational cross-cultural kids', who comprise local children attending an international school. This is an important distinction for DDL in that Karras (2016) claims that TCK learners, in particular, are atypical of most secondary EFL learners, as there may be "a tripartite relationship between the TCK experience, attending an international school, and their linguistic and academic prowess" (p. 182). This tripartite relationship may result in increased motivation to try new approaches when learning second languages, including the kind of autonomous, constructivist learning practices associated with direct DDL.

In terms of improving grammar, Moon and Oh (2018) explored the use of DDL with Korean middle school EFL learners to "unlearn" (p. 48) the overgeneration of the copula before thematic verbs (e.g. *he is dance very well*), a common error in Korean L2 English. Almost 200 students were divided into either a traditional textbook-based instructional group or an experimental DDL group, who received printed concordances from a graded reader corpus composed of articles written for Time Magazine for Kids (www.timeforkids.com) as well as from a learner corpus generated from the learners' own writings, before consulting these corpora hands-on using Wordsmith Tools (Scott, 2008). Learners taking the DDL treatment produced significantly fewer redundant copula post-training than the control group. In particular, the authors stress the importance of exposing learners to negative evidence of erroneous forms via consulting a learner corpus generated from their own writings, as seen in Crosthwaite (2017). Additionally, in a study focusing on the Greek EFL context, Michali and Patsala (2020) used a combination of printed concordance handouts and instructional materials on querying the British National Corpus and COCA to aid English grammar teaching with 36 students at junior high school. After just two teaching hours, the young learners reported very positive opinions about the use of corpora for learning about both grammar and vocabulary, although reported that the examples taken from the two online corpora were above their level of proficiency.

25.5 Future directions of research

One of the major issues still facing those who wish to increase DDL adoption in YL contexts is simply a lack of empirical data on its effectiveness in the classroom. Whenever writing grant applications involving corpus consultation for YLs, I always seem to receive feedback along the lines of "but there is no evidence that it works", despite the wealth of evidence now available for how older learners can and do benefit from DDL. Of the few DDL studies that have been performed in YL contexts, and aside from the empirical studies reported in the section above, most studies deal with aspects of teacher training for YL or YL teachers' reactions to corpus use, leaving data from students themselves sorely lacking. This situation is likely because teacher training contexts are as far as most researchers have been able to penetrate into pre-tertiary school systems to conduct DDL research, due to the numerous ethical and bureaucratic complexities involved in actually getting access to young children from whom to collect data. In addition, of the studies already cited in this chapter involving YL teacher training (e.g. Kim, 2019; Schaeffer-Lacroix, 2019), despite initial positivity during such training, many teachers remain sceptical of how YLs will react to or engage with corpus use, and given the vast range of other workload demands placed on primary and secondary teachers, many are still unwilling to take the risk of even partial classroom implementation during actual teaching periods. These rational fears (Boulton, 2009) are potentially preventing the kind of large-scale funded projects required to empirically test the affordances of DDL with YLs from getting off the ground, and it may take more significant developments involving DDL with older learners in mainstream education before the pendulum can eventually swing to increased opportunities for YLs.

Another area for future research is that while many DDL studies have been conducted in technologically-rich Western or East Asian countries, the benefits of DDL are yet to be realised in regions such as the Middle East, S.E. Asia, and Africa. As a result, little is currently known about teacher trainees' or educators' acceptance of or preparation for DDL in these regions. This situation may be reflective of a digital divide (Lozano & Izquierdo, 2019) between relatively ICT-poor countries and their richer neighbours. Reporting on teachers of YLs' attempts to implement CALL technology into the classroom in the Middle East, Taghizadeh & Yourdshahi (2020) claim that a large number of teachers receive little to no CALL training within initial teacher education. In addition, limited ICT infrastructure and a lack of support from schools were major barriers to teachers' willingness to undertake appropriate professional development to remedy their technological or pedagogical shortcomings. The above-mentioned work by Soruç and Tekin (2017) is the first DDL study that I am aware of that has tested the affordances of DDL in the African context. Crosthwaite *et al.* (2021) and Crosthwaite (2020) used Zoom workshops to introduce DDL to trainee L2 English teachers at a teacher training facility in Indonesia. Generally, positive perceptions of DDL were reported for secondary school trainees, while primary school trainees were more negative in their views. More studies (aside from those already mentioned in this chapter) from other contexts including South America, Africa, and S.E. Asia are of course welcome. Additionally, it would also be beneficial for the field as a whole if more DDL studies involving YLs were conducted where the target language is other than English. While Di Vito (2019) investigated the acquisition of L2 French within the Italian YL context, and Schaeffer-Lacroix's (2019) looked at teachers of L2 German in the French context, there is a significant need for DDL studies featuring YLs for languages other than English. This is highlighted as a key factor in Vyatkina's (2020) explanation for the underutilisation of corpora in mainstream education, where she calls for a broadening of contexts for DDL beyond EFL/ESL, broadening access to DDL resources, increased scaffolding of DDL for teachers, and an increase in open DDL resources and corpora for general use.

Further reading

Braun, S. (2007). Integrating corpus work into secondary education: From data-driven learning to needs-driven corpora. *ReCALL, 19*(3), 307–328. Despite being written over a decade ago, Braun's case study of DDL for YLs at the secondary education level has been cited over 150 times. The paper presents a valuable overview of the pedagogical requirements for corpus integration in secondary schools, before arguing for novel corpora and corpus activities based on the specific needs of secondary-age language learners.

Crosthwaite, P. (2019). *Data-driven learning for the next generation: Corpora and DDL for pre-tertiary learners.* Routledge. This is the first edited volume of DDL studies specifically targeting research involving YLs. The book is organised into three sections, with the first dealing with overcoming challenges for DDL with YLs, the second on applying new DDL methods with YLs, while the third section covers a small number of empirical studies involving YLs corpus use at the primary and secondary levels of education.

Sealey, A., & Thompson, P. (2004). 'What do you call the dull words?' primary school children using corpus-based approaches to learn about language. *English in Education, 38*(1), 80–91. This is one of the very few studies dealing with DDL for primary school education, exploring the potential for teaching Key Stage 2 pupils in the UK context using corpus materials. The study includes valuable examples of the teaching activities used, as well as extracts of discussions between the researcher and two groups of pupils as they attempt to use corpora to learn the distinction between open and closed word classes.

References

Alsop, S., & Nesi, H. (2009). Issues in the development of the British Academic Written English (BAWE) corpus. *Corpora, 4*(1), 71–83. https://doi.org/10.3366/E1749503209000227

Asher, J. (2009). *Learning another language through actions: The complete teacher's guidebook* (7th ed.). Sky Oaks Productions.

Baisa, V., & Suchomel, V. (2014, December). SkELL: Web interface for English language learning. In *RASLAN* (pp. 63-70).

Bax, S. (2003). CALL—Past, present and future. *System, 31*(1), 13–28.

Beauchamp, G., & Kennewell, S. (2010). Interactivity in the classroom and its impact on learning. *Computers & Education, 54*(3), 759–766. https://doi.org/10.1016/j.compedu.2009.09.033

Bernardini, S. (2001). Corpora in the classroom: An overview and some reflections on future developments. In J. Sinclair (Ed.), *How to use corpora in language teaching* (pp. 15–36). Benjamins.

Biggs, J. (1996). Enhancing teaching through constructive alignment. *Higher Education, 32*(3), 347–364.

Bingimlas, K. A. (2009). Barriers to the successful integration of ICT in teaching and learning environments: A review of the literature. *Eurasia Journal of Mathematics, Science & Technology Education, 5*(3), pp. 235–245. https://doi.org/10.12973/ejmste/75275

Boontam, P., & Phoocharoensil, S. (2018). Effectiveness of English preposition learning through data-driven learning (DDL). *The Southeast Asian Journal of English Language Studies, 24*(3), 125–141. http://doi.org/10.17576/3L-2018-2403-10

Boulton, A. (2009). Data-driven learning: Reasonable fears and rational reassurance. *Indian Journal of Applied Linguistics*, *35*(1), 81–106.

Boulton, A. (2010). Data-driven learning: On paper, in practice. In T. Harris & M. Moreno Jaén (Eds.), *Corpus linguistics in language teaching* (pp. 17–52). Peter Lang.

Boulton, A. (2019). Foreword. In P. Crosthwaite (Ed.), *Data-driven learning for the next generation: Corpora and DDL for pre-tertiary learners* (pp. xiv–xx). Routledge.

Boulton, A., & Cobb, T. (2017). Corpus use in language learning: A meta-analysis. *Language Learning*, *67*(2), 348–393. https://doi.org/10.1111/lang.12224

Braun, S. (2007). Integrating corpus work into secondary education: From data-driven learning to needs-driven corpora. *ReCALL*, *19*(3), 307–328. https://doi.org/10.1017/S0958344007000535

Butler, Y. G. (2019). Teaching vocabulary to young second-or foreign-language learners: What can we learn from the research. *Language Teaching for Young Learners*, *1*(1), 4–33. https://doi.org/10.1075/ltyl.00003.but

Chambers, A., Conacher, J. E., & Littlemore, J. (Eds.). (2004). *ICT and language learning*. A & C Black.

Chen, M., Flowerdew, J., & Anthony, L. (2019). Introducing in-service English language teachers to data-driven learning for academic writing. *System*, *87*, 102148. https://doi.org/10.1016/j.system.2019.102148

Clark, E. (1993). *The lexicon in acquisition*. Cambridge University Press. https://doi.org/10.1017/CBO9780511554377

Cobb, T. (1999). Applying constructivism: A test for the learner-as-scientist. *Educational Technology Research & Development*, *47*, 15–33. https://doi.org/10.1007/BF02299631

Cobb, T. (2005). *The Compleat Lexical Tutor for data-driven learning on the web*. [Web-based suite of programs]. University of Quebec. http://lextutor.ca/

Coffey, S. (2018). Differentiation in theory and practice. In M. Maguire, S. Gibbons, M. Glacking, D. Pepper, & K. Skilling (Eds.), *Becoming a teacher: Issues in secondary education* (5th ed.) (pp. 197–209). Open University Press.

Crosthwaite, P. (2017). Retesting the limits of data-driven learning: Feedback and error correction. *Computer Assisted Language Learning*, *30*(6), 447–473.

Crosthwaite, P. (2019). Data-driven learning and younger learners: Introduction to the volume. In P. Crosthwaite (Ed.), *Data-driven learning for the next generation: Corpora and DDL for pre-tertiary learners* (pp. 1–10). Routledge. https://doi.org/10.4324/9780429425899-1

Crosthwaite, P. (2020). Taking DDL online: Designing, implementing and evaluating a SPOC on data-driven learning for tertiary L2 writing. *Australian Review of Applied Linguistics*, *43*(2), 169–195. https://doi.org/10.1075/aral.00031.cro

Crosthwaite, P., Luciana, & Schweinberger, M. (2021). Voices from the periphery: Perceptions of Indonesian primary vs secondary pre-service teacher trainees about corpora and data-driven learning in the L2 English classroom. *Applied Corpus Linguistics*, *1*(1), 100003.

Crosthwaite, P., & Stell, A. (2019). "It helps me get ideas on how to use my words": Primary school students' initial reactions to corpus use in a private tutoring setting. In P. Crosthwaite (Ed.), *Data driven learning for the next generation: Corpora and DDL for pre-tertiary learners* (pp. 150–170). Routledge. https://doi.org/10.4324/9780429425899-9

Davies, M. (2009). *Exploring English with online corpora: An introduction*. Palgrave Macmillan.

Di Vito, S. (2019). Teaching French to younger learners through DDL. In P. Crosthwaite (Ed.), *Data driven learning for the next generation: Corpora and DDL for pre-tertiary learners* (pp. 171–186). Routledge. https://doi.org/10.4324/9780429425899-10

Eng, T. S. (2005). The impact of ICT on learning: A review of research. *International Education Journal*, *6*(5), 635–650.

Flowerdew, L. (2009). Applying corpus linguistics to pedagogy. *International Journal of Corpus Linguistics*, *14*(3), 393–417. https://doi.org/10.1075/ijcl.14.3.05flo

Gabrielatos, C. (2005). Corpora and language teaching: Just a fling or wedding bells? *TESLEJ*, *8*(4), 1–37.

Gatto, M. (2019). Query complexity and query refinement: Using web search from a corpus perspective with digital natives. In P. Crosthwaite (Ed.), *Data driven learning for the next generation: Corpora and DDL for pre-tertiary learners* (pp. 106–130). Routledge. https://doi.org/10.4324/9780429425899-7

Glover, D., Miller, D., Averis, D., & Door, V. (2007). The evolution of an effective pedagogy for teachers using the interactive whiteboard in mathematics and modern languages: An empirical analysis from the secondary sector. *Learning, Media and Technology*, *32*(1), 5–20. https://doi.org/10.1080/17439880601141146

Hirata, E. (2016). The development of multi-modal corpus tool for teaching English to young learners. *Fukuoka Jo Gakuin University Bulletin. Faculty of International Career Development, 2*, 19–32.

Hirata, E. (2019). The development of a multi-modal corpus for young EFL learners: A case study on the integration of DDL in teacher education. In P. Crosthwaite (Ed.), *Data driven learning for the next generation: Corpora and DDL for pre-tertiary learners* (pp. 88–105). Routledge. https://doi. org/10.4324/9780429425899-6

Johns, T. (1997). Contexts: The background, development and trialling of a concordance-based CALL program. In A. Wichmann, S. Fligelstone, T. McEnery, & G. Knowles (Eds.), *Teaching and language corpora* (pp. 100–115). Longman.

Karras, J. N. (2016). The effects of data-driven learning upon vocabulary acquisition for secondary international school students in Vietnam. *ReCALL, 28*(2), 166–186.

Kennedy, C., & Miceli, T. (2010). Corpus-assisted creative writing: Introducing intermediate Italian learners to a corpus as a reference resource. *Language Learning & Technology, 14*(1), 28–44. http:// dx.doi.org/10125/44201

Kim, H. (2019). The perception of teachers and learners towards an exploratory corpus-based grammar instruction in a Korean EFL primary school context. *Primary English Education, 25*(1), 123–152.

Koehler, M., & Mishra, P. (2009). What is technological pedagogical content knowledge (TPACK)? *Contemporary Issues in Technology and Teacher Education, 9*(1), 60–70.

Latif, M. M. A. (2021). Corpus literacy instruction in language teacher education: Investigating Arab EFL student teachers' immediate beliefs and long-term practices. *ReCALL, 33*(1), 34–48.

Lee, H., Warschauer, M., & Lee, J. H. (2019). The effects of corpus use on second language vocabulary learning: A multilevel meta-analysis. *Applied Linguistics, 40*(5), 721–753. https://doi.org/10.1093/ applin/amy012amy012

Lee, S. (2011). Challenges of using corpora in language teaching and learning: Implications for secondary education. *Linguistic Research, 28*(1), 159–178.

Leńko-Szymańska, A. (2017). Training teachers in data driven learning: Tackling the challenge. *Language Learning & Technology, 21*(3), 217–241.

Lin, L. C. (2014). Learning word meanings from teachers' repeated story read-aloud in EFL primary classrooms. *English Language Teaching, 7*(7), 68–81. https://doi.org/10.5539/elt.v7n7p68

Liontou, T. (2019). The effect of data-driven learning activities on young EFL learners' processing of English idioms. In P. Crosthwaite (Ed.), *Data driven learning for the next generation: Corpora and DDL for pre-tertiary learners* (pp. 208–227). Routledge. https://doi.org/10.4324/9780429425899-12

Long, M. (1991). Focus on form: A design feature in language teaching methodology. In K. De Bot, R. Ginsberg, & C. Kramsch (Eds.), *Foreign language research in cross-cultural perspectives* (pp. 39–52). Benjamins. http://dx.doi.org/10.1075/sibil.2.07lon

Lozano, A. A., & Izquierdo, J. (2019). Technology in second language education: Overcoming the digital divide. *Emerging Trends in Education, 2*(3), 52–70. https://doi.org/10.19136/etie.a2n3.3250

Michali, M., & Patsala, P. (2020). Learning experiences in secondary education: A study exploring Greek EFL learners' attitudes towards corpus-based teaching, *INTED2020 Proceedings*, 6871–6881. https://doi.org/10.21125/inted.2020.1827

McKenney, S., & Visscher, A. (2019). Technology for teacher learning and performance. *Technology, Pedagogy and Education, 28*(2), 129–132. https://doi.org/10.1080/1475939X.2019.1600859

Meunier, F. (2019). A case for constructive alignment in DDL: Rethinking outcomes, practices and assessment in (data-driven) language learning. In P. Crosthwaite (Ed.), *Data driven learning for the next generation: Corpora and DDL for pre-tertiary learners* (pp. 13–31). Routledge. https://doi.org/ 10.4324/9780429425899-2

Montag, J. L., Jones, M. N., & Smith, L. B. (2015). The words children hear: Picture books and the statistics for language learning. *Psychological Science, 26*(9), 1489–1496. https://doi.org/10.1177 %2F0956797615594361

Moon, S., & Oh, S. Y. (2018). Unlearning overgenerated be through data-driven learning in the secondary EFL classroom. *ReCALL, 30*(1), 48–67. https://doi.org/10.1017/S0958344017000246

Özbay, A. S., & Olgun, O. (2017). The application of DDL for teaching preposition collocations to Turkish EFL learners. *The International Journal of Research in Teacher Education, 8*(3), 1–10.

Pérez-Paredes, P. (2019a). A systematic review of the uses and spread of corpora and data-driven learning in CALL research during 2011–2015. *Computer Assisted Language Learning*. https://doi.org/10.1080 /09588221.2019.1667832

Pérez-Paredes, P. (2019b). The pedagogic advantage of teenage corpora for secondary school learners. In P. Crosthwaite (Ed.), *Data driven learning for the next generation: Corpora and DDL for pre-tertiary learners* (pp. 67–87). Routledge. https://doi.org/10.4324/9780429425899-5

Piaget, J. (1970). *Science and education and the psychology of the child.* Orion Press.

Prensky, M. (2001). Digital natives, digital immigrants. *On the Horizon, 9*(5), 1–6.

Roberts, T. A. (2008). Home storybook reading in primary or second language with preschool children: Evidence of equal effectiveness for second-language vocabulary acquisition. *Reading Research Quarterly, 43*(2), 103–130. https://doi.org/10.1598/RRQ.43.2.1

Saeedakhtar, A., Bagerin, M., & Abdi, R. (2020). The effect of hands-on and hands-off data-driven learning on low-intermediate learners' verb-preposition collocations. *System, 19*, 102268.

Schaeffer-Lacroix, E. (2019). Barriers to trainee teachers' corpus use. In P. Crosthwaite (Ed.), *Data driven learning for the next generation: Corpora and DDL for pre-tertiary learners* (pp. 47–64). Routledge. https://doi.org/10.4324/9780429425899-4

Scott, M. (2008). *WordSmith tools (version 5).* Liverpool: Lexical Analysis Software.

Shintani, N. (2011). A comparative study of the effects of input-based and production-based instruction on vocabulary acquisition by young EFL learners. *Language Teaching Research, 15*, 137–158. https://doi.org/10.1177/1362168810388692

Soruç, A., & Tekin, B. (2017). Vocabulary learning through data-driven learning in an English as a second language setting. *Educational Sciences, Theory and Practice, 17*(6), 1811–1832. https://doi.org/10.12738/estp.2017.6.0305

Taghizadeh, M., & Hasani Yourdshahi, Z. (2020). Integrating technology into young learners' classes: Language teachers' perceptions. *Computer Assisted Language Learning, 33*(8), 982–1006. https://doi.org/10.1080/09588221.2019.1618876

Tekin, B., & Soruç, A. (2016). Using corpus-assisted learning activities to assist vocabulary development in English. *The Turkish Online Journal of Educational Technology, Special Issue*, 1270–1283.

Thompson, P. (2013). The digital natives as learners: Technology use patterns and approaches to learning. *Computers & Education, 65*, 12–33. https://doi.org/10.1016/j.compedu.2012.12.022

Tyne, H. (2012). Corpus work with ordinary teachers: Data-driven learning activities. In J. Thomas & A. Boulton (Eds.), *Input, process and product: Developments in teaching and language corpora* (2nd ed.) (pp. 707–712). Routledge.

Vajjala, S., & Meurers, D. (2012). On improving the accuracy of readability classification using insights from second language acquisition. In *NAACL HLT '12 Proceedings of the Seventh Workshop on Building Educational Applications Using NLP* (pp. 163–173), Montreal, Canada, June 07, 2012

Voogt, J., Knezek, G., Cox, M., Knezek, D., & ten Brummelhuis, A. (2013). Under which conditions does ICT have a positive effect on teaching and learning? A call to action. *Journal of Computer-Assisted Learning, 29*(1), 4–14. https://doi.org/10.1111/j.1365-2729.2011.00453.x

Vyatkina, N. (2020). Corpora as open educational resources for language teaching. *Foreign Language Annals, 53*(2), 359–370. https://doi.org/10.1111/flan.12464

Whyte, S., & Schmid, E. C. (2018). Classroom technology for young learners. In S. Garton & F. Copland (Eds.), *The Routledge handbook of teaching English to young learners* (pp. 338–355). Routledge.

Wicher, O. (2019). Data-driven learning in the secondary classroom: A critical evaluation from the perspective of foreign language didactics. In P. Crosthwaite (Ed.), *Data driven learning for the next generation: Corpora and DDL for pre-tertiary learners* (pp. 31–46). Routledge. https://doi.org/10.4324/9780429425899-3

Yılmaz, E., & Soruç, A. (2015). The use of concordance for teaching vocabulary: A data-driven learning approach. *Procedia-Social and Behavioral Sciences, 191*, 2626–2630. https://doi.org/10.1016/j.sbspro.2015.04.400

26

HOW LEARNERS USE CORPORA

Pascual Pérez-Paredes

26.1 Introduction

The focus of this chapter is the analysis and discussion of learners' use of corpora, leading to an increased understanding of how language learners' interaction with corpora and data-driven learning (DDL) can be traced to aid such research. In the context of this chapter, DDL and corpus use are understood broadly as "foreign or second language (L2) learners [working] with written or spoken corpus data" (Boulton & Cobb, 2017, p. 349). The present chapter focuses on methods that can help us understand how learners use corpora, and, accordingly, not on the outcomes or the pedagogical uses of DDL.

As Hafner and Candlin (2007) put it, "there is a lack of direct evidence of students' self-directed use of corpus tools" (p. 304). In fact, there is a lack of different types of evidence of both self-directed and teacher-led use of corpora. Chambers and Sullivan (2004) noted that "studies involving corpus consultation by learners are few in number, there is as yet no clearly defined methodology on which one can rely" (p. 161). Pérez-Paredes *et al.* (2011) observed that the studies reflecting the resources consulted by learners, exact queries, search results, or even discoveries are still "very few in number" (p. 235). In a recent study, Crosthwaite *et al.* (2019) noted that there are few studies that track the students' actual engagement with corpora for DDL.

One of the main challenges involved in the analysis of learners' uses of corpora is that the operationalisation of these uses in concrete, measurable ways has so far not been given appropriate attention. The phrase "uses of corpora" is often too vague, and it is used as a proxy to denote that learners make use of corpora in generic or undefined ways. However, Gaskell and Cobb (2004) noted that it is essential to understand what real learners do when exposed to concordancing and DDL: "It is often noted that the various educational uses of concordancing are more talked about than tested with real learners" (p. 317).

Research that specifically describes how corpus uses have been operationalised as well as ways in which future research can apply alternative methods are discussed in this chapter. In the context of our analysis, our starting point is to discuss the meta-analyses carried out by Boulton and Cobb (2017), and Lee *et al.* (2018), as well as the systematic literature review in Pérez-Paredes (2019). This chapter outlines a framework where specific uses of corpora can be pinned down and identifies the methodologies and research areas that can advance our

DOI: 10.4324/9781003002901-31

knowledge about these uses. Section 26.2 offers a critical perspective on how to understand learners' engagement with the technological and linguistic affordances of corpora. Section 26.3 discusses how logs can be operationalised to research such uses. Section 26.4 examines alternative sites where corpus uses may be explored and offers a discussion on the role of method triangulation in researching learners' use of corpora.

26.2 Uses of corpora: A critical ecological perspective

This section discusses how corpus uses are shaped by the microsystem where they occur, including learners, tools, artefacts, and semiotic resources.

Uses of corpora do not occur in a social vacuum. Chun *et al.* (2016) have shown that uses of technology for language learning imply reflection on and awareness about the symbolic and virtual realities of classroom technologies, including new literacies and learners' agency. Inspired by Bronfenbrenner's (1979) analysis of interpersonal relations, and more recently by the Douglas Fir Group (2016), learners can be seen as operating in micro, meso, and macro (ecological) systems. Computer-assisted language learning (CALL) ecosystems consist of "interacting components including language learners, teachers [...] technological devices, applications [and] material/semiotic artefacts and resources, all of which participate in a language learning [...] as well as the social processes and semiotic practices that characterise the way the human actors interact with one another and with other components of the system" (Blin, 2016, p. 39). An understanding of how these systems interface can only benefit our comprehension of how learners use corpora. In the next paragraphs, we argue that this area needs further analysis and attention.

Most DDL (Johns, 1990) research has looked at microsystems and learners' interactions with corpus data in instructed settings. Thus, corpus use has been conceptualised attending to different criteria that vary from site to site. Perhaps, the most widely spread conceptualisation is to equate corpus use with the aim(s) of the corpus query, as in Crosthwaite (2017), where the learners used the corpus to correct errors of word choice, word form, collocations, and phrasing. Similarly, Tono *et al.* (2014) instructed learners to correct errors using a corpusbased tool by way of a revision manual. They categorised the learners' corrections into omission, addition, and misformation corrections. This is a top-down approach where corpus uses are mediated by the overall design of the task and learners' uses are seen as the result of the researchers' analysis. In this type of conceptualisation, DDL uses are mediated by the target language form or skill selected by researchers. An alternative conceptualisation uses a bottom-up approach to examine corpus uses that are interpreted in the light of learners' uses of the affordances of the corpus tools and data used in the research design. These approaches make use of logs, either manual or computer logs, and are treated in the next section. Other ways to conceptualise uses are by exploring directed vs. self-directed uses or by looking at meta-uses (learning how to use corpora) vs. applied uses (using corpora to complete a task).

Comparatively, much less attention has been paid to meso- and macro-systems that explore language learning, particularly in pre-tertiary educational levels. For example, mesosystems involve how institutions and communities shape language learning contexts, a topic rarely discussed in the DDL literature. Similarly, macrosystems deserve further attention in the specialised literature if we are to understand some prevailing values and attitudes to, among others, the role of data in language learning and societal attitudes to language learning (Noguera-Díaz & Pérez-Paredes, 2020). From an ecological perspective, the examination of these three levels is expected to shed light on socially situated experiences of language learning.

The fact that DDL research has primed the analysis of microsystems may have contributed to a representation of learners' uses of corpora that is fundamentally driven by research designs in tertiary education contexts and, for example, not so much by the analyses of how institutional practices or how researcher-driven learning goals may impact our understanding of the field. These concerns have been voiced by researchers such as Yoon and Jo (2014), who claim that a learner needs-based approach to corpus use in L2 writing instruction is essential when using corpora in classrooms, and O'Sullivan (2007), who holds that corpus-consultation literacy needs to be framed in process-oriented approaches to language learning.

26.2.1 Who are the learners that use corpus resources for language learning?

The DDL literature reveals that learners' uses of corpora are fundamentally designed and tested by researchers in university contexts (Boulton & Cobb, 2017; Pérez-Paredes, 2019). Put simply, learners' corpus uses are afforded by research designs. The uses of corpora in the research analysed in Boulton and Cobb (2017) can be classified as corpus use either for language learning or for reference purposes. Both purposes yield large to medium effect sizes, which showcases the effectiveness of DDL. Paradoxically, language teachers other than researchers play a minor role in DDL, which may contribute to the widely spread idea that learners' corpus use has failed to become normalised (Bax, 2003) across language classrooms and levels (Chambers, 2019; Mukherjee, 2004; Pérez-Paredes *et al.*, 2018). For example, in the 2018 Chicago TESOL convention, the largest forum for TESOL worldwide, only 1.1% of all presentations (N=900) examined the uses of corpora in English teaching. None dealt with language learners' uses of corpora.

When learners do engage with corpus uses in semi-autonomous ways, they do so either because they follow the directions provided by researchers such as in Bernardini (2000), Lee and Swales (2006), Hafner and Candlin (2007) or, among others, Charles (2012). Evidence of learners' self-directed, autonomous uses of corpora are scarce and, arguably, need further attention in the literature. Research carried out by Charles (2012, 2014) has been successful in identifying a locus in EAP courses where directed and (semi) self-directed types of uses seem to have worked well. However, learners in DDL studies are rarely depicted as having negotiated their learning goals with their teachers or with the researchers involved. This is somewhat worrying as adult learners may be represented and treated in DDL research as passive stakeholders that do not show agency (Leung & Scarino, 2016) in using corpus tools.

26.2.2 Resources

Understanding the tools, artefacts, and the semiotic resources used in DDL is essential to account for learners' uses of corpora. Boulton and Cobb (2017) conclude that the most widely researched skill in DDL is writing (20 out of 24 studies in pre- and post-test designs without counting the seven studies devoted to translation and categorised as a skill), whereas the language aspects favoured the most by researchers are lexicogrammar, vocabulary, grammar, and discourse. Pérez-Paredes (2019) shows that in the 2011–2015 period, research examined the use of a loosely defined set of learners' abilities instrumental in completing DDL activities. These abilities are to consult an online learner dictionary quickly and efficiently; to make generalisations about usage; to edit grammatical errors from (learners') writing; and to use L2 collocations. However, the author notes that cognitive abilities are not usually the main focus of research. In other words, more weight is given to learning outcomes and purposes behind the use of corpora than to the learners' actual uses. In fact, many of the uses of corpora are conceptualised in terms of the affordances that the corpus tools and the corpora themselves present. Boulton (2017b) suggests that the specialised literature is dominated by an artefact-centric view of DDL in language education. Many of the uses researched are interactions with either representative corpora of English or bespoke applications. Thus, while 35% of the research uses representative corpora like the BNC or COCA, 44% of the research makes use of either ad hoc software or ad hoc corpora (Pérez-Paredes, 2019). This is a particular strength of DDL research as researchers show both initiative and agency in developing software and data-analysis solutions that adapt to different learning scenarios.

The semiotic resources that are exploited in DDL research favour a conception of language as "a bounded system of formal rules" (Douglas Fir Group, 2016, p. 21). Language learning, as conceptualised in the area of learner corpus research and DDL, does not seem to favour an idea of learning as encompassing social and emotional facets as language learning is seen as a solely cognitive phenomenon. While this may be seen as a criticism to DDL, the fact is that the understanding of language as a complex lexico-grammatical semiotic resource (Hoey, 2004a, 2004b; Sinclair, 2003; Sinclair & Mauranen, 2006) has favoured the exploitation of language properties that were not present in other language learning approaches. These resources include discrete features such as linking adverbials or tenses, metadiscourse, and composite features such as lexical sophistication (Pérez-Paredes & Mark, 2021). All three categories fall within Hoey's (2004b) textual extension of colligation and, arguably, it is the main contribution of DDL to the study of language-related semiotic resources in instructed second language acquisition (SLA). O'Keeffe (2020) has suggested that closer collaboration with SLA research will benefit DDL by expanding the link between the above-mentioned semiotic resources with other variables that can address outstanding learning concerns such as the degree of mediation (teacher- or peer-led) relative to learning or the types of data curated for learners. The investigation of learner uses of corpora provides a window into some of the most substantial areas that impact and condition language learning in DDL. Section 26.3 below looks at how logs and computer tracking can help us understand how to explore learners' uses of corpora.

26.3 Examining learners' interaction with DDL

Very few DDL researchers have tried to analyse what exactly students do when they use corpora, either in hands-on or in using paper-based activities. One of the reasons that may explain the lack of research in this area is the emphasis of DDL research on producing evidence of its effectiveness (Pérez-Paredes *et al.*, 2011). This emphasis characterised the early days of computer-assisted language learning (CALL) research. Johansson (2009) claimed that "there is little evidence to suggest that direct corpus consultation is coming to be seen as a complement or alternative to consultation of a dictionary, course book, or grammar by the majority of learners" (p. 41), an opinion that has been recently echoed in Chambers (2019). She has confirmed a lack of engagement with the vast majority of learners and language teachers outside Higher Education (HE). Despite this criticism, the meta-analyses carried out by Boulton and Cobb (2017) and Lee *et al.* (2018) have cast robust results on the benefits of DDL. Boulton and Cobb have found average effect sizes of 1.50 for pre/post-test designs and 0.95 for control/experimental designs. As the effect size measures the magnitude of a treatment effect, these results show that, irrespective of the research design, DDL has a strong positive impact on learning outcomes. Lee *et al.* (2018) have reported a medium-sized effect of corpus use on vocabulary learning. Overall, these are medium or large effect sizes that support the use of DDL for language learning. What leaners do when engaged with DDL activities merits further attention, though. This will be explored in the following section.

26.3.1 DDL uses

Despite the wide scope of learning outcomes and targets such as English for general, academic, and specific purposes (Boulton & Cobb, 2017), DDL research has actually focused on a limited set of learning contexts and learning targets. The research published in top-quality journals has favoured the study of Higher Education (HE) learners, 94% of the studies are situated in tertiary education (Pérez-Paredes, 2019), and most of them foster writing skills (Boulton & Cobb, 2017). These authors argue that "the DDL approach seems to be most effective when using a concordancer hands-on [...] [and] tailor-made local corpora may be somewhat more effective than large public corpora" (p. 385). Interestingly, these findings endorse the approach in Reppen (2010) where hands-on activities are recommended as they do not only favour a stronger learner engagement but also are said to be "more enjoyable" (p. 53). We could see Reppen's recommendations as the basis for the learners' uses that corpus-based materials promote. She advises language teachers to (1) follow a clear step-by-step direction, (2) walk students through the process, and (3) recommend learners to open just one website (that is the concordance) to avoid distractions. Her rationale behind the use of concordance lines is that learners, teachers, and researchers can explore co-occurrence patterns. She offers a range of DDL sample activities:

- vocabulary for pre-reading. Examination of word lists
- examination of registers, particularly frequency lists in academic and conversation texts
- examination of discourse level. Analysis of situational and textual features across a variety of texts
- examination of lexical bundles in micro-textual functions such as topic shift and asking for clarification in conversations

As we can see, examination and analysis play a major role in DDL activity design. These two cognitive processes lie at the heart of what researchers and teachers may expect from the learners' engagement with corpora. However, how exactly learners examine and analyse corpus data is an entirely different question. The following paragraphs show ways as to how to study hands-on uses of corpora.

26.3.2 Tracking learners' uses

Knowing what learners do and how they interact with corpus resources is challenging. Corpus-query tracking seeks to understand the process embraced by language learners when interacting with hands-on activities and resources. Some of the research that has examined learner-corpus interaction has made use of manual logs where the students note down search words and their findings. Ma (1994) asked 18 students to complete a concordance diary with their search strings, the information obtained, and the conclusions drawn. The author asked the learners to "fill out the form in the greatest possible detail" (p. 7) emphasising that they should record every search. Chambers and O'Sullivan (2004) examined the use of corpora of eight university learners of French. The authors looked at the changes implemented in the writing of these learners as a result of corpus consultation. After receiving unfocused feedback, the learners were trained to query corpora, compile their own corpus, and use WordSmith Tools (Scott, 2008). They were given two lab hours to examine this feedback and check out corpus resources: "[the students] had to study the words and phrases underlined in their text, search the corpus for ways to help them improve these phrases, look at the results of the concordance and decide if they wanted to change their text" (p. 163).

Manual logs rely heavily on the subjects' understanding of the task and the adherence to the instructions provided. Chambers and O'Sullivan (2004) note that the experience was successful as the language requiring improvement had been indicated on the text which was returned to the learners. However, the researchers did not analyse the learners' strategies and cognition when querying the corpus as their research question rested within the scopes of error correction and the viability of corpus consultation as a supporting writing aid. Recently, Gatto (2019) has examined the use of web searchers as a linguistic resource. She uses manual logs to analyse their students' searches and concludes that a more refined understanding of how web searches can inform intuition is needed.

Manual logs have met some relevant criticism. In the field of education, Cohen *et al.* (2018) have noted that observations, in general, tend to be selective and may be inaccurate. They argue that systematic, repeated observations, together with triangulation of methods, can help researchers improve the validity of this data collection procedure. In computer science, the examination of log quality issues is common as the success of the analysis depends on the quality of the collected data (Suriadi *et al.*, 2017). Computer activity tracking responds to criticism by Hafner and Candlin (2007) that few studies offer direct evidence of learners' use of corpus tools due to a reliance on indirect observation methodologies, including self-report and the analysis of tasks related to the corpus consultation. In the context of error correction in writing, Gaskell and Cobb (2004) used IP numbers of submitting machines to verify that searches were taking place. These IP numbers are assigned to the devices (laptops, tablets, etc.) connected to a network that uses the Internet. The authors concluded that the procedure was not totally satisfactory and that a "a finer grained tracking system for a follow-up that would match learners and behaviours more precisely" (Gaskell & Cobb, 2004, p. 311) was necessary. Hafner and Candlin (2007) made use of logs of the student searches, structured interviews with nine students, samples of legal writing of a selection of students, as well as the learning journals of four students. The authors put together a small corpus of legal cases and integrated corpus use and consultation as one of the tools at the disposal of the students. During the first year, only 21% of the students checked out the corpus, while during the second year of the experience 35% turned to the corpus as a way to improve their writing. The analysis of the search logs revealed that most students seemed confused as the object of the search and thus searched for full documents rather than words or patterns. The authors found that some of the students preferred to test their hypotheses using Google even when they were aware of the existence of a specialised corpus. The following is of particular relevance:

> [...] students need considerable additional help in order to make sense of the lin-
> guistic data presented in concordance lines or collocation lists. This help should be
> in the form of methodological help: for example, what questions is it appropriate to
> ask of the corpus? [...] Such help could also be applied to exploit the tendency of
> students to browse the web for language patterns, often in an unfocused manner.
> For students to use existing web search engines to understand the use of language
> patterns effectively, they need to be able to understand and interpret output from
> web search engines in terms of its particular discursive functions in context. (Hafner
> & Candlin, 2007, p. 315).

These findings were corroborated in the studies carried out by Pérez-Paredes *et al.* (2011) and Pérez-Paredes *et al.* (2012). These two studies used computer tracking to examine the search patterns and behaviour of HE students of general English in the context of focus-on-form instruction. The approach in both studies seeks to overcome some of the short-coming in other data gathering methods (Fischer, 2007), such as manual logs, interviews, or diaries. Pérez-Paredes *et al.* (2011) argue that direct observation methods can offer a faithful, unmediated account of how learners interact with corpus interfaces and DDL activities. Computer tracking increases the validity of experiments as the researchers can know for sure whether some of the research conditions such as consultation or search criteria were satis-fied by the informants. For example, Pérez-Paredes *et al.* (2011) found that the majority of their participants in their experimental group (EG) actually accessed the materials that were supposed to read in order to complete the activities. One of the 15 learners, however, did not. Two others did not perform BNC searches despite completing the activities and completing a survey offering an evaluation of their corpus experience. They were removed from the dataset as a consequence. Computer tracking can reveal, among others, the following:

* the resources used (corpora queried, online dictionaries, and other www resources)
* time spent querying
* exact queries
* search results
* answers and attempts provided.

Computer-generated logs are used in process-oriented data mining to construct models that aim to provide insights into a variety of processes. Pérez-Paredes *et al.* (2011) used a between-groups research design to examine the uses of DDL under guidance and non-guidance conditions. The learners had to complete tasks dealing with it-cleft (*It was Jane that drove all night*) and subject-verb inversion (*No sooner had dad closed the door*) structures. The researchers used Sinclair's (2003) corpus consultation stages, in particular the initiate-interpret-consolidate-report steps, which were reformulated into observe – search the corpus – rewrite stages. Figure 26.1 sums up the approach advocated by the authors.

The researchers set up a web debugging proxy for internet browsers in the computer lab where the experiment was carried out. The tool that was used in this research, Fiddler, is a web debugging tool which logs HTTP(S) traffic between the computers in the lab and the Internet, capturing traffic from applications. The learners in the guided condition used resources as intensively as those in the control group despite having less time as they had to go

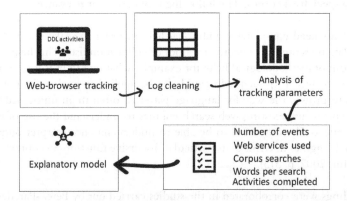

Figure 26.1 Tracking learners' uses of corpora, based on Pérez-Paredes *et al.* (2011)

through guided-consultation information provided by the researchers. All the learners used a variety of resources and not just the BNC. In the control group (CG), the students scored a mean of 9.09 for browser events (left-click, right-click, keydown, submit, etc.) while in the experimental group (EG) the mean was 12.5; that is, the EG visited either more sites or searched those sites more frequently than the CG. The students in both groups used online dictionaries or search engines such as Google. Many of these searches involved looking up grammar-related terms, such as emphasis, cleft, or even corpus. The students in the EG searched the BNC three times more often than their classmates in the CG (a mean of 5.4 BNC searches per learner and 1.42 per learner and activity, respectively). This difference was statistically significant. The low rate of BNC searches confirms some sort of resistance to make use of corpus resources when other alternatives such as Google are provided. The explanatory model that emerges from this experiment is one that suggests that online guided instruction favours more intensive search both in corpus resources but also in non-corpus resources such as Google and online dictionaries, used by 82% and 63% of the learners in the EG, respectively.

Pérez-Paredes *et al.*'s (2012) follow-up study examined search types and search efficiency. Using a similar research design and DDL activities as in their previous work (Figure 26.2), the authors tracked web-browser actions and captured all the web pages visited, the information typed in, the searchers performed as well as the information returned by the web services, including the Moodle activity reports. The authors operationalised learner behaviour into search actions. These are the queries performed in any resource, whether corpora (e.g. BNC) or not (e.g. Google). Researchers first identified the sequential search pattern followed by the learner in terms of the order and number of searches, the emerging patterns, and how they correlated with the learners' activity performance. Analysing the number and types of queries performed in each resource can contribute to understanding how DDL principles are translated into concrete actions that can inform DDL practice.

Three distinct patterns emerged from the analysis. Pattern A was endorsed by 41.7% of the students. Only one BNC search was enough to complete the activity. Pattern B was followed by 12.5% of the learners. In this pattern, the learners used Google or a similar resource after their initial corpus query. Pattern C was endorsed by 45.8% of the learners. In this pattern, learners checked either the BNC consultation guidelines or Google or a similar service after their initial search. A further, final corpus search was performed by the learners before completing the activity. Individuals that used patterns B and C outperformed those that followed

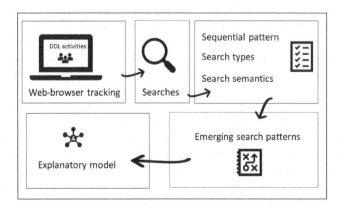

Figure 26.2 Search patterns in DDL, based on Pérez-Paredes *et al.* (2012)

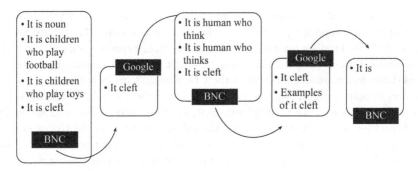

Figure 26.3 An instance of a pattern C mixed search, adapted from Pérez-Paredes *et al.* (2012)

pattern A. In fact, 67.2% of the learners that followed pattern C obtained the highest marks in the search the corpus activity, while only 25% of those that made use of pattern A managed to get such marks. Contrary to the more mature subjects in Ma (1994), learners rarely made use of wildcards or tags. Figure 26.3 sheds some light on the underlying cognitive processes followed by learners when approaching DDL activities. In this case, a student was asked to induce cleft-sentences patterns in English.

Computer tracking allowed the researchers to problematise the operationalisation of the search/induction construct, an infrequently discussed area of analysis. Figure 26.3 shows how a learner, despite the explicit instruction received, finds it difficult to choose the right term to query the corpus. This stage corresponds with the initiate stage. Sinclair (2003) defines it as the starting point to read and interpret concordance lines. He stresses the difficulties involved in deciding on the strongest pattern and acknowledges that the decision is a matter of judgment. The learner here is struggling to find the search terms that can help them complete the activity and combines a range of highly specific linguistic patterns with metalanguage. The search logs show that the learner finds it hard to grasp the kind of item that may trigger the search results that are somehow expected by those that designed the DDL activity. As pointed out in Ma (1994, p. 18), "it is [...] necessary that students should learn to develop enquiry-based, relevant and successful searches, or that this development should be speeded up in some way by the teacher".

Extensive tracking of searches such as those above, or the ones in Crosthwaite *et al.* (2019), can inform DDL researchers and language teachers about, for example, how nodes are used. The choice of search nodes that language pattern-C learners made in Pérez-Paredes *et al.* (2012) was not particularly sophisticated but proved to be enough to sort out the right context and provide a valid answer to the question proposed by the researchers. Flowerdew (2009) has suggested that different approaches to DDL, and, more generally, work with concordances, may prompt different ways to favour how the information in a group of concordance lines can be processed acted upon by learners. Flowerdew (2009) holds that truncated concordance lines promote a bottom-up processing of the information and suggests that a more discursive approach will help both top-down and bottom-up processes to cooperate. She suggests that Lee and Swales' (2006) study is a good example that combines both approaches. Tracking learners' events and interactions with DDL and concordance lines can inform the sort of pedagogical transfer that is appropriate across these two approaches (bottom-up vs top-down) and how they are shaped up across the many different micro learning classroom contexts (Ballance, 2017; Pérez-Paredes, 2010). Recent research such as Saeedakhtar *et al.* (2020) has proved that both hands-on and hands-off concordancing is effective to teach collocations as long as the nodes are provided to the learners, which opens up a further debate about the different forms of DDL most appropriate across different emic perspectives.

26.4 Current contributions to research

DDL research is transitioning from a stage where the effectiveness and the perceived usefulness of DDL for language learning are evidenced (Boulton & Cobb, 2017; Lee *et al.*, 2018), to one where there is an emphasis on an increased understanding of how the technological, social, and language affordances of the DDL microsystem interact to offer situated learning experiences to language learners (O'Keeffe, 2020; Pérez-Paredes *et al.*, 2019). So far, these interactions have not been fully explored. However, DDL is extraordinarily well positioned to offer researchers, teachers, and language learners opportunities to explore the contributions of digital and data-supported language learning.

The research reviewed in both Boulton and Cobb (2017), and Pérez-Paredes (2019) has paid little attention to the operationalisation of learner uses of corpora. Such operationalisation may require both a re-appraisal of the foci of DDL research and a research-informed discussion on the role of human-data interactions in language education. An excellent starting point to do this is Ballance (2017), who operationalised the notion of concordancing after observing that (a) looking for repetition is a cognitively complex task likely to involve quantities and qualities of data that may be inappropriate for learners that may be (b) exacerbated by the truncated KWIC formatting and the presence of (c) concordances of large heterogeneous corpora. We agree with Ballance (2017) in that learners' use of concordances "should draw more upon a pedagogical model of concordance use" (p. 279). Ballance found that very frequent users of concordancing seem to do well when examining KWIC contexts, while infrequent users persisted in finding obstacles along the way. Two of his suggestions for further research are that sentence formats are more widely used and that researchers facilitate the priming of relevant examples.

In this section, we discuss how the contributions of triangulation, particularly method triangulation, and the analysis of new sites of language learning engagement can contribute to a refined understanding of learners' uses of corpora.

26.4.1 Method triangulation

Research that makes use of triangulation methods favours not only the generation of more reliable evidence but also the exploration of the interconnectedness of some of the features that characterise the DDL microsystem discussed above, including the roles of teachers, learners, language learning, and how semiotic resources interact with all of them. The reason is that the triangulation of methods encourages the examination of a variety of theories, paradigms, axiologies, and research designs (Cohen *et al.*, 2018). This can potentially help us readdress how learners' uses of corpora can contribute to the expansion of the scope of DDL across a wider representation of language learners and teachers alike.

Method triangulation has already been useful in widening the scope of DDL research. An overreliance on indirect observation based on questionnaires and interviews (Bernardini, 2002; Chambers, 2005; Lee & Swales, 2006; Ma, 1994) in the past has reflected not so much what learners "do" but their attitudes towards the corpora and the DDL approach, their evaluation of the activity, and their self-perceived difficulties. Charles (2012) has highlighted the fact that the overlapping roles of researchers and teachers may impact the students' drive to be polite to their teachers and, accordingly, show more positive attitudes to what can be understood as coursework that will be evaluated by their teachers. On a similar note, Chapelle and Mizuno (1989), and Fischer (2007) have pointed out the risks of assuming that what students report they are doing or what we believe they are doing uncovers their actual behaviour. However, the assumption can be extended to researchers' interpretation of one single dataset or one single method. The following case studies show how the triangulation of methods can be instrumental in conceptualising corpus use. They show ecological perspectives that discuss the roles of teachers and learners, the affordances of concordances across hands-on and paper-based uses, the cognitive aspects behind corpus searches as well as the role of vocabulary learning, errors, and writing in contemporary university settings.

Yoon and Yo (2014) looked at learning strategies in corpus-based writing revision in four Korean EFL students with the interest of "corpus use on error correction, error correction patterns, and learning strategies" (p. 96). Among other data collection methods, the authors used think-aloud protocols and learning journals. They concluded that learners made use of four strategies when correcting errors: affective strategies (i.e. lowering anxiety), meta-cognitive strategies (i.e. self-evaluation), social strategies (i.e. asking for clarification), and cognitive strategies (i.e. using materials, association, grouping, translation). Particularly interesting in this research design is the use of think-aloud protocols as a way to access learners' cognitions.

Lee *et al.* (2020) is an excellent example of how DDL research can be further explored by using a combination of methods. The authors used robust measures of constructs such as working memory and think-aloud protocols as well as vocabulary and reading tests. Using paper-based concordances, the learners were invited to use lexical inferencing strategies when working out meanings. It was found that 12 strategies were used by the learners. These strategies were further grouped into four categories: form-focused strategies, meaning-focused strategies, evaluating strategies, and, the most frequently used, DDL-focused strategies. Three DDL strategies, exploring, double-checking, synthesising, were found to contribute largely to L2 vocabulary acquisition, which confirms previous studies (Cho, 2016; O'Sullivan, 2007; Pérez-Paredes *et al.*, 2012) that stated that cognitive factors involved in concordance reading are key in explaining the successful implementation of DDL activities.

Crosthwaite (2017) examined the errors that students corrected using corpora so, following a common research design in DDL studies, offered HE students DDL training and collected their writing. What is of interest in this research is that Crosthwaite triangulates the results of the students' error correction, a learners' questionnaire, and the correction provided to the students with the researchers glosses over the actions performed by the students. Crosthwaite (2017) offers a much-needed reflection in our field on negative evidence: "while students use corpora to correct (mainly lexical) issues of collocation, word choice and word form, students do not typically use corpora to resolve errors of morphosyntax or deletion and only correct errors of omission with corpora 50% of the time" (p. 464).

Despite the important methodological contributions in these three studies, they look at HE learners exclusively. In the following section, alternative sites of engagement are explored.

26.4.2 Under-researched sites of engagement

This section showcases some studies that have engaged with learners' uses of corpora in two alternative sites: cooperative corpus consultation and mobile DDL. They explore possible uses of corpora in sites that examine interactions with semiotic resources in sites where technology plays a role, either because of the type of interactions promoted among users or because of the increased agency vested in self-directed uses of Mobile-Assisted Language Learning (MALL).

The first site of engagement is classrooms where collaboration and group work are fostered. Collaborative consultation has been suggested to facilitate corpus use (O'Sullivan, 2007). This approach fits well with the emphasis on group work across different stages and levels of compulsory education across the world. While some researchers have identified challenges in this type of interaction (Vannestål & Lindquist, 2007), Cho (2016) found that collaborative work facilitates DDL tasks that focus on so-called conceptual tasks that explore semantic differences among synonymous items. More recently, Kulsitthiboon and Pongpairoj (2018) used the term cooperative corpus consultation to explore DDL where the interaction of a group of learners is a prerequisite for completing an activity. The authors encouraged positive interdependence, individual accountability, promotive interaction, use of social skills, and group processing. Their results are encouraging and show a way into the integration of collaborative DDL in language learning. Studies like this one could pave the way for uses in primary and secondary education where group work and collaboration are part of the classroom ecology.

A second site for engagement is MALL. The use of DDL in mobile devices has scarcely been explored. Quan (2016) tested an app that provided academic concordance lines to learners. The emphasis of this research rested upon the perceived affordances of the app and, unfortunately, there was no room for the exploration of some of the defining features of MALL such as ubiquitousness and the opportunities for non-formal learning. The author found that the combined use of concordance lines and dictionaries seemed to work well for the learners in the study. However, learners reported that concordance lines were difficult to interpret and added little to the learning experience. Pérez-Paredes *et al.* (2019) probed into the design and learners' uses of a mobile app that provided an environment where learners could evaluate their own writing depending on their target competence level. Learners in focus groups said that the use of the app had increased their language awareness by (1) having easy access to collocation, synonym, and regular dictionaries and (2) by checking the classification of each word into Common European Framework of Reference for Languages (CEFR) frequency bands. The learners reported that they would have liked to have a personal dashboard and a more gamified experience. Given the massive use of apps of MALL for self-directed language learning (Zhang & Pérez-Paredes, 2019), this area is expected to gain traction in the forthcoming years.

26.5 Future directions of research

In this chapter, learners' uses of corpora have been situated in an ecological microsystem (Figure 26.4) that has tried to account for the scope of the research carried out in the field so far. Microsystems are defined by the roles and characteristics of the agents involved and by the type of tools and resources used to facilitate learning. We have identified two elements that have driven the research on the uses of corpora: researchers' aims and the cognitive nature of language learning (represented as rectangles in Figure 26.4). A substantial part of the research in DDL uses has been driven by the researchers' agenda to probe into the benefits of language corpora (Boulton & Cobb, 2017) for language education.

If we want to gain a more critical understanding of how learners' uses of corpora are embedded in emic sites of engagement, it is necessary that DDL research expands its current focus and examines learners' uses in ecological models where teachers, institutions, and learners play a more active role. The circles in Figure 26.4 represent areas that can be operated in order to promote a more diverse use (and research on the uses) of DDL. They include a more diverse type of learners in research designs (professionals, non-tertiary students, occasional language learners); a more diverse range of learning sites including mobile devices and technology-enriched language learning environments that do not entail steep curves of

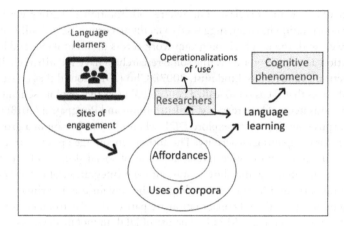

Figure 26.4   An ecological micro system for DDL

learning when manipulating data representation or visualisation (a.k.a. corpus searches), and a more diverse integration of tools that combine the affordances of corpora with the affordances of MALL and data processing and machine-human interaction. The arrows represent areas that future research will need to examine. The operationalisation of corpus use as a construct calls for the collaboration between research methods and data analysis approaches. The use of think-aloud protocols fits in well with the use of psycholinguistic experiments (Ellis, 2017) that make use of robust methods that are used in cognitive science, including eye-tracking, online experiments that involve interaction tracking, and magnetic resonance imaging (MRI) studies. A closer dialogue with cognitive scientists will benefit the field (Varela *et al.*, 2016).

Another arrow in Figure 26.4 calls for a re-appraisal of how language learning is conceptualised in DDL research. While irreplaceable contributions to our understanding of the theoretical implications behind DDL have been produced (Ballance, 2017; Chambers, 2005; Flowerdew, 2009; Hoey, 2004b), further research needs to explore how the microsystem represented in Figure 26.4 relates to the meso and macro systems where it is situated. This calls for an evaluation of corpus-mediated focus-on-form in language learning (O'Keeffe, 2020) across a variety of contexts and sites, an examination of the role of institutions in implementing data-driven learning, the so-called 21st-century skills (Pérez-Paredes *et al.*, 2019; Vyatkina, 2020) and, among many others, an analysis of the values and attitudes to language learning methodology for an entire new generation of learners (Crosthwaite *et al.*, 2019).

Further reading

Crosthwaite, P., Wong, L. C., & Cheung, J. (2019). Characterising postgraduate students' corpus query and usage patterns for disciplinary data-driven learning. *ReCALL*, *31*(3), 255–275. https://doi.org/10.1017/S0958344019000077. This is a mixed-methods study that examines the tracking of 327 learners' corpus use in a large postgraduate disciplinary thesis writing program. The authors gathered learner information concerning corpus usage history, query syntax, query function (frequency lists, concordance sorting, collocation, et.), and query filters (searches by faculty, discipline, or thesis section).

O'Keeffe, A. (2020). Data-driven learning – A call for a broader research gaze. *Language Teaching*, *54*(2), 259–272. https://doi.org/10.1017/S0261444820000245. Anne O´Keeffe argues that there is a need for greater critical engagement with the pedagogical underpinnings in the form of theories of learning and theories of language acquisition. She holds that it is essential that we devise methods to research how learners engage with corpus use.

Pérez-Paredes, P., & Sánchez Hernández, P. (2018). Uptake of corpus tools in the Spanish higher education context: A mixed-methods study. *Research in Corpus Linguistics*, *6*, 51–66. https://doi.org/10.32714/ricl.06.05. This research presents negative evidence about the usefulness of corpora. The paper looks at corpus consultation in the course of 'Introducing Research Articles (RA) Writing', a 12-hour module that offered university researchers from different disciplines the opportunity to gain insight into writing RAs. While most learners found corpus tools of great use when writing their research articles, the delayed questionnaire and subsequent delayed interviews (n = 5) revealed that the use of corpora had had limited or no impact on the writing practices of these researchers.

References

Ballance, O. J. (2017). Pedagogical models of concordance use: Correlations between concordance user preferences. *Computer Assisted Language Learning*, *30*(3–4), 259–283. https://doi.org/10.1080/09588221.2017.1307228

Bax, S. (2003). CALL—Past, present and future. *System*, *31*(1), 13–28. https://doi.org/10.1016/S0346-251X(02)00071-4

Bernardini, S. (2000). Systematising serendipity: Proposals for concordancing large corpora with language learners. In L. Bumard & T. McEnery (Eds.), *Rethinking language pedagogy from a corpus perspective* (pp. 225–234). Peter Lang.

Blin, F. (2016). Towards an 'ecological' CALL theory. In F. Farr & L. Murray (Eds.), *The Routledge handbook of language learning and technology* (pp. 39–54). Routledge.

Boulton, A. (2017a). Corpora in language teaching and learning. *Language Teaching*, *50*(4), 483–506. https://doi.org/10.1017/S0261444817000167

Boulton, A. (2017b). Data-driven learning and language pedagogy. In S. Thorne & S. May (Eds.), *Language, education and technology: Encyclopedia of language and education* (pp. 181–192). Springer.

Boulton, A., & Cobb, T. (2017). Corpus use in language learning: A meta-analysis. *Language Learning*, *67*(2), 348–393. https://doi.org/10.1111/lang.12224

Bronfenbrenner, U. (1979). *The ecology of human development*. Harvard University Press.

Chambers, A. (2005). Integrating corpus consultation in language studies. *Language Learning & Technology*, *9*(2), 111–125.

Chambers, A. (2019). Towards the corpus revolution? Bridging the research–practice gap. *Language Teaching*, *52*(4), 460–475. https://doi.org/10.1017/S0261444819000089

Chambers, A., & O'Sullivan, Í. (2004). Corpus consultation and advanced learners' writing skills in French. *ReCALL*, *16*(1), 158–172.

Chapelle, C., & Mizuno, S. (1989). Students' strategies with learner-controlled CALL. *CALICO Journal*, *7*, 25–47.

Charles, M. (2012). Proper vocabulary and juicy collocations: EAP students evaluate do-it-yourself corpus-building. *English for Specific Purposes*, *31*(2), 93–102. https://doi.org/10.1016/j.esp.2011.12.003

Charles, M. (2014). Getting the corpus habit: EAP students' long-term use of personal corpora. *English for Specific Purposes*, *35*, 30–40. https://doi.org/10.1016/j.esp.2013.11.004

Cho, H. (2016). Task dependency effects of collaboration in learners' corpus consultation: An exploratory case study. *ReCALL*, *28*(1), 44–61. https://doi.org/10.1017/S0958344015000130

Chun, C., Smith, B., & Kern, R. (2016). Technology in language use, language teaching, and language learning. *The Modern Language Journal*, *100*(1), 64–80.

Cohen, L., Manion, L., & Morrison, K. (2018). *Research methods in education*. Routledge.

Crosthwaite, P. (2017). Retesting the limits of data-driven learning: Feedback and error correction. *Computer Assisted Language Learning*, *30*(6), 447–473. https://doi.org/10.1080/09588221.2017.1312462

Crosthwaite, P. (Ed.). (2019). *Data-driven learning for the next generation: Corpora and DDL for pre-tertiary learners*. Routledge.

Crosthwaite, P., Wong, L. C., & Cheung, J. (2019). Characterising postgraduate students' corpus query and usage patterns for disciplinary data-driven learning. *ReCALL*, *31*(3), 255–275. https://doi.org/10.1017/S0958344019000077

Douglas Fir Group. (2016). A transdisciplinary framework for SLA in a multilingual world. *The Modern Language Journal*, *100*(1), 19–47. https://doi.org/10.1111/modl.12301

Ellis, N. C. (2017). Cognition, corpora, and computing: Triangulating research in usage-based language learning. *Language Learning, 67*(1), 40–65. https://doi.org/10.1111/lang.12215

Fischer, R. (2007). How do we know what students are actually doing? Monitoring students' behaviour in CALL. *Computer Assisted Language Learning, 20,* 409–442. https://doi.org/10.1080/09588220701746013

Flowerdew, L. (2009). Applying corpus linguistics to pedagogy: A critical evaluation. *International Journal of Corpus Linguistics, 14*(3), 393–417. https://doi.org/10.1075/ijcl.14.3.05flo

Gaskell, D., & Cobb, T. (2004). *Can learners use concordance feedback for writing errors? System, 32*(3), 301–319.

Gatto, M. (2019). Using web search from a corpus perspective with digital natives. In P. Crosthwaite (Ed.), *Data-driven learning for the next generation: Corpora and DDL for pre-tertiary learners* (pp. 106–129). Routledge.

Hafner, C. A., & Candlin, C. N. (2007). Corpus tools as an affordance to learning in professional legal education. *Journal of English for Academic Purposes, 6*(4), 303–318. https://doi.org/10.1016/j.jeap.2007.09.005

Hoey, M. (2004a). Textual colligation: A special kind of lexical priming. In K. Aijmer & B. Altenberg (Eds.), *Advances in corpus linguistics* (pp. 169–194). Rodopi.

Hoey, M. (2004b). The textual priming of lexis. In G. Aston, S. Bernardini, & D. Stewart (Eds.), *Corpora and language learners* (pp. 21–41). Benjamins.

Johansson, S. (2009). Some thoughts on corpora and second-language acquisition. In K. Aijmer (Ed.), *Corpora and language teaching* (pp. 33–44). Benjamins.

Johns, T. (1990). From printout to handout: Grammar and vocabulary teaching in the context of data-driven learning. *CALL Austria, 10,* 14–34.

Kulsitthiboon, S., & Pongpairoj, N. (2018). Cooperative corpus consultation for acquisition of adjective+ preposition collocations. *GEMA Online Journal of Language Studies, 18*(3), 57–72. http://dx.doi.org/10.17576/gema-2018-1803-04

Lee, D., & Swales, J. (2006). A corpus-based EAP course for NNS doctoral students: Moving from available specialized corpora to self-compiled corpora. *English for Specific Purposes, 25*(1), 56–75. https://doi.org/10.1016/j.esp.2005.02.010

Lee, H., Warschauer, M., & Lee, J. H. (2018). The effects of corpus use on second language vocabulary learning: A multilevel meta-analysis. *Applied Linguistics, 40*(5), 721–753. https://doi.org/10.1093/applin/amy012

Lee, H., Warschauer, M., & Lee, J. H. (2020). Toward the establishment of a data-driven learning model: Role of learner factors in corpus-based second language vocabulary learning. *The Modern Language Journal, 104*(2), 345–362. https://doi.org/10.1111/modl.12634

Leung, C., & Scarino, A. (2016). Reconceptualizing the nature of goals and outcomes in language/s education. *The Modern Language Journal, 100*(1), 81–95. https://doi.org/10.1111/modl.12300

Ma, B. K. (1994). Learning strategies in ESP classroom concordancing: An initial investigation into data-driven learning. In L. Flowerdew & A. Tong (Eds.), *Entering Texts*, (pp. 197–214). Hong Kong University of Science and Technology Language Centre.

McEnery, T., & Wilson, A. (1993). The role of corpora in computer-assisted language learning. *Computer Assisted Language Learning, 6*(3), 233.

Mukherjee, J. (2004). Bridging the gap between applied corpus linguistics and the reality of English language teaching in Germany. In U. Connor & T. Upton (Eds.), *Applied corpus linguistics: A multidimensional perspective* (pp. 239–250). Rodopi.

Noguera-Díaz, Y., & Pérez-Paredes, P. (2020). Teaching acronyms to the military: A paper-based DDL approach. *Research in Corpus Linguistics, 8*(2), 1–27. https://doi.org/10.32714/ricl.08.02.01

O'Keeffe, A. (2020). Data-driven learning – A call for a broader research gaze. *Language Teaching, 54*(2), 259–272. https://doi.org/10.1017/S0261444820000245

O'Sullivan, Í. (2007). Enhancing a process-oriented approach to literacy and language learning: The role of corpus consultation literacy. *ReCALL, 19*(3), 269–286. https://doi.org/10.1017/S095834400700033X

Pérez-Paredes, P. (2010). Corpus linguistics and language education in perspective: Appropriation and the possibilities scenario. In T. Harris & M. Jaén (Eds.), *Corpus linguistics in language teaching* (pp. 53–73). Peter Lang.

Pérez-Paredes, P. (2019). A systematic review of the uses and spread of corpora and data-driven learning in CALL research during 2011–2015. *Computer Assisted Language Learning, 35,* 36–61 https://doi.org/10.1080/09588221.2019.1667832

Pérez-Paredes, P., & Mark, G. (2021). What can corpora tell us about language learning? In A. O'Keeffe & M. McCarthy (Eds.), *The Routledge handbook of corpus linguistics* (2nd ed.). Routledge.

Pérez-Paredes, P., Ordoñana Guillamón, C., & Aguado Jiménez, P. (2018). Language teachers' perceptions on the use of OER language processing technologies in MALL. *Computer Assisted Language Learning, 31*(5–6), 522–545. https://doi.org/10.1080/09588221.2017.1418754

Pérez-Paredes, P., Ordoñana Guillamón, Van de Vyver, J., Meurice, A., Aguado-Jiménez, P., Conole, G., & Sánchez Hernández, P. (2019). Mobile data-driven language learning: Affordances and learners' perception. *System, 84*,145–159. https://doi.org/10.1016/j.system.2019.06.009

Pérez-Paredes, P., Sánchez-Tornel, M., Alcaraz Calero, J. M., & Aguado Jiménez, P. (2011). Tracking learners' actual uses of corpora: Guided vs non-guided corpus consultation. *Computer Assisted Language Learning, 24*(3), 233–253. https://doi.org/10.1080/09588221.2010.539978

Pérez-Paredes, P., Sánchez-Tornel, M., & Alcaraz Calero, J. M. (2012). Learners search patterns during corpus-based focus-on-form activities: A study on hands-on concordancing. *International Journal of Corpus Linguistics, 17*(4), 482–515. https://doi.org/10.1075/ijcl.17.4.02par

Quan, Z. (2016). Introducing "mobile DDL (data-driven learning)" for vocabulary learning: An experiment for academic English. *Journal of Computers in Education, 3*(3), 273–87.

Reppen, R. (2010). *Using corpora in the language classroom*. Cambridge University Press.

Saeedakhtar, A., Bagerin, M., & Abdi, R. (2020). The effect of hands-on and hands-off data-driven learning on low-intermediate learners' verb-preposition collocations. *System, 91*, 102268. https://doi.org/0.1016/j.system.2020.102268

Scott, M. (2008). Developing WordSmith. *International Journal of English Studies, 8*(1), 95–106.

Sinclair, J. (2003). *Reading concordances: An introduction*. Longman.

Sinclair, J., & Mauranen, A. (2006). *Linear unit grammar: Integrating speech and writing*. Benjamins.

Suriadi, S., Andrews, R., Ter Hofstede, A. H. M., & Wynn, M. T. (2017). Event log imperfection patterns for process mining: Towards a systematic approach to cleaning event logs. *Information Systems 64*, 132–150. https://doi.org/10.1016/j.is.2016.07.011

Tono, Y., Satake, Y., & Miura, A. (2014). The effects of using corpora on revision tasks in L2 writing with coded error feedback. *ReCALL, 26*(2), 147–162. https://doi.org/10.1017/S095834401400007X

Vannestål, M., & Lindquist, H. (2007). Learning English grammar with a corpus: Experimenting with concordancing in a university grammar course. *ReCALL, 19*(3), 329–350. https://doi.org/10.1017/S0958344007000638

Varela, F. J., Thompson, E., & Rosch, E. (2016). *The embodied mind: Cognitive science and human experience*. MIT Press.

Vyatkina, N. (2020). Corpora as open educational resources for language teaching. *Foreign Language Annals, 53*(2), 359–370. https://doi.org/10.1111/flan.12464

Yoon, H., & Jo, J. (2014). Direct and indirect access to corpora: An exploratory case study comparing students' error correction and learning strategy use in L2 writing. *Language Learning & Technology, 18*(1), 96–117.

Zhang, D., & Pérez-Paredes, P. (2019). Chinese postgraduate EFL learners' self-directed use of mobile English learning resources. *Computer Assisted Language Learning, 34*, 1128–1153. https://doi.org/10.1080/09588221.2019.1662455

27

CORPORA AND AUTONOMOUS LANGUAGE LEARNING

Maggie Charles

27.1 Introduction

As early as 2001, Aston (2001) made the following claim: "Perhaps the greatest attraction of corpora for language pedagogy is their potential for autonomous learning" (p. 41). This chapter examines the extent to which this potential has been realised. It takes as its starting point the ground-breaking work of Holec, who defined autonomy in language learning as "the ability to take charge of one's own learning" (1979, p. 3). Putting the concept of autonomous learning into practice brings with it a shift in emphasis away from teaching and onto learning. Thus the learner's involvement in and responsibility for decisions affecting their own learning are central elements of the approach. However, Holec stresses that the ability to take charge of one's own learning is not innate, but acquired; as a result, learners may exercise different degrees of autonomy under different pedagogical circumstances, and their ability to assume responsibility for their own learning can be fostered and developed over time.

Holec (1979) sets out two important conditions which are essential for autonomous learning to take place and which have far-reaching consequences not only for learners, but also for teachers and institutions. First, learners must know how to make decisions. However, in order to acquire such knowledge, learners need experience of decision-making, which can only be achieved through a concomitant relaxation of teacher control. Thus, it becomes the task of the teacher to offer learners opportunities for taking charge of aspects of their own learning and to provide guidance and support as learners learn how to do so.

Holec's (1979) second condition is that learners must have the possibility of exercising autonomy. This implies that the institutional circumstances of the learning also have to be conducive to this major shift in approach. Thus, for example, if syllabuses, curricula, and materials are rigidly prescribed, there is little or no scope for the exercise of autonomy by either teachers or learners. As Yi (2017) points out, the development of autonomous learning for students necessitates a measure of teacher autonomy, which, in turn, requires institutional managers to relinquish some of their control. Thus the success of an autonomous learning approach depends on establishing shared understandings and achieving a delicate balance of autonomy and control among these three interdependent groups of actors.

The discussion in this chapter addresses three aspects of the topic: corpora and autonomous learning in relation to (1) learners, (2) teachers, and (3) resources. Each section highlights

DOI: 10.4324/9781003002901-32

some of the core issues that currently concern members of the field, while the final section indicates areas that are under-represented in the literature and provides suggestions for future research. It should be noted, however, that studies of corpus use do not tend to address the development of autonomy specifically. Rather, their focus is on the development of language proficiency; autonomy, if mentioned at all, is positioned as a positive side-effect. This leads to a somewhat restricted conception of the notion of autonomy, which is reflected in much of the literature discussed below.

27.2 Corpora, autonomy, and learners

This section focuses on the role of corpus use by learners and the extent of autonomy it affords. Most of the research in this area is concerned with the development of writing skills, including e.g. lexico-grammatical knowledge, vocabulary-building, and error correction. Accordingly, we address research on writing instruction first; we then briefly consider the opportunities for autonomy presented by corpus work in other areas.

A concern with autonomous learning can be traced back to early reports on students' use of corpora. It is central to Johns' (1991) approach of 'data-driven learning' (DDL), in which learners are confronted directly with the corpus data they need for learning the language. Johns regards the language learner as a linguistic researcher and argues that DDL stimulates inductive learning strategies. His students suggested issues to investigate, conducted investigations, and formulated their own conclusions. Thus, the learners exercised considerable autonomy throughout the learning process, while the teacher's role was to facilitate and support their efforts. This approach is aptly characterised by the "Illustration-Interaction-Induction" procedure advocated by Carter and McCarthy (1995, p. 155). At the Illustration stage, learners examine corpus data for the feature studied; in Interaction, students discuss their findings; finally, in Induction the group puts forward its own rule to explain the point they have examined.

As this procedure indicates, corpus consultation involves a wide range of cognitive and meta-cognitive processes such as noticing, analysing, interpreting, hypothesising and verifying (O'Sullivan, 2007). Case studies of individual corpus users show evidence of these processes in practice and thus reveal how corpus consultation fosters an active role in learning (Park, 2012; Yoon, 2016b). These findings also support the view that corpus use can result in increased learner autonomy.

However, as noted earlier, autonomous learning has to be developed, and classwork can have a considerable role in the process. Reinders (2010, p. 46) provides a useful eight-stage framework for the application of autonomous learning in the classroom and recommends the involvement of the learner at each stage: (1) Identifying needs; (2) Setting goals; (3) Planning learning; (4) Selecting resources; (5) Selecting learning strategies; (6) Practice; (7) Monitoring progress; and (8) Assessment and revision. Central to this sequence of stages is stage 6 (Practice), in which language use occurs, while stages 1–5 prepare for practice and stages 7 and 8 evaluate outcomes. Accounts of corpus-based classwork often reveal a shared responsibility between teacher and learner in which teachers tend to control decisions at the macro-level which impact the whole class, while individual learners may exercise autonomy at the micro-level, affecting their own learning. Thus, learner autonomy in corpus use can be seen as existing on a cline (Mukherjee, 2006), with its endpoints designated as 'hard' and 'soft' DDL (Gabrielatos, 2005).

The notion of a hard/soft cline raises two issues that are closely related to learner autonomy: the implementation of inductive and/or deductive procedures and the amount and type of teacher input. Simply put, inductive approaches ask students to derive generalisations from corpus data, while deductive approaches present rules for which learners seek supporting corpus evidence. Thus, inductive approaches tend to have less teacher input and to be closer to the more autonomous or "hard" end of the cline, while deductive approaches are likely to have greater teacher input and to be situated towards the less autonomous "soft" end of the cline. However, this distinction is by no means clear-cut (Flowerdew, 2009) and DDL work may combine the two, or progress from guided work to assignments which allow students more autonomy (Cresswell, 2007).

The extent of autonomy appropriate for a specific learner group depends on a number of contextual factors, including instructional aims, institutional arrangements, students' English level, maturity, and educational background. Thus, it has been argued that considerable teacher mediation or scaffolding is necessary for corpus use to be successful for lower levels and/or less mature learners (Karras, 2016; Moon & Oh, 2018), while greater autonomy is likely to be more appropriate for advanced-level adults. For example, Bernardini's (2000) advanced language students successfully carried out self-directed corpus browsing with minimal teacher input. Nonetheless, she later (2002) argued that self-directed learning should be practised within a structured environment, thereby assigning teachers an important role in developing learners' autonomy.

Since the amount and type of teacher mediation affects the exercise of learner autonomy, it is important to examine the ways in which this scaffolding occurs. Johansson (2009) suggested a "guided inductive approach" (p. 42), which combines inductive and deductive elements and is adapted to the pedagogical context. Testing the efficacy of this method, Smart (2014) reported that guided induction led to greater gains in grammar learning. However, Lee and Lin (2019) found inductive and deductive approaches to be equally effective for learning vocabulary and concluded that less time-consuming deductive methods were preferable. Pedagogic mediation was also advocated by Flowerdew (2009), who added an optional Intervention stage to the Illustration-Interaction-Induction procedure, thereby enabling teachers to offer guidance to students during the learning process. Scaffolding can also be provided by presenting the corpus data on paper. This method not only eliminates technical problems, but also allows teachers to select relevant data and/or modify them for ease of use (Boulton, 2012). Comparing hands-on or direct corpus consultation with paper-based, indirect DDL, Yoon and Jo (2014) found that, while indirect work was more effective for error correction, students preferred direct autonomous corpus use. It seems likely, then, that although greater teacher input implies less autonomy for the learner, in certain pedagogical circumstances, for example with beginners, a blended approach may be more suitable (Chujo & Oghigian, 2012). While the main purpose of the teacher input in these studies may well be to facilitate corpus consultation, such mediation also provides ample opportunities for developing students' autonomy.

Pérez-Paredes *et al.* (2011) aimed to determine empirically whether the provision of guidance on corpus use made a difference to learners' corpus consultation. Search-log tracking software was employed, which showed that guidance was associated with the use of more corpus resources and a greater number of searches. This finding indicates that student-corpus interaction can be facilitated and enhanced through appropriate scaffolding, a result consistent with Yoon and Hirvela's (2004) study, which showed that students who experienced teacher mediation became more enthusiastic corpus users than those who worked autonomously without teacher support. There is, then, a delicate balance to be struck between teacher control and learner autonomy, which requires in-depth knowledge of the learners and their pedagogical circumstances in order to determine the extent and type of support to offer.

Corpus work can provide opportunities for autonomous learning at several stages of Reinders' (2010) framework. During the preparation phase, learners can be asked to build their own corpora; they thereby assume responsibility for the data on which their learning is based. This commitment not only enables students to learn how to evaluate and select appropriate language resources, but also gives them increased motivation, a sense of ownership of the corpus, and the ability to adapt it as their needs change. In English for Academic Purposes (EAP), the approach was introduced by Lee and Swales (2006) and has been successfully used with graduates by Charles for learning discourse functions (2012, 2014) and for editing purposes (2018), and by Smith (2020) for vocabulary-building. Small specialist corpora have also been compiled by general English students for writing extended assignments on self-chosen topics (Gavioli, 2009; Smith, 2011).

At the practice stage, learner autonomy may also be fostered when students are offered a range of resources and asked to revise their writing by selecting and applying the most suitable tool. The choice may be between corpus and non-corpus resources (Bridle, 2019; Dolgova & Mueller, 2019) or between multiple corpora (Gilmore, 2008; Luo & Liao, 2015). Alternatively, corpus resources may be supplied, and students are required to identify errors and formulate suitable corpus queries to address them (Crosthwaite, 2017; Mull & Conrad, 2013). Such tasks offer many opportunities for autonomous decision-making.

Learner autonomy can also be designed into courses through the careful scaffolding and sequencing of corpus activities. Examples include three programmes for graduates: Chen and Flowerdew's (2018b) workshops on writing for research publication; Crosthwaite's (2018) introductory online corpus course and Crosthwaite *et al.*'s (2019) thesis-writing programme. These courses focus specifically on developing autonomy since they aim to provide know-how and resources for learners to consult throughout their academic careers. The approach can also be successful at undergraduate level, as indicated by Crosthwaite and Cheung's (2019) course on the language of dentistry.

Turning to the evaluation stages, students' assessments of DDL are generally positive (Chen & Flowerdew, 2018a) and they express appreciation of the autonomy it affords (Charles, 2017; Soruç & Tekin, 2017). Ongoing autonomous use is reported in Charles (2014), which found that 71% of students consulted their corpora one year after their corpus course, with 38% doing so at least once a week. However, it is not clear how much students' assessments contribute to the ongoing revision and development of courses. Further, although many studies claim that autonomy has been fostered by DDL, few attempt to quantify its extent. One attempt found increased self-efficacy in students who experienced classes with 60% DDL work (Lin, 2016). Using a more rigorous quantitative analysis, Mizumoto *et al.* (2015) developed and validated a psychometric scale for the measurement of students' perceived benefits and preferences of DDL. After testing on Japanese lower-level learners, the authors claim that their scale offers a new and more reliable way to measure student attitudes, including the attitude to autonomy.

Although the majority of accounts of autonomous corpus use target writing improvement, Allan (2009) reported using DDL and a corpus of graded readers with lower level students and suggested that such a resource could be used autonomously. Working with a similar corpus and students, Hadley and Charles (2017) aimed to enhance extensive reading, but reported little success in either independent or class work. By contrast, Gordani (2013) successfully integrated DDL into a vocabulary-building course for reading comprehension and the students expressed their appreciation of the autonomy afforded by corpus work. In Curado Fuente's (2007) study using a corpus of tourism advertisements, students worked individually on scaffolded tasks to develop their reading skills. DDL learners recorded higher reading comprehension scores than those traditionally taught. In a later course, using keywords to understand news reports, the majority of students stated that they would use the approach autonomously (Curado Fuentes, 2015).

There are also some accounts illustrating the use of spoken/multimedia corpora for oral production which describe initiatives to develop autonomy. Braun (2007) specifically designed her multimedia corpus of interviews for autonomous use by teachers and learners; similarly, Ackerley and Coccetta (2007) suggest that their multimedia corpus on general topics could be used independently by advanced students. In EAP, learners performed autonomous corpus searches after instruction on spoken pragmatic routines (Bardovi-Harlig *et al.*, 2015; Bardovi-Harlig *et al.*, 2017), while Aston (2015) provided activities for autonomous users to learn spoken phraseology. Geluso and Yamaguchi's (2014) DDL course also focused on spoken formulaic language; it allowed students considerable autonomy in selecting topics and content resources, identifying relevant formulaic language and giving student-led sessions to teach it. Despite the valuable contribution of these studies on reading and oral skills, it is clear that the potential of autonomous DDL in these areas is under-developed.

This section has shown that the use of corpora provides opportunities for students' autonomy through the degree of control they can exercise over the selection of resources, the choice of search items and techniques, and the application of corpus findings to their own work. However, the achievement of learner autonomy requires learners and teachers to work together to develop the necessary competencies and strategies. In practice, then, some form of semi-autonomous corpus-based learning is likely to be most widely and successfully implemented.

27.3 Corpora, autonomy, and teachers

This section discusses three ways in which teachers, corpora, and autonomy are closely interconnected. First, it addresses the impact of DDL and learner autonomy on teachers' roles; next it considers how corpus use can enhance autonomy for teachers; finally, it focuses on the function of teacher education in developing autonomy for both teachers and learners.

It has been pointed out that the use of DDL, with its aim of learner autonomy, entails a corresponding change in the role of the teacher towards becoming a "director and co-ordinator" (Johns, 1991, p. 3). As Benson and Voller (2013) point out, "Changing roles in autonomous learning are closely bound up with changes in the distribution of power within the learning process" (p. 9). In this case, teachers hand over some of their power to students, thereby relinquishing the role of authority, and taking on that of facilitator. This change involves a change in identity and may therefore be difficult, especially for teachers who are used to operating within a more traditional pedagogy (Lin, 2019). However, a teacher may exercise both linguistic and professional authority. Thus, although some linguistic authority may be given up in favour of corpus findings, the exercise of professional authority is likely to be changed in nature, but not in extent.

As facilitators, teachers perform a series of tasks which are characteristic of DDL classes and which are crucial to their success. In terms of planning, they have to determine which teaching points are amenable to DDL, select or build suitable corpora, retrieve, study and perhaps modify the data to create suitable materials. Drawing on their knowledge of the students and the pedagogical context, the teacher has to decide on the extent of mediation necessary, and judge whether the corpus material is best presented on paper or through hands-on access.

While the learners study the corpus data, the teacher's task is to monitor their work, motivating students to perform unfamiliar and demanding DDL tasks and providing guidance, if necessary. Finally, the teacher has to draw together the threads of students' discussions so that the group can come to a set of guidelines that represent the results of their learning. These tasks require the careful exercise of professional authority and expertise and involve considerable autonomous decision-making by the teacher. For further discussion of the challenges involved, see Chambers *et al.* (2011) and Frankenberg-Garcia (2012b).

Teachers' perceptions of their professional roles and responsibilities in relation to autonomous learning were investigated as part of a large-scale study in Hong Kong (Chan, 2003). Chan found that teachers considered two of the most important aspects of their task of developing autonomy to be methodological decision-making and student motivation. Although Chan does not deal with the use of corpora, it is clear that the tasks of the DDL teacher as described above correspond well with the teachers' perspectives she uncovered: they demand a high level of competence both in methodological decision-making and student motivation. They also require the teacher to relax sufficient control to allow students room for experimentation, debate, and differing opinions. The process of DDL can be messy and unpredictable and for many teachers, learning to adapt to this level of uncertainty is difficult. Lin (2019) suggests that "the course of becoming a DDL teacher is a complex, radical and continuous series of transformations" (p. 70). Teachers' success in accomplishing such role modifications has important implications for autonomous learning.

Although the majority of research has emphasised the benefits of DDL for student autonomy, the ability to use corpus data is equally empowering for teachers, particularly those with L2 English. Tsui's (2004) study of over 1,000 language queries raised by Hong Kong English teachers, showed how corpus evidence could provide appropriate responses for use with their students, covering issues such as distinguishing between synonyms and explaining collocations. Tsui argues that access to corpus data enabled teachers to question previously held assumptions and to raise their overall language awareness. The potential of corpora to address teachers' needs was also highlighted by Römer (2009), who administered a questionnaire to German secondary teachers. Like their Hong Kong counterparts, many German teachers felt uncertain about their English; they also judged their reference resources to be inadequate and were critical of their teaching materials. In both cases, access to corpora could help teachers address their problems more autonomously, by decreasing their reliance on L1 English speakers and enabling them to become more discerning and judicious users of reference materials.

A further benefit for teachers is that with current freeware and minimal training, they can build corpora of their students' writing and use corpus methods to examine the data. Working with a local learner corpus is not only motivating for students (Cotos, 2014; Moon & Oh, 2018), but also constitutes a valuable resource for teachers (Granger, 2009). Learner corpora enable recurrent problems to be identified and numerous authentic examples to be found quickly and easily, thereby providing abundant material for tailored tasks. Examples of small-scale teacher-led projects include work by Seidlhofer (2000) and Millar and Lehtinen (2008). Access to a corpus of learners' work can help teachers increase student motivation and target learning resources more precisely. Thus, by decreasing reliance on published materials, the use of local learner corpora can widen teachers' scope for autonomy.

Teachers' own experience of autonomous corpus use is an important factor in the development of learner autonomy. As Reinders and Balcikanli (2011) point out, the extent to which learners achieve autonomy is likely to be greatly influenced by teachers' understanding and support of autonomous learning and their ability to implement it in the classroom.

Investigating the treatment of autonomy in 11 teacher education textbooks, they find almost no discussion of the approach and therefore no training in how to foster its development. The absence of the topic from textbooks reveals a significant gap in teacher education and suggests that the promotion of autonomy is accorded little importance. In McCarthy's (2021) terms it does not seem to be part of the "invisible orthodoxy" of English language teaching (p. 126). Stressing teachers' role as learners of teaching, Smith (2000) argues that examining the extent and nature of their own autonomy as learners would enable teachers to better meet the challenges of developing autonomy in their learners.

Smith (2000) is not concerned with training for DDL, but Breyer (2009) takes a similar view in her account of an education programme for corpus use with pre-service secondary teachers. Her aim was to provide participants with a course which positioned them simultaneously as learners and teachers. As learners, participants were asked to reflect on their experience of learning corpus techniques, while as teachers they had to evaluate the potential of the approach for their future pedagogical practice. Breyer makes the point that training in corpus methods and DDL facilitates a re-examination of methodology and pedagogical assumptions, leading not only to increased language awareness, but also to "teaching awareness" (p. 167). Putting the teacher in the position of the DDL learner enables them to experience the benefits and downsides of autonomous learning; in this way, DDL training can support and indeed exemplify training for autonomy.

The education programme devised by Hüttner *et al.* (2009) for pre-service teachers of English for Specific Purposes (ESP) also aimed to foster teachers' ability to operate autonomously. During the course, learners acted as linguistic researchers in order to develop their ability to analyse and teach unfamiliar genres. Evaluation of the course by participants and employers was positive, indicating that it was successful in enhancing teachers' capacity for working autonomously. The course described by Leńko-Szymańska (2014, 2017) also aimed to prepare pre-service teachers to perform autonomously, but despite positive participant evaluations, she suggests that the approach "does not produce autonomous corpus users and corpus-using teachers" (2017, p. 234) and calls for a wider engagement with corpora across all pre-service teacher education. It should be noted, however, that the prime concern of these studies on teacher education is not with autonomous learning as conceived by Holec (1979), but rather with the ability to use corpora independently. Thus, their scope is much narrower, focusing on the practicalities of corpus use without necessarily situating it within the wider context of the task of developing autonomous learners.

This section has highlighted the interconnections between corpora, learner autonomy, and teacher autonomy. It has shown how corpus use enables greater autonomy for teachers, indicating that training in DDL has an important role to play in the development of both teacher and learner autonomy.

27.4 Corpora, autonomy, and resources

The third perspective taken here is to examine the role of corpora as resources for promoting autonomous learning. This section focuses particularly on the contribution of online resources to both learner and teacher autonomy.

Corpus resources consist of two elements: the corpus itself i.e. the collection of texts, and the tools used to examine the data. Although these two elements are often packaged together, they may also be accessed separately and then combined according to the user's need. This flexibility is an advantage for the autonomous learner/teacher, allowing them the option to compile their own corpora and examine them with a tool of their own choosing.

Anthony's freeware, including the concordancer AntConc (Anthony, 2019a) and the corpus-builder AntCorGen (Anthony, 2019b) have been widely used to facilitate the construction of the highly specialised corpora needed in ESP/EAP (Asano, 2018; Charles, 2018). In addition to its corpus-building capability, Sketch Engine (Kilgarriff *et al.*, 2004) gives access to the British Academic Written English Corpus (BAWE) (Heuboeck *et al.*, n.d.) and includes the "word sketch" tool, which is especially helpful for autonomous users as it presents the frequent collocations and patterns associated with a search item. Highlighting the need for an application that is accessible, simple, and customisable, Lee *et al.* (2015) describe a new open-source online concordancer which can be run from teachers' laptops and is designed for autonomous use.

There is a wide range of corpora with built-in tools, which offer multiple affordances for exploitation by the independent learner/teacher. Initial instruction and ongoing support may be required, however, for autonomous users to derive maximum benefit from these corpora (Chang & Sun, 2009). Two of the most frequently consulted are the British National Corpus (BNC) (n.d.) and the Corpus of Contemporary American English (COCA) (Davies, 2008); both are large general corpora covering several different registers, including journalism, academic texts, and spoken language. Consulted autonomously by teachers, these resources can provide material for DDL tasks (Frankenberg-Garcia, 2012a), but they can also be examined independently by students, for example as a means of improving writing (Bridle, 2019; Chang, 2014). In EAP/ESP, specialised corpora such as the Michigan Corpus of Upper-level Student Papers (MICUSP) (2009) are often used (Römer, 2012); discipline- or topic-specific corpora may also be constructed by learners/teachers and used for autonomous learning, in-class or outside. Examples include corpora of legal English (Fan & Xu, 2002; Hafner & Candlin, 2007) and of business topics (Poole, 2017; Smith, 2020).

One way of providing scaffolding for learners is through the tools themselves. Rather than simply retrieving unsorted concordance lines, the software may perform further analyses in response to the user's search. For example, the corpus data may be grouped into lexico-grammatical patterns as in Just the Word (n.d.) and Word Neighbours (Milton & Cheng, 2010), developed in Hong Kong for L1 Chinese speakers. Frequency data may also be given in an easily interpreted graphical form such as the word clouds in Sketch Engine for Language Learning (SkELL, n.d.) (Baisa & Suchomel, 2014; Kilgarriff *et al.*, 2015). Phraseological competence is the goal of two newly developed tools. Based on data from a corpus of research articles (RAs), ColloCaid offers "just in time" collocation assistance during writing (Frankenberg-Garcia *et al.*, 2019). Similarly, Mizumoto *et al.*'s (2017) tool provides an auto-complete feature which suggests frequent lexical bundles associated with the section of the RA being written. For lesson preparation or self-study it is particularly useful for the learner/teacher to be able to input their own texts, a feature provided by Word and Phrase, which compares self-selected texts to results from COCA, and VersaText (Thomas & Baisa, n.d.), which offers word clouds, concordancing, and vocabulary profiling.

Another way of providing corpus data to students is by using links to concordance lines which are inserted into the learner's text where an error occurs. These links offer tailored input to students as they revise their writing, thereby taking advantage of the immediacy of the student's need. An early example was Gaskell and Cobb's (2004) Link Extractor, designed for lower-level learners. The concordance links enabled successful correction of the majority of errors and there was evidence that the procedure stimulated autonomous corpus consultation. The Quicklinks (n.d.) project, based on data from BAWE, offers a more recent example of this technology, providing targeted help for specialised EAP learners (Vincent & Nesi,

2018). The re-usable links highlight phraseological issues and can provide not only concordance lines, but also word sketches, with collocation and colligation information.

Several resources for autonomous work in EAP writing implement a combined corpus and genre approach. Assistance with composing abstracts is provided by WriteAhead (Liou *et al.*, 2012), which gives contextualised, discipline-specific help, while Hsieh and Liou (2009) provide online materials for applied linguistics abstracts. However, the genre most often targeted is the RA. Sun's (2007) Scholarly Writing Template provides genre information and language support in the form of concordances, while Chang and Kuo's (2011) online material is designed for learning to write computer science RAs. Drawing on a multidisciplinary corpus of 900 RAs, The Research Writing Tutor (Cotos, 2016; Cotos *et al.*, 2017) analyses students' texts, colour-coding and classifying each sentence according to its genre function, and giving macro- and micro-level feedback. The functionality of such resources, then, goes beyond addressing the traditional lexico-grammatical concerns of DDL and demonstrates the potential of corpora to help students work autonomously at the levels of content, discourse and genre as well.

Although self-directed access to corpus resources is rarely discussed or quantified in the literature (Flowerdew, 2010), some resources mentioned in this section were set up specifically with autonomous use in mind (e.g. Cotos *et al.*, 2017), while work on advanced writing courses has also provided data on students' self-directed corpus use (e.g. Charles, 2014; Chen & Flowerdew, 2018b).

Resources like those described above provide a high degree of support to help users notice significant features in the retrieved data. While it could be argued that such scaffolding might decrease the depth of cognitive engagement by learners, such tools are easier to use than simple concordancers, which makes it more likely that they can be employed successfully by autonomous users. Moreover, the affordances of these new tools demand the active participation of the learner. As Yoon (2016a) points out, "students should realise that the greater autonomy afforded by reference resources comes with a greater responsibility for their own writing and learning." (p. 224).

27.5 Future directions of research

There are still many under-developed aspects of corpus-based autonomous learning. Most accounts focus on Reinders' (2010) practice stage, and greater learner involvement could be encouraged at stages 1–5 and 7–8, in the preparation and evaluation of DDL programmes. Moreover, autonomous approaches to DDL have been applied most frequently to writing instruction, while the development of reading and spoken language skills have been somewhat neglected. Reports on the use and evaluation of autonomous DDL in these areas would make a valuable contribution to widening the scope of corpus-based pedagogy. Further, although DDL is often claimed to facilitate the development of learner autonomy, more research is necessary to refine the concept and measure its extent.

Areas for investigation can also be suggested in relation to teachers and corpus-based autonomy. Attention has focused on pre-service teachers and their training for DDL, but less is known about the training, practices, and attitudes of serving teachers in a range of pedagogical contexts. Finally, it is encouraging to see the many significant advances that have taken place in corpus tools for autonomous learning. It is likely that these developments will continue in response to users' needs and it is hoped that more of these resources can be made available free so that learners and teachers can make extensive use of them autonomously.

Further reading

Godwin-Jones, R. (2019). Riding the digital wilds: Learner autonomy and informal language learning. *Language Learning & Technology, 23*(1), 8–25. https://doi.org/10125/44667. Limitations of space meant that this chapter did not deal with informal language learning, but this article gives an excellent overview of the issue in relation to the use of new technologies.

Johns, T. (1991). Should you be persuaded: Two samples of data-driven learning materials. *English Language Research Journal, 4,* 1–16. This is a foundational text for those concerned with DDL and lays the groundwork for much of the thinking on autonomous corpus use.

Reinders, H. (2017). *Autonomy bibliography.* https://innovationinteaching.org/free-tools/autonomy-bibliography.php. This is an easily searchable comprehensive bibliography of about 2,400 references on learner autonomy.

References

Ackerley, K., & Coccetta, F. (2007). Enriching language learning through a multimedia corpus. *ReCALL, 19*(3), 351–370. https://doi.org/10.1017/S0958344007000730

Allan, R. (2009). Can a graded reader corpus provide 'authentic' input? *ELT Journal, 63*(1), 23–32. https://doi.org/10.1093/elt/ccn011

Anthony, L. (2019a). *AntConc* (Version 3.5.8) [Computer software]. Waseda University. https://www.laurenceanthony.net/software

Anthony, L. (2019b). *AntCorGen* (Version 1.1.2) [Computer Software]. Waseda University. https://www.laurenceanthony.net/software

Asano, M. (2018). Construction of medical research article corpora with AntCorGen: Pedagogical implications. *Japanese Association for English Corpus Studies, 25,* 101–115.

Aston, G. (2001). Learning with corpora: An overview. In G. Aston (Ed.), *Learning with corpora* (pp. 7–45). CLUEB.

Aston, G. (2015). Learning phraseology from speech corpora. In A. Leńko-Szymańska & A. Boulton (Eds.), *Multiple affordances of language corpora for data-driven learning* (pp. 65–84). Benjamins. https://doi.org/10.1075/scl.69.04ast

Baisa, V., & Suchomel, V. (2014). SkELL: Web interface for English language learning. In A. Horák & P. Rychlý (Eds.), *Proceedings of Recent Advances in Slavonic Natural Language Processing* (pp. 63–70). NLP Consulting.

Bardovi-Harlig, K., Mossman, S., & Vellenga, H. (2015). Developing corpus-based materials to teach pragmatic routines. *TESOL Journal, 6*(3), 499–526. https://doi.org/10.1002/tesj.177

Bardovi-Harlig, K., Mossman, S., & Su, Y. (2017). The effect of corpus-based instruction on pragmatic routines. *Language Learning & Technology, 21*(3), 76–103. http://llt.msu.edu/issues/october2017/bardovi-harligmossmansu.pdf

Benson, P., & Voller, P. (2013). Introduction: Autonomy and independence in language learning. In P. Benson & P. Voller (Eds.), *Autonomy and independence in language learning* (pp. 1–12). Routledge. https://doi.org/10.4324/9781315842172-1

Bernardini, S. (2000). Systematising serendipity: Proposals for concordancing large corpora with language learners. In L. Burnard & T. McEnery (Eds.), *Rethinking language pedagogy from a corpus perspective* (pp. 225–234). Peter Lang.

Boulton, A. (2012). Hands-on/hands-off: Alternative approaches to data-driven learning. In J. Thomas & A. Boulton (Eds.), *Input, process and product: Developments in teaching and language corpora* (pp. 152–168). Masaryk University Press.

Braun, S. (2007). Designing and exploiting small multimedia corpora for autonomous learning and teaching. In E. Hidalgo, L. Quereda, & J. Santana (Eds.), *Corpora in the foreign language classroom* (pp. 31–46). Rodopi. https://doi.org/10.1163/9789401203906_004

Breyer, Y. (2009). Learning and teaching with corpora: Reflections by student teachers. *Computer Assisted Language Learning, 22*(2), 153–172. https://doi.org/10.1080/09588220902778328

Bridle, M. (2019). Learner use of a corpus as a reference tool in error correction: Factors influencing consultation and success. *Journal of English for Academic Purposes, 37,* 52–69. https://doi.org/10.1016/j.jeap.2018.11.003

British Academic Written English Corpus (BAWE) (n.d.). https://www.sketchengine.eu/british-academic-written-english-corpus/

British National Corpus (BNC) (n.d). http://www.natcorp.ox.ac.uk/

Carter, R., & McCarthy, M. (1995). Grammar and the spoken language. *Applied Linguistics, 16*(2), 141–158. https://doi.org/10.1093/applin/16.2.141

Chambers, A., Farr, F., & O'Riordan, S. (2011). Language teachers with corpora in mind: From starting steps to walking tall. *Language Learning Journal, 39*(1), 85–104. https://doi.org/10.1080/09571736.2010.520728

Chan, V. (2003). Autonomous language learning: The teachers' perspectives. *Teaching in Higher Education, 8*(1), 33–54. https://doi.org/10.1080/1356251032000052311

Chang, C.-F., & Kuo, C.-H. (2011). A corpus-based approach to online materials development for writing research articles. *English for Specific Purposes, 30*, 222–234. https://doi.org/10.1016/j.esp.2011.04.001

Chang, J.-Y. (2014). The use of general and specialized corpora as reference sources for academic English writing: A case study. *ReCALL, 26*(2), 243–259. https://doi.org/10.1017/S0958344014000056

Chang, W.-L., & Sun, Y.-C. (2009). Scaffolding and web concordancers as support for language learning. *Computer Assisted Language Learning, 22*(4), 283–302. https://doi.org/10.1080/09588220903184518.

Charles, M. (2012). 'Proper vocabulary and juicy collocations': EAP students evaluate do-it-yourself corpus-building. *English for Specific Purposes, 31*(2), 93–102. https://doi.org/doi10.1016/j.esp.2011.12.003

Charles, M. (2014). Getting the corpus habit: EAP students' long-term use of personal corpora. *English for Specific Purposes, 35*, 30–40. https://doi.org/10.1016/j.esp.2013.11.004

Charles, M. (2017). Do-it-yourself corpora in the classroom: Views of students and teachers. In L. Wong & K. Hyland (Eds.), *Faces of English education: Students, teachers and pedagogy* (pp. 107–123). Routledge. https://doi.org/10.4324/9781315205618-8

Charles, M. (2018). Corpus-assisted editing for doctoral students: More than just concordancing. *Journal of English for Academic Purposes, 36*, 15–25. https://doi.org/10.1016/j.jeap.2018.08.003

Chen, M., & Flowerdew, J. (2018a). A critical review of research and practice in data-driven learning (DDL) in the academic writing classroom. *International Journal of Corpus Linguistics, 23*(3), 335–369. https://doi.org/10.1075/ijcl.16130.che

Chen, M., & Flowerdew, J. (2018b). Introducing data-driven learning to PhD students for research writing purposes: A territory-wide project in Hong Kong. *English for Specific Purposes, 50*, 97–112. https://doi.org/10.1016/j.esp.2017.11.004

Chujo, K., & Oghigian, K. (2012). DDL for EFL beginners: A report on student gains and views on paper-based concordancing and the role of L1. In J. Thomas & A. Boulton (Eds.), *Input, process and product: Developments in teaching and language corpora* (pp. 169–182). Masaryk University Press.

Cotos, E. (2014). Enhancing writing pedagogy with learner corpus data. *ReCALL, 26*(2), 202–224. https://doi.org/10.1017/S0958344014000019

Cotos, E. (2016). Computer-assisted research writing in the disciplines. In S. Crossley & D. McNamara (Eds.), *Adaptive educational technologies for literacy instruction* (pp. 198–210). Routledge. https://doi.org/10.4324/9781315647500-15

Cotos, E., Link, S., & Huffman, S. (2017). Effects of DDL technology on genre learning. *Language Learning and Technology, 21*(3), 104–130. http://llt.msu.edu/issues/october2017/cotoslinkhuffman.pdf

Cresswell, A. (2007). Getting to 'know' connectors? Evaluating data-driven learning in a writing skills course. In E. Hidalgo, L. Quereda & J. Santana (Eds.), *Corpora in the foreign language classroom* (pp. 267–287). Rodopi. https://doi.org/10.1163/9789401203906_018

Crosthwaite, P. (2017). Retesting the limits of data-driven learning: Feedback and error correction. *Computer Assisted Language Learning, 30*(6), 447–473. https://doi.org/10.1080/09588221.2017.1312462

Crosthwaite, P. (2018, June 8). *Scaling up DDL: Challenges of bringing DDL to an online SPOC format* [Paper presentation]. 2nd BAAL Corpus Linguistics SIG Conference, Coventry, UK.

Crosthwaite, P., & Cheung, L. (2019). *Learning the language of dentistry: Disciplinary corpora in the teaching of English for specific academic purposes.* Benjamins. https://doi.org/10.1075/scl.93

Crosthwaite, P., Wong, L., & Cheung, J. (2019). Characterising postgraduate students' corpus query and usage patterns for disciplinary data-driven learning. *ReCALL, 31*(3), 255–275. https://doi.org/10.1017/S0958344019000077

Curado Fuentes, A. (2007). A corpus-based assessment of reading comprehension in English for tourism studies. In E. Hidalgo, L. Quereda, & J. Santana (Eds.), *Corpora in the foreign language classroom* (pp. 309–326). Rodopi. https://doi.org/10.1163/9789401203906_020

Curado Fuentes, A. (2015). Exploiting keywords in a DDL approach to the comprehension of news texts by lower-level students. In A. Leńko-Szymańska & A. Boulton (Eds.), *Multiple affordances of language corpora for data-driven learning* (pp. 177–198). Benjamins. https://doi.org/10.1075/scl.69.09cur

Davies, M. (2008). *The Corpus of Contemporary American English (COCA)* https://corpus.byu.edu/coca/

Dolgova, N., & Mueller, C. (2019). How useful are corpus tools for error correction? Insights from learner data. *Journal of English for Academic Purposes, 39*, 97–108. https://doi.org/10.1016/j.jeap.2019.03.007

Fan, M., & Xu, X. (2002). An evaluation of an online bilingual corpus for the self-learning of legal English. *System, 30*(1), 47–63. https://doi.org/10.1016/s0346-251x(01)00052-5

Flowerdew, L. (2009). Applying corpus linguistics to pedagogy. *International Journal of Corpus Linguistics, 14*(3), 393–417. https://doi.org/10.1075/ijcl.14.3.05flo

Flowerdew, L. (2010). Using corpora for writing instruction. In A. O'Keeffe & M. McCarthy (Eds.), *The Routledge handbook of corpus linguistics* (pp. 444–457). Routledge.

Frankenberg-Garcia, A. (2012a). Integrating corpora with everyday language teaching. In J. Thomas & A. Boulton (Eds.), *Input, process and product: Developments in teaching and language corpora* (pp. 36–53). Masaryk University Press.

Frankenberg-Garcia, A. (2012b). Raising teachers' awareness of corpora. *Language Teaching, 45*(04), 475–489. https://doi.org/10.1017/S0261444810000480

Frankenberg-Garcia, A., Lew, R., Roberts, J., Rees, G., & Sharma, N. (2019). Developing a writing assistant to help EAP writers with collocations in real time. *ReCALL, 31*(1), 23–39. https://doi.org/10.1017/S0958344018000150

Gabrielatos, C. (2005). Corpora and language teaching: Just a fling or wedding bells? *TESL-EJ, 8*(4), 1–35.

Gaskell, D., & Cobb, T. (2004). Can learners use concordance feedback for writing errors? *System, 32*, 301–319. https://doi.org/10.1016/j.system.2004.04.001

Gavioli, L. (2009). Corpus analysis and the achievement of learner autonomy in interaction. In L. Lombardo (Ed.), *Using corpora to learn about language and discourse* (pp. 39–71). Peter Lang.

Geluso, J., & Yamaguchi, A. (2014). Discovering formulaic language through data-driven learning: Student attitudes and efficacy. *ReCALL, 26*(2), 225–242. https://doi.org/10.1017/S0958344014000044

Gilmore, A. (2008). Using online corpora to develop students' writing skills. *ELT Journal, 63*(4), 363–372. https://doi.org/10.1093/elt/ccn056

Gordani, Y. (2013). The effect of the integration of corpora in reading comprehension classrooms on English as a foreign language learners' vocabulary development. *Computer Assisted Language Learning, 26*(5), 430–445. https://doi.org/10.1080/09588221.2012.685078

Granger, S. (2009). The contribution of learner corpora to second language acquisition and foreign language teaching: A critical evaluation. In K. Aijmer (Ed.), *Corpora and language teaching* (pp. 13–32). Benjamins. https://doi.org/10.1075/scl.33.04gra

Hadley, G., & Charles, M. (2017). Enhancing extensive reading with data-driven learning. *Language Learning and Technology, 21*(3), 131–152. http://llt.msu.edu/issues/october2017/hadleycharles.pdf

Hafner, C., & Candlin, C. (2007). Corpus tools as an affordance to learning in professional legal education. *Journal of English for Academic Purposes, 6*(4), 303–318. https://doi.org/10.1016/j.jeap.2007.09.005

Heuboeck, A., Holmes, J., & Nesi, H. (n.d.). *The BAWE corpus manual.* http://www.reading.ac.uk/internal/appling/bawe/BAWE.documentation.pdf

Holec, H. (1979). *Autonomy and foreign language learning.* Pergamon Press.

Hsieh, W.-M., & Liou, H.-C. (2009). A case study of corpus-informed online academic writing for EFL graduate students. *CALICO Journal, 26*(1), 28–47.

Hüttner, J., Smit, U., & Mehlmauer-Larcher, B. (2009). ESP teacher education at the interface of theory and practice: Introducing a model of mediated corpus-based genre analysis. *System, 37*, 99–109. https://doi.org/10.1016/j.system.2008.06.003

Johansson, S. (2009). Some thoughts on corpora and second-language acquisition. In K. Aijmer (Ed.), *Corpora and language teaching* (pp. 34–44). Benjamins. https://doi.org/10.1075/scl.33.05joh

Johns, T. (1991). Should you be persuaded: Two samples of data-driven learning materials. *English Language Research Journal, 4*, 1–16.

Just the word (n.d.) http://www.just-the-word.com/

Karras, J. (2016). The effects of data-driven learning upon vocabulary acquisition for secondary international school students in Vietnam. *ReCALL*, *28*(2), 166–186. https://doi.org/10.1017/S0958344015000154

Kilgarriff, A., Marcowitz, F., Smith, S., & Thomas, J. (2015). Corpora and language learning with the sketch engine and SkELL. *Revue Française de Linguistique Appliquée*, *XX*(1), 61–80. https://doi.org/10.3917/rfla.201.0061

Kilgarriff, A., Rychlý, P., Smrz, P. & Tugwell, D. (2004). The Sketch Engine. In G. Williams & S. Vessier (Eds.), *Proceedings of the eleventh Euralex international congress* (pp. 105–116). Université de Bretagne-Sud.

Lee, D., & Swales, J. (2006). A corpus-based EAP course for NNS doctoral students: Moving from available specialized corpora to self-compiled corpora. *English for Specific Purposes*, *25*(1), 56–75. https://doi.org/10.1016/j.esp.2005.02.010

Lee, J., Lee, H., & Sert, C. (2015). A corpus approach for autonomous teachers and learners: Implementing an on-line concordancer on teachers' laptops. *Language, Learning and Technology*, *19*(2), 1–15. http://llt.msu.edu/issues/june2015/emerging.pdf

Lee, P., & Lin, H. (2019). The effect of the inductive and deductive data-driven learning (DDL) on vocabulary acquisition and retention. *System*, *81*, 14–25. https://doi.org/10.1016/j.system.2018.12.011

Leńko-Szymańska, A. (2014). Is this enough? A qualitative evaluation of the effectiveness of a teacher-training course on the use of corpora in language education. *ReCALL*, *26*(2), 260–278. https://doi.org/10.1017/S095834401400010X

Leńko-Szymańska, A. (2017). Training teachers in data-driven learning: Tackling the challenge. *Language Learning & Technology*, *21*(3), 217.

Lin, M. (2016). Effects of corpus-aided language learning in the EFL grammar classroom: A case study of students' learning attitudes and teachers' perceptions in Taiwan. *TESOL Quarterly*, *50*(4), 871–893. https://doi.org/10.1002/tesq.250

Lin, M. (2019). Becoming a DDL teacher in English grammar classes: A pilot study. *The Journal of Language Teaching and Learning*, *9*(1), 70–82.

Liou, H.-C., Yang, P.-C., & Chang, J. (2012). Language supports for journal abstract writing across disciplines. *Journal of Computer Assisted Learning*, *28*(4), 322–335. https://doi.org/10.1111/j.1365-2729.2011.00446.x

Luo, Q., & Liao, Y. (2015). Using corpora for error correction in EFL learners' writing. *Journal of Language Teaching and Research*, *6*(6), 1333–1342. https://doi.org/10.17507/jltr.0606.22

McCarthy, M. (2021). *Innovations and challenges in grammar*. Routledge.

Michigan Corpus of Upper-level Student Papers (MICUSP). (2009). The Regents of the University of Michigan. https://micusp.elicorpora.info/

Millar, N., & Lehtinen, B. (2008). DIY local learner corpora: Bridging gaps between theory and practice. *The JALT CALL Journal*, *4*(2), 61–72. https://doi.org/10.29140/jaltcall.v4n2.63

Milton, J., & Cheng, V. (2010). A toolkit to assist L2 learners become independent writers. In *Proceedings of the NAACL HLT 2010 Workshop on Computational Linguistics and Writing* (pp. 33–41). Association for Computational Linguistics.

Mizumoto, A., Chujo, K., & Yokota, K. (2015). Development of a scale to measure learners' perceived preferences and benefits of data-driven learning. *ReCALL*, *28*(2), 227–246. https://doi.org/10.1017/S0958344015000208

Mizumoto, A., Hamatani, S., & Imao, Y. (2017). Applying the bundle-move connection approach to the development of an online writing support tool for research articles. *Language Learning*, *67*(4), 885–921. https://doi.org/10.1111/lang.12250

Moon, S., & Oh, S.-Y. (2018). Unlearning overgenerated *be* through data-driven learning in the secondary EFL classroom. *ReCALL*, *30*(1), 48–67. https://doi.org/10.1017/S0958344017000246

Mukherjee, J. (2006). Corpus linguistics And language pedagogy: The state of the art – and beyond. In S. Braun, K. Kohn, & J. Mukherjee (Eds.), *Corpus technology and language pedagogy* (pp. 5–24). Peter Lang.

Mull, J., & Conrad, S. (2013). Student use of concordancers for grammar error correction. *ORTESOL Journal*, *30*, 5–14.

O'Sullivan, Í. (2007). Enhancing a process-oriented approach to literacy and language learning: The role of corpus consultation literacy. *ReCALL*, *19*(3), 269–286. https://doi.org/10.1017/s095834400700033x

Park, K. (2012). Learner-corpus interaction: A locus of microgenesis in corpus-assisted L2 writing. *Applied Linguistics*, *33*(4), 361–385. https://doi.org/10.1093/applin/ams012

Pérez-Paredes, P., Sánchez-Tornel, M., Alcaraz Calero, J. & Aguado Jimenez, P. (2011). Tracking learners' actual uses of corpora: Guided vs non-guided corpus consultation. *Computer Assisted Language Learning, 24*(3), 233–253. https://doi.org/10.1080/09588221.2010.539978

Poole, R. (2017). "New opportunities" and "Strong performance": Evaluative adjectives in letters to shareholders and potential for pedagogically-downsized specialized corpora. *English for Specific Purposes, 47*, 40–51. https://doi.org/10.1016/j.esp.2017.03.003

Quicklinks (n.d.) https://bawequicklinks.coventry.domains/

Reinders, H. (2010). Towards a classroom pedagogy for learner autonomy: A framework of independent language learning skills. *Australian Journal of Teacher Education, 35*(5), 39–55. https://doi.org/10.14221/ajte.2010v35n5.4

Reinders, H., & Balcikanli, C. (2011). Learning to foster autonomy: The role of teacher education materials. *Studies in Self-Access Learning Journal, 2*(1), 15–25. https://doi.org/10.37237/020103

Römer, U. (2009). Corpus research and practice: What help do teachers need and what can we offer? In K. Aijmer (Ed.), *Corpora and language teaching* (pp. 83–97). Benjamins. https://doi.org/10.1075/scl.33.09rom

Römer, U. (2012). Corpora and teaching academic writing: Exploring the pedagogical potential of MICUSP. In J. Thomas & A. Boulton (Eds.), *Input, process and product: Developments in teaching and language corpora* (pp. 70–82). Masaryk University Press.

Seidlhofer, B. (2000). Operationalizing intertextuality: Using learner corpora for learning. In L. Burnard & T. McEnery (Eds.), *Rethinking language pedagogy from a corpus perspective* (pp. 207–223). Peter Lang. https://doi.org/10.1075/lllt.6.14sei

Sketch Engine for English Language Learning (SkELL) (n.d.). https://skell.sketchengine.co.uk/run.cgi/skell

Smart, J. (2014). The role of guided induction in paper-based data-driven learning. *ReCALL, 26*(2), 184–201. https://doi.org/10.1017/S0958344014000081

Smith, R. (2000). Starting with ourselves: Teacher-learner autonomy in language learning. In B. Sinclair, I. McGrath & T. Lamb (Eds.), *Learner autonomy, teacher autonomy: Future directions* (pp. 89–138). Longman.

Smith, S. (2011). Learner construction of corpora for general English in Taiwan. *Computer Assisted Language Learning, 24*(4), 291–316. https://doi.org/10.1080/09588221.2011.557024

Smith, S. (2020). DIY corpora for accounting & finance vocabulary learning. *English for Specific Purposes, 57*, 1–12. https://doi.org/10.1016/j.esp.2019.08.002

Soruç, A., & Tekin, B. (2017). Vocabulary learning through data-driven learning in an English as a second language setting. *Educational Sciences: Theory and Practice, 17*(6), 1811–1832. https://doi.org/10.12738/estp.2017.6.0305.

Sun, Y.-C. (2007). Learner perceptions of a concordancing tool for academic writing. *Computer Assisted Language Learning, 20*(4), 323–343. https://doi.org/10.1080/09588220701745791

Thomas, J., & Baisa, V. (n.d.) *VersaText* [Computer software]

Tsui, A. (2004). What teachers have always wanted to know – and how corpora can help. In J. Sinclair (Ed.), *How to use corpora in language teaching* (pp. 39–61). Benjamins. https://doi.org/10.1075/scl.12.06tsu

Vincent, B., & Nesi, H. (2018). The BAWE Quicklinks project: A new DDL resource for university students. *Lidil, 58*, 1–17. https://doi.org/10.4000/lidil.5306

Yi, W. (2017). When teacher autonomy meets management autonomy to enhance learner autonomy. *Chinese Journal of Applied Linguistics, 40*(4), 392–409. https://doi.org/10.1515/cjal-2017-0023

Yoon, C. (2016a). Concordancers and dictionaries as problem-solving tools for ESL academic writing. *Language Learning & Technology, 20*(1), 209–229. http://llt.msu.edu/issues/february2016/yoon.pdf

Yoon, C. (2016b). Individual differences in online reference resource consultation: Case studies of Korean ESL graduate writers. *Journal of Second Language Writing, 32*, 67–80. https://doi.org/10.1016/j.jslw.2016.04.002

Yoon, H., & Hirvela, A. (2004). ESL student attitudes toward corpus use in L2 writing. *Journal of Second Language Writing, 13*(4), 257–283. https://doi.org/10.1016/j.jslw.2004.06.002

Yoon, H., & Jo, J. (2014). Direct and indirect access to corpora: An exploratory case study comparing students' error correction and learning strategy use in L2 writing. *Language Learning & Technology, 18*(1), 96–117. https://doi.org/doi:10125/44356

28

DDL FOR ENGLISH LANGUAGE TEACHING IN PERSPECTIVE

Ivor Timmis and Jane Templeton

28.1 Introduction

The term *data-driven learning* (DDL) was coined by Johns (1991), who is generally credited with pioneering this language learning technique. The main principle of Johns' (1991) conception of DDL is summarised thus by Naismith (2016): "in essence, DDL advocates that learners access corpus data in the classroom, typically through computer software, to notice features of language and to draw conclusions about its usage" (p. 274). In its simplest form, DDL involves learners interacting directly with corpora (collections of texts) and corpus tools (online applications or concordancing software). DDL has shifted its shape over the years and now seems to encompass the cline (Gilquin & Granger, 2010) between pre-prepared corpus output (indirect use) and direct access to corpora (direct use) (Römer, 2006).

DDL, as so conceived, has certainly gained some ground in ELT over the years. There has, for example, been a steady flow of articles mentioning DDL in the journal *ReCALL* (The Journal of the European Association for Computer Assisted Language Learning), the earliest in 1994, and the latest in 2019. In addition, papers on DDL regularly feature at the biennial TALC conference (Teaching and Language Corpora). It cannot, however, be said that DDL is in widespread use in ELT. Mukherjee (2004) reported that 80% of English teachers in Germany did not even know what corpus linguistics was, let alone DDL. More recently, Meunier (2020, p. 423) speaks of "a lack of uptake and sustainable practices in DDL" (p. 423).

There is a tendency in language teaching for debates about the value of innovative methods or techniques to become polarised between enthusiastic proponents and sceptical opponents. While DDL is no exception, we argue that the question at this stage should not be whether an innovation such as DDL is intrinsically good or bad, but who might benefit from it, in what context and for what purpose. As far as possible, this appraisal should be empirically based in terms of both learner and teacher attitudes and attested learning gains. We aim to offer such an appraisal so that teachers can decide what DDL might have to offer them in their teaching and learning context. In addition, we make a series of recommendations for teachers as to how they might most fruitfully apply DDL.

DOI: 10.4324/9781003002901-33

28.2 Review of current state of research

Empirical research in DDL has focused, and continues to focus, both on learners' and teachers' attitudes to DDL and on empirical evidence of learning gains from real-world applications of DDL. In this section, we review these three kinds of study.

28.2.1 Learners' attitudes

There have been a number of studies into learners' attitudes to DDL, mostly carried out by researchers or practitioners with expertise in this field rather than teachers experimenting with the technique. Götz and Mukherjee (2006), working with university students in Germany, note that overall, learners found DDL "interesting, useful and fun" (p. 49). While some found the autonomous aspect of DDL "positive" and "refreshing", Götz and Mukherjee (2006) report that "most of them would have preferred a more thorough introduction" (p. 59). Among the negative evaluations were comments that DDL was "confusing" and "laborious" and that instructions were "too vague" (Götz & Mukherjee, 2006, p. 56). Interestingly, the study found that even those students who saw the potential of DDL did not actually feel they had made real learning gains through their exposure to DDL.

An experiment was carried out by Adel (2010) where the students investigated how experienced writers expressed certain functions such as exemplification. The outcome of the experiment, Adel (2010) reports, was "mixed" but "primarily positive" (p. 43). More specifically, the students enjoyed inductive learning and the novelty of using computers, though a serious limitation was that it was a one-off experiment with no follow-up (Adel, 2010). A consideration in all such experiments, we would note, is the unknown factor of how far the element of novelty influences attitudes, and how long this effect lasts. In an experiment designed to help Chinese college students with their writing, Luo (2016) got students to work with the British National Corpus (BNC) (BNC Consortium, 2007) and found that their attitudes were positive, although an important reservation was that DDL had to be supplemented by other activities to support the writing process.

For readers who teach other languages, it is worth noting that DDL research has been conducted outside ELT (Jablonkai *et al.*, 2020). Yao (2019), for example, working with students of Spanish as a Foreign Language, found that her learners "generally favoured DDL and adopted a positive attitude towards its future application to Spanish learning" (p. 18). Her research is of particular interest because, unlike many studies, she reports learners' reactions to specific aspects of DDL: most of her learners liked the KWIC format, finding it comprehensible and useful for differentiating between synonyms, while all agreed that the format "provided a rich context for the target vocabulary" (Yao, 2019, p. 35).

A systematic approach to integrating corpus work in an undergraduate course is described by Varley (2009), who observes that "most of the students indicated they are likely to use concordancers in the future and this interest is strongest amongst those students who have clear goals for their language learning" (p. 133). Asik *et al.* (2016) researched learners' reactions to using DDL techniques for lexical development in a Turkish context. The learners were positive about DDL for some aspects of lexical awareness but were critical of technical problems and the time-consuming nature of the tasks. In a Saudi university context, Alsolami and Assrar (2020) investigated the reactions of learners to using corpus tools to improve their academic writing. Although a few learners commented that they needed more time to get to grips with corpus tools, learners' overall reaction was positive and they highlighted four benefits: increased confidence in writing; great language awareness, exposure to relevant input, and greater autonomy (Alsolami & Assrar, 2020).

The overall impression from the literature is of mixed attitudes to DDL, though with a preponderance of positive responses. As Kennedy and Miceli (2001) observe, it is not just a question of differences between learners: individual learners can also have mixed attitudes, finding DDL "helpful and confidence boosting, but sometimes also discouraging, time-consuming and frustrating" (p. 80). It seems, then, that learners see the potential benefits of DDL, at least for some aspects of language learning, though complaints, as Chambers (2010) notes, about the time-consuming and sometimes tedious and laborious nature of the tasks are quite common. Many of the evaluations of DDL are at a quite general level, and it would be useful to have more studies which investigate in detail the kind of tasks which are well received and the kind of language work for which DDL is most suited.

28.2.2 Teachers' attitudes

There have been several studies of the attitudes of teachers, particularly teachers in training, to DDL. In a Taiwanese context, Lin (2016) introduced DDL to early career teachers who were positive about it and judged it to have a positive effect on their learners' attitudes to learning grammar, even though they had technical difficulties in implementing DDL and found that it increased their workload.

A particularly detailed study was carried out by Breyer (2009) with student teachers who followed a short course in DDL and prepared their own materials. It is a most interesting and nuanced study, concluding that "despite the reported difficulties [...] the student teachers presented very interesting learning activities and expressed their enthusiasm for the task" (Breyer, 2009, p. 167). Naismith (2016) also introduced trainee teachers to corpus tools and reported that "interest in the corpus tools was consistently high, as evidenced by the questionnaire answers and tutor observations, and regardless of whether trainees even used the corpus tools" (p. 278).

Chen *et al.* (2019) carried out a research project which involved introducing English language teachers in Hong Kong to the use of corpora in teaching academic writing. They found that the teachers generally responded positively though their responses were influenced by a number of variables: prior knowledge of corpora; prior experience in using corpora; motivation for professional development and teaching experience. An overall positive response, with some reservations, was also observed by Leńko-Szymańska (2014) working with graduate teacher trainees in Poland. The participants felt, however, that they needed more time to master the resources and tools and greater awareness of the pedagogical issues of DDL.

The difficulties and challenges commonly faced by teachers fall into two principal categories, as summarised by Gilquin and Granger (2010): logistical considerations, including the equipment and preparation time required, and those relating to teacher expertise and confidence.

28.2.3 Specific learning gains from real-world applications of DDL

It is more difficult to quantify learning gains than it is to gauge attitudes, but empirical evidence of gains will be crucial in persuading teachers that DDL has something to offer. It is very helpful for our purposes that a number of meta-analyses have been conducted over the years which collate the empirical studies to date. Via these, we can trace the increasing body of work.

A meta-analysis of 64 DDL studies (Boulton & Cobb, 2017) paints quite a bright picture. These studies showed significant effects on learning; we should also note that the gains were not limited to specific kinds of contexts, corpus, activity, or learner:

> learners seem able to perceive language patterns despite the lines chopped off the concordance output and [...] DDL activities are not confined to advanced learners, nor exclusively to simplified corpora or mediated data, nor to hands-off or paper-based activities, nor for learning goals limited to vocabulary and collocation. The evidence on all these seems clear. (Boulton & Cobb, 2017, p. 386)

Lee *et al.* (2017) carried out a meta-analysis of 29 studies with specific reference to vocabulary learning, which "found an overall positive medium-sized effect of corpus use on L2 vocabulary learning for both short-term [...] and long-term periods" (p. 721). It is worth noting that they pinpointed a number of variables which influenced effectiveness: "learners' L2 proficiency and several features of corpus use (i.e. interaction types, corpus types, training, and duration)" (Lee *et al.*, 2017, p. 721). In a Japanese context, Mizumoto and Chujo (2015) carried out a meta- analysis of 14 DDL studies. They found that DDL worked well for vocabulary and basic grammar items but made little impact on overall proficiency measures.

Luo and Zhou (2017) carried out what they term "an overview of empirical DDL research in writing published from 2010 to 2016" (p. 182). As is the case with so many studies, they found great potential in DDL, but they also expressed an interesting reservation: learners found traditional reference tools or online dictionaries better for some purposes than corpus tools. Accordingly, they suggest that a platform which offers access to both a corpus and other electronic resources might be the way forward.

The studies consulted, we argue, suggest strongly that there is enough empirical evidence of learning gains, and enough evidence of positive learner and teacher attitudes, to merit further principled exploration of DDL with the aim of maximising the attested potential for learning and autonomy.

28.3 Critical issues in DDL

Despite the seemingly promising empirical picture which emerges from the literature cited above, Vincent and Nesi (2018) maintain that "[DDL] still continues to meet with resistance from teachers and learners" (p. 2). We need to consider, then, the issues which might cause such resistance.

28.3.1 DDL and basic learning principles

While there is a temptation to treat DDL as "sui generis", we believe it is important to hold it to the same fundamental criteria we would with other techniques or materials. Accordingly, we begin by considering DDL in the light of Tomlinson's (2011) three basic criteria for language learning materials. They should:

a. be motivating and relevant to the learners
b. present an achievable level of challenge
c. draw attention to selected features of the input

In this section, we consider how far DDL meets these criteria.

28.3.1.1 Motivation and relevance

Since DDL has not yet made its way into most mainstream textbooks (Vincent & Nesi, 2018) and many teachers are likely to be unfamiliar with it (Naismith, 2016), it seems safe to assume that DDL will be a new way of learning for many learners. This means that they may easily be de-motivated by tasks which appear unattractive or inaccessible.

In terms of relevance, authentic corpora will inevitably yield results from a variety of contexts which will include irrelevant or confusing data. Working with data extracts drawn from random contexts, or, in the case of concordance lines, no meaningful context, is often seen as challenging; working with decontextualised data which has no intrinsic interest can be very dispiriting (Gilquin & Granger, 2010). While there may be analytical learners who are motivated simply by the cognitive challenge presented by typical DDL activities, it is likely, we would argue, that many need the hook of language or techniques they perceive as relevant to draw them in. An inclination to notice features of language in the input may depend on this motivational hook, but exposure to multiple examples of a target feature in a colour-coded KWIC format certainly gives learners the opportunity to notice specific aspects of the use of the feature.

There is plenty of potential for learners to be motivated, as evidenced by the positive comments from learners in Section 28.2. However, the nature of the DDL task can have a significant impact on motivation. Activities perceived as tedious, laborious, or time-consuming (Asik *et al.*, 2016; Chambers, 2010; Gilquin & Granger, 2010; Götz & Mukherjee, 2006) are unlikely to be engaging.

Overall, then, while DDL can indeed be highly motivating, we should not take motivation for granted, nor assume that DDL will be intrinsically interesting or appear useful to all learners.

28.3.1.2 Achievable level of challenge

Clearly, in order for learners to be motivated and for learning to occur, it is important that learners are able to do the DDL activity.

In direct corpus use, acquiring the data requires digital access and technical skills, and there are many potential issues: internet access, device malfunction or user error, and the functionality of the corpus tool. Not all students have devices they can use in class, nor do all classrooms have reliable internet access. Technical difficulties are not uncommon, as reported in Asik *et al.* (2016).

Making inductive discoveries from concordance lines requires the ability to read and interpret concordance lines, which is not an intuitive skill (Sripicharn, 2010). The vertical format of concordance lines can present difficulties to some learners (Chambers, 2010). In both direct and indirect use, the presence of confusing and irrelevant results can make it difficult to identify relevant data. It is also possible for learners to drown in data even when it is relevant. If a corpus search generates hundreds of concordances of the target feature, then the task of making inductive discoveries from concordance lines can be overwhelming. Even in a relatively small corpus, the most frequent words can occur too frequently for the concordances alone to be accessible. Learners, therefore, need additional skills in order to be able to refine searches and filter results. If the instructions are unclear, as in Götz and Mukherjee (2006), this will also negatively affect learners' ability to do the task.

There are tools which have been designed to make the data easier to interpret. For example, the colour-coding by part of speech on the search tool integrated into the Corpus of Contemporary American English (COCA) (Davies, 2008) can make it easier to identify relevant results and spot patterns. However, such tools can present barriers to learners with certain attributes, e.g. visual impairment, dyslexia, and neurodiversity. For example, the wealth of information provided by Voyant Tools (Sinclair & Rockwell, 2016), which features a range of visualisations of data from user-provided text, can be immensely helpful for some learners but distracting or overwhelming for others.

At the same time, it is important not to exaggerate the difficulty of corpus literacy (Bernardini, 2001). It is generally accepted that DDL involves inductive, discovery learning, and this, as Boulton (2009), remarks, "exploits processes that humans have evolved to be naturally good at exposure to information, detection of patterns, extrapolation to other cases" (pp. 39–40). Similarly, it should not be assumed that learners will lack the necessary digital skills. As Boulton and Cobb (2017) argue, DDL taps into practices and processes at which learners are already adept through everyday use of ICT.

Overall, we would argue that it is certainly possible for learners to do DDL – there is no reason why most learners should not be able to. But there is a real danger that learners may not take to it quickly, as there are many factors that can make the challenge too difficult to be achievable.

28.3.1.3 Noticing features of the input

While KWIC concordance lines are designed to draw attention to features of the input, learners need to be motivated to notice these features. Tomlinson (2011) argues that learners will be best disposed to notice features of the input if they are engaged by the text. If we take 'text' to mean the corpus or the results of the search, learners may be engaged by the text if it is relevant to them, e.g. if they have made their own corpus or if they are looking in a genre-specific corpus and they want to produce text in that genre. They may be visually engaged by the KWIC format or visualisation tools, e.g. Voyant Tools (Sinclair & Rockwell, 2016) or WordWanderer (Dörk & Knight, 2015). They may also be cognitively engaged if they want to know the answers that the corpus yields. In all of these cases, noticing is likely to occur. Conversely, it follows that noticing may well not occur if these conditions are not met. Therefore, it should not be assumed that learners will automatically notice the intended features of the language in question.

28.3.2 DDL is not suitable for all learners in all contexts

Even if we accept that DDL has much to recommend it, it is clear from the literature that it is not suitable for all learners. Not all learners enjoy or respond well to inductive learning (Gilquin & Granger, 2010). Some learners require additional resources in order to develop their language skills (Luo, 2016), while some learners prefer traditional reference tools for some purposes (Luo & Zhou, 2017).

Additionally, learners need to be trained in corpus literacies. While DDL does indeed exploit natural processes (Boulton, 2009), it does not follow that it is intuitive. Learners need to be trained to read concordance lines (Sripicharn, 2010), and as Götz and Mukherjee (2006) and Adel (2010) found, one exposure to DDL may not be enough. Alsolami and Assrar (2020) also reported that some learners needed more time to develop facility with corpus tools. This requires there to be time within a syllabus for training, which may not be possible in all contexts. There is clearly great potential for learners to be motivated by DDL and for the activity to be successful, but this is not guaranteed and requires careful calibration of tasks and scaffolding of learning.

28.3.3 Materials and training

There may be a gap between the research literature on DDL and the practical needs of teachers waiting to take their first steps in DDL without the benefit of specific prior training. As Naismith (2016) points out, trainees on one of the best-known pre-service training courses, the Cambridge Certificate in English Language Teaching for Adults (CELTA), had low familiarity with corpus tools even in cases where they had previous teaching experience. Moreover, even when they had been introduced to corpus tools, they lacked the confidence to use them live in class. As we noted in Section 28.3.2, it takes time to develop this confidence and familiarity: the teachers in Leńko-Szymańska's (2014) study, for example, felt that they needed more time to master the resources and tools and develop greater awareness of the pedagogical issues of DDL.

It also takes time to prepare materials, which increases workload. This issue is reported by teachers even though they express positive attitudes to DDL (Lin, 2016; Naismith, 2016). While there are recommendations and practical examples of activities in the literature (e.g. Friginal, 2018; Poole, 2018; Vyatkina, 2020), published DDL materials are still relatively scarce (Vyatkina, 2020), and the context-specific nature of DDL means that in many cases teachers will need to design their own activities. While it is logical that open access resources may act as exemplars for teachers to design their own materials (Vyatkina, 2020), this may be daunting for inexperienced teachers.

Faced with issues of workload and confidence in their technological skills, teachers inexperienced in DDL may choose to play safe and avoid it.

28.3.4 DDL challenges traditional views of language and the role of the teacher

Corpus findings have challenged traditional views of language as a fixed set of rules and patterns (Cook, 1998; Sinclair, 1991). It can be unsettling when certainties are thrown into question, and this may be one reason why teachers shy away from corpora. Corpus research can certainly challenge received wisdom about discourse and grammar (Timmis, 2015), throwing into doubt, for example, long-cherished notions of EAP, such as the topic sentence (Hoey & O'Donnell, 2007). "Loss of expertise" (Gilquin & Granger, 2010, p. 366) is a common reason for negative evaluations of DDL. The role of the teacher changes somewhat in DDL from that of expert to co-researcher (Lin, 2019), which can be daunting for inexperienced teachers.

Overall, there are many plausible reasons for not using DDL and many potential pitfalls that can deter the inexperienced teacher. In the following section, we explain how to avoid or mitigate these pitfalls.

28.4 Recommendations for practice

In the light of the issues discussed above, we make recommendations in this section as to how DDL might successfully be applied in a way which exploits its undoubted potential while also addressing its equally undoubted challenges.

28.4.1 Design appropriate tasks for your learners

It seems clear that if DDL is to be motivating to learners and effective in terms of learning, good task design is essential. There are several important considerations for teachers, which we outline below.

28.4.1.1 Consider the kinds of query that might appeal to your learners

In each iteration of DDL, there should be a question whose answer is relevant to most of the learners. This may be a linguistic query about how a specific language feature patterns or is used in a particular context. Alternatively, the query can be technical: How do I find out how noun patterns with prepositions? How do I find out the most frequent verb collocates of a noun? How do I find examples of this phrase used in my target genre? Starting with a relevant query is the key to choosing the appropriate tools.

28.4.1.2 Consider the most appropriate corpus for your learners

The choice of an appropriate corpus for the learners in question is crucial to the success of DDL. While the proliferation in the number and range of corpora available in recent years can be seen as positive for DDL, it may also bewilder those new to the field. It is important, therefore, to consider the range of options available to the teacher. A summary of the main types of corpus and their applications follows.

The type of corpus to use depends on your language query and whether it can be answered using existing corpora. For general language queries where the context is not of particular relevance, e.g. if you were interested in which prepositions can follow *present*, large online corpora such as the BNC (BNC Consortium, 2007) and their subdomains are useful, both for preparing material for indirect use and for direct access in class. An example of using such a corpus can be found in Luo (2016).

Where the context is relevant, e.g. if you were looking for how *present* is used in Medicine, genre-specific corpora can be used. ESP and EAP are well served by such corpora, e.g. the British Academic Written English Corpus (BAWE) (Vincent & Nesi, 2018). Work with these corpora is well represented in the literature. Curado Fuentes (2002, 2003) discusses the classroom exploitation of Business English corpora, while Fan and Xunfeng (2002) consider the use of online corpora in the learning of legal English. There is an extensive discussion of the use of corpora in ESP by Gavioli (2005), while Boulton (2012) offers an empirical review of corpora in ESP.

Teaching-oriented corpora (Leech, 1997) are useful because they are specially designed for language learners. They are typically small enough for the learners not to drown in data, and are based on a homogenous collection of texts dealing with topics likely to motivate the learner (Braun, 2005). They may also be available in audio-visual format and are often annotated for pedagogic rather than research purposes. Perhaps most importantly for teachers, they include guidance notes and practical examples of activities. One excellent example is the English Language Interview Corpus as a Second Language (ELISA), a collection of video interviews where native speakers of different varieties of English talk about their professional careers (Braun, 2006).

Where internet access is not available or reliable in class, or when you want to investigate language use in an area of interest too specific to be represented by existing corpora, you can build your own and analyse it using concordancing software, e.g. AntConc (Anthony, 2019).

One type of build-your-own corpus is a "pedagogic corpus", which is gradually built up from the texts and materials the learners have used in the natural course of their classroom activities (Willis, 2003). The advantage of such a corpus is that when learners access it either directly or indirectly, they will already be familiar with the co-text when they look at their search results (Willis, 2003). A somewhat similar proposal is made by Allan (2009), who suggests compiling a corpus from a set of graded readers. Her comment about the value of such a corpus could well be applied *mutatis mutandis* to all teaching-oriented corpora:

> Learners are less likely to be overwhelmed by the data, and more likely to be able to understand it and draw conclusions from it. Learning can be staged in a way that it cannot be through an authentic corpus, with learners introduced to a limited number of senses and uses of a particular word or phrase, just as they would be through a learner dictionary or textbook; moving through levels of learner corpora would allow them. (Allan, 2009, p. 300)

Another option is for teachers to compile their own corpora for their classes, which allows control over both size and content. Corpora can be compiled from published texts or from more esoteric sources. Flowerdew (1993), for example, created a corpus of lectures attended by the students, while Timmis (2015) reports improvising a corpus of music teaching English from a collection of music examiners' reports. Alternatively, corpora can be compiled from learners' writing, which can be very useful for focusing on accuracy and identifying systemic issues (see Granger, 2017, for an overview of learner corpora).

Finally, learners can compile their own corpora with texts from their area of interest, thus ensuring relevance. Lee and Swales (2006), for example, asked postgraduate students to create their own corpus of texts relevant to their specific discipline. Charles (2018) has shown that students can use 'DIY corpora' of texts in their own bibliography, or of their own chapters, to edit the language, content and organisation of their theses or dissertations.

Compiling a small corpus is a straightforward process which does not require advanced technical skills (e.g. Jablonkai, this volume; Koester, 2010; Timmis, 2015). It requires merely the conversion of texts into a format that the concordancing software can read, typically plain text, which can be done with a few mouse clicks. In some cases, it may be desirable to clean up the corpus, e.g. by removing references from journal papers (Charles, 2018) or other metadata, but this is not essential. Tribble's (1997) concept of a 'quick and dirty corpus' is an important consideration here. The only function which may need additional effort is that of searching by colligation, i.e. the association of a word with a grammatical structure, as is it not possible to do this unless the corpus is tagged, i.e. each word is labelled by part of speech. Using the online freeware CLAWS (http://ucrel.lancs.ac.uk/claws/) (Garside, 1987), a corpus can be automatically tagged in a matter of moments with an accuracy rate of around 95%. However, teachers should not be deterred by the absence of tagging from using concordancing software with learners, as it is not necessary for a corpus to be tagged in order for searches to yield a wealth of useful information.

28.4.1.3 Design tasks which are appropriately calibrated to your learners

It is crucial that DDL tasks are carefully calibrated in terms of the level of challenge they present to a given set of learners. Gilquin and Granger (2010) note that DDL activities "may be located along a cline ranging from teacher-led to learner-led e.g. from cloze tests to free browsing" (p. 363). Teachers should, therefore, experiment with different kinds of task. Götz (2012), for example, found that her learners reacted better to tightly structured tasks rather than fully autonomous discovery tasks, but that might not be the case in all contexts. The order in which tasks are sequenced can also be significant. Tekin and Soruc (2016), following the work of Thurstun and Candlin (1998), introduced four target words to the students, initially through concordance lines. This procedure was supplemented by activities in which the learners had to manipulate or use the words. Learners' responses, both in the qualitative and quantitative data, were very positive.

There are several options for using DDL principles and techniques without using concordance lines. Voyant Tools (Sinclair & Rockwell, 2016), for example, includes a word cloud feature among its visualisations. Word clouds are an effective way of easily identifying keywords within a text and introducing learners to the idea that frequent is useful (Naismith, 2016) and can be combined with manual concordancing from the text in question. The embedded tool in COCA (Davies, 2008) shows the collocates of a word in the COCA corpus, as well as textually related topics, while Word Wanderer (Dörk & Knight, 2015) shows the collocates of a word in user-provided text. Such tools may suit lower-level learners, or those who are encountering DDL for the first time.

28.4.1.4 Allow for differentiation in levels and abilities

Although Boulton and Cobb (2017) argue that L2 proficiency is no barrier to learning from DDL methods, Lee *et al.* (2017) suggest that it can have an impact. The level of difficulty of DDL tasks can be quite carefully calibrated to be appropriate for lower-level or inexperienced learners, as Aston (2001, p. 43) argues, by designing tasks which:

- do not cause too many problems of precision and recall: 'precision' refers to the degree to which a search will retrieve only the search item; 'recall' refers to the degree to which a search will retrieve all instances of the search item. For a more detailed discussion of this, see Aston (2001)
- require little manipulation of the input
- do not require all the data to be classified
- require relatively superficial interpretation
- encourage learners to collaborate
- include elements that can be delegated to stronger learners

28.4.1.5 Allow for differentiation in engagement

It is important to bear in mind when designing tasks that, in any class, there may be learners who do not enjoy inductive learning, are not interested in the target feature(s), find concordance lines difficult to interpret, have technical or access issues, and find DDL tedious. However, if the language query is appropriate, learners should be interested in the answer even if they are not interested in this particular methodology for obtaining it. Therefore, teachers can design alternative tasks, e.g. learners could answer the query using a different method or resource.

28.4.2 Train the learners in corpus literacy and scaffold their learning

We believe that the ultimate aim of DDL should be to equip learners with the tools and skills to carry out searches to answer their own language queries. That this is a key benefit from learners' perspectives is borne out in the literature: in several studies (e.g. Boulton & Cobb, 2017; Charles, 2018; Luo, 2016) the potential for independent use was highlighted in learners' evaluations. Turnbull and Burston (1998) carried out a longitudinal study with two postgraduate students who were encouraged to use concordancing techniques to work on errors in their written texts. They conclude that concordancing can be very useful for such students, but extensive training is needed which needs to be carefully calibrated to students' experience of inductive learning and of working with computers. Charles (2018) trained learners over several weeks in how to use the various features of AntConc (Anthony, 2019) to improve their PhD theses. The importance of learner training in corpus use is also stressed by Gilmore (2009).

Given that learners require training, a gradual progression with DDL tasks and activities seems appropriate. Chambers (2010) argues that learners might progress from teacher-prepared concordances to consultation of easy-to-use online resources, and then to independent corpus analysis. Varley's (2009) systematic approach to integrating corpus work in an undergraduate course led learners to use concordancing independently. In similar vein, Boulton (2016) discusses the systematic integration of corpus tools and techniques into an ESP course. Corino and Onesti (2019) argue that DDL can be used as a scaffolding methodology for both ESP and CLIL classes.

28.4.3 *Develop your own technical skills and corpus literacy*

Corpus literacy is not an all-or-nothing attribute and there is a lot to be said for learning a particular skill at point of need. Equally, there is much to be said for keeping one step ahead of the learners. In terms of reference material, O'Keeffe and McCarthy (2010) have several chapters dealing with both compiling a corpus and with basic analytical techniques. Timmis (2015) also has a chapter dealing with straightforward search techniques. The BNC (BNC Consortium, 2007) has a very useful five-minute tour which introduces you to all the basic search possibilities. It is worth pointing out that teachers do not need expertise in all the available tools, or experience of all the available corpora. There is nothing to fear but fear itself.

28.4.4 *Be prepared to adjust your perspective and your role*

As Aston (2001) emphasises, teachers (and learners) may well need to modify their conceptions of the nature of language and language learning. The key message is to adopt a critical perspective: to question assumptions about language, to accept that there is not one correct answer, and to be comfortable with uncertainty.

Clearly, then, it may be necessary for some teachers to modify their understanding of their role and their expectations of their learners, and to help their learners make the transition. This may be a leap of faith for some, but we strongly urge it, because it can be very liberating not to have to know all the answers. Once the teacher has shed the burden of expertise, there is no expectation that everything will go perfectly. Every interaction with a corpus can be a learning experience – failing to find the answer to a query is a very useful way of gaining knowledge about the types of searches likely to yield appropriate results. Turning the responsibility of finding out over to the learners and adopting the role of guide can be a daunting step, but a very fruitful one.

28.5 Future directions of research

There is a need, we would argue, for more empirical research on the lines of that carried out by Boulton and Cobb (2017) which seeks to evaluate actual learning gains from the application of DDL. Empirical research could narrow down to focus on specific issues, e.g.

1. Does DDL seem to be more effective for lexis or grammar?
2. What kind of DDL tasks seem to be effective for what kind of learner?

3. When learners access corpora autonomously, what kind of questions are they seeking to address, what kind of searches are they carrying out, and how successful are they in answering their own queries? Pérez-Paredes *et al.* (2011; 2012) and Crosthwaite (2017) have pioneered work in this area.
4. What kind of corpus interface seems to be the most user-friendly for teachers and learners?

Research into the precise nature of corpus literacy is also needed. As Götz and Mukherjee (2006) observe, "if DDL activities are to be included in the English language curriculum, it is essential to identify the analytical and methodological competencies that learners need to acquire when working with – and learning from – corpora" (p. 1).

There is also a need for research into how corpus findings can best inform materials and how data-supported learning can be integrated into a course. It would also be good to involve teachers in DDL research, encouraging them to carry out action research projects which involve experimenting with DDL, and evaluating the experience both from their own and their learners' perspectives.

We have sought in this chapter to provide a critical review of what DDL has to offer teachers and learners. It seems to us that the potential of DDL has been firmly established through empirical research. However, there comes a time when we need to stop talking about potential and to focus on how gains from DDL can be optimised. What is needed now is more nuanced empirical research which seeks to establish the DDL resources and tasks which best suit given learning contexts, and more consideration of how DDL can be aligned with learners' and teachers' real world needs (Meunier, 2020). DDL is not a panacea for all ills, but there are times when it will be the most effective prescription for a particular learning need. In the final analysis, DDL is a tool like any other, which can be used highly effectively for particular purposes. It should, then, be a staple on teacher training and education courses so that teachers are conversant with the theory which underpins DDL and the techniques required to apply it. Crucially, they should also have the critical awareness to know when the teaching context calls for it.

Further reading

O'Keeffe, A., McCarthy, M., & Carter, R. (2007). *From corpus to classroom*. Cambridge University Press. This book provides a very accessible summary of findings from spoken corpora which are of potential value in the classroom.

O'Keeffe, A., & McCarthy, M. (2022). *The Routledge handbook of corpus linguistics*. Routledge. Section 1 has chapters on building different types of corpora e.g. spoken or written. Section 2 has chapters on carrying our corpus research for different purposes e.g. lexis or grammar. Section 3 offers chapters relating to corpora and language pedagogy and language acquisition.

Timmis, I. (2015). *Corpus linguistics for ELT: Research and practice*. Routledge. This book covers corpus research in various domains, e.g. lexis and grammar, and has a chapter on using corpora in the classroom. It also has tasks for readers to carry out and points for discussion.

References

Adel, A. (2010). Using corpora to teach academic writing: Challenges for the direct approach. In M. C. Campoy-Cubillo, B. Belles-Fortuno, & L. Gea-Valor (Eds.), *Corpus-based approaches to English language teaching* (pp. 39–55). Continuum.

Allan, R. (2009). Can a graded reader corpus provide 'authentic' input? *ELT Journal, 63*(1), 23–32. https://doi.org/10.1093/elt/ccn011_23

Alsolami, T., & Assrar, A. (2020). Saudi EFL learners' perceptions of the use of corpora in academic writing teaching. *Studies in English Language Teaching, 8*(4), 94–111. https://doi.org/10.22158/selt.v8n4p94

Anthony, L. (2019). AntConc (Version 3.5.8) [Computer Software]. Waseda University. https://www. laurenceanthony.net/software

Asik, A., Vural, A. S., & Akpinar, K. D. (2016). Lexical awareness and development through Data Driven Learning: Attitudes and beliefs of EFL learners. *Journal of Education and Training Studies,* *4*(3), 87–96.

Aston, G. (Ed.). (2001). *Learning with corpora.* Athelstan.

Bernardini, S. (2001). Spoilt for choice: A learner explores general language corpora. In G. Aston (Ed.), *Learning with corpora* (pp. 220–249). Athelstan.

BNC Consortium. (2007). British National Corpus (version 3, BNC XML ed.). https://www.english-corpora.org/bnc/

Boulton, A. (2009). Testing the limits of data-driven learning: Language proficiency and training. *ReCALL, 21*(1), 37–54. https://doi.org/10.1017/S0958344009000068

Boulton, A. (2012). Corpus consultation for ESP: A review of empirical research. In A. Boulton, S. Carter-Thomas, & E. Rowley-Jolivet (Eds.), *Corpus-informed research and learning in ESP: Issues and applications* (pp. 261–291). Benjamins. https://doi.org/10.1075/scl.52.11bou

Boulton, A. (2016). Integrating corpus tools and techniques in ESP courses. *La Revue de Geras, 16,* 113–137. https://doi.org/10.4000/asp.4826

Boulton, A., & Cobb, T. (2017). Corpus use in language learning: A meta-analysis. *Language Learning,* *67*(2), 348–393. https://doi.org/10.1111/lang.12224

Braun, S. (2005). From pedagogically relevant corpora to authentic language learning contents. *ReCALL, 17*(1), 47–64. https://doi.org/10.1017/S0958344005000510

Braun, S. (2006). ELISA – A pedagogically enriched corpus for language learning purposes. In S. Braun, K. Kohn, & J. Mukherjee (Eds.), *Corpus technology and language pedagogy: New resources, new tools, new methods* (pp. 25–47). Peter Lang.

Breyer, Y. (2009). Learning and teaching with corpora: Reflections by student teachers. *Computer Assisted Language Learning, 22*(2), 153–172. https://doi.org/10.1080/09588220902778328

Chambers, A. (2010). What is data-driven learning? In A. O'Keeffe & M. McCarthy (Eds.), *The Routledge handbook of corpus linguistics* (pp. 345–359). Routledge. https://doi.org/10.4324/9780203856949

Charles, M. (2018). Corpus-assisted editing for doctoral students: More than just concordancing. *Journal of English for Academic Purposes, 36,* 15–25. https://doi.org/10.1016/j.jeap.2018.08.003

Chen, M., Flowerdew, J., & Anthony, L. (2019). Introducing in-service English language teachers to data-driven learning for academic writing. *System, 87.* https://doi.org/10.1016/j.system. 2019.102148

Cook, G. (1998). "The uses of reality". A reply to Ron Carter. *ELT Journal, 52*(1), 57–63. https://doi.org/10.1093/elt/52.1.5

Corino, E., & Onesti, C. (2019). Data-driven learning: A scaffolding methodology for CLIL and LSP teaching and learning. *Frontiers of Education, 19,* 1–12. https://doi.org/10.3389/feduc.2019.00007

Crosthwaite, P. (2017). Retesting the limits of data-driven learning: Feedback and error correction. *CALL, 30*(6), 447–473. https://doi.org/10.1080/09588221.2017.1312462

Curado Fuentes, A. (2002). Exploitation and assessment of a business English corpus through language learning tasks. *ICAME Journal, 26,* 5–32. http://gandalf.aksis.uib.no/icame/ij26/curadofuen.pdf

Curado Fuentes, A. (2003). The use of corpora and IT in a comparative evaluation approach for oral business English. *ReCALL, 15*(2), 189–201. https://doi.org/10.1017/S0958344003000521

Davies, M. (2008). Corpus of Contemporary American English. https://www.english-corpora.org/coca/

Dörk, M., & Knight, D. (2015). WordWanderer: A navigational approach to text visualisation. *Corpora,* *10*(1), 83–94. https://doi.org/10.3366/cor.2015.0067

Fan, M., & Xunfeng, X. (2002). An evaluation of an online bilingual corpus for the self-learning of legal English. *System, 30*(1), 47–63. https://doi.org/10.1016/S0346-251X(01)00052-5

Flowerdew, J. (1993). Concordancing as a tool in course design. *System, 21*(2), 231–244. https://doi.org/10.1016/0346-251X(93)90044-H

Friginal, E. (2018). *Corpus linguistics for English teachers: Tools, online resources, and classroom.* Routledge.

Garside, R. (1987). The CLAWS word-tagging system. In R. Garside, G. Leech, & G. Sampson (Eds.), *The computational analysis of English: A corpus-based approach.* Longman. https://doi.org/10.1016/0306-4573(89)90051

Gavioli, L. (2005). *Exploring corpora for ESP learning.* Benjamins. https://doi.org/10.1075/scl.21

Gilmore, A. (2009). Using online corpora to develop students' writing skills. *ELT Journal, 63*(1), 363–372. https://doi.org/10.1093/elt/ccn056

Gilquin, G., & Granger, S. (2010). How can data-driven learning be used in language teaching? In A. O'Keeffe & M. McCarthy (Eds.), *The Routledge handbook of corpus linguistics* (pp. 359–371). Routledge. https://doi.org/10.4324/9780203856949

Götz, S. (2012). Testing task types in data-driven learning: Benefits and limitations. In K. Biebighäuser, M. Zibelius, & T. Schmidt (Eds.), *Aufgaben 2.0 - konzepte, materialien und methoden für das fremdsprachenlehren und lernen mit digitalen medien* (pp. 249–276). Narr.

Götz, S., & Mukherjee, J. (2006). Evaluation of data-driven learning in university teaching: A project report. In S. Braun, K. Kohn, & J. Mukherjee (Eds.), *Corpus technology and language pedagogy: New resources, new tools, new methods.* Peter Lang.

Granger, S. (2017). Learner corpora in foreign language education. In S. Thorne & S. May (Eds.), *Language, education and technology. Encyclopedia of language and education* (3rd ed.) (pp. 427–440). Springer. https://doi.org/10.1007/978-3-319-02237-6_33

Hoey, M., & O'Donnell, M. B. (2007). Death to the topic sentence: How we really paragraph. In L. Yiu-nam (Ed.), *Selected papers from the sixteenth international symposium on English teaching* (pp. 60–76). English Teachers' Association/ROC.

Jablonkai, R., Forti, L., Castello, M., Salengros-Iguenane, I., Schaeffer-Lacroix, E., & Vyatkana, N. (2020). Data-driven learning for languages other than English: The cases of French, German, Italian, and Spanish. In K. M. Frederiksen, S. Larsen, L. Bradley, & S. Thouësny (Eds.), *CALL for widening participation: Short papers from EUROCALL 2020* (pp. 132–137). Research-publishing.net. https://doi.org/10.14705/rpnet.2020.48.1177

Johns, T. (1991). Should you be persuaded: Two samples of data-driven learning materials. In T. Johns, & P. King (Eds.), *Classroom concordancing* (pp. 1–16). Centre for English Language Studies, University of Birmingham.

Kennedy, C., & Miceli, T. (2001). An evaluation of intermediate students' approach to corpus investigation. *Language Learning and Technology, 5*(3), 77–90. https://dx.doi.org/10125/44567

Koester, A. (2010). Building small specialized corpora. In A. O'Keeffe & M. McCarthy (Eds.), *The Routledge handbook of corpus linguistics* (pp. 66–79). Routledge. https://doi.org/10.4324/9780203856949

Lee, D., & Swales, J. (2006). A corpus-based EAP course for NNS doctoral students: Moving from available specialized corpora to self-compiled corpora. *ESP, 25*(1), 56–75. https://doi.org/10.1016/j.esp.2005.02.010

Lee, H., Warschauer, M., & Lee, J. H. (2017). The effects of corpus use on second language vocabulary learning: A multilevel meta-analysis. *Applied Linguistics, 40*(5), 721–753. https://doi.org/10.1093/APPLIN/AMY012

Leech, G. (1997). Teaching and language corpora: A convergence. In A. Wichmann, S. Fligelstone, A. McEnery, & G. Knowles (Eds.), *Teaching and language corpora* (pp. 1–23). Addison Wesley Longman.

Leńko-Szymańska, A. (2014). Is this enough? A qualitative evaluation of the effectiveness of a teacher-training course on the use of corpora in language education. *ReCALL, 18*(1), 83–104. https://doi.org/10.1017/S095834401400010X

Lin, H. M. (2016). Effects of corpus-aided language learning in the EFL grammar classroom: A case study of students' learning attitudes and teachers' perceptions in Taiwan. *TESOL Quarterly, 50*(4), 871–893. https://doi.org/10.1002/tesq.250

Lin, M. (2019). Becoming a DDL teacher in English grammar classes: A pilot study. *The Journal of Language Teaching and Learning, 1,* 70–82.

Luo, Q. (2016). The effects of data-driven learning activities on EFL learners' writing development. *Springer Plus, 5,* 1–13. https://doi.org/10.1186/s40064-016-2935-5

Luo, Q., & Zhou, J. (2017). Data-driven learning in second language writing class: A survey of empirical studies. *iJET, 12*(3), 182–196. https://doi.org/10.3991/ijetv12/2i03.6523

Meunier, F. (2020). Data-driven learning: From classroom scaffolding to sustainable practices. *EL.LE, 8*(2), 423–434. https://doi.org/10.30687/ELLE/2280-6792/2019/02/010

Mizumoto, A., & Chujo, K. (2015). A meta-analysis of data-driven learning approach in the Japanese EFL classroom. *English Corpus Studies, 22,* 1–18.

Mukherjee, J. (2004). Bridging the gap between applied corpus linguistics and the reality of English language teaching in Germany. In U. Connor & T. Upton (Eds.), *Applied corpus linguistics – A multidimensional perspective* (pp. 239–50). Rodopi. https://doi.org/10.1163/9789004333772_014

Naismith, B. (2016). Integrating corpus tools on intensive CELTA courses. *ELT Journal, 71*(3), 273–283. https://doi.org/10.1093/elt/ccw076

O'Keeffe, A., & McCarthy, M. (2010). *The Routledge handbook of corpus linguistics.* Routledge. https://doi.org/10.4324/9780203856949

Pérez-Paredes, P., Sánchez-Tornel, M., Calero, J., & Jiménez, P. (2011). Tracking learners' actual uses of corpora: Guided vs non-guided corpus consultation. *Computer Assisted Language Learning, 24*(3), 233–53. https://doi.org/10.1080/09588221.2010.539978

Pérez-Paredes, P., Sánchez-Tornel, M., & Alcaraz Calero, J. M. (2012). Learners' search patterns during corpus-based focus-on-form activities. *International Journal of Corpus Linguistics, 17*, 483–516. https://doi.org/10.1075/ijcl.17.4.02par

Poole, R. (2018). *A guide to using corpora for English language learners.* Edinburgh University Press. https://doi.org/10.13136/2281-4582/2020.i15.644

Römer, U. (2006). Pedagogical applications of corpora: Some reflections on the current scope and a wish list for future developments. *ZAA, 54*(2), 121–134. https://doi.org/10.1515/zaa-2006-0204

Sinclair, J. (1991). *Corpus, concordance and collocation.* OUP. http://dx.doi.org/10.4236/jcc.2016.44010

Sinclair, S., & Rockwell, G. (2016). Voyant Tools. [Web]. http://www.voyant-tools.org/

Sripicharn, P. (2010). How can we prepare learners for using language corpora? In A. O'Keeffe & M. McCarthy (Eds.), *The Routledge handbook of corpus linguistics* (pp. 371–385). https://doi.org/10.4324/9780203856949

Tekin, B., & Soruc, A. (2016). Using corpus-assisted learning activities to assist vocabulary development in English. *The Turkish Online Journal of Educational Technology,* 1270–1283.

Thurstun, J., & Candlin, C. N. (1998). Concordancing and the teaching of the vocabulary of academic English. *English for Specific Purposes, 17*, 267–280.

Timmis, I. (2015). *Corpus linguistics for ELT: Research and practice.* Routledge. https://doi.org/10.4324/9781315715537

Tomlinson, B. (2011). (Ed.). *Materials development in language teaching* (pp. 1–35). Cambridge University Press.

Tribble, C. (1997). Improvising corpora for ELT: Quick-and-dirty ways of developing corpora for language teaching. In J. Melia & B. Lewandowska-Tomaszczyk (Eds.), *PALC '97: Proceedings.* Lodz University Press. http://www.ctribble.co.uk/text/Palc.htm

Turnbull, J., & Burston, J. (1998). Towards independent concordance work for students: Lessons from a case study. *ON-CALL, 12*(2), 10–22. http://www.cltr.uq.edu.au/oncall/turnbull122.html

Vincent, B., & Nesi, H. (2018). The BAWE Quicklinks Project: A new DDL resource for university students. *Lidil, 58*, 1–18. https://doi.org/10.4000/lidil.5306

Willis, D. (2003). *Rules, patterns and words: Grammar and lexis in ELT.* Oxford University Press. https://doi.org/10.1017/CBO9780511733

Varley, S. (2009). I'll just look that up in the concordancer: Integrating corpus consultation into the language learning environment. *Computer Assisted Language Learning, 22*(2), 133–15. https://doi.org/10.1080/09588220902778294

Vyatkina, N. (2020). Corpora as open educational resources for language teaching. *Foreign Language Annals, 53*(2), 359–370. https://doi.org/10.1111/flan.12464

Yao, G. (2019). Vocabulary learning through data-driven learning in the context of Spanish as a foreign language. *Research in Corpus Linguistics, 7*, 18–46. https://doi.org/10.32714/ricl.07.02

PART V

Corpora and corpus tools for English language teaching

29
EVALUATING CORPUS ANALYSIS TOOLS FOR THE CLASSROOM

Clinton Hendry and Emily Sheepy

29.1 Introduction

Learning a language is a challenging proposition. Corpora can provide both metrics and materials needed to personalize instruction according to students' needs (Hendry & Sheepy, 2019). Corpus tools empower teachers to incorporate authentic language material (Boulton & Cobb, 2017), and students find them useful for learning vocabulary, collocations, and register awareness (Pérez-Paredes, 2019). However, many corpus-based tools are costly or not user-friendly, presenting a challenge for teachers and students (Pérez-Paredes, 2019).

In this chapter, we present a practical demonstration of a low-cost method of evaluating corpus-based language learning tools before selecting them for use in the classroom. We will first present key concepts and definitions from human-computer interaction and educational technology literature relevant to evaluating educational software and briefly review evidence of the importance of usability in the adoption and effectiveness of educational software. Next, we apply a general-purpose usability heuristic evaluation method to describe the interfaces of three freely available online corpus-based tools. These illustrative cases demonstrate how heuristic evaluation can be applied to systematically evaluate the affordances of corpus-based tools and make recommendations for their application in instructional contexts.

29.2 Review of current state of research

In this section, we first define usability as a construct, then discuss the impact of usability on the adaption and effectiveness of educational software in relation to Cognitive Load Theory (Sweller *et al.*, 1998). Next, we briefly review instructional applications of corpus tools in vocabulary learning.

29.2.1 Usability of educational software

Research into corpus linguistics and data-driven learning has shown that learners can benefit from using corpus-based language learning tools (Boulton & Cobb, 2017). However, learners will only use a tool as long as it helps them to reliably achieve their goals. Thus, usability limits how much a learner can benefit from computer-assisted learning. Usability, or ease of use, is a multidimensional construct that is well researched by software engineering and human-computer interaction specialists. The International Standards Organization defines usability as "The extent to which a product can be used by specified users to achieve specified goals with effectiveness, efficiency and satisfaction in a specified context of use" (ISO, 2018). Poor usability increases the effort required on the part of the user to complete their tasks. Sweller *et al.*'s (1998) Cognitive Load Theory (CLT) predicts that this additional effort, or cognitive load, negatively impacts learning. CLT has two key assumptions: (1) that humans have limited cognitive processing resources (i.e., working memory), and (2) that memory limitations can be overcome with the support of cognitive structures (schema) and automation.

CLT proposes three categories of cognitive load in learners: intrinsic, extraneous, and germane cognitive load (Sweller *et al.*, 1998). Intrinsic cognitive load directly arises from the complexity of the target learning task; this type of cognitive load cannot be reduced without compromising understanding and is moderated by learner expertise (Sweller *et al.*, 1998). Germane cognitive load describes the effort the learner expends as they construct new knowledge, for example, when consciously searching for patterns in learning materials, or when applying metacognitive processes such as problem construction and self-monitoring (Schnotz & Kürschner, 2007). Extraneous cognitive load describes the cognitive resource demand caused by the instructional design, including the materials and learning environment (Sweller *et al.*, 1998). Bad design presents information inappropriately or requires students to complete irrelevant activities, drawing processing power away from the target task (Hollender *et al.*, 2010). Ideally, the instructional design should minimize extraneous cognitive load on the learner.

Hollender *et al.* (2010) proposed that CLT be modified to account for two sources of extraneous cognitive load: (1) load induced by the instructional design and (2) load caused by software usage. CALL practitioners can proactively reduce extraneous demands arising from the design of the software by evaluating and mitigating potential sources of user error and frustration. These concerns go beyond merely inconveniencing learners. Poor usability cannot only prevent a learner from benefiting from their time on task, but also create inequity in the classroom. Educational software that is difficult to use disproportionately harms students with special accessibility needs, low technological competency, and low reading ability (Damarin, 2000).

29.2.2 Instructional applications of corpus tools

Corpora have been used to research a variety of linguistic structures for pedagogical and research purposes. For example, corpora informed the development of instructional materials and have been used directly by learners to explore language in context (Timmis, 2015). For this chapter, we focus on applications of corpus tools in vocabulary instruction because vocabulary is a strong predictor of language proficiency in general, and reading proficiency in particular (Nation, 2006). Vocabulary instruction is often minimized in the classroom because of the daunting number of words a person needs to learn to speak a language, the time required to properly teach vocabulary, and because many instructors believe there are easier ways to learn vocabulary besides explicit instruction (Nation, 2012). However, explicit vocabulary instruction of high-frequency or domain-specific technical vocabulary can lead to early gains for learners, enabling them to achieve sufficient reading comprehension to continue reading on their own (Nation, 2012). Like Nation (2012), we argue that corpus-informed vocabulary instruction can help learners to acquire vocabulary quickly and efficiently by selecting relevant target vocabulary based on student needs. As corpus tools become more accessible, teachers can instruct their students in their use, allowing learners to use them to improve through self-regulated learning, which has been associated with higher overall academic achievement (Winne, 2018).

Boulton and Cobb (2017) describe two major purposes instructors have for using corpus analysis tools: (1) to decide what to teach based on frequency of occurrence and typical usage and (2) to use as a source of authentic language samples for use in teaching and assessment. The authors also conclude that learners can use corpus analysis tools to support vocabulary acquisition (1) as a reference to identify important words to study, (2) as a reference to check for patterns in typical usage in authentic texts, and (3) to evaluate their own writing by comparing their work with authentic examples of language in use. We will briefly review four forms of corpus analysis that support vocabulary learning: frequency analysis and keyword analysis, useful for identifying target vocabulary; and concordance analysis and collocation analysis, useful for providing samples of typical usage.

29.2.2.1 *Identifying target vocabulary with frequency and keyword analysis*

Frequency analysis involves ranking vocabulary by the number of times a word appears in a text, corpus, or entire language. Frequency analysis is useful for anticipating learner needs, and for generating instructional materials sensitive to vocabulary demands. The more frequent a word is in a language, the more likely a learner is to have encountered it, so word prevalence estimates from large corpora can be used to test readability (Nation, 2006). The frequency of a word in a specific text can also be used to predict whether a word appears enough times in a text for incidental learning to take place (Cobb, 2007; Hendry & Ruivivar, 2019). Finally, removing low-frequency vocabulary from a text can make it easier to read, a strategy employed when developing graded readers (Cobb, 2007).

Instructors can use frequency data to generate lists of target vocabulary to be provided as reference materials or incorporated into interactive resources such as flashcards. Alternatively, learners can be taught how to select their own vocabulary (Boulton & Cobb, 2017). These targeted lists can also be used to generate samples of low-frequency or technical vocabulary in authentic texts using concordance analysis.

Another instructional application of ranked frequency data is to evaluate learners' vocabulary use; a corpus composed of learner writing samples can be used to compare students' language use with that of native speakers to identify areas of weakness, or to monitor development. Keyword analysis automatically compares ranked frequency lists to identify words that appear with greater frequency in one corpus when compared with a reference corpus (Brezina & Gablasova, 2018). Keyword analysis is a straightforward method for instructors or students to efficiently identify vocabulary that are of particular importance within a certain context. For example, Tongpoon-Patanasorn (2018) combined keyword analysis with expert evaluation to identify technical vocabulary in Business English.

29.2.2.2 *Identifying typical word environments with concordancing and collocation analysis*

Concordancers are common corpus analysis tools that search texts based on a word or phrase provided by the user, then provide every instance of that word in context. The tools output concordance lines, presenting the target word or phrase and a number of words on either side. One public and easy to use concordancing tool is available for the Corpus of Contemporary American English (COCA; see Figure 29.1).

Clinton Hendry and Emily Sheepy

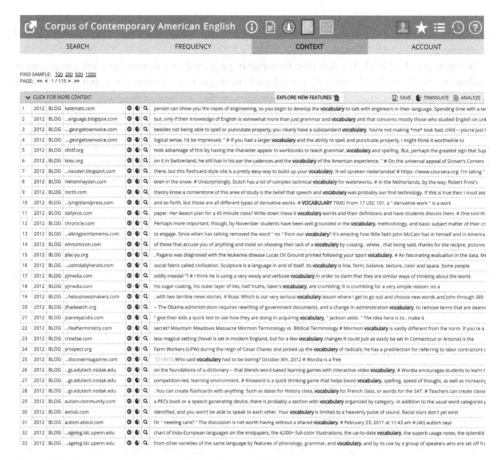

Figure 29.1   The concordancer for COCA (Davies, 2008)

In data-driven learning (DDL), learners directly use corpora to search for authentic examples of language to better understand how a word is used or its grammatical properties (Timmis, 2015). Nation (2012) argues that to learn a word requires that a learner knows its form, meaning, and use, and that understanding a word's use requires knowledge of its functions, frequency, and *collocations*. Corpus tools that facilitate collocation identification can help learners improve their knowledge of target vocabulary or increase correct collocation use in their writing. Concordance lines and collocation visualization tools in corpus analysis software can both help learners recognize and remember collocations.

DDL approaches promote deep processing of vocabulary and therefore support long-term retention, but also place high cognitive load on learners (Boulton & Cobb, 2017; Lee & Lin, 2019). DDL research has shown that without teacher instruction, concordancing interfaces can be difficult to comprehend (Boulton & Cobb, 2017). Some theorists argue that the cognitive load intrinsic to inductive vocabulary learning can be reduced by providing learners references such as lists of word meanings and usage guidelines to learners to guide their exploration with the corpus analysis tool (Chan & Liou, 2005; Lee & Lin, 2019). Some suggest that the cognitive load intrinsic to inductive vocabulary learning can be reduced by providing

440

reference materials such as definitions and usage guidelines to learners in addition to access to the corpus analysis tool (Chan & Liou, 2005; Lee & Lin, 2019). They argue that this can reduce learner anxiety and reduce the time required to generalize patterns that they observe in the corpus (Lee & Lin, 2019). While their recommendation offers a means of reducing the intrinsic complexity of learning with a corpus, it does not address the need to reduce or eliminate extraneous cognitive load deriving from the usability of the DDL tool.

29.3 Core issues: Usability of CALL tools

Language instruction has begun to move ever more into online spaces, requiring more knowledge and skills from teachers to facilitate their students' learning (Godwin-Jones, 2015). However, teachers can find computer-driven learning uncomfortable in general (Boulton & Cobb, 2017), and lack of training contributes to teacher reluctance to adopt new technologies (Godwin-Jones, 2015). Therefore, evaluating the usability of teaching tools is important to promote DDL and other corpus-based approaches to pedagogical practitioners.

Chapelle's (2001) evaluation framework for CALL instructional designs considers language learning potential, learner fit, meaning focus, authenticity, impact, and practicality of the proposed instructional intervention. Chapelle recommends evaluating the "practicality" of a CALL application using expert evaluation to assess whether or not the hardware, software, and personnel resources available are sufficient for the learning task to succeed (Chapelle, 2001). However, Chapelle's framework does not provide a specific protocol for assessing practicality. Consequently, we recommend that practitioners look to the usability engineering literature for principled and well-researched guidelines for evaluating software.

Poor usability can limit the adoption of new instructional technologies by negatively affecting the perceived usefulness of a tool (Venkatesh & Davis, 2000). Davis' (1989) Technology Acceptance Model (TAM) aims to predict whether people will reject or accept new technologies; in this model, intention to use new technology is most strongly predicted by perceived usefulness – the user's perception that technology will enhance their job performance and perceived ease-of-use – the perception that the technology can be used with minimal effort (Venkatesh & Davis, 2000). Since then, the TAM model has been found effective in a wide number of contexts (Granić & Marangunić, 2019; Venkatesh & Davis, 2000), including CALL and MALL environments (e.g., Barret *et al.*, 2020; Kim & Lee, 2016). Poor perceived ease-of-use lowers perceived usefulness, in turn lowering users' intention to use tools in the future (Venkatesh & Davis, 2000). This suggests that though corpus tools have demonstrated practical and pedagogical benefits, the literature suggests that if they are (1) hard to use or (2) perceived to be hard to use, then widespread adoption is not likely.

29.3.1 Heuristic evaluation

There are many different methods and metrics employed to evaluate usability, including experimental designs, field studies, and surveys. Metrics such as error rates, task completion times, and satisfaction ratings can be used to monitor effectiveness, efficiency, and user satisfaction. However, many empirical methods for evaluating usability are too costly and time-consuming to deploy easily.

Heuristic evaluation was developed in software engineering as one of multiple low-cost predictive usability evaluation techniques developed to identify likely sources of inefficiency, error, and user frustration before a tool is used in the field. Heuristic evaluation requires the evaluators to examine the user interface of a tool and comment on its compliance with a set of usability principles (Nielsen, 1995). Though first developed for usability engineering, the method has been adopted to evaluate a variety of instructional tools such as educational games and simulations (Vieira *et al.*, 2019), learning management systems (Salas *et al.*, 2019), and mobile learning applications (Kumar & Mohite, 2018). It is also a recommended evaluation approach for teachers to use when evaluating instructional tools for use in the classroom (Squire & Preece, 1999).

Many heuristic evaluation frameworks have been developed, but heuristic sets vary widely in quality and are often developed through informal methods (Anganes *et al.*, 2016). In the future, validated CALL-specific frameworks for usability evaluation may become more abundant, and evaluators may benefit from tools such as the Heuristic Quality Scale, developed to help evaluators select appropriate heuristic sets (Anganes *et al.*, 2016). However, at the moment, no heuristic evaluation frameworks are as well documented and widely cited as Nielsen's (1995) framework for evaluating graphical user interfaces.

29.3.1.1 Nielsen's usability heuristics

In a heuristic evaluation, a small group of evaluators judge to what extent a software interface complies with recognized usability principles. The aim is to identify likely sources of user error and frustration (Nielsen, 1995). Nielsen's framework comprises ten interface design principles known to impact users' effectiveness, efficiency, and satisfaction. Table 29.1 presents Nielsen's ten heuristics, with examples of comments reviewers might give in applying the criteria to an instructional tool.

We highly recommend that practitioners refer to the online resource library offered by Nielsen Norman Group, which includes many articles and videos that define and illustrate these principles (https://www.nngroup.com/topic/heuristic-evaluation/). Nielsen (1995) recommends inviting 3–5 evaluators to participate in the process; the goal is to document as many varied observations as possible, and each evaluator may provide a unique perspective. However, even a single evaluator can produce valuable insights (Nielsen, 1995). Note that different task flows within the same software tool can yield different ratings, even for a single evaluator. Functions offered within the tool may be delivered using a variety of dialogs and with varied levels of support documentation.

29.3.2 An adapted usability heuristic evaluation protocol for CALL practitioners

Below, we propose a modified evaluation protocol that adapts Nielsen's general-purpose protocol for practical application in the CALL context.

1. Select instructional goals and methods of interest.

    For example, your goal as an instructor may be to offer targeted vocabulary instruction focused on workplace discourse for nurses. To achieve that objective, your goal might be to create a list of relatively low-frequency words that are of importance in the medical context.

2. Select tools that support those learning outcomes.

    These will be the subject of your evaluation.

Table 29.1 Usability heuristics adapted from Nielsen (1995)

1.1 Heuristic	1.2 Sample positive comment	1.3 Sample negative comment
Visibility of system status 1.4 The system should always keep users informed about what is going on, through appropriate feedback within reasonable time.	1.5 "Status updates appear at the bottom of the screen while files are processing".	1.6 "The system shows a status bar while things are processing, but if you have multiple files to process, you can't tell how many have been processed".
Match between system and the real world 1.7 Use words, phrases, and concepts familiar to the user. Make information appear in a natural and logical order.	1.8 "Requires very little technical vocabulary for understanding [the interface]. Anybody familiar with Windows will find it intuitive".	1.9 "Terms and labels may be familiar if you do corpus research, but most of the names [of functions] are obscure".
User control and freedom 1.10 Users often choose functions by mistake and need a clearly marked "emergency exit." Support undo and redo.	1.11 "When you [click] "back," your previous settings are still in place".	1.12 "You can't save your settings".
Consistency and standards 1.13 Users should not wonder whether different words, situations, or actions mean the same thing. Follow platform conventions.	1.14 "You load the corpus the same way for all functions in the tool".	1.15 "This tool doesn't follow UI conventions used by most websites".
Error prevention 1.16 Prevent problems from occurring in the first place. Either eliminate error-prone conditions or check for them and present users with a confirmation option.	1.17 "Many warnings are given in advance (e.g., maximum size of text files)".	1.18 "The side-to-side arrangement of the checkbox options makes it hard to tell where to click - this may lead to errors".
Recognition rather than recall 1.19 Minimize the user's memory load by making objects, actions, and options visible. Users should not have to remember information. Instructions for use of the system should be visible or easily retrievable.	1.20 "The options are all visible on the screen and are grouped".	1.21 "When you switch to another corpus you can't see all the options without clicking first".
Flexibility and efficiency of use 1.22 The system should cater to both inexperienced and experienced users. Allow users to tailor frequent actions.	1.23 "It's efficient. You can save settings to a file, and you can save or export your results for simple import into Excel or other tools".	1.24 "There's an advanced search button and dialogue but no shortcut to advanced settings for more experienced users."
Aesthetic and minimalist design 1.25 Dialogues should not contain irrelevant information.	1.26 "Looks like a generic visual basic program. Clean, easy to find things. More advanced options are in tabs such as File, Settings (which is fine)".	1.27 "There's a lot of information on the screen and it's not always clear that there's information unrelated to the task you're working on".

(Continued)

Table 29.1 Usability heuristics adapted from Nielsen (1995) *(Continued)*

1.1 Heuristic	*1.2 Sample positive comment*	*1.3 Sample negative comment*
Help users recognize, diagnose, and recover from errors 1.28 Error messages should be expressed in plain language, precisely indicate the problem, and suggest a solution.	1.29 "Many warnings are given in advance (e.g., Maximum size of text files). [...] If the text file is too big, eventually the website may say so".	1.30 "There are no error messages. I wouldn't have any idea what I was doing wrong".
Help and documentation 1.31 Help and documentation should be easy to search, and list concrete steps to be carried out.	1.32 "There is a question mark icon that always takes you to the help information for that tool".	1.33 "Instructions are incorporated on the screen. The instructions are task-focused but the language may not be obvious to novice users because there's a lot of jargon".

3. Select a heuristic set.

   We recommend Nielsen's general-purpose heuristic set because it is a well-documented and recognized set of design principles characteristic of interfaces that are easy to use. Note that most widely used heuristic sets are intended to identify technical problems that are likely to arise when using software. The appropriate fit of your instructional goals and methods for the learners and subject matter of interest must be evaluated using other methods.

4. Identify benchmark tasks.

   Apply CALL and pedagogical expertise to identify typical tasks users are expected to complete. Articulate expected outcomes grounded in instructional goals. By identifying specific tasks to perform, you ensure that the evaluator visits the interface dialogues that the target users (students or instructors) are likely to encounter.

5. Train the evaluators.

   While it is best to include a usability expert, evaluators with domain expertise and even end users can be trained to apply heuristics. Together, the evaluators should review the list of heuristics, discuss definitions in relation to illustrative examples, and review the task list to ensure that each evaluator understands what outcomes are expected.

6. Conduct independent evaluations of the tools.

   Each evaluator independently reviews the interfaces required to complete each task flow, identifying potential problems, and recording ratings. Raters can fill out a reporting form or speak aloud to a notetaker.

7. Debrief.

   The evaluators compare and discuss their observations. They should discuss any difficulty they had in evaluating each task flow, or in applying the criteria effectively. Areas of strong discrepancy in ratings should be examined in greater detail to examine what experiences and observations informed each rater.

8. Synthesize and report your overall recommendations for practice.

The evaluators should then negotiate heuristic ratings for each task. Problems identified during the review should be discussed and documented with a statement about the severity of the issue. Finally, overall recommendations about the strengths and weaknesses of each tool with respect to the benchmark tasks should be reported.

29.3.2.1 Limitations of the protocol

Heuristic evaluation is a predictive method intended to uncover strengths and potential problems that may impact users' effectiveness, efficiency, and satisfaction with a tool; the outcomes should not be generalized to other tools, or to all users. It is a process that facilitates principled judgment of a tool's suitability for classroom use. The evaluators predict that certain features will be easier or harder to use in practice, and recommendations and concerns that emerge can be empirically validated with learners and teachers in laboratory and field studies.

This application of the framework uses the heuristic set to guide review and conversation. It is very important for the evaluators to discuss and to compare their observations, as each person may have had quite different experiences of the software: a single piece of software may provide multiple methods of completing the same task, system errors may occur at random, or human factors such as visual acuity and fatigue might affect how evaluators rate a tool.

29.4 Recommendations for practice: Heuristic evaluation of three corpus tools for the classroom

In this section, we present three case studies to demonstrate the application of this usability evaluation protocol to evaluate three free corpus-based tools for use in vocabulary instruction.

We selected Lextutor, AntConc, and LancsBox for evaluation. They are available for free online, and all have potential applications in vocabulary instruction. In what follows we briefly introduce each tool.

Lextutor (v.8.3)

Lextutor (Cobb, 2020) is a website developed by Tom Cobb. It is designed to be a free and efficient tool for data-driven learning and corpus-based research, is regularly updated, and is compatible with a variety of operating systems and web browsers (Cobb, 2020). Lextutor enables instructors to generate word usage examples using concordance lines in up to four languages and to evaluate vocabulary demands for texts to support personalized instruction (Cobb, 2020).

AntConc (3.5.9)

AntConc (Anthony, 2020) is a free, downloadable corpus analysis tool. The tool allows instructors to rank vocabulary within a document based on frequency, create concordance lines, create word lists of target vocabulary, and more (Anthony, 2020). Unlike Lextutor, AntConc requires that corpora for analysis be uploaded.

LancsBox (5.0.1)

LancsBox (Brezina *et al.*, 2020), created by researchers at Lancaster University, is a free, downloadable corpus tool which provides lexical frequency analysis tools, concordance, and collocation analysis tools. Similar to AntConc, the user must upload the corpora for analysis, and it can perform similar analyses. However, LancsBox has a unique graphical interface that may be easier for some to use.

29.4.1 Definition of the benchmark tasks

Based on our review of instructional applications of corpus analysis tools, a CALL subject matter expert identified instructional goals and benchmark tasks for use in the evaluation. Table 29.2 summaries the tasks and indicates whether each task is supported in each of the three tools.

Because the three tools use different names for these functions, we identified the relevant task flows specific to each tool, to ensure that the two evaluators would review the same interfaces.

29.4.2 Procedure

Following the protocol outlined in "An adapted usability heuristic evaluation protocol for CALL practitioners" (see Section 29.3.2), we began by identifying our instructional goals and methods. We are interested in improving learner vocabulary instruction through corpus analysis using

Table 29.2 Instructional goals and benchmark tasks for the heuristic evaluation

Instructional goal	Benchmark Task	Functionality required	Lextutor	AntConc	LancsBox
Improve vocabulary targets for instruction	Create a word list from a reference corpus using frequency	Frequency analysis	Yes "VocabProfile"	Yes "Word List"	Yes "Words"
Improve vocabulary targets by identifying technical vocabulary.	Refine a word list by removing non-target vocabulary	Frequency analysis	Yes "VocabProfile"	Yes "Word List"	Yes "Words"
Improve vocabulary targets by identifying technical vocabulary.	Create a list of keywords	Keyword analysis	No	Yes "Keyword List"	Yes "Words"
Provide learners with examples of target vocabulary use	Create a list of concordance lines	Concordance analysis	Yes "Web concordance"	Yes "Concordance"	Yes "KWIC"
Provide learners with information on vocabulary use	Automatically identify collocations of target vocabulary	Collocation analysis	No	Yes "*Collocates*"	Yes "GraphColl"

four common corpus analysis methods: frequency analysis, concordance analysis, keyword analysis, and collocation analysis (Brezina & Gablasova, 2018). We selected three corpus tools for evaluation: Lextutor, AntConc, and LancsBox, and Nielsen's usability heuristics (1995) as our heuristic set.

One usability expert and one domain expert (the authors) acted as evaluators. After reviewing the benchmark tasks and heuristic definitions, each evaluator independently reviewed the tools. For each task (Frequency analysis, Keyword analysis, Concordance analysis, and Collocation analysis) performed using each software (Lextutor, AntConc, and LancsBox), each evaluator provided a score and written explanation for analysis. This was followed by a debrief and a report.

The evaluators applied a five-point scoring system to indicate a tool's compliance with each of the ten Nielsen criteria, where one indicated very poor compliance and five indicated excellent compliance. In the engineering context, Nielsen's framework is typically applied in a purely qualitative fashion, where issues are identified, listed, and each violation is rated for the severity of its impact on the user. In our protocol, we instead assigned overall scores pertaining to the level of compliance for each heuristic within each feature or workflow. Though our use of scoring was effectively a qualitative exercise, we have reported Cohen's linear-weighted kappa as an index of inter-rater agreement; this index is recommended as an indicator of how closely judges agree when assigning ratings on an ordinal scale (Cohen, 1968). However, in most practical applications calculating inter-rater agreement is not necessary. Our aim in using a scoring strategy was to enable us to quickly identify areas of consensus and strong disagreement, to facilitate further discussion and negotiation of our final evaluations.

29.4.3 Usability ratings of the selected corpus tools

Now we will present observations of the usability of each tool when performing the benchmark tasks using Nielsen's usability heuristic framework (Nielsen, 1995). We will compare their strengths and weaknesses and our overall evaluation for the use of these tools in instructional applications.

29.4.3.1 Lextutor

The web-based corpus analysis suite Lextutor (Cobb, 2020) provides many tools. We narrowed our evaluation to completing two benchmark tasks: (1) creating a word list based on lexical frequency data, and (2) creating concordance lines with the word "vocabulary" in the Academic General corpus. Table 29.3 presents our negotiated ratings.

Table 29.3 Overall negotiated ratings for Lextutor using Nielsen's (1995) usability heuristic framework

Heuristic (Nielsen, 1995)	Negotiated rating
Visibility of system status	3
Match between system and the real world	3
User control and freedom	4
Consistency and standard	3
Error prevention	3
Recognition rather than recall	3.5
Flexibility and efficiency of use	4
Aesthetic and minimalist design	2
Help users recognize, diagnose, and recover from errors	2.5
Help and documentation	2.5

Note: 1 = "Poor compliance", 3 = "Satisfactory compliance", 5 = "Excellent compliance". Cohen's linear-weighted κ = .4286 (95% CI, .1446 to .712) indicated "moderate" agreement between the two evaluator's judgments of compliance with the usability heuristics.

Freq. Level	Families (%)	Types (%)	Tokens (%)	Cumul. token (%)
K-1 :	384 (60.7)	496 (64.33)	2345 (86.7)	86.7
K-2 :	114 (18.0)	124 (16.08)	180 (6.7)	93.4
K-3 :	40 (6.3)	44 (5.71)	57 (2.1)	95.5
Coverage 95				
K-4 :	34 (5.4)	36 (4.67)	38 (1.4)	96.9
K-5 :	14 (2.2)	16 (2.08)	19 (0.7)	97.6
K-6 :	17 (2.7)	17 (2.20)	19 (0.7)	98.3
Coverage 98				
K-7 :	6 (0.9)	6 (0.78)	7 (0.3)	98.6
K-8 :	7 (1.1)	7 (0.91)	7 (0.3)	98.9
K-9 :	6 (0.9)	6 (0.78)	6 (0.2)	99.1
K-10 :	4 (0.6)	4 (0.52)	4 (0.1)	99.2
K-11 :	2 (0.3)	2 (0.26)	2 (0.1)	99.3
K-12 :	1 (0.2)	1 (0.13)	1 (0.0)	
K-13 :	2 (0.3)	2 (0.26)	4 (0.1)	99.4
K-14 :	1 (0.2)	1 (0.13)	1 (0.0)	
K-15 :				
K-16 :				
K-17 :	1 (0.2)	1 (0.13)	1 (0.0)	
K-18 :				
K-19 :				
K-20 :				
K-21 :				
K-22 :				
K-23 :				
K-24 :				
K-25 :				
Off-List:	??	8 (1.04)	14 (0.52)	99.92
Total (unrounded)	633+?	771 (100)	2705 (100)	≈100.00

Figure 29.2 Lextutor VocabProfile output

The VocabProfile tool within Lextutor is one of the simplest and most powerful tools available in Lextutor. It is an adaptation of Heatley *et al.* (2002) Range program. It can take a text file of up to 1 million words, and rank those words based on their frequency within various reference corpora, such as the Corpus of Contemporary English (COCA). Performing the analysis is relatively straightforward; the user inputs the target text and presses *Submit*. Figure 29.2 illustrates an output from Lextutor's VocabProfile tool.

Lextutor provides concordancers in four languages (English, French, German, and Spanish), with a variety of reference corpora to search from. The *Web Concordance* interface does not follow typical interface conventions. If the user follows the instructions from left to right (Figure 29.3), the tool outputs concordance lines using preloaded reference corpora on topics from general academic vocabulary to Shakespeare (Figure 29.4).

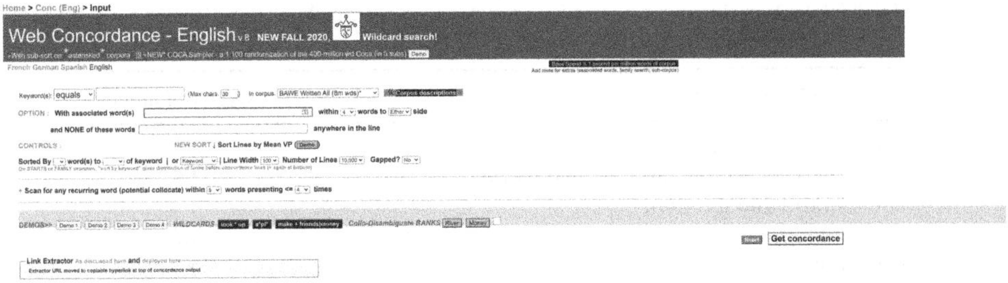

Figure 29.3 Concordancer menu from Lextutor (2020)

Figure 29.4 Lextutor concordancer results for the word *vocabulary* in the Academic General corpus

29.4.3.2 *AntConc*

AntConc (Anthony, 2020) supports a variety of functions including N-gram analysis that were not evaluated here. AntConc was evaluated with respect to three benchmark tasks: (1) creating a vocabulary list based on word frequency, (2) generating a Keyword list, and (3) generating examples of the environment in which a target word appears in a text. Table 29.4 presents our negotiated ratings.

Note that there was a significant discrepancy indicated by the low kappa coefficient. This difference attributable to a real difference in the experiences of the two evaluators. Although both evaluators were testing AntConc Build 3.5.9, we realized that the Windows and macOS versions did not have the same menu structure, and the Mac user was unable to access the Help documentation, and so assigned much lower ratings on the help and support dimension.

Table 29.4 Overall negotiated ratings for AntConc using Nielsen's (1995) usability heuristic framework

Heuristic (Nielsen, 1995)	Negotiated rating
Visibility of system status	4
Match between system and the real world	4.5
User control and freedom	3
Consistency and standard	4.5
Error prevention	3
Recognition rather than recall	3.5
Flexibility and efficiency of use	4.5
Aesthetic and minimalist design	4.5
Help users recognize, diagnose, and recover from errors	1
Help and documentation	3

Note: 1 = "Poor compliance", 3 = "Satisfactory compliance", 5= "Excellent compliance". Cohen's linear-weighted κ = .173 (95% CI, .1019 to .3728) indicates "slight" agreement between the two evaluator's judgments.

AntConc generates a ranked frequency list based on an uploaded text or corpus. These frequency lists describe how often each token appears within the text and allows one to compare tokens to each other. After uploading a corpus, the user must only go to the Word List tab and press start, and AntConc will then generate a word list (Figure 29.5).

AntConc's keyword function creates a word list of the most uniquely frequent words in a target corpus when compared to a reference corpus. The user clicks the Keyword List tab and loads the text. The steps for loading a reference corpus are unintuitive, requiring that the user select "Tool Preferences" from the Settings menu rather than the main menu. After the

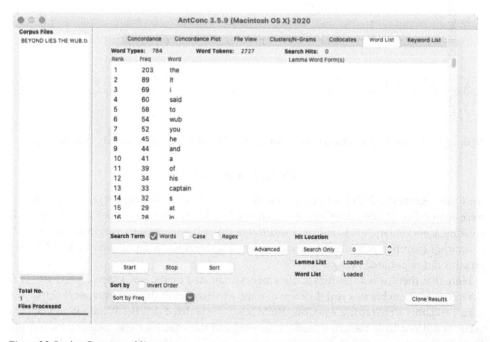

Figure 29.5 AntConc word list output

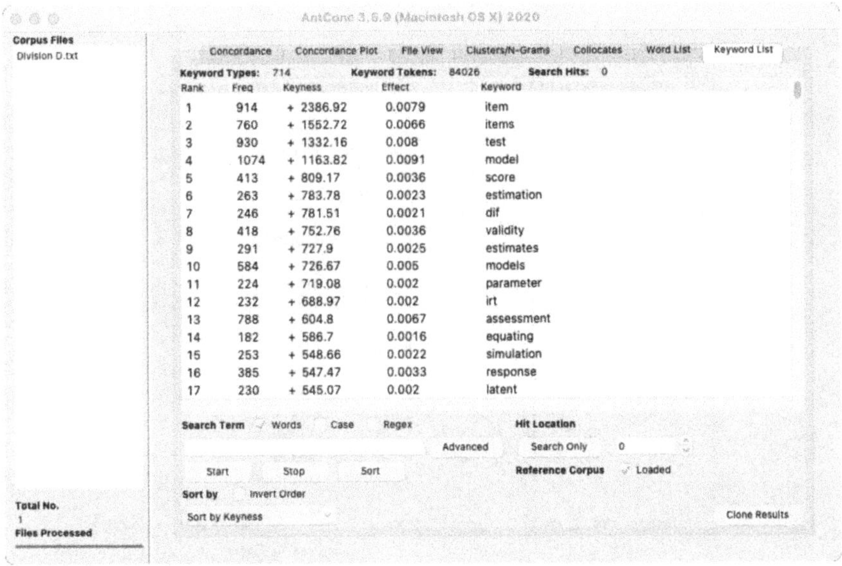

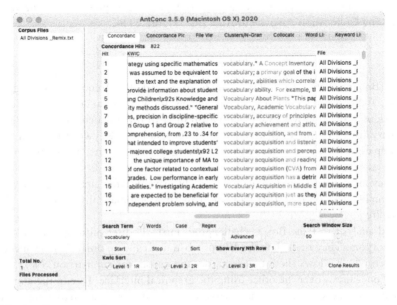

Figure 29.6 AntConc Keyword List output

reference corpus is loaded, the user only needs to return to the main menu and press Start to generate a Keyword list (Figure 29.6).

Concordance analysis is relatively simple in AntConc. The user can type in a target word into the Concordance tab search bar or click on a target word generated from any other analysis (such as a Word List). AntConc then generates a concordance list for the target word. Figure 29.7 illustrates the output obtained using Concordance in AntConc. The option to explore words identified through previous analyses is highly efficient.

Figure 29.7 AntConc concordance output

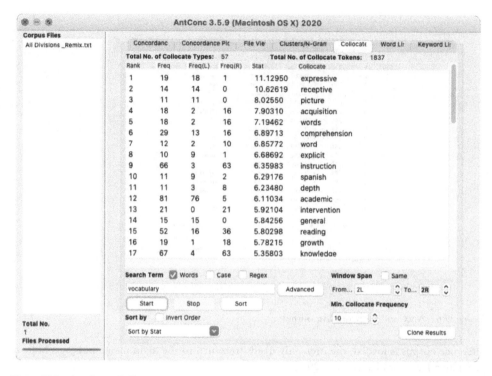

Figure 29.8 AntConc Collocates output

Collocation analysis is also a straightforward task in AntConc. The user must first choose the Collocates tab, then type in the target word (node) and press Start. The output was obtained using Collocation Analysis in AntConc (Figure 29.8).

29.4.3.3 LancsBox

LancsBox (Brezina *et al.*, 2020) offers many features, including frequency ranking, word list generation, and concordancing. This tool uniquely allows users to create data visualizations of collocations. LancsBox was evaluated with respect to three benchmark tasks: (1) creating a vocabulary list based on word frequency, (2) generating a Keyword list, and (3) generating examples of the environment in which a target word appears. Table 29.5 presents our negotiated ratings.

Frequency analysis in LancsBox is very straightforward. After uploading a target corpus, the user simply clicks on the *Words* tab, and LancsBox automatically generates a Word List ordered by frequency (Figure 29.9).

Keyword analysis in LancsBox is challenging. First, the user must upload the target and reference corpora. They then click the Words tab and expand an unlabeled tab at the bottom of the screen which allows them to select a second corpus for comparison. Next, they drag the icon of one corpus over the other using the graphical interface. Due to the complexity of the procedure, learners will require access to the support documentation to complete the task. The output is easy to interpret (Figure 29.10).

Table 29.5 Overall negotiated ratings for LancsBox using Nielsen's (1995) usability heuristic framework

Heuristic (Nielsen, 1995)	Negotiated rating
Visibility of system status	4
Match between system and the real world	2.5
User control and freedom	4.5
Consistency and standard	3.5
Error prevention	2.5
Recognition rather than recall	3
Flexibility and efficiency of use	4.5
Aesthetic and minimalist design	4
Help users recognize, diagnose, and recover from errors	2
Help and documentation	4.5

Note: 1 = "Poor compliance", 3 = "Satisfactory compliance", 5 = "Excellent compliance". Cohen's linear-weighted κ = .3412 (95% CI, .1887 to .4937) indicates "fair" agreement between the evaluator's judgments.

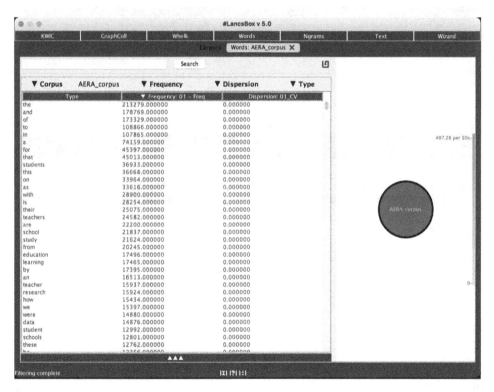

Figure 29.9   LancsBox words output

LancsBox users can view concordance lines using the KWIC (keyword in context) tool (Figure 29.11).

LancsBox users can visualize collocation relationships using the GraphColl tool (Figure 29.12). GraphColl allows users to manipulate collocation data visually (Brezina *et al.*, 2020). It is simple to operate; the user clicks the GraphColl tab, then types the target word in the search bar.

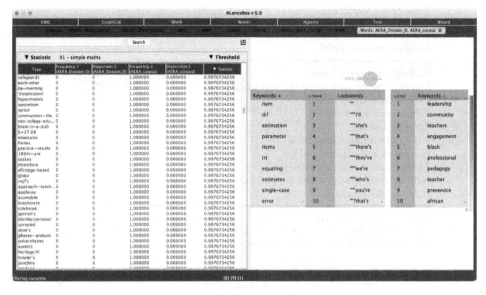

Figure 29.10 LancsBox keyword analysis output

Figure 29.11 LancsBox KWIC output

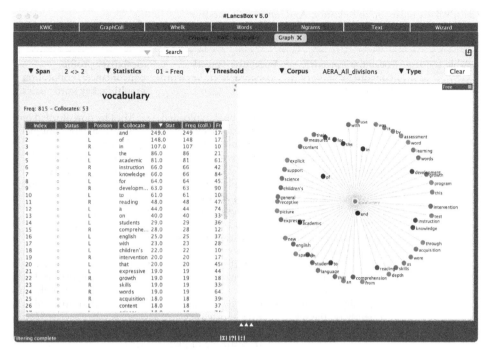

Figure 29.12 LancsBox GraphColl output

29.4.4 Comparison of the three tools

Lextutor, AntConc, and LancsBox have different strengths. Table 29.6 presents a summary of the strengths and weaknesses of each tool identified through our evaluation process.

29.4.4.1 Lextutor

Lextutor is best suited for educators who would like to quickly evaluate texts or generate exercises using authentic texts. For the researcher, Lextutor provides many essential functions for preparing corpora, such as the tag stripper, familizer, and the corpus builder. However, it is less flexible and user-friendly for analysis of a fully assembled corpus. We recommend it as a complementary tool for preprocessing materials. Lextutor's range of tools offers extremely efficient analysis without requiring download or installation. This allows for relatively easy and quick analysis on any number of platforms, especially when the target text for analysis is available online. However, the interface does not follow recognizable interface conventions, and there are violations of the principle of "aesthetic and minimalist design" which could lead to confusion. Instructions for the various tools are provided in the interface, but not in consistent locations. Explicit training on where functions are located would greatly help to prepare teachers or learners for using it successfully.

29.4.4.2 AntConc

AntConc is suitable for learners and instructors. AntConc follows standard interface design and is relatively accessible to new users for simpler tasks and is particularly helpful for wordlist

Table 29.6 Comparison of Lextutor, AntConc, and LancsBox

	Lextutor (Cobb, 2020)	AntConc (Anthony, 2020)	LancsBox (Brezina et al., 2020)
Notable features	Vocabulary profiler, concordancer, corpus builder, cloze task generator	Vocabulary profile, concordancer, keyword analysis	Vocabulary profile, concordancer, collocation graphing, keyword analysis
Strengths	• No download required • Provides access to a variety of reputable reference corpora in one place • Offers a variety of tools for generating instructional materials • Most tasks can be completed using just a few clicks • Instructions are typically available directly on the relevant page	• Must be downloaded but is available for multiple platforms • Intuitive workflow for working with multiple corpora • Offers ability to save settings and easily repeat processes • Users can save results in a text file for import into other data management tools • Instructions and advice for most aspects of AntConc are available in PDF and on the web	• Must be downloaded but is available for multiple platforms • Provides efficient tools, including a report generating function and tools not available elsewhere • Able to quickly process multiple corpora • Produces easily interpreted outputs • The written and video tutorial support for this tool is very comprehensive and well-constructed
Weaknesses	• Interfaces are not standardized, and some pages contain a lot of content; novices may struggle to identify relevant options • The structure and colors used in the interface may pose an accessibility barrier	• Interfaces are not standardized, and some pages contain a lot of content; novices may struggle to identify relevant options • The structure and colors used in the interface may pose an accessibility barrier	• First-time users will need to consult the manual or tutorials to complete basic tasks (however, the support materials are very good)

creation. It also offers the simplest and most intuitive interface for use by learners to view concordances. It supports complex searching and filtering of corpora and has excellent support for analysis of custom corpora.

AntConc offers good flexibility of use. AntConc is downloadable and capable of manipulating and analyzing corpora of varied sizes. Although the interface follows a consistent pattern, more advanced operations can be challenging to locate, but help documentation and YouTube tutorials provide excellent guidance to support task completion. Lastly, due to violations of the "Visibility of system status" principle, it can also be difficult to determine whether AntConc is in the process of completing a task or has crashed. We recommend that practitioners provide explicit instruction to new users, including information about what to expect when AntConc is performing a new or unfamiliar task. The evaluation also revealed that AntConc's experiences are not the same on Mac and Windows platforms. Practitioners may prefer to hold class in a computer lab to ensure that all learners are using the same version on the same platform to reduce training and troubleshooting requirements.

29.4.4.3 LancsBox

LancsBox is also suitable for both instructors and learners. It provides a highly consistent experience across functions within the tool. Of the three tools, LancsBox provides the most comprehensive set of tools for analyzing and comparing corpora, with especially powerful tools for keyword analysis and inspecting collocations. It offers a clean and highly consistent interface for learners to view concordance lines and use its visualization tool to explore collocations. The analysis suggests that novice users will require support from the user manual and some training to get started, because the labels in the interface assume a base level of knowledge of corpus analysis terminology.

LancsBox provides flexibility for advanced users by allowing you to save your settings. It also allows for multiple modes of interaction, using the visual interface, keyboard commands, batch processing, and a report wizard. We recommend that instructors take advantage of the excellent user manual and YouTube tutorials posted on the LancsBox homepage (http://corpora.lancs.ac.uk/lancsbox/). Help and documentation for this tool were exceptionally supportive, although it does not include much troubleshooting information. Note that the help buttons in the application link to online support resources; learners who do not have internet access at home should be advised to download the relevant manuals.

29.5 Future directions for research

As the evidence for the efficacy of using corpus tools in the classroom grows, and tools are more widely adopted, evaluating the tools that become available will become an important duty for instructors and departments. Future design-based research in CALL can incorporate heuristic evaluation and empirical usability testing methods to predict, verify, and propose remediation for usability barriers that impede the use and adoption of corpus-based tools in the classroom. Incorporating cognitive load theory into evaluation frameworks around corpus-based instruction and data-driven learning could lead to important explorations of how individual differences such as reading ability can affect the usability and perceived utility of corpus analysis tools in instruction. Because high cognitive load can interfere with efficient self-regulation (de Bruin & van Merriënboer, 2017), future research can also clarify how corpus tool designers can incorporate cognitive load theory to better design corpus tools to maximize learner benefits from self-regulation.

Further research inspired by the technology acceptance model can also explore the learner experience, including learner access to, awareness of, and intention to use corpus tools. In particular, there is a need to expand research on self-regulated learning using corpus analysis tools beyond DDL and concordancers, to include creating individualized word lists or collocation lists.

In this chapter, we demonstrated how to apply a low-cost adapted usability heuristic evaluation methodology to evaluate three freely available online tools that have previously been recommended for use in CALL practice. We provided a detailed breakdown of our evaluation followed by recommendations for teachers who may want to use these tools for teaching or research. Our hope is that practitioners can adapt this evaluation model for their own context, so that they can more systematically evaluate the affordances of corpus analysis tools for classroom use and ground their recommendations in best practices for corpus tool design.

Further reading

Chapelle, C. A. (2001). *Computer applications in second language acquisition.* Cambridge University Press. https://doi.org/10.1017/CBO9781139524681. Chapelle's seminal work on computer-assisted language learning, which provides great discussion of the effective use of software in language teaching, as well as a variety of evaluation criteria.

Corpus-aided Platform for Language Teachers (CAP) (n.d.). The Education University of Hong Kong. https://corpus.eduhk.hk/cap/index.php. This website is an excellent resource for educators developed by the Department of Linguistics and Modern Language Studies at the Education University of Hong Kong. It provides background reading, sample resources, tutorial videos, and teaching cases.

Granić, A., & Marangunić, N. (2019). Technology acceptance model in educational context: A systematic literature review. *British Journal of Educational Technology, 50*(5), 2572–2593. Granić and Marangunić provide an insightful and contemporary look into TAM's effectiveness in an educational context. It further supports TAM's core variables as effective measurements for predicting the acceptance of new learning technologies.

Nation, I. S. P. (2012). *Learning vocabulary in another language.* Cambridge University Press. https://doi.org/10.1017/CBO9781139524759. Nation offers an in-depth overview of research on L2 vocabulary acquisition. It is an excellent resource for teachers interested in the pedagogical benefits of vocabulary instruction.

References

Anganes, A., Pfaff, M. S., Drury, J. L., & O'Toole, C. M. (2016). The heuristic quality scale. *Interacting with Computers, 28*(5), 584–597. https://doi.org/10.1093/iwc/iwv031

Anthony, L. (2020). AntConc (Version 3.5.9) [Computer Software]. Waseda University. https://www.laurenceanthony.net/software

Boulton, A., & Cobb, T. (2017). Corpus use in language learning: A meta-analysis: Meta-analysis of corpus use in language learning. *Language Learning, 67*(2), 348–393. https://doi.org/10.1111/lang.12224

Brezina, V., & Gablasova, D. (2018). The corpus method. In J. Culpeper, P. Kerswill, R. Wodak, T. McEnery, & F. Katamba (Eds.), *English language: Description, variation and context* (2nd ed.) (pp. 595–609). Palgrave Macmillan.

Brezina, V., Weill-Tessier, P., & McEnery, A. (2020). #LancsBox v. 5.x. [Computer Software]. https://corpora.lancs.ac.uk/lancsbox

Chan, T.-P., & Liou, H.-C. (2005). Effects of web-based concordancing instruction on EFL students' learning of verb–noun collocations. *Computer Assisted Language Learning, 18*(3), 231–251. https://doi.org/10.1080/09588220500185769

Chapelle, C. A. (2001). *Computer applications in second language acquisition.* Cambridge University Press. https://doi.org/10.1017/CBO9781139524681

Cobb, T. (2007). Computing the vocabulary demands of L2 reading. *Language Learning & Technology, 3*(11), 38–63. https://doi.org/10125/44117

Cobb, T. (2020). *Compleat Lexical Tutor.* https://www.lextutor.ca/

Cohen, J. (1968). Weighted kappa: Nominal scale agreement provision for scaled disagreement or partial credit. *Psychological Bulletin, 70*(4), 213–220. https://doi.org/10.1037/h0026256

Damarin, S. K. (2000). The 'digital divide' versus digital differences: Principles for equitable use of technology in education. *Educational Technology, 40*(4), 17–22. https://www.jstor.org/stable/44428620

Davies, M. (2008). *The Corpus of Contemporary American English.* www.english-corpora.org/coca/.

Davis, F. D. (1989). Perceived usefulness, perceived ease of use and user acceptance of information technology. *MIS Quarterly, 13*(3), 319–339. https://www.jstor.org/stable/249008

de Bruin, A. B. H., & van Merriënboer, J. J. G. (2017). Bridging cognitive load and self-regulated learning research: A complementary approach to contemporary issues in educational research. *Learning and Instruction, 51*, 1–9. https://doi.org/10.1016/j.learninstruc.2017.06.001

Godwin-Jones, R. (2015). The evolving roles of language teachers: Trained coders, local researchers, global citizens. *Language Learning & Technology, 19*(1), 10–22. http://doi.org/10125/44395

Granić, A., & Marangunić, N. (2019). Technology acceptance model in educational context: A systematic literature review. *British Journal of Educational Technology: Journal of the Council for Educational Technology, 50*(5), 2572–2593. https://doi.org/10.1111/BJET.12864

Heatley, A., Nation, I.S.P., & Coxhead, A. (2002). RANGE and FREQUENCY [Computer software]. http://www.victoria.ac.nz/lals/staff/paul-nation.aspx

Hendry, C., & Ruivivar, J. (2019). MOOCs as environments for learning spoken academic vocabulary. In F. Meunier, J. Van de Vyver, L. Bradley, & S. Thouësny (Eds.), *CALL and complexity – Short papers from EUROCALL 2019* (pp. 180–186). https://doi.org/10.14705/rpnet.2019.38.9782490057542

Hendry, C., & Sheepy, E. (2019). Creating your own corpus-driven CALL materials. Workshop session presented at EUROCALL 2019, Louvain-la-Neuve, Belgium.

Hollender, N., Hofmann, C., Deneke, M., & Schmitz, B. (2010). Integrating cognitive load theory and concepts of human–computer interaction. *Computers in Human Behavior, 26*(6), 1278–1288. https://doi.org/10.1016/j.chb.2010.05.031

International Organization for Standardization. (2018). Ergonomics of human-system interaction—Part 11: Usability: Definitions and concepts (ISO Standard No. 9241:2018). https://www.iso.org/standard/63500.html

Kim, G. M., & Lee, S-J. (2016). Korean students' intentions to use Mobile-Assisted Language Learning: Applying the Technology Acceptance Model. *International Journal of Contents, 12*(3), 47–53.

Kumar, B. A., & Mohite, P. (2018). Usability of mobile learning applications: A systematic literature review. *Journal of Computers in Education, 5*(1), 1–17. https://doi.org/10.1007/s40692-017-0093-6

Nation, I. (2006). How large a vocabulary is needed for reading and listening? *Canadian Modern Language Review, 63*(1), 59–82. https://doi.org/10.3138/cmlr.63.1.59

Nation, I. S. P. (2012). *Learning vocabulary in another language.* Cambridge University Press. https://doi.org/10.1017/CBO9781139524759

Nielsen, J. (1995, April 24). 10 Usability Heuristics for User Interface Design. Nielsen Norman Group. https://www.nngroup.com/articles/ten-usability-heuristics/

Lee, P., & Lin, H. (2019). The effect of the inductive and deductive data-driven learning (DDL) on vocabulary acquisition and retention. *System, 81,* 14–25. https://doi.org/10.1016/j.system.2018.12.011

Pérez-Paredes, P. (2019). A systematic review of the uses and spread of corpora and data-driven learning in CALL research during 2011–2015. *Computer Assisted Language Learning, 35,* 1–26. https://doi.org/10.1080/09588221.2019.1667832

Salas, J., Chang, A., Montalvo, L., Núñez, A., Vilcapoma, M., Moquillaza, A., & Paz, F. (2019). Guidelines to evaluate the usability and user experience of learning support platforms: A systematic review. In *Communications in computer and information science* (pp. 238–254). Springer International Publishing. https://doi.org/10.1007/978-3-030-37386-3_18

Schnotz, W., & Kürschner, C. (2007). A reconsideration of cognitive load theory. *Educational Psychology Review, 19*(4), 469–508. https://doi.org/10.1007/s10648-007-9053-4

Squires D., & Preece, J. (1999). Predicting quality in educational software: Evaluating for learning, usability and the synergy between them. *Interacting with Computers, 11,* 467–.483.

Sweller, J., van Merrienboer, J. J. G., & Paas, F. G. W. C. (1998). Cognitive architecture and instructional design. *Educational Psychology Review, 10,* 251–296. https://doi.org/10.1023/A:1022193728205

Timmis, I. (2015). *Corpus linguistics for ELT: Research and practice.* Routledge.

Tongpoon-Patanasorn, A. (2018). Developing a frequent technical words list for finance: A hybrid approach. *English for Specific Purposes, 51,* 45–54. https://doi.org/10.1016/j.esp.2018.03.002

Venkatesh, V., & Davis, F. D. (2000). A theoretical extension of the technology acceptance model: Four longitudinal field studies. *Management Science, 46*(2), 186–204. https://doi.org/10.1287/mnsc.46.2.186.11926

Vieira, E. A. O., da Silveira, A. C., & Martins, R. X. (2019). Heuristic evaluation on usability of educational games: A systematic review. *Informatics in Education, 18*(2), 427–442. https://doi.org/10.15388/infedu.2019.20

Winne, P. H. (2018). Cognition and metacognition within self-regulated learning. In D. H. Schunk & J. A. Greene (Eds.), *Routledge handbook of self-regulation of learning and performance* (pp. 36–48). Routledge. https://doi.org/10.4324/9781315697048

30

BUILDING CORPORA FOR ELT

Reka R. Jablonkai

30.1 Introduction

One of the key issues in corpus-based studies is the creation of the corpus itself. It is crucial as all the conclusions drawn on the basis of the analysis of the corpus can only be interpreted in light of the collection of texts examined. How big should the corpus be? How many texts should be included? What genres and text types should be represented in the corpus? Should the corpus be made up of whole texts or excerpts of texts of a predetermined size? If we are to include excerpts how long should these be? These are some of the important questions that need to be addressed when designing and building corpora for teaching and research purposes. Ever since corpora have been used for linguistic research, the "how" and "what" of corpus building have always been discussed. Theoretical considerations have been suggested (Biber *et al.*, 1998; Clear, 1992; McEnery & Hardie, 2012; Sinclair, 2005), practical problems raised, and solutions proposed (Friginal, 2018; Nelson, 1996; Weisser, 2016) for systemising the way of compiling a corpus. The present chapter will review these most important theoretical and practical considerations of corpus building and will propose a comprehensive framework for corpus design and creation. The proposed framework attempts to integrate guiding principles and practices and includes the essential elements of the corpus building process necessary for sound corpus research primarily for various pedagogic purposes.

Corpus research has served the following broad pedagogic purposes over the course of its history (see also Xu, this volume):

a. to study large English language general corpora to inform learner dictionaries, grammar books, and textbooks about the general linguistic features of English, that is, to study the use of English in a wide range of contexts with various communicative purposes and modes (e.g. Biber *et al.*, 1999);

b. to study specialised corpora of particular language varieties determined by specific contextual, situational, and disciplinary characteristics to inform syllabus and materials design by identifying typical language patterns, for example, in casual conversations (McCarthy & McCarten, this volume) or pedagogically relevant vocabulary in texts collected from specific professional contexts (Coxhead, this volume);

 DOI: 10.4324/9781003002901-36

c. to gain a better understanding of the language development of English language learners by analysing learner corpora comprising examples of learners' written and spoken production (e.g. Granger, 2012; Paquot, this volume);

d. to facilitate discovery learning and promote learner autonomy with a data-driven approach by allowing learners to access general, specialised, or purpose-built pedagogic corpora (e.g. Braun, 2005; Charles, this volume).

The present chapter aims to provide an overview of debated issues relating to the compilation of corpora, some of which are more relevant for large general corpora. The practical considerations, however, will primarily focus on building smaller, specialised, learner, and pedagogic corpora. A general corpus aims to capture as wide a range of varieties of language use as possible and, therefore, it includes a wide variety of texts and text types of different domains. It is usually large and is typically used as a baseline for comparison with specialised corpora and to produce reference materials (Hunston, 2002; McEnery & Hardie, 2012). Specialised corpora focus on one particular type of text, genre, or language variety (Clancy, 2010; Koester, 2010). Learner corpora include written and spoken texts produced by language learners either as part of their courses or completing tasks specifically designed for the purposes of corpus compilation (e.g. Lu & Ai, 2015; Meunier *et al.*, 2020). Finally, pedagogic corpora are aimed to be used in language teaching and, therefore, are designed with pedagogic purposes in mind (Pérez-Paredes, 2019; Willis, 2011).

The present chapter will start with an overview of the current state of research concerning corpus building and will discuss the main steps of corpus design and corpus creation. Using these steps as a starting point, a comprehensive framework for corpus design and creation will be proposed. The framework includes theoretical issues such as questions of size, representativeness and sampling, and practical issues concerning data collection, data entry, and legal matters.

30.2 Review of guidelines and principles

One of the influential sets of principles for corpus building was proposed by Clear (1992). In order to avoid an undisciplined collection of texts for linguistic analysis and to ensure a sound basis for comparability across corpora, he suggested the following guiding principles for building a corpus of general English:

"P1: The notion of a "core" of language is useful". (p. 27)

Extending the idea of a core vocabulary in applied linguistics to all levels of language use, he suggested that corpus building should deal with the central and typical.

"P2: The corpus may be a sample corpus or a monitor corpus". (p. 28)

The distinction between sample and monitor corpora is based on the corpus collection approach and practice. A monitor corpus refers to a corpus with a large or in some cases infinite size (e.g. the Bank of English). A sample corpus, however, is of a finite size, and the collection of texts is strictly controlled (McEnery & Hardie, 2012).

"P3: The definition of a "text type" should be fairly clear and objective". (Clear, 1992, p. 28)

Although some intuitive text categories which are used to classify printed and spoken pieces of language exist, they are often related to the communicative purpose of a text within a specific discourse community rather than based on general theoretical criteria. As a text is a "very complex socio-linguistic artefact" (Clear, 1992, p. 29), the types of texts typically vary according to different social contexts.

> "P4: The definition of "text types" should distinguish internal criteria from external". (Clear, 1992, p. 29)

Clear (1992) introduced the internal and external criteria of text types which should also be a factor when building a corpus for linguistic analysis. Internal criteria are essentially text-internal, linguistic characteristics, e.g. to categorise a text as formal/informal is based on its linguistic features. External criteria, on the other hand, are based on text-external, non-linguistic characteristics, e.g. to classify texts according to the gender of their authors or the time of publication.

> "P5: The corpus will help us to discover new aspects of language use and will provide evidence to confirm (or refute) provisional hypotheses". (Clear, 1992, p. 29)

In his description, Clear emphasised the danger of selecting certain texts because they have particular linguistic features, that is, applying exclusively internal criteria. Xiao (2010) also highlights that the circular nature of using internal criteria for text selection is problematic as this might result in strengthening the hypotheses of language use rather than testing them. While we acknowledge that other scholars (e.g. Biber, 1995) define text types based on internal linguistic criteria alone and call a corpus balanced when a sufficient number of different genres or registers (i.e. Clear's definition of text-types) are included (see discussion on representativeness in Section 30.3.1), we adopt Clear's framework for the purposes of this chapter.

> "P6: Decisions concerning corpus quality should be based whenever possible on assessment of existing corpus resources". (p. 30)

A cycle of corpus creation was introduced under this principle. The value of a corpus is not only in processing and presenting data based on them, but also in reviewing and refining our methods of text collection. Clear (1992) suggested that corpus building be based on experience gained from earlier corpora not only in respect of linguistic description, but also concerning methodology. Although these principles were primarily formulated for building general English corpora they can be considered as basic guidelines for corpus building in general.

As technology has developed, a greater variety of corpus types are possible and available, however, the basic principles and fundamental design and compilation considerations remain the same. Sinclair (2005), as well as Friginal (2018), suggests that corpus building has two almost inseparable stages: design and collection. In practical terms, these two stages can be divided into further individual steps along the main considerations and decisions that need to be made throughout the corpus building process. A summary of these steps is given in Figure 30.1. As it is outlined in the following sections, one single step also includes several procedures to consider and many decisions to make. In Step 1, the most important decision about the corpus is its ultimate purpose; that is, it should serve the research or pedagogic aims of the project it is

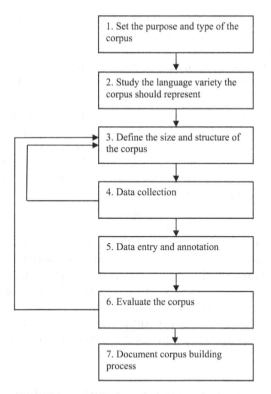

Figure 30.1   Main steps of corpus design and creation

designed for (Reppen, 2010; Xiao, 2010). It will influence all subsequent decisions and will be a decisive factor in all steps and aspects of corpus design and creation.

Closely related to the purpose of the corpus is the decision on the type of the corpus. Depending on the research and pedagogic aim, building a specialised corpus of a language variety or a pedagogic corpus for DDL might be more appropriate than a general corpus. Several corpora are developed and made available each year. Therefore, it should be considered whether any of the existing corpora can serve the purposes of the intended study before starting to compile a new corpus (Reppen, 2010). Friginal (2018) and Timmis (2015) provide lists of online corpus resources and directories. Probably the most extensive list including corpora and corpus tools is the Corpus-Based Linguistics Links maintained by Martin Weisser (Weisser, 2016). Databases, for example, CLARIN (https://www.clarin. eu), ELRA Catalogue of Language Resources (http://catalogue.elra.info), and IRIS (https:// www.iris-database.org) are also places to start searching for available corpora.

In Step 2, the language variety and the population of texts to be investigated need to be defined and extensively studied so that relevant text categories are determined. In Step 3, the decisions on the size, structure, and contents of the corpus should be made based on the selected text categories and their proportions. Step 4, the data collection phase will very much be influenced by practical constraints (Friginal, 2018), indicated by the arrow coming from Step 4 back to Step 3 in Figure 30.1. Friginal (2018) emphasised the importance of a clear understanding of the feasibility of corpus collection before embarking on the potentially time-consuming journey of corpus building. Despite careful preparation of theoretically well-based content and selection criteria, all accounts of corpus creation report on the practical difficulties of data collection. Such practical constraints might cause a slight distortion of the proportion of text types and genres in a corpus, or in some cases, the exclusion or inclusion of certain text categories and other changes to the originally planned structure and contents (Alsop & Nesi, 2009; Kennedy, 2014; Nelson, 2010; Prieto Ramos *et al.*, 2019).

Step 5 is data entry that does not only involve decisions on the methods of entering the data into the database, but also decisions on creating a storage and retrieval system and whether any form of mark-up or annotation is required (Friginal, 2018; Weisser, 2016).

A crucial step in corpus building is to evaluate the extent to which the corpus represents the diversity and balance of relevant text categories and the linguistic variability that is characteristic of the language variety under investigation. This evaluation in Step 6 might reveal deficiencies or limitations of the corpus and if so, it might be necessary to repeat Steps 3–5 (Egbert, 2019; Phillips & Egbert, 2017).

The final step is documentation. Thorough documentation of the decisions made during the corpus building process can be reported in research articles (e.g. Alsop & Nesi, 2009; Braun, 2005) or corpus manuals (e.g. MICASE Manual, 2003). Such documentation should ideally include descriptions of metadata that provide information about the context and speakers or writers of the texts the corpus includes (Burnard, 2005; Meunier *et al.*, 2020). It is crucial that this information is made available to potential future corpus users so that they can make informed decisions whether the corpus is suitable for their purposes (Egbert, 2019).

In the following sections, issues and considerations relating to these basic steps of corpus design and creation are presented and discussed as elements of a framework for pedagogical corpus building.

30.2.1 A framework for corpus building

At the advent of corpus research, teams of linguists created the first corpora for linguistic studies (Xu, this volume). Since then, technology has developed and individual researchers (Ghadessy *et al.*, 2001; Reppen, 2010), language teachers (e.g. Bi, 2020; Hunston, 2002) and translators (e.g. Biel *et al.*, 2018) can create their own corpora for their own purposes. In order to make the findings of these research projects comparable and meaningful, the way their corpora are created should be theoretically well-founded. Scholars in the field of corpus-based research published descriptions of earlier studies (Alsop & Nesi, 2009; Kennedy, 2014), guiding principles, and practical advice (Clear, 1992; Friginal, 2018; Phillips & Egbert, 2017; Sinclair, 2005; Weisser, 2016) for corpus development. The currently proposed framework aims to combine the theoretical and practical considerations necessary to systematic corpus building, primarily with pedagogic purposes in mind.

A summary of the elements of the framework is presented in Table 30.1. Issues and considerations are arranged according to the seven main steps of the corpus building process. The third column gives the sources where the information necessary for the decisions can be gained from. In the last column, the most common examples for the relevant issues are enumerated. A visual representation of the framework can be seen in Figure 30.2. In what follows, issues and considerations are discussed in detail, outlining theoretical underpinnings for the decisions that need to be made in each step.

30.3 Core issues and recommendations for practice

The first and foremost decision about a corpus is what it will be used for. Not all investigations into language and language varieties can be conducted with a corpus. Although there are

Table 30.1 A framework for corpus building

Steps	Considerations	Sources of information	Examples
1.1 Define the aim and purpose of the corpus	• Aims of the research project • Pedagogic aims	• Earlier corpus-based studies • Manuals of corpus-analysis software	
1.2 Define the type of the corpus	• The planned types of analysis • Pedagogic considerations	• Earlier corpus-based studies	• Specialised corpus • Learner corpus • Pedagogic corpus for DDL • Parallel corpus • Multimodal corpus • Comparable corpus
2. Study the language or language variety the corpus aims to represent	• Representativeness • Define a sampling frame • Set external criteria for text selection • Sampling methods: random, stratified	• Findings of social sciences and other relevant fields of research • Findings of earlier linguistic research • Needs analyses • Statistical information	• Time period when the texts were produced • Mode of text: written, spoken, electronic • The location where the texts were produced • Types of texts, genres: letter, book, journal, presentation, etc.
3.1 Define the structure of the corpus	• Relevant text categories • Proportion of text categories • Balance of text categories • Diversity of topics • Homogeneity	• Findings of Step 2	
3.2 Define the size of the corpus	• Total number of running words in the corpus • Number of samples • Number of running words of samples • Whole texts • Feasibility of analysis • Comparability with earlier corpus-based studies • Pedagogic aims	• Similar earlier corpus-based studies	
4. Data collection	• Adequate sources of texts • Feasibility, availability • Systematic collection and selection procedure • Legal and ethical issues • Confidentiality	• Language users • Publications • World Wide Web	

(Continued)

Table 30.1 A framework for corpus building *(Continued)*

Steps	Considerations	Sources of information	Examples
5. Data entry	• Electronic versions • Mark up system	• Earlier corpus-based studies • Standards	• Methods: keyboarding scanning transcription
6. Evaluate the corpus	• Representativeness in terms of text categories and their proportion • Representativeness in terms of linguistic variability • Fit for pedagogic purpose	• Findings of the preliminary analysis of the language variety in Step 2 • Findings of needs analysis	
7. Document the corpus building process	• Detailed documentation of the design and collection process • Metadata		

more and more types of analyses that can be carried out with the help of corpora as computer technology advances, there are certain research queries for which a corpus approach is the best fit. Three main types of corpus-based studies for pedagogic purposes can be distinguished: lexical, syntactic, and discoursal. Word frequency and collocational patterns in specialised corpora is often a research aim in ESP for pedagogic purposes (e.g. Bi, 2020; Green & Lambert, 2018). Corpus-based research can also inform language teachers and researchers about semantic associations of certain words (Jablonkai, 2020; Nelson, 2006). Secondly, both descriptive and pedagogic corpus research can focus on sentence-level features like verb forms,

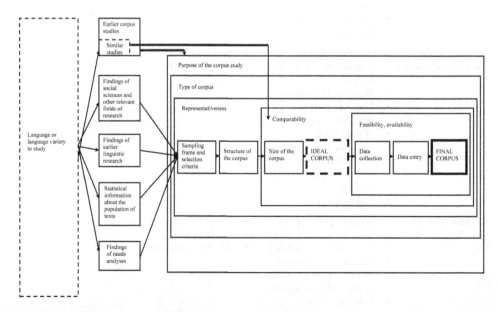

Figure 30.2 Framework for corpus building

use of prepositions or conjunctions in disciplinary discourse, or in language learner written or spoken production (Lu & Ai, 2015). Finally, corpus-based discourse studies focus on rhetorical patterns (Henry & Roseberry, 2001) or moves (Upton & Connor, 2001) of specific genres, analyse how texts are structured (Csomay, 2005; Csomay & Wu, 2020), or investigate metadiscourse and the use of specific discourse markers (Hyland, 2017). Earlier corpus-based studies, manuals of corpus analysis software, and studies that evaluate specific corpus tools (Anthony, 2013; Ari, 2006; Hendry & Sheepy, this volume; Hockey, 2001; Reppen, 2001) can be the sources of information for deciding whether a corpus-based methodology can best serve a particular research or pedagogic purpose.

30.3.1 Representativeness

An essential issue to consider when compiling a corpus is representativeness, which can only be discussed in the light of the purpose of a particular corpus (Friginal, 2018; Reppen, 2010). A corpus is more than a mere collection of texts in that it is created to represent a language or a language variety determined by situational characteristics, or a specific genre or register determined by the communicative purpose, demographic factors, or time period, for example. As Leech (1991) puts it, "In practical terms a corpus is 'representative' to the extent that findings based on its contents can be generalized to a larger hypothetical corpus" (p. 27). Biber (1993) approaches representativeness from a statistical point of view where the sample is representative of the population and defines it as "the extent to which a sample includes the full range of variability in a population" (p. 243).

What does this mean for corpus design? The appropriate way to create a corpus is based on what the corpus aims to represent and what linguistic or pedagogic purposes it will serve. Therefore, the criteria adopted to achieve representativeness can be very different in the case of general, specialised, and pedagogic corpora. The representativeness of the corpus determines what type of analyses can be carried out and also the extent to which findings can be generalised. For example, results of an analysis on a corpus of exclusively written texts would not allow generalisation on language use as a whole. Furthermore, if we are investigating the use of slang words in conversations of teenagers, our findings will not be characteristic of conversations in general (Biber *et al.*, 1998). Phillips and Egbert (2017) distinguish between target domain representativeness and linguistic representativeness. The former captures the variability in terms of text types per Clear's (1992) definition, that is, whether the corpus includes all relevant types of text in an appropriate proportion, and the latter focuses on linguistic variability that is, whether the full range of linguistic features can be found in the corpus.

Although issues of representativeness are crucial in corpus linguistics, creating a perfectly representative corpus is impossible (Egbert, 2019; Hunston, 2002; Kennedy, 2014). Leech (1991) was hoping for statistical and other models to measure the representativeness of a corpus, however, there have not been major developments in this respect (Xiao, 2010). Phillips and Egbert (2017) recommended to use the split-half method to evaluate the linguistic representativeness of corpora. Applying this method, corpus compilers can measure whether a linguistic feature is represented reliably by randomly selecting two groups of texts of the corpus and comparing the relevant linguistic features in the two groups. No major differences between the frequencies of the features would suggest that the corpus is a fairly reliable sample for the analysis of the specific linguistic feature.

Representativeness is often achieved by balance (Kennedy, 2014; Xiao, 2010) and diversity (Biber *et al.*, 1998) of corpus content. Balance refers to the proportion of different sections of corpora, for example, different genres and topic areas (Kennedy, 2014; Xiao, 2010), and diversity ensures that a language variety is represented in its entirety with all its different registers, genres, topics or other relevant categories.

In case of specialised and pedagogic corpora, corpus researchers highlight the need to prioritise different aspects, pedagogic rather than linguistic representativeness. Such corpora typically pursue specific pedagogic aims and are often topic-driven and consider diversity or homogeneity of addressees, text types, topic relevance, currency, and recency as relevant in corpus design (Braun, 2005; Krausse, 2005; Pérez-Paredes, 2019). Furthermore, the requirements for representativeness do not have to be as strict in case of pedagogic corpora compiled primarily for teaching purposes. A realistic aim in this case can be a balanced corpus that represents the lexico-grammatical and discoursal features characteristic of the language variety and relevant in the specific teaching context (Friginal, 2018).

30.3.1.1 Sampling methods

As it is usually unrealistic to include all the texts of a language or language variety in a corpus, sampling methods are used to achieve the appropriate degree of representativeness, balance, and diversity (Xiao, 2010). Random sampling is a standard way of selecting subjects for analysis in many areas of science and social sciences. Random sampling, however, is in most cases impossible for corpus building as texts of naturally occurring language are usually not fully accessible (Phillips & Egbert, 2017). Another drawback of random sampling is that it might result in a corpus that does not represent specific or relevant text categories. Stratified sampling has proven to be more suitable for corpus building as it ensures that text categories pertinent to the investigated language variety, for example, specific genres or sub-genres, are all included in the final corpus (Biber, 1993; Friginal, 2018).

The starting point for stratified sampling is the clear definition and thorough understanding of the language variety to be investigated. There are several ways to define the sampling frame. In the case of general corpora, a comprehensive bibliographical index can be used. For example, for the creation of the LOB corpus, the British National Bibliography and Willing's Press Guide were used (Xiao, 2010). Statistical information on publications, e.g. how many books, journal articles, pieces of law, was published in a given time period or about a specific topic area can also be used. In case of specialised corpora for ESP that often focus on the technical language use of a discipline, findings of that particular discipline or results of linguistic analyses of the language variety are essential to define the sampling frame. Members of the particular discourse community are useful informants (Sinclair, 1991), especially in the case of designing corpora of situationally defined language varieties. A suitable and yet underexploited method to gain an understanding of the population of texts and relevant text categories from subject specialist informants is needs analysis (Jablonkai, 2020). The two main reasons for using needs analysis techniques to inform the design of specialised corpora for ESP purposes are (a) learner needs are a fundamental element in ESP course and materials design; (b) subject-specialists can inform the corpus design process about the range and relevance of particular text categories. Despite the established strengths of needs analysis in ESP, to our knowledge, there are only a handful of corpus-based studies in ESP that based their corpus creation on the systematic analyses of the target situation (Jablonkai, 2020).

In summary, the potential sources of information that can inform the sampling frame for corpus design include (a) findings of social sciences and other relevant fields of research, (b) findings of earlier linguistic research of the language variety, (c) statistical information about the population of texts, and (d) needs analyses (Friginal, 2018; Jablonkai, 2020; Phillips &

Egbert, 2017). These are represented by the boxes in the second column on the left of the visual representation of the framework in Figure 30.2.

30.3.1.2 Structure of the corpus

Clear (1992) also emphasised the significance of extra-linguistic or external factors, such as social and situational variables, for the definition of text types. For example, variables such as age, gender, level of education, language background were defined and recorded in the text collection procedure for the International Corpus of English (ICE) (Nelson, 1996). In this respect, in Step 2 of corpus building, a set of criteria have to be established in order to help develop the structure and contents of the corpus (see Table 30.1 and Figure 30.2).

In general, in large reference corpora, representativeness is attempted to be achieved by a rigorous selection procedure and by the large amount of data. In the case of specialised corpora, external selection criteria are often used to ensure representativeness. The number of these criteria should, however, be limited and the criteria themselves should be easy to establish in order to avoid complications at the text selection stage (Sinclair, 2005).

In some projects, the structure of the corpus, that is, the relevant text categories and their proportions were defined partly by intuition and statistical information, e.g. ICE project (Nelson, 1996). In the case of specialised and pedagogic corpora, members of the relevant discourse community or potential future users of the corpus are often best placed to inform decisions on the corpus structure. The text categories used for compiling a corpus of written English European Union (EU) texts, for example, were determined by a needs analysis including interviews and a questionnaire survey among the discourse community of Hungarian EU professionals. The initial text categories were identified based on the interviews and publicly available text repositories of written EU documents. In a follow-up online questionnaire, EU professionals were asked to indicate how frequently they used specific text types and how relevant they felt these were for their jobs. The questionnaire results then determined the proportions of the different text types and genres in the corpus (Jablonkai, 2010).

Another example of defining the structure of a specialised corpus is Nelson's (2000) Business English Corpus. He started out by defining the discourse community of Business English as native speakers of English "who use English in the pursuit, transaction and discussion of business, trade and commerce" (Nelson, 2000, p. 240). The external criteria he used to closely define the population included gender, regional varieties, levels of respondent in business, type of business. Decisions on which text categories and genres to include in the corpus were based on the literature and earlier findings about the language of Business English. Based on these considerations Nelson created the content specification of his ideal Business English Corpus.

However, it is generally accepted that initial classification and categorisation of texts might turn out to be too rigid for the purposes of a study, therefore corpus building procedures should allow certain flexibility, for example, by including sub-categories or merging some categories (Kennedy, 2014; Nelson, 1996).

30.3.2 Corpus size: The bigger the better?

After designing the structure of the corpus, decisions on its overall size have to be made. Choices about the size of a corpus involve decisions on the total number of words, the number of text types, the number of samples of each text type, and also the size of each sample (Biber

469

et al., 1998; Egbert *et al.*, 2020; Kennedy, 2014; Pan *et al.*, 2020). The issue of size has been heavily debated among scholars in corpus linguistics. The main guiding principle that "bigger means better" (Leech, 1991, p. 9) seems to be abandoned and more recently, smaller corpora are also compiled and analysed.

On the basis of their size, Leech (1991) distinguishes three generations of corpora. Examples of the first generation are the Brown Corpus and its British counterpart the Lancaster-Oslo-Bergen (LOB) Corpus with one million running words, which seemed almost unsurpassable at that time. In the 1980s, the second generation appeared with ten to thirty million running words. This generation can be represented by the Cobuild project, by the work of John Sinclair and his team at the University of Birmingham, and by the Longman/Lancaster English Language Corpus. The third generation of corpora already consists of hundreds of millions of words and they also apply advanced computer technologies. The main reason for arguing for big corpora is the uneven pattern of occurrence of words in texts. Sinclair (1991) suggested that "in order to study the behaviour of words in texts, we need to have available quite a large number of occurrences" (p. 18). General corpora, the aim of which is to describe the language in general, therefore, typically includes many text types, genres, written and spoken texts, and texts of several subject matter. The British National Corpus (BNC) with 100 million words and the Corpus of Contemporary American (COCA) with many hundred million words are examples of general corpora.

Although the prevailing view had been that large corpora are best, this view was already challenged in the early 1990s by Leech and later by other researchers as well (Hunston, 2002; Kennedy, 2014; Leech, 1991). Researchers raised concerns relating to the overwhelming amount of data that large corpora generate (Hunston, 2002). Kennedy (2014), for example, points out that "although it is the case that for descriptive adequacy of low-frequency phenomena such as collocations very large corpora are necessary, there is no point in having bigger and bigger corpora if you cannot work with the output" (p. 68).

Hunston (2002) suggested that in order to gain a manageable amount of information from corpora we have two options: (a) to use software to select data randomly or, on the basis of certain important characteristics, for example, frequency or (b) to use a smaller corpus. These considerations are even more relevant in the case of pedagogic corpora.

30.3.2.1 Small can be beautiful too

During the last couple of decades, a new movement among scholars in corpus linguistics has emphasised the importance of small corpora (Ghadessy *et al.*, 2001; Nelson, 2000). Corpus types other than general corpora are typically of smaller size. The aim of a specialised corpus, for example, is to investigate a particular linguistic variety or one single genre and this delimits the types of texts one can include in such corpora. A few examples of the abundant number of specialised corpora include CANCODE, a collection of informal registers of British English with 5 million words (Hunston, 2002), the Michigan Corpus of Academic Spoken English with 1.8 million words (MICASE, http://quod.lib.umich.edu/m/micase/), the Michigan Corpus of Upper-level Student Papers with 2.6 million words (MICUSP, https://elicorpora.info/, Römer & O'Donnel, 2011) and the Computer Science Textbook Corpus (Bi, 2020) with around 7 million words. Specialised corpora of very small sizes have also been created for specific pedagogic purposes. A corpus of 40 letters of application and 20 'introduction to speaker' speeches were, for example, used to identify key lexical and rhetorical elements of a genre for teaching purposes (Henry & Roseberry, 2001).

Learner corpora and pedagogic corpora are also typically small in size. For example, the sub-corpora based on the learners' mother tongue in the International Corpus of Learner English on average comprised 230,000 words. A recent learner corpus, the Multilingual Traditional, Immersion, and Native Corpus (MulTINCo) altogether consist of 493,861 words with sub-corpora according to task types and learners' mother tongue ranging from 2,153 to 80,237 words (Meunier *et al.*, 2020). Braun (2005) recommends that pedagogic corpora be of a similar small size ranging from 20,000 to 200,000 words so that learners search a manageable amount of data. Examples here include the ELISA corpus that comprises in total around 60,000 words of conversations (Braun, 2005) and the SACODEYL-EN corpus that includes 53,090-word of video interviews (Pérez-Paredes, 2019).

An additional factor to consider when setting the size of a corpus is comparability. Pan *et al.* (2020), for example, found that lexical bundle use across corpora of different sizes, number of texts, and length of texts showed considerable difference even though the corpora were matched for discipline, writer expertise, and audience. A box with the heading 'Comparability' represents this factor in the framework including all the following phases of the design and implementation process (see Figure 30.2).

30.3.2.2 Sample size

As regards the size of samples in a corpus, two main approaches are usually taken. The first is to compile extracts of a predetermined number of words from the carefully selected texts. These are very often extracts of 2000 words following the traditions of the LOB and Brown corpora; the International Corpus of English (Nelson, 1996) is an example of this method. Other scholars suggest that 2000-word extracts are not sufficient to represent a text type or genre as linguistic features are not evenly distributed within texts, and with random selection, certain characteristics might be lost. Therefore, a sample size of 20,000 words was suggested as an appropriate size to provide statistically reliable results (Kennedy, 2014; Nelson, 2000). An example for this method is the Business English Corpus by Nelson (2000).

The second approach is to include whole texts. Sinclair (1991), a strong advocate of whole texts in corpora, argues that whole texts allow a wider range of linguistic analysis. To include whole texts is especially important when studying genre and discourse features, as results of earlier research in these fields suggest that certain linguistic characteristics are typical of certain parts of a text (Csomay, 2005; Csomay, 2013; Csomay & Wu, 2020). Egbert *et al.* (2020), for example, found that lexical dispersion was strongly influenced by the corpus unit it was measured across and therefore argue that corpus samples that represent linguistically meaningful units for a specific research aim (e.g. texts, genres, registers) should be considered in corpus design.

Decisions and considerations in Steps 2 and 3 (see Figure 30.2) lead up to an ideal structure, contents, and size of the corpus which, as many corpus linguists have acknowledged, is almost impossible to achieve (Biber *et al.*, 1998; Nelson, 2000). It is, however, a common feature of all types of corpus creation that these theoretically well-founded decisions and criteria have to be applied in a flexible way because of practical constraints (Biber *et al.*, 1998; Friginal, 2018).

30.3.3 Data collection

In the corpus building process and after the theoretical considerations outlined above, there come the implementation phases of data collection and data entry. Issues in Steps 4 and 5 (see Figure 30.2 and Table 30.1) include the difficulties of collecting pieces of language of authentic sources, entering the data into the corpus, and gaining permission for copying entire texts or extracts from copyright holders.

One of the sources for a corpus study is publicly available data. These include, for example, newspapers, journals, sites on the Internet, and magazines. It should be noted that the fact that certain texts are available publicly does not mean that they are free from copyright and permission might be needed to use them (Section 30.3.3.1). Advantages of these sources are that these texts are often available in an electronic form and are easily accessible. A disadvantage, however, is that usually they only reflect certain limited aspects of language use. For example, when creating the Business English Corpus, Nelson (2000) found that publicly available sources provided texts talking about business, but they did not reflect the actual process of doing business. Therefore, he also included texts from more private sources, for example, business letters, handwritten notes, and recordings of personal conversations to better represent the language use in the field of business. Several difficulties might occur while gathering private data, as they are not easy to access and special permissions are necessary for using them in research (Nelson, 2000).

30.3.3.1 Ethical and legal issues

As in all types of research in corpus research, there are also certain ethical and legal issues to consider. One of the most important ones is getting permission for using texts for research or pedagogic purposes. The difficulties involved in gaining copyright permissions are well recognised among scholars (e.g. Friginal, 2018; Weisser, 2016). The general experience is that although copyright holders are usually willing to grant permission, the whole process to obtain permission takes quite a long time, and it is recommended that more samples for the different categories be collected than originally planned as copyright holders might be very slow to react to requests or do not permit the use of their texts (Friginal, 2018; Kennedy, 2014). In general, it is advisable to enquire about the relevant copyright rules before the start of the data collection as these might differ from country to country (Weisser, 2016).

Another important issue as in any other research study is confidentiality. Corpus compilers have to make every effort not to invade personal privacy in any way. When using personal documents and recordings names of individuals and institutions might need to be deleted or changed. In case of spoken texts, participants need to be informed about being recorded and should have the right to listen to the recordings before giving their consent to any analysis (Friginal, 2018; Weisser, 2016).

30.3.3.2 Data entry

The second issue among practical considerations is data entry. This concerns the way in which texts will be converted into a machine-readable format. There are technically three ways to do this. The first is keyboarding, that is, typing the texts manually into the computer database, which is probably the most time-consuming method but necessary if the document is not available in an electronic form. The second way is scanning. In this case, it is important to make sure that the scanned text matches the original because in some cases (like bad photocopies) the quality is not good enough for scanning. The third way is adapting texts that are originally available in an electronic format. Even such texts might need to be converted into a format that the corpus tool or file storage system can manage. For example, typically, texts on the Internet are in HTML, pdf, or Word format and they need to be converted to plain text files for corpus analysis (Friginal, 2018; Weisser, 2016). The final format of texts, as regards character sets and language encoding, is also determined by the corpus analysis tool to be used. Some tools can only handle one type of character set others can decode several types and most of the times, it can be set under a settings function in the analytical software which character set was used for encoding the texts in the corpus. This information can usually be found in user manuals (e.g. Scott, 2020). AntConc, for example, requires files to be in UTF-8 character encoding (Anthony, 2014). Many freeware programs are available to help with encoding and conversion (e.g. AntFileConverter, Anthony, 2017). In the case of spoken language data, the tedious job of creating the transcription has to be added to the steps of data entry.

Practical considerations of data entry also involve decisions on the whole data storage system and ways to provide metadata. When creating the database one has to bear in mind that the data have to be easily retrievable. A straight-forward way for small corpora is to use a file manager for this purpose. Sub-corpora can be created by putting the texts into the same folder or merging several text files into a single text file (Friginal, 2018; Reppen, 2010). Such techniques should, however, be used cautiously as valuable information might be lost when merging files. Coded file names can also be helpful for selecting relevant texts from the whole corpus for certain analyses.

Corpus compilers can also encode their texts in order to signpost different parts of the texts such as word boundaries, hesitation in spoken texts, or line numbers. In the 1990s, the need for an agreement on what features about a text should be encoded arose, and the Text Encoding Initiative Guidelines, a complex application of SGML, were designed. The TEI Guidelines help establish standards among scholars creating their electronic corpora regardless of the language of the corpus. This flexible encoding system gives assistance to researchers on what and how to mark up a text, but it also gives the freedom to the individual scholar to decide how detailed the markup in the given corpus should be (Kennedy, 2014; Guidelines for Electronic Text Encoding and Interchange, 2002).

Probably the most widely used coding of corpora is POS (part-of-speech) tags. There are automatic taggers available, but for reliably tagging a corpus, automatic tagging might need to be corrected manually. Sketchengine (Kilgarriff, 2013), for example, POS tags corpora when they are uploaded to the platform. Wmatrix (Rayson, 2013) provides two layers of annotation: POS tags and semantic tagging. Researchers who analyse syntactic, pragmatic, and discourse features and functions might need to manually annotate their corpora. Crosthwaite *et al.* (2017), for example, used the UAMCorpustool (O'Donnell, 2008) to annotate a learner corpus and a professional corpus of dentistry reports for stance markers in order to compare expert and novice writers' presentation of stance. For the purposes of pedagogic corpora, Braun (2005) proposed to include teaching-oriented annotations regarding the following: content-related categories (e.g. keywords and topics), L2-related categories (e.g. lexical, grammatical, pragmatic, and discourse properties), and learner-related categories (level of proficiency, relevant knowledge requirements, skills which can be practised, challenges and difficulties). In addition, she argued for enriching pedagogic corpora with additional materials, for example, frequency lists, pre-prepared concordances, and tasks and exercises.

A further decision at the data entry stage is to determine what type of metadata will be provided and in what form. Metadata essentially provides the contextual information that the actual texts do not include and, thus, it is critical for analysing, interpreting, and comparing corpus data (Burnard, 2005). Metadata can be stored in a separate file or database. Alternatively, it can be integrated into individual texts in a header typically between angle brackets (<...>). The documentation and reporting should give detailed information of metadata for future reference and future corpus studies (Phillips & Egbert, 2017). MICASE, for example, offers ten categories of metadata at their website including speech event, academic discipline, native speaker status, gender, age, academic role, etc. (MICASE Manual, 2003).

30.4 Future directions

Overall, the main principles of corpus building formulated in the early days of corpus linguistics are still relevant today. To date, guidelines primarily concentrate on building general, specialised, and learner corpora. These guidelines could be developed further to clarify several aspects of corpus building. For example, more detailed guidance would be required for (a) evaluating corpora, (b) determining an appropriate size for analysing different linguistic features and applying specific analytical frameworks, and (c) integrating metadata into corpora. We also argued for the application of needs analysis as a method to involve subject specialist informants in the corpus building process especially for future pedagogically motivated specialised corpora. This will ensure that the text categories and their proportions are determined by their relevance in the specific discourse community. The area, however, that future pedagogically motivated studies of corpus building should primarily focus on is the design, compilation, and annotation of pedagogic corpora. This will most probably require the co-operation of applied linguists, programmers, experts in education technology, corpus linguists, and language educators. Such co-operation will hopefully result in more learner-friendly pedagogic corpora. Thus, allowing that corpora not only inform learner dictionaries and course and materials design, but are applied in teaching on a wider scale.

Further readings

Ädel, A. (2020). Corpus compilation. In P. Magali & S. Gries (Eds.), *A practical handbook of corpus linguistics* (pp. 3–24). Springer. The author provides an overview of the key elements of corpus compilation covering considerations of representativeness, balance, ethics, and metadata. It also covers the technical aspects of formatting and annotation.

Friginal, E. (2018). *Corpus linguistics for English teachers.* Routledge. Chapter B2 in this book provides an overview of the corpus building process specifically for teaching purposes. It highlights relevant aspects to consider during the preparation and collection phases.

O'Keefe, A., & McCarthy, M. (Eds.). (2022). *The Routledge handbook of corpus linguistics* (2nd ed). Routledge. Section II of this handbook includes six chapters that focus on the principles and practicalities of corpus building of different types of corpora, for example, spoken, written, and specialised.

Weisser, M. (2016). *Practical corpus linguistics.* Blackwell. The author discusses several issues relating to corpus design, compilation, and preparation for analysis. Technical details of file formats, corpus tools and annotation are given in a very accessible manner including practical exercises with solutions and comments.

References

Alsop, S., & Nesi, H. (2009). Issues in the development of the British Academic Written English (BAWE) corpus. *Corpora, 4*(1), 71–83. https://doi.org/10.3366/e1749503209000227

Anthony, L. (2013). A critical look at software tools in corpus linguistics. *Linguistic Research, 30*(2), 141–161. https://doi.org/10.17250/khisli.30.2.201308.001

Anthony, L. (2014). AntConc (Version 3.4.3) [Computer Software]. Waseda University. Available: www.laurenceanthony.net

Anthony, L. (2017). AntFileConverter (Version 1.2.1) [Computer Software]. Waseda University. https://www.laurenceanthony.net/software.

Ari, O. (2006). Review of three software programs designed to identify lexical bundles. *Language Learning & Technology, 10*(1), 30–37.

Bi, J. (2020). How large a vocabulary do Chinese computer science undergraduates need to read English-medium specialist textbooks? *English for Specific Purposes, 58*, 77–89.

Biber, D. (1993). Representativeness in corpus design. *Literary and Linguistic Computing, 8*(4), 243–257.

Biber, D. (1995). *Dimensions of variation. A cross-linguistic comparison.* Cambridge University Press.

Biber, D., Conrad, S., & Reppen, R. (1998). *Corpus linguistics. Investigating language structure and use.* Cambridge University Press.

Biber, D., Johansson, S., Leech, G., Conrad, S., & Finegan, E. (1999). *Longman grammar of spoken and written English.* Longman.

Biel, L., Biernacka, A., & Jopek-Bosiacka, A. (2018). The glossary of EU English competition collocations and terms. In S. Marino, L. Biel Lucja, M. Bajcic, & V. Sosoni (Eds.), *Language and law* (pp. 249–274). Springer.

Braun, S. (2005). From pedagogically relevant corpora to authentic language learning contents. *ReCALL, 17*(1), 47–64.

Burnard, L. (2005). Metadata for corpus work. In M. Wynne (Ed.), *Developing linguistic corpora: A guide to good practice* (pp. 30–46). AHDS.

Crosthwaite, P., Cheung, L., & Jiang, F. K. (2017). Writing with attitude: Stance expression in learner and professional dentistry research reports. *English for Specific Purposes, 46*, 107–123. https://doi.org/10.1016/j.esp.2017.02.001

Csomay, E. (2005). Linguistic variation within university classroom talk: A corpus-based perspective. *Linguistics and Education, 15*(3), 243–274.

Csomay, E. (2013). Lexical bundles in discourse structure: A corpus-based study of classroom discourse. *Applied Linguistics, 34*(3), 369–388.

Csomay, E., & Wu, S. M. (2020). Language variation in university classrooms. A corpus- driven geographical perspective. *Register Studies, 2*(1), 131–165.

Clancy, B. (2010). Building a corpus to represent a variety of language. In A. O'Keefe & M. McCarthy (Eds.), *The Routledge handbook of corpus linguistics* (pp. 80–92). Routledge.

Clear, J. (1992). Corpus sampling. In G. Leitner (Ed.), *New directions in English language corpora* (pp. 21–31). Mouton de Gruyter.

Egbert, J. (2019). Corpus design and representativeness. In T. B. Sardinha & M. V. Pinto (Eds.), *Multi-dimensional analysis: Research methods and current issues* (pp. 27–42). Bloomsbury.

Egbert, J., Burch, B., & Biber, D. (2020). Lexical dispersion and corpus design. *International Journal of Corpus Linguistics, 25*(1), 89–115. https://doi.org/10.1075/ijcl.18010.egb

Friginal, E. (2018). *Corpus linguistics for English teachers.* Routledge.

Ghadessy, M., Henry, A., & Roseberry, R. L. (Eds.). (2001). *Small corpus studies and ELT.* Benjamins.

Granger, S. (2012). How to use foreign and second language learner corpora. In A. Mackey & S. M. Gass (Eds.), *Research methods in second language acquisition: A practical guide* (pp. 7–29). Wiley-Blackwell. https://doi.org/10.1002/9781444347340.ch2

Green, C., & Lambert, J. (2018). Advancing disciplinary literacy through English for academic purposes: Discipline-specific wordlists, collocations and word families for eight secondary subjects. *Journal of English for Academic Purposes, 35*, 105–115.

Guidelines for Electronic Text Encoding and Interchange by the Text Encoding Initiative Consortium. (2002). www.tei-c.org

Henry, A., & Roseberry, R. L. (2001). Using a small corpus to obtain data for teaching a genre. In M. Ghadessy, A. Henry, & R. L. Roseberry (Eds.), *Small corpus studies and ELT* (pp. 93–134). Benjamins.

Hockey, S. (2001). Concordance programs for corpus linguistics. In C. R. Simpson & J. M. Swales (Eds.), *Corpus linguistics in North America. Selections from the 1999 symposium* (pp. 58–97). The University of Michigan Press.

Hunston, S. (2002). *Corpora in Applied Linguistics.* Cambridge University Press.

Hyland, K. (2017). Metadiscourse: What is it and where is it going. *Journal of Pragmatics, 113*, 16–29.

Jablonkai, R. (2010). Towards an English EU discourse corpus. In T. Frank & K. Károly (Eds.), *Gateways to English* (pp. 231–247). Eötvös University Press.

Jablonkai, R. R. (2020). Leveraging professional wordlists for productive vocabulary knowledge. *ESP Today, 8*(1), 2–24.

Kennedy, G. (2014). *An introduction to corpus linguistics.* Routledge.

Kilgarriff, A. (2013). SketchEngine [Computer Software]. Available from http://www. sketchengine. co.uk/.

Koester, A. (2010). Building small specialised corpora. In A. O'Keefe & M. McCarthy (Eds.), *The Routledge handbook of corpus linguistics* (pp. 66–79). Routledge.

Krausse, S. (2005). Testing the validity of small corpus information. *ESP World, 4*(1). http://esp-world.7p.info/Articles_9/testing_the_validity.htm

Leech, G. (1991). The state of the art in corpus linguistics in. In K. Aijmer & B. Altenberg (Eds.), *English Corpus linguistics* (pp. 8–29). Longman.

Lu, X., & Ai, H. (2015). Syntactic complexity in college-level English writing: Differences among writers with diverse L1 backgrounds. *Journal of Second Language Writing, 29,* 16–27. https://doi.org/10.1016/j.jslw.2015.06.003

McEnery, T., & Hardie, A. (2012). *Corpus linguistics.* Cambridge University Press.

Meunier, F., Hendrikx, I., Bulon, A., Goethem, V., & Naets, K., H. (2020). MulTINCo: Multilingual traditional immersion and native corpus. Better-documented multiliteracy practices for more refined SLA studies. *International Journal of Bilingual Education and Bilingualism.* https://doi.org/10.1080/13670050.2020.1786494

MICASE Manual (2003). https://ca.talkbank.org/access/0docs/MICASE.pdf

Nelson, G. (1996). The design of the corpus. In S. Greenbaum (Ed.), *Comparing English worldwide: The International Corpus of English.* Clarendon Press.

Nelson, M. (2000). *A corpus-based study of Business English and Business English teaching materials.* Unpublished PhD Thesis, University of Manchester, Manchester. http://www.kielikanava.com/thesis.html

Nelson, M. (2006). Semantic association in Business English: A corpus-based analysis. *English for Specific Purposes, 25,* 217–234.

Nelson, M. (2010). Building a written corpus: What are the basics? In A. O'Keefe & M. McCarthy (Eds.), *The Routledge handbook of corpus linguistics* (pp. 53–65). Routledge.

O'Donnell, M. (2008). The UAM CorpusTool: Software for corpus annotation and exploration. In C. M. Bretones Callejas, J. F. F. Sánchez, J. R. I. Ibáñez, M. E. García Sánchez, et al. (Eds.), *Applied Linguistics now: Understanding language and mind* (pp. 1433–1447). Universidad de Almería. http://www.corpustool.com/index.html

Pan, F., Reppen, R., & Biber, D. (2020). Methodological issues in contrastive lexical bundle research. *International Journal of Corpus Linguistics, 25*(2), 215–229.

Pérez-Paredes, P. (2019). The pedagogic advantage of teenage corpora for secondary school learners. In P. Crosthwaite (Ed.), *Data driven learning for the next generation: Corpora and DDL for pre-tertiary learners* (pp. 67–87). Routledge.

Phillips, J., & Egbert, J. (2017). Advancing law and corpus linguistics: Importing principles and practices from survey and content-analysis methodologies to improve corpus design and analysis. *Brigham Young University Law Review, 25*(6), 1589–1619.

Prieto Ramos, F., Cerutti, G., & Guzmán, D. (2019). Building representative multi-genre corpora for legal and institutional translation research. *Translation Spaces, 8*(1), 93–116. https://doi.org/10.1075/ts.00014.pri

Rayson, P. (2013). *Wmatrix.* [Computer Software]. http://ucrel.lancs.ac.uk/wmatrix/

Reppen, R. (2001). Review of MonoConc Pro and WordSmith tools. *Language Learning & Technology, 5*(3), 32–36.

Reppen, R. (2010). Building a corpus: What are key considerations. In A. O'Keefe & M. McCarthy (Eds.), *The Routledge handbook of corpus linguistics* (pp. 31–37). Routledge.

Römer, U., & Donnell, M. B. O. (2011). From student hard drive to web corpus (part 1): The design, compilation and genre classification of the Michigan Corpus of Upper-level Student Papers (MICUSP). *Corpora, 6*(2), 159–177. https://doi.org/10.3366/corp.2011.0011.

Scott, M. (2020). *WordSmith tools version 8,* Stroud: Lexical Analysis Software. http://www.lexically.net/wordsmith/

Sinclair, J. (1991). *Corpus, concordance, collocation.* Oxford University Press.

Sinclair, J. (2005). Corpus and text – basic principles. In M. Wynne (Ed.), *Developing linguistic corpora: A guide to good practice* (pp. 1–16). Oxbow Books. http://ahds.ac.uk/linguistic-corpora/

Timmis, I. (2015). *Corpus linguistics for ELT: Research and practice.* Routledge.

Upton, T. A., & Connor, U. (2001). Using computerized corpus analysis to investigate the textlinguistic discourse moves of a genre. *English for Specific Purposes, 20*, 313–329.

Weisser, M. (2016). *Practical corpus linguistics*. Blackwell.

Weisser, M. (2016). Corpus-based Linguistics Links. http://martinweisser.org/corpora_site/CBLLinks.html

Willis, J. (2011). Concordances in the classroom without a computer: Assembling and exploiting concordances of common words. In B. Tomlinson (Ed.), *Materials development in language teaching* (pp. 51–77). Cambridge University Press.

Xiao, R. (2010). Corpus creation. In N. Indurkhya & F. Damerau (Eds.), *The handbook of Natural Language Processing* (pp. 147–165). Taylor and Francis.

31

PARALLEL CORPORA IN ELT

Laura M. Hartwell and Olivier Kraif

31.1 Introduction

Since the Rosetta stone, multilingual texts have been essential for understanding other languages, notably bilingual editions for ancient Greek and Latin, as well as for European literature, such as the French *Les Belles Lettres* or *l'Aubier* (Chartier & Martin, 1986). "Dual language" or "bilingual" books are used positively for foreign or second language learning by children and adults in and outside of the classroom (Ernst-Slavit & Mulhern, 2003). Instead of reading full texts in more than one language displayed side-by-side as for bilingual books, a parallel corpus query allows users to consult multiple occurrences of a keyword or sequence and their translations, relying upon statistical measures to identify the likelihood of those constructions.

Much of parallel corpora research stems from human and machine translation studies. In her evaluation of the usefulness and usability of parallel corpora for research and translation needs, Rabadán (2019, p. 17) offers "action points" also relative to teaching and learning: determining clear questions, reviewing available corpora and their reliability, building upon existing resources, being creative, contributing, and sharing resources. Translation studies and teaching draw upon parallel corpora to determine how best to render an enunciation from a source to a target language. Language learning requires understanding and expressing one's self in a target language. The border between translation and teaching is blurred as professionals and students increasingly rely upon available automatic translators. However, expressing one's self extends beyond translation equivalents, requiring attention to both audience and cultural differences. Thus, parallel corpora invite new means to examine how language works across languages and across cultures.

A parallel corpus is composed of source texts aligned with their translations by word, chunk, sentence, or paragraph in one or more other languages. The order of the languages in the translation process may be either unidirectional (i.e. from one language to another), bidirectional or "reciprocal" (i.e. translations from and to both languages), multidirectional (i.e. the source and/or translations including a range of languages), or translation via a third language (for example, a source document in Swahili, translated to English, before translation to Italian). Translations have typically come from available fictional works, governmental records, business needs, and film subtitles. This availability reflects societal advancements and

 DOI: 10.4324/9781003002901-37

has largely influenced both the creation of parallel corpora and the possibilities for research (Doval & Sánchez Nieto, 2019). Essential to translation and translation studies, parallel corpora are increasingly consulted directly or in mediated forms for foreign and second language teaching and learning (Frankenberg-Garcia, 2012a).

In this chapter, we review current research that relies considerably on available existing sources, notably institutional productions, and translation studies. We discuss how the availability of tools and languages define factors of core issues. Based on these factors, we focus on language teaching and learning, including three case studies illustrating the interest of parallel corpora. We conclude with perspectives and recommendations. First, we highlight the differences between parallel corpora and similar resources.

31.1.1 *Difference from comparable multilingual corpora and dictionaries*

A parallel corpus differs from a comparable multilingual corpus. A comparable corpus is a collection of independent texts in two or more languages, containing no translations from the other language. For example, the corpus Étude interdisciplinaire et interlinguistique du discours académique (EIIDA) (Carter-Thomas & Jacques, 2017) is a comparable corpus of research articles and conference transcripts in either English or in French. All of the articles and transcripts in the EIIDA corpus are in their original language, allowing comparisons, such as word frequency, pronoun use, or overall structure across languages. A comparable corpus contains no translations of the original documents, thus making automatic alignment at the word or sentence level impossible. This automatic alignment is a key technical element of parallel corpora as it allows users to scrutinise languages at the word or sentence level.

Within lexicology, Teubert and Čermáková (2004) explain how parallel corpora differ from multilingual dictionaries by their larger variety of translation equivalents that reduce ambiguity:

> Even the largest bilingual dictionary will present only a tiny segment of the translation equivalents we find in a not too small parallel corpus. Because the ordering principle of printed dictionaries is alphabetical, based on mostly single-word entries, bilingual dictionaries do not record larger and more complex units of meaning in a methodical way. Neither do they tell us which of the equivalents they offer belong in which contexts. [...] From parallel corpora, we can extract a larger variety of translation equivalents embedded in the contexts, which make them unambiguous. This is what makes parallel corpora so attractive. (p. 123).

31.1.2 *An overview of technical considerations*

Parallel corpora share commonalities with unilingual corpora in their reliance upon technical advances. The early 1970s marked the first multilingual corpus, the Yugoslav-Serbo-Croatian-English Contrastive corpus compiled by Filipovac (Doval & Sánchez Nieto, 2019). However, the birth of parallel corpora was the English-Norwegian Parallel corpus, of which the English-Swedish Parallel Corpus built upon the same design and many of the same English documents (ibid., p. 2). The original corpus was compiled between 1994 and 1997, later tagged for parts of speech and enlarged with texts in German, Dutch, and Portuguese, especially extracts from novels and non-fictional books, as part of the password-protected Oslo Multilingual Corpus (Johansson, 2008).

Creating parallel corpora remains more technically complex than creating unilingual corpora. Beyond the issue of gathering quality bilingual sources, issues of alignment (i.e. by word, chunk, sentence, or page) to the corresponding translation raises further issues, as we will discuss, since translations are not simple word-to-word correspondences and have possibly different alphabetic or character systems.

31.2 Review of current sources inspiring research

The field of parallel corpora research is young and inextricable from the creation of consequential parallel corpora. Researchers rely upon sufficiently large authentic bilingual or multilingual resources. The compilation of these corpora precedes and determines the current research, as discussed next.

31.2.1 Governmental and intergovernmental sources

Governing bodies publish high-quality documents in many languages allowing their community to access key legal and other documents. Thus, the United Nations' official records are available as parallel corpora in Arabic, Chinese, English, French, Russian, and Spanish. These and other documents, such as those of the European Parliament, are valuable downloadable multilingual data sources. They are also incorporated within research-oriented platforms.

One early source is the Canadian government's collection of laws and other governmental documents in both English and French since 1978, including 'Hansards' (official records). These Hansards were incorporated into initial systems of bilingual aligning, notably within the Bitextes Anglais-Français corpus, one of the first multi-genre sentence-aligned parallel corpus, which also served to benchmark original aligning techniques (Simard, 1998). Today, chunk-aligned Hansards of the 36th Canadian Parliament are freely available for download.

Another key source for reliably translated documents is from the European Union. Its European Commission oversees the *Joint Research Center*, which offers their sentence-aligned parallel corpus JRC-Acquis (Steinberger *et al.*, 2012) covering 22 languages (all official European languages except Croatian and Irish) and 231 language pairs totalling 1.5 million documents (1.37 billion words, of which 103,458,996 words are in English) related to debates, press releases, reports, and other parliamentary documents. The European Commission's Directorate-General for Translation also publishes its 24-language 'Translation Memory' (approximately 1.9 million translation units per language) of the legal documents of the Acquis Communautaire (DGT-TM). The original language is not recorded, but 72% were initially drafted in English, before translation by "highly qualified human translators specialised in specific subject domains" and a multi-step verification (Steinberger *et al.*, 2012, p. 455), thereby assuring the high quality of both languages, a key factor for language learning.

31.2.2 Disciplinary contributions

Other major sources of parallel corpora stem from the needs related to human and machine-based translation. Translation memories are databases recording previous translated segments, with the intention of facilitating translations by humans or machines. They may include essential terminological, linguistic, and contrastive stylistic information. Despite the great wealth of translation memories, Simard (2020) notes that they are "anchored in time and space". Thus, for example, while the French term *pêcheur* was previously translated as *fisherman*, it now calls for the gender-neutral *fisher* (p. 87). While these sources tend to be reserved for private use, exceptions are the DGT-TM (*supra*), MyMemory and the Translation Automation User Society (TAUS), a language industry association that offers a repository of documents provided by members and totalling 35 billion words. However, many of the TAUS documents pertain to machine or automatic translation and may not be pertinent for general English or other domains. Other sources related to language engineering or information technology, which may nevertheless meet certain pedagogical needs, include the European Language Resources Association, the Common Language Resources and Technology Infrastructure (CLARIN), and the mostly fee-based Linguistic Data Consortium (LDC) at the University of Pennsylvania.

Parallel-corpus research also contributes to translation teaching, lexicology, pragmatics, and contrastive analysis. Frérot (2016) describes their use by teachers of translation to target difficulties, as well as for in-class activities, reflecting both academic and professional environments, notably as a complement to translation memory systems. Aijmer (2020) describes the use of parallel corpora for contrastive pragmatics across languages and genres, which attends to a form's function in varying linguistic, social, cultural, and historical contexts. These include cognates, such as her study of *absolutely* and the Swedish *absolut*, as well as pragmatic markers, speech acts, information structure, and politeness. Drawing upon the field of contrastive analysis and the Europarl corpus, Granger (in press) highlights the interest of n-gram analysis of learner and expert corpora with identifiable translation directions. Identifying differences, she highlights the under- or overuse of lexical bundles in translated or "third code" texts, thereby contributing to our knowledge of both translation studies and the interlanguage of foreign-language learners, as a 'third code' "arises out of the bilateral consideration of the matrix and target codes: it is, in a sense, a sub-code of each of the codes involved" (Frawley, 1984, p. 168).

31.2.3 Other sources for current research

Literary works, legal documents, and movie or television subtitles constitute other reliable sources for parallel corpora. One easy-to-use corpus combining these genres is the Translation Equivalents Database (TREQ), built automatically from the InterCorp parallel corpus including texts in Czech and 27 other languages. The current TREQ interface allows users to select the genre and any of the original languages before translation into either English or Czech, with other languages projected (Škrabal & Vavřín, 2017). Queries may target sequences or include fragments of words, while results are listed by frequency with access to context. The InterCorp corpus (Čermák & Rosen, 2012), containing fictional works, political commentaries, European Parliament documents, and subtitles produces "translation candidates" based on unreviewed automatic excerption and word-level alignment results. InterCorp can also be queried via the interface Kontext equipped with various tools according to availability of the original corpus: tokenisers, morphological analysers, taggers, and lemmatisers (Čermák, 2019), laying the groundwork for future projects.

Illustrative of the societal need for translated legal documents, Fan and Xu (2002) compiled a 100-file corpus of primarily legal and documentary texts in English (300,000 words) and Chinese (500,000 characters). At the beginning of each sentence, manually inserted hyperlinks permit navigation to a corresponding sentence in the other language. To analyse its usefulness, 63 translation students in Hong Kong were asked to consult the corpus for legal responses related to inheritance and divorce. The legal vocabulary was found to be a veritable hurdle, such as the Chinese literal equivalent to *non-land real property*, deemed more obscure than the English *personal chattels*. The authors conclude, "the corpus provides instant access to both language versions and since students rely on both languages for comprehension (albeit with Chinese dominant), [...] a bilingual corpus of legal language is pedagogically useful" (Fan & Xu, 2002, p. 62). Another larger Chinese-English parallel corpus offering a range of categories (including law, spoken discourse, academic theses) is the downloadable UM-Corpus (15 million aligned sentences) available on the OPUS platform (Tiedemann, 2016) and the Natural Language Processing and Portuguese-Chinese Machine Translation Laboratory (Tian *et al.*, 2014).

Another well-represented genre is patent documentation because of international needs. Utiyama and Isahara (2008) compiled a Japanese-English corpus of some two-million-sentence pairs from patent applications They confirmed that lexical translations were more dependable and easier to treat than long sentences. The Statistical Natural Language Processing Group at the University of Heidelberg created the downloadable Japanese-English BoostCLIR corpus of patent abstracts and German-English or French-English Patent Translation Resource corpora. These patent corpora reflect how financed corporate needs influence the availability of data for international research and student use.

Offering an oasis within the dearth of oral corpora, the public OpenSubtitles repository of movie and television subtitles ranges across many languages and genres, representing slang, narrative and expository discourses. Lison and Tiedemann (2016) treated, notably by algorithms, some 3.36 million-subtitle files representing 2.6 billion sentences distributed across 60 languages before making them available via the OPUS platform. Subtitles, in blocks of 50 characters maximum, were aligned using timing information, plus other corrections and metadata to assure quality.

Finally, academic parallel corpora are rare, but are of considerable interest to teaching language in higher education. A recent addition is the English-French, syntactically annotated ParaSHS corpus incorporating some 1,000 research articles in the Humanities (Kraif, 2018).

31.3 Tools and corpora defining core issues for teaching and learning

More so than for other corpus studies, core issues are defined in function with query tools. The underlying or accessible tools largely influence the type and results of a query. Parallel corpora resources announce their document sources and tools, which is not necessarily the case for well-known resources such as Linguee, ReversoTranslation, and WordReference. Rabadán (2019, p. 59) notes that they often lack information on the language data or the tools serving for alignment or reference to frequency. These absences may affect the reliability of query results, especially as related to frequency and genre (Hartwell, 2020), which is not the case for parallel corpora. To illustrate how tools and document availability condition teaching and learning possibilities, we now examine some key sources.

31.3.1 Tools

Queries rely upon tools common to analysing many of the same elements as monolingual corpora: keyword in context, frequency lists, collocates, search grammars. There are several levels of query: immediate consultation of an online interface, downloading a corpus for query with a separate tool, or creating one's own corpus using free aligning tools, such as Hunalign, LF aligner, or Web Align Toolkit. These tools offer a predictive power for cross-language consultation surpassing the word-to-word translations often found in dictionaries.

One of the most advanced on-line user-friendly sources is OPUS, a database of 34 languages in a range of genres, as well as a collection of downloadable bilingual or multilingual corpora. It relies upon the open-source architecture Corpus Workbench, designed at the University of Stuttgart and used for the British National Corpus, later influencing Sketch Engine (Evert & Hardie, 2011). On OPUS, users first select either the aligned-sentence interface or the lexical correspondence interface, built upon translation probability and parallel concordancing. After selecting a corpus, such as OpenSubtitles2018, Tatoeba, or TedTalks, then the source and target language, users may query an individual item or sequence, lemma, or part of speech. Thus, users can relatively easily access complex language data within a specific genre or field.

In contrast, other sources must be downloaded. The European Parliament includes a downloadable tool to query their parallel corpus. Another option is Sketch Engine, requiring a paid individual or institutional subscription, which allows users to query a parallel corpus acquired elsewhere, such as those found on OPUS, via the "Create Corpus" option. Other, more targeted initiatives continue to be created, such as the 280,000-word sentence-aligned European Parliament Translation and Interpretation Corpus (EPTIC) integrating cleaned transcriptions, interpretations, translations, and additional uncleaned transcriptions (including metadata) of parliamentary speeches in English, French, and Italian, as well as access to time-synced video documents (Ferraresi & Bernardini, 2019). The EPTIC corpus illustrates the possibilities offered by advanced uses of tools and available documents.

31.3.2 Language availability

Another key factor determining core issues is the availability of quality language translations. Although both OPUS and CLARIN (86 downloadable multilingual parallel corpora) declare the objective of incorporating a wider range of languages, documents in European languages continue to constitute the bulk of available data. Other projects seek to compile bilingual corpora with often diverging alphabets or scriptural traditions, which raises new questions of automatic analysis, tagging, or alignment. For instance, languages such as Arabic or Chinese need dedicated tools for word and sentence segmentation, as blank spaces, capital characters, and punctuation marks do not constitute reliable clues for these tasks.

Mikhailov and Cooper (2016) detail some 30 parallel corpora, most of them including English. Among these are the publicly available Amsterdam Slavic Parallel Aligned Corpus of literary texts, the Svrokorpus collection of Slovene-based bilingual texts, the Multilingual Corpora for Cooperation (nine European languages) of comparable financial newspapers plus the *Journal of the European Commission*, the paragraph-aligned Multilingual Corpus of Legal Documents Corpus (English, Finnish, Swedish, Russian), and the Russian National Corpus including literary classics and their translations.

To remedy the lack of representation of certain languages, one project underway is the King Saud University's 10-million word Arabic–English Bidirectional Parallel Corpus, targeting eight themes, from biographical, medical, or scientific. Manually compiled, cleaned, and aligned at the sentence level, one of the major hurdles has been the lack of programs capable of compiling such resources (Alotaibi, 2017).

Within a context of increasingly present language technology, many African languages remain digitally underrepresented. However, the part-of-speech tagged, lemmatised, and sentence-aligned 1.2-million-word downloadable Swahili-English SAWA Corpus draws upon dictionary exemplars, the Kenyan Constitution, Kenyan investment reports, movie subtitles, non-governmental organisation leaflets, United Nations documents, and religious texts (De Pauw *et al.*, 2011). Difficulties resulting from the morphologically more complex nature of Swahili were lessened by morphologically deconstructing Swahili words (De Pauw *et al.*, 2011, p. 337).

Another response to enlarging language availability in addition to English is Tatoeba, a collaborative and open collection of sentences and their translations into a multitude of languages, each sentence tagged with the contributor's name. Some 365 languages are supported, including over 37,000 sentences in Toki Pona, 22,000 in Persian, and 3,000 in Thai. Attention is given to source, for example the word *Enkosi!* ("Thank you" in Xhosa) is listed as initially translated into four languages, before translating these for some 141 new languages. Although without a precise research objective, the site is remarkably clear and easy-to-use, as well as being controlled for quality, all of which are key issues for language learning.

31.3.3 Current contributions to teaching and learning

The access to tools and languages are initial considerations for any teacher wishing to query parallel corpora. As for unilingual corpora, classroom applications may favour data-driven learning (DDL). Illustrating a "good example" of DDL, Cobb (2019, p. 195) cites Chan and Liou (2005) who asked students to complete gap-fill exercises by querying a Chinese-English parallel corpus in order to generalise about language patterns, typically verb-noun collocations, such as *set fire*. Further illustrating computer-assisted language learning, Johns *et al.* (2008) found that incorporating Chinese translations into the corpus consulted by a Taiwanese secondary school English literature class allowed students to rely on their first language for comprehension, thereby surpassing reductive word-to-word translation.

Both direct computer-based and indirect paper-based queries contribute to DDL. Chujo and Oghigian (2012) drew upon a Japanese-English newspaper corpus, comprised of 150,000 aligned translation pairs accessible via the concordancer Paraconc, to propose both computer concordancing and paper concordance data to Japanese engineering students learning basic English. Students discovering both mediums showed greater capacity to identify and to produce noun and verb phrases, than the control group. Overall, approximately three-quarters of the students declared that the computer-based DDL (1) offered more necessary translations, (2) provided a sensation of security, (3) helped to translate a specific sentence, and (4) helped to grasp word meaning compared to half or less of the students who found this true for the paper-based DDL translations. The authors suggest adopting a blended approach beginning with paper-based exercises to control for focus before introducing computer-based DDL to reinforce learning. They conclude that "students faced with non-vetted computer-based DDL use the parallel translation to confirm the meaning so that they can focus on the grammatical structure" (Chujo & Oghigian, 2012, p. 180). Thus, learning can be enhanced by alternating between paper and numeric supports and also by alternating attention between form and meaning.

Friginal (2018) details a teaching unit in which pre-Intermediate Japanese students of English consult the sentence-aligned Japanese-English WebParaNews Corpus of news articles from a bilingual newspaper to notice, through hands-on concordancer queries, the different uses of synonyms such as *start/begin* and *big/large*. Then, students edited their own written production by replacing certain words with more "natural-sounding" ones using the same concordancer techniques. Once students are comfortable employing these techniques on the user-friendly but smaller WebParaNews Corpus, they move on to a more complex, tool-equipped unilingual corpus.

Frankenberg-Garcia (2012a) explains "it takes time and substantial training to become a proficient corpus user, but learners needn't become experts in corpus linguistics. Simple demonstrations of how corpora can be utilised to answer authentic questions that emerge in class will do" (p. 50). In 15 minutes, she created a paper handout of Compara and OpenSubtitles concordance data for students to examine the Portuguese *segurança,* equivalent to either "security" or "safety", allowing them to identify contextual differences mandating use. Verification of lexical use is one of the most accessible benefits of parallel corpora.

The difficulty of identifying lexical differences between languages is also highlighted by the authors of the sentence-aligned Russian Learner Translator Corpus (2.3 million English or Russian tokens) produced by translation students from 14 Russian universities. This corpus can be queried for individual items or sequences, lemmas, or parts of speech and covers ten genres, including news reports, letters, and interviews. They suggest investigating challenging English lemmas lacking immediate counterparts in Russian such as *overqualified* or *lock-in,* and *faux amis,* such as *actual, decade,* or *economical.* In another example of confusing multiple lexical translations, Frankenberg-Garcia and Santos (2003) queried the English-Portuguese parallel Compara Corpus to help students understand that *actualmente* does not translate to the English cognate "actually", but rather terms such as "now", "nowadays", "at the moment" (pp. 387–388). These current contributions serve as foundations for future projects and contribute to better teaching practices.

31.4 Case studies

Building upon these studies, we now explore the pertinence of parallel corpora in advanced language learning environments through three case studies. The first study illustrates the importance of the resource for identifying accurate meaning, the second examines false cognates across multiple parallel corpora, and the third delves into the capacity to examine complex constructions.

31.4.1 Case study 1: Existing multilingual resources

This analysis illustrates how the data of a resource, whether general data from the Internet or from specific corpora, influences the quality of lexical resources. We compare several well-known on-line dictionaries, Linguee, ReversoTranslation, and WordReference, which Doval and Sánchez Nieto (2019, p. 3) define as dictionaries "enlarged with multilingual online resources" and one parallel corpus platform, Tradooit.

In order to test the reliability of these sources, we analysed proposed translations of the expression *third degree* into French. The two terms 'third' and 'degree' are also frequently found together to describe a burn, an assault or a status in computer science. However, the expression *third degree* takes on a specific meaning in a legal context, as found in the United States Supreme Court's opinion for Miranda v. Arizona (1966), "it is clear that police violence and the 'third degree' flourished [during the 1930s]". According to the *Merriam-Webster dictionary,* 'third degree' refers only to "the subjection of a prisoner to mental or physical torture to extract a confession". The *Cambridge dictionary* which also has an entry for 'third-degree burn', considers it to be "asking serious questions and/or giving someone rough treatment to get information".

Linguee proposes *troisième degré,* but also *troisième diplôme,* building upon 'degree' as a university diploma. Wordreference also first refers to medical burns, followed by 'getting and giving the third degree' with the weaker translation *interroger* ("to interrogate") and the idiomatically appropriate *cuisiner* ("to cook"). ReversoDictionary offers the medically-based example "third degree atrioventricular block". ReversoContext highlights two possible uses, *troisième degré* and *interrogatoire* ("interrogation"). *Troisième degré* is illustrated by a reference to the severity of burns and the example "No wonder I'm getting the third degree", which does not aid understanding. In ReversoContext, *interrogatoire* ("interrogation") is contextualised by the bilingual Example (1), in which the 'suggested translation' (ST) in French, containing the ambiguous *interrogation,* is clarified by the adjective *severe,* as reflected in the 'literal translation' (LT), included here for greater comprehension of the French counterparts.

(1) The suspect was given the third degree until he confessed his crime.

(ST: "Le suspect avait eu un interrogatoire sévère avant qu'il n'avoue son crime" (ReversoContext))

(LT: "The suspect had a severe interrogation before confessing his crime")

Tradooit, one of the rare sources to offer the option to select and identify corpus data, proposes the translations *troisième degré, interrogatoire* and *inquisiteur* ("inquisition") as well as the relevant *passage a tabac* ("a violent beating") and *cuisinage* ("to cook"). In contrast, the vast majority of TAUS references apply to informatics or computer science, such as "Does not export entities as third-degree B-splines". Finally, the OpenSubtitles Corpus offers 151 English-French matches, many of which apply to policing: *interrogatoire musclé* ("muscled interrogation") and *les flics m'ont donné toutes sortes de traitement de choc* ("the police made me undergo all sorts of shock treatments").

These resources are easy to use and accessible on a mobile device or computer. However, as we have seen, the results are only as reliable as the quality of the language of the corpora they draw upon. In other words, a source that relies heavily upon general English may not offer the formal language required for academics. The capacity to deal with multi-word sequences or the verification by community members are both important. The subject domain of the corpus is determinant, as, for example, noted for the computer-science oriented TAUS. In the Supreme Court opinion, "third degree" was within quote marks to signal its informal character. This informality is characteristic of fictional films and television programs, as exemplified in the results found here. The results for *third degree* exemplify how the qualities of the data influence results. General language data does not always respond well to specific needs and may actually mislead scholarly users.

31.4.2 Case study 2: False cognates

Drawing upon Frankenberg-Garcia and Santos (2003), we queried three corpora for several well-known French/English false cognates: the online interfaces Tradooit and TREQ, plus the downloaded GlobalVoice available on OPUS and queried via Sketch Engine. By comparing the translation results from French to English of the "false friends", *actuellement, demande, évidence,* and *réalisation,* we hope to illustrate the technical and corpus differences of these options. TradooIT allows users to choose from a range of corpora (Europarl, UN, subtitles, etc.). Here, we have selected the entire corpora, which offers higher frequency, but without attention to genre.

All three sources give simultaneous "keyword in context" (KWIC) results, simultaneously listing both the French and English equivalents. TradooIT only searches one word form at a time, here the keyword's singular form. TREQ and Sketch Engine are case sensitive and thus show frequencies for *obviously* and *Obviously.* They all offer the option to view frequency. In order to access frequencies via Sketch Engine, the user must first search for the keyword in the source language, identify the recurrent translations in the target language and include these in a second query. Frequencies can be viewed according to word form, lemma, or part of speech.

Table 31.1 Lexical comparison

	GlobalVoices	TradooIT	TREQ
actuellement	now (6421), current (1725), Now (1322), currently (1090), moment (907), present (848)	currently (21504), now (6922), is (5384), current (2819), present (1347), presently (1250), today (1027)	currently (4016), now (723), present (599), current (407), moment (237), today (118), being (117)
demande	asks (255), demand (209), wonder (154), request (15830), wonders (141), asked (131), demands (119)	demand (16819), request (15830), asked (10544), application (9871), wonder (3783), calls (2910), apply (2570)	request (9056), application (7331), demand (3466), ask (1543), applications (1023), wonder (922), calls (805)
évidence	obviously (44), clearly (33), Obviously (27), obvious (14), highlights (14), highlight (13), evidence (11)	obviously (7501), clearly (4024), highlight (2697), evidence (1089), obvious (817), shows (817), identified (388)	obviously (220), highlighted (152), clearly (134), highlight (97), Obviously (95), Clearly (88), obvious (88),
réalisation	achievements (38), project (10), achievement (8), implementation (7), carry (3), realisation (3), completion (2), achieved (2), achieve (2)	achievement (2825), achieving (2676), project (2415), carrying (884), delivery (829), conduct (815), implementation (731)	achievement (731), achieving (463), completion (337), implementation (323), realisation (212), achieve (193), attainment (182)

Table 31.1 lists the top seven translations and their frequency by word form, although actual query results may include supplementary data.

The results vary according to the corpora database and the tools, as can be understood by observing the results. For *actuellement,* GlobalVoices has a greater frequency of the culturally-associated equivalent *moment,* also found in the Cineurope and the OpenSubtitles Corpus integrated into TradooIT. Although *request* or *ask* are frequent equivalents of *demande, application* is listed by both TradooIT and TREQ, due to their incorporation of governmental sources. TradooIT queries respect singularity or plurality, but not capitalisation, thereby giving rise to less repetition (within the first seven results) of target-words often beginning a sentence, such as *évidence.* In contrast, GlobalVoices and TREQ list both *obviously* and *Obviously,* splitting the frequencies of this term. Finally, for *realization, conduct* occurs notably within TradooIT's incorporation of documents from the Canadian Nuclear Safety Commission, while TREQ's *attainment* originates primarily from the Acquis Communautaire corpus. Thus, these frequency results may help learners explore a range of unexpected equivalents, especially according to genre.

31.4.3 Case study 3: Complex phenomena

Parallel corpora also offer possibilities to examine complex and non-intuitive phenomena, which are of direct interest to language learners. For example, Frankenberg-Garcia (2012b) relates a study concerning the appropriateness of ending a business letter with either *I look forward to hearing from you* or *I am looking forward to hearing from you.* A query of the one-million-word English-only Business Letter Corpus of American and British letters confirmed that both are acceptable, but that the former is more conventional. It is possible to undertake such an investigation thanks to a parallel corpus. To illustrate the technical possibilities, we introduce here the results of a sequence query.

Learners often have difficulty grasping when past tense forms should be used. This is true for francophone learners because a present tense form is used in French even when evoking events beginning in the past. Furthermore, in English, time can be introduced by either *for* or *since*. The interest of consulting a parallel corpus for differentiating between *since* or *for* is also highlighted on the Russian Learner Translator Corpus platform. In French, both of these prepositions are translated as "depuis", thus rendering a direct word-to-word translation impossible. To help learners notice differences in French, a query of the sequence containing a first-person pronoun, a verbal part of speech (pos), and the preposition *depuis* ("since/for") could take the form of Example 2:

(2) je [pos=V.★] depuis
LT: ("I [pos=V.★] since|for")

A query of Europarl.v7 on OPUS produces 86 matches, with 36 varying lexical verbs. These sequences show repeatedly that while the French verbs are in the present tense, the English versions take a past tense form. In Example 3, the lexical verb *faire* takes a singular present tense form: *fais* ("do/make"). However, the proposed equivalent is *have been doing*, as a simple present tense would be incorrect in English.

(3) Peut-être le mieux est-il encore de s'en tenir à ce que **je fais** *depuis* quinze ans
(LT: "Maybe the best is still to carry on as **I do** *for* 15 years")
(ST: "Perhaps the best all-round solution is to carry on as **I have been doing** *for* the past 15 years" (Europarl.v7))

Example 4, also from Europarl.v7, displays multiple non-intuitive phenomena of a French sequence. First, the more frequent French ambiguous pronoun of the collocation *on sait* ("one knows") serves to generalise the source of the information by its inclusive nature (Hartwell & Jacques, 2014) and is translated here by "as you all know". Once again, the central lexical verbal collocation *je plaide* ("I plead") is in the present tense in French, but takes the present perfect continuous tense in English, "have been calling for".

(4) **On** sait que **je plaide** depuis…
(LT: "**One** knows that **I plead** for/since…")
(ST: "As you all know, **I have been calling for**…" (Europarl.v7))

Example 5 confirms that the equivalent of a French present tense *souligne* ("underline") is a present perfect continuous tense in English, more often translated as "have been highlighting". Also notable for English language learners is the translation of *depuis* to "since" instead of "for", followed by a date. Learners can benefit from seeing that *since* is followed by a date, but *for* by a period of time.

(5) Il subsiste certaines préoccupations, **que je souligne depuis** 1999.
(LT: "It exists certain concerns that **I underline since** 1999".)
(ST: "There are still areas of concern that **I have been highlighting since** 1999". (Europarl.v7))

A query of the GlobalVoices Corpus on OPUS of Example 2 results in 20 occurrences. Among the pertinent ones, example 6 offers a more complex translation of the French *je fais depuis* (LT: "I do/make for"), by adopting a new grammatical category: "the critique that

I make" becomes simply "my critique". Furthermore, *depuis longtemps* ("for a long time") becomes the compact *long standing*.

(6) qui confirme la critique que **je fais depuis** longtemps des arts plastiques en Jamaïque
(LT: "which confirms the criticism that **I make for** a long time about plastic arts in Jamaica")
(ST: "which bears out **my long-standing** critique of visual art in Jamaica" (GlobalVoices)

Thus, these examples allow language learners to visualise the multiple ways of formulating meaning in different languages. Language rules, such as the use of a present or past tense, become more explicit to language learners as they view a compiled set of occurrences. Corpus queries offer condensed collections of input, thus illustrating rules and making patterns more apparent. Reliable bilingual data allow learners to concentrate on language differences or patterns, with less cognitive load related to comprehension.

31.5 Recommendations for teaching and learning

31.5.1 Caveats of corpora

Many of the caveats for teaching and learning with parallel corpora are similar to those decried for corpora in general, notably, the necessary time, training, technical, and ergonomic accessibility. As Frankenberg-Garcia (2016) notes, mastering how to select a corpus or to query and interpret concordances, word lists, collocations or other data is a first step. Transposing this expertise to the classroom is a second, for "corpus-based teaching aids must be relevant, useful and accessible to the particular group of learners" (Frankenberg-Garcia, 2016, p. 394).

However, these observed difficulties are exasperated by reduced availability of parallel corpora and, for some queries or corpora, increased technical needs. Students tend to access certain common resources, such as Linguee, despite the existence of free corpus-based and user-friendly sites, such as TradooIT. The current shortages of existing parallel corpora depend greatly on research funding benefitting or not a given language community. However, community endeavours, such as GlobalVoices and Tatoeba, are new conduits between less represented languages and English language learning.

31.5.2 Simplification and over-normalisation

Another weakness of calling upon parallel corpora is the issue of the quality of the target language found in translated texts and the phenomenon known as "translationese" (Aijmer, 2020; Baker, 1998). Quality translations stretch beyond word-to-word translations to adopt more complex equivalents, such as a change in grammatical category (Example 6). This is why many parallel corpora are aligned at the sentence level instead of by word. Understanding subtle connotation is also a learning challenge, as Kübler (2011) highlights, for example as related to the neutral *to cause* and the French *causer*, the latter introducing a negative result. She suggests that consulting corpora and specifically specialised corpora may help students to "avoid using *causer* as the translation equivalent of those English verbs of causation that do not have a negative semantic prosody" (Kübler, 2011, p. 77).

Furthermore, relying upon unique data sources of corpora increases the risk of an unwanted normalisation, such as "eurolect", a manifestation of converging terminology and linguistic interferences within European Parliament documents (Torrellas Castillo, 2009). Cultural, social, and political histories influence subject matter and the associated discursive patterns across communities. For English language learning, the student population as well as their academic and professional discursive needs should also be taken into account. Kubota and Chiang (2013) confirm that "it is necessary to explore contextual understanding of *needs* by taking into consideration how learner's gender, race, class, and other backgrounds shape social practices in a specific professional context" (p. 495). Thus, teaching activities and materials incorporating parallel corpora should build upon language learners' diverse needs as related to learners' first language, with attention to the corpora's underlying content and socio-political positioning. Corpora, like language, is not neutral, meriting a teacher's attention to possibly problematic content or the normalisation of diverse learners' needs.

31.6 Future directions of research

Machine translation tools provide solutions based on corpora and statistical probability models. Systems incorporating machine translation tools offer an indirect way of accessing parallel corpora, as these systems essentially rely on existing translation corpora. Until the early 2010s, Statistical Machine Translation systems (Koehn *et al.*, 2003) suggested a translation by coupling word- or phrase-level translation probabilities and probabilities linked to the model of the target language. This coupling improves the idiomatic character of the suggested translations. The knowledge introduced by these language and translation models were, to some extent, made explicit by the corresponding probability measures.

In more recent models based on deep-learning techniques (Bahdanau *et al.*, 2015), sentences are translated, not by combining translation fragments, but on the basis of a global representation of their meaning, thereby offering significant improvements especially as related to the idiomaticity. However, accessing the information encoded by the neural network remains difficult, as the parallel corpora feeding the abstract network is not always easily identified. As we have seen, the source data is essential to the quality of the results.

In the future of artificial intelligence, modulating the suggested translations according to the textual genre of the parallel texts would be an important step forward. For example, Chambers (2010) comments that the 87 occurrences of the verb *connaître* (commonly, "to know") in the Chambers-Le Baron Corpus of French research articles refer to "doing an experience". Thus, a unilingual corpus helps to identify meaning often within a specific genre, but does not suggest translations, as does a parallel corpus such as the ParaSHS English-French parallel corpus of research articles in the humanities (Example 7). Here, *connaîtrons* is translated as "experiencing", which mirrors Chamber's (*ibid*) understanding of the word in an academic context.

(7) **Connaîtrons**-nous alors une mutation des liens entre **moi** et corps et, corrélativement, une mutation de l'imaginaire tel que le définit Lacan? (ParaSHS)
(ST: Are we thus **experiencing** a change in the relations between the **self** and the body and, by correlation, of the imaginary as Lacan defines it? (ParaSHS)

The Tradooit automatic neuronal translator based on Canadian governmental documents also adopts of form of ("experience") to translate the verb *connaître* (Example 7). However, it proposes ("me") instead of the psychological notion of "self".

(8) Would we then **experience** a mutation in the bonds between **me** and body and, consequently, a mutation of the imagination as defined by Lacan? (Tradooit)

If Deepl (Example 8) correctly identifies *moi* as the ("self"), it suggests the frequent general English verb ("know"), which does not ring true.

(9) (ST: Would we then **know** a mutation of the links between **self** and body and, correlatively, a mutation of the imaginary as defined by Lacan? (Deepl))

Thus, parallel corpora and automatic translation systems evolve synchronically. Automatic translations rely upon the quality and type of data. Parallel corpora expand according to the evolution of tools as well as the academic, societal, corporate capacities, and projects.

Technological advances corresponding to greater accessibility and ease-of-use – as well as teacher training in corpus use – will influence the future of parallel corpora for language teaching. Actual academic and professional practices of consulting these resources should modify their introduction and role in the classroom as a strategy for lifelong learning. The acquisition of core vocabulary or grammatical understanding should accompany the capacity to consult critically and successfully available resources, such as parallel corpora. This can be done by combining direct consultation or indirect study from chosen output. For non-native learners of English, the capacity to consult a set of corresponding English, their language occurrences targeting a specific lexical or grammatical question is a great advantage especially when adapted to language level. This advantage complements and enforces theoretical explanations or decontextualised data. Consulting parallel corpora can focus on meaning and form. Thus, understanding teacher, learner, material designers, and professional practices of consulting parallel corpora is another area for future research.

Further reading

Doval, I., & Sánchez Nieto, M. T. (2019). *Parallel corpora for contrastive and translation studies.* Benjamins. This collective work offers an overview of parallel corpora, notably for translation.

Fan, M., & Xu, X. (2002). An evaluation of an online bilingual corpus for the self-learning of legal English. *System, 30,* 47–63. A study confirming the pedagogical interest for translation students to consult a Chinese-English legal corpus containing navigational hyperlinks to corresponding sentences in the other language.

Frankenberg-Garcia, A., & Santos, D. (2003). Introducing COMPARA the Portuguese-English parallel corpus. In F. Zanettin, S. Bernardini, & D. Stewart (Eds.), *Corpora in translator education* (pp. 71–87). St. Jerome. One of several articles about the ground-breaking Portuguese-English parallel corpus and of the many uses of parallel corpora for teaching and learning applicable across languages.

Corpus and interface links:
Bitextes anglais-français corpus: http://rali.iro.umontreal.ca/rali/?q=fr/BAF
Canadian Parliament Hansards: https://www.isi.edu/natural-language/download/hansard/
Common Language Resources and Technology Infrastructure: www.clarin.eu/content/language-resource-inventory
Compara: www.linguateca.pt/COMPARA
Deepl: https://www.deepl.com
EIIDA: https://corpora.aiakide.net/scientext20/?do=SQ.setView&view=corpora
English-Norwegian Parallel corpus: https://tekstlab.uio.no/glossa2/saml?licence=ACA-NC-LOC-LRT-ND_OMC;back=https%3a%2f%2ftekstlab.uio.no%2fglossa2%2fomc4
European Commission's Translation Memory: https://data.europa.eu/euodp/en/data/dataset/dgt-translation-memory
European Language Resources Association: www.elra.info/en/about/elra/
European Parliament corpus: https://ec.europa.eu/jrc/en/language-technologies/dcep
European Research Infrastructure Consortium: https://www.clarin.eu/resource-families/parallel-corpora
Linguistic Data Consortium: www.ldc.upenn.edu/about

MyMemory: https://mymemory.translated.net/
OPUS: http://opus.nlpl.eu/
ParaSHS: http://phraseotext.univ-grenoble-alpes.fr/lexicoscope_2.0
Russian Learner Translator Corpus: https://rus-ltc.org/static/html/about.html
Sketch Engine: https://www.sketchengine.eu/guide/setting-up-parallel-corpora/
Statistical Natural Language Processing Group: https://www.cl.uni-heidelberg.de/statnlpgroup/
Translation Automation User Society: https://data-app.taus.net/
Translation Equivalents Database: http://portal.clarin.nl/node/18403
UM-corpus: http://nlp2ct.cis.umac.mo/um-corpus/index.html
United Nations corpus: https://conferences.unite.un.org/UNCORPUS/en/DownloadOverview
Tatoeba: https://tatoeba.org/eng
Web Align Toolkit: http://phraseotext.univ-grenoble-alpes.fr/webAlignToolkit

References

Aijmer, K. (2020). Contrastive pragmatics and corpora. *Contrastive Pragmatics*, *1*, 28–57. https://doi.org/10.1163/26660393-12340004

Alotaibi, H. M. (2017). Arabic-English parallel corpus: A new resource for translation training and language teaching. *Arab World English Journal*, *8*(3), 319–337. https://dx.doi.org/10.24093/awej/vol8no3.21

Bahdanau, D., Cho, K. H., & Bengio, Y. (2015). *Neural machine translation by jointly learning to align and translate* [Paper presentation]. 3rd International Conference on Learning Representations, ICLR 2015, San Diego, United States. https://arxiv.org/pdf/1409.0473.pdf

Baker, M. (1998). Réexplorer la langue de la traduction: Une approche par corpus. *Meta: Translators' Journal*, *43*(4), 480–485.

Carter-Thomas, S., & Jacques, M.-P. (Eds.). (2017). *CHIMERA. Romance corpora and linguistic studies*, *4*(1). https://revistas.uam.es/index.php/%20chimera/article/view/6948

Čermák, F. (2019). InterCorp: A parallel corpus of 40 languages. In I. Doval & M. T. Sánchez Nieto (Eds.), *Parallel corpora for contrastive and translation studies* (pp. 93–102). Benjamins.

Čermák, F., & Rosen, A. (2012). The case of InterCorp, a multilingual parallel corpus. *International Journal of Corpus Linguistics*, *17*(3), 411–427.

Chambers, A. (2010). L'apprentissage de l'écriture en langue seconde à l'aide d'un corpus spécialisé. *Revue Française de Linguistique Appliquée*, *XV*, 9–20.

Chan, T. P., & Liou, H. C. (2005). Effects of web-based concordancing instruction on EFL students' learning of verb-noun collocations. *Computer Assisted Language Learning*, *18*(3), 231–251.

Chartier, R., & Martin, H.-J. (1986). *Histoire de l'édition française*, 4. Fayard.

Chujo, K., & Oghigian, K. (2012). DDL for EFL beginners: A report on student gains and views on paper-based concordancing and the role of L1. In J. Thomas & A. Boulton (Eds.), *Input, process and product: Developments in teaching and language corpora* (pp. 169–182). Masaryk University Press.

Cobb, T. (2019). From corpus to CALL: The use of technology in teaching and learning formulaic language. In A. Siyanova-Chanturia & A. Pellicer-Sanchez (Eds.), *Understanding formulaic language: A second language acquisition perspective* (pp. 192–210). Routledge.

De Pauw, G., Wagacha, P. W., & de Schryver, G.-M. (2011). Exploring the SAWA corpus: Collection and deployment of a parallel corpus English-Swahili. *Language Resources & Evaluation*, *45*, 331–344. https://doi.org10.1007/s10579-011-9159-7

Ernst-Slavit, G., & Mulhern, M. (2003). Bilingual books: Promoting literacy and biliteracy in the second language and mainstream classroom. *Reading Online*, *7*(2), 1–15.

Evert, S., & Hardie, A. (2011). *Twenty-first century corpus workbench: Updating a query architecture for the new millennium* [Paper presentation]. Corpus Linguistics 2011, University of Birmingham, UK. https://www.birmingham.ac.uk/documents/college-artslaw/corpus/conference-archives/2011/Paper-153.pdf

Ferraresi, A., & Bernardini, S. (2019). Building EPTIC: A multi-sided, multi-purpose corpus of EU parliament proceedings. In I. Doval & M. T. Sánchez Nieto (Eds.), *Parallel corpora for contrastive and translation studies* (pp. 123–139). Benjamins.

Frankenberg-Garcia, A. (2012a). Integrating corpora with everyday language teaching. In J. Thomas & A. Boulton (Eds.), *Input, process and product: Developments in teaching and language corpora* (pp. 36–53). Masaryk University Press.

Frankenberg-Garcia, A. (2012b). Raising teacher's awareness of corpora. *Language Teaching, 45*(4), 475–489.

Frankenberg-Garcia, A. (2016). Corpora in the classroom. In G. Hall (Ed.), *Routledge handbook of English language teaching* (pp. 383–398). Routledge.

Frawley, W. (Ed.). (1984). *Translation: Literary, linguistics and philosophical approaches.* University of Delaware Press.

Frérot, C. (2016). Corpora and corpus technology for translation purposes in professional and academic environments. Major achievements and new perspectives. *Cadernos de Tradução, 36*(1), 36–61. https://doi.org/10.5007/2175-7968.2016v36nesp1p36

Friginal, E. (2018). *Corpus linguistics for English teachers: New tools, online resources, and classroom activities.* Routledge.

Granger, S. (in press). Tracking the third code: A cross-linguistic corpus-driven approach to metadiscursive markers. In A. Čermáková & M. Mahlberg (Eds.), *Corpus as discourse.* Benjamins.

Hartwell, L., & Jacques, M.-P. (2014). Authorial presence in French and English: Pronoun + verb patterns in biology and medicine research articles. *Discourse, 15, 1-21.* https://doi.org/10.4000/discours.8941

Hartwell, L. (2020). A didactic comparison of online French-English lexical resources. *Études en Didactique des Langues, 34*, 7–24.

Johansson, S. (2008). *Contrastive analysis and learner language: A corpus-based approach.* University of Oslo. https://www.hf.uio.no/ilos/forskning/grupper/English_Language_and_Corpus_Linguistics_Research/papers/contrastive-analysis-and-learner-language_learner-language-part.pdf

Johns, T., Lee, H.-C., & Wang, L. (2008). Integrating corpus-based CALL programs in teaching English through children's literature. *Computer Assisted Language Learning, 21*(5), 483–506.

Koehn, P., Och, F.-O., & Marcu, D. (2003). Statistical phrase-based translation. In *Conference of the North American Chapter of the Association for Computational Linguistics on Human Language Technology (NAACL): Proceedings,* Volume 1 (pp. 48–54).

Kraif, O. (2018). Constitution et traitement d'un corpus bilingue d'articles scientifiques: Exemple de mise en oeuvre automatique avec une architecture légère en perl. In M. Mangeot & A. Tutin (Eds.), *Actes des journées LTT 2018.* Grenoble.

Kübler, N. (2011). Working with different corpora in translation teaching. In A. Frankenberg-Garcia, L. Flowerdew, & G. Aston (Eds.), *New trends in corpora and language learning* (pp. 62–80). Continuum.

Kubota, K., & Chiang, L. T. (2013). Gender and race in ESP research. In B. Paltridge & S. Starfield (Eds.), *The handbook of English for specific purposes* (pp. 481–499). Wiley-Blackwell.

Lison, P., & Tiedemann, J. (2016). OpenSubtitles2016: extracting large parallel corpora from movie and TV subtitles. In *Proceedings of the 10th international conference on language resources and evaluation.* https://www.semanticscholar.org/paper/OpenSubtitles2016%3A-Extracting-Large-Parallel-from-Lison-Tiedemann/e11edb4201007530c3692814a155b22f78a0d659

Mikhailov, M., & Cooper, R. (2016). *Corpus linguistics for translation and contrastive studies: A guide for research.* Routledge.

Rabadán, R. (2019). Working with parallel corpora: Usefulness and usability. In I. Doval & M. T. Sánchez Nieto (Eds.), *Parallel corpora for contrastive and translation studies* (pp. 57–78). Benjamins.

Simard, M. (2020). Corpora in the classroom. In M. O'Hagan (Ed.), *Routledge handbook of translation and technology* (pp. 78–90). Routledge.

Simard, M. (1998). The BAF: A corpus of English-French bitext. *Proceedings of the First International Conference on Language Resources and Evaluation* (pp. 489–494), Granada, Spain. http://www.mt-archive.info/LREC-1998-Simard.pdf

Škrabal, M., & Vavřín, M. (2017). The Translation Equivalents Database (Treq) as a lexicographer's aid. In I. Kosek, et al. (Eds.), Proceedings of the eLex 2017 conference: Electronic lexicography in the 21ˢᵗ century (pp. 124–137).

Steinberger, R., Eisele, A., Klocek, S., Pilos, S., & Schlüter, P. (2012). DGT-TM: A freely Available Translation Memory in 22 Languages. *Proceedings of the Eighth International Conference on Language Resources and Evaluation* (pp. 454–459), Istanbul.

Teubert, W., & Čermáková, A. (2004). Directions in corpus linguistics. In K. Halliday (Ed.), *Lexicology and corpus linguistics* (pp. 113–165). A&C Black.

Tian, L., Wong, D. F., Chao, L. S., Quaresma, P., Oliveira, F., Li, S., Wang, Y., & Lu, Y. (2014). UM-Corpus: a large English-Chinese parallel corpus for statistical machine translation. *Proceedings of the Ninth International Conference on Language Resources and Evaluation, Reykjavik*, Iceland.

Tiedemann, J. (2016). OPUS - Parallel corpora for everyone. *Baltic Journal of Modern Computing, 4*(2), 923–926.

Torrellas Castillo, M. (2009*). Les interférences linguistiques dans les textes en espagnol des institutions de l'Union Européenne: Étude fondée sur le corpus bilingue massif aligné de l'acquis communautaire.* [Unpublished doctoral dissertation]. Université de Poitiers.

Utiyama, M., & Isahara, H. (2008). Mining patents for parallel corpora. In C. Goutte, N. Cancedda, M. Dymetman, & G. Foster (Eds.), *Learning machine translation.* MIT Press. https://direct.mit.edu/books/chapter-pdf/228866/9780262255097_cab.pdf

32

AUTOMATED SYNTACTIC ANALYSIS FOR ELT

Xiaofei Lu, J. Elliott Casal and Yingying Liu

32.1 Introduction

Recent advances in natural language processing (NLP) and corpus linguistics research have led to the development of computational tools for automating different types of syntactic analysis of first (L1) and second language (L2) texts (Lu, 2014). For example, a number of syntactic parsers are now available for analyzing the syntactic structures of sentences or the relations among different elements of a sentence (e.g. Honnibal & Johnson, 2015; Manning *et al.*, 2014), and several syntactic complexity analyzers can now be used to assess the degree of complexity of the syntactic structures used in spoken or written production (e.g. Biber *et al.*, 1999; Kyle, 2016; Lu, 2009, 2010; McNamara *et al.*, 2014). Such tools have dramatically increased the scope and scale of computational, theoretical, as well as applied linguistics research that involves analyzing the syntactic structures or complexity of spoken or written texts. At the same time, they have also inspired useful practical applications in language pedagogy (Lu, 2018; Lu & Bluemel, 2020).

This chapter starts with a brief overview of the state-of-the-art NLP technologies for automated syntactic analysis (ASA) and then systematically discusses three strands of current and potential innovative applications of such technologies in language teaching and learning. The first strand draws upon the theoretical proposals of focus on form (Long, 1991) and input enhancement (Sharwood Smith, 1991) and uses ASA to identify occurrences of target syntactic structures in pedagogical texts, make those occurrences textually salient, and create in-text exercises on the target structures to promote learners' acquisition of those structures. The second strand also builds on the notion of input enhancement but focuses on promoting learners' overall syntactic awareness rather than their acquisition of specific structures. This is done by reformatting pedagogical texts in such a way that makes the clausal and phrasal structures of each sentence visually explicit in order to facilitate learners' syntactic processing and subsequently the development of their reading skills and potentially other language skills, too. The third strand is informed by the emerging line of research in corpus-based genre analysis aimed at systematically mapping linguistic features to the rhetorical functions they are used to realize in texts of different genres. This strand integrates ASA with rhetorical and functional analysis of texts to promote learners' awareness of genre-specific mappings between syntactic forms and rhetorical functions as well as their ability to deploy complex syntactic structures in functionally effective and genre-appropriate ways. The chapter concludes with a discussion of future directions of ASA-informed language pedagogy.

32.2 NLP technologies for automated syntactic analysis: An overview

At the core of NLP technologies for ASA are computational tools designed to automate the analysis of syntactic categories (e.g. part-of-speech categories and phrasal categories) and relations (e.g. hierarchical constituency relations and dependency relations). Results of these core types of syntactic analysis can facilitate further explorations that tap into categorical and/ or relational information. This section introduces the analytical steps involved in ASA and the tools for automating them without delving too deeply into the algorithmic details of the NLP technologies behind them.

A necessary first step in ASA is the segmentation of the text under investigation into individual words and sentences, as the subsequent steps in identifying the categories of and relations among syntactic elements and the overall structures of sentences necessitate clear demarcation of word and sentence boundaries. While sentence boundaries are generally delimited by a small number of punctuation marks, the presence of one such punctuation mark does not always denote the end of a sentence. In English, for example, a period may be used to denote an abbreviation or a decimal point, among other possibilities. Sentence segmentation, thus, primarily involves determining whether each occurrence of a sentence-final punctuation mark denotes the end of a sentence or not. Word segmentation may appear to be straightforward for languages that use white space between words. At the same time, even in these languages, decisions need to be made with respect to whether contracted forms such as *I've* and hyphenated words such as *life-threatening* should be analyzed as one word or multiple words. In languages that do not use white space between words, such as Chinese, word segmentation is a more complicated task, as there may be abundant ambiguity in which elements form a word with each other (e.g. Lu, 2006).

Once a text has been segmented into sentences and words, the next step in ASA is often to determine the part-of-speech (POS) category of each word in each sentence, as POS information is necessary for analyzing the syntactic relations among words. The primary challenges for this process involve disambiguating words that belong to multiple POS categories (e.g. *book* as a verb or noun) and determining the POS categories of new words that have not been previously used, such as new names (e.g. Google when the name was first used in written form).

The structure of a sentence can be analyzed in various ways, depending on the underlying syntactic theory or grammar. In phrase structure grammars, for example, sentence structure is understood in terms of constituency relations (e.g. Bies *et al.*, 1995). A constituent is a word or word grouping (e.g. a phrase or clause) that can function as a single unit in a sentence (e.g. a noun phrase that serves as the subject of the sentence), and constituents are hierarchically related in the sense that a constituent may be part of a larger constituent (e.g. a prepositional phrase may be part of a noun phrase). Phrase structure grammars generally contain a set of rules that specify how different types of sentences and their constituents can be formed. ASA based on such grammars thus involves determining the boundaries and categories of and the hierarchical relations among the constituents of a sentence. In dependency grammars, sentence structure is analyzed in terms of dependency relations between pairs of words in the sentence. Specifically, a word may be said to depend on or be governed by another word in a specific way. For example, in *his sister*, the word *his* can be said to depend on the word *sister*, and the specific grammatical relation between them is one of possessive modification (e.g.

De Marneffe & Manning, 2008). ASA based on dependency grammars, thus, involves determining which words enter into what types of dependency relations in a sentence.

A number of computational tools can be used to perform these analyses automatically with a fairly high level of accuracy, such as the Stanford CoreNLP National Language Processing Toolkit (Manning *et al.*, 2014) and spaCy (Honnibal & Johnson, 2015). For example, given the sentence in (1), the Stanford CoreNLP Toolkit can generate both a phrase structure analysis and a dependency analysis, represented in (2)[1] and (3)[2], respectively.

1. I have a dream.
2. (ROOT
          (S
          (NP (PRP I))
          (VP (VBP have)
          (NP (DT a) (NN dream)))
          (..)))
3. nsubj(have-2, I-1)
          root(ROOT-0, have-2)
          det(dream-4, a-3)
          dobj(have-2, dream-4)

In (2), the ROOT node represents the top level of a single, complete sentence. If we had multiple sentences in a text, each sentence would be denoted by a separate ROOT node, corresponding to the outcome of the sentence segmentation process. In terms of word segmentation, notice that the sentence has been broken down into five tokens, including four words and a period, as indicated by the five pairs of brackets that enclose them, namely, (PRP I), (VBP have), (DT a), (NN dream), and (..). The POS category of each token is indicated by a POS tag to the left of the token. The boundaries of and hierarchical relations among the constitutes of the sentence are marked through indentation and bracketing, and the category of each constituent is indicated by a tag immediately following each opening bracket. For example, (NP (PRP I)) indicates that the personal pronoun *I* alone makes up a noun phrase, (NP (DT a) (NN dream)) indicates that the determiner *a* and the noun *dream* make up another noun phrase, and (VP (VBP have) (NP (DT a) (NN dream))) indicates that the verb *have* and the noun phrase *a dream* together make up a verb phrase. The subject NP (i.e. *I*) and the VP (i.e. *have a dream*) make up a simple declarative sentence, as indicated by the same level of indention of these two constituents below S.

In (3), each triplet indicates the grammatical relation between a pair of words, with the first element denoting the grammatical relation, the second element the governor word, and the last element the dependent word. The numbers following the words correspond to the positions of the words in the sentence, and ROOT-0 simply denotes the entire sentence. The four triplets each reads: "*I* is the nominal subject of *have*", "*have* is the root of the sentence", "*a* is the determiner of *dream*", and "*dream* is the direct object of *have*". For readers who prefer visual representations of such grammatical relations, GrammarScope[3] provides a graphic user interface to the phrase structure and dependency relation analyses generated by the Stanford CoreNLP National Language Processing Toolkit that is user-friendly and intuitive to use.

The results from these or similar analyses can be used to determine the presence and frequency of different types of syntactic structures used in language production. Tregex (Levy & Andrew, 2006), for example, is a tool that can be used to query syntactically annotated texts to extract and count sentences, clauses, or phrases containing particular syntactic structures of interest to the user (e.g. noun phrases with a post-modifying prepositional phrase). Results from sentence structure analyses have many useful applications, such as the development of tools for grammar checking (e.g. Grammarly[4]) and learning (e.g. the iGE app[5]). Several grammatical or syntactic complexity analyzers use such results to assess the degree of variation, elaboration, and sophistication of the syntactic structures used in language production in different ways, including the Biber Tagger[6] (Biber *et al.*, 1999), Coh-Metrix (Graesser *et al.*, 2004), L2 Syntactic Complexity Analyzer (L2SCA) (Lu, 2010), and the Tool for the Automatic Analysis of Syntactic Sophistication and Complexity (TAASSC) (Kyle, 2016).

32.3 Textual enhancement and grammar acquisition

The first strand of research into the pedagogical applications of ASA that we will discuss in this chapter has to do with its use in textual enhancement to promote grammar acquisition. This line of research draws on the theoretical proposals of focus on form (Long, 1991), which posits that learners' noticing of linguistic forms is a prerequisite for learner intake, and on input enhancement (Sharwood Smith, 1991), which postulates that making target linguistic forms salient in the input can facilitate learners' noticing of those forms. Based on these proposals, input texts can be enhanced in various ways to help learners notice the occurrences and contexts of the use of target linguistic forms in those texts, such as vocabulary items, collocations, phraseological units, and grammatical structures, among others. NLP technologies can be used to analyze input texts, identify occurrences of such target linguistic forms, and subsequently make those forms salient in the input texts in some way (e.g. by using a larger size or different color). When it comes to grammatical categories (e.g. vocabulary items of a specific POS category in a text, or adjectives modifying a particular noun in a text) and structures (e.g. finite relative clauses or non-finite dependent clauses), ASA technologies become highly useful for identifying their occurrences in the input texts.

The visual input enhancement of the Web (VIEW) system[7] developed by Meurers *et al.* (2010) is an excellent example of how ASA can be used to analyze and enhance input texts to facilitate learners' noticing of target grammatical forms. VIEW is an extension that can be added to Firefox, Chrome, or Opera to automatically enhance authentic Web texts by highlighting occurrences of the grammatical category or structure that learners choose to work with out of a set of available choices. In addition, following the notion that learners need to act on the forms they notice in the input in order for acquisition to occur (Sharwood Smith, 1981), VIEW goes beyond making the target grammatical forms salient in the input text and integrates the capability to generate several types of exercises for learners to practice recognizing and producing those forms within the Web texts they are reading.

Specifically, after installing the VIEW extension in a compatible web browser, the learner can navigate to any Web text in any of the supported languages (English, German, Russian, and Spanish), specify the language of the Web text, the target grammatical structure to work with, and the desired activity type, and then submit the Web text for enhancement. The grammatical structures available for the four languages vary. For English, for example, learners can choose to work with articles, determiners, gerunds vs. infinitives, noun countability, phrasal verbs, and prepositions. For all languages and all available grammatical structures, four types of activities are available. The first activity, Colorize, is a traditional input enhancement activity that highlights all occurrences of the target grammatical structure in the Web text with a different color. The second activity, Click, is a recognition activity that asks the learner to click on occurrences of the target grammatical structure one at a time. The third is a Multiple Choice activity that requires the learner to choose the right form for each occurrence of the target structure out of a list of choices (e.g. the correct preposition in a particular context). The fourth activity, Practice, asks the learner to provide the right form for each occurrence of the target structure in a blank. All activities occur within the Web text in the browser window. With the exception of the Colorize activity, feedback is given to the learner by turning the color of the clicked, selected, or produced text green if the response is correct and red if wrong. In addition to Web texts, learners can also open local text files in a compatible Web browser and utilize the functions of VIEW in the same way. It is probably not difficult to see that the role of ASA technologies in the realization of the functionalities of VIEW lies in the automatic analysis of the syntactic structures of the sentences in the text in question and the identification of occurrences of the target grammatical structures in the text. Based on the theoretical claims of focus on form and input enhancement, the types of textual enhancement and recognition and production activities provided in VIEW constitute useful supplementary opportunities for learners to notice and potentially acquire target grammatical structures while reading authentic texts.

Few studies have examined the effect of these types of textual enhancement and activities enabled by ASA technologies on learners' grammatical acquisition. Ruiz *et al.* (2019) used the activities in the VIEW system in their investigation of how individual differences in working and declarative memory may interact with the condition of instruction (form-focused vs. meaning-focused) to affect L2 learners' acquisition of English phrasal verbs. They divided 127 advanced-level adult L1 German learners of English into two groups. One group read news articles online while completing multiple choice activities for phrasal verbs generated by VIEW (form-focused group) for two weeks, and the other read news articles online for the same period of time without completing any additional exercises. They found that working memory predicted learning in the form-focused condition but not in the meaning-focused condition, while declarative memory as measured by the Continuous Visual Memory Task predicted learning in both conditions. Their study did not directly compare the effects of the condition of instruction on learning per se but contributed useful insights into whether and how individual differences may affect learning in different conditions of instruction supported by NLP technologies.

32.4 Visual-syntactic text formatting and syntactic processing

In addition to its use in textual enhancement to promote the acquisition of specific grammatical features (as discussed in Section 32.3), ASA has also been used to parse pedagogical texts and modify their formats of presentation in an effort to reveal the overall syntactic structure of each input sentence and subsequently facilitate learners' development of reading skills and potentially other language skills as well. For language learners, particularly low-proficiency and L2 learners, processing the syntactic structures present in pedagogical materials in standard block format can be challenging, due to such adverse factors as limited syntactic awareness, inadequate syntactic processing skills, and L1-L2 differences, among others. Grounded also on the notion of input enhancement (Sharwood Smith, 1991), some researchers hypothesized that manipulating the format of presentation of the input text in a way that makes the overall structure of each sentence in the text salient to learners may help raise their syntactic awareness, facilitate their syntactic processing and reading comprehension, and positively affect the development of their syntactic knowledge and reading skills in the long run (e.g. Jandreau & Bever, 1992; Park & Warschauer, 2016; Tate *et al.*, 2019; Walker *et al.*, 2005).

One particular approach to text format modification for the purpose of syntactic enhance-ment favors reformatting texts in standard block format into shorter syntactic segments. Two techniques have fared prominently in this approach, namely, simple phrase-segmented for-matting (e.g. Bever *et al.*, 1990; Jandreau & Bever, 1992) and visual-syntactic text formatting (VSTF) (Walker *et al.*, 2005). With the first technique, extra spaces are inserted between phrasal and clausal units in each sentence, so that texts are chunked into shorter syntactic segments. VSTF is a more complex technique in that it not only inserts additional spaces between smaller chunks, but also presents them in a cascading hierarchy based on the syn-tactic relations among them. We focus our discussion on the VSTF technique in the rest of this section.

VSTF was designed by Walker *et al.* (2005) to assist with both visual and syntactic pro-cessing in reading. Legge *et al.* (1997) showed that human eyes can only capture a limited span at each fixation – 9–15 characters to be exact. To help readers reduce eyestrains and focus their attention to visual processing, Walker *et al.* (2005) limited the length of each lin-guistic element to no more than two fixation eye spans and presented one linguistic element per line. Syntactic processing has to do with the mental processes involved in uncovering abstract hierarchical structures behind a linear sequence of words and plays a critical role in the construction of meaning of the text (e.g. Goldberg, 1995). By pre-segmenting sentences into smaller, meaningful linguistic elements, and capturing the hierarchical relations among those elements through line indentions, VSTF was expected to support learners' accurate and fast syntactic processing. Furthermore, the reduction in the cognitive demand for syntactic processing was also expected to free up more cognitive resources for other comprehension-related activities and lead to better comprehension of the text. The example in (4) illustrates how a sentence from this section may be presented in VSTF format, generated by Live Ink[8], the online tool made available by the VSTF developers.

4. While VSTF
    was initially designed primarily
      to promote syntactic processing
        and reading skill development,
  some researchers
    suggested
      that it
    may potentially facilitate
      the development
    of other language skills.

Walker *et al.* (2005) empirically validated the effects of VSTF on promoting reading com-prehension, retention, and proficiency. A short-term lab experiment with college students and a year-long classroom research with ninth-grade students revealed that, compared to the standard block format, VSTF led to greater improvement in all three areas. Notably, participants of their lab experiment spent more time reading the VSTF passages but achieved a 25% higher reading efficiency, assessed as the reading comprehension score divided by reading time, than those reading passages in the standard block format.

While VSTF was initially designed primarily to promote syntactic processing and reading skill development, some researchers suggested that it may potentially facilitate the develop-ment of other language skills. For example, Park and Warschauer (2016) claimed that VSTF could help promote learners' writing skill development. Specifically, they argued that as learners' syntactic awareness improves through VSTF reading, they would be able to derive more syntactic knowledge from the input and subsequently write in more syntactically appropriate ways. Park (2018) pointed out that VSTF may positively affect vocabulary development as it helps readers identify the grammatical functions and meanings of words in context.

Researchers from the Digital Learning Lab at University of California, Irvine have conducted a series of large-scale classroom experiments to assess the efficacy of VSTF in promoting adolescent learners' reading and writing (Park & Warschauer, 2016; Tate *et al.*, 2019; Warschauer *et al.*, 2011). Participants in their studies were L1-English and L2-English students from sixth to eighth grade in California. The pedagogical interventions adopted in their studies were well integrated into the established curriculum of the participating classes and have implications for language teachers in a wide range of contexts. Park and Warschauer (2016), for instance, divided 282 sixth-grade L2 students of English in two suburban school districts in Southern California into a VSTF group and a control group. The two groups read the same textbook in different formats for one school year, one in VSTF format on the laptop and the other in regular block format in print. The researchers used mixed methods of data collection and analysis, including class observation notes, semi-structured interviews with class instructors, and quantitative analysis of pre- and post-test scores to examine the effects of the two formats on the participants reading and writing performance. The participant's scores on the English language arts subtests of the California Standards Tests in the two consecutive years before and after the treatment were used as their pre- and post-test scores, respectively. Results suggested that VSTF promoted the participants' overall syntactic awareness, knowledge of vocabulary analysis, and knowledge of syntactic structures, and that low-proficiency students benefited more from VSTF than high-proficiency students.

Park and Warschauer's (2016) study demonstrated how VSTF can be integrated into an established curriculum and implemented in language classrooms. Textbooks and other reading materials can be easily converted to the VSTF format online using LiveInk, although a subscription is required for converting more than 1000 characters per request. Another practical issue with applying VSTF in classrooms is the requirement for digital devices (i.e. computers, laptops, iPads, Chromebooks, cellphones, etc.). Tate *et al.* (2019) showed that using iPads or Chromebooks resulted in no significant difference in the effect of the VSTF treatment and recommended that districts or schools make their digital device selection based on their needs and financial resources.

32.5 Mapping syntactic features to rhetorical functions of genre

The final application of ASA to language pedagogy discussed in this chapter draws on an emerging line of corpus-based genre analysis research that investigates the linguistic features used in the rhetorical functions of different genres (Le & Harrington, 2015; Lu *et al.*, 2020; Omidian *et al.*, 2018; Yoon & Casal, 2020). Such research integrates automated and semi-automated corpus-based approaches to linguistic analysis with qualitative analysis of writers' rhetorical goals, largely adopting Swales' (1990, 2004) groundbreaking rhetorical move analysis. These integrative studies are motivated by a growing understanding within Applied Linguistics that language development entails more than the acquisition of isolated forms, as well as current conceptions of genre that emphasize the use of linguistic features in genre-appropriate ways.

With an emphasis on the domain-specific linguistic form-rhetorical function mappings of various genre practices, it is unsurprising that the vast majority of corpus-based genre analysis aims to analyze academic disciplinary genre practices from an English for Academic

Purposes (EAP) perspective with the explicit aim of impacting genre-based EAP pedagogy (particularly writing). Much of this research has targeted research article writing practices (e.g. Cortes, 2013; Durrant & Mathews-Aydınlı, 2011; Le & Harrington, 2015; Lim, 2010; Lu *et al.*, 2021), while others have examined the construction of academic conference abstracts (e.g. Omidian *et al.*, 2018; Yoon & Casal, 2020), with most adopting a phraseological lens to analyze recurring formulaic or semi-formulaic sequences in terms of the genre-specific rhetorical goals that writers utilize them for.

Lu *et al.* (2020) represent a major step in advancing the adoption of ASA and rhetorical analysis to inform and support the teaching of domain-specific language skills, such as disciplinary academic writing, as they examined both the variable use of syntactically complex structures across rhetorical steps of text and the rhetorical functions of the most complex sentences for each of their target measures. Data consisted of 600 research article introductions balanced across six social science disciplines (Anthropology, Applied Linguistics, Economics, Political Science, Psychology, and Sociology) published in major journals from 2012 to 2016 (513,688 total words; M = 856; SD = 476). In their analysis, the authors adopted five previously established syntactic complexity measures across global, clausal, and phrasal dimensions (see Table 32.1) and an adapted rhetorical move framework based on Swales' (2004) Revised Creating a Research Space model. A team of seven researchers (including the authors) annotated the entire corpus for rhetorical moves and steps with high interrater reliability (Cohen's Kappa .81), placing codes at sentence boundaries even when rhetorical steps were larger blocks of text. The complexity indices were assessed and mapped to rhetorical codes using a custom python script on move-annotated, syntactically parsed, and part-of-speech tagged versions of the corpus. The authors then used one-way multivariate analysis of variance (MANOVA) and graphical analysis of means (ANOM) to identify and report rhetorical moves that differed significantly in terms of mean complexity for each measure, and they used simple linear regression to identify rhetorical moves that demonstrated a greater proportion of complex sentences for each measure (identified as the third quartile and higher) than would be expected based on frequency.

The results of Lu *et al.*'s (2020) analysis have important implications for EAP writing pedagogy and for the role of ASA more broadly in language pedagogy. The authors found that the language that writers produced in the realization of distinct rhetorical goals differed significantly along many dimensions of syntactic complexity and that the most complex sentences for each measure were significantly more likely to further specific rhetorical

Table 32.1 Syntactic complexity indices from Lu et al. (2020)

Index	Description
Sentence length	Number of words in the sentence (Lu, 2010)
Nominalizations	Number of words with one of the following five suffixes: *-ity*, *-ment*, *-ness*, *-sion* or *-tion* (Biber *et al.*, 1999) or included in Nomlex (Macleod *et al.*, 2001)
Finite dependent clauses	Number of finite dependent clauses, either nominal, adjectival, or adverbial (Lu, 2010)
Non-finite dependent clauses	Number of nonfinite dependent clauses with gerund, infinitive, or past participles (Biber *et al.*, 2011)
Left-embeddedness	Number of words before the main verb of the sentence (McNamara *et al.*, 2014)

goals. For example, gap building moves were characterized by significantly greater degrees of left-embeddedness on average than many other rhetorical moves/steps, and a disproportionately large number of the most left-embedded sentences had a gap-building rhetorical function. Closer manual examination suggested that this tendency was associated with the face-saving practice of including brief positive introductions to sentences that included negative evaluations or types of gap-statements, which highlights an important connection between linguistic and rhetorical choices that writers make in situated writing practices. Similarly, it was found that a disproportionately large number of long sentences had an "announcing aims" rhetorical function. The authors connected writers' tendency to pack large numbers of descriptors and modifiers related to methods, theories, and analytical procedures in their purpose statements, perhaps to provide a more complete aim statement. These two findings highlight the potential for ASA and rhetorical analysis to inform educators and materials designers in selecting pedagogical foci in a move towards targeting the intersection of formal and rhetorical thinking, rather than teaching rhetorical and formal teachers in isolation.

Pedagogically oriented ASA studies that integrate formal and rhetorical perspectives are scarce, but the findings of Lu *et al.* (2020) have had an influence on syllabus design in L2 graduate writing courses in their research context, and a number of recent contributions have adopted similar genre-based corpus analysis approaches with distinct linguistic features. For example, Chen and Flowerdew (2018) recruited 473 graduate student writers in Hong Kong to participate in an EAP-based pedagogical intervention that included (1) a workshop on corpus techniques, (2) workshops on rhetorical move analysis and the use of AntConc (Anthony, 2019) to examine their linguistic realizations in discipline-specific corpora, and (3) self-directed corpus-building and analysis projects. Similarly, 30 master's students in mechanical and electrical programs at a major Chinese university participated in Dong and Lu's (2020) similar EAP-based pedagogical intervention that involved the co-compilation of specialized engineering corpora by students and an instructor, the co-annotation of those corpora for rhetorical moves, and a collaborative analysis of linguistic realization. Both studies (Chen & Flowerdew, 2018; Dong & Lu, 2020) present overall positive learner evaluations of the usefulness of this approach. Moreover, Dong and Lu (2020) also present evidence of writing development through manual analysis of learner texts.

Taken together, both dimensions of the corpus-based genre analysis research presented here – those which aim to analyze community-specific genre practices and those which aim to bring formal and rhetorical analyses into learning contexts as pedagogical activities themselves – constitute potentially profound implications for applying ASA in genre-sensitive language learning environments. Studies that integrate ASA and rhetorical move analysis, such as Lu *et al.* (2020), have the potential to reveal genre- and community-specific common syntactic patterns and to explore the use of these syntactic features in the realization of rhetorical goals. This can both inform syllabus design (i.e. what to teach) and materials design through, for example, the identification and extraction of complex sentences. Studies such as Chen and Flowerdew (2018) and Dong and Lu (2020), which bring the linguistic and rhetorical analysis into pedagogical spaces as learning activities themselves, expand the scope of data-driven approaches to language learning by highlighting form-function mappings within a genre-based approach. While pedagogically oriented ASA and rhetorical move analysis-based approaches will in some cases require tools beyond the scope of those mentioned above (e.g. AntConc), many features can be explored even through concordance-based interaction.

32.6 Future directions of research

Multiple directions for future research into the pedagogical applications of ASA technologies exist for the three research strands discussed above. For the first strand, the number of languages supported and the range of grammatical structures available for each supported language may both be expanded, and research can examine how the textual enhancement and exercise generation functionalities can be best used to support and promote learners' grammar acquisition. A number of important questions remain unanswered for the second strand, too. For example, prior research focused mostly on VSTF with adolescent students in L1 English or English as a Second Language contexts, while relatively little is known about the efficacy of VSTF in English as a Foreign Language contexts, for learners in other age groups, or for languages other than English. The relationship between the efficacy of VSTF and readers' language proficiency also needs further examination, given the concerns that VSTF may slow down advanced learners' reading speed and that high-proficiency learners tend to benefit less from this format than low-proficiency learners (e.g. Park & Warschauer, 2016; Walker *et al.*, 2005; Yu & Miller, 2010). The effect of VSTF on other language skills, such as listening comprehension, can also be explored (see Park, 2018). For the third strand, the integrated approach has, thus, far been implemented for a small number of academic genres in EAP contexts only. Further efforts can be made to expand this line of corpus-based genre analysis research into novel genres within and beyond the bounds of English-language academic disciplinary communities. Meanwhile, integrated ASA and rhetorical analysis of genre practices can be used to inform syllabus design, teacher training, and in-class corpus work with systematic descriptions and concrete examples of form-function mappings for context-specific language education, particularly in Language for Specific Purposes contexts.

There exist various other directions for future research to apply ASA technologies in language teaching, learning, and assessment. First, ASA technologies can be used to assess the degree of linguistic complexity and reading difficulty of pedagogical texts and to inform the selection of reading materials for learners at different grade or proficiency levels (e.g. Chen & Meurers, 2019). Relatedly, it can also be used to inform the adaptation of authentic reading materials to fit learners at different proficiency levels (e.g. Jin & Lu, 2018; Jin *et al.*, 2020). Second, ASA technologies can be used to analyze learners' spoken or written production to evaluate the quality of such production (e.g. Biber *et al.*, 2016; Kyle & Crossley, 2018; Lu, 2017; Yang *et al.*, 2015; Yoon *et al.*, 2020) as well as to identify issues in such production and provide useful feedback to learners (e.g. Ai, 2017; Ai & Lu, 2018; Lu & Bluemel, 2020).

Notes

1 ROOT = top of the sentence, S = simple declarative clause, imperative, infinitive, NP = noun phrase, PRP = personal pronoun, VP = verb phrase, VBP = verb, non–third-person singular present, NP = noun phrase, DT = determiner, NN = noun, singular or mass (Bies *et al.*, 1995).
2 nsubj = nominal subject, root = root, det = determiner, dobj = direct object (de Marneffe & Manning, 2008).
3 GrammarScope is accessible at http://grammarscope.sourceforge.net/.
4 Grammarly is accessible at https://www.grammarly.com/.
5 iGE is accessible at https://www.ucl.ac.uk/english-usage/apps/ige/)
6 The Biber Tagger does not directly produce grammatical complexity indices, but the tagged output can be further analyzed generate such indices (e.g. Biber *et al.*, 2011).
7 VIEW is accessible at http://sifnos.sfs.uni-tuebingen.de/VIEW/. Other syntax highlighters exist (e.g. the English Syntax Highlighter at https://english.edward.io/), generally with more limited functionalities.
8 LiveInk is accessible at http://www.liveink.com/index.php.

Further reading

Chen, M., & Flowerdew, J. (2018). Introducing data-driven learning to PhD students for research writing purposes: A territory-wide project in Hong Kong. *English for Specific Purposes, 50*, 97–112. The authors presented a large-scale data-driven learning approach to academic writing instruction which involved interaction with general and discipline-specific course corpora and construction of personal corpora. The researchers also examined learners' evaluations of the workshop, which were positive.

Lu, X. (2014). *Computational methods for corpus annotation and analysis.* Springer. This book offers an accessible introduction to the state-of-the-art computational tools that can be used to automate the annotation and analysis of natural language texts. The book includes two chapters on syntactic annotation and analysis that provide useful background information for the use of automatic syntactic analysis in language research and pedagogy.

Lu, X., Casal, J. E., & Liu, Y. (2020). The rhetorical functions of syntactically complex sentences in social science research article introductions. *Journal of English for Academic Purposes, 44*, 100832. The authors adopted five previously established measures of syntactic complexity to analyze the use of syntactically complex structures across rhetorical steps and the rhetorical functions of the most syntactically complex sentences in a move-annotated corpus of 600 social science research article introductions. The authors found significant differences in the syntactic complexity of language furthering different rhetorical aims of authors and clear rhetorical patterns for the most complex sentences.

Park, Y., Xu, Y., Collins, P., Farkas, G., & Warschauer, M. (2019). Scaffolding learning of language structures with visual-syntactic text formatting. *British Journal of Educational Technology, 50*(4), 1896–1912. The authors investigated the effects of visual-syntactic text formatting on the English literacy of fourth- and sixth-grade students through a one-year intervention in English language arts and social studies classes. The authors found no significant for fourth-graders but confirmed a significant positive effect for the six-grade treatment group.

Tate, T., Collins, P., Xu, Y., Yau, J., Krishnan, J., Prado, Y., Farkas, G., & Warschauer, M. (2019). Visual-syntactic text format: Improving adolescent literacy. *Scientific Studies of Reading, 23*(4), 287–304. The authors implemented a one-year digital intervention in seventh- and eighth-grade English language arts classes to examine the extent to which visual-syntactic text formatting (VSTF) could help improve students' reading and writing performance. The authors reported beneficial effects of VSTF on reading and writing, although such effects were largely limited to students with middle-level baseline scores.

References

Ai, H. (2017). Providing graduated corrective feedback in an intelligent computer-assisted language learning environment. *ReCALL, 29*(3), 313–334. https://doi.org/10.1017/S095834401700012X

Ai, H., & Lu, X. (2018). Exploring the interdisciplinary synergy between sociocultural theory and intelligent computer-assisted language learning. In J. P. Lantolf, M. E. Poehner, & M. Swain (Eds.), *The Routledge handbook of sociocultural theory and second language development* (pp. 409–421). Routledge.

Anthony, L. (2019). *AntConc* (Version 3.5.8) [Computer Software]. Waseda University. https://www.laurenceanthony.net/software

Bever, T., Burwell, R., Jandreau, S., Burwell, R., Kaplan, R., & Zaenen, A. (1990). Spacing printed text to isolate major phrases improves readability. *Visible Language, 25*(1), 74–87.

Biber, D., Gray, B., & Poonpon, K. (2011). Should we use characteristics of conversation to measure grammatical complexity in L2 writing development? *TESOL Quarterly, 45*(1), 5–35. https://doi.org/10.5054/tq.2011.244483

Biber, D., Gray, B., & Staples, S. (2016). Predicting patterns of grammatical complexity across language exam task types and proficiency levels. *Applied Linguistics, 37*(5), 639–668. https://doi.org/10.1093/applin/amu059

Biber, D., Johansson, S., Leech, G., Conrad, S., & Finegan, E. (1999). *Longman grammar of spoken and written English.* Longman.

Bies, A., Ferguson, M., Katz, K., MacIntyre, R., Tredinnick, V., Kim, G., Marcinkiewicz, M. A., & Schasberger, B. (1995). *Bracketing guidelines for Treebank II style Penn Treebank project*. Linguistic Data Consortium. http://languagelog.ldc.upenn.edu/myl/PennTreebank1995.pdf

Chen, M., & Flowerdew, J. (2018). Introducing data-driven learning to PhD students for research writing purposes: A territory-wide project in Hong Kong. *English for Specific Purposes, 50*, 97–112. https://doi.org/10.1016/j.esp.2017.11.004

Chen, X., & Meurers, D. (2019). Linking text readability and learner proficiency using linguistic complexity feature vector distance. *Computer Assisted Language Learning, 32*(4), 418–447. https://doi.org/10.1080/09588221.2018.1527358.

Cortes, V. (2013). *The purpose of this study is to*: Connecting lexical bundles and moves in research article introductions. *Journal of English for Academic Purposes, 12*(1), 33–43. https://doi.org/10.1016/j.jeap.2012.11.002

De Marneffe, M.-C., & Manning, C. D. (2008). *Stanford typed dependencies manual*. Stanford University. https://nlp.stanford.edu/software/dependencies_manual.pdf

Dong, J., & Lu, X. (2020). Promoting discipline-specific genre competence with corpus-based genre analysis activities. *Journal of English for Academic Purposes, 58*, 138–154. https://doi.org/10.1016/j.esp.2020.01.005

Durrant, P., & Mathews-Aydınlı, J. (2011). A function-first approach to identifying formulaic language in academic writing. *English for Specific Purposes, 30*(1), 58–72. https://doi.org/10.1016/j.esp.2010.05.002

Graesser, A. C., McNamara, D. S., Louwerse, M. M., & Cai, Z. (2004). Coh-Metrix: Analysis of text on cohesion and language. *Behavior Research Methods, Instruments, & Computers, 36*, 193–202. https://doi.org/10.3758/BF03195564

Goldberg, A. E. (1995). *Constructions: A construction grammar approach to argument structure*. University of Chicago Press.

Honnibal, M., & Johnson, M. (2015). An improved non-monotonic transition system for dependency parsing. In *Proceedings of the 2015 Conference on Empirical Methods in Natural Language Processing* (pp. 1373–1378). Association for Computational Linguistics. https://doi.org/10.18653/v1/D15-1162

Jandreau, S., & Bever, T. G. (1992). Phrase-spaced formats improve comprehension in average readers. *Journal of Applied Psychology, 77*(2), 143–146. https://doi.org/10.1037/0021-9010.77.2.143.

Jin, T., & Lu, X. (2018). A data-driven approach to text adaptation in teaching material preparation: Design, implementation and teacher professional development. *TESOL Quarterly, 52*(2), 457–467. https://doi.org/10.1002/tesq.434

Jin, T., Lu, X., & Ni, J. (2020). Syntactic complexity in adapted teaching materials: Differences among grade levels and implications for benchmarking. *The Modern Language Journal, 104*(1), 192–208. https://doi.org/10.1111/modl.12622

Kyle, K. (2016). Measuring syntactic development in L2 writing: Fine grained indices of syntactic complexity and usage-based indices of syntactic sophistication [Doctoral dissertation, Georgia State University]. ScholarWorks @ Georgia State University. https://scholarworks.gsu.edu/alesl_diss/35/

Kyle, K., & Crossley, S. A. (2018). Measuring syntactic complexity in L2 writing using fine-grained clausal and phrasal indices. *Modern Language Journal, 102*(2), 333–349. https://doi.org/10.1111/modl.12468.

Le, T. N. P., & Harrington, M. (2015). Phraseology used to comment on results in the discussion section of applied linguistics quantitative research articles. *English for Specific Purposes, 39*, 45–61. https://doi.org/10.1016/j.esp.2015.03.003

Legge, G. E., Ahn, S. J., Klitz, T. S., & Luebker, A. (1997). Psychophysics of reading—XVI. The visual span in normal and low vision. *Vision Research, 37*(14), 1999–2010. https://doi.org/10.1016/S0042-6989(97)00017-5

Levy, R., & Andrew, G. (2006). Tregex and Tsurgeon: Tools for querying and manipulating tree data structures. In *Proceedings of the Fifth International Conference on Language Resources and Evaluation* (pp. 2231–2234). European Language Resources Association. https://www.aclweb.org/anthology/L06-1311/

Lim, J. M. (2010). Commenting on research results in applied linguistics and education: A comparative genre-based investigation. *Journal of English for Academic Purposes, 9*(4), 280–294. https://doi.org/10.1016/j.jeap.2010.10.001

Long, M. H. (1991). Focus on form: A design feature in language teaching methodology. In K. De Bot, C. Kramsch, & R. Ginsberg (Eds.), *Foreign language research in cross-cultural perspective* (pp. 39–52). Benjamins. https://doi.org/10.1075/sibil.2.07lon

Lu, X. (2006). *Hybrid models for Chinese unknown word resolution* [Doctoral dissertation, The Ohio State University]. OhioLINK Electronic Theses and Dissertations Center. http://rave.ohiolink.edu/etdc/view?acc_num=osu1154631880

Lu, X. (2009). Automatic measurement of syntactic complexity in child language acquisition. *International Journal of Corpus Linguistics, 14*(1), 3–28. https://doi.org/10.1075/ijcl.14.1.02lu

Lu, X. (2010). Automatic analysis of syntactic complexity in second language writing. *International Journal of Corpus Linguistics, 15*(4), 474–496. https://doi.org/10.1075/ijcl.15.4.02lu

Lu, X. (2014). *Computational methods for corpus annotation and analysis.* Springer. https://doi.org/10.1007/978-94-017-8645-4

Lu, X. (2017). Automated measurement of syntactic complexity in corpus-based L2 writing research and implications for writing assessment. *Language Testing, 34*(4), 493–511. https://doi.org/10.1177/0265532217710675

Lu, X. (2018). Natural language processing and intelligent computer-assisted language learning (ICALL). In J. I. Liontas (Ed.), *The TESOL encyclopedia of English language teaching.* Blackwell. https://doi.org/10.1002/9781118784235.eelt0422

Lu, X., & Bluemel, B. (2020). Automated assessment of language. In S. Conrad, A. Hartig, & L. Santelmann (Eds.), *The Cambridge introduction to applied linguistics* (pp. 86–93). Cambridge University Press.

Lu, X., Casal, J. E., & Liu, Y. (2020). The rhetorical functions of syntactically complex sentences in social science research article introductions. *Journal of English for Academic Purposes, 44*, 1–16. https://doi.org/10.1016/j.jeap.2019.100832

Lu, X., Yoon, J., & Kisselev, O. (2021). Matching phrase-frames to rhetorical moves in social science research article introductions. *English for Specific Purposes, 61*, 63–83. https://doi.org/10.1016/j.esp.2020.10.001

MacLeod, C., Grishman, R., Meyers, A., Barrett, L., & Reeves, R. (2001). *Nomlex.* New York University. https://nlp.cs.nyu.edu/nomlex/

Manning, C. D., Surdeanu, M., Bauer, J., Finkel, J., Bethard, S. J., & McClosky, D. (2014). The Stanford CoreNLP natural language processing toolkit. In *Proceedings of the 52nd Annual Meeting of the Association for Computational Linguistics: System Demonstrations* (pp. 55–60). Association for Computational Linguistics. https://doi.org/10.3115/v1/P14-5010

McNamara, D. S., Graesser, A. C., McCarthy, P. M., & Cai, Z. (2014). *Automated evaluation of text and discourse with Coh-Metrix.* Cambridge University Press.

Meurers, D., Ziai, R., Amaral, L., Boyd, A., Dimitrov, A., Metcalf, V., & Ott, N. (2010). Enhancing authentic web pages for language learners. In *Proceedings of the Fifth Workshop on Innovative Use of NLP for Building Educational Applications* (pp. 10–18). Association for Computational Linguistics. https://www.aclweb.org/anthology/W10-1002

Omidian, T., Shahriari, H., & Siyanova-Chanturia, A. (2018). A cross-disciplinary investigation of multi-word expressions in the moves of research article abstracts. *Journal of English for Academic Purposes, 36*, 1–14. https://doi.org/10.1016/j.jeap.2018.08.002

Park, Y. (2018). Syntactic enhancement: Bootstrapping for second language reading. *Journal of Cognitive Science, 18*(4), 473–509. https://doi.org/10.1007/s40299-018-0389-y

Park, Y., & Warschauer, M. (2016). Syntactic enhancement and second language literacy: An experimental study. *Language Learning & Technology, 20*(3), 180–199. http://dx.doi.org/10125/44488

Ruiz, S., Rebuschat, P., & Meurers, D. (2019). The effects of working memory and declarative memory on instructed second language vocabulary learning: Insights from intelligent CALL. *Language Teaching Research, 25*(4), 510–539. https://doi.org/10.1177/1362168819872859

Sharwood Smith, M. (1981). Consciousness-raising and the second language learner. *Applied Linguistics, 2*(2), 159–168. https://doi.org/10.1093/applin/II.2.159

Sharwood Smith, M. (1991). Speaking to many minds: On the relevance of different types of language information for the L2 learner. *Second Language Research, 7*(2), 118–132. https://doi.org/10.1177/026765839100700204

Swales, J. M. (1990). *Genre analysis: English in academic and research settings.* Cambridge University Press.

Swales., J. M. (2004). *Research genres: Explorations and applications.* Cambridge University Press.

Tate, T., Collins, P., Xu, Y., Yau, J., Krishnan, J., Prado, Y., Farkas, G., & Warschauer, M. (2019). Visual-syntactic text format: Improving adolescent literacy. *Scientific Studies of Reading, 23*(4), 287–304. https://doi.org/10.1080/10888438.2018.1561700

Walker, S., Schloss, P., Fletcher, C. R., Vogel, C. A., & Walker, R. C. (2005). Visual-syntactic text formatting: A new method to enhance online reading. *Reading Online, 8*(6), 1–27.

Warschauer, M., Park, Y., & Walker, R. (2011). Transforming digital reading with visual- syntactic text formatting. *The JALT CALL Journal, 7*(3), 255–270. https://doi.org/10.29140/jaltcall.v7n3.121

Yang, W., Lu, X., & Weigle, S. C. (2015). Different topics, different discourse: Relationships among writing topic, measures of syntactic complexity, and judgments of writing quality. *Journal of Second Language Writing, 28*, 53–67. https://doi.org/10.1016/j.jslw.2015.02.002

Yoon, J., & Casal, J. E. (2020). P-frames and rhetorical moves in applied linguistics conference proposals. In U. Römer, V. Cortes, & E. Friginal (Eds.), *Advances in corpus-based research on academic writing: Effects of discipline, register, and writer expertise* (pp. 282–305). Benjamins. https://doi.org/10.1075/scl.95.12yoo

Yoon, S.-Y., Lu, X., Zechner, K., & Zechner (2020). Features measuring vocabulary and grammar. In K. Evanini (Ed.), *Automated speaking assessment: Using language technologies to score spontaneous speech* (pp. 123–137). Routledge.

Yu, C., & Miller, R. C. (2010). Enhancing web page readability for non-native readers. In *Proceedings of the 28th International Conference on Human Factors in Computing Systems* (pp. 2523–2532). Association for Computing Machinery. https://doi.org/10.1145/1753326.1753709

33

TRAINING TEACHERS AND LEARNERS TO USE CORPORA

Agnieszka Leńko-Szymańska

33.1 Introduction

As the present volume illustrates, corpus data are used in language education in a variety of ways and they are implemented by different parties involved in teaching and learning. Römer (2011) provided a useful review of the areas in which corpora are being exploited in language pedagogy. On the one hand, large text collections are very helpful to researchers and materials writers. They enable them to observe interesting but little-known facts about target language use, which later find their way into syllabi, reference works (dictionaries and grammars), and teaching materials (coursebooks and supplementary resource books). Corpora are also a limitless source of authentic citations featured in pedagogical resources. Römer (2011) labels these uses of corpora indirect applications. On the other hand, text collections can be consulted directly by language teachers and learners without the mediation of a researcher. This can take the form of students accessing a corpus or working with corpus data pre-selected and pre-processed by their teachers. Such interactions make it possible for teachers to prepare tasks and materials tailored precisely to their students' specific needs, and for learners to study the language relevant to their interests. Direct corpus applications can also provide students with opportunities to become researchers themselves who are capable of observing, analysing, and drawing conclusions from examples of real language use. This mode of learning promotes a pro-active attitude, autonomy, and language awareness (Römer, 2011). The author calls such direct consultations of corpora by language teachers and students data-driven learning (DDL), echoing the term coined by Tim Johns (1991), which was originally reserved only for cases of students' inductive and hands-on experience with text collections (Karlsen & Monsen, 2020).

In the last two decades, great progress has been made in the development of indirect applications of corpora. However, despite its advantages, as asserted by enthusiasts and confirmed by empirical evidence (Boulton & Cobb, 2017), data-driven learning has been scarcely implemented in language classrooms, a fact that is frequently lamented in the literature (cf. a recent review by Chambers, 2019). This scarcity has prompted researchers to, on the one hand, probe into the reasons for this lack of popularity, and, on the other hand, fervently advocate active promotion of direct applications of corpora in language pedagogy (Chambers, 2019; Römer, 2009). One important form of such promotion is effective teacher and student training in exploiting large text collections in order to support foreign language learning.

DOI: 10.4324/9781003002901-39

33.2 Core issues and topics in teacher and student training in DDL

33.2.1 Surveys of direct corpus applications

Over the last 20 years, a number of surveys have been conducted to query the implementation of corpora by language teachers. These surveys attempted to establish the extent to which language instructors make use of corpora. Some of these studies also attempted to establish the specific uses of corpora by educators in their practice as well as to uncover perceived obstacles in the application of corpora in language instruction.

One of the first such surveys was a questionnaire administered by Mukherjee (2004). He queried 248 English teachers in German secondary schools about their experience with large text collections. He discovered that almost 80% of them were unfamiliar with the term corpus linguistics and only 10% of the respondents had had some contact with corpus linguistics, although this did not necessarily entail having used corpus data in their teaching in any way. Almost 15 years later, the study was replicated in the same educational context by Callies (2019), who used a more detailed instrument to gather information on the instructors' practices with corpora and their attitudes towards the benefits of corpus use for themselves and their students. Although only 26 teachers responded to his questionnaire, the results did demonstrate that almost half of the participants (42%) had not encountered the term corpus linguistics during their university studies and one quarter (23%) declared very little exposure to this methodology during their tertiary education. In addition, 80% of participants had no contact with corpora during their subsequent in-service teacher training. Nevertheless, a vast majority (70%) of the respondents declared having used corpora for various purposes, but frequently this use was very limited and their familiarity with corpus resources remained low. Among the respondents who acknowledged employing corpora in their teaching, the most frequent application was for reference (65%), that is, to look up individual words, phrases, or grammatical points. Fewer teachers used corpora for designing their own materials (46%), and even fewer encouraged their students to engage with corpus data (19%). Callies' results, although not fully reliable due to the small sample size, illustrate that the direct applications of corpora in language instruction remain very scarce.

Tribble's (2015) survey had a more international reach and included 560 respondents from 63 countries, with the largest numbers from the US, UK, and China. Three-quarters of respondents to his survey declared using corpora in their teaching. Although this figure appears encouraging, Tribble acknowledges that the channels selected for the distribution of the questionnaire might have resulted in a sample skewed towards corpus enthusiasts. It should also be noted that a large majority of Tribble's respondents worked in a different context than the language instructors queried by Mukherjee (2004) and Callies (2019). Half of them were scholars (lecturers and researchers) and almost 80% taught languages at the tertiary level. The most frequent use of corpora reported in the questionnaire was the production of teaching materials in various forms: electronic (19%), paper-based (16%), and coursebooks (7%). Interestingly, the applications involving the instructor's personal reference were almost equally frequent as students' reference (both a little over 20%). However, corpus consultations in student-led DDL activities were rare (a little over 10%).

A particularly relevant aspect of Tribble's study for the issues discussed in this chapter is the respondents' answers concerning the reasons why some teachers did not exploit corpora in their practice. Two obstacles were most frequently selected among several explanations: a lack of time to develop corpus-based materials and a lack of knowledge of the potential of corpora

Because they	**don't know how**	to use corpora in teaching
.... but	**don't know how**	to put it to good use
... but we	**don't know how**	to use them effectively

Figure 33.1 Selected concordances from the answers to an open question on the reasons for not using corpora in the classroom (Tribble, 2015, p. 56)

(both over 20%). A few concordance lines drawn from the answers to an open question in Figure 33.1 confirm the perceived lack of teachers' competence related to the exploitation of corpora.

On the whole, Tribble's results, although generally optimistic, reveal that, in spite of the increasing level of implementation of corpora in tertiary-level language education, instructors do not take advantage of the full potential of this medium for language learning. In addition, they believe that they do not have sufficient expertise in how to integrate corpus data into their practice.

No comparable wide-ranging surveys on corpus use have been conducted among language learners. If students are ever queried on their experience with corpora, this is usually in questionnaires distributed to control and experimental groups in studies into the effectiveness of different aspects of DDL. Such samples are usually small-scale and opportunistic, and not representative of larger student populations; nevertheless, their responses shed some light on learners' familiarity with corpus resources and tools. For example, in a recent study set in the Iranian context (Saeedakhtar *et al.*, 2020), almost none of 60 students declared previous contact with corpus resources. In a more comprehensive project, Karlsen and Monsen (2020) queried 154 Norwegian students in four secondary schools and taught by four teachers who had been trained in corpus linguistics during their university studies. In response to an open question about the digital resources consulted for language learning, none of the students mentioned a corpus-based tool or a text collection in any format. Only 6% of the students declared familiarity with the concept of a corpus and only two of them attempted to explain the notion. However, in a multiple-choice question, the respondents admitted having heard of the most popular corpus resources: BNC (15% of the students), COCA (11%), SKELL (8%), Just-the-word.com (6%), and AntConc (3%).

The responses to the surveys distributed among language instructors and students indicate that the information on corpora and their affordances in language education has had a limited reach. In addition, the respondents' answers suggest that merely "spreading the word" about corpora, as recommended by Römer (2009, p. 84), may not be sufficient for their major uptake in education. Both teachers and learners need a systematic and dedicated training in DDL in order to take advantage of this medium in the classroom.

33.2.2 Skills needed for data-driven teaching and learning

Two types of skills are indispensable for language students to engage in data-driven learning: technical and corpus-analytical. First, it is necessary for learners to have technical skills of operating corpus tools efficiently, which involves being aware and capable of using different functionalities offered by language processing software – for example, wildcards, sorting concordance lines, or generating lists of collocates. Second, learners need to have acquired the skills of corpus analysis, even if only implicitly. This entails recognising the kind of information that can be searched in a corpus (e.g. contexts, patterns of use, variation), knowledge how to retrieve this information successfully (building effective queries), and an ability to interpret search results (by focusing on relevant information and identifying interesting patterns). The need for some of these skills can be reduced by teachers who preselect appropriate citations from corpora and guide their students in the process of their analysis and interpretation. However, instructors have to be fully proficient in these competences, as well as in corpus-related pedagogical skills necessary for the creation of interesting, varied, relevant and instructionally-valid materials and tasks that are well integrated into lessons and syllabi (Callies, 2019; Leńko-Szymańska, 2017; Mukherjee, 2004). Both teachers and learners require assistance in developing these necessary sets of skills in courses, workshops, and seminars aimed at training teachers and students in DDL.

33.2.3 Models of teacher and student training

Promoting the potential of data-driven learning must begin with teachers since it is from their instructors that learners are most likely to hear of, get exposure to, and learn to manipulate and interpret corpus data (Mauranen, 2004). Therefore, effective teacher training is the key element in popularising direct uses of corpora in language education. In the last decade, several books for language educators have been published showcasing multiple uses of corpora in the classroom (e.g. Flowerdew, 2012; Friginal, 2018; Poole, 2018; Reppen, 2010). In addition, a number of teacher training courses have been described in the literature (e.g. Leńko-Szymańska, 2014, 2015, 2017; Zareva, 2017). These courses targeted either practicing instructors or teacher trainees. Training in-service and pre-service teachers differs due to the instructional setting. The former is usually only available for short intensive courses. Seminars designed for the latter group are often interwoven with other teacher training classes and can span over a longer period.

Three approaches to designing teacher-training courses in data-driven learning can be identified in the literature. One type of training – offered to both pre-service and in-service teachers – are courses focusing on corpus linguistics (Abdel Latif, 2021; Ebrahimi & Faghih, 2017). Such classes start with introducing fundamental concepts in the field such as definition of a corpus, collocation, or concordance, and then participants are presented with different ways of querying text collections by using a range of tools for language analysis. These courses can supplement or expand on training in general linguistics or information-technology for language teachers. Their main objective is to help trainees become aware of the types of information that can be searched in a corpus and the types of analyses that can be performed with corpus tools. The syllabus is often constructed around available resources and software and emphasises the development of technical and corpus-analytical skills in language teachers. However, this approach does not always cater for the development of pedagogical skills related to designing data-driven activities.

Another approach to popularising data-driven learning among language teachers is making them use corpus resources and tools in their foreign language or language awareness classes (Callies, 2016; Farr, 2008; Heather & Helt, 2012). This option is mainly available to preservice teachers for whom improving language proficiency or awareness is often an integral part of their teacher training programmes. For example, Zareva (2017) reported on a semester-long course in English grammar with a substantial corpus component offered to TESOL teacher trainees enroled in an MA programme at an American university. As part of the coursework, the participants completed a corpus-based project on a selected grammatical issue and prepared an in-class presentation as well as a written report on their findings.

The main premise behind this approach is that before language instructors can be expected to use corpora in their teaching, they need to have contact with data-driven education as language learners. The training follows the syllabus of a language course, i.e. trainees focus on issues related to various aspects of language such as grammar, vocabulary, or discourse structure. Yet, instead of using traditional materials, they are guided to consult corpora. This way pre-service teachers not only get acquainted with a variety of resources, tools, and their functions (technical skills), and learn to analyse and interpret corpus data (corpus-analytical skills) but they also get first-hand experience of the relevance of information derived from corpora for language learning. The benefits of such experience have been highlighted by Breyer (2011) who notes: "If teacher trainees can discover the potential of corpora for their own learning, then this may foster intrinsic motivation to make use of corpora in their profession as teachers. It also allows teacher trainees to explore and address the challenges that such an approach entails" (p. 230).

However, the efficiency of such training for language instructors has been questioned by some researchers due to its neglect of the DDL-related pedagogical skills (Leńko-Szymańska, 2017). As Breyer (2009) observes, "recognising that there is a significant difference between learning and teaching with corpora, as well as providing student teachers with the required skills, is of great importance" (p. 156). Thus, the third approach to teacher training in data-driven learning has emerged. It recognises the indispensability of corpus-related pedagogical skills in preparing teachers to exploit text collections in their classrooms (Breyer, 2009, 2011; Hüttner *et al.*, 2009; Leńko-Szymańska, 2014, 2015, 2017). In these courses, teachers not only learn how to query corpora for relevant information and how to analyse and interpret search results, but also how to transform these results into pedagogically-sound and valuable language teaching materials and tasks. The syllabus covers typical language teaching problems and participants discover how corpora can assist learners in studying and mastering these points. An example of such a course addressed to pre-service teachers enrolled in a Master's of Education programme at a German university was described by Le Foll (2020). The course was built around a collective project whose aim was to create *A practical guide to using corpora for EFL teachers*. The guide was meant to showcase various applications of corpora for teaching a range of language elements and skills to students at different educational levels. Each trainee (co-) worked on one chapter built around a topic of their choice. The chapters included step-by-step instructions on how to query a selected corpus or how to build and analyse a custom corpus for specific purposes, as well as a sample of corpus-related instructional materials related to the selected topic.

Learners also require special training in order to successfully engage in DDL. Language instructors frequently assume that students' technical and corpus-analytical skills are gradually fostered whenever they come into contact with corpora in or outside the classroom. Instances of courses in which students are exposed to corpus data are abundant in the literature (e.g. Aston, 2015; Crosthwaite *et al.*, 2019; Geluso & Yamaguchi, 2014; Vyatkina, 2016). In some DDL classes, students are presented with corpus materials offline – for example in the form of selected corpus citations or printed concordance lines, which they must examine and interpret (Boulton, 2010; Huang, 2014; Szudarski, 2019). In other courses, learners can directly consult a corpus but they are provided with specific instructions on how to build a query and what information to consider when scrutinising the results (Moles-Cases & Oster, 2015; Yoon & Hirvela, 2004). Such activities are claimed to have the benefit of exposing students to examples of authentic examples of language use to help them discover characteristics often disregarded in traditional teaching materials such as course books, dictionaries, or grammar books. They are also believed to raise students' language awareness (Gilquin & Granger, 2010; Römer, 2011).

Yet, it can be argued that exposing language learners to corpus data may be insufficient for the development of all the skills necessary for data-driven learning. Some educators claim that students should be explicitly taught these skills (Gilquin & Granger, 2010; Sripicharn, 2010). Bernardini (2002) summarised this approach to student training as follows "[i]n such frameworks, it is the rationale and/or methodology/ies of corpus linguistics that are put to didactic use, whilst the role of descriptively-adequate corpus-derived knowledge remains in the background" (p. 165). She calls this approach corpus-aided discovery learning and advocates giving control to students in the process of working with a corpus. The instructor creates a rich learning environment but has no influence over the language analysed and learned in class. Instead, their task is to accompany students "as a guide, not telling them what to do but advising them on how to pursue their own interests, suggesting alternative ways to proceed, other interpretations of the data or possible ways forward" (p. 166). In effect of such training, learners are expected not only to be capable of searching for, analysing, and interpreting corpus data on their own, but more importantly to "develop a frame of mind in which detours and distractions are not stigmatised, but valued as potential sources of unexpected serendipitous encounters" (p. 180).

Several such student-training courses have been reported in thematic volumes and academic journals. In the seminar offered by Bernardini (2002), students in English Studies worked with a variety of large reference corpora and corpus tools in order to discover the patterned quality of language. Doctoral students enrolled in the course described by Lee and Swales (2006) were encouraged to build their own domain-specific corpus of research articles and a corresponding corpus made of their own academic writing. The students subsequently examined the two collections to identify the differences related to a range of language use aspects. The majority of DDL courses are directed at advanced learners in the tertiary-level education. However, recent increased attempts to target younger learners include Crosthwaite and Stell (2019) who described the process of instructing two ten-year-old primary school students in the use of two corpus-based resources for revising lexical errors in their writing. All these student-training courses aimed not only at the improvement of the participants' linguistic knowledge, but equally importantly at the development of their technical and corpus-analytical skills, thus enabling the students to apply data-driven learning techniques in their own learning outside the classroom.

33.3 Review of current state of research on the effectiveness of teacher and student training

33.3.1 Methodology for evaluating the effectiveness of teacher and learner training

The effectiveness of DDL teacher and learner training courses as well as more generally teachers' and learners' perceptions of DDL techniques have been scrutinised with a range of methods. The most popular instrument to gather relevant data has been the questionnaire. Questionnaires have been distributed before a course (e.g. Le Foll, 2020; Leńko-Szymańska, 2014; Mukherjee, 2004) in order to probe participants' prior knowledge of and experience in corpus linguistics. They may also give an insight into reasons for selecting an elective course. Questionnaires administered directly after a training, on the other hand, give information on teachers' as well as learners' attitudes to corpus applications in language education

(Leńko-Szymańska, 2014, 2015). Respondents may declare how difficult or time-consuming they found the new techniques. They may also express their opinions on the benefits and drawbacks of corpus-based teaching and learning. Finally, participants may also be queried about their intentions to use corpora in the future. Delayed questionnaires, circulated several months, or even years after the course offer an insight into teachers' and students' actual DDL practices (Charles, 2012; Farr, 2008). Respondents may also relate their unprompted and unguided corpus use or provide reasons for abandoning consultation of text collections.

Instead of predominantly quantitative data collected through questionnaires, reflective essays, and individual or focus group interviews may provide qualitative data on teachers' or learners' attitudes towards DDL as well as the effectiveness of teacher and learner training (Abdel Latif, 2021; Karlsen & Monsen, 2020; Le Foll, 2020). These instruments make it possible to examine teachers' and learners' perceptions and actual practices in a more detailed and nuanced way but, as for most qualitative methods, are limited to a smaller group of participants.

In addition to the methods based on teachers' and learners' reports and declarations, other, more evidence-based procedures of evaluating the effectiveness of instruction in DDL have been proposed. One of them is a systematic analysis of trainees' and learners' assignments or projects produced to meet course requirements (Breyer, 2011; Charles, 2015; Heather & Helt, 2012; Leńko-Szymańska, 2017). Such assignments are meant to explore the knowledge and skills acquired and developed by participants during the course and identify which sets of necessary competences are easier or more difficult to master. Other methodologies offering a great potential for researching actual use of corpus-based materials – in particular by language learners – are logs, screen captures, and use histories (Crosthwaite *et al.*, 2019; Pérez-Paredes, this volume, Pérez-Paredes *et al.*, 2011; Schaeffer-Lacroix, 2019). The application of eye-trackers has been advocated by O'Keeffe (2020), but so far no studies have exploited these instruments to collect data.

33.3.2 Results of the research into the effectiveness of teacher and learner training

Overall, the research into the effectiveness of teacher and student DDL training to date has produced ambiguous and difficult-to-interpret results. On the one hand, the questionnaires, reflective essays, focus groups, and interviews reveal generally positive reactions to corpora by pre-service teachers (Farr, 2008; Leńko-Szymańska, 2015), practicing instructors (Chen *et al.*, 2019; Lin, 2016), and learners (Geluso & Yamaguchi, 2014; Yoon & Hirvela, 2004). The responses also confirm teachers' and students' recognition of the advantages of DDL such as access to examples of authentic language use and rich contextual information, fostering language awareness, and supporting autonomy (Szudarski, 2019; Zareva, 2017). Learners perceive the usefulness of DDL for studying formulaic language (Geluso & Yamaguchi, 2014), lexico-grammatical information (Szudarski, 2019); grammar (Zareva, 2017); and writing and reading (Charles, 2015; Cotos, 2014). However, at the same time, several drawbacks of this approach are frequently mentioned.

One group of these drawbacks pertain to technological challenges, such as limited access to computers and an adequate internet connection, and a lack of local IT support (Farr, 2008). In more recent surveys, these concerns have become less prominent; for example, technological difficulties were mentioned by less than 5% of respondents in Tribble's (2015) survey. Nevertheless, hardware and software availability remains an obstacle in some educational contexts (Ebrahimi & Faghih, 2017). The technical complexity of software and a lack of sufficient technical skills are also a challenge mentioned by respondents (Farr, 2008; Zareva, 2017). Another issue frequently raised is a dearth of suitable resources and tools meeting teachers' and learners' needs (Karlsen & Monsen, 2020; Schaeffer-Lacroix, 2019).

Another group of problems voiced by respondents is the high demands that corpus-based activities pose on time and cognitive involvement. Teachers complain that preparing suitable DDL materials and tasks is time-consuming (Tribble, 2015). Learners assert that the very process of analysing corpus data also takes a long time (Charles, 2012). Moreover, both instructors and students report that in spite of the received training, they lack appropriate corpus-analytical skills. Respondents frequently declare that corpus methods continue to be taxing as they require high cognitive involvement related to building appropriate queries, analysing the data, and interpreting the results (Zareva, 2017). In addition, corpora can be linguistically challenging even for advanced students (Charles, 2012, 2015) and the format of corpus results, i.e. truncated concordance lines, tables, and numbers, can be difficult for examination (Geluso & Yamaguchi, 2014; Zareva, 2017).

Finally, language teachers feel insecure about their DDL-related pedagogical skills such as designing corpus activities and integrating them into regular instructional practice. The responses to the questionnaires and interviews as well as the analyses of trainees' assignments reveal that during the training teachers develop some idea of the ways in which corpora can be used for studying lexis and phraseology; however, designing DDL activities related to grammatical and pragmatic issues is more problematic, as such tasks require more abstract and complex queries and present more challenges in interpreting the data (Heyvaert & Laffut, 2008). Analyses of trainees' assignments also highlight the need for more guidance in pedagogical aspects of DDL. This implies shifting the focus in training courses from corpus linguistics to such pedagogical aspects as lesson planning and materials design which would enable teachers to produce pedagogically-sound learning resources that are incorporated well into the syllabus (Le Foll, 2020; Leńko-Szymańska, 2017).

All these challenges result in declarations of some instructors in their post-course questionnaires and interviews that despite the training they have received, they do not plan to incorporate DDL techniques in their classrooms (e.g. 30% of respondents in the study by Le Foll, 2020). The inquiry into instructors' actual practices carried out several years after completing a corpus training confirms that this is frequently the case (Karlsen & Monsen, 2020).

33.4 Current contributions to the research on teacher and student training in DDL

This section will present in more detail two DDL training courses discussed in the literature: one designed for pre-service teachers and one offered to advanced learners in an academic context. The courses' content and methods were described exhaustively in a series of publications which also included thorough analyses of the effects of the instruction examined with a range of instruments. Both cases can serve as typical examples of the kinds of issues addressed in teacher and student training and the methodology employed for determining its effectiveness.

33.4.1 An example of a teacher-training course

The course designed by Leńko-Szymańska (2014, 2015, 2017) is an elective offered to students enrolledin a Master's programme in applied linguistics at the University of Warsaw. The course has been running annually in either a winter or summer semester for the last eleven years. It consists of 13–15 90-minute sessions divided into three non-consecutive modules. The first module introduces the participants to the fundamental concepts of corpus linguistics and presents samples of research in this area. The next module focuses on the exploitation of large general L1 corpora for teaching language elements and skills. The third module presents the implementation of small purpose-built collections for instruction in language for special purposes. The majority of sessions adopt a workshop format.

During the workshops, the participants perform guided corpus queries and analyse their results. However, these corpus consultations are frequently accompanied by lead-in or follow-up language activities which do not involve interactions with a corpus, such as reading a text, dictionary searches, gap-filling exercises, or group discussions. An example of such a task is provided in Figure 33.2. In addition, trainees are requested to evaluate the corpus-based activities through individual guided reflection, class discussions or short writing assignments, focusing on the instructional value of the completed tasks. The combination of these assignments ensures that the participants learn to use different corpus resources and tools, while discovering how to analyse corpus data and interpret the results. They can also

---

1. Read the text at http://www.guardian.co.uk/international/story/0,,1182857,00.html.

   There are a number of events mentioned in the text. Arrange them in chronological order.

2. What are the synonyms of the word *coup*. Go to the following address to find more:

   http://www.wordandphrase.info/frequencyList.asp

3. Study the information (frequency in different genres, collocates and word patterns of each of the synonyms) available in different widows on the page. Pay particular attention to frequent preposition following the synonyms.

4. Which of the synonyms found in the corpus were used in the text?

5. Find words and expressions in the text that are related to putsches and revolutions.

6. Which nouns are followed by the preposition *against*? List as many as you can find.

   Now check in a corpus by following the procedure described below. Study the first 30 items on the list. Can you see any similarities in meaning between these nouns? Can you group them in semantic fields? If necessary, study these words in context.

7. Work in pairs. Tell your partner about any familiar putsch or revolution you are familiar with. If you cannot think of any historical or political event, recount the putsch described in the text you have just read.

Figure 33.2 A DDL vocabulary task

observe how to merge corpus explorations with other types of classroom activities and develop critical evaluation skills of the merits and drawbacks of the proposed DDL techniques. In this manner, the course caters for the development of the three types of skills needed for the implementation of DDL in language teaching: technical, corpus-analytical, and pedagogical. The trainees are also provided with an opportunity to put the newly acquired competence and skills into practice. For the final course assignment, students are requested to compile a small (ca. about 30K word) corpus of specialised language texts, analyse it for teaching purposes and build a coherent lesson around their findings (see a sample DDL vocabulary task in Figure 33.2). In addition to corpus documentation and the results of an unassisted exploration of the data, the assignment must include a detailed lesson plan and all teaching materials.

Leńko-Szymańska (2014, 2015, 2017) evaluated the effectiveness of the course through two questionnaires administered at the end of two editions of the course as well as through an analysis of 53 end-of-the-semester projects collected from five trainee cohorts. The two questionnaires showed somewhat conflicting results. The first group of respondents had a less positive judgment of their skills in manipulating corpora, as well as of their ability to use corpora for their own language study and for teaching. One year later, a different cohort showed more confidence in these respects, but mainly in corpus-based analyses and teaching of lexis and phraseology, and less so in relation to grammar and discourse problems. More importantly, most of the trainees also declared recognition of the benefits of corpora in language teaching, especially of general corpora but also, to a lesser extent, of small purpose-built specialised corpora. The results revealed that the respondents saw a greater value of corpora as a tool for teachers in creating general language and ESP teaching materials than in having language learners engage directly in data-driven activities. However, the study also showed that a few participants had developed negative attitudes to the value of corpus-based activities in language teaching.

A subsequent analysis of the trainees' final course projects (Leńko-Szymańska, 2017) produced more disappointing results. It showed that the participants did not develop the expected level of expertise in direct applications of corpora for language teaching. The projects contained only the simplest analyses prescribed in the instructions (selection of specialised terminology and interesting clusters), which demonstrated that in unguided contact with a corpus the trainees lacked intuitions about the selection of pedagogically-valid language points suitable for corpus-based explorations. Corpus data was integrated into the projects' teaching materials chiefly as a source of examples for presentation and controlled practice activities such as gap-filling and matching. The lesson plans contained almost no hands-on activities engaging potential learners in the analysis of corpus data in a printed or electronic format. Leńko-Szymańska (2017) concluded that if teacher-trainees contact with corpora is limited to one course, the pre-service teachers are not likely to develop a sufficient expertise in the three types of skills indispensable for implementing DDL techniques in their classrooms.

33.4.2 An example of a student-training course

Charles (2012, 2014, 2015) provided a description of a DDL student-training course offered for several years at the Oxford University Language Centre. The course was addressed to graduate students in multiple disciplines and focused on the development of their skills in academic writing through investigating grammar and rhetorical functions in discipline-specific texts. It consisted of six weekly two-hour optional and non-assessed sessions. In the more recent editions of the course, the first class served as an introduction to the concept of

Carry out the following tasks and make notes of the information.

a. How frequently does 'that' collocate on the RIGHT of the verb? FREQUENCY =

b. Is 'show* that' a frequent pattern of this verb in your corpus? YES/NO

c. Which nouns and pronouns collocate most frequently on the LEFT of the verb? Are any of these likely to construct claims?

d. Look at the concordances and original files to check the function of the collocates and fill in the table below.

e. Write down one typical example for each noun/pronoun. Choose examples which will be useful in your own writing. An example is given below.

f. Compare your findings with those of another student. Discuss any similarities or differences you see and try to explain them.

Figure 33.3   Example of a guided discovery task on making and modifying claims (Charles, 2015, p. 154)

hands-on concordancing and its usefulness for improving the quality of learners' writing, as well as to the relevance of small self-compiled corpora for investigating rhetorical conventions used in domain-specific academic texts. In the subsequent sessions, students explored individual functionalities offered by text analysis packages – represented by AntConc in the course – for searching information on selected language points. In this way, students were simultaneously practising the technical skills of operating the software and the corpus-analytical skills of examining and interpreting retrieved data. Each class started with the instructor's short presentation of a selected type of analysis based on a small corpus of theses. Subsequently, all students received identical tasks which they completed by querying their own specialised collections. Finally, the participants were given an opportunity to compare their results with their fellow students from other disciplines and discuss the significance of their findings for their own writing practices. Figure 33.3 presents an example of such a task, focusing on the behaviour of the verb *show* to perform the rhetorical function of making and modifying claims and studied with the help of the Collocates function.

The effects of the course were examined with several instruments. Immediate course evaluation questionnaires were completed by the participants after each of the four editions of the course. The overall results showed an overwhelmingly positive response. The students perceived the main strength of the course in working with discipline-related corpora, which ensured the relevance of the findings for their own particular needs. They also felt that corpus consultations helped them improve their writing. Interestingly, 9 out 42 students (Charles, 2015) mentioned the benefit of discovering discourse studies as a field of academic inquiry. Some reservations were voiced about the size of the self-compiled corpora, which were too small to return a sufficient amount of data to some queries and about their inadequately cleaned format which obscured the results. The answers also indicated that non-native authorship of the texts selected for the personal collections undermined the trust in the obtained results. In addition, several students reported some linguistic problems with reading concordance lines and complained about the time necessary to process large amounts of language data.

Forty students from one cohort of the course (Charles, 2012) answered a delayed questionnaire probing their long-term use of the self-compiled corpora. Seventy percent of the participants declared some use of their collections in the period of 12 months after the course. Interestingly, five of the declared non-users stated their intentions to consult their corpora once they started working on their dissertations and two other non-users queried large general resources (the BNC) instead. One-third of the students used their corpora at least once a week, with 10% declaring consultations several times a day. In addition, 30% of the respondents made modifications to their personal collections after the course, which involved adding and/or deleting files.

Finally, Charles (2015) conducted a qualitative analysis of a sample of students' written answers on the worksheets submitted after each class. The results demonstrated that the guided discovery techniques used in the course enabled the students to discover important and relevant facts about grammar and discourse conventions used in their own disciplines. In addition, comparisons with fellow peers as well as class discussions helped them understand the specificity of the writing in their domains and reinforced their confidence as autonomous language investigators, the abilities which – according to Charles – would not only foster the quality of their written language but also their general intellectual development as researchers. Charles (2015) summarised the effects of the tasks in the following words:

The 'same task, different corpus' approach allows students to check the findings of research against data from a specialised corpus in their own field. This problematizes established accounts of academic writing, which paves the way for students to adopt a more nuanced and critical attitude towards such descriptions. Being able to refer to highly specific corpus data not only builds students' knowledge of the norms of usage in their own field, but enables them to back up their intuitions with evidence and thus increases their confidence in their own judgements. (p. 139)

Charles (2012, 2015) results confirm that her students acquired the sufficient levels of technical and corpus-analytical skills which enabled them to become independent corpus users.

33.5 Future directions of research

Although direct applications of corpora by teachers and students remain scarce, we can observe, over the last two decades, a growing awareness of the availability and expediency of corpora in language education. An increasing number of instructors apply corpus resources in their everyday practice. Yet, a closer look into the responses from various surveys among language teachers and learners indicates that data-driven learning is not equally popular in all educational settings. It is primarily used by instructors who are corpus researchers themselves and who work in academic contexts, particularly in language-related programmes such as translation. This observation has led researchers to voice the need for promoting DDL, particularly among 'ordinary' teachers working in pre-tertiary settings. A number of accounts of teacher- and learner-training courses have indeed appeared in the literature. However, the research into their effectiveness has produced somewhat discouraging results. Although both instructors and students develop positive attitudes to corpora and recognise their benefits in language education, neither party acquires sufficient skills to become fully autonomous corpus users.

Three principal problems hindering successful implementation of DDL have been identified: high time demands, complexity of the required skills, and a lack of pedagogic integration. Future developments in the area should address these specific concerns. First, teachers and learners need pedagogically-relevant resources and tools as well as off-the-shelf DDL materials and tasks (Chambers, 2019; Gilquin & Granger, 2010). Such solutions contradict some of the argued advantages of corpora – authenticity and relevance to students' specific needs. However, it seems that without some compromises instructors and students will continue to turn towards conventional resources such as coursebooks, dictionaries, and reference grammars, which do not require onerous and time-consuming searches. Second, beyond highly specialised corpus linguistics or DDL courses, corpus use must have greater representation in language, linguistics, and general teaching methodology classes. Only then will DDL likely reach a tipping point resulting in the mastery and constant reinforcement of the complex technical and corpus-analytical skills necessary for querying and analysing corpus data. Finally, more research and training should support the successful integration of DDL into the language learning process and the development of teachers' corpus-related pedagogical skills. Consequently, instructors and students will become aware of how to successfully combine corpus activities with other effective pedagogic techniques and learning strategies. Meeting these conditions – admittedly not unproblematic – will finally bring about a change not just in teachers' and learners' perceptions and attitudes, but in their routine DDL practice.

Further reading

Chambers, A. (2019). Towards the corpus revolution? Bridging the research–practice gap. *Language Teaching*, *52*(4), 460–475. https://doi.org/10.1017/S0261444819000089. This article overviews the current issues in direct uses of corpora and suggests some solutions for teacher and learner training.

Chen, M., Flowerdew, J., & Anthony, L. (2019). Introducing in-service English language teachers to data-driven learning for academic writing. *System*, *87*, 102–148. https://doi.org/10.1016/j.system.2019.102148. In addition to describing a teacher training workshop in direct applications of corpora for academic writing instruction, the authors analyse teachers' individual characteristics that may lead to their endorsing or rejecting the approach.

Kennedy, C., & Miceli, T. (2017). Cultivating effective corpus use by language learners. *Computer Assisted Language Learning*, *30*(1–2), 91–114. https://doi.org/10.1080/09588221.2016.1264427. This paper describes an interesting approach to learner training in DDL which encourages students to copy ready-made chunks of language into their own production rather than analyse and retrieve rules from corpus data.

Meurice, A., & Meunier, F. (2020). Designing in-service teacher training for computer- and mobile-assisted foreign language learning: A mixed-methods and SWOT analysis of the TELL-OP training module for language professionals. In A. Adujar (Ed.), *Recent Tools for computer- and mobile-assisted foreign language learning* (pp. 289–306). IGI Global. The authors move beyond the use of corpora in the classroom and describe the process of designing a teacher-training course in the use of natural language processing (NLP)-based tools in language education.

Wicher, O. (2019). Data-driven learning in the secondary classroom. A critical evaluation from the perspective of foreign language didactics. In P. Crosthwaite (Ed.), *Data-driven learning for the next generation. Corpora and DDL for pre-tertiary learners* (pp. 31–46). Routledge. https://doi.org/10.4324/9780429425899-3. Although this paper does not deal with teacher and learner training per se, it is recommended to instructors as it stresses the importance of implementing DDL in language education in accordance with the current theories of language instruction and the models of lesson stages.

References

Abdel Latif, M. M. M. (2021). Corpus literacy instruction in language teacher education: Investigating Arab EFL student teachers' immediate beliefs and long-term practices. *ReCALL, 33*(1), 34–48. https://doi.org/10.1017/S0958344020000129

Aston, G. (2015). Learning phraseology from speech corpora. In A. Leńko-Szymańska & A. Boulton (Eds.), *Multiple affordances of language corpora for data-driven learning* (pp. 63–84). Benjamins. https://benjamins.com/catalog/scl.69.04ast

Bernardini, S. (2002). Exploring new directions for discovery learning. In B. Kettemann & G. Marko (Eds.), *Teaching and learning by doing corpus linguistics. Papers from the fourth international conference on teaching and language corpora, Graz 19-24 July 2000* (pp. 165–182). Rodopi.

Boulton, A. (2010). Data-driven learning: Taking the computer out of the equation. *Language Learning, 60*(3), 534–572. https://doi.org/10.1111/j.1467-9922.2010.00566.x

Boulton, A., & Cobb, T. (2017). Corpus use in language learning: A meta-analysis of corpus use in language learning. *Language Learning, 67*(2), 348–393. https://doi.org/10.1111/lang.12224

Breyer, Y. (2009). Learning and teaching with corpora: Reflections by student teachers. *Computer Assisted Language Learning, 22*(2), 153–172. https://doi.org/10.1080/09588220902778328

Breyer, Y. (2011). *Corpora in language teaching and learning: Potential, evaluation, challenges.* Peter Lang.

Callies, M. (2016). Towards corpus literacy in foreign language teacher education: Using corpora to examine the variability of reporting verbs in English. In R. Kreyer, S. Schaub, & A. Gulderning (Eds.), *Angewandte linguistik in schule und hochschule* (pp. 391–414). Peter Lang.

Callies, M. (2019). Integrating corpus literacy into language teacher education. The case of learner corpora. In S. Götz & J. Mukherjee (Eds.), *Learner corpora and language teaching* (pp. 245–263). Benjamins. https://benjamins.com/catalog/scl.92.12cal

Chambers, A. (2019). Towards the corpus revolution? Bridging the research–practice gap. *Language Teaching, 52*(4), 460–475. https://doi.org/10.1017/S0261444819000089

Charles, M. (2012). 'Proper vocabulary and juicy collocations': EAP students evaluate do-it-yourself corpus-building. *English for Specific Purposes, 31*(2), 93–102. https://doi.org/10.1016/j.esp.2011.12.003

Charles, M. (2014). Getting the corpus habit: EAP students' long-term use of personal corpora. *English for Specific Purposes, 35*, 30–40. https://doi.org/10.1016/j.esp.2013.11.004

Charles, M. (2015). Same task, different corpus. In A. Leńko-Szymańska & A. Boulton (Eds.), *Multiple affordances of language corpora for data-driven learning* (pp. 129–154). Benjamins. https://benjamins.com/catalog/scl.69.07cha

Chen, M., Flowerdew, J., & Anthony, L. (2019). Introducing in-service English language teachers to data-driven learning for academic writing. *System, 87*, 102148. https://doi.org/10.1016/j.system.2019.102148

Cotos, E. (2014). Enhancing writing pedagogy with learner corpus data. *ReCALL, 26*(2), 202–224. https://doi.org/10.1017/S0958344014000019

Crosthwaite, P., & Stell, A. (2019). "It helps me get ideas on how to use my words": Primary school students' initial reactions to corpus use in a private tutoring setting. In P. Crosthwaite (Ed.), *Data-driven learning for the next generation: Corpora and DDL for pre-tertiary learners* (pp. 150–170). Routledge. https://doi.org/10.4324/9780429425899-9

Crosthwaite, P., Wong, L. L. C., & Cheung, J. (2019). Characterising postgraduate students' corpus query and usage patterns for disciplinary data-driven learning. *ReCALL, 31*(3), 255–275. https://doi.org/10.1017/S0958344019000077

Ebrahimi, A., & Faghih, E. (2017). Integrating corpus linguistics into online language teacher education programs. *ReCALL, 29*(1), 120–135. https://doi.org/10.1017/S0958344016000070

Farr, F. (2008). Evaluating the use of corpus-based instruction in a language teacher education context: Perspectives from the users. *Language Awareness, 17*(1), 25–43. https://doi.org/10.2167/la414.0

Flowerdew, L. (2012). *Corpora and language education.* Palgrave Macmillan. https://doi.org/10.1057/9780230355569

Friginal, E. (2018). *Corpus linguistics for English teachers: Tools, online resources, and classroom activities.* Routledge.

Geluso, J., & Yamaguchi, A. (2014). Discovering formulaic language through data-driven learning: Student attitudes and efficacy. *ReCALL, 26*(2), 225–242. https://doi.org/10.1017/S0958344014000044

Gilquin, G., & Granger, S. (2010). How can data-driven learning be used in language teaching? In A. O'Keeffe & M. McCarthy (Eds.), *The Routledge handbook of corpus linguistics* (pp. 359–370). Routledge. https://doi.org/10.4324/9780203856949.ch26

Heather, J., & Helt, M. (2012). Evaluating corpus literacy training for pre-service language teachers: Six case studies. *Journal of Technology and Teacher Education, 20*(4), 415–440.

Heyvaert, L., & Laffut, A. (2008). Corpora in the teaching of English in Flemish secondary schools: Current situation and future perspectives. In A. Frankenberg-Garcia, T. Rkibi, M. R. Cruz, R. Carvalho, C. Direito, & D. Santos-Rosa (Eds.), *Proceedings of TaLC 8—Lisbon, 8th teaching and language corpora conference* (pp. 400–409). Associação de Estudos e de Investigação do ISLA-Lisboa.

Huang, Z. (2014). The effects of paper-based DDL on the acquisition of lexico-grammatical patterns in L2 writing. *ReCALL, 26*(2), 163–183. https://doi.org/10.1017/S0958344014000020

Hüttner, J., Smit, U., & Mehlmauer-Larcher, B. (2009). ESP teacher education at the interface of theory and practice: Introducing a model of mediated corpus-based genre analysis. *System, 37*(1), 99–109. https://doi.org/10.1016/j.system.2008.06.003

Johns, T. (1991). "Should you be persuaded": Two samples of data-driven learning materials. *Classroom Concordancing ELR Journal, 4*, 1–16.

Karlsen, P., & Monsen, M. (2020). Corpus literacy and applications in Norwegian upper secondary schools: Teacher and learner perspectives. *Nordic Journal of English Studies, 19*(1), 118–148.

Le Foll, E. (2020, July). *Development and evaluation of a corpus linguistics seminar in pre-service teacher training.* 14th Teaching and Language Corpora (TaLC 2020), Perpignan.

Lee, D., & Swales, J. (2006). A corpus-based EAP course for NNS doctoral students: Moving from available specialized corpora to self-compiled corpora. *English for Specific Purposes, 25*(1), 56–75. https://doi.org/10.1016/j.esp.2005.02.010

Leńko-Szymańska, A. (2014). Is this enough? A qualitative evaluation of the effectiveness of a teacher-training course on the use of corpora in language education. *ReCALL, 26*(2), 260–278. https://doi.org/10.1017/S095834401400010X

Leńko-Szymańska, A. (2015). A teacher-training course on the use of corpora in language education: Perspectives of the students. In A. Turula, B. Mikolajewska, & D. Stanulewicz (Eds.), *Insights into technology enhanced language pedagogy* (pp. 135–150). Peter Lang. https://doi.org/10.3726/978-3-653-04995-4

Leńko-Szymańska, A. (2017). Training teachers in data-driven learning: Tackling the challenge. *Language Learning, 21*(3), 217–241.

Lin, M. H. (2016). Effects of corpus-aided language learning in the EFL grammar classroom: A case study of students' learning attitudes and teachers' perceptions in Taiwan. *TESOL Quarterly, 50*(4), 871–893. https://doi.org/10.1002/tesq.250

Mauranen, A. (2004). Spoken corpus for an ordinary learner. In J. Sinclair (Ed.), *How to use corpora in language teaching* (pp. 89–105). Benjamins.

Moles-Cases, T., & Oster, U. (2015). Webquests in translator training. In A. Leńko-Szymańska & A. Boulton (Eds.), *Multiple affordances of language corpora for data-driven learning* (pp. 199–224). Benjamins. https://benjamins.com/catalog/scl.69.10mol

Mukherjee, J. (2004). Bridging the gap between applied corpus linguistics and the reality of English language teaching in Germany. In U. Connor & T. A. Upton (Eds.), *Applied corpus linguistics. A multidimensional perspective* (pp. 239–250). Rodopi. https://doi.org/10.1163/9789004333772_014

O'Keeffe, A. (2020). Data-driven learning – A call for a broader research gaze. *Language Teaching, 54*(2), 259–272. https://doi.org/10.1017/S0261444820000245

Pérez-Paredes, P., Sánchez-Tornel, M., Calero, J. M. A., & Jiménez, P. A. (2011). Tracking learners' actual uses of corpora: Guided vs non-guided corpus consultation. *Computer Assisted Language Learning, 24*(3), 233–253. https://doi.org/10.1080/09588221.2010.539978

Poole, R. (2018). *A guide to using corpora for English language learners.* Edinburgh University Press.

Reppen, R. (2010). *Using corpora in the language classroom.* Cambridge University Press.

Römer, U. (2009). Corpus research and practice: What help do teachers need and what can we offer? In K. Aijmer (Ed.), *Corpora and language teaching* (pp. 83–98). Benjamins. https://doi.org/10.1075/scl.33.09rom

Römer, U. (2011). Corpus research applications in second language teaching. *Annual Review of Applied Linguistics, 31*, 205–225. https://doi.org/10.1017/S0267190511000055

Saeedakhtar, A., Bagerin, M., & Abdi, R. (2020). The effect of hands-on and hands-off data-driven learning on low-intermediate learners' verb-preposition collocations. *System, 91*, 102268. https://doi.org/10.1016/j.system.2020.102268

Schaeffer-Lacroix, E. (2019). Barriers to trainee teachers' corpus use. In P. Crosthwaite (Ed.), *Data-driven learning for the next generation. Corpora and DDL for pre-tertiary learners* (pp. 47–64). Routledge. https://doi.org/10.4324/9780429425899-4

Sripicharn, P. (2010). How can we prepare learners for using language corpora? In A. O'Keeffe & M. McCarthy (Eds.), *The Routledge handbook of corpus linguistics* (pp. 399–412). Routledge. https://doi.org/10.4324/9780203856949-38

Szudarski, P. (2019). Effects of data-driven learning on enhancing the phraseological knowledge of secondary-school learners of L2 English. In P. Crosthwaite (Ed.), *Data-driven learning for the next generation: Corpora and DDL for pre-tertiary learners* (pp. 133–149). Routledge. https://doi.org/10.4324/9780429425899-8

Tribble, C. (2015). Teaching and language corpora: Perspectives from a personal journey. In A. Leńko-Szymańska & A. Boulton (Eds.), *Multiple affordances of language corpora for data-driven learning* (pp. 37–82). Benjamins. https://benjamins.com/catalog/scl.69.03tri

Vyatkina, N. (2016). Data-driven learning for beginners: The case of German verb-preposition collocations. *ReCALL, 28*(2), 207–226. https://doi.org/10.1017/S0958344015000269

Yoon, H., & Hirvela, A. (2004). ESL student attitudes toward corpus use in L2 writing. *Journal of Second Language Writing, 13*(4), 257–283. https://doi.org/10.1016/j.jslw.2004.06.002

Zareva, A. (2017). Incorporating corpus literacy skills into TESOL teacher training. *ELT Journal, 71*(1), 69–79. https://doi.org/10.1093/elt/ccw045

INDEX

Note: Page references in *italics* denote figures, in **bold** tables and with "n" endnotes.

Academic Collocation List 209

academic corpus resource: EAP 179–180; ESP 179–180

Academic Formulas List (AFL) 208–209

Academic General corpus 447, *449*

Academic Vocabulary List (AVL) 49, 151, 194, 209, 213

Academic Word List (AWL) 44, 139, 183, 212, 215, 241

accent 90, 98; pitch 94; and scaffolding 302

Acquis Communautaire corpus 480, 487

active listenership 4, 108–109, 300

agent-oriented *vs.* speaker-oriented modals 63–65

Amsterdam Slavic Parallel Aligned Corpus 483

annotation: multimodal 254–258; phonological, of corpora 94

AntConc 123, 134, 137, 180, 187, 198, 222, 228, 240, 427, 430, 445, 455–457, 511, 519; collocation analysis 452, *452*; concordance analysis 451, *451*; *vs.* LancsBox **456**; *vs.* Lextutor **456**; overall negotiated ratings for **450**; usability rating of 449–452; word list output *450*, 450–451

AntCorGen 187, 198, 237, 413

AntGram 222

AntWordProfiler 13, 18

Anvil 253, 362, 367

Arabic–English Bidirectional Parallel Corpus 483

"armchair" approach 13

Asian Corpus of English (ACE) 162

authentication of language 103

authenticity: DDL 346–347; and spoken academic discourse 249

automated syntactic analysis (ASA) 6; for ELT 495–504; future directions of research 504; grammar acquisition 498–499; mapping syntactic features to rhetorical functions 501–503; NLP technologies for 496–498; overview 495–496; syntactic processing 499–501; textual enhancement 498–499; visual-syntactic text formatting 499–501

automatic tagging of corpora: continue working for ultimate goal of 68; for pragmatic features 68

autonomous language learning 406–414

autonomy: and corpora 407–414; and learners 407–410; and resources 412–414

Aviation English (AE): case study 138–142; CL for materials development in 133; curriculum developed for 133; lexicon, teaching 139–141, *140*; lexicon in pilot-ATC communication 142; plain English 138; radiotelephone (RTF) 138; standardized phraseology 138; teaching of 137–138; training curricula 138–139

AWL vocabulary 152

BACKBONE (Corpora for Content and Language Integrated Learning) 364

Backbone (BB) project 334–335, 339

BASIC Vocabulary 13

BoostCLIR corpus 482

British Academic Spoken English Corpus (BASE) 74, 155, 180, 188, 251

British Academic Written English (BAWE) 179, 182, 212, 234, 236, 267–268, 413

British Association for Lecturers in English for Academic Purposes (BALEAP) 184–185

British National Corpus (BNC) 14, 16, 28, 62, 75, 105, 235, 385, 470, 483, 511
British National Spoken Corpus 74
Brown Corpus 11, 13, 470
Business English Corpus (BEC) 147, 156, 469, 471–472
business textbooks 152; *see also* textbooks
BYU-COCA corpus platform 379, 382, 384

CALL tools: heuristic evaluation 441–442; heuristic evaluation protocol 442–445, **443–444**; limitations of protocol 445; Nielsen's usability heuristics 442; usability of 441–445
Cambridge and Nottingham Corpus of Discourse in English (CANCODE) 75, 83, 470
Cambridge Certificate in English Language Teaching for Adults (CELTA) 426
Cambridge Learner Corpus (CLC) 29, 285, 292n1, 314, 316, 318
Canadian Nuclear Safety Commission 487
CARLA 77, 84
case studies: Aviation English (AE) 138–142; complex phenomena 487–489; concordance, redefining 362–365; English modal verbs 61–67; existing multilingual resources 485–486; false cognates 486–487; gender minorities 126–128, **127**; investigation of multisemiotic genres 367–371; issues in corpora evaluation of coursebooks 155–157; of Micro Corpus projects 121–128; online multimodal corpora 365–367; parallel corpora 485–489; refugee crisis 122–125, **123**; student-led construction of video corpora 367–371
Centre for English Corpus Linguistics (CECL) 35
Chambers-Le Baron Corpus of French research articles 490
Chinese-English parallel corpus 482, 484
CityU Corpus of Essay Drafts of English Language Learners 291
classroom: corpus analysis tools for 437–457; DDL in 330–332; heuristic evaluation of three corpus tools for 445–457
cognitive fluency 89
Cognitive Load Theory 437
Coh-Metrix 18, 498
ColloCaid project 19, 50, 267
collocation: collocational frameworks 210; defined 206–207; direct corpus use for teaching 211; future of corpora for teaching 216–217; issues for teaching ESP 211–213; knowledge and second language (L2) 207–208; and mutual information (MI) score 207, 208–210; use of corpora for teaching 208–211
collocational frameworks 210
Common European Framework of Reference for Languages (CEFR) 282, 297, 311–312

Common Language Resources and Technology Infrastructure (CLARIN) 91, 463, 481, 483
communication: intercultural (*see* intercultural communication (IC)); study in textbooks 154–155
"comparative fallacy" 313
Compleat Lexical Tutor 75
Complex Dynamic System Theory (CDST) 30
comprehensibility 90, 94–95, 97–98, 382
comprehension corpora 249
computer-assisted language learning (CALL) 49, 50, 132, 393; technologies 379–380; tools 441–445; and written learner corpora 290–291; and YLs 381–382, 385
Computer Science Textbook Corpus 470
concordance: analysis, AntConc 451, *451*; redefining 362–365
contrastive interlanguage analysis (CIA) 19–20, 31–33, *32*
conversation: management of 110; in second language (L2) learning 103–105; study and corpora 105–107; and syllabuses 108
conversational grammar 106
conversational syllabus *see* syllabuses
conversation analysis (CA) 105–106
coordinate phrases 168, **169**
corpora: analysis of grammar-in-discourse 56–68; Asian Corpus of English (ACE) 162; automatic tagging of 68; and autonomous language learning 406–414; and autonomy 407–414; British Academic Spoken English Corpus (BASE) 74, 155, 251; British Academic Written English (BAWE) 179, 182, 212, 234, 236, 267–268, 413; British National Corpus (BNC) 14, 16, 28, 62, 75, 105, 235, 385, 470, 483, 511; British National Spoken Corpus 74; building, for ELT 460–474; Business English Corpus (BEC) 147, 156, 469, 472; Cambridge Learner Corpus (CLC) 29, 285, 292n1, 314, 316, 318; caveats of 489; for classroom activities 131–132; Corpus of Academic Learner English (CALE) 235; critical ecological perspective 391–393; current trends in 134, **135**; defined 1, 93; for development of reference books 14–17; for EAP writing 234–244; Google as 336, 397; in instructed second language pragmatics 71–85; learner (*see* learner corpora); and learners 390–402, 407–410; for listening comprehension 259n1; Longman Learners' Corpus 282; for materials design 131–143; MicroConcord Corpus 236; multilingual 479; multimodal 5, 20, 97, 113, 253–254, 346; Oxford Corpus of Academic English (OCAE) 251; parallel (*see* parallel corpora); pedagogic 2, 6, 332–334, 382–383, 467–471, 473–474; phonological annotation of 94; Published Materials Corpus

(PMC) 155–157; Published Research Article Corpus (PRAC) 227, **227**; for research and instructional purposes 238–242; and resources 412–414; for revising and referencing purposes 242–243; role in English language teaching and learning 1–3; small 61, 226, 235, 252, 255, 259n2, 331, 470–471; as sources of authentic language for pragmatics 74–75; and speaking skills 89–99; Spoken Open American National Corpus (SOANC) 105, 107, 109; structure of 469; and study of conversation 105–107; and teachers 410–412; for teaching and learning vocabulary in ESP 193–203; for teaching social conversation 102–113; and textbooks 148–149; as tools for instructional pragmatics 75; training teachers and learners to use 509–521; types of 2; of university-level written feedback 270–273; use, in teaching and learning vocabulary 49–50; uses of 391–393; in the Web 2.0 era 266–270; *see also specific entries*
corpus analysis tools: comparison of 455–457; definition of benchmark tasks 446; future research 457; heuristic evaluation of 445–457; instructional applications of 438–441; procedure 446–447; review of current state of research 437–441; target vocabulary with frequency and keyword analysis 439; typical word environments 439–441; usability of CALL tools 441–445; usability of educational software 437–438; usability ratings of 447–455
corpus-based autonomous learning 414
corpus-based materials 79; development of course materials 17–18; in ESP 184–186; and pedagogical approaches 17–20
corpus-based vocabulary research: into ESP classrooms 202; for testing in ESP 202
corpus building: core issues 464–474; corpus size 469–471; data collection 471–474; data entry 472–474; ethical and legal issues 472; framework for 464, **465–466**, *466*; future directions 474; guidelines and principles 461–464; overview 460–461; recommendations for practice 464–474; representativeness 467–469
corpus consultation, and younger learners 378–379
corpus design: and L2 speaking 93–95; and learner corpora 93–95
corpus-informed analyses of grammar-in-discourse 57–59
corpus-informed materials: EAP/ESP 4, 184–186; lexical bundle analyses 240–241
corpus-informed teaching 2, 85; English language 20–21
corpus linguistics (CL) 11, 56, 131, 329, 495; analysis of grammar-in-discourse 56–57; and CA 105–106; to foster intercultural

competence 119–120; and intercultural communicative competence skills 116; for materials development in Aviation English 133; representations and othering 118–119; role of 90
corpus literacy 349, 430; training learners in 429–430
Corpus of Academic Learner English (CALE) 235
Corpus of Contemporary American English (COCA) 28, 56, 74, 75, 85, 137, 235, 385, 413, 470, 511; application of 242; -based frequency dictionary 14; *see also* corpora
Corpus of London Teenage Language (COLT) 75
Corpus of Pilot and Air Traffic Controller Communications (CORPAC) 139
Corpus of Repository of Writing (CROW) 235
corpus size 469–471; sample size 471; small corpora 470–471
corpus spots 284, 290
Corpus Workbench 482
coursebooks: defined 148; issues in corpora evaluation of 155–157; *see also* textbooks
Create A Research Space (CARS) model 181, 185
critical discourse analysis (CDA): to foster intercultural competence 119–120; Micro Corpus, projects to promote ICC development 120–128
cryptotechnical words 194, 201
cultural identity 121
culture: corpora for teaching 116–130; problematisation of 120; 'third culture kids' 384
curriculum: developed for Aviation English 133; developer 141, 143; *vs.* syllabuses 102

data collection: corpus building 471–474; data entry 472–474; ethical and legal issues 472
data-driven learning (DDL) 1, 5, 18–19, 56, 184–185, 235; achievable level of challenge 424–425; adjusting perspective and role 430; alignments and contentions 332–334; authenticity 346–347; and basic learning principles 423–425; case study from Norway 334–336; in classroom 330–332; and corpora for materials design 132–133; critical issues in 423–426; current issues 347–350; defined 49, 186; design appropriate tasks for learners 426–429; digital turn 349–350; and education 348; for ELT in perspective 420–431; examining learners' interaction with 393–399; fundamentals of 345–347; future directions 338–339; future research 356–357; hands-off 2; hands-on 2; lack of engagement with SLA theory 348–349; and learner autonomy 273; learner-centredness 347; and learner corpora 285–286; learning

from real-world applications of 422–423; materials and training 426; metalinguistic awareness 345; motivation and relevance 424; multimodal corpora and concordancing in 361–372; overview 329–330; preparing teachers-in-training for 67–68; proxy for frequency effects 346; recommendations for practice 350–356; revamping 347–350; and role of the teacher 426; sample activities 394; skills needed for 511–512; stand-alone DDL activities 350–356; teacher education context 336–338; technical skills and corpus literacy 430; traditional views of language 426; training learners in corpus literacy 429–430; in upper secondary classroom 334–336; use with mixed disciplinary group of students 186; and vocabulary 49–50; for younger learners 377–386

dictionaries: COCA-based frequency 14; development of 16–17; learner 283–284

digital humanities 11

digital technology, affordances of 344–357

direct corpus use 384, 424; defined 211; for teaching collocation 211

disciplinary vocabulary 44

discourse: instructional (*see* instructional discourse); study in textbooks 154–155

do-it-yourself (DIY) corpora 2, 50, 187, 332, 346, 428

Dual Coding Theory 349

EAP writing: citation practices 238; corpora for research and teaching of 234–235; issues and debates in using corpora for 237; keywords 241–242; lexical bundles 240–241; reporting verbs 238; Swalesian move structure patterning 239–240

educational software 437–438

ELAN 253–255, 367

ELRA Catalogue of Language Resources 463

Engineering Lecture Corpus (ELC) 84

English as a Foreign Language (EFL) learners 28, 35, 161, 504

English as a Lingua Franca (ELF) corpora 19–20, 62, 243; academic writing, core issues and topics 162–163; implications, of teaching English academic writing 170; overview 161; research 162; research articles **167**, 167–168; syntactic features of 167–169

English as a Lingua Franca in Academic Settings (ELFA) 161, 162; accommodation to conventions in writing 165–167; non-conventional use of lexical forms 165, **166**; syntactic features of 167–169; writing, lexical features of 164–167; written discourse, lexical features in **165**

English as a native language (ENL) 163

English for Academic Purposes (EAP) 177; academic corpus resource 179–180; coursebooks 18, 44; disciplinary variation 178–179; EGAP *vs.* ESAP 178; lexical bundles in 220–232; writing, corpora for 234–244

English for General Academic Purposes (EGAP) 178, 234

English for Occupational Purposes (EOP) 177

English for Research Publication Purposes (ERPP) 240

English for Specific Academic Purposes (ESAP) 178, 234

English for Specific Purposes (ESP) 44, 177; academic corpus resource 179–180; collocation, issues for teaching 211–213; corpora for teaching and learning vocabulary in 193–203; corpora for teaching collocation in 216–217; corpus-based materials in 184–186; corpus-based studies on vocabulary in 195, 196–197; corpus-based vocabulary research 202; corpus-informed materials in 184–186; defined 206; disciplinary variation 179; high-, mid-, and low-frequency vocabulary 194; size of technical vocabulary in 197; specialized vocabulary in 193–194; technical vocabulary in 195–196

English frequency lists: during 1920s–1940s 13–14; compilation of 11–14; lexical frequency lists 12

English Language Interview Corpus as a Second Language (ELISA) 334, 364, 427

English language teaching and learning (ELT): automated syntactic analysis for 495–504; building corpora for 460–474; case study 61–67; core issues 60–61; and corpus analysis 1; corpus analysis of grammar-in-discourse for 56–68; corpus-informed 20–21; corpus-informed analyses of grammar-in-discourse 57–59; corpus linguistics and grammar-in-discourse 56–57; course materials 17–18; current state of research 421–423; DDL for 420–431; English modal verbs 61–67; future research 67–68, 430–431; learners' attitudes 421–422; parallel corpora in 478–491; real-world applications of DDL 422–423; recommendations for practice 426–430; role of corpora in 1–3; teachers' attitudes 422

English modal verbs 61–67; agent-oriented *vs.* speaker-oriented modals 63–65; background on 62–63; use in questions 65–67

English-Norwegian Parallel corpus 479

English-only Business Letter Corpus of American and British letters 487

English Profile Project 282, 289, 314–315, 318–319

English-Swedish Parallel Corpus 479

ethical/legal issues, in corpus building 472

Étude interdisciplinaire et interlinguistique du
discours académique (EIIDA) corpus 479
European Commission 480
European Corpus of Academic Talk
(EuroCoAT) 302, 303
European Language Resources
Association 481
European Parliament Translation and
Interpretation Corpus (EPTIC) 483
European Science Foundation Second Language
SLA Bank 92
European Union 209, 480
European Union Science Hub 349
Exemplary Empirical Research Articles
(EXEMPRAES) corpus 243
EXMARaLDA 367
"Exploring Your Own Discourse World" 136
extraneous cognitive load 438, 441

feedback: corpora of university-level written
270–273; defined 264; generic 264; before
the Web 2.0 era 265–266; in the Web 2.0 era
266–270
"feedback sandwich" effect 272–273
fluency: cognitive 89; perceived 89; utterance 89
foreign language learners *see* second language
learners
Foreign Language Teaching (FLT) 311–312
formulaic language 45–46
French-English Patent Translation Resource
corpora 482
French Learner Language Oral Corpora
(FLLOC) 92
frequency-based descriptions of vocabulary
42–44, *44*
"A Frequency Dictionary of the German
Language" *see Häufigkeitswörterbuch der deutschen
Sprache* (Kaeding)
frequency information 42, 45, 58, 78, 90, 183

GEC Cool Edit 290
general learner corpora 319; application to LTA
314–315; defined 314
General Service List (GSL) 13, 153
German-English Patent Translation Resource
corpora 482
GlobalVoices Corpus 488
Google: as concordancer 352–353, **353**; as a
corpus 336, 397; use as dictionary 338, 397
governmental sources 480
Graded Examinations in Spoken English (GESE)
314
Graded Readers Corpus 383
grammar: acquisition, and textual enhancement
498–499; conversational 106; corpus studies
in textbooks 149–151; pedagogical 11, 14–16,
150, 299

grammar-in-discourse: automatic tagging of
corpora 68; corpus-informed analyses of
57–59; corpus linguistics and analysis of
56–57; preparing teachers-in-training
for DDL 67–68; unified theory of tense and
aspect 67
Grammarly 504n4
GrammarScope 497, 504n3

hands-off DDL 2
hands-on DDL 2
heuristic evaluation: of corpus tools 445–457;
instructional goals and benchmark tasks for
446; overview 441–442; protocol for CALL
practitioners 442–445
high-frequency vocabulary 194
Hong Kong Corpus of Spoken English (HKCSE)
154
hyperlinks 266–268

IBM 11
idioms 154
illustration, and spoken language 111
IMRD (Introduction-Methods-Results-
Discussion) structure 181, 183
induction, and spoken language 111–112
Information and Communication Technology
(ICT) 378–380, 385, 425
instructed second language acquisition (ISLA)
71
instructed second language pragmatics: corpora
in 71–85; current research 79–83; current state
of using corpora 74–79; future research 83–85;
historical perspectives on 72–74; using corpora
to teach pragmatics 79–83
instructional discourse: corpus-based research
on 249–252; defined 249; large-scale projects
249–251; and listening comprehension 252–
254; multimodal 252–254; small-scale research
251–252; *see also* discourse
instructional pragmatics 72; corpora as tools for
75; and ISLA 71
Integrated Contrastive Model (ICM) *32*, 32–33
integrated corpus-supported teaching and
learning 2
intelligibility 90, 94, 95, 97–98
interaction: and spoken language 111; study in
textbooks 154–155
InterCorp corpus 481
intercultural communication (IC):
combining CL and CDA to foster 119–120;
conceptualising 117–118; corpora for teaching
116–130; and corpus linguistics 116; defined
117; development of 116
intercultural communicative competence (ICC):
development, Micro Corpus CDA projects
to promote 120–128; representations and

othering 118–119; skills and corpus linguistics 116; theory 117–118
intergovernmental sources 480
interlanguage corpora 90
International Civil Aviation Organization (ICAO) 138, 139
International Corpus Network of Asian Learners of English (ICNALE) projects 20, 298
International Corpus of English (ICE) 74, 469, 471
International Corpus of Learner English (ICLE) 20, 234, 235, 282, 288, 312, 314
International Listening Association 252
International Standards Organization 438
International Teaching Assistants corpus (ITAcorp) 299
intradisciplinary variation 182, 188
intrinsic cognitive load 438
IRIS databases 463
iWeb 362, *363*

Japanese learner English Corpus (NICT JLE Corpus) 314

keywords 241–242; application to pedagogy 242; defined 241; grammatical 241
KWIC (key-word-in-context) concordancing program 236

L2 Syntactic Complexity Analyzer (L2SCA) 498
Lancaster-Oslo-Bergen (LOB) Corpus 470
LancsBox 446, 457; *vs.* AntConc **456**; *vs.* Lextutor **456**; usability rating of 452–455
language availability, and parallel corpora 483–484
language learners: direct applications of corpus data by 51; lexical bundles for 223; and pragmatic competence 71; second (*see* second language learners); use of Google as concordancer 352; using corpora to teach pragmatics 74–79
language learning textbooks 2; corpus-based evaluation of 147–158; *see also* textbooks
Languages and Social Networks Abroad Project (LANGSNAP) 92, 93, 306
language testing and assessment (LTA) 311; applications of learner corpora to 315–318; approaches to using learner corpora in **316**; general learner corpora 314–315; importance of learning context variables for 321–322; learner corpora used to inform 313–315
language tests: learner corpora compiled from 313–314; learner corpora to develop 320–321
learner-centredness, and DDL 347
learner corpora 2, 6; application to LTA 314–315; compiled from language tests 313–314; core

issues and topics 313–318; and corpus design 93–95; and customisation 282; data, nature of 320; and data-driven learning 285–286; defined 27, 281; descriptor scales and learner corpus research 320; English Profile Project 318–319; and foreign language teaching 287; future research 319–322; issues associated with 286–287; and language teacher 287; language testing and assessment 313–315; and language tests 320–321; and learner dictionaries 283–284; learning context variables for LTA 321–322; and metadata 31, 282; nature of data 320; pedagogical resources based on 284–285; review of current state of research 312–313; role in teaching 281–292; and SLA 27–28, 34–35, 91; speaking skills and SLA 93–95; as specialised corpora 297; and teaching research 91; testing and assessment 311–322; types of applications of 315–318; *see also* corpora
learner corpus research (LCR) 19, 27–28, 312–313; and individual variation 96; and issues in SLA 34; and language teaching 283; MuPDAR(F) in 33; refinement of contents in descriptor scales based on 320; and spoken learner corpora 299
learner dictionaries 283–284
learners: attitudes, and ELT 421–422; and autonomy 407–410; and corpora 407–410; design appropriate tasks for 426–429; interaction with DDL 393–399; tracking learners' uses 394–399; use of corpora 390–402
learners' uses of corpora: current research 399–401; future research 401–402; learners' interaction with DDL 393–399; method triangulation 399–400; resources 392–393; tracking learners' uses 394–399; under-researched sites of engagement 400–401; using corpus resources for language learning 392
Lexical Approach 18–19
lexical bundles: analyses, and corpus-informed materials 240–241; characteristics of 220–221; defined 222; in EAP 220–232; EAP writing 240–241; function in academic lectures 223; function in academic prose **224**; function in research articles **225**; identification 222–223; issues with functions of 223–227; pedagogical potential of 230–231; and range 221; three-word 227–229
lexical frequency profiles (LFP) 46, 48
lexical profiling 46–48
lexical selection, in textbooks 151–154
Lexical Syllabus 18–19
lexico-grammatical chunks 106–107
lexicography 283–284
Lextutor 19, 46–47, 85, 236, 274n1, 445, 455; *vs.* AntConc **456**; *vs.* LancsBox **456**; overall

negotiated ratings for **447**; usability
rating of 446–449; VocabProfile tool
448, **448**
Limerick-Belfast Corpus of Academic Spoken
English (LI-BEL) 74
Linguee 482, 485, 489
linguistic analysis 255
Linguistic Data Consortium (University of
Pennsylvania) 481
listening: comprehension 252–254; defined 252;
multimodal 252–253; *see also* communication
Live Ink 500, 501, 504n8
Longitudinal Database of Learner English
(LONGDALE) project 20, 315
Longman/Lancaster English Language Corpus 470
Longman Learners' Corpus 282
Louvain Corpus of Native English Essays
(LOCNESS) 286, 288
Louvain EAP dictionary (LEAD) (Granger and
Paquot) 16, 236
Louvain International Database of Spoken
English Interlanguage (LINDSEI) 20, 91, 93,
298, 314, 320
low-frequency vocabulary 43, 194, 439

machine translation tools 490
Marburg Intermediate Learner English (MILE)
corpus 315
materials: development, and vocabulary 49; and
syllabus 110–112; teaching, using corpora to
develop 136
materials design: corpora for 131–143; current
trends in 134, **135**; data-driven learning
(DDL) and corpora for 132–133; teacher
perspectives and recommendations for corpora
in 136–137
MEDAL2 project 289
mediation: of data 107; pedagogic 242, 408; and
syllabus 110–112; teacher 408
Medical Academic Vocabulary List 213
metadata 27, 30–31, 35–36, 282, 314, 364, 473–474
metalinguistic awareness, and DDL 345
metaphors 21, 61, 151, 154
methodology: illustration 111; induction 111–112;
interaction 111; and spoken language 111; and
syllabus 110–112
method triangulation 399–400
MICASE Handbook 84
Michigan Corpus of Academic Spoken English
(MICASE) 74, 75, 78–79, 84, 85, 178, 250–251,
299, 473–474
Michigan Corpus of Upper-Level Student Papers
(MICUSP) 179, 236–237, 413, 470
*Michigan series in English for Academic and
Professional Purposes* (Swales and Feak) 18
MicroConcord Corpus 236, 265
micro corpora 2, 121

Micro Corpus projects 116–117; case studies of
121–128; definition of Micro Corpus 121; to
promote ICC development 120–128
mid-frequency vocabulary 43–44, 194
Mobile-Assisted Language Learning (MALL)
331, 400–402
modals: agent-oriented *vs.* speaker-oriented
63–65; verb use in questions 65–67
Moder 196
Multidimensional Analysis (MDA) model 243
Multilingual Academic Corpus of Assignments:
Writing and Speech (MACAWS) 298
multilingual corpora 479
Multilingual Corpora for Cooperation 483
Multilingual Corpus of Legal Documents
Corpus 483
Multilingual Student Translation (MUST)
learner translation project 20
Multilingual Traditional, Immersion, and Native
Corpus (MulTINCo) 471
multimodal analysis 255–258
Multimodal Analysis Video 254, 362, 367
multimodal annotation 367; corpus and analysis
254–255; integrating corpus tools with
254–258; linguistic analysis 255; multimodal
analysis 255–258
multimodal concordancing: concordance,
redefining 362–365; current contribution
of research to DDL approaches to 362–371;
multisemiotic genres 367–371; online
multimodal corpora 365–367; student-led
construction of video corpora 367–371
multimodal corpora 5, 20, 97, 113, 253–254,
346; and concordancing in DDL 361–372;
current research 371–372; DDL approaches to
multimodal concordancing 362–371; future
research 372; online 365–367; overview 361–362
multimodal literacy 249, 252, 372
multimodal video corpora 367, 372
multisemiotic genres 367–371
multiword constructions (MWC) 153
MuPDAR(F) (Multifactorial Prediction and
Deviation Analysis using Regression/random
forests) 33–34
mutual information (MI) score 207, 208–210
MWSWeb platform 368

National Education Association (NEA) 12
National Institute of Information and
Communications Technology 314
native corpus 281, 286–288, 312
native speakers 19, 33, 59, 76, 89, 96; *vs.* learners
317; from MICUSP 236; pronunciation 162;
use of collocations 213
'natural' language 27
natural language processing (NLP) 495; for
automated syntactic analysis 496–498

Natural Reader 352
Newcastle Corpus of Academic Spoken English (NUCASE) 74
New London Group 252
Nielsen Norman Group 442
Norway: case study from 334–336; DDL in upper secondary classroom 334–336
noun postmodifiers 169

Online Corpus of Academic Lectures (OnCAL) 84–85
On Speaking Terms: Real Language for Real Life 17
OpenSubtitles Corpus 486, 487
OPUS platform 482–483, 486, 488
Oslo Multilingual Corpus 479
othering: and corpus linguistics 118–119; defined 118
Oxford Corpus of Academic English (OCAE) 251

paper-based DDL 2
parallel corpora 2, 6; case studies 485–489; caveats of corpora 489; Chinese-English 482, 484; and comparable multilingual corpora 479; contributions to teaching and learning 484–485; and dictionaries 479; disciplinary contributions 480–481; in ELT 478–491; future research 490–491; governmental and intergovernmental sources 480; language availability 483–484; overview 478–480; recommendations for teaching and learning 489–490; review of current sources inspiring research 480–482; simplification and over-normalisation 489–490; sources for current research 481–482; technical considerations 479–480; tools 482–485
ParaSHS English-French parallel corpus 490
pedagogical approaches: and corpus-based materials 17–20; data-driven learning 18–19; ELF corpora 19–20; Lexcial Syllabus 18–19; Lexical Approach 18–19
pedagogical grammars 11, 14; and corpus-based studies 150; use of corpora by 299; writings of 15–16
pedagogically-oriented corpora 50
pedagogic corpora 2, 6, 332–334, 382–383, 467–474; early versions of 334; and language teaching 461; learner-friendly 474
perceived fluency 89
Phrasalstein 354, *354*
phrasal structures 168
Phrasalverb Machine 354
phrasal vocabulary 45–46
plain English 138, 139, 142
pragmalinguistic knowledge 71–72
pragmatic competence: defined 71; and second language learners 71

pragmatics: ability 90; and corpora 4; corpora as sources of authentic language for 74–75; corpora as tools for instructional 75; defined 71; testing effects of using corpora to teach 79–83
Process Corpus of English in Education (PROCEED) 35, 291–292
pronunciation 90; and accent 90; and comprehensibility 90; and intelligibility 90
psychological collocates 207
Published Materials Corpus (PMC) 155–157
Published Research Article Corpus (PRAC) 227, **227**

questions: modal verb use in 65–67; multiple choice 320
The Quirk Corpus 15

radiotelephone (RTF) 138
Radiotelephony Plain English Corpus (RTPEC) 139
random sampling 61, 237, 468
Range 13, 18, 47
reference corpora: defined 28; examples of 28; linguistic information derived from 28–29; and SLA 27, 28–29, 36; *see also* corpora
Reference Language Varieties (RLVs) 31
Reference Level Descriptions (RLDs) 312–313, 317–319
replication studies 202–203
reporting verbs 18, 56, 106, 238, 284
representations: and corpus linguistics 118–119; and intercultural communicative competence 118–119
representativeness: corpus building 467–469; sampling methods 468–469; structure of the corpus 469
research-practice gap 3, 51
Research Writing Tutor (RWT) 186, 414
resources: and autonomy 412–414; and corpora 412–414; learners' uses of corpora 392–393
ReversoTranslation 485
Russian Learner Translator Corpus 485, 488
Russian National Corpus 74, 483

SACODEYL corpus 334, 364
SACODEYL-EN corpus 471
sampling: methods 468–469; random 61, 237, 468; scientific 14; stratified 468
Santa Barbara Corpus of Spoken American English 74–75
Secondary Vocabulary Lists (SVL) 213, 215
Second Language Acquisition (SLA) 312; characteristics of 26; core issues and topics 29–31; current state of research 27–29; future research 34–37; and learner corpora 27–28, 34–35; observations 26–27; and reference corpora 27, 28–29, 36; researchers and teachers

94–95; research methods 31–34, *32*; study designs 27

second language learners 4, 29, 71; and learner corpora 27, 281; and pragmatic competence 71; and vocabulary in ESP 194

second language (L2) learning: and "bilingual" books 478; conversation in 103–105; use of texts as tools 120

second language (L2) speaking: and corpus design 93–95; and language knowledge 89; speaking skills and SLA 93–95

self-compiled corpora 2, 241, 519–520

self-directed DDL 2, 392

semantic frequency lists 12, 13

semantic motifs 182

semantic sequences 182

short private online course (SPOC) 19, 270

Sketch Engine for Language Learning (SkELL) 17, 19, 269, 335, 379, 511

SLA theory: data-driven learning (DDL) 348–349; lack of engagement with 348–349

small corpora 61, 226, 235, 252, 255, 259n2, 331, 470–471

small-scale corpus-based research 251–252

social conversation: characteristics of 108; corpora for teaching 102–113; defined 102; design of syllabuses for teaching 102; syllabus for 108–110; *see also* conversation

sociopragmatic knowledge 71

Spanish Learner Language Oral Corpora (SPLLOC) 92

speaking skills: and corpora 89–99; fluency 89; pronunciation 90; and spoken learner corpora 95–97

specialised corpora 241, 251, 331, 413, 461, 470, 489; and AntCorGen 237; and corpus linguistics 116, 119; for ESP 468; learner corpora as 297; *vs.* micro corpora 121; *see also* corpora

specialized vocabulary: in ESP 193–194; studies on 197–198

spoken language: and illustration 111; and induction 111–112; and interaction 111; and methodology 111

spoken learner corpora 98; core issues and topics 301–303; direct uses, in language pedagogy 300–301; future research 306; indirect uses, in language pedagogy 299; for language teaching 296–306; overview 296; and speaking skills 95–97; *see also* corpora

Spoken Open American National Corpus (SOANC) 105, 107, 109

standardized phraseology 138

Stanford CoreNLP National Language Processing Toolkit 497

Statistical Machine Translation systems 490

stratified sampling 468

StringNet 19

student: defined 206; -led construction of video corpora 367–371; -training course 518–520

suppression, defined 127

Survey of English Usage project 15

surveys of direct corpus applications 510–511

Swahili-English SAWA Corpus 483

Swalesian move structure patterning 239–240

syllabus design: for teaching social conservation 102; and vocabulary 49

syllabuses: active listenership 109; constructing and organizing your own talk 109; and conversation 108; *vs.* curriculum 102; defined 102; items and features 112; language learning 102; management of the conversation 110; for social conversation 108–110; taking account of the listener(s) 109

syntactic complexity indices **502**

syntactic processing: skills 499; visual-syntactic text formatting and 499–501; and VSTF 500

Tatoeba 483–484, 489

teacher and student training: core issues and topics in 510–514; current research on 516–520; evaluating the effectiveness of 514–515; future research 520–521; models of 512–514; overview 509; research into effectiveness of 515–516; skills needed for data-driven 511–512; student-training course 518–520; surveys of direct corpus applications 510–511; teacher-training course 516–518; *see also* student

teacher-created corpus data 266–268

teacher education: data-driven learning (DDL) 336–338; and personal corpora 50; pre-service 412

teachers: attitudes, and ELT 422; and autonomy 410–412; and corpora 410–412; -in-training for DDL 67–68; *see also* teacher and student training

teacher-training course 516–518

teaching: -oriented corpora 427; parallel corpora 489–490; pragmatics 74–79; tools and corpora defining core issues for 482–485; traditional 347, 513

teaching-oriented corpus *see* pedagogic corpora

technical vocabulary 44; in ESP 195–196; in plumbing 199–200, **200**; size, in ESP 197; *see also* vocabulary

Technology Acceptance Model (TAM) 441

TED Corpus Search Engine (TCSE) 366, *366*

TED Talks 365, 483

TESOL Quarterly 73

textbooks: and corpora 148–149; corpus studies of communication in 154–155; corpus studies of discourse in 154–155; corpus studies of grammar in 149–151; corpus studies of interaction in 154–155; corpus studies of lexis in 151–154; and English language teaching

147; *if-clause* in 151; verb tense usage 150–151; *see also* coursebooks

textual enhancement 498–499

three-word lexical bundles 227–229; functional classification of **229**; PRAC sub-section used for **227**; structural classification of **228**; *see also* lexical bundles

TLCHub 305, 306

TOEFL 2000 Spoken and Written Academic Language (T2K-SWAL) Corpus 250

Tool for the Automatic Analysis of Syntactic Sophistication and Complexity (TAASSC) 498

traditional teaching 347, 513

Tradooit 485–487, 489–490

Translation Equivalents Database (TREQ) 481, 486–487

Tregex 497

Trinity Lancaster Corpus (TLC) 92, 95, 297, 298, 302, 303–305, 314

t-score 207–208

unified theory of tense and aspect 67

Université Catholique de Louvain's Center for English Corpus Linguistics (CECL) 91

upper secondary classroom 334–336

usability: of CALL tools 441–445; defined 438; of educational software 437–438

usability heuristic framework: negotiated ratings for AntConc **450**; negotiated ratings for Lextutor **447**, **453**

USTVRI Corpus 62, *63*, *64*, 64–66

utterance fluency 89

vague category markers (VCMs) 107

Varieties of English for Specific Purposes Database (VESPA) 235

Verb-Argument Constructions (VACs) 30

video corpora: multimodal 367, 372; student-led construction of 367–371

Vienna-Oxford International Corpus of English (VOICE) 20, 162, 303

visual-syntactic text formatting (VSTF) 499–501, 504

VocabProfiler 47, *47*

vocabulary: corpora and pedagogical approaches to 48; corpora for teaching and learning, in ESP 193–203; corpora use in teaching and learning 49–50; corpus-assisted analysis of 46–48; corpus-based analysis of 42–46; and data-driven learning 49–50; frequency-based descriptions of 42–44, *44*; indirect use of corpora in learning 46–49; indirect use of corpora in teaching 46–49; loading 153; mid-frequency 43–44, 194; phrasal 45–46; specialized, in ESP 193–194; syllabus design and materials development 49; use in specific contexts 44–45; *see also* grammar

"Vocabulary Control Movement" 13

vocabulary research: core issues in corpus-based 42–50; current state of 41–42; future directions of 51–52

Web 2.0 era: corpora in 266–270; feedback before 265–266; feedback in 266–270

WebCorp 362, 365

WebParaNews Corpus 484

Web (VIEW) system 498–499

Wikipedia system 179

Word Association Lists 214, **214**

Word Book (Thorndike) 13

WordReference 482, 485

WordSmith Tools 156, 236, 265, 365, 394

Write Like a Chemist (Robinson) 143

written learner corpora: and computer-assisted language learning 290–291; and language teaching 283; and learner dictionaries 283–284; overview 281–282; role in teaching 287–292; writing process 291–292; *see also* corpora; learner corpora

younger learners (YL): classroom, corpora into 379–383; and corpus consultation 378–379; current contributions and research 383–385; current state of research 377–378; DDL for 377–386; future research 385–386

Yugoslav-Serbo-Croatian-English Contrastive corpus 479